Spain After Franco

Spain After Franco

The Making of
a Competitive Party System

Richard Gunther
Giacomo Sani
and
Goldie Shabad

University of California Press
BERKELEY • LOS ANGELES • LONDON

University of California Press
Berkeley and Los Angeles, California

University of California Press, Ltd.
London, England

Printed in the United States of America
1 2 3 4 5 6 7 8 9

LIBRARY OF CONGRESS CATALOGING IN PUBLICATION DATA
Gunther, Richard.
Spain after Franco.

Bibliography: p.
Includes index.
1. Political parties—Spain.   2. Spain—Politics and
government—1975–   .   3. Representative government
and representation—Spain.   I. Sani, Giacomo.
II. Shabad, Goldie.   III. Title.
JN8395.A2G86   1985   324.246   84-16172
ISBN 0-520-05183-1

For Elizabeth
Laura and Giulia
Ariel and Mira

Contents

Tables

Illustrations

FIGURES

MAP

Acknowledgments

LIKE NEARLY ALL STUDENTS of contemporary Spanish politics, we owe an enormous debt of gratitude to Juan Linz. His research of the past two decades has provided an invaluable foundation upon which this and many other studies have been based. In addition, he was most generous with his time, comments, and advice, all of which helped in the design and analysis portions of this study. We are also most grateful to DATA S.A., and, in particular, Manuel Gómez-Reino, Darío Vila Carro, and Francisco Andrés Orizo. Aside from the excellent work they did in carrying out our mass-level survey, we benefitted greatly from their technical advice, their insights into contemporary Spanish politics, and their friendship. We also wish to thank Antonio Pons Puig, Maite González Royo, Nuria de Loresecha Sánchez, Guillermo Pacheco del Olmo, and Nicolás García Muñoz of DATA for their assistance during different phases of the project.

Kristi Andersen, Roger Blough, and James Warhola of Ohio State University made valuable contributions to the study in varying ways. Pilar del Castillo Vera, Robert Fishman, Stanley Payne, Hans-Jürgen Puhle, and José Ramón Montero also made valuable comments and criticisms concerning various portions of the manuscript.

This study would not have been possible without the generous cooperation of national- and provincial-level leaders of Spain's political parties. Although space does not permit a listing of all those interviewed, we would like to express our special thanks to the following, some of whom were interviewed several times: José María Alkain, Santiago Alvarez, Oscar Alzaga, Rafael Arias Salgado,

Xabier Arzallus, Juan María Bandrés, Heribert Barrera, Gerardo Bujanda, Enrique Curiel, Leopoldo Calvo Sotelo, Antonio Carro, Iñigo Cavero, Josep María Cullell, Manuel Fraga, Jesús Fuentes, Felipe González, José Manuel González Páramo, Alfonso Guerra, Miguel Herrero de Miñón, Pello de Irujo, Joaquín Leguina, José Lladó, José Luis Malo de Molina, Jaime Mayor Oreja, Juan Antonio Ortega y Díaz Ambrona, Antonio Palomares, Gregorio Peláez, Félix Pastor Ridruejo, Miguel Angel Pino, Javier Rupérez, Luis Solana, Jordi Solé Tura, Adolfo Suárez, Josep María Trías de Bes, Javier Tusell, Jorge Verstrynge, and Federico Ysart. In addition, we are grateful to Fernando Jáuregui, General Manuel Gutiérrez Mellado, José María Maravall, Luís Sánchez Merlo, and Amando de Miguel for the insights they provided in extensive informal conversations.

Generous financial assistance was provided by the National Science Foundation under grants Nos. SOC77–16451 and SES-8309162. The opinions, findings, and conclusions expressed in this book, however, are those of the authors and do not necessarily reflect the views of the National Science Foundation. The 1982 survey was undertaken (in collaboration with Juan Linz, José Ramón Montero, and Hans-Jürgen Puhle) with support from the Stiftung Volkswagenwerk of West Germany. Richard Gunther would also like to thank the Comité Conjunto Hispano-Norteamericano para Asuntos Educativos y Culturales, whose travel grant helped make possible a third round of interviews with political elites in 1981, the College of Social and Behavioral Sciences of The Ohio State University, whose research fellowship greatly aided in the writing of this manuscript, and the Fundación José Ortega y Gasset, which arranged for extensive follow-up interviews with Felipe González and Adolfo Suárez in May 1984. We also wish to acknowledge the assistance of Ohio State University's Polimetrics Laboratory, Valentina Rojo for her superb transcription of taped elite interviews, Barbara Williams for typing the manuscript, and Lynn Maurer for preparing the index.

Finally we would like to thank Linda Gunther, Marina Dotti-Sani, and Robert Krivoshey for their support and patience.

Abbreviations

ACL	Acción Ciudadana Liberal
AP	Alianza Popular
BEAN	Bloc d'Esquerra d'Alliberament Nacional de Catalunya
BNPG	Bloque Nacional Popular Gallego
CCOO	Comisiones Obreras
CC-UCD	Centristes de Catalunya, CC-UCD
CDC	Convergència Democràtica de Catalunya
CEDA	Confederación Española de Derechas Autónomas
CiU	Convergència i Unió (coalition of CDC and Unió Democràtica de Catalunya)
CNT	Confederación Nacional del Trabajo
CSUT	Confederación de Sindicatos Unitarios de Trabajadores
EE	Euskadiko Ezkerra
ERC	Esquerra Republicana de Catalunya
ETA	Euskadi ta Askatasuna
FDC	Federación Demócrata Cristiana
FPDL	Federación de Partidos Demócratas y Liberales
HB	Herri Batasuna
HOAC	Hermandades Obreras de Acción Católica
JOC	Juventudes Obreras Católicas
ORT	Organización Revolucionaria de Trabajadores
PCE	Partido Comunista de España
PDC	Pacte Democràtic per Catalunya (coalition of CDC and PSC-Reagrupament)

PNV	Partido Nacionalista Vasco
PSA	Partido Socialista de Andalucía – Partido Andaluz
PSC-Congrés	Partit Socialista de Catalunya – Congrés
PSC-PSOE	Socialistes de Catalunya
PSC-Reagrupament	Partit Socialista de Catalunya – Reagrupament
PSG	Partido Socialista de Galicia
PSOE	Partido Socialista Obrero Español
PSP	Partido Socialista Popular
PSPV	Partit Socialista del País Valencià
PSUC	Partit Socialista Unificat de Catalunya
PTE	Partido del Trabajo de España
SU	Sindicato Unitario
UCD	Unión de Centro Democrático
UDE	Unión Democrática Española
UDPE	Unión del Pueblo Español
UG	Unidade Galega
UGT	Unión General de Trabajadores
UNE	Unión Nacional Española
US	Unidad Socialista (PSP-US)
USO	Unión Sindical Obrera

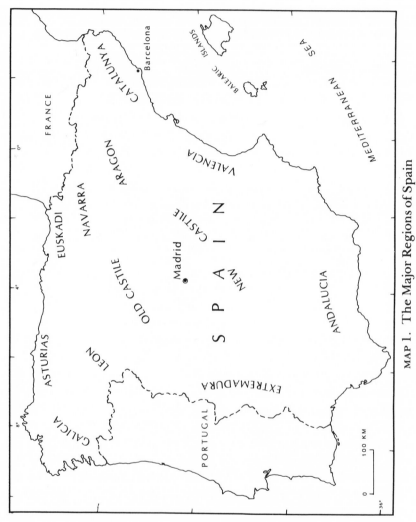

MAP 1. The Major Regions of Spain

CHAPTER ONE

Introduction

IN THE SPRING of 1979 Enrique Tierno Galván, a prominent Socialist opposition leader during the Franquist era, was elected mayor of Madrid. In Barcelona, Spain's second largest city, a Catalán Socialist, Narcis Serra, assumed the responsibilities of heading the municipal government. At the same time, the newly elected mayor of San Sebastián was the Basque nationalist José María Alkain. Representatives of the centrist Unión de Centro Democrático (UCD) and of the Spanish Communist party (PCE) were chosen to head municipal administrations in Santander and Córdoba, respectively. In total, over 60 thousand persons were democratically elected to serve as mayors or city councilmen in Spain's local governments.

The municipal elections held in April 1979 were perhaps less important than the legislative elections and the two referenda held between December 1976 and March 1979, but the election to office of thousands of Spanish citizens (some of whom had been jailed or exiled under the previous regime, and the vast majority of whom had never been active in politics before) was of symbolic significance: it represented the implantation even at the local level of a competitive party system. Barely three and a half years before, nothing remotely comparable existed. When Francisco Franco died, he left behind the decaying remnants of an authoritarian regime in which not even the official political organization, the *Movimiento*, could be properly called a party.

The process through which a competitive party system emerged in post-Franco Spain is the subject of this book. Our main focus is on

1

the formation and gradual institutionalization of parties, on the relationships among parties, and on the linkage between party elites and the mass public. We view the outcome—the party system that evolved—as being in large measure an act of creation, the product of conscious decisions made by political elites. But we also argue for the importance of the social, political, and historical context within which these decisions were made. This context provided the raw materials for the decisions made by elites, as well as for the constraints on the response of the mass public to the alternatives posed by politicians. We also view the outcome as being indeterminate at the beginning of the transition period when many fundamental choices were still to be made. The alternatives chosen at several crucial junctures became constraints on the decisions to be made in subsequent stages, leading to a structuring of the process and making the outcome progressively more determinate.

A NEW PARTY SYSTEM

At the end of a successful transition to democracy in Spain, a competitive party system was well on its way to consolidation. By the time of the second general election in early 1979, a moderately fragmented and polarized party system, with four major nationwide parties and several significant micronationalist forces, appeared to have taken root.

Many elements contributed to the peaceful transformation of the regime, among them a favorable international climate, the generally acquiescent posture of *los poderes fácticos* (the powers that be—armed forces, Church, business community), a widely shared desire among both elites and the masses to avoid the bitter confrontations of the past, the positive role played by the monarch, and the modernization of Spanish society. All of these were influential in contributing to the emergence of democratic politics, but the specific characteristics of the party system were the product of the interaction among three factors: the beliefs of the electorate, the strategies adopted by political elites, and the institutions established during the transition.

The social context within which parties attempted to take root was clearly relevant to the structure of the new party system. In our analysis, we focus on three societal cleavages that have been of particular significance for Spain in the past and that contributed to the failure of earlier democratic experiments: class conflicts, differences over the proper role of the Church in social and political life, and struggles between some regional micronationalist movements and the centralist tendencies of Spanish nationalists. But political ideas often have a life of their own. Thus, we examine a fourth critical dimension of the Spanish context in the 1970s: the general political orientations and ideological predilections of the Spanish populace. These mass beliefs are clearly pertinent to voting decisions in a newly emerging party system, particularly insofar as they interact with class, religious, or center-periphery cleavages.

Mass-level characteristics alone, however, do not provide a satisfactory explanation of the basic features of the party system that emerged in Spain in the late 1970s. Mass-level divisions are best regarded as the bases of potential political conflict. They are not automatically translated into overt political behavior, let alone into a particular pattern of interparty competition. The configuration of partisan forces in a new democratic system is, in large measure, the product of the perceptions, values, calculations, strategies, and behavior of political elites as they attempt to attract electoral support. The specific societal cleavages likely to be channeled into an emergent party system will depend greatly on the identity of the social groups that party leaders seek to mobilize and the issues that they choose to emphasize.

It makes a great deal of difference for the dynamics of partisan competition if party elites define their target groups narrowly or broadly, that is, whether they prefer to attract a homogeneous clientele or pursue "catch-all" strategies; or whether they opt for the preservation of ideological purity over the maximization of votes. Once these target groups have been identified, party leaders must formulate and implement strategies for attracting support. First, decisions must be made concerning the kind of image the party should project to the general public—a particularly crucial decision in founding parties in the age of television. Second, choices must be made concerning the creation of an organizational structure designed to penetrate into society and to convey the party's messages to potential voters or future party activists. Success in these endeavors can create important electoral resources. A large base of party members, for example, can provide additional funding for the organization, lower the cost of campaign activities through the use of voluntary labor, and add the personal influence of militants to the party's arsenal of campaign weapons. Third, party leaders must decide whether to establish ties to secondary organizations. The manner in which party elites seek to create supportive organizations throughout the country or to link up with existing voluntary associations will greatly affect their success in mobilizing various social groups. In sum, an understanding of the emergence of partisan alignments requires, in Sartori's words, that one assess "to what extent parties are dependent variables reflecting social stratification and cleavages, and, *vice versa,* to what extent these cleavages reflect the channelling imprint of a structured party system."[1] Clearly, through their ideologies, strategies, and organizational tactics, parties contribute greatly to the configuration of partisan alignments.

In making crucial decisions about these matters, Spanish party elites had a great deal of leeway because they were operating in a highly fluid political environment. Although Spain in the late 1970s was not an electoral tabula rasa, it is clear that the voting decisions of Spanish citizens in the first elections were far less determined by force of habit than those of electors in older democracies. Most contemporary Spaniards had not yet been born at the time of the last competitive election in February 1936. Even for those who had cast ballots under the Second Republic, their experience with democracy had been brief. It was therefore unlikely that long-standing party loyalties or stable party identifications would influence the choices of many voters. The malleability of the Spanish electorate with regard to specific partisan preferences provided party elites with enhanced opportunities to be creative and flexible in the design of their electoral strategies.

However, in making these crucial decisions the emerging political elites were not totally unconstrained. Three of the six largest parties during the period 1977 to 1982 had deep historical roots: the Partido Socialista Obrero Español (PSOE), the Partido Comunista de España (PCE), and the Partido Nacionalista Vasco (PNV) had existed under the Second Republic and, clandestinely, throughout the Franquist era. Thus, these parties inherited from those earlier periods organizational structures and formal ideologies or (in the case of the PNV) programmatic committments. In addition, voters' perceptions and evaluations of these parties were profoundly affected by "historical memories"—it would be particularly difficult for the PCE, for example, to overcome the divisive image it had acquired during the Civil War. Even newly created parties, such as the UCD and the Alianza Popular (AP), were affected by such memories, albeit of a more recent historical period. Most of the founding members of the AP, for instance, had been government ministers under the Franco regime and thus were often regarded as *los continuadores del régimen* (those who would perpetuate the former regime). Due to these historical constraints, potentially advantageous options were sometimes precluded by inherited structural or ideological factors. For other parties, attempts to alter the formal content of their ideologies or organizational structures and practices to better adapt to contemporary circumstances generated intraparty tensions, pitting those favoring change against those opposed to it. And, in virtually all cases, electoral strategies sought either to erase, or to capitalize on, public images inherited from the past.

Because basic decisions concerning party ideologies, organizational structures, and electoral images were made by party elites over an extended period of time, the points at which specific choices were made had a definite impact on the degree to which different parties were successful. For some parties, many of these traits had already been determined during the Second Republic or the Franquist era. In other cases, particularly that of the UCD, basic decisions were not made until the eve of the 1977 elections. Those made at earlier times (either clandestinely or during the beginning phases of the transition to democracy) were formulated in the face of great uncertainty.

At the time of Franco's death, for example, it was not known how (or even if) a transition to democracy would take place—by an abrupt and possibly violent *ruptura* or via legal and peaceful *reforma*. Neither did elites know which parties would be legalized and permitted to take part in elections, what the characteristics (and the biases) of the electoral law would be, or even who would be in power at the time of the first election. Strategies formulated early in the transition could turn out to be totally inappropriate for the conduct of a successful election campaign, depending on how each of these uncertainties were resolved. Conversely, strategies adopted at later stages of the transition, when indeterminacy had been progressively reduced, were formulated with a better knowledge of the circumstances under which interparty competition would take place. Decision making later in this process, however, proved to be a mixed blessing: such choices were more sharply constrained by recent political developments, and certain options were precluded. Thus, the temporal dimension, in and of itself, emerged as a critical factor.

Finally, as the transition proceeded and institutional arrangements were made, the political environment became gradually more structured and less fluid; both political elites and masses were progressively constrained by the newly created institutions stemming from the Political Reform Law approved in late 1976, by the electoral law passed in early 1977, and, eventually, by the Constitution promulgated at the end of 1978. Thus, while the electoral system chosen, for example, by no means predetermined a specific outcome, it did affect the chances of representation for small nationwide parties and, at the same time, favored the emergence of micronationalist forces. Thus, on one hand, the rules of the game contributed to a lesser degree of fragmentation than might otherwise have been the case. On the other hand, it enhanced the probability that the center-periphery cleavage would become a major component of the new democratic polity.

DEMOCRATIC STABILITY

The prospect for stability of the new Spanish democracy is the second concern of this book. From the beginning of the post-Franco era, questions were often raised about the durability of the new regime. Such concerns were voiced by many politicians from different political quarters who stressed the importance of learning from the tragic mistakes of the past. As Manuel Fraga, leader of one of the major political groups put it in a 1978 statement,

> We must learn the lesson of our not-very-successful earlier constitutional experiments; elaborate and well-intentioned theories, an interminable procession of brilliant speeches, but all without convincing results. None of our constitutions secured popular assent [or even] minimal duration, the respect of time, the value of efficacy.[2]

The fundamental task facing the founders of the new regime was to create a political system capable of managing deep-seated conflicts through institutional channels. Success in this endeavor would depend on both the intensity of politically relevant cleavages in the society and the extent to which leaders working through the newly created institutions—the party system among them—would be able to find mutually acceptable solutions.

In the mid-1970s the new political class confronted the same basic cleavages that had played a disruptive role in the past. But, with the passage of time, changes had occurred that served in some cases to soften and in others to exacerbate these historic divisions. The socioeconomic development of Spain over the preceding three decades had profoundly altered many aspects of its social structure, mitigating somewhat the divisive potential of class conflict. Insofar as high levels of literacy and urbanization and the existence of a large middle class are prerequisites for a stable democracy, these changes have contributed to the new regime's chances for success. The bases of some traditionally explosive social problems, moreover, have been substantially altered: the number of landless peasants in Andalucía and Extremadura, for example, had been reduced as the result of massive migration to industrial centers in other parts of Spain or Western Europe. In other respects, however, social and economic problems actually have become greater in recent years: a serious recession throughout Spain and much of the rest of Western Europe greatly increased unemployment after 1975 and brought about the massive repatriation of migrant workers. Thus, just as in the 1930s,

Spain's political leaders had to deal with a major economic crisis at the same time that they were trying to establish a new regime.

Similarly, mixed conclusions can be drawn about changes affecting the religious cleavage. On one hand, the decline of religious practice and the more progressive stance of the Spanish Church following Vatican II had contributed to a softening of anticlerical sentiments in some segments of the population. On the other hand, it was unlikely that this source of division within Spanish society had disappeared, especially because the Church had so closely embraced the Franquist regime in its early phases (and in return its traditional privileges had been restored and maintained until well into the post-Franco transition).

Finally, there were reasons to suppose that, with the reestablishment of an open polity, tensions would flare up between the Spanish state and previously repressed micronationalist movements in Catalunya and, especially, Euskadi. As a reaction against the former regime's centralizing excesses and crude attempts to crush out regional languages and cultures, regional nationalist movements entered the transition to democracy with great strength, and terrorist violence escalated steadily throughout this period. At the same time, significant segments of Spanish society were hostile to what they perceived as demands for the dismemberment of the Spanish state.

These divisions became salient for the new regime almost immediately, because they had to be addressed in the course of writing a new constitution. Particularly critical was the manner in which Church-state relations would be altered and the Spanish state decentralized. Indeed, Church hostility to the Second Republic was the direct product of the constituent process itself: the Constitution drafted in 1931 bitterly alienated religious Spaniards from the new regime. Of equal or greater significance would be the extent to which agreement could be reached over Basque and Catalán demands for regional autonomy. The absence of consensus over the basic structure of the state could undermine the legitimacy of the new regime, as well as contribute to further polarization between micronationalist groups and right-wing traditionalist elements in the armed forces.

The depth of these cleavages at the mass level certainly affected efforts to resolve them—or at least to regulate them within institutional channels. But, again, the manner in which political elites dealt with these matters constituted an important factor in determining the intensity of political conflict. Elite behavior was crucial for two reasons. First, party leaders elected to the Cortes in 1977 had to come to terms with these issues in writing the new Constitution. Second, because their political parties (in varying degrees) reflected the divisions in Spanish society—and in many instances posed as spokesmen for the particular interests of various social groups—the manner in which they chose to articulate conflicting social demands could greatly affect the level of hostility among social groups, as well as the possibility of securing compromise resolution of the differences among them.[3]

More generally, elite political culture in and of itself was likely to play a critical role. Many students of politics have argued that the manner in which party elites view the rules of political competition has a significant effect on the level of polarization of a political system.[4] When elites perceive competition as an activity fraught with unacceptable risks, or when they regard compromise as evil and demeaning, or politics as a zero-sum game, the likelihood of the existence of an extremely polarized and potentially unstable system is high.[5] Moreover, when party elites view political competition as a matter of "life or death," they are likely to influence the general public and thereby reinforce the level of polarization at the mass level.[6] However, when political elites view compromise and cooperation as desirable, the potential for the viability of a democracy is greater, even though a high degree of polarization may exist at the mass level.

THE DATA

Given the importance of both mass and elite political attitudes and behavior, as well as the activities of political parties during the first years of the democratic regime, we used several different kinds of data in this study. These included in-depth interviews with national- and provincial-level party leaders; a national survey of the Spanish electorate; materials gathered during observation of the 1979 parliamentary election campaign; party programs and other documents; informal interviews with a small number of Madrid residents in spring 1979; press coverage of political events in 1977–1979; and social, economic, and political data aggregated at the provincial level.

In-depth interviews were undertaken with national- and provincial-level leaders of the then-largest political parties: the UCD, the PSOE, the PCE, the AP, the Convergència Democràtica de Catalunya (CDC), and the PNV. Four waves of interviews were conducted by Richard Gunther: 72 preelection interviews were held between April and July 1978; 52 postelection interviews were conducted in June and July 1979; 15 follow-up interviews were held in Madrid in 1981; and another 59 interviews were undertaken in June and July 1983. Finally, extensive follow-up interviews with Felipe González and Adolfo Suárez were conducted in May 1984.

The purpose of interviews with national-level leaders (some of whom are listed in the acknowledgments) was to acquire information about their "historical memories," their assessments of the stability of the new regime, and how these affected their party-building strategies; the manner in which they (in the case of UCD and AP elites) forged elite-level coalitions in the early stages of creating their respective parties; and, in all cases, the party models that guided their efforts, as well as the actual processes by which they extended their party organizations into the provinces. Interviews with national-level party leaders also focused on the ideological stands, electoral strategies, and tactics employed in the 1979 parliamentary election campaign, and the nature of the parties' relations with various secondary organizations (most importantly, religious associations and trade unions). Finally, whenever an elite respondent had played an important role in the writing of the Constitution or a regional autonomy statute (e.g., Adolfo Suárez, Manuel Fraga, Alfonso Guerra, Rafael Arias Salgado, Jordi Solé Tura, Xabier Arzallus, Pello de Irujo,

José María Alkain, and Josep María Cullell), interviews dealt with those decision-making processes, as well as the values, calculations, and perceptions that underlay those decisions.

Interviews with provincial-level party leaders (see appendix C) focused on the processes through which party branches were created or, in the cases of the PCE, PSOE, and PNV, the histories of clandestine provincial party branches during the Franquist regime. They were also aimed to assess the degree of institutional development and organizational resources at the disposal of each branch (total number of party members; proportion of members who pay dues, attend party meetings, and contribute voluntary labor during election campaigns; etc.). Provincial-level interviews also dealt with the manner in which party strategies and tactics were adjusted to fit with local circumstances and with the characteristics of that province itself (e.g., whether its clergy was progressive or conservative). Provincial-level respondents proved to be excellent sources of information about intraparty conflicts of various kinds—topics that some national-level leaders were hesitant to discuss. Finally, in those regions within which support for micronationalist movements or demands was widespread (most importantly, Catalunya and Euskadi, but also Galicia, Andalucía, Navarra, and Valencia), interviews dealt with the dynamics of each regional party system, as well as the nature and origins of support for regional challenges to the state.

The mass survey of 5,439 Spaniards was carried out in April and May of 1979 by DATA S. A. of Madrid. The protocols (see appendix E) included a common segment that was administered to all respondents and five distinct sections used in the regions of Euskadi, Catalunya, Galicia, Navarra, and Valencia, where the regional autonomy issue was important. The sample was stratified by both region and size of community (see appendix D). The questionnaire included both closed and open-ended items. In addition to a number of standard sociodemographic characteristics of the respondents, the questions dealt with the political relevance of religion, class, and orientations regarding regional autonomy; evaluations of political

institutions and politicians; partisanship; ideological predispositions; images of parties; definitions of left and right; attitudes toward
democracy; and degrees of political participation.

To gain a better understanding of voters' perceptions of politics
and the motivations behind their electoral choices, Giacomo Sani
conducted informal taped interviews with about 80 Madrid residents in spring 1979. These persons by no means constituted a representative sample, but the men, women, and young people interviewed belonged to different social groups and had widely different
political leanings. These conversations covered a wide range of topics, including evaluations of the new democratic institutions and of
the new and old political class, sources of political information, feelings toward parties, reasons for voting choices, attitudes toward labor unions and other important social groups, and assessments of
the future. The information provided by these interviews was used
to illustrate and enrich the findings based on the nationwide survey.

Finally, the activities of the four major parties during the last
month of the 1979 campaign in Madrid were observed by Giacomo
Sani and Goldie Shabad. The authors attended party rallies, viewed
television broadcasts by leaders of all political parties, and collected
campaign-related materials.

CHAPTER TWO

Past as Prologue

In his opening speech before the newly elected democratic Cortes on July 22, 1977, King Juan Carlos stated to the Cortes (parliament), "We must strive to eliminate forever the historic causes of our confrontations."[1] Indeed, Spain has experienced great difficulties in sustaining stable democratic regimes. Both of its previous experiments in democracy, the Restoration Monarchy of 1874–1923 and the Second Republic of 1931–1936, culminated in the establishment of authoritarian regimes. The collapse of the Second Republic was particularly traumatic, insofar as it was accompanied by a long and bloody civil war (1936–1939).

This is not the place for a thorough analysis of the origins of the Civil War, a description of the Franquist regime, or a detailed account of the events that brought about the transition from authoritarianism to the present democracy.[2] An understanding of the problems encountered in creating a competitive party system, however, requires some familiarity with the historical context from which partisan institutions and voting patterns emerged. This chapter sets forth a brief description of the most salient features of two of these three recent historical periods, especially those most relevant to the mass-level, elite-level, and institutional factors on which we focus in our exploration of the founding of the post-Franco party system. Some knowledge of the Republican era is necessary for understanding contemporary political behavior, insofar as the deep-rooted cleavages in Spanish society that led to the collapse of the democratic regime are still present (albeit in modified form), and insofar as "historical memories" shaped perceptions and interpretations of the events of

13

recent years. During the Franquist era, a profound transformation of the Spanish economy and society occurred, and the roots of many political and quasi-political institutions of today were laid down. Finally, the peaceful, evolutionary character of the post-Franco transition contributed greatly to the stability of the current democratic regime and partly determined which of the many emerging political parties would survive into the 1980s.

THE SECOND REPUBLIC

The Second Republic was weakened and ultimately toppled by deep-rooted social conflict, by destabilizing characteristics of basic political institutions, by various aspects of the Spanish political culture, and by certain features of the international political environment. Specifically, that democratic regime collapsed because it could not adequately regulate conflicts that arose out of three historic cleavages in Spanish society—those involving the social and political roles of the Catholic Church, class differences, and struggles for autonomy from the Castilian state on the part of Basque and Catalán nationalists.[3] Conflict resolution was further hampered by a highly fragmented party system and by an electoral law that greatly distorted the popular vote, produced dramatic changes in the partisan composition of the Cortes from one election to the next, and thereby undermined prospects for incremental conflict resolution. These conflicts were exacerbated by the rancorous and uncompromising behavioral styles of key sectors of the Spanish political elite of the era,[4] by the ascendency of fascism in many European countries, and by the economic crisis of the 1930s.

The relationship between politics and religion in Spain has been both long and tumultuous. Formal ties between Church and state can, in fact, be traced as far back as the Visigothic era.[5] But that association was subjected to serious challenges beginning in the eighteenth century. Over the next 150 years, in particular, conflicts over the proper role of the Catholic Church in Spanish society were so intense as to have given rise to numerous outbreaks of anticlerical violence. The founding of the Second Republic in 1931 coincided with a particularly virulent upsurge of anticlerical sentiments. Its constitution represented a clear victory for anticlerical forces in this struggle. It abruptly disestablished the Church, cut off subsidies to religious organizations, secularized cemeteries, legalized divorce, confiscated Jesuit properties, excluded religious orders from participation in the education system and threatened some of them with expulsion, and posed a direct threat to the continued existence of the private sector of education. As a result, it alienated religious Spaniards from that democratic regime.[6] These tensions were clearly reflected in the party system of the Second Republic: bourgeois anticlerical parties (such as Manuel Azaña's Left Republicans) and left-wing parties (the largest being the Spanish Socialist Workers' Party—PSOE) were arrayed against the right-wing CEDA (Confederación Española de Derechas Autónomas, led by José María Gil Robles) and other clerical forces. The venomous rancor of some of the antagonists in this conflict polarized opinion concerning these issues and encouraged the outbreak of clerical versus anticlerical violence.[7] Ultimately these religious-based conflicts could not be regulated successfully, and they contributed decisively to the outbreak of the Civil War.

Similarly, the manner in which class conflicts were articulated during the Second Republic greatly intensified intergroup hostilities and destabilized the regime. One factor that contributed to polarization was that both urban workers (in the industrial zones of Catalunya, Euskadi, and Asturias, and in Madrid) and the rural working classes (particularly in the latifundist areas of Andalucía and Extremadura) were represented by trade unions which often preferred maximalist rhetoric to pragmatic bargaining and which sometimes engaged in direct, violent action as a means of securing social and political objectives. This was particularly true of the anarchosyndicalist Confederación Nacional del Trabajo (CNT), which had between 1.5 and 2 million members, concentrated principally in the latifundist south and in Catalunya.[8] Its formal ideology rejected representative democracy, favoring instead direct, violent strike action as a means of bringing about social revolution.[9] The formal ideology of the socialist Unión General de Trabajadores (UGT) (which also had about 2 million members, most of them in Asturias, Euskadi, Madrid, and, increasingly after 1933, in rural areas of the south)[10] was, by comparison, minimalist and reformist in tone.[11] Under the leadership of Francisco Largo Caballero (referred to by many of his followers as "the Spanish Lenin"),[12] however, important segments of the UGT shifted to maximalist political and social demands after 1933. This culminated in a bloody revolt in Asturias, which, to some extent, can be regarded as a dress rehearsal for the Civil War. These manifestations of conflict were rooted in the inegalitarian structure of Spanish society and dismal living conditions for workers, particularly for landless day laborers in the agricultural south.[13] Employers and their allies in government, moreover, sometimes used violent means of stifling working-class dissent: the 1934 revolt in Asturias, for example, was put down by the army and police with an extreme degree of brutality.[14]

The third major social cleavage divided the Castilian center of the Spanish state from regions with distinctive languages and cultural traditions. Ever since its creation, Spain has been a multilingual, multicultural society: the vast majority of the population of Galicia (see map 1) speak Gallego, the parent tongue of modern Portuguese; several closely related dialects derived from medieval Occitan (the most important being Catalán, Valenciano, and Mallorquín) are spoken in Catalunya, Valencia and the Balearic Islands; and Euskera (the Basque language) is not an Indo-European language.[15] Powerful micronationalist movements began to emerge toward the end of the nineteenth century in Catalunya and Euskadi that directly challenged the centralized Castilian state.[16] These movements (represented in Euskadi mainly by the PNV, and in Catalunya by the left-wing Esquerra and the conservative Lliga) demanded the decentralization of the Spanish state and the restoration of regional self-government, which had been progressively reduced or eliminated during the eighteenth and nineteenth centuries.[17] Tensions arising out of the centralizing tendencies of the government in Madrid had, in fact, given rise to four civil wars (in 1640, 1700–1715, 1835–1839, and 1876) prior to the establishment of the Second Republic. To some extent, the Civil War of 1936–1939 may be regarded as yet another manifestation of this long-term struggle between center and periphery: Catalán and Basque nationalists opposed the rising by the Spanish army mainly because they wanted to defend or reestablish semi-autonomous regional governments.

The severity of these three social cleavages would have posed a grave challenge to any democratic regime. Dealing with these conflicts was made even more difficult by certain features of the party system of the Second Republic, which were, in turn, partly a result of its peculiar electoral law. In order to facilitate the formation of governing majorities in the Cortes, that law permitted voters in each of the 60 electoral districts[18] to cast as many votes as were defined as a "majority" of seats in that district.[19] In effect, this gave the parties or local-level coalitions that received a plurality of popular votes between 75 and 80 percent of the seats in most districts. The second largest party or coalition in each constituency received all the remaining seats. In the Madrid municipal district, for example, there were 17 total seats, and each voter could cast 13 votes. In the 1933 election, this meant that the Socialists, with 175 thousand popular votes, won 13 seats. The conservative coalition received 170 thousand votes but was allocated only 4 seats, while the Left Republicans and Radicals, with 100 thousand votes, received no parliamentary representation at all.[20]

This electoral law had several undesirable consequences. It favored the formation of broad electoral alliances within each district or region, rather than the merger or consolidation of parties at the national level. This, in turn, facilitated the proliferation of independent parties and produced a highly fragmented party system. In each of the three legislatures of the Second Republic (1931–1933, 1933–1935, and February–July 1936) more than 20 parties received parliamentary representation, with at least 11 parties in each session having ten or more seats.[21] In none of those legislatures did a single party control more than 23 percent of the seats. This meant that broad-based multiparty coalitions were required for the formation of a government. As one might expect, this led to considerable cabinet instability: during the 25 months of the 1933–1935 Cortes session, for example, there were 13 government crises.[22] This extreme fragmentation may also have reinforced the uncompromising behavioral style characteristic of important Republican political leaders. Sartori has argued that "beyond a certain limit, the more the number of parties increases, the more their identification becomes a problem; and the remedy to which each party has recourse in order to be perceived as distinct is a punctilious ideological and principled rigidity."[23] If this analysis is correct, then the "fragmentation" of the Second Republic's party system may have greatly reduced the prospects for satisfactory management of the deep-rooted social conflicts described above.

A second serious defect of that electoral law was that, by so distorting the parliamentary representation of each political group, it created the illusion within the Cortes of an overwhelming mandate in favor of the policy proposals of the victorious coalition, when, in fact, that coalition may have received a bare plurality of the popular vote. In the 1936 election, for example, the Popular Front coalition received only 34.3 percent of the popular vote but controlled a substantial majority of the seats in the Cortes (263 out of 474).[24] This distorting influence was particularly apparent in the composition of the constituent Cortes, within which anticlerical forces held a massive majority. The effect of the electoral law (despite its description by a prime minister of that time as "capricious and arbitrary")[25] contributed to the belief that compromise was unnecessary in making such fundamental decisions as writing a constitution.[26]

Finally, the great sensitivity of the electoral law to slight shifts in public opinion produced changes of landslide proportions from one legislature to the next. Accordingly, parties of the left received 299 seats in the constituent Cortes, fell to 100 in the 1933–1935 legislature, but then surged to 280 in the Popular Front election. These drastic pendular swings in the ideological composition of the parliament produced abrupt reversals in certain crucial public policies. As the balance of power shifted from the anticlerical, center-left legislature of 1931–1933 to the proclerical, center-right governments of 1933–1935, and then back to the anticlerical left in 1936, policy decisions pertaining to each of the three crucial cleavages discussed above were reversed. The Catalán regional government (the Generalitat), created in 1932, was suspended in 1934, but then reinstated in 1936. Implementation of the pro–public education and anticlerical legislation passed in 1931–1933 was halted during the following biennium and was then accelerated in 1936.[27] The land reform undertaken in 1932–1933 was stopped in its tracks by the succeeding government but then revived and drastically increased in 1936.[28] And labor and social reform legislation enacted in 1931–1933 was effectively replaced by government inaction, increased unemployment, and a decline in the standard of living of the working classes under the conservative coalitions.[29]

The effects of these pendular swings were twofold. First, the rejection of legislation enacted under the previous Cortes meant that serious issues would not be sequentially and incrementally dealt with and resolved. Instead, they remained open policy questions and became increasingly salient to competing groups. But these abrupt shifts had a direct influence on mass politics as well: they produced an alternation of sentiments veering from greatly increased hopes to frustration and despair, and vice versa. Evidence suggests that this phenomenon may have contributed to the massive land seizures in the latifundist south and the increased political violence throughout Spain in the months immediately preceding the outbreak of the Civil War.

Finally, the Europe of the 1930s did not constitute an environment that would have facilitated the creation of a new democratic regime. The economic depression contributed to a worsening of class conflict and reduced the volume of resources available to governmental elites.[30] The rise to power of fascist governments in Germany and Italy, moreover, legitimated somewhat the expression of nondemocratic or antidemocratic attitudes and provided models for emulation by the enemies of the newly emerging Second Republic.

Thus, Spain's most recent democratic experiment was unsuccessful because long-standing social conflicts—between believer and anticlerical, between employer and industrial worker, between landless peasant and latifundist landowner, and between Spanish nationalist and Basque and Catalán nationalists—could not be adequately dealt with through institutional channels. The electoral system permitted a proliferation of parties such that all possible shades of opinion concerning basic issues were represented[31] but also intensified conflict over them and impeded their resolution. A hostile international environment further complicated the already difficult task of founding a new regime.

THE FRANQUIST REGIME

The regime created by General Franco and the Nationalist forces in the aftermath of the Civil War represented a drastic swing of the pendulum.[32] The Franquist regime was, in many respects, the mirror image of the final government of the Second Republic—that of the Popular Front. Where the Popular Front parties were anticlerical, the Franquist regime and its dominant elites were overwhelmingly favorable to the Catholic Church. Where the Popular Front government had restored the Catalán Generalitat and hastily (following the outbreak of the Civil War) granted autonomy to Euskadi, the state under Franco was rigidly centralized and Spanish nationalist in its "mentality." Where the principal working-class and leftist organizations of the Republican era (the PSOE, the communist PCE, the Trotskyite Partido Obrero de Unificación Marxista, and the anarchosyndicalist CNT) militarily opposed the generals' rebellion, the Franquist state administration was upper class in sociodemographic composition and conservative in its political predilections. Finally, where the Second Republic was democratic, the Franquist regime was authoritarian.

In a drastic reversal of the anticlerical values and policies of the left and center-left government of the Second Republic, and even of the Republican constitution, the Franquist regime restored the Catholic Church to its earlier privileged position in Spanish society.[33] Catholicism once again held the status of an official religion and was subsidized by the state from taxes and other revenues. All anticlerical legislation passed under the Republic was repealed, and divorce was abolished. In addition, the Church was given a dominant role in the education system. Most schools at the intermediate level were directly operated by the Church,[34] and religious instruction became a required part of the curriculum from the elementary through the university levels, in both public and private schools.

The founders of the Franquist regime also reacted against what they perceived to be the decomposition of a nation-state under the Second Republic. Regional government bodies, such as the Generalitat, were abolished, and virtually all important government decisions, including the appointment of heads of local governments (mayors and provincial civil governors), were made by the highly centralized state administration. But Franquist hostility toward regionalism went beyond merely restructuring institutions of government. Systematic campaigns were waged against the Basque and Catalán languages (whose public use was banned during the early years of the regime) and against symbols of cultural distinctiveness: displays of Basque and Catalán flags were illegal, the dancing of the Catalán *sardana* was suppressed, Basque names were forcibly Castilianized, and even Basque tombstones were scraped clean. Needless to say, only Castilian was used in the education system and by the media.

Because the Franquist regime was founded by a coalition of social groups opposed to a leftist Popular Front government claiming to represent the working class, it is not surprising that the social composition of its political and administrative elites was top-heavy, and the values of government officials were overwhelmingly conservative.[35] Accordingly, upper social strata had favored access to decision makers in the formulation of public policy, and the regime's economic policies (such as its highly regressive taxation system) tended to benefit these same groups.[36] The regime's propaganda network, moreover, waged a ceaseless campaign against Marxists and, particularly, Communists, who, along with Freemasons, were regarded as posing a grave threat to Spanish civilization.[37]

Above all, the Franquist regime represented a reaction against the democratic institutions and procedures of the Second Republic. Franco believed that the collapse of civil order in Spain under that regime had been brought about by the self-serving behavior of elected officials, and that competing political parties had divided Spain into warring camps. Thus, the Franquist regime was authoritarian. It was based on an explicit rejection of mass suffrage as a source of legitimacy and as a means of elite recruitment. Francisco Franco, as "Generalísimo of the Army, Chief of State, and, by the Grace of God, Caudillo of Spain and of the Crusade," was the ultimate repository of legitimate authority.[38] All key decision makers (the Council of Ministers, civil governors, mayors of large cities, high-ranking bureaucrats, and others) were either directly or indirectly appointed by, and responsible to, him. Moreover, even though he rarely played an active role in the actual formulation of public policy, he imposed constraints on the range of possible policy options available to the state administration, thereby preserving the basic characteristics of that regime until his death in 1975.[39]

"Representative" institutions within an "organic democracy" were created, but they were by no means comparable to legislative bodies in democratic states. These organizations—the Cortes, *diputaciones provinciales* (provincial legislatures), and *ayuntamientos* (city councils)—were much weaker and less independent than their democratic counterparts: the Council of Ministers, for instance, was neither invested by the Cortes nor could it be toppled by a vote of no confidence. Most legislative matters were to be ratified by the Cortes, but the government's ability to control its internal deliberations and to enact a wide range of legislation by decree meant that the Cortes would not perform a "transformative" role in the legislative process.[40] (To some extent, however, the Cortes did serve as a conservative "watchdog," deterring some bureaucrats from introducing legislation that could be regarded by the Franquist "inner circle" as too progressive.)[41]

These "representative" bodies were also different from democratic legislatures insofar as they were largely constituted along "corporatist" lines. In keeping with the corporatist philosophies that were so widespread in the 1930s, the regime explicitly rejected the concept of social class, which it regarded as inherently conducive to social disintegration. Instead of being based on notions of "class interest" or "group interest," representation formulas all involved "organic" or "natural" social units. Accordingly, the "horizontal" trade unions of the Second Republic were outlawed and were replaced by 27 "vertical" syndicates, representing the various sectors of the economy, such as "chemicals," "education," and "metals." All persons employed in each sector—from managers and technicians to common laborers—were to be represented by a single syndicate. Labor conflict, most importantly in the form of strike activity, was made illegal, but in return workers were granted a high degree of job security. Inconsistent with corporatist philosophy (but understandable, in light of the social bases of support for the regime), organizations representing upper-class interests, such as professional and trade associations, were permitted to remain independent and entirely outside of the syndical structure. This inconsistency, coupled with frequent and severe crackdowns on emerging underground trade unions, led sociologist José María Maravall to describe the Franquist regime as a "labor-repressive," "dictatorial capitalist state."[42] The Cortes was also reconstituted largely along corporatist lines, but with some departures from those principles—the most important of which was the direct election of "family representatives" after 1967.[43]

Throughout the life of the regime, political parties were outlawed, and the underground vestiges of Socialist and Communist parties were subjected to sometimes brutal police repression. Even *procuradores* (members of parliament) in the Cortes were prevented from forming factions or even informal caucuses, although some "family representatives" acted individually in a semi-opposition role at times.[44] The only "political party" formally sanctioned by the regime was the Movimiento Nacional (National Movement)—a greatly diluted version of the fascist Falange, some of whose leaders, prior to 1942, had aspirations of forming a revolutionary, totalitarian, single-party state.[45] Franco's basic conservatism and lack of ideological commitment (other than to Spanish nationalism and Roman Cathol-icism), coupled with opposition from the other segments of the Na-tionalist coalition, led to the quashing of such aspirations, and to the transformation of the Falange's revolutionary fascist ideology.[46] By the end of this process, José Luís de Arrese (who headed the party from 1940 to 1945) could summarize its "ideology" by stating simply, "We believe in God, Spain and Franco."[47] Not only did the Falange (renamed the Movimiento Nacional in 1958) fail to secure its revolu-tionary objectives, but by the 1960s it had even ceased to be a channel of elite recruitment. It also failed to exert a significant influence in the formulation of public policy. Virtually all that was left for the party was management of the massive syndical bureaucracy, of a chain of newspapers, and of occasional propaganda campaigns against Communists and other "enemies of Spain." In the end the Movimiento was reduced to "a noisy propaganda machine, an over-grown bureaucracy, and a few immature students."[48]

THE ROOTS OF CHANGE

Although the political institutions of the Franquist regime re-mained as an anachronism in the Western Europe of the 1960s and 1970s, Spanish society had undergone a profound transformation. Stanley Payne has written that, "on the basis of civic culture, literacy rates and economic development, it might be hypothesized that by 1930 Spain was at the level of England in the 1840s and 50s or France in the 1860s or 70s."[49] This lag was dramatically reduced, if not en-tirely eliminated, by the 1970s. By that time Spain had become a major industrial power,[50] and its gross national product per capita had risen to a level comparable to those of other Western European countries. Most of this economic development took place during a relatively short period of time: between 1964 and 1973 the Spanish economy grew in real terms at a rate of 7.3 percent per year—a growth rate second only to that of Japan among major Western econ-omies.[51] Gross national product per capita rose from less than $300 in 1960[52] to $3,260 in 1977, a figure just short of Italy's $3,530, but well above those for Portugal ($1,840), Greece ($2,950), and Ireland ($3,060).[53] During this period, rapid social change took place. The percentage of the labor force engaged in agriculture, forestry, hunting, and fishing, for example, declined from over 46 percent in 1930[54] to 24.8 percent in 1970.[55]

This shift was accompanied by a considerable urbanization of the Spanish populace: the percentage of Spain's population residing in municipalities over 100 thousand in size increased from 14.8 percent in 1930 to 36.8 percent in 1970.[56] Because Spanish industry is concentrated in Catalunya, Euskadi, and Madrid, this change was accompanied by a massive interregional migration. Between 1931 and 1970, over 1.5 million persons left Andalucía;[57] 1.1 million migrated from the provinces of León and Old Castile;[58] 0.75 million left the rural provinces of New Castile;[59] over 500 thousand left Galicia;[60] and more than 600 thousand migrated from Extremadura.[61] Meanwhile, Madrid and Barcelona were each recipients of 1.5 million migrants, and the Basque provinces of Vizcaya and Guipúzcoa received over 400 thousand and Valencia over 300 thousand.[62] The impact of this migration, coupled with the natural population growth, is that Catalunya, Madrid, Valencia, and Euskadi have nearly doubled in population since 1930, while the populations of Old Castile, León, and Galicia have remained static, and that of Extremadura has actually declined.[63] In general terms, by the mid-1970s the rural areas were becoming depopulated, while Madrid and the industrial north and northeast were burgeoning.

In conjunction with the socioeconomic modernization that occurred during the decades preceding the 1970s, Spanish literacy levels and consumption habits became more like those of other Western European countries. The extent of illiteracy in Spain in 1930 was strikingly high, with estimates ranging between 26 and 31 percent.[64] By 1970 nine out of ten Spaniards could read.[65] Similarly, by 1975 there was one automobile in circulation for every seven Spaniards, and 85 percent of Spanish households had television sets. This would seem to indicate that Spain had become a mass-consumption society, even if it did lag somewhat behind its wealthier European neighbors.[66]

Although the economic miracle of the 1960s and early 1970s may have irrevocably altered the structure of Spanish society and enriched its economy, the benefits of that economic growth were by no means evenly distributed. In fact, a 1975 study concluded: "The economic development of this past decade . . . is not contributing to the diminution of social inequalities; on the contrary, it is tending to make them ever greater."[67] Indeed, Gini coefficients (measuring inequality in the distribution of income) increased from .378 in 1964, to .446 in 1967, and to .487 in 1970.[68] By 1970, the top 1.23 percent of the Spanish population in terms of income possessed a larger portion of the total national income (22.39 percent) than did the bottom 52.2 percent of the population (who possessed only 21.62 percent of the national income),[69] and by 1976, "The richest 10 percent were nearly twice as rich as their opposite numbers in the U.K."[70] The uneven pattern of Spanish economic development also contributed to great interregional imbalances in the possession of wealth. In 1977 Spain's five richest provinces (the three Basque provinces, Barcelona, and Madrid) had per capita incomes over twice as great as those of the five poorest provinces (Lugo, Orense, Granada, Badajoz, and Jaén).[71]

At the same time that the Spanish economy was developing, the Franquist regime was subjected to serious new internal stresses. Indeed, it could be argued that economic development and social change were the direct cause of several emerging challenges to the authoritarian political institutions of that regime. Maravall, for instance, argues that the abandonment of autarchy, the entry of Spain into the international capitalist order, and rapid economic development after 1958 greatly stimulated the reemergence of clandestine "horizontal" trade union organizations and a massive increase in illegal strike activity.[72] Under the original corporatist system of labor relations, workers were prevented from striking, and wage levels were established by the Ministry of Labor; but, in return, employers were prevented from firing their employees and could transfer them to new tasks only with great difficulty. Faced with new competition from foreign producers after 1958, employers came to believe that these job-security provisions undermined productivity to such an extent that they more than offset the benefits derived from this system. Consequently, during the 1960s and 1970s employers entered into de facto collective bargaining with worker representatives, offering them better pay and fringe benefits than were officially sanctioned by the labor ministry, in exchange for greater flexibility in reallocating their labor forces and other productivity-related provisions. This paved the way for the reemergence of trade unions, such as the Comisiones Obreras (Workers' Committees), the Unión Sindical Obrera (USO), and the UGT, which in turn, facilitated the reemergence of political party activity.

The abandonment of autarchy and the encouragement of temporary emigration by unemployed and underemployed workers after 1960 gave rise to other challenges to the regime as well: extended periods of residence in democratic Western European societies exposed Spanish workers to models for emulation that were incompatible with Franquist authoritarianism. In many instances these migrants became members of Socialist or Communist trade unions and political parties while resident in the host country. Upon their return to Spain they were quickly integrated into the corresponding party or trade union, then reorganizing in clandestinity. The impact of this experience abroad was by no means negligible: between 1960 and 1973 over 1.5 million Spaniards emigrated in search of work to other European countries (mainly West Germany, France, and Switzerland). It is estimated that, in 1975, 850 thousand workers (8 percent of the labor force) were residing outside of Spain.[73]

The desire to encourage economic development even undermined ideological consensus within the state administration itself. After 1957 the technical expertise required to manage an advanced capitalist economy and a rapidly changing social structure led increasingly to the recruitment of relatively apolitical technocrats to staff the middle and upper positions of the bureaucracy.[74] Many of these officials did not share the conservative and/or authoritarian social values of the original Nationalist coalition, which they gradually displaced from positions of power, and they ultimately played important roles in dismantling the Franquist regime.

Finally, it could be argued that socioeconomic modernization it-self produced the most direct long-term challenge to the Franquist regime by mobilizing large numbers of previously passive Spaniards for more active roles in politics. One of the most well-substantiated hypotheses in the social sciences is that socioeconomic change cre-ates protoparticipatory orientations within populations; as societies modernize, their populations tend to become more politically active or, at least, to expect and demand more active roles in the political system.[75] Even within relatively developed societies, those individ-uals who possess more of those attributes commonly associated with modernity (e.g., higher education levels or urban residence) tend to be the most active participants.[76] Consistent with this interpretation, overt protest activity in the form of strikes and demonstrations in-creased greatly among industrial workers and the most "modern" sector of society—university students—following' the economic "take-off" in the early 1960s. Student demonstrations and the begin-nings of massive protests in Euskadi were so severe as to lead the government to declare a "state of emergency" on three separate oc-casions between 1968 and 1970.[77]

Other changes in the Spanish political environment of the 1960s and 70s had little or nothing to do with social modernization per se. The most important of these was the modified stance of the Spanish Catholic Church following Vatican Council II. By the late 1960s the Franquist regime could no longer count on the Church for undi-vided loyalty and support, as it did during the 1940s and early 1950s. Indeed, among the regime's most active opponents were many young priests and some influential members of the Church hierarchy itself.

Vatican II brought about a greater concern on the part of the Church for the plight of the poor, as well as a tacit acceptance of social activism by the clergy. These new attitudes and committments facilitated a significant shift in the political orientations of the Span-ish clergy, especially among younger priests. A poll of the Spanish clergy undertaken by the Joint Assembly of Bishops and Priests in 1971 clearly revealed the extent of this change.[78] In that survey of over 15 thousand priests (about 85 percent of the total Spanish clergy), the political preference that received the greatest support was "socialism" (24.8 percent of those polled), while "workers' movements" followed in third place (12.6 percent). It is clear that this change from the Church's past political conservatism occurred largely along generational lines: 47 percent of the youngest priests most highly favored "socialism," while among the oldest priests in this sample only 3.9 percent expressed such a preference. At that same assembly, motions were passed that called for a significant revision of the existing relationship between the Church and the Franquist state in the direction of greater institutional "autonomy and independence" and the progressive elimination of "every real or apparent situation of mutual concession of privileges."[79]

Church opposition activities were not strictly limited to these legal and public manifestations: religious officials were sometimes involved in "alegal" and even illegal behavior as well. The most significant form of this involvement was the use of religious organizations (which, in accord with the 1953 Concordat, were protected from police interference or harassment) as a façade behind which overt political opposition activities could take place. Catholic lay organizations, such as the HOAC (Hermandades Obreras de Acción Católica) and the JOC (Juventudes Obreras Católicas), sometimes served as infrastructures for labor protests (including massive strikes on occasion), which otherwise would have been vigorously suppressed. The preference of some priests for the reemergence of a competitive party system following the death of Franco also led them to collaborate with illegal party organizations. As a provincial-level Communist leader explained in an interview in June 1978, "During clandestinity they protected us. Most of our meetings took place in church buildings, with the consent of Church officials." One of the most vivid manifestations of such covert partisan involvement occurred in Catalunya: the principal Catalán nationalist party, the CDC, was founded (according to a party official) at a clandestine meeting held at the monastery of Montserrat. Some priests assumed even more direct roles in opposition to the Franquist regime. A Communist leader claimed in a June 1979 interview in Navarra that in his province "priests gave an important impetus to the opposition struggle, even from the pulpit—that is, the weekly sermons of some priests were more political anecdotes than elements of religious meditation." Ultimately, some priests and lay members of religious organizations became leaders of partisan organizations of the left in the post-Franco era—including the Workers' Committees (CCOO), the PCE, the Maoist Partido del Trabajo de España (PTE), and the Maoist/anarchist Organización Revolucionaria de Trabajadores (ORT). In fact, the ORT was led by a former Jesuit priest!

The extent of these changes should not be exaggerated, however. The Spanish Catholic Church did not as a collectivity move sharply to the left during this period. Indeed, many older priests and several bishops remained steadfastly right-wing in both their social and political views. These changes within the Church did mean, however, that by the final decade of the Franquist era the Church could by no means be regarded as a homogeneously conservative institution.

A similar mixture of attitudes favorable and resistant to change existed among the general public as indicated by survey data gathered in the early 1970s.[80] On the one hand, a large majority of Spaniards preferred election over appointment for selecting public officials (82 percent).[81] There were also large majorities who expressed support for other important aspects of a more liberal regime, such as freedom of the press (74 percent), religious freedom (71 percent), and freedom of association for trade unions (58 percent).[82] Furthermore, when people were asked to state their political preferences, fewer than two adults in ten said that they would vote for the Movimiento or the Falange in case of an election.[83] Desire for change was also evident in popular preferences concerning the structure of the Spanish state: 24 percent of those interviewed in a 1975 survey favored regional autonomy; 10 percent, a federal state; and 2 percent, complete independence for certain regions. In Catalunya and the Basque country, in particular, those who expressed a desire for varying degrees of autonomy substantially outnumbered those who were in favor of the status quo.[84] Overall, many Spaniards were in favor of transforming the Spanish political system into something similar to those of its Western European neighbors.[85]

On the other hand, there were significant segments of the population who continued to believe that "it is better for a distinguished man to have authority and decide for us" (36 percent), or "in Spain, the most important thing is to maintain peace and order" (80 percent), or "what we Spaniards need is discipline" (52 percent).[86] Moreover, only 37 percent of respondents in a 1973 survey favored freedom of association for political parties.[87] In that same study, spontaneous answers to a question about "what ought to be done in Spain" indicated that most people were much more concerned with economic and social problems than with politics or political change: only 5 percent of those persons interviewed mentioned "political change," and another 5 percent referred to "political development."[88] Overall, the level of demand for change was far lower at the mass level than among the more articulate layers of public opinion.

There was, moreover, no clear consensus concerning the desired direction or focus of change among those who favored a transformation of the Franquist regime. Respondents in a 1975 study were asked to state their preference among several political systems. Of those who indicated a desire for a regime other than *Franquismo*, 43 percent said that a liberal democracy would be desirable for Spain; 17 percent favored other kinds of regime; and 40 percent said that they did not know or refused to answer.[89]

The policies and behavior of some of the most prominent figures within the Franquist regime itself contributed to this inconsistency and uncertainty of opinion about the future evolution of Spain's political system. Two policy initiatives during the regime's final decade were particularly significant insofar as they partially liberalized Spanish society and gave rise to hopes for more substantial political change. The first was the Press Law enacted in 1966 under the guidance of Minister of Information and Tourism Manuel Fraga Iribarne. This legislation terminated prior censorship of published materials, although publishers were still subject to post hoc suspension or closure for various offenses (as the daily newspaper *Madrid* discovered in 1971). The net effect of this law was to permit daily newspapers and journals, such as *Informaciones, Ya,* and *Cambio 16,* to publish numerous criticisms of the existing regime and calls for reform throughout the early 1970s. Press liberalization also stimulated the publication of materials in regional languages, particularly Catalán.[90] The regime's relaxation of control over the exchange of ideas was particularly pronounced in the universities. As Maravall writes, "Tolerance at the ideological level was unquestionable.... From 1967 to 1975 it was possible to find publications of all varieties of Marxism in Spain."[91] Prominent intellectuals and university professors (such as the ex-Falangist social democrat Dionisio Ridruejo, the leftist Christian Democrat Joaquín Ruíz Giménez, and the socialist Enrique Tierno Galván) openly criticized the regime and called for political reform.

This liberalization did not, however, extend to the realm of political activity. One could think, write and (if properly cautious) publish almost anything; but attempts to translate verbal criticisms into overt political activities were vigorously suppressed. In fact, at the very time that Fraga was implementing his Press Law, the regime was substantially increasing its efforts to snuff out opposition activities in all significant arenas: the CCOO were declared illegal in 1968 and harshly suppressed thereafter; Socialist and Communist provincial party leaders reported in interviews that mass arrests of clandestine party executive committees were most numerous in 1968–1969; and Carr and Fusi write that "police were in permanent occupation of the universities between 1968 and 1973."[92] They further describe the period of political ascendancy of Luis Carrero Blanco as one of "bleak authoritarian rule."[93]

A second significant development began with the December 1973 assassination of the ultraconservative Carrero Blanco and his replacement as prime minister by Carlos Arias Navarro (who served in that capacity until July 1976). Arias was by no means a progressive reformist. He did favor restrained institutional reforms, but only those that would not alter the basic character of the Franquist regime. Arias' most important act in this regard was his announcement, in a televised speech before the Cortes on February 12, 1974, that "the national consensus in support of the regime must in the future be expressed in the form of participation," and that there must be an "increase in the representativeness of its institutions," which would reflect the "real political pluralism of our society."[94] According to Arias, "associations" would not constitute full-fledged political parties, however, and the entire reform process would unfold within a "scrupulous respect for the fundamental principles" of the regime.[95] "Associationism" ultimately proved to be a dead end on the road to democracy. As a result of fierce opposition from the more reactionary segments of the Franquist elite, this reform proposal was scaled back below even the levels that Arias favored: the Statute of Associations enacted in December 1974 required that all associations support the Fundamental Principles of the Movimiento, gave the Movimiento Nacional authority to license (or veto) the formation of associations, and required endorsement of each such group by the signatures of 25 thousand persons residing in at least 15 provinces. Only one association ever met all the above criteria, and only eight groups ever bothered to register as associations.[96]

Nevertheless, associationism was highly significant for the transition. At a crucial point during the final days of the regime, a Franquist government placed on the policy agenda a serious consideration of a substantial political reform proposal. The "spirit of February 12" raised expectations concerning the prospects for political change and immediately stimulated a lively debate within the regime's administrative elite between *aperturistas* (those favoring an opening up of the regime) and those with more conservative political goals. Perhaps more importantly, enactment of the Statute of Associations by the political institutions of the regime while Franco was still alive set a precedent, which was more successfully used by Arias' successor, Adolfo Suárez, and helped pave the way for the use of those same institutions for the purpose of dismantling the regime itself.

By the time of Franco's death in November 1975, it had become clear that socioeconomic and institutional change, as well as modifications in political beliefs at both the mass and elite level of Spanish society had eroded away the underpinnings of his authoritarian regime. At the same time, they provided no definitive clues as to what kind of regime would be created in its place or how it might be brought into existence, and even fewer inklings of what kind of party system might emerge.

THE TRANSITION TO DEMOCRACY

For nearly a year following the death of Francisco Franco, it was entirely unclear how (or even if) a successful transition to democracy could be achieved. The fundamental question was whether it would be possible to establish a democratic regime through an evolutionary process of *reforma*, or whether the old regime could only be dislodged through a more abrupt and probably tumultuous *ruptura*, forced by the mass mobilization of segments of Spanish society. The nature of the transition would greatly affect the degree of polarization in the new system and would have profound consequences for the success or failure of emerging parties. An abrupt, revolutionary break with the former regime, such as had recently occurred in Portugal, could polarize public opinion and could initially benefit the parties that had successfully organized in clandestinity (e.g., the Portuguese Communist party). Conversely, a peaceful, evolutionary transformation of the Franquist regime into a democracy could reinforce the moderate character of mass-level political attitudes and could increase the popularity of reformist groups.

The lack of significant progress toward democratization under the second Arias Navarro government (December 1975 through June 1976), coupled with the existence of institutional obstacles to reform set in place before the Caudillo's death (e.g., the corporatist Cortes and the Council of the Realm),[97] gave rise to pessimism over the prospects for a peaceful *reforma*. Assuming that change could only be brought about through a *ruptura democrática*, most major parties of the clandestine opposition formed broad-based coordinating councils and began to collaborate with each other in their efforts to topple the Franquist regime.[98] They demanded total amnesty for and immediate release of all political prisoners, prompt legalization of all political parties,[99] formation of a provisional government, and immediate elections to a constituent assembly. From the standpoint of the legitimating formula underpinning the process of transition, the most important of their demands were those that called for a complete break with all Franquist institutions and a referendum on the future of the monarchy. The resulting institutional discontinuity would have made impossible a formally legal transition to democracy, thereby precluding a temporary "backward legitimation" of a new regime.[100] In more concrete terms, this might have alienated from the new regime those with lingering sympathies for *franquismo* and heightened the anxieties of those who feared an impending collapse of law and order. Such worries were further amplified by the tactics used by some parties of the illegal opposition. In support of their demands for a *ruptura democrática*, they organized an ever-increasing number of public demonstrations and strikes. Their success in organizing politically motivated strikes by workers was most impressive: Maravall claims that the number of strikes grew from 931 in 1973, to 2,290 in 1974 to 3,156 in 1975, and to 17,731 in 1976, and the number of man-hours lost through such activities increased more than tenfold, from 14.5 million in 1975 to 150 million in 1976.[101] In short, a significant mass mobilization of opposition forces was taking place, and a showdown with the defenders of the Franquist state seemed inevitable. Even though most Spaniards preferred evolutionary reforms over abrupt change, 79 percent of a sample of workers polled in early 1977 also believed that "the egoism of the powerful will make any reform impossible."[102]

Instead, rapid progress toward democratization was made following the dismissal of Carlos Arias Navarro and the appointment of a new government in July 1976. The key to this reform process was the leadership of Adolfo Suárez, a young and relatively unknown product of the Movimiento Nacional, who had previously served under Franco as director general of the state-run television network, and in the first post-Franco government as minister of the Movimiento. In an impressive display of political skill (and with the close collaboration of the King and Torcuato Fernández-Miranda, President of the Cortes and of the Council of the Realm), Suárez persuaded the corporatist Cortes to commit institutional suicide by approving the Political Reform Law in October 1976, which established procedures for future political reforms to be undertaken by a new, democratically elected Cortes. In rapid succession other crucial reforms were enacted: hundreds of political prisoners were granted pardons in July 1976 and March 1977; the Movimiento was disbanded and political parties legalized; the vertical labor syndicates were abolished and replaced by independent trade unions; an electoral law that set the rules for electoral competition was negotiated with opposition political forces; and, despite fierce opposition from certain sectors of the military, the PCE (the Spanish Communist party) was admitted as a legitimate contender in the new political arena.

The evolutionary nature of this transition to democracy was, for several reasons, of great political significance. It contributed to the legitimacy of the new regime in the eyes of many Franquistas by initiating political change according to formal procedures established by the Franquist regime itself. Thus, important sectors of the Franquist regime would play active roles in the reform process, rather than sitting on the sidelines as embittered opponents of change or as vengeful victims of a political purge. The evolutionary nature of the transition also ensured that change would take place within a relatively stable political and institutional environment, and not within a chaotic political vacuum. The Catalán Communist leader Jordi Solé Tura writes that, by way of comparison, "the three great constituent moments of a democratic variety in our constitutional history [1810, 1869, and 1931] took place within a common situation of an institutional vacuum, a radical break with dynastic power, a sudden irruption of important sectors of the populace into the political scene, a military crisis, and a correlation of forces favorable to those groups with the most radical transformative desires."[103] The thoroughness of Suárez's political reforms[104] was also crucial from the standpoint of the regime's viability. The release of political prisoners and the relatively unrestricted licensing of political parties may have had some drawbacks,[105] but those decisions represented positive contributions to the new regime insofar as they brought many potential regime opponents into the democratic game of politics and encouraged them to perform as loyal and trustworthy regime supporters.

CHAPTER THREE

The Emergence of Political Parties

IN THE FORMATIVE STAGES of a democratic regime, a large number of groups are likely to appear on the political scene. Few, however, can realistically expect to survive the test of political competition. The experience of Spain in the transition from authoritarianism to democracy provides a good illustration both of the surfacing of many groups with political ambitions and of the "weeding out" that occurs as a result of the first electoral contest. In 1976 and 1977 over 150 parties, representing an entire spectrum of political positions, came into existence. After the votes were counted and the seats in the new Cortes distributed, it became clear that only a few had obtained parliamentary representation. The response by the mass public to the alternatives posed by competing political groups had eliminated most would-be protagonists but conferred a significant role on others. With the 1977 election the Spanish party system moved from a fluid and magmatic stage to a more definite configuration.

Spain's party system, from the time of that first democratic election until late 1982, was dominated by two relatively moderate political groups—the UCD (Unión de Centro Democrático) and the PSOE (Partido Socialista Obrero Español). Between them they garnered almost 63 percent of the votes cast on June 15, 1977, and over 80 percent of the seats in the lower house (the Congress of Deputies) of the constituent Cortes. The center to center-right UCD received 34 percent of the popular vote and controlled 165 seats in the Congress of Deputies, just 11 short of an absolute majority. On that basis, it was able to form a minority government. The socialist PSOE clearly emerged as the principal party of opposition, with 28.9 percent of the vote and 118 seats. Two other political groups, the PCE (Spanish Communist Party) and the rightist AP (Alianza Popular) fared less well (table 1) but still gained enough votes to insure for themselves a significant role in the new parliament. The remaining few seats were distributed among smaller parties, the most prominent of which were two regional groups, the PDC (Catalán Democrats), a coalition which received 11 seats, and PNV (Basque Nationalist Party), which received 8 seats.

TABLE 1
RETURNS OF THE 1977 ELECTION,
CONGRESS OF DEPUTIES (CORTES ESPAÑOLAS)

Parties	Valid votes	Percentage of valid votes cast	Number of seats	Percentage of seats
UCD	6,309,991	34.0	165	47.1
PSOE	5,371,466	28.9	118	33.7
PCE-PSUC	1,709,870	9.2	20	5.7
AP	1,488,001	8.0	16	4.6
PSP-US	816,582	4.4	6	1.7
PDC	514,647	2.8	11	3.1
PNV	314,272	1.7	8	2.3
UCDCC	172,791	0.9	2	0.6
EC	143,954	0.8	1	0.3
EE	64,039	0.3	1	0.3
DC	257,152	1.4	0	0.0
SD	206,238	1.1	0	0.0
Others	1,217,267	6.5	2[a]	0.6
Total	18,586,270		350	

UCD   Unión de Centro Democrático
PSOE   Partido Socialista Obrero Español and Socialistes de Catalunya
PCE-PSUC   Partido Comunista de España and Partit Socialista Unificat de Catalunya
AP   Alianza Popular
PSP-US   Partido Socialista Popular– Unidad Socialista
PDC   Pacte Democràtic per Catalunya
PNV   Partido Nacionalista Vasco
UCDCC   Coalición Electoral Unió del Centre i la Democracia Cristiana de Catalunya
EC   Esquerra de Catalunya
EE   Euskadiko Ezkerra (includes "Independent" slate #14 in Alava)
DC   Equipo de la Democracia Cristiana, Federación de la Democracia Cristiana, Democracia Cristiana Vasca-Euskal Kristan Demokrasia, Equipo Demócrata Cristiana e Social Democracia Galega, Partido Popular Gallego, Unión Democrática Cristiana, Unión Democrática del País Valenciá, Democracia Cristiana Aragonesa, Democracia Social Cristiana de Catalunya
SD   Alianza Socialista Democrática, Partido Socialista Democrático Español, Centro Izquierda de Albacete, ASD-Centro Izquierda, Reforma Social Española, PSOE (H), and (in Soria only) Independientes.

Source: Ministerio de la Gobernación, Dirección General de la Política Interior, *Elecciones Generales 1977: Resultados Congreso por Provincias.*
[a]Two deputies representing "others" are of Candidatura Aragonesa Independiente de Centro and Candidatura Independiente de Centro in Castellón.

From one perspective, then, what emerged after the death of Franco could be regarded as (what Spanish politicians and journalists called) an "imperfect two-party system."[1] In most of the provinces of Spain it was dominated by two relatively moderate parties, with secondary roles played by two smaller parties farther from the center of the political spectrum. Such a conceptualization, however, fails to take into consideration the existence of two regional party subsystems, within which the dynamics of partisan competition were entirely different from that of the rest of Spain, mainly because of the salience of the center-periphery cleavage. In Euskadi and Catalunya it was the UCD that was reduced to a secondary role, with much of its "political space" occupied by relatively moderate Basque and Catalán nationalist parties. In Euskadi, moreover, a much more fragmented party system emerged, and the level of polarization was much greater than in the rest of Spain. Given the complexity of these regional phenomena, the party systems of Euskadi and Catalunya (as well as of Galicia, for purposes of comparison) will be analyzed separately in a later chapter.

What factors account for the emergence of this particular party system with its two distinct regional subsystems? In our view this development can best be understood as the product of an interacting set of forces operating at three different levels: the institutional, the mass, and the elite levels.

The institutional factor most directly relevant to our explanation of the outcome of the 1977 election and that of 1979 is the electoral law established in March 1977. Any electoral law, and particularly those provisions dealing with the "translation" of popular votes into seats, constitutes a forcing device that affects, to a greater or lesser degree, the fate of different political groups. In a newly emerging party system, the "underrepresentation" or "overrepresentation" of parties is especially important and greatly affects their ability to survive until the next electoral contest. Parties that are denied seats in the first democratic election quickly become invisible to the electorate and may be susceptible to electoral claims by their competitors that continuing popular support for these smaller groups would produce only "wasted votes." However, parties that receive sizable blocs of seats in a constituent parliament will be the subjects of extensive press coverage that, given the importance and the excitement of creating a new political regime, may have a profound impact on public opinion. The highly visible presence of a party in legislative or governmental arenas may thereby contribute to its chances for survival over the long term.

Another institutional factor that affects the viability of parties is the financial resources at their disposal. If, as in Spain, the activities of parties are partly financed out of state tax revenues, then the formula by which those funds are allocated may determine whether a party will go bankrupt or will survive to fight another day.[2]

Political predispositions at the mass level constituted a second important determinant of the emerging party system. (In subsequent chapters, we will deal extensively with the influence of class, religious, and center-periphery cleavages on the structure of partisan competition.) In the years preceding the first democratic election, increasing numbers of Spaniards adopted general attitudes about the desirable degree of political and social change, placed themselves on the left-right spectrum, and identified with various political families—Communist, Socialist, social democratic, liberal, Christian democratic, conservative, etc. The distribution of such attitudes among the electorate meant that certain options offered to voters in the 1977 election would be reduced to relative insignificance, while others would emerge as major political protagonists. At the same time, the political elites' awareness of the overall shape of these general predispositions, coupled with the lack of firmly held partisan preferences at the mass level, meant that the parties that fell within the most populated portion of the political spectrum would have some room to maneuver in fashioning their programmatic committments and electoral strategies.

The third set of important factors influencing the shape of the Spanish party system involves the images, behavior, and strategic decisions of political elites. Before the first democratic election, these individuals had already made several crucial choices, which affected the electoral fates of their respective parties. One set of decisions implicitly or explicitly established or modified the party's position on the political spectrum. Another set pertained to the creation of an organizational infrastructure through which each party could make its electoral appeals: this involved fund raising, choices among various organizational models, the attraction and mobilization of party militants, and the recruitment of candidates for the new Cortes. Finally, and most importantly, party elites played key roles in the transition to democracy, in the course of which they had to make choices that would affect the basic institutions, the legitimacy, and the viability of the new regime.

The behavior of party elites in the transition to democracy not only was significant from the standpoint of the stability of the new regime but affected the electoral fortunes of their respective parties in several ways. As the principal protagonists in the transition, their highly visible activities affected their popularity among voters. In addition, their behavior largely determined the nature of the political environment within which the first democratic elections were held. Strategic or organizational choices made by party leaders may fit well with one kind of political environment but may be inappropriate for another. A mass-mobilization strategy, for example, may be well-suited for an abrupt revolutionary break with the former regime but would be irrelevant or even counterproductive within a stable or moderate electoral context.

The stage during the transition when these various decisions were made also emerges as a significant factor affecting each party's degree of success in attracting votes. All strategic decisions made by party-building elites were made in the face of varying degrees of uncertainty about the ultimate outcome of the transition and, hence, about the electoral utility of those decisions. Uncertainty was greatest at the beginning of the transition, when the issue of *reforma* versus *ruptura* was totally unresolved; it was progressively reduced as the first democratic election drew near. Thus, party-building strategies formulated later in the transition were less likely to be confounded by uncertainty, while the groups that organized earlier sometimes found themselves locked into strategies ill-suited for the political environment that actually evolved. This temporal factor, however, cut both ways. With the passage of time, the political environment also became progressively more structured, and some strategic options were no longer available. Thus, party-building elites were sometimes forced to adopt a course of action that initially may not have been regarded as optimal and that, over the long term, proved to have significant drawbacks.

In making these choices, parties were also constrained by their origins and basic characteristics. (A discussion of regional parties will be deferred until chapter 9.) Among the four nationwide parties to be analyzed here, two, the PCE and PSOE, had existed as antisystem movements throughout the Franquist regime and thus entered the transition to democracy with previously established ideologies, organizational hierarchies, public images, significant levels of affiliation, and historical traditions. The range of strategic choices open to their leaders was, therefore, relatively restricted. Their principal tasks during the transition were to expand as organizations, to modify their public images to fit with their perceptions of voter preferences, and, most importantly, to undertake the transformation from illegal, clandestine antisystem movements to vote-maximizing political parties as quickly and with as little internal disruption as possible. On the other hand, such parties as the UCD, the AP, and, in many respects, the Christian democratic and social democratic alliances were created during this transitional period, and thus had no previous organizations, ideologies, programs, or public images. Consequently, the range of options available to their founders was greater, the decisions were more complex, and their impact on the electoral outcome was more decisive. For the most part, these decisions consisted of choices of coalition partners who would transform tiny clusters of friends or ideological allies into broader-based parties. Implicit in these choices was the definition of the ideological space to be occupied by the new party, which would profoundly affect its electoral appeal.

THE ELECTORAL LAW

Selection of an electoral law prior to the first democratic contest in the life of a new regime is of great importance. In purely partisan terms, political groups will favor adoption of differing electoral systems in accord with their estimations of the size and geographical distribution of their respective blocs of supporters. Thus, parties who believe that they will receive pluralities or near-pluralities of popular votes (such as AP in early 1977) will favor electoral laws that magnify that advantage into larger pluralities or even a majority of seats in parliament. Conversely, smaller parties with geographically dispersed bases of support (such as the PCE) will favor proportional representation formulas. And purely regional parties (such as the Basque and Catalán nationalist parties) will be greatly concerned with the manner in which the boundaries of electoral districts are drawn. The selection of an electoral system is (and is widely regarded as) crucial, insofar as it directly affects each party's prospects for staking out a dominant or at least visible position on the political scene.

But the choice of a particular electoral system is also of great significance from the standpoint of the legitimacy and viability of the new regime itself. A difficult balance must be struck between the need to create a party system conducive to stable government and the need to represent the interests of significant political and social groups. On one hand, excessive fragmentation of the new party system must be reduced in order to facilitate the formation of governments that have the ability to enact legislation and to carry out those programs over reasonable periods of time. This was particularly true of Spain in early 1977, when over 100 political "parties" came into existence. On the other hand, the exclusion of significant political forces from a constituent parliament could threaten the legitimacy of the new regime. Groups excluded from deliberations over establishment of the basic institutions and procedures of a new democracy may, simply because of their exclusion, reject whatever constitution may be produced. In contrast, groups who take part in the constituent process are more likely to conclude that they have a stake in preserving the new regime that they have helped to create.[3] The electoral law ultimately adopted in 1977 represents a reasonable compromise among these competing concerns and conflicting partisan demands.

Decisions concerning the electoral law were made in two steps, both of which entailed negotiations or consultations between the Suárez government and representatives of various political parties. Some features of the new electoral system were contained in the Political Reform Law of 1976. In keeping with the government's initial preferences, proportional representation principles were endorsed. In order to secure Cortes approval of the reform law, however, prime minister Suárez depended on the votes of many *procuradores* affiliated with AP. This enabled the latter to bargain successfully for inclusion in the electoral law of "correctives," designed to reduce party-system fragmentation and, as a byproduct, to reduce the proportionality of representation in the future Congress of Deputies. Thus, the reform law stipulated that the lower house (the only one that will be discussed here) would have 350 members; that a minimum threshold of votes would be required to obtain parliamentary representation; that electoral districts would normally coincide with the 50 provinces; and that each province would be entitled to a minimum number of representatives.[4] The "corrective" influence of the relatively small size of the Congress, coupled with the large number of electoral districts and the guaranteed minimum number of representatives for even the least populous provinces, will be examined below.

These general principles were made specific in a royal decree enacted on March 18, 1977. This decree was promulgated after extensive discussions between the Suárez government and representatives of various opposition groups.[5] These talks were not formal negotiations, per se, and never resulted in a formal agreement between government and opposition forces. Instead, Suárez listened to the appeals of the various parties and, as described by one of the participants, "skillfully translated our demands into the terms of the decree law." The result was the creation of an electoral system that would be (in Suárez's words) "acceptable to all."

The 1977 electoral law resolved several issues left open by the reform law of the previous year. One such provision determined that the D'Hondt method of seat allocation would be used, and another set a minimum of 3 percent as a provincial-level threshold below which a party would not obtain a seat. The most important provision concerned the minimum number of seats to be assigned to each province: at least 2 seats would be awarded in each province, plus 1 additional seat for every 144,500 inhabitants or fraction over 70 thousand inhabitants.[6] In practice, this meant that the smallest provinces obtained 3 seats, and the largest over 30 seats (Barcelona elects 33 deputies, and Madrid, 32). The distribution of provinces by size of congressional delegation is shown in table 2.

The stated purposes of the electoral law were "to avoid excessive fragmentation" and to obtain "a greater territorial equilibrium in representation."[7] But the "correctives" inherent within this proportional representation system also introduced substantial representational biases. The contribution of the smaller districts to the elective assembly would be very significant and out of proportion to their populations. The seven smallest districts, with a combined population of approximately 1.1 million inhabitants, had 21 seats in the Congress of Deputies, while the province of Oviedo, with a roughly similar population of about 1.1 million, could elect only 10 representatives. As can be seen in table 2, the mean number of inhabitants per seat varies considerably and increases systematically as one moves from the smaller to the larger districts. Thus, there is 1 deputy for every 34,636 residents of Soria, while it take 139,569 Madrileños to elect 1 deputy. This distortion in favor of certain districts would not be politically significant if the size of a province's population had nothing to do with political preferences. But in Spain, as elsewhere, this is not the case. The less populated provinces also tend to be rural, agricultural, and less economically developed and thus constitute a better basis of support for conservative or moderate parties

TABLE 2
POPULATION AND NUMBER OF SEATS
OF SPANISH ELECTORAL DISTRICTS

Province	Population	Number of seats	Inhabitants per seat
Avila	187,725	3	62,575
Guadalajara	139,524	3	46,508
Huesca	216,345	3	72,115
Palencia	186,710	3	62,237
Segovia	151,620	3	50,540
Soria	103,908	3	34,636
Teruel	155,449	3	51,816
Albacete	331,390	4	82,848
Alava	238,233	4	59,558
Burgos	349,347	4	87,337
Cuenca	222,306	4	55,577
Lérida	349,233	4	87,300
Logroño	240,736	4	60,184
Salamanca	349,843	4	87,461
Zamora	230,787	4	57,697
Almería	386,776	5	77,355
Cáceres	425,667	5	85,133
Castellón	411,129	5	82,226
Ciudad Real	481,212	5	96,242
Gerona	441,990	5	88,398
Huelva	400,104	5	80,021
Lugo	390,062	5	78,012
Navarra	483,867	5	96,773
Orense	404,945	5	80,989
Santander	490,249	5	98,050
Tarragona	484,583	5	96,917
Toledo	464,226	5	92,845
Valladolid	450,670	5	90,134
Baleares	633,016	6	105,503
Las Palmas	707,330	6	117,888
León	526,496	6	87,749
Badajoz	640,850	7	91,550
Córdoba	717,005	7	102,429
Granada	736,045	7	105,149
Guipúzcoa	682,517	7	97,502
Jaén	645,524	7	92,218
Tenerife	686,958	7	98,137
Cádiz	952,328	8	119,094
Málaga	919,251	8	114,906
Murcia	884,073	8	110,509
Pontevedra	825,607	8	103,201
Zaragoza	802,031	8	100,254
Alicante	1,060,601	9	117,845
La Coruña	1,042,880	9	115,876
Oviedo	1,099,418	10	109,942

TABLE 2 (CONTINUED)

Province	Population	Number of seats	Inhabitants per seat
Vizcaya	1,150,593	10	115,059
Sevilla	1,375,540	12	114,628
Valencia	1,939,488	15	129,299
Madrid	4,466,218	32	139,569
Barcelona	4,506,284	33	136,554

Sources: Except for Madrid and Barcelona, the figures are drawn from the table annexed to the Royal Decree of January 4, 1977, reported in Legislación Electoral, pp. 109–110. The figures for Barcelona and Madrid did not include population numbers; population figures used are from Instituto Nacional de Estadística, Anuario Estadístico 1981, population estimates as of July 1977, pp. 452–55.

than the larger districts, especially those containing large urban or metropolitan centers.

The political impact of the existence of many small districts is compounded by the "D'Hondt" system of seat allocation. Under this method seats are assigned to parties on the basis of the "highest average," which is obtained by dividing the number of votes received by a party by the number of seats already received plus one. Because at the beginning no seats have been assigned, the denominator is one, and the highest average is equal to the total number of votes received by each party. The party with the highest average is awarded the first seat and the distribution then continues until there are no more seats to be assigned. In general, this formula "will penalize small parties in the extreme unless district magnitude is very large or the party system is highly fractionalized."[8] In the Spanish case, the first of these mitigating conditions was eliminated a priori for most districts. There were only six provinces in which ten or more representatives were to be elected, and only the districts of Madrid and Barcelona could be said to be "very large." There remained, therefore, only the second mitigating factor, the degree of fractionalization or, to again use the words of Douglas Rae, "the extent to which competitive strength is concentrated in one party or divided among many."[9] But for this second condition to work, the number of seats to be distributed must be at least as large as the number of parties that are of approximately equal strength.

The impact of the D'Hondt formula can be illustrated by examining different patterns of vote distribution in three Spanish provinces in 1977. The returns of the first, Soria, gave the largest party (UCD) a wide margin over the second party (PSOE), while AP and other groups were even further behind. (See table 3.) Computation of the "highest average" leads to the attribution of the first, second, and third seat to the largest party (35,324, 17,662, 11,774 are, respectively, the values of the highest average for the first 3 seats). Had there been more seats to be distributed, the fourth would have gone to the PSOE, the fifth, sixth, and seventh again to the UCD, and the eighth again to the Socialists. The third party would have come into the picture only if there had been 12 seats at stake. But Soria was a very small district with only 3 seats, and thus not even the second largest party managed to elect a representative. Clearly, in the presence of low fragmentation and small district size, the D'Hondt formula produces devastating results for all but the largest group.

A second pattern of vote distribution is illustrated by the returns in the province of Albacete (table 3). In this case the two largest parties were relatively equal in terms of popular support and were well ahead of other groups. Analysis of the number of votes received shows that the four seats available would be given to the UCD (the first and the third) and to the PSOE (the second and the fourth). The third party, AP, would receive a seat only if the districts had at least eight representatives. As to the fourth largest party, the PCE, its average would become the highest only if there were at least ten seats at stake. This second pattern indicates that, in the context of a relatively small district, the D'Hondt formula is rewarding for, at most, the two largest parties.

The third pattern exemplifies the case of a relatively fractionalized party system. In the province of Tarragona, the vote was dispersed in relatively equal shares among several parties, as table 3 shows. Under these conditions and with five seats at stake, the electoral method provided representation to all four major parties. To be sure, the D'Hondt formula resulted in the overrepresentation of the UCD (two seats), and it denied representation to the fifth party (AP).

TABLE 3
ALLOCATION OF SEATS IN THREE PROVINCES ACCORDING TO THE D'HONDT METHOD

	Seat Assignment Rounds											
	1	2	3	4	5	6	7	8	9	10	11	12
SORIA												
UCD	35,324	17,662	11,774	8,831	8,831	7,065	5,887	5,046	5,046	4,415	3,924	3,532
PSOE	10,757	10,757	10,757	10,757	5,379	5,379	5,379	5,379	3,586	3,586	3,586	3,586
AP	3,792	3,792	3,792	3,792	3,792	3,792	3,792	3,792	3,792	3,792	3,792	3,792
ALBACETE												
UCD	64,603	32,302	32,302	21,534	21,534	16,151	16,151	12,921	12,921	12,921		
PSOE	56,332	56,332	28,166	28,166	18,777	18,777	14,083	14,083	14,083	11,266		
AP	16,005	16,005	16,005	16,005	16,005	16,005	16,005	16,005	8,003	8,003		
PCE	13,623	13,623	13,623	13,623	13,623	13,623	13,623	13,623	13,623	13,623		
TARRAGONA												
UCD	69,014	34,507	34,507	34,507	34,507							
PSOE	59,926	59,926	29,963	29,963	29,963							
PSUC	41,345	41,345	41,345	20,673	20,673							
PDC	37,146	37,146	37,146	37,146	18,573							
AP	15,216	15,216	15,216	15,216	15,216							

Source: Election data from Ministerio de la Gobernación, *Elecciones Generales: Resultados Congreso por Provincias*.
Note: Italicized figures are the "highest average" in each round. Boxed rounds corrspond to the number of seats actually assigned to the three provinces.

In spite of the fact that district size was limited, however, the electoral system did not favor only the two largest parties.

Given these properties of the electoral formula, it is clear that its overall impact would depend on which of these three patterns would turn out to be the most common. If the first two were to prevail, the advantage for the largest and, to a lesser extent, second largest party would be overwhelming. If the more common pattern turned out to be the fractionalized distribution, the smaller parties would be penalized to a lesser degree. In the 1977 election, the "One-Party Dominant" pattern occurred in 18 provinces, and the "High Fractionalization" pattern, in 14 districts (table 4).

Thus, the adoption of this electoral system led to the overrepresentation in most parts of the country of two large parties and the underrepresentation of smaller parties. The outcome could have been different only if the strength of the parties had differed greatly from one part of the country to another, so that a party dominant in one area might have been quite small in another (as in Canada), or if the vote had been highly fractionalized in a large number of districts, that is, if it had been distributed in fairly equal shares among several parties. This second condition occurred only in about a quarter of the districts, mostly in areas where regional parties were strong. The first condition did not occur; the UCD and the PSOE turned out to be the first or the second largest party in an overwhelming number of districts. The UCD garnered more votes than any other party in 37 districts and was the second party in another 9 provinces, while the Socialists were the largest party in 9 districts and the second largest in 37. Thus, in most districts the two major protagonists were the same. The predominance of these two groups meant that other parties could get into the picture only in large districts or in the few provinces where they had an unusually high level of support. This second factor worked to the benefit of the regional parties of Euskadi and of Catalunya. Smaller parties with geographically dispersed bases of support, however, could normally receive seats only in large districts. (See table 5.)

We can thus say that this institutional factor made a significant

TABLE 4
PROVINCIAL DISTRIBUTION OF VOTES AND SEATS IN CONGRESS OF DEPUTIES, 1977

Province	Largest	Second largest	Third largest	Fourth largest	Fifth largest	Sixth largest	Seventh largest
			One-Party Dominant (18 cases)				
Avila	68%(3)	14%	7%	5%	2%	2%	1%
Las Palmas	66 (5)	14 (1)	6	6	3	3	1
Orense	62 (4)	13 (1)	13	2	2	2	2
Soria	59 (3)	18	8	6	5	2	2
Pontevedra	57 (6)	16 (1)	12 (1)	5	3	2	2
Segovia	59 (2)	21 (1)	9	6	2	1	0
Salamanca	56 (3)	23 (1)	8	6	3	3	0
Cuenca	56 (3)	23 (1)	8	6	2	2	2
Tenerife	52 (5)	19 (2)	10	5	4	3	2
Teruel	50 (2)	18 (1)	16	4	3	2	0
La Coruña	50 (6)	18 (2)	11 (1)	5	4	4	3
Lugo	52 (4)	22 (1)	12	6	2	2	2
Cáceres	55 (4)	26 (1)	9	3	2	2	2
Baleares	52 (4)	23 (2)	9	5	5	4	0
Guadalajara	49 (2)	21 (1)	16	7	4	3	1
León	51 (4)	24 (1)	12 (1)	5	3	2	2
Palencia	51 (2)	26 (1)	14	4	3	1	0
Burgos	48 (3)	24 (1)	15	3	3	3	2
			Two-Party Balance (18 cases)				
Almería	50 (3)	27 (2)	8	6	3	3	1
Huesca	46 (2)	28 (1)	11	6	6	2	1
Málaga	43 (4)	27 (3)	12 (1)	8	5	2	1
Badajoz	47 (4)	34 (3)	7	7	2	1	1
Huelva	48 (3)	34 (2)	5	5	3	2	2

(Continued on the following page)

TABLE 4 (CONTINUED)

Province	Largest	Second largest	Third largest	Fourth largest	Fifth largest	Sixth largest	Seventh largest
Granada	44 (4)	32 (3)	10	7	4	1	1
Valladolid	43 (3)	31 (2)	8	6	3	3	3
Murcia	41 (4)	35 (4)	7	7	5	2	2
Jaen	39 (4)	33 (3)	10	8	4	2	1
Ciudad Real	41 (3)	32 (2)	13	6	5	1	0
Albacete	38 (2)	33 (2)	9	8	7	3	1
Santander	40 (3)	26 (1)	14 (1)	5	5	3	2
Alicante	39 (4)	36 (4)	9 (1)	7	4	2	1
Navarra	29 (3)	21 (2)	9	9	7	5	4
Sevilla	37 (5)	33 (5)	13 (2)	6	5	3	1
Cádiz	37 (4)	27 (2)	10 (1)	10 (1)	5	3	3
Valencia	37 (7)	31 (5)	10 (1)	6 (1)	5	3	3
Guipúzcoa	31 (3)	28 (3)	9	8	6	5	5
Fractionalization (14 cases)							
Zamora	46 (2)	24 (1)	20 (1)	4	2	2	1
Logroño	41 (2)	26 (1)	15 (1)	3	3	2	2
Castellón	35 (2)	29 (2)	14 (1)	6	6	3	2
Madrid	32 (11)	32 (11)	11 (4)	11 (3)	9 (3)	1	1
Zaragoza	32 (3)	26 (3)	11 (1)	10 (1)	8	5	3
Toledo	38 (2)	32 (2)	17 (1)	8	3	2	0
Oviedo	32 (4)	31 (4)	14 (1)	10 (1)	7	2	2
Córdoba	34 (3)	33 (3)	17 (1)	9	4	2	1
Barcelona	31 (11)	20 (7)	15 (6)	15 (5)	6 (2)	5 (1)	3 (1)
Vizcaya	31 (4)	25 (3)	16 (2)	7 (1)	5	5 (1)	3
Alava	31 (2)	28 (1)	18 (1)	6	3	3	3
Tarragona	27 (2)	24 (1)	16 (1)	15 (1)	6	3	3
Lérida	25 (2)	25 (1)	15 (1)	12	10	8	4
Gerona	27 (2)	25 (2)	18 (1)	10	10	5	6

Source: Ministerio de la Gobernación, Dirección General de la Política Interior, Elecciones Generales 1977.
Note: The "one-party dominant" category is differentiated from two-party balance provinces on the basis of the magnitude of the difference in vote shares between the largest and second largest parties in each district. The "fractionalization" category is based on a more subjective assessment of the vote share differences among the top three or four parties in each district.

contribution to the configuration of the new Spanish party system. But the impact of the electoral law—its predisposition toward the emergence of two stronger political groups and two or three smaller ones—was compatible with several political alternatives. In addition to the pattern that actually emerged, two large parties flanked by smaller ones (fig. 1, A), the electoral formula could have produced other configurations: for example, a pattern similar in some respects to the one of the Italian party system, that is, with a Communist party larger than the Socialist group (fig. 1, B). Similarly, the system was compatible with an outcome (fig. 1, C) giving the largest blocs of seats to the PSOE and the AP (as occurred in the 1982 elections). It could also have produced a polarized pattern, that is, two larger groups separated by the two smaller ones as depicted in figure 1, D. The formula was also compatible with a configuration in which parties of the center-right would be the largest groups (fig. 1, E). A sixth possibility, a mirror image of the fifth, would be less likely in view of the fact that the electoral law overrepresented the smaller, more conservative districts. Why, then, was it the first pattern that emerged and not one of the others also compatible with the electoral system? Part of the answer can be found in the political orientations of the Spanish electorate.

POLITICAL ORIENTATIONS OF THE ELECTORATE

It is difficult to speak of partisan identification or party preferences before the actual emergence of parties on the political scene,

TABLE 5
SEATS IN CONGRESS OF DEPUTIES AWARDED
TO MINOR STATEWIDE PARTIES BY SIZE OF DISTRICT

	PCE-PSUC	PSP-US	AP
Large districts (12 or more)	14	4	5
Medium districts (7–10)	5	2	4
Small districts (3–6)	1	0	7

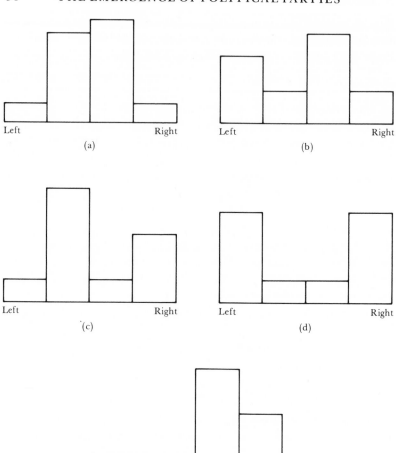

FIGURE 1.   Alternative Configurations of the Spanish Party System

because the objects of those mass-level orientations do not yet exist or, for most citizens, appear as confused and indistinct objects. This is even more likely to be the case in a society in which political parties have been banned for a long time and where the groups that did survive existed only in exile or clandestinity. One would also expect a population to be even less oriented toward parties if the preceding regime had done its utmost to extirpate and denigrate the very notion of partisanship and to depoliticize society. From a methodological standpoint, one should also expect that, prior to the restoration of full political freedom, individual citizens would be reluctant to disclose their political leanings in a society in which partisan ties could be seen as threatening or dangerous and in which political activism was repressed.

For these reasons, it is not surprising to find that, before the first democratic election, few Spaniards held (or were willing to express) strong attitudes in support of specific political parties or groups. As late as January 1977, fewer than two survey respondents out of ten said that they had thought about which party they might vote for in the forthcoming elections.[10] As a measure of the extent to which the Franquist regime had successfully depoliticized Spanish society, moreover, the levels of interest in, and knowledge about, politics were very low. Only 4 percent of those interviewed in a preelection study claimed that they were well informed about political events, while 71 percent admitted that they were "little" or "not at all" informed about "what happens in politics."[11]

This should not, however, be taken to mean that there was a total absence of political orientation among the Spanish electorate. In spite of the lack of clearly visible and identifiable political organizations, large segments of the Spanish population were able to identify with various political tendencies. The overwhelming majority of those surveyed in two large-scale studies of the transition to democracy had no difficulty in classifying themselves in left-right terms. About eight out of ten of those interviewed in July 1976 and in January 1977 were able to place themselves on an ideological scale ranging from one (extreme left) to ten (extreme right).[12] Other evidence suggests that the electorate was steadily increasing in its levels of attachment to specific political groups. In 1975 only half of those interviewed could name a generic "political family" (Socialists, Christian democrats, liberals, Communists, Falange, etc.) that they liked and believed would best defend their interests.[13] By January 1977, 70 percent were able to do so.[14] The reluctance to openly discuss politics during the early stages of the transition may partly account for the lower response rate in 1975, but the increase in partisan orientation may also indicate that Spaniards were progressively learning about politics and identifying themselves with one or another political group throughout this period.

The distribution of these gradually crystallizing political orientations greatly affected the prospects for success of the parties that were being created or emerging from clandestinity at this same time. In general, the moderate nature of public opinion meant that voters would be more likely to support relatively centrist parties than more extremist political options. As can be seen in figure 2, self-locations on the left-right continuum by respondents in two studies indicated that the most heavily populated segments were those near the center. In both 1976 and 1977 a majority of voters could be classified as belonging to the moderate left or the moderate right (positions 4–5 and 6–7, respectively).[15] Other survey data confirm these general findings. In the 1977 study, future voters were asked to choose among politically relevant terms represented as dichotomies (*franquismo/anti-franquismo, marxismo/no-marxismo,* clericalism/anticlericalism, etc.). Their responses suggest that terms associated with the less moderate or more extreme options were not very popular: "Franquismo" was chosen by only 29 percent of the respondents; "Marxism," by 9 percent; and "revolution," by a mere 2 percent.[16] Although the visible manifestations of politics during this period made Spain appear to have been rather polarized—strikes and demonstrations against the Franquist "bunker," for example—this evidence suggests that at the mass level there was a relatively moderate pattern of political leanings.

The increasing levels of support expressed for moderate parties or "political families" reaffirm this basic electoral predisposition. As can be seen in table 6, the relatively moderate Christian democratic, socialist, and social democratic groups were increasingly favored, while the level of support for more extremist options was low. But

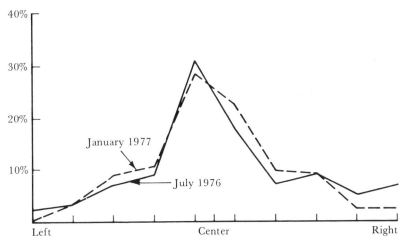

FIGURE 2.   Distribution of Spaniards on the Left-Right Continuum, July
             1976 and January 1977

Source: Based on FOESSA 1981: 372.

partisan orientations among the Spanish electorate during this period included negative attitudes as well as positive feelings. Indeed,
as Linz et al. point out, future Spanish voters had much clearer ideas
about what they disliked than about which political groups they preferred.[17] When asked if there were parties for which respondents
"would never vote," only 17 percent failed to mention at least one.
And the groups which were singled out most frequently as the objects of these negative partisan evaluations were those located toward the extreme ends of the political spectrum. (See table 6.)

The implications of this evidence about political leanings at the
mass level are clear. Within both the left and the right segments of the
political spectrum, the outcome was likely to favor the more moderate
of the options offered to the voters. Moreover, the data indicate that on
the left the communist option would be handicapped by a lingering
strong hostility toward the PCE and that, on the right, the options
closely associated in the mind of the voters with *Franquismo* would do

TABLE 6
POSITIVE AND NEGATIVE
PARTISAN PREDISPOSITIONS, 1975 AND 1977

	Which group best liked (%)		Would never vote for (1977) (%)
	1975	1977	
Revolutionaries	0	1	66
Communists[a]	1	2	63
Socialists	5	15	16
Social democrats	6	13	9
Liberals	3	4	16
Christian democrats	14	16	11
Conservatives	0	4	28
Carlists[b]	1	1	34
Continue regime[c]	15	12	44
Falange	4	2	42
None	7	10	10
No answer; don't know	43	20	7
N	(4,399)	(8,837)	(8,837)

Sources: Juan Linz, Manuel Gómez-Reino, Francisco Andrés Orizo, and Darió Vila, Informe Sociologico sobre el Cambio Político en España 1975–1981, IV Informe, FOESSA, Madrid, Editorial Euroamérica, 1981, pp. 14 and 162.
[a] In 1975, included Communists, Maoists, and others.
[b] In 1975, included Carlists and Traditionalists.
[c] Continuadores del Régimen de Franco; in 1975, Movimiento.

less well than those offered by political groups characterized by a moderate or centrist image.

We have seen that the electoral law was likely to strengthen the two larger parties. Analysis of the orientations existing at the mass level suggested that these two larger groups would not be extreme groups but more moderate forces.[18] Neither the electoral law nor mass orientations, however, can account for the success of some moderate parties and for the failure of others. For this we must turn to the third element in our model: the calculations, strategies, and behavior of party-building elites.

PARTIES OF THE LEFT: THE PCE, PSOE, AND PSP

In the 1977 election three significant nationwide parties competed for the support of voters on the left of the political spectrum: the PCE,[19] the PSOE, and the Partido Socialista Popular (PSP). The

PSOE emerged from that election as the dominant party of the left, and the PSP was consigned to political oblivion. This outcome was the result of several factors: party images inherited from the past, their respective organizational resources, their ideological stands, and, to a lesser degree, the assistance given by parties in other Western European countries.

THE COMMUNIST PARTY (PCE)

The PCE was born on April 15, 1920, as the product of a schism within the PSOE and its affiliated organizations.[20] It remained electorally unimportant throughout the Second Republic, but, following the outbreak of the Civil War, grew enormously in size and political influence within the Republican camp.[21] Under Franco it maintained a continuity in leadership as well as clandestine organizational structures throughout the country. By the time of Franco's death, it had become the largest and best organized opposition group in Spain.

Although institutional continuity is an important characteristic of the PCE (some consequences of which will be discussed below), perhaps more important were the significant changes in immediate political objectives, ideology, organizational structure, and behavioral style that took place within the party during the last 20 years of *Franquismo*. In this period the PCE gradually evolved from a "devotee party"[22] into what we shall refer to as a "mass-mobilization party." These two types of party are alike insofar as they both involve mobilization for the purpose of conducting antigovernment or antisystem activities in various extraparliamentary arenas. They differ, however, in that "mass-mobilization" parties combine protest activities with electoral efforts to come to power legally, while "devotee" parties place little real emphasis on such purely electoral objectives. From this basic functional distinction stems a series of organizational and strategic differences.

The "devotee" model conceives of the party as an elite "vanguard," whose objective is to lead an overthrow of the existing political regime and bring about a revolutionary change in society. Given these revolutionary aspirations, such parties are usually illegal and must function in clandestinity. This implies that the party must be a relatively closed organization: membership is highly selective and is compartmentalized organizationally into isolated and semisecret cells. Such parties are authoritarian, highly centralized in decision making, and intolerant of opinions and behavior that clash with their official policy. This gives rise to expulsions of dissidents and a strictly enforced ideological homogeneity.

One reason for the initially close approximation to this model by the PCE is obvious: as an affiliate of the Third International, it had no choice but to adhere to Lenin's 21 Points, among which are such concepts as the "vanguard" revolutionary party, democratic central-ism, and the "dictatorship of the proletariat" (and, hence, a lack of real concern for conformity with bourgeois-democratic "rules of the game"). But the principal objectives and strategic calculations of the party after defeat in the Civil War, coupled with the realities of clan-destine existence under the Franquist regime, were also compatible with these organizational structures and practices.

From 1941 until the early 1950s the main efforts of the party were directed to conducting guerrilla warfare against the Franquist re-gime. It was believed that *Franquismo* was not sufficiently popular or institutionalized to survive such attacks, and that, in any case, the Allies would invade Spain immediately after World War II and put Franco to rout, just as they had done to Hitler and Mussolini. This strategy dictated close adherence to a "devotee" party model. Such military activities require strict secrecy, and, because they can be carried out by relatively small numbers of people, do not require a massive recruitment of new party members. Clandestinity per se was also conducive to this type of organization. Maravall writes:

> Selectivity of recruitment was very much a requirement in a political situation where secrecy was necessary for survival. Proselytism was restricted to those potential recruits who, because of their families or because of their personal connections with militants, presented no risk to the organizations from the point of view of secrecy. Recruit-

ment under those conditions also involved slow and careful indoctrination, a period of apprenticeship, lengthy training through seminars of ideological and political initiation.[23]

Several PCE officials have claimed that clandestinity also led to the adoption of an authoritarian decision-making style: "In a clandestine congress there is no room for elections," argued Ramón Tamames (who would later resign from the PCE in 1980 in protest against what he regarded as the persistence of such authoritarianism).[24] More directly to the point, PCE Secretary General Santiago Carrillo frequently stated that "inner democracy and an open structure would have been luxuries facilitating the work of the police."[25] This need for cohesion frequently led to the expulsion of dissidents. As Ignacio Gallego (a close associate of Santiago Carrillo) said of the expulsion of Enrique Lister and others of the pro-Soviet and anti-Carrillo faction in 1971: "In a clandestine party, it is impossible to accept ambiguity regarding a question of this kind. . . . In these conditions, we cannot allow ourselves to be carried away by an absurd liberalism."[26]

After the failure of the *guerrilla* war (which, in fact, proved to be counterproductive),[27] the PCE turned to a different strategy, one based on "the possibility of replacing Franco by peaceful means."[28] This strategy, initially referred to as the Policy of National Reconciliation, was placed before the executive committee of the party in 1956 by Santiago Carrillo (who would not formally become secretary general until 1960). In his first exercise of dominance of the party apparatus, he gained the committee's approval of that new strategy. The new policy implied a totally different set of organizational imperatives, in accord with which the party's structures and procedures began to evolve, over a period of two decades, toward the "mass-mobilization" party model.

Like devotee parties, mass-mobilization parties may first emerge in clandestinity, and they often use extraparliamentary means of pressing for radical change. In anticipation of electoral politics in a post-authoritarian system, however, they strive to avoid ideological narrowness and place great emphasis on openness and the attraction of a broader range of supporters. Thus, the secret "cell" structure is replaced by the more open "branch" as the primary organizational unit. Membership expands, becoming much less selective, and indoctrination is less rigorous. Hence, mass-mobilization parties are less ideologically homogeneous than are devotee parties.[29] The quality of militancy also changes: as Tamames argued, when parties are small and clandestine, it may be necessary for militants to devote 50 percent of their time to the party, while expanded party membership can enable a mass-mobilization party to accomplish many of the same political goals, demanding only 10 percent of their members' time.[30] Nonetheless, militancy in mass-mobilization parties is much more demanding than is membership in purely electoral parties. The party is not merely active at election time; because it seeks to apply extraparliamentary mass pressure on government in order to secure radical reforms, it requires the year-round devotion of party activists. In order to sustain such militancy, mass-mobilization parties must stress ideology more than do purely electoral parties: there must, after all, be some "higher purpose" to justify the sacrifices of time, effort, and money, as well as occasional imprisonment. In combination with the greater heterogeneity and internal democratization of such parties (as compared with devotee parties), this stress on ideology sometimes produces intense internal struggles and instability.

The Policy of National Reconciliation (further elaborated and renamed the *Pacto por la Libertad* in 1970) marked a departure from previous PCE strategies in several respects. First, while the *guerrilla* war may be regarded as a continuation of the Civil War, the new policy was tantamount to a proclamation of peace by the party:

> The Policy of National Reconciliation . . . signifies the end of the spirit of civil war, of the division between victors and vanquished. The war was lost by all the people in their totality, on both sides. The PCE rejects all desires for revenge . . . and will continue to try in the future to erase from the horizon in our country the spectre of a civil war.[31]

Second, the policy identified a much broader range of possible allies in the march toward socialism. Not only would the party seek to attract the working classes, but also "the middle classes and the forces of culture. Marxism is not the exclusive patrimony of Communists," argued Carrillo in 1956, "we must also count on the armed forces. We are not asking them for a coup d'état, but only that they cease to be supporters of the dictatorship."[32] Even the Church was included in Carrillo's list of potential allies in the struggle against *Franquismo*.[33] Finally, the Policy of National Reconciliation drastically altered the short-term and intermediate objectives and basic strategy of the party: socialism was to be secured only through a gradual process and by democratic means. The most immediate goal of the party would, in fact, be the establishment of a democratic regime. As Carrillo argued:

> Later on we'll raise the problem of the march toward socialism. Once that has been achieved we'll break from capitalism. We don't want to socialize everything overnight. First it is necessary to create an anticapitalist, anti-monopolist and anti-latifundist democracy. . . . Alongside the public sector will continue to exist for some time a sector of private, capitalist property. We do not want to overburden society with the nationalization of the enormous number of small and medium-sized businesses of this country. The poor would suffer from our haste. This will be a very long process, which at first we will not even regard as socialist.[34]

Despite the formal proclamation of this new policy, changes in the party's ideological declarations and organizational structures and practices were slow in coming. The concept of the "dictatorship of the proletariat" was not repudiated until the Eighth Party Congress in 1972, and its Catalán affiliate (PSUC) did not abandon that concept until 1977.[35] The "cell" structure of the party was not replaced by open *agrupaciones territoriales* (neighborhood branches) as the party's basic unit of organization until August 1976 (when the central committee endorsed this change at a plenary session in Rome). The party did not remove the term "Leninist" from its self-designation until April 1978 (nearly a year after the first democratic elections). And "democratic centralism" continued to function sporadically as a decision-making principle into the 1980s. Overall, the process that Santiago Carrillo set in motion by the national reconciliation policy of 1956 succeeded in transforming the PCE from a devotee party into a predominantly mass-mobilization party by the late 1960s.

One principal means employed by the party in its efforts to create a broad-based coalition of forces in opposition to the Franquist regime was to work through secondary organizations. This was beneficial in two respects: first, the legality of many such organizations provided a façade behind which opposition activities could be conducted; and, second, the party could take advantage of the organized structure of some of these groups and thus would not face the difficulties inherent in attempts to create them from scratch. The first foci of these activities were labor and student organizations. Following the first outbursts of antiregime protests by students in 1956, the PCE played a significant role in organizing or working through existing student opposition groups. By the early 1960s, party members were also active in organizing de facto trade unions, often using as an important organizational infrastructure the regime's own system of "vertical" *sindicatos* (trade unions). (PCE trade union activities will be discussed in chapter 5.) By the early 1970s, the party was encouraging its members to join and play leadership roles within a much broader array of secondary organizations. Thus,

> PCE members became more involved in legal associations [such as] housewives' groups, consumer pressure groups, parent-teacher associations, neighborhood groups—and party lawyers were prominent in the defense of trade unionists on trial for their activities. All of this constituted, within the limits of the dictatorship, an attempt to emulate the successes of the Italian Communists in municipal government, a demonstration that Communists were efficient and reliable.[36]

While a principal purpose of these activities was to gain the respect of a wide variety of social groups and to forge long-term alliances with them, an important function in the short term was to use these groups for popular mobilizations against the regime. There were several waves of such protest activity. The first involved the organization of massive strikes by workers and began in 1962 by taking advantage of dissatisfaction with the social consequences of the austere stabilization plan implemented by the regime. Party leadership of illegal trade union protests was consolidated throughout the 1960s.[37] Student protest activities in which party militants played an important role also increased during this period, with a pronounced radicalization of student involvement in response to the killing of two students by police in 1967 and 1969. Maravall writes: "From 1967 to 1970, political action was in the form of violent demonstrations, commandos breaking windows, stopping traffic, setting up barricades, hurling Molotov-cocktails."[38] Although these activities failed to topple the regime, they did succeed in frightening the governing political elite, who responded with university closures, declarations of states of emergency, and police occupation of campuses.[39]

The final period when protest demonstrations were particularly widespread and politically important occurred during the first six months after Franco's death. In light of the complete absence of progress toward democratization under the government of Arias Navarro, the PCE (as well as other opposition groups) mobilized its supporters in a campaign of strikes and demonstrations designed to force democratization via *ruptura*. A great wave of politically motivated strikes broke out. In total, over 150 million man-hours of labor were lost in 1976—as compared with just 14.5 million in 1975, which itself had been a record high.[40]

Throughout this period, party membership grew enormously, and the PCE was transformed from a closed vanguard party into a sizable mass-mobilization party. Maravall points to 1965 as the period in which this transformation became most apparent. The size, recruitment procedures, and degree of ideological homogeneity of the party were all affected by this transformation, at least within the university community:

> The importance of careful screening of potential recruits, the long and intensive novitiate periods, ideological training, decreased due to

the new importance of sheer numbers.... After 1965 any chap who was seen as somewhat active was recruited. If you entered the university and became involved in . . . [student politics], without preparation, without careful precautions and training, you could be a member of the Spanish Communist party in two weeks.[41]

The net result was that by Franco's death the PCE had become by far the largest political party organization in Spain. And the rate of increase in membership accelerated as the 1977 elections approached: the number of party members increased from 15 to 20 thousand in 1975,[42] to 90 to 100 thousand in 1976–1977.[43]

This increase in membership went together with an expansion of organizational infrastructure that would be of considerable benefit to the party in the 1977 elections. At a minimum, it meant that the PCE or one of its regional affiliates would be able to field candidates in all constituencies. According to party officials, the PCE, unlike rival parties on the left, had succeeded in maintaining some kind of organization in virtually all Spanish provinces throughout the Franquist era (although in some areas, such as Old Castile and Galicia, this organizational presence may have consisted of nothing more than a few isolated cells).[44] More importantly, the PCE could count on the massive support of party militants in undertaking campaign activities in the most populous provinces, which would send sizable blocs of delegates to the Congress of Deputies, and in which the electoral chances of the PCE were relatively good. In Madrid and Barcelona, for example, PCE campaign activities in 1977 were manned by 15 thousand volunteers each. (By way of comparison, the newly formed UCD had only 237 members in Madrid by the end of that year.)[45] Thus, the PCE's long history of opposition to *Franquismo* provided the party with organizational resources useful for campaign activities.

The party's past opposition activities were not, however, an unambiguously beneficial legacy. To be sure, some people were attracted to the PCE precisely because it had served as the principal clandestine political organization. In the words of one historic Communist leader, the party gained some prestige because it had kept alive "the sacred flame" of opposition to Franquist authoritarianism.[46] But, for several reasons, other aspects of the party's history had decidedly negative electoral consequences. Some older voters who had supported other parties on the Republican side continued to harbor hostility toward the PCE because of the manner in which it had progressively eliminated its socialist, Trotskyite, and anarchosyndicalist rivals for power during the Civil War. Although the massive demographic turnover since the Republican era meant that the number of persons with direct personal knowledge of such events was small, lingering historical memories probably colored perceptions of the party among a larger number of voters. This was partly a result of the presence in leadership positions of such persons as Santiago Carrillo and Dolores Ibárruri ("Pasionaria") who had played prominent and controversial roles in the Civil War.

A larger segment of the electorate was, perhaps, led to adopt a negative stance toward the PCE as a result of the extensive propaganda campaign undertaken over several decades by the Franquist regime itself. That campaign was so pervasive that Carr and Fusi were moved to write, "After 1939 anticommunism became the "raison d'être" of Francoism."[47] Two aspects of this propaganda were particularly damaging to the party. The first painted a demonic image of the party and its program. As described by one Communist official in a 1979 interview, "it had been the policy for 40 years that everything that happened was blamed on the Communists—that we are inhuman, that we are monsters, that we have no other desires than for revenge." Another PCE official in a rural area said, "We still have the image that we will take away peasants' land, their cows, and who knows what." A third official in another area claimed that such propaganda "had some repercussions on the entire population" and created a distorted public image of the party, its program, and its ultimate intentions.

A second aspect of Franquist anticommunist propaganda was particularly damaging insofar as it seemed to fit with the public perceptions of the party's mass mobilizations against the Franquist regime. As Pérez Ledesma has written, "Franquist propaganda untiringly repeated that the Uprising (by the Nationalists) was a response to a Communist plot hatched in 1936. . . . Against them weighed the accusation of having been in part responsible for the conflict."[48] For many Spaniards, concerned less with abstract goals like democratization than with the maintenance of tranquility in their daily lives, the PCE's opposition to *Franquismo* was disruptive and counterproductive: they believed that the party's "antifranquist struggle had created agitation and disorder in the country, and had contributed indirectly to the lack of *apertura* [an opening-up or gradual democratization of the old regime] and to the maintenance of a dictatorial regime."[49] This "trouble-maker" image fit particularly well with perceptions of the intensive protest activities of 1976.

The great uncertainty about the nature and ultimate outcome of the post-Franco transition exacerbated this problem and presented the PCE with a strategic dilemma. As a high-ranking leader of the party said in an interview: "We had many problems in confronting the new situation of political change (since) we had to face a situation that was not that which we had foreseen, with a correlation of forces that was unfavorable to us. As we were thinking, all of our policies revolved about the theme of the *ruptura democrática,* and [instead] we had to adapt ourselves to the *reforma.*" The PCE was convinced throughout much of the transition that the only way by which a democratic regime could be created was through a *ruptura.* Hence, it was regarded as necessary to mobilize party supporters and collaborators to confront the regime with massive protests in order to force it to accept political changes which it otherwise would reject. Even in the absence of a *ruptura,* these mass mobilizations were regarded by some as essential, because, as Maravall contends, "it is more than doubtful that the reformist policy would have been successful, faced with the resistance of Franquist groups, if these pressures from below had not existed."[50] A final source of uncertainty (not resolved until the legalization of the party just two months before the June elections) was whether or not the party would be permitted to field candidates in that contest. Even after ratification of the reform law in the referendum of December 1976, the party continued to believe that it would not be legalized until after the parliamentary elections (if then).[51] Under these circumstances, there seemed to be no alternative but to continue its campaign of mass mobilizations. Unexpectedly rapid progress under the Suárez government toward thorough democratization of the political system meant, in effect, that the Communist party had committed itself to a strategy ill-suited to meet the demands of an election campaign in a peaceful and predominantly moderate social setting.

Once the PCE was legalized in April, 1977, the party leadership moved quickly to adjust to the new situation. Immediate steps were taken to moderate the PCE's image and program proposals. In one respect, the party had little choice but to embark on this moderate path: an abandonment of certain of its radical and revolutionary demands was implicitly imposed on the party by Adolfo Suárez as a condition for its legalization. Suárez has claimed that he always favored legalization of the PCE, and, indeed, that he feared the political consequences of a continuation of its clandestine status.[52] But for tactical reasons, he delayed until the very last moment before lifting the ban on the party. The principal objective of this tactic was to placate the military, whose tolerance was necessary for the success of the transition to democracy, but whose staunch anticommunism meant that an early decision to legalize the PCE might provoke opposition to the entire process. The conversion of the PCE into a party of "loyal opposition" also constituted an important objective in its own right. Pursuit of these dual objectives was manifested in Suárez's behavior at a crucial meeting with the military chiefs of staff on September 8, 1976, at which his plans for political reform were endorsed. As expected, the prime minister was asked about his intentions concerning the PCE. Suárez responded by saying, "Given the statutes of the PCE, its legalization is impossible." Military officers left the meeting convinced that Suárez would not legalize the party. Instead, his ambiguous response was intended both to assuage military fears of an impending PCE legalization, as well as to use the conditional clause concerning "the statutes of the PCE" to coerce the party into moderating its stance. Through an emissary and later through a long discussion with Santiago Carrillo, Suárez conveyed to the PCE leadership his proposal to legalize the party in exchange for changes in its statutes and programmatic proposals.

Prompt moderation of the party's image was also undertaken for short-term electoral reasons. "Carrillo decided to go into the elections projecting an image of 'the party of order,'" writes Pedro J. Ramírez.[53] In accord with this strategy, the PCE set forth a moderate election program and went to great efforts to defuse the demonic and *revanchiste* image associated with the party by four decades of Franquist propaganda: the color red and the hammer and sickle were largely absent from the party's billboards and posters; the national flag adopted by Franco replaced the Republican tricolor at party rallies; efforts were made to attract Catholics to the party and erase its anticlerical image; and the PCE exerted pressure on its trade union ally, the CCOO, to abstain from strike activities during the campaign. But for many Spanish voters, this campaign of moderation was too little, too late.

Thus, the fate of the PCE in the election of 1977 was strongly influenced by the legacy of four decades of opposition to *Franquismo*. The party benefitted from that experience through its sizable membership base, its "presence" in all parts of the country and in many secondary organizations, and the continuity, experience, and discipline of its leadership. Its electoral prospects were harmed, however, by the public image it had acquired through its clandestine activities. These perceptions, exploited by other political groups, pushed the PCE away from the moderate majority of Spanish voters.

THE SOCIALISTS: PSOE AND PSP

The PSOE, founded in 1879, is the oldest of Spain's political parties. During the Second Republic, it was also the largest party of the left, both in terms of its share of the vote (16.4 percent of the votes cast in the 1936 election), and in terms of membership—the UGT (its affiliated trade union) claimed a membership of 1.4 million in 1933.[54] In spite of its deep historical roots, however, the PSOE was by no means as large or as well institutionalized as the PCE during the final decade of the Franquist era. For a "mass-mobilization party," its levels of affiliation were, in fact, strikingly low: in the early 1970s the PSOE's membership within Spain did not exceed two thousand, and by 1975 its membership (including those residing abroad) totaled four thousand.[55] Moreover, despite efforts to maintain its clandestine opposition to the Franquist regime, all traces of PSOE organization had been eliminated from a considerable number of Spanish provinces by the 1940s.[56]

To some extent, strategic errors and structural defects in the PSOE contributed to its almost complete eradication under the Franquist regime. Unlike the PCE (which, as described by Maravall, was "smaller, better protected, with a rigidly centralized leadership and important financial support"),[57] the PSOE retained its "mass-mobilization" character. Its basic unit of party organization was the relatively open *agrupación,* not the closed and secret cell. It attempted to maintain its own UGT structure, rather than infiltrate and use various legal and alegal organizations through more subtle means, which might have afforded greater protection from police harassment. Given this vulnerable organizational structure, moreover, a confession to police by a single militant could lead to the arrest of the entire executive committee of the party or the trade union. Maravall reports that by 1954 seven complete UGT executive committees had "fallen" in this manner: "Every time an executive committee fell, the whole organization crumbled, and it was extremely hard to rebuild it." Only "in proletarian areas (with) traditions of militancy and a homogeneous working class," such as the mining zones of Asturias and the heavily industrialized portions of Vizcaya, did the Socialist party manage to maintain a sizable underground UGT structure throughout the Franquist era.[58]

In response to the frequent collapse of party executive committees, the PSOE moved its statewide leadership structure into exile after 1945. This only compounded the party's difficulties in maintaining a clandestine organization in the so-called "interior." Problems of communication and coordination increased as a result of the physical separation of the party leadership from its clandestine organizations and members. A more serious consequence of this bifurcation was that "the leadership in exile increasingly lost contact with what was occurring in the interior."[59] In an interview in Madrid in June 1981, a former social-democratic politician said that "the *históricos* [as the exiled leaders were called] lived in the political world of the 1930s: their [analytical framework] was useless for trying to understand anything, and they were not connected with reality." In spite of this, the leadership in exile continued to exercise "a very strict control over socialist groups in the interior."[60] PSOE members remaining in Spain were not even permitted to vote at party congresses until 1972. There was confusion, lack of coordination, lack of ideological and programmatic consensus, and increasing conflict between leaders in the interior and in exile over basic strategies and tactics. One particularly divisive issue concerned whether party members should be permitted to cooperate with the PCE in organizing opposition to the Franquist regime, a tactic that was forbidden by the staunchly anticommunist *históricos*. As a result, the Socialists had been displaced by the Communists as the principal party organization on the left by the 1950s.

Socialist fortunes began to change as the leadership in exile was gradually replaced by officials operating within Spain. This process began in 1970 with the entry into the executive committee of a majority of representatives of the interior (drawn largely from the three areas in which the party was strongest—Madrid, Vizcaya, and Andalucía).[61] Two years later, following the party congress at Toulouse, it was decided that executive committee meetings would henceforth be held in Spain. Finally, at the 1974 party congress at Suresnes, Felipe González, with the backing of Willy Brandt and the Socialist International, replaced Rodolfo Llopis as party secretary general. Debate concerning this impending change had already produced a split in the party. Most of the former leaders in exile refused to recognize the new executive committee and formed a rival socialist party, which appeared on the ballots as the PSOE-Histórico.

Following the change in leadership, recruitment of new militants increased significantly: membership quadrupled between 1974 and 1976, reaching eight thousand by December 1976.[62] Accompanying this increase in membership, the party extended its reach into all parts of Spain by establishing branches in provinces from which such organizations had disappeared under the Franquist regime. The exact manner by which such provincial branches were created varied from province to province. In the most common pattern, party representatives from core areas in which the PSOE was well institutionalized visited neighboring provinces in order to assist in founding party organizations. Party militants from Madrid, for instance, played crucial roles in establishing branches in nearby Toledo and Segovia. Felipe González, Alfonso Guerra, Guillermo Galeote, and other "sevillanos," to cite another example, actively assisted in the development of party structures in other provinces of Andalucía. Another pattern was the spontaneous formation of party branches on the basis of historical memories of the PSOE. Several politically active students in Galicia, for example, had been attracted by the PSOE tradition and, after an extended series of informal conversations among themselves, decided to create a branch of the party. Perhaps the best illustration of the drawing power of such historical traditions is the Baleares branch of the PSOE. As a party official said in an interview in Palma de Mallorca in June 1978:

> This branch of the party was born out of the merger of two very small groups which had sprung up spontaneously in different parts of Palma without knowing about each other. In one group there were six persons led primarily by Emilio Alonso, our present deputy. . . . The second group, which was formed in a different part of the city at about the same time, was led by Felix Pons, our second deputy in this province. . . . The two groups existed in clandestinity without knowing about the existence of each other until 1974 or 1975.

Finally, many individuals joined the PSOE because of their ties to socialist parties or trade unions in other Western European countries in which they had lived as emigrant workers. Thus, even though the PSOE had been unable to maintain party branches in all parts of Spain, its historical tradition, its ties to the Socialist International, and its organizational continuity in some strongholds provided it with a basis on which to rebuild.

"The PSOE," in the words of Maravall, "was reborn as a socialist party of a radical character."[63] At the Suresnes congress the party opposed "any reform, continuation or transformation of the regime."[64] The strategy of the party was thenceforth to be the securing of "particles of liberty through mobilizations, pressures and negotiations with the objective of securing a *ruptura democrática*."[65] Although such activities of mass-mobilization parties are often detrimental to their electoral prospects, it is likely that PSOE involvement in strikes and demonstrations (particularly in 1976) did not have as much of a negative impact on the outcome of the 1977 election as did similar activities by the PCE. The PSOE had not been such a prominent object of propaganda attacks by the Franquist regime, and, thus, citizens who disapproved of disruptive political activities were not predisposed to blame the Socialists. The party was, moreover, much smaller and had been a less significant opposition force during the preceding decade. As one observer wrote, the PSOE was "more free from accusations concerning its behavior during the war, [and] benefitted from the renovation of its leadership and from its almost total absence of activity during Franquismo."[66] Thus, it is likely that the PSOE paid less of a price for adopting the same *ruptura democrática* strategy as the PCE.

The "radical" character of the reborn PSOE was also evident in the ideology and programmatic declarations drafted at the 1976 congress. The resolutions adopted at the PSOE Twenty-Seventh Party Congress, in fact, represented a "Bad Godesberg in reverse" insofar as it included in the party's self-description the term "Marxist" for the first time in PSOE history. The PSOE declared itself to be a "class party, and therefore of the masses, Marxist and democratic." Its principal objective was stated as "the overcoming of the capitalist means of production through the seizure of economic and political power, and the socialization of the means of production, distribution and exchange by the working class." The party rejected "any path of accommodation with capitalism or the simple reform of that system."[67] Its economic program called for nationalization of the ten largest banks (which control 80 percent of total financial resources) and 50 of the largest industrial firms in a wide variety of sectors.[68] Temporarily resigning from the party in protest, PSOE economist Miguel Boyer (later to become the first socialist minister of finance of the post-Franco era) attacked this economic program as "archaic and more extreme than that of the French Socialist Party or of the Italian Communist Party."[69] Other programmatic declarations called for elimination of the private (i.e., religious) sector of education and for the creation of a republic.

Despite its radical ideology and strategy, in the 1977 election the PSOE sought to project an image of moderation. Its media campaign focused on the attractive personality of Felipe González, whose speeches totally avoided demands for extensive nationalizations, etc., and focused instead on noncontroversial issues, such as "the need to elaborate a new Constitution, proposals to improve the quality of life of citizens, and the opportunity for integration of Spain in Europe."[70] Maximalist rhetoric could be found at party rallies, but, as Roskin reported, "Most voters did not go to these rallies, and news reports concentrated on González's moderate statements on free public education, national medical care, etc. The PSOE's net public image, therefore, was less radical than a closeup image."[71] The party's success in projecting this moderate image enabled it to appeal much more effectively than the PCE to voters near the modal center of the Spanish electorate. Given the large number of parties active in the campaign, uncertainty concerning which parties would present the greatest electoral threat, and the disproportionate attention focused on the AP in the 1977 campaign, other parties were not particularly successful in pointing to the great inconsistencies between the PSOE's formal program and the content of its campaign statements.

Finally, the PSOE benefitted from formal recognition and financial support from the Socialist International and, in particular, the West German social-democratic party (SPD). The exact amount of financial assistance from the SPD is unknown,[72] but the severe scarcity of funds at the disposal of its rivals on the left of the political spectrum meant that the PSOE gained a distinct advantage from such aid.[73] Perhaps more importantly, the PSOE benefitted greatly from practical advice volunteered by their more experienced German colleagues concerning such important matters as management of party finances, conduct of the campaign, and organization of public meetings.

The financial resources, provincial implantation, historical tradition, and mass membership of the PSOE were particularly helpful in efforts to overcome the challenges posed by rival socialist parties, the most important of which was the PSP (Partido Socialista Popular) of Enrique Tierno Galván. The origins of the PSP can be traced back to the University of Salamanca in 1954, where a group of professionals and academics clustered around "the old professor" Tierno began to organize in opposition to the Franquist regime, and to collaborate with the newly emerging student movement. Claiming that "socialism had virtually disappeared from the country" after the exile of the PSOE,[74] their activities culminated in the founding of the Socialist Party of the Interior in 1964, which was renamed the PSP in 1974. The PSP defined itself as a "socialist party of the left . . . a vanguard party in the current conception of the revolutionary struggle against capitalism."[75] Its leaders usually compared the PSP to other left socialist parties, such as the French PSU (Parti Socialiste Unifié) and the Italian PSIUP (Partito Socialista Italiano di Unità Proletaria).[76] Its program called for the nationalization of large firms in the industrial, agricultural, and service sectors of the economy, for workers' self management, and for a "radical transformation of Spanish society."[77] Although the party included some social democrats within its ranks, its ideology formally embraced the "Marxist conception of historical evolution,"[78] and its two principal leaders, President Tierno Galván and Secretary General Raul Morodo, both professed orthodox Marxist beliefs, asserting that the party's ideology was most notable for its "radical criticism of social democracy."[79]

The PSP differed from the PSOE in several important respects. First, it never attempted to create a trade union of its own. Most of its members who were affiliated with a trade union belonged to the CCOO, and the rest were dispersed among the USO (Unión Sindical Obrera), the UGT, and other *sindicatos*. Given the nearly hegemonic position of the PCE within the CCOO in most parts of the country, this meant that the PSP lacked a separate organizational link to the working classes. This, coupled with the elitist image frequently projected by its leaders, hindered the PSP in its attempts to extend its reach beyond the universities and intellectual communities which were its core areas of support.[80] Second, the PSP entered the 1977 election as part of a broad coalition named Unidad Socialista (US), rather than under its relatively well-recognized party label. Perhaps as a means of compensating for its infrastructural weakness (which will be discussed in chap. 4), the party joined with several regional socialist parties (the most important of which was the PSA [Partido Socialista de Andalucía]), which had previously formed a Federación de Partidos Socialistas. Although this alliance may have increased the PSP's voter appeal in a few areas (such as Cádiz), it is probable that the accompanying last-minute change of party label undercut the appeal that Tierno and the PSP could have derived from their decades of prominent opposition activity.[81] A third difference between the two principal socialist parties concerned their international orientations. As described by Raul Morodo: "While the PSOE, through its connection with the Socialist International, which is a social-democratic International, has great and intimate ties especially to German social democracy, the PSP maintains a very independentist line, a line more of the Mediterranean, more of the socialism of the south."[82] The PSP's "clear Third World vocation"[83] was reinforced by even stronger attitudes on the part of several of its coalition partners in the 1977 elections, some of whom were reportedly close to Libya.

The absence of an infrastructural base outside of the universities, the undercutting of what "historic" appeal could be derived from the names of Tierno and the PSP, and the inappropriateness of a "Third World" image for the Spain of the late 1970s all contributed to that party's poor showing in the 1977 election. The final element in its demise was the uneven campaign performance by many of its leaders. Pedro J. Ramírez has argued that after projecting a very radical image during the first part of the campaign (during which Tierno threatened to return to violence in the streets if the AP won), the PSP made an abrupt about-face, calling itself the "party of responsibility." This change was attacked by other parties as demogogic, and, in Ramírez's view, damaged the party's electoral chances.[84]

THE ALIANZA POPULAR (AP)

The AP was created under the leadership of Manuel Fraga Iribarne on October 9, 1976. It was born as a political party with a quasi-federal structure as the product of a merger of several separate political and personalistic groupings: Fraga's Reforma Democrática, the Unión del Pueblo Español of Cruz Martínez Esteruelas, Acción Democrática Española of Federico Silva Muñoz, Laureano López Rodó's Acción Regional, the Democracia Social under Licinio de la Fuente, the Unión Nacional Española of Gonzalo Fernández de la Mora, and the Unión Social Popular of Enrique Thomás de Carranza. These individuals, referred to in the press as "the Magnificent Seven," had all served as high-ranking officials in various Franquist governments: Martínez Esteruelas had been minister of education and science; Licinio de la Fuente had been minister of labor; Silva and Fernández de la Mora had each served as minister of public works; López Rodó had been minister of development planning (and for some time functioned as "superminister" for economic policy);[85] and Fraga had been minister of information and tourism. Only Thomás de Carranza had not risen to the rank of minister, but he had served as a civil governor, director of Radio Nacional, head of the Movimiento in Toledo, and had held three different posts at the rank of director general.

The emergence and electoral fate of the AP from 1976 to 1977 is a story of frustrated intentions and ambitions, which clearly underscore the risks involved in formulating party-building strategies in an uncertain political environment. The party that emerged was distinctly different, in many important respects, from the one Fraga initially had hoped to create. Instead of a reformist center-right party, the AP appeared to the electorate in 1977 as a party of the far right, which, to some, represented a last-ditch attempt to maintain the basic character of the Franquist regime through electoral means. Instead of a modern, broad-based, "catch-all" party, the AP more closely resembled the "clientelistic" party networks of the late nineteenth century. And instead of becoming a party of government, the AP was relegated to an opposition role, finishing in fourth place, behind even the recently legalized PCE.

Building on the reformist reputation he had acquired as minister of information and tourism (as the author of the press liberalization law), Fraga had hoped to take the lead in the creation of a competitive party system via *reforma*. In several publications in the early 1970s, he set forth the argument that Spain should change its political institutions to fit with the characteristics of other developed, industrialized societies: "Two aims must be gradually pursued: an opening of alternative choices (liberalization, associations) and greater participation at all levels (representation, democratic legitimacy)."[86] This process of reform should be guided by what Fraga and other AP leaders called the "center." For Fraga and other AP leaders, the "center" did not refer to the exact middle of the political spectrum, but rather to the "isolation of the extremes—an extreme right which does not believe in democracy, (and) an extreme left which doesn't believe in it either."[87] This notion of "the center," therefore, is rather broad and includes the democratic right-wing of Spanish politics. Fraga's conception of political change was described in a formal ideological declaration, as follows:

> Reformism is a policy of the center which accepts the reality of change and attempts to direct it, in a balanced manner and within certain ethical values, toward the obtaining of the greatest improvements possible without, thereby, renouncing what may be positive in various situations, past and present. Between immobilism and revolution, it aspires in a reasoned manner to a profound transformation of political, social and economic structures, based on the majoritarian consensus, which banishes violence and demands the use of the authority of a strong state to guarantee the rights of citizens vis-à-vis those minorities who, by one means or another, attempt to destroy them.[88]

As minister of the interior in the first post-Franco government, Fraga was in a position to attempt to implement these reformist designs. His record, however, was mixed. On the one hand, "he initiated concessions to regional susceptibilities, provided the drive for institutional reform and allowed political parties greater freedom to function."[89] On the other hand, "his police imprisoned opposition politicians and continued their war against the Basques."[90] During the first half of 1976, there were several instances of excessive brutality by the various police units under Fraga's authority. His failure to contain those excesses (such as the killing of five demonstrators at a protest in Vitoria) seriously tarnished his reputation as a reformer. Leaders of other parties also objected to his inflexibility and insensitivity in informal contacts and negotiations with the opposition. Ramón Tamames, representing the PCE in these discussions, attacked Fraga's "political manipulation" of other parties and accused him of trying to "model the aspirations of the Spanish people according to his own pretentions."[91] The most serious setback for Fraga's strategy of reformism was the product of events not under his control. Due largely to the lack of adequate support for reform from Arias Navarro himself and to certain tactical errors (which enabled the Cortes and the National Council of the Movimiento to reject important pieces of reform legislation), the resulting lack of progress toward democratization led the king to dismiss the Arias Navarro government and start anew under a different prime minister—Adolfo Suárez. Fraga's absence from the succeeding cabinet deprived him of the political benefits of having played a leading role in the process of political change and enabled the future leader of a rival party "to steal our program of reforms" (as a collaborator of Fraga's put it).[92]

Similarly, Fraga was frustrated in his efforts to bring into existence the kind of party he had initially envisaged. Both the organizational structure and the ideological center of gravity of the AP fell short of his expectations. The original objective was to forge an alliance among groups of the "center and center-right, and lay down the bases of a future party like the British Conservatives and the American Republicans" (interview with AP official, June 1981). This was to be "a great, modern, liberal-conservative party—that is, a *sui-generis* centrism, clearly polarized on (matters of) order and security, but, at the same time, clearly reformist in social matters and clearly democratic."[93] It would be a key actor in what was envisaged by Fraga as a two-party system, "with the extremes of the left and right excluded [and with] one great group of the center-right and one group of the center-left" (interview with AP official, June 1981). The "ideological space" to be occupied by his ideal party would range from the "democratic right" to non-Marxist social democrats: "Our party is open to all Spaniards who are not Marxists, not separatists and not reactionary"; the ideological center of gravity of the party, however, "must be clearly that of the center-right" (interview with AP official, May 1978).

The "modern" party structure that Fraga had in mind was close to what Otto Kirchheimer calls the "catch-all party."[94] These parties are purely electoral organizations whose overriding (or only) objective is the maximization of votes at election time. Given this purpose, catch-all parties in societies in which the distribution of public opinion (on a left-right continuum) is, and is believed to be, unimodal and centrist will strive to appear to be moderate in their policy preferences and modes of behavior. If such parties draft formal ideological statements, they will tend to be vague, moderate, and eclectic. The behavior and public pronouncements of all those who claim to represent the party (government officials, candidates, party bureaucrats, and party militants) should be consistent with this moderate image, so as not to frighten away centrist voters. Lacking an explicit ideology, such parties may emphasize the attractive personal attributes of their most prominent candidates, and the nomination of those candidates will be largely determined by the electoral resources at their disposal, rather than by other criteria, such as years of experience in, or service to, the party organization. Finally, the party's campaign will strive to attract votes from a wide variety of social groups and will not emphasize ideological claims to represent the particularistic interests of any specific class or set of social groups.

Even before the death of Franco, and even while serving as the Spanish ambassador to the United Kingdom, Fraga worked tirelessly to found a political party of this kind. Carr and Fusi have written: "After December 1974 Fraga became the center of political life. His energy is enormous; his industry prodigious. The press followed breathlessly his visits to Madrid, his meetings with Arias, his ministers, and the leading figures of the political class."[95] His initial design was to found a political association consistent with the liberalization first suggested in the Arias Navarro speech of February 1974. Given the harsh constraints imposed on the formation of political associations, however, Fraga soon abandoned that effort and opted instead for the creation of "study groups"—the first, a rather heterogeneous group (which included some individuals who would later play roles in the formation of the UCD) called FEDISA, then a smaller group of his own, called GODSA, intended to function as a supportive and collaborative staff in the drafting of a formal party program. Fraga's main efforts involved transforming his extensive personal contacts into an organizational network. A large number of persons who later became AP officials had personally known and collaborated with Fraga in the late 1960s and early 1970s, as revealed in interviews with AP officials in 13 provinces. The product of these efforts was the establishment in early 1976 of the Reforma Democrática—a small, "reformist" party, based on "a desire to preserve public order, to maintain the authority of the state, and to achieve social justice."[96]

Fraga's personal contacts and labors on behalf of Reforma Democrática, however, were insufficient to transform it into the "great party of the center and center-right." Such a party might have been feasible while its leader retained the post of minister of the interior (in which case civil governors and others in the state administration might have reinforced the party's infrastructure throughout the country), but the dismissal of the second Arias Navarro government terminated those prospects. Faced with a deficient provincial infrastructure and a severe shortage of funds,[97] Fraga had little choice but to seek out allies and merge with other parties or factions.

This process of proto-party coalescence was greatly affected by uncertainty over the course of the transition, which contributed to misperceptions and miscalculations. Decisions concerning the selection of coalition partners were complicated, multifaceted, and dependent on factors outside the control of these party-builders, such as the electoral law. The choice of coalition partners at this early stage in the transition dramatically affected the nature of the party's organization, its ideology, and its public image. Long-term difficulties arose because the characteristics of the different coalition partners were often incompatible.

One such difficulty was ideological incompatibility. For many potential coalition partners near the center of the political spectrum, the inclusion of conservative *Franquistas,* or of those whose commitment to democracy was suspect, was unthinkable. In negotiations during the summer of 1976 with centrists, such as José María de Areilza and Pío Cabanillas (who subsequently founded the Partido Popular—a precursor of the UCD), this matter was of paramount importance. Areilza and Cabanillas refused to consider prominent right-wing *Franquistas* as potential coalition partners. Fraga's insistence that many of them would greatly contribute to the strength of a center-right party, in fact, led to the collapse of those efforts to forge an alliance.[98] Similarly, Fraga's inclusion within the AP of right-wingers led the Christian democratic Unión Democrática Española (UDE) to rebel against the leadership of its founder, Federico Silva, and to refuse to enter the AP with him.[99] Thus, Fraga's decision to coalesce with such persons as Fernández de la Mora and Thomás de Carranza reduced the "ideological space" occupied by the party and shifted its ideological center of gravity much farther to the right than had been desired initially. The refusal of centrist groups to enter the coalition meant that Fraga, rather than standing near the middle of a broad-based party, would instead be one of the most progressive members of a very right-wing coalition.

Why, then, include conservative *Franquistas* in the coalition? Several factors were involved. The first is that AP leaders misperceived the true center of gravity of the Spanish electorate, believing it to be farther to the right than it actually was. There was also a discrepancy between their own "centrist" positions (as they saw them) and their right-wing images in the eyes of both other political elites and the general public. Elite interviews indicated that while such image misperceptions were common, in the case of the AP these distortions were more pronounced. Since most of the founders of the AP had been government officials under Franco, it is likely that they had become accustomed to evaluating the ideological stands of individuals according to their relationship to other members of the Franquist political elite. This basis of comparison was highly misleading, because Franquist governments consisted almost exclusively of persons with conservative political values.[100] Thus, such political figures as Fraga and Licinio de la Fuente were described by some AP officials as progressive centrists, or even to the left of center, while these individuals were perceived by the general public as being much farther to the right.

The creation of AP was also greatly affected by uncertainty about the future electoral law. Fraga and his coalition partners expected the adoption of a single-member constituency system of either the British "first past the post" or the French Fifth Republic two-ballot variety. They believed that such electoral mechanisms would promote a two-party or two-bloc system, within which a center-right party would benefit: given a choice between a moderately conservative party or coalition, on the one hand, and a left-of-center coalition (including Communists and other Marxists), on the other, most Spaniards would prefer the former. Such expectations were not entirely unreasonable, given the small percentage of self-identified Marxists[101] and the antipathy toward communism that had built up over the preceding decades. The division of Spain into single-member constituencies was also expected to maximize the voter-mobilization capacities of the various members of the AP through their connections with local notables, and would allow them to capitalize on the name recognition of those leaders. These miscalculations concerning the electoral law had serious detrimental effects. The eventual selection of a modified proportional-representation electoral law contributed to the emergence of a multiparty system, and AP found itself outflanked by more centrist political forces. The latter, moreover, were able to use the anti-Marxist appeals that had initially been a major element of the AP campaign strategy. Thus, many of the strategic decisions taken by the founders of the AP turned out to be inappropriate for the conditions under which the 1977 campaign was actually conducted.

Another source of difficulties for the AP was the contradiction between the "catch-all" model initially envisaged by Fraga and its excessive reliance on patron-client relationships, which led to AP's actual emergence as a "clientelistic party." This kind of political party is a loose confederation of notables, each with his own geographical or clientelistic base of support. Such a party typically has a weak organization and places little or no stress on program or ideology. Its principal function is to coordinate the individual campaign efforts of notables for the purpose of securing power at the national level. Their campaign activities, in turn, are based on hierarchical chains of interpersonal relationships of a quasi-feudal variety.[102] Central to these hierarchical relationships are what are referred to in Spain as *caciques*—local notables who perform the crucial role of "transmission belt between local interests and the administration."[103] Under conditions of geographical isolation from a dominant center of government, coupled with low levels of functional literacy and poorly developed transportation and communications media, a localized patron-client relationship of this kind can be mutually beneficial. A party official in Galicia described the *cacique* as

> the vehicle by which the citizen can resolve his problems. The citizen—who is worried about resolving problems with the doctor or the school, or the problem of difficult or nonexistent communication, or the problem of an unjust accusation before the courts, or of delinquency in paying his taxes to the state, etc.—the citizen, the peasant, in these dispersed nuclei of population, has recourse to an intermediary. That intermediary is the *cacique,* who can intercede on his behalf, but in exchange for pledging his very conscience and his vote.[104]

Although such political relationships flourished in the past,[105] they have diminished in importance as a consequence of socioeconomic modernization. Javier Tusell argues in several studies of Spanish politics of the Restoration era that "the generalized demobilization of the electorate, especially in rural environments," is a prerequisite for this variety of political activity.[106] As socioeconomic modernization proceeds—as rural populations become increasingly literate, exposed to mass communications media, and "mobilized" politically—the utility of the *cacique* as an intermediary declines, and his attempts to influence voting decisions are increasingly perceived as objectionable interference.[107]

Nonetheless, this kind of party remained relevant to Spain in the late 1970s for several reasons. First, in certain regions, such as Galicia (the region of origin of both Manuel Fraga and Gonzalo Fernández de la Mora), the socioeconomic and geophysical prerequisites for *caciquismo* were met. A large proportion of Galicia's 2.5 million people are widely scattered among 40 thousand separate nuclei of habitation, which, because of the mountainous terrain and a poor transportation infrastructure, are relatively isolated. This geophysical factor interacts with the relatively low level of education and literacy in Castilian to produce a passive, "unmobilized" population, within which *caciquismo* persists. Hence, while a clientelistic party may be inappropriate for most of modern Spain, it remained a viable option in certain areas. Second, if political demobilization is a necessary mass-level prerequisite for the survival of clientelistic party structures, then the intentional and systematic demobilization of the Spanish population under the Franquist regime facilitated the reappearance of such parties.[108] Third, elite-level *personalismo* and clientelism were widespread within political institutions and the state administration during the Franquist era.[109] Hence, nearly four decades of familiarity with clientelism as a normal means of conducting business led party leaders with considerable past experience in these government institutions to conceive of the process of party-building as one primarily concerned with extending clientelistic networks and loosely linking them together at the national level. It also led them to overestimate the importance of such personalistic linkages as electoral resources. Finally, the Franquist regime was one within which ideological differences were intentionally suppressed both at the mass and the elite level. Gonzalo Fernández de la Mora went so far as to proclaim in *Twilight of Ideologies* (and on other occasions)[110] that all ideologies were outmoded and would soon disappear from politics. Party-builders holding such views were therefore attracted to the nonideological nature of a clientelistic party. At a minimum, they paid insufficient attention to the ideologies or public images of their future coalition partners in the process of forging alliances.

Clientelism was an important criterion in all of the basic decisions involved in founding the AP. It influenced the negotiations that culminated in mergers of the formerly independent proto-parties, the strategies and methods used in creating a provincial-level infrastructure, and the recruitment of candidates for the 1977 elections.

Negotiations over the alliance of Fraga's Reforma Democrática with other groups took place in the summer of 1976. Following the collapse of discussions with the centrists Areilza and Pío Cabanillas, Fraga turned his attention to the various groups in the Federación de Asociaciones del Movimiento-Organización—that is, those "associations" which had been created in accord with Arias Navarro's "reforms." These included the UDPE of Martínez Esteruelas, Silva's UDE, the UNE of Fernández de la Mora, Acción Regional of López Rodó, and Raimundo Fernández Cuesta's Frente Nacional Español. All but one eventually joined the AP. As an indication of the ideological heterogeneity of these groups, Fernández Cuesta opted for an attempt to resurrect the Falange and moved into an alliance with other extreme right-wing parties led by the charismatic fascist Blas Piñar.

Fraga entered into this coalition partly out of his appreciation of the electoral benefits to be derived from the pooling of the personal followings of his collaborators:

> At a moment like this, in which it is necessary to mobilize a population which has spent many years demobilized politically, it is indeed natural that a party can present various fronts, various tentacles, can we say, various pseudopods to reach out and attract.... For example, we can, through Licinio de la Fuente, direct ourselves to some fronts which are different from those which, on the other hand, Laureano can touch, etc. I can reach others different from those which Gonzalo can touch.[111]

Further elaborating on the influence of personalistic ties on the formation of the AP, it was stated in a 1981 interview, "That always occurs—personal relations—especially in a process which starts from the nonexistence of parties. But these personal connections are not purely personal . . . they were not friendships based on a golf club or a business, but rather involved mutual political propositions."

The second criterion that entered into these decisions involved electoral resources of a different kind. It was believed that many Spanish banks would be more willing to contribute generously to a broad-based right-wing alliance than to individual conservative factions. *Cambio 16* reported on September 27, 1976, that a consortium of banks had pledged to such a coalition an annual contribution of 1,000 million pesetas—a sum that would ultimately exceed the reported 1977 campaign expenditures of all other Spanish parties. In addition to these financial resources, it was further believed that a party such as the AP could count on the support of the Movimiento's extensive infrastructure throughout the country.[112] Wildly optimistic electoral projections were published shortly before the formal announcement of the creation of the Alianza Popular. An account in *Cambio 16* (ibid.) claimed that, under certain conditions, the AP would receive 66 percent of the votes of the Spanish electorate. Another account (ibid.) estimated that a right-wing party with Movimiento support could so totally dominate the electoral process in Spain's 28 least populous, rural conservative provinces that "the opposition could hope to elect none of its candidates. These are close to 90 seats, without any contest."

On the basis of these miscalculations of strength, and in order to capitalize on its projected support in conservative, rural provinces, members of the AP and their allies in the last corporatist Cortes demanded that the electoral law proposed by the Suárez government be substantially altered. AP *procuradores* first insisted on adoption of a single-member constituency system,[113] as conservative parties have done in Spanish politics.[114] When it became clear that the Suárez government would not abandon its attempt to create a proportional representation system, AP representatives demanded that, in exchange for their votes in favor of the government's Political Reform Law, "correctives" would have to be made to reduce the proportionality of representation.[115] Specifically, they insisted that even the least populous rural province should be guaranteed a minimum of five seats in the new Congress of Deputies.[116]

At the provincial level, the personalistic nature of this party-building process was even more apparent. Lacking the kind of historical tradition or organizational continuity that facilitated the infrastructural development of the Socialist and Communist parties, personal ties and outright clientelism played disproportionate roles in the establishment of provincial branches of the AP. In virtually all of the provinces included in our elite-interview sample, the AP executive committee members who had joined the party in its early stages reported that they had been induced to play active roles in politics because of personal ties to one or more of the national-level founders of the party. As one AP provincial executive committee member said in an interview in July 1978: "Most were personal friends or collaborators of those national leaders. They had established contacts while those national leaders were ministers of Franco." On this basis, each of the founders of the AP had established provincial branches of their respective proto-parties. The most widespread of these were branches of Fraga's Reforma Democrática, but several other national leaders had also been reasonably successful in organizing small clusters of supporters in a large number of Spanish provinces. The alliance forged at the national level in October 1976 was followed by mergers at the provincial level among the embryonic party organizations previously established. Representatives of each of the proto-parties present in the province were given seats on the newly created executive committee of AP, at least until a party congress could be held to democratically elect provincial party leaders.

The national-level merger between Fraga's Reforma Democrática and the other six parties to form AP did succeed in augmenting the organizational and, especially, the financial resources available for the 1977 campaign. But, in securing these objectives, the image of Manuel Fraga and his party had been severely damaged. In some instances (particularly with regard to the populist Licinio de la Fuente), the individuals drawn into the coalition fit with the reformist center-right image Fraga initially wished to project. Even the inclusion of Federico Silva appeared, at the time, to be consistent with a professed committment to democratization of the Spanish political system.[117] But the presence of such right-wingers as Thomás de Carranza, López Rodó, and, especially, Fernández de la Mora gave the AP a decidedly right-wing character. (It should be remembered that Fernández de la Mora, as late as autumn 1976, attempted to alter the Suárez reform law to provide for the creation of a *corporatist* upper legislative house.)

The selection of candidates at the provincial level further damaged whatever remained of AP's "reformist" image. In most provinces *caciques* and local notables with close ties to the Franquist past were chosen, and in some cases persons on the extreme right stood as AP candidates. This was in part a result of the personalistic nature of the AP and its loose, quasi-confederal structure. Several persons close to Fraga had wished to screen candidates carefully to preclude the nomination of those who might damage the party's image, but they were largely prevented from doing so by other faction leaders acting as patrons.[118] Provincial executive committees—on which the more progressive Reforma Democrática representatives were often outnumbered by supporters of the more conservative proto-parties—had a great deal of autonomy in the formulation of electoral lists. In contrast with the dominant role played by national leaders of other parties, the role played by Fraga and the AP central office in this process was restricted to resolving disputes at the provincial level. And in provinces in which the "Magnificent Seven" stood as candidates, the AP central office was excluded from the process altogether. Thus, in Catalunya candidates selected by López Rodó displaced Reforma Democrática members who had labored to establish a viable branch of that proto-party,[119] Fernández de la Mora determined the selection of candidates in Pontevedra, and so on.[120] In other provinces, there was jealous jockeying among the original proto-parties for the most favored positions on the electoral lists. As an embittered president of a provincial branch of the AP said in an interview in Andalucía in May 1978, each of the leaders of the seven original parties "wanted their own representatives to head the list. We did not undertake an adequate study of the candidates. We did not sufficiently examine their backgrounds nor make intelligent decisions about what kinds of candidates would project a desirable image." As a result, too many of the candidates nominated in that province were "aristocrats. This was a terrible mistake—it subjected us to a brutal propaganda campaign on the part of all the other parties, and it is for that reason that we did so poorly in the election. We needed instead to attract candidates from the middle class, ordinary persons, people in industry. We must avoid the temptation of attracting persons of high social status." Even Manuel Fraga's sister warned him that, because of the public images of the candidates nominated in her province (Sevilla, where most AP candidates had been members of Fernández de la Mora's UNE), the AP would receive very few votes.[121]

Perhaps the most serious mistake in the selection of candidates was the nomination of Carlos Arias Navarro as an AP candidate for the Senate. As Ramírez has claimed, "The announcement of the candidacy of Carlos Arias was for the AP the point of no return." For the average voter, it irrevocably converted the party into "a purely and simply continuist party, purely and simply Franquist."[122] Despite the fact that Arias never attempted to conceal his political preferences (he claims that, when asked to stand as an AP candidate, he told Fraga that he felt a "dogged loyalty to the Caudillo"),[123] Fraga suggested his candidacy because, in Arias' words, "for a sector of the Spanish people my image could be important."[124] But, for the majority of voters, the inclusion of Arias was decidedly negative. In spite of requests from the AP campaign committee[125] and from Fraga himself that he "speak more of the future and less of the past,"[126] Arias frequently expressed his pride in the accomplishments of the old order, and often provoked crowds at AP rallies to break out in chants of "Franco, Franco, Franco. . . ." Possibly the most serious damage to the AP campaign was inflicted by Arias' appearance on nationwide television, during which he explicitly mentioned the name of Franco 7 times, and made 14 additional allusions to him.[127]

Finally, Fraga himself contributed to the disastrous erosion of the reformist image he had originally wished to project. Perhaps as a product of the strains and frustrations of the campaign, his behavior at campaign rallies and on national television became increasingly immoderate. At one party rally, for example, he unexpectedly charged into the crowd in angry pursuit of a cluster of hecklers who had disrupted his speech.[128] His agitated appearance during the final televised speech of the campaign, moreover, did little to calm the fears of moderate voters suspicious of the party's stability and committment to democracy.[129]

Despite the relatively moderate and reformist electoral platform of the AP (90 percent of which was virtually identical to that of the UCD),[130] the appearance on Alianza Popular lists of diehard *Fran-*

quistas, the frequent favorable references to the old regime at campaign rallies, the alarmist, authoritarian language used by many candidates, the nomination of *caciques* and elitist elements in many provinces, and even Fraga's short temper—all contributed to the electorate's perception of the AP as a reactionary, clientelistic party, rather than the reformist, catch-all party first envisaged by its principal creator. With this public image, it succeeded in attracting only 8.3 percent of the popular vote and in electing only 16 deputies.

This bitterly disappointing outcome was the product of attempting to create a political party at an early stage in the transition, in the face of uncertainty concerning both the ultimate outcome of that transition and the efficacy of different kinds of electoral resources in a new democratic regime. As a close collaborator of Manuel Fraga's lamented on these frustrated intentions in an interview in July 1979:

> During the summer [of 1976] he moved precipitously, instead of waiting. He moved precipitously and created a political party rooted fundamentally in the essences of *Franquismo*—when he himself was not like that. He was a man of the center. He had invented "the center" and had always spoken of the center. He had, of course, collaborated with Franco, but from a reformist position. And instead of maintaining himself in that position. . . . As I say: in politics one must be authentic. He was not authentic, was not loyal to his convictions and his very being. He joined with López Rodó, who had been his traditional enemy under *Franquismo,* and with Fernández de la Mora. That was clearly an act of inauthenticity. And that had to explode in some manner. . . . The birth of Alianza Popular had its original sin.

THE CENTER

With the PSOE and PCE staking out the left of the political spectrum and the AP appealing primarily to conservative voters, there remained the center. There was no lack of contenders for dominance over this segment of the political space. But only one party, the UCD, emerged as the victor. The crucial question is, why did it do so well and others fare so poorly? The key factor, although not the only one, in the UCD's success was its ability to bring together the moderate opposition to *Franquismo* and the reformists who held official posts within the regime itself. "Moderate opposition," as described by Javier Tusell, "does not mean to say that it was timid but refers to the existence of another kind of opposition which would attempt to alter the very bases of social and economic organization, or would utilize violent means, or does not believe in democratic formulas for the organization of the state."[131]

The moderate opposition, then, excluded various Marxist parties and referred to a wide variety of liberal, social democratic, Christian democratic, and even monarchist groups, which began to form in the final two decades of the Franquist regime. None of these groups ever came close to attaining the levels of mass membership or penetration into society that had been achieved by the Socialist and Communist parties. They did, however, serve as nuclei of potential political leaders. In the early 1970s moderate opposition groups proliferated and expanded.

These proto-parties began to emerge at the time of the first major outbreak of antiregime protest demonstrations in 1956. Among the most important were the Democracia Social Cristiana of José María Gil Robles (former leader of the clerical, right-wing CEDA of the Second Republic), the Izquierda Demócrata Cristiana of Manuel Giménez Fernández (who had also served as a minister under the Republic), the Unión Española of Joaquín Satrústegui (a liberal monarchist), and the social democratic Partido Social de Acción Democrática of Dionisio Ridruejo. Although these groups were illegal, they were not persecuted, as were the Socialists and Communists. Only when their leaders took part in highly visible protests against the regime were they subjected to arrest and imprisonment.[132]

As the death of Francisco Franco approached, moderate opposition parties began to emerge in great numbers. This was particularly true of the 1974–1976 period, when numerous liberal and social democratic parties, in particular, began to form or function more openly. Among the new liberal parties were the Federación de Partidos Demócratas y Liberales (FPDL) of Joaquín Garrigues Walker and Antonio Fontán, the Partido Liberal of Enrique Larroque, and Ignacio Camuñas' Partido Demócrata Popular (PDP). Several social democratic parties were created such as the Grupo Izquierda Social Democrática, founded by Luís González Seara, Rafael Arias Salgado, and Francisco Fernández Ordóñez, and the Partit Socialista de Catalunya-Reagrupament (PSC-R) of Josep Pallach. In addition some evolved out of Ridruejo's original Partido Social de Acción Democrática, including the Partido Socialista Democrático Español of Antonio García López and Manuel Gómez-Reino, the Partido Social Demócrata (PSD) and the Unión Social Demócrata Española (USDE). Christian democratic groups also proliferated. Aside from Gil Robles' Democracia Social Cristiana (renamed the Federación Popular Democrática) and the Izquierda Demócrata Cristiana (by this time under the leadership of former Franquist Education minister Joaquín Ruiz Giménez) were the various "Tácitos,"[133] some of whom joined a political association named the Unión Democrática Española (UDE), initially created in accord with Arias Navarro's "reforms" by Federico Silva and the former Franquist finance minister Alberto Monreal Luque. Others, such as Iñigo Cavero and Fernando Alvarez de Miranda, chose to work temporarily through Fraga's "study group" (Federación de Estudios Independientes, S.A.), and then with Ruiz Giménez. During the summer of 1976, Cavero and Alvarez de Miranda created their own Partido Popular Demócrata Cristiano (PPDC).

The most significant stage in this process of forming centrist parties began with coalescence among the tiny proto-parties within each political family. In 1976 Fernández Ordóñez led the social democratic Izquierda Social-Demócrata Española, PSD, and USDE in founding a Federación Socialdemócrata (FSD). Similarly, the FPDL of Garrigues entered into a loose Alianza Liberal with Satrústegui's Unión Española and Larroque's Partido Liberal. And, following the entry of Federico Silva into the AP, most of his UDE merged with the PPDC of Cavero and Alvarez de Miranda to form the Partido Demócrata Cristiano (PDC).

The second phase of coalescence involved formal mergers among parties of different ideological families. The first product of this process was the Partido Popular, created in December 1976, which included Christian democrats, liberals, social democrats, and others. The leadership of the Partido Popular also reflected a link between reformist sectors of the state administration and moderate groups identified with the illegal opposition. Both of the most prominent leaders of the Partido Popular had held prominent official positions under the old regime, but both had fallen from Franquist favor: José María de Areilza had been Spain's ambassador to Washington and to Paris but after 1970 had begun to play a highly visible quasi-opposition role; and Pío Cabanillas had been a minister but had been fired by Franco in 1975 for favoring press liberalization. Several of the conservative Christian democratic Tácitos were early members of the Partido Popular, as were several previously unaffiliated social democrats and liberals. The creation of Partido Popular was important in several different ways. First, it established a precedent of collaboration among parties from different centrist political families, thus laying the groundwork for the emergence of a catch-all party. As such, it precluded close and explicit ties between the party and particularistic secondary organizations, like religious or business groups. Accordingly, despite their clericalism, the Tácitos involved in founding the PP acknowledged that it would not be a confessional party. The Partido Popular was the driving force behind the formation of a still-broader coalition, the Centro Democrático.

This larger coalition was led by Areilza and Cabanillas. By early 1977 it had attracted, in addition to the Partido Popular, the liberal parties of Garrigues and Camuñas, the Christian democratic PDC, and most of the social democratic factions which had formed the FSD, and, thus, covered a broad segment of the Spanish political spectrum. Although some important Christian democratic, social democratic and liberal parties were excluded, those three political families were represented, and the coalition spanned the ideological space from center-left social democracy to conservative Christian democracy. In addition, the Centro Democrático bridged the gap between the moderate opposition and the former regime. It included persons with past involvement within the Franquist State (such as Fernández Ordóñez, Areilza, Cabanillas, several Tácitos and many former members of the UDE), others who had kept their distance from that regime (e.g., Garrigues), and still others who had opposed the regime and even had been confined for their activities (e.g., Alvarez de Miranda and Cavero).

The Centro Democrático was seriously deficient in one respect. It lacked an adequate presence in all parts of the country, and, even in those areas where it was strongest, its penetration into Spanish society was very shallow. Indeed, while all of the groups merging to form the CD called themselves parties, formulated ideologies, elected officers, etc., in no case did they constitute anything more than "groups of notables"[134] with their respective personalistic followings, who happened to share certain basic notions about politics and wished to play important roles within the new democratic regime. According to a member of the UCD provincial executive committee in an interview in Granada in May 1978, in this period of party formation, "the parties which made up the coalition consisted of nothing more than prominent persons at the national level. They had only a small circle of influence in specific areas. They could not by any stretch of the imagination be called national parties." In most provinces, "branches" of these political parties consisted of little more than "personal contacts with national leaders. There was virtually no core of militants within these parties" (ibid.). As a party official for Málaga bluntly described it in an interview in May 1978: "The national leaders had their own peons in the provinces." Those who had been most instrumental in founding a party branch in their province were primarily "friends of Fernández Ordóñez and the rest," and what they succeeded in establishing was little more than a network of "personal contacts totally lacking any organizational means" (ibid.).

In addition to organizational weaknesses, the Centro Democrático suffered from a shortage of funds and lacked the kind of financial means necessary to run a modern election campaign.[135] The resources needed to compensate for these weaknesses would have to come from other quarters.

ADOLFO SUÁREZ AND THE "INDEPENDENTS"

In early 1977 the most popular politician in Spain was, without any doubt, prime minister Adolfo Suárez.[136] Suárez's popularity stemmed from his crucial role in the creation of a new democratic system. In sharp contrast to the lack of progress toward democratization of the previous government of Arias Navarro, Suárez had moved quickly and decisively to dismantle the Franquist regime immediately after his appointment as prime minister in July 1976. Given his long history of association with the Movimiento Nacional and the Franquist state apparatus, Suárez's appointment was at first greeted unfavorably by all opposition forces. Even Areilza had such grave doubts about Suárez's reformist intentions that he rejected an offer of a ministerial post in the new government.[137] Such expectations were soon confounded, however, by the prompt introduction and enactment of the Political Reform Law, legalization of competing political parties and class-based trade unions, abolition of the Movimiento and the vertical labor syndicates, and legalization of the Communist party.

In addition to his enormous prestige and popularity, Adolfo Suárez had other resources of great value to a political party. As President of the Government, Suárez presided over the state's bureaucratic apparatus, which could be used to compensate for the lack of party organization in many provinces. A further asset was his fund-raising ability. Voluntary contributions, particularly from business groups, could be expected to be greater if they were solicited by a party representing the incumbent government.[138] But in addition to the more-or-less proper and legal financial benefit of incumbency, it was widely alleged that funds from the state budget could be used for electoral purposes.[139] Thus, Suárez possessed many favorable attributes that could be greatly beneficial for a political party. By spring 1977 it was also becoming clear to the prime minister that he could derive advantages from collaboration with a coalition like the CD.

Such a course of action was not, however, Suárez's initial preference. Immediately after approval of the Political Reform Law in the

December 1976 referendum, he wished to found a progressive-centrist or center-left party, which would have been much less heterogeneous ideologically than the future UCD.[140] (Such a party might have been somewhat less successful over the short term in attracting votes from a broad spectrum of political families but over the long term would have been more ideologically coherent and perhaps more stable.) Suárez was prevented from founding a party at that time, however, by strong opposition from a powerful sector of Spanish society. With Cortes President Torcuato Fernández-Miranda acting as an intermediary, one of the *poderes fácticos* warned Suárez that he was regarded as too ambitious and that the launching of his own party at that time could have destabilizing consequences for the regime. Suárez was thus forced to wait until spring 1977, by which time centrist proto-parties had begun to emerge in great numbers, and the Centro Democrático had been formed.

Even though collaboration with those groups had not been his first choice as a party-building method, Suárez had little alternative but to adjust his strategy to fit with the altered circumstances of the political environment. In addition, cooperation with those centrist "taxi parties" (so-called because, in most cases, they were so small that all their members could fit comfortably inside a single taxi) could offset some of Suárez's weaknesses. The most serious of these was his lack of credibility as a convert to democracy. Given his Franquist background, some political sectors were suspicious of his ultimate objectives and regarded with incredulity the process of transition to democracy under his leadership. This image problem could be alleviated through an alliance with persons who had unimpeachable credentials as democrats and with political groups tied to liberal, social democratic, and Christian democratic parties in other democratic countries. Such an alliance would not only improve his own electoral prospects but would increase interparty trust, which would be essential to the next stage of the transition to democracy following the June 1977 elections.

In early spring, informal consultations began concerning the possible entry of Suárez into the Centro Democrático. These overtures took on an added note of urgency as the election approached, and as fears mounted over a victory (or at least a strong showing) by AP. A public opinion poll leaked to the press in April 1977 indicated that the AP had a 20-point lead over the Centro Democrático. Of those expressing a party preference in that poll, "over 40 percent would be in favor of Alianza Popular, while 20 percent would vote for the Centro Democrático."[141] Half of those favoring the AP, however, regarded themselves as centrists and thus might be induced to support a different party. Additional encouragement could be drawn from the finding that many voters (about 40 percent) said they had not yet decided which party they favored.

Negotiations over a merger between Suárez and the centrist parties, however, generated considerable tension within the CD concerning the future leadership of the party. Alfonso Osorio argued that Suárez was the true architect of political reform and that "if the Centro Democrático is going to play the political game of solidarity or understanding with the reform policies of the President, then there can be no other leader than the President."[142] Hurt by what he perceived to be a cabal against his leadership, Areilza resigned on April 24 and withdrew from active involvement in the 1977 campaign. The way was now clear for Suárez to join and take control of the center coalition.

The integration of Adolfo Suárez and his followers within the new Unión de Centro Democrático (UCD) was not accomplished without additional conflict and angry resignations. In exchange for contributing his prestige, popularity, infrastructural support, and financial resources to the new party, Suárez demanded and received full authority to draw up the various provincial lists of UCD candidates for the Congress of Deputies and the Senate. As his collaborator Leopoldo Calvo Sotelo (to whom Suárez delegated responsibility for selecting candidates) indelicately stated to the assembled leaders of the Centro Democrático, "You will have to sign documents that are not negotiable."[143] One of these statements gave considerable authority to Suárez and enabled him (actually, Calvo Sotelo) to add to electoral lists the names of numerous individuals not initially associated with the Centro Democrático:

> Unión de Centro Democrático proposes to offer to the voters a moderate position similar to that represented by the non-Marxist parties preponderant in Europe, of Christian democratic, liberal and social democratic filiation, in order to support in the next Cortes the policy of President Suárez, for the peaceful and definitive consolidation of a stable democracy in Spain. In this sense, numerous requests have been received from independent personalities who wish to be included in the candidacies of the coalition.[144]

Accordingly, Calvo Sotelo and Suárez drastically revised the lists of candidates initially proposed by the Centro Democrático. In doing so, they shaped the basic character of the new party, as well as determined the identity of its elites.

The electoral lists presented to the assembled party leaders on May 6 provoked considerable disappointment and anger. Only about one-half of the 350 candidates for the Congress of Deputies had been members of the original Centro Democrático parties: 54 had been members of the Partido Popular; 39 belonged to the Christian democratic PDC; 49 were liberals from the FPDL or the PDP; and 20 were PSD social democrats.[145] Among those added to the lists by Calvo Sotelo and Suárez were representatives of small regional parties, such as the Partido Social Liberal Andaluz of Manuel Clavero Arévalo, the Partido Gallego Independiente, the Unión Democrático Murciana, Acción Regional Extremeña and the Unión Canaria, as well as of the rump of the Federación Social Demócrata which had earlier refused to join the CD with Fernández Ordóñez and his PSD. But the bulk of the UCD's candidates were "independents"— "the President's men"—many of whom had been associated with the Movimiento Nacional or the vertical *sindicatos* of the Franquist regime.[146] The displacement of large numbers of CD candidates, coupled with the inclusion of former *Franquistas* whose commitment to democracy was open to challenge, nearly led to the breakdown of the coalition.[147] Particularly questionable was the appearance of two conservative *Franquistas* among the top nine names on the electoral lists for Madrid—a province where there was very little need for "infra-structural reinforcement," and where their presence could do significant damage to the progressive centrist image the party wished to project.[148] Serious conflicts broke out in other provinces as well.[149] Some frustrated CD leaders resigned in protest over the low positions on electoral lists that they were allocated. Among them were Enrique Larroque (head of the small Partido Liberal) and Antonio de Senillosa (a close associate of Areilza in the Partido Popular).

In the face of such intense opposition, why were so many "independents" incorporated within the party? The most important reason (as described by one of the party's founders in an interview in July 1983) was that

> they were persons with government experience. That was very important at a time like that. . . . Political life [at that time] had such dynamism; the opposition was so strong; the attacks on the very process [of transition to democracy] were very serious. In those days time, for me, was not a matter of months, it was a matter of seconds. . . . [Thus] the incorporation of those persons was so that the ministries under their control would not function poorly. The reason for the incorporation of Martin Villa, etc., was their efficacy, their capacity to govern: the capacity to take a seat in a ministerial department and begin to act, without having to pass through a period of apprenticeship.

A second major reason for the incorporation of "independents" within the UCD coalition was that they possessed organizational resources which could compensate for the infrastructural weaknesses of the original CD parties. With their many years of service in the Franquist state apparatus, prominent "independents" had established personal relationships with local elites throughout the country. Rodolfo Martin Villa, in particular, was at the center of an extensive personalistic network, of which Jaúregui and Soriano write:

> [It] was nothing more and nothing less than the personal contacts built up in the course of nearly two decades of public life, in various posts in the administration. Men of the vertical Organización Sindical, for the most part, or the remains of the Sindicato Español Universitario. Men who were going to prove themselves to be so useful in assembling a party—starting from a group of friends and notables—that would win the elections of 1977.[150]

In the course of the 1977 campaign, assistance from notables with extensive personalistic networks or (if accusations by opposition parties are to be believed) from the office of the civil governor was indeed of much benefit in offsetting infrastructural weakness in some areas. This was particularly true in certain rural provinces—such as in Galicia, Old Castile, and Leon[151]—where levels of political activity were insufficient to have created well-organized party branches. The centrist coalition also benefitted from governmental intervention in Catalunya. There the coalition was weak because, as Tusell argues, the Catalán nationalist orientation of moderate opposition groups inhibited collaboration with their statewide counterparts, and the region totally lacked a reformist Franquist tradition.[152] Thus, as a UCD official in Barcelona explained in an interview in July 1978:

> There was great concern at the national level of the UCD about this absence of success in forming a party in Barcelona. One week before the formal closure of lists prior to the June election, Suárez acted boldly and suddenly, and instructed [an individual in the office of the civil governor] . . . to put together a party list for the UCD within 48 hours. This was a stroke of genius by Suárez, which succeeded brilliantly. Given that there was no party structure and an imposed party list, we nonetheless succeeded in electing five deputies from this province.

This kind of partisan intervention by individuals within or close to the state apparatus led to outraged cries of protest from other parties. Some described the UCD as nothing more than a "syndicate of power."[153] Others claimed "that the UCD is an official party led by a government. If the government had not formed this party, it would not have received 5 percent of the vote in the last election."[154] Although accusations of this kind may have been exaggerated for partisan reasons, they clearly reveal the widespread belief among political elites that the UCD gained significant benefit from the activities of Adolfo Suárez and his "independents."

Finally, the inclusion of "independents" within the UCD coalition helped to bridge the gap between collaborators and supporters of the Franquist regime, on the one hand, and its opponents, on the other. These considerations were not paramount among the decision-making criteria of the founders of the UCD,[155] but other studies have shown that the incorporation in the governing party of persons with past ties to the old regime helped to legitimate the new regime.[156] In addition, for those voters with lingering sympathies toward the old regime, as well as those fearful of abrupt political change, their inclusion provided a modicum of comforting continuity, thereby enhancing the electoral appeal of the UCD.

At the same time, the presence within the UCD of persons with Franquist backgrounds was not as great a liability as one might have expected. Among voters hostile to the former regime, the UCD benefitted from the highly salient presence in the campaign of the AP, which functioned as a lightning rod for such anti-Franquist sentiments. The behavior of the two parties during the campaign highlighted the differences in their public images in this regard. Where AP candidates spoke of the accomplishments of the Franquist regime, the UCD could claim that it had dismantled it and had created a democracy in its place.[157] Several AP leaders (such as Arias Navarro) used alarmist, authoritarian language in warning of the impending breakdown of order and stability; the UCD never articulated such themes.

The personal backgrounds of AP and UCD candidates also contributed to their differing images. Although the UCD included both persons from reformist sectors of the Franquist regime and from the moderate opposition, AP lists included no representatives of any opposition group. Thus, the presence of persons active in the moderate opposition, as well as of those who had been uninvolved in politics under the former regime, precluded any widespread perception of the UCD as a Franquist party.

An analysis of the backgrounds of AP and UCD candidates elected to the Congress of Deputies in 1977 reveals further differences between the two parties: the elected representatives of AP, in general, were older than most UCD representatives (see appendix A). AP deputies had achieved higher official positions in the Franquist state, over a more extended period of time, than had UCD candidates with ties to the state administration. Of the AP's 16 deputies, 7 had served as government ministers prior to 1975, and their terms in office averaged over six years. Only 1 of the 165 UCD deputies had reached such a high rank while Franco was still alive—he served for less than one year and was fired for his "excessive" liberalism. The other 24 UCD deputies who had held official positions within the state administration prior to 1975 were lower in rank and, therefore, less visible to the general public (5 had served as subsecretaries, 5 as directors general, 8 as subdirectors general or service chiefs, and 6 as section chiefs). Several prominent UCD figures achieved ministerial rank prior to the first democratic elections (including Suárez, Fernando Abril, Rudolfo Martín Villa, Leopoldo Calvo Sotelo, and Landelino Lavilla), but their briefer tenure in office during the July 1976–June 1977 period did not identify them with Franquism as much as did longer service in high office during an earlier, unambiguously Franquist period. Indeed, service in that transitional government was translated into a distinct political advantage, because it had been responsible for passage of the Political Reform Law and other liberalization measures. These widely advertised reformist postures greatly assisted the UCD in distracting the electorate from the personal backgrounds of other UCD candidates who had been closely associated with the Movimiento, the vertical *sindicatos,* and other Franquist institutions.[158]

A VAGUE AND ECLECTIC "IDEOLOGY"

In preparing for the 1977 election, the founders of the UCD coalition never seriously attempted to formulate a precise declaration of ideological or programmatic principles. Indeed, the UCD issued only one "ideological" document during the campaign, *Manual para Vientidos Millones de Electores,* which was released just five days before the election and committed the coalition to nothing more specific than the pursuit of "reform, moderation, democracy, liberty and, as the soul of all this, justice."[159] In ideological terms, what emerged from the 1977 campaign was "an omnibus party,"[160] whose vague, eclectic, ideological predispositions were simply inherited from stands taken by the proto-parties who comprised the original coalition.

That inheritance included elements of liberalism, social democracy, Christian democracy, and other less clearly defined ideological positions associated with each of the political families in the coalition. The social democratic component (led by Francisco Fernández Ordóñez and Rafael Arias Salgado) was comparable to moderate social democrats in other Western European politics. It favored "a process of reforms in capitalist society. . . . Social democracy is a gradual interpretation of the socialist project, a socialism whose utopia is confined by the possible reality. . . . But social democracy is also a deepening of the concept of liberty, and that explains its connection with the liberal thought of the left."[161] Similarly, the Christian democrats in the UCD coalition were much like their European counterparts. They opposed legalization of divorce and abortion, favored "the preservation of the family," and insisted on the continued subsidization of the religious sector of education. On economic issues, most of them were conservative,[162] but several were centrists in economic questions, and a few were decidedly to the left of center.

The liberals, as described by a UCD official in a 1978 interview, were "very progressive concerning social matters (such as legalization of divorce), but very, very conservative regarding economic matters. They are liberals in the classic nineteenth-century sense of the term." Indeed, as Joaquín Garrigues Walker described his ideology: "The three pillars which support our ideological edifice are: defense of a real liberty for all, limitation of the ever more all-inclusive power of government, and the guarantee of initiative and private property as the motors of economic activity."[163] Contemporary Spanish liberalism, however, departs from the classic model of the nineteenth century in that it is totally devoid of anticlericalism. As the ideological declaration of Garrigues' FPDL states, "Relations with the Catholic Church, professed by the majority of Spaniards and united with our national history, will be established on the principles of mutual respect and independence."[164] In sharp contrast with the anticlerical liberalism of the past, several prominent members of Garrigues' party were members of Opus Dei.

Finally, even those "independents" brought into the party by Suárez who had histories of involvement in the Movimiento and the vertical *sindicatos* were noteworthy because of their lack of ideological uniformity. A common erroneous assumption, especially in 1976–1977, was to think that past association with the Movimiento was synonymous with right-wing social and political values. Although many "independents" were indeed right wingers, the most important of them—Suárez, Fernando Abril, and their immediate collaborators—were not. Eventually Suárez emerged as the principal figure on the left wing of the party and was attacked by conservatives within his own ranks for his progressive social views (e.g., support for legalized divorce and for a progressive tax reform).

No steps were taken prior to the 1977 election toward drafting a more precise and coherent party ideology for two reasons. First, it was regarded as electorally useful (at least over the short term) to issue vague and eclectic appeals. The eclecticism of the UCD's "ideology" enabled it to appeal to different segments, or political families, within the politically informed strata of the Spanish electorate. The vagueness of its stands fits well with the belief that most voters were not particularly interested in political ideologies of any kind. As a former UCD secretary general explained in a 1983 interview:

> You must not forget that at that time the Spanish people had a very limited political culture and were not ideological. There were persons who regarded themselves as of the left, and knew that historically the left was identified with the Socialist and Communist parties. But aside from them, for most persons of the center, it was very difficult to explain the differences between Christian democracy, or a liberal party, or moderate social democracy.... [Under the Franquist regime] the average citizen had been converted to consumerism; as long as he didn't get mixed up in politics nobody would bother him. There had been no politicization of the country. A welfare consumerism had been created. Faced with this lack of political awareness, it was very difficult to launch an undertaking of ideological parties.

For some other UCD leaders, the reasons for not staking out clear ideological stands transcended the particular circumstances of post-Franco Spain. Asked in a 1978 interview to describe the UCD's ideology, a member of the national executive committee replied:

> Do American parties have ideologies? Do they? Ideologies are synthetic creations. They close out options. There is no reason to close

out options; we want to be open, to take a little from one and a little from another. Ideologies are conducive to Messianism. That style of politics is not acceptable to the man of today. That leads to dogmatic argument. We want to be an integrative party. We accept certain basic principles but are open to all shadings of meaning within those basic principles. To write a specific ideology would be to enter into a period of contraction. We don't believe in ideologies—we don't want to have our own catechism. But we certainly want to remain true to the basic principles of liberty, equality, justice, solidarity, and integration.

Apart from reasons of electoral efficacy and the lack of time between the formation of the coalition and the 1977 election, there were other reasons for maintaining a vague ideological stance: in several respects, the ideological tenets of the political families making up the original coalition were inconsistent with one another. These incompatibilities became increasingly clear after the 1979 elections and contributed to the ultimate breakup of the party. Over the short term, they simply made it difficult (if not impossible) for UCD elites to reach agreement on a clear statement of ideological principles before the 1977 election campaign.

Common agreement could easily be reached, however, concerning one matter of overriding importance in that first democratic contest—the nature of the transition to a new democratic regime. "There was one adhesive element," a former UCD minister said in a 1983 interview, "and that was that political change should take place by means of a process other than *ruptura*, which was the position initially taken by the Socialist party, or than the continuist mode favored by AP in 1977: the fundamental task which joined these distinct groups together was to undertake political change via *reforma*." In his view, the transition to democracy was the raison d'être of the UCD.

THE DEMISE OF OTHER MODERATE PARTIES

Several moderate political parties disappeared as a consequence of the 1977 election. The most important of these were the Izquierda Demócrata Cristiana of Ruiz Giménez and the Federación Popular Democrática of Gil Robles (which had joined forces in the Federación de la Democrácia Cristiana [FDC]). A complete explanation of their demise involves a wide variety of factors related to one fateful decision: the refusal to join or remain within a broader electoral coalition. Failure to do so meant that in some cases (e.g., several liberal and social democratic groups) the party occupied too narrow a niche on the political spectrum, and in all cases the party suffered from an inadequate organizational infrastructure and a serious shortage of funds.

The disappearance of the two largest Christian democratic parties was the most striking example of this phenomenon. In the months preceding the election, public opinion polls indicated that a plurality of Spaniards expressed a partisan preference for these Christian democratic groups.[165] These parties had relatively long organizational histories and enjoyed considerable visibility and prestige, both domestically and internationally. As early as 1965 they had been recognized by the Christian Democratic International, which meant that they received financial subsidies, advice, and even outright physical assistance during the election.[166] In the early stages of the 1977 campaign, this involved the active participation of such dignitaries as Aldo Moro, Leo Tindemans, Kai Uwe von Hassel, and other leading figures of European Christian democracy.[167] The West German Christian Democratic Union (CDU) also contributed financially to their campaign.[168]

The parties of the FDC, however, failed to heed the advice offered by the CDU, which had urged them to seek out alliances with a broader array of political groups.[169] Gil Robles was particularly opposed to this strategy, because he had always preferred to keep his Christian democratic party independent from other ideological factions.[170] He was also utterly opposed to collaboration with individuals linked to the political institutions of the Franquist regime, regardless of how progressive their current political beliefs might be.[171] Gil Robles had even opposed collaboration with the Partido Popular and the UDE for that reason, arguing on January 20, 1977, that "This is the heroic hour of testimonial purity."[172] Ruiz Giménez also initially opposed alliances with the Partido Popular and the UDE, but for a slightly different reason. As a former minister during the Franquist regime, he could not reasonably argue against contacts with persons linked to the Franquist past. By 1977, however, Ruiz Giménez's political beliefs had shifted substantially to the left, and he came to oppose cooperation with the Partido Popular and the UDE because of their relative conservatism.[173] By late April, however, Ruiz Giménez reluctantly reached the conclusion that coalition with the newly emerging UCD was essential. During the preceding month he had been contacted both by Suárez and the leaders of the Centro Democrático concerning his possible entry into the coalition.[174] Thus a proposal for integration with the UCD was set before the political council of the FDC. Representatives of Ruiz Giménez's Izquierda Democrática voted 29 to 15 in favor of integration, but Gil Robles' FPD opposed that proposal by a margin of 15 to 4. Because it had previously been decided that such a decision must be reached by a positive vote of two-thirds of the membership of the political council, the proposal was defeated. Thus, the FDC contested the election for the Congress of Deputies in accord with Gil Robles' initial preferences—"to maintain the democratic purity and the Christian democratic identity of the party, even at the cost of converting itself into a merely testimonial force."[175] The FDC did form an alliance (called the Equipo Demócrata Cristiano del Estado Español) with several regional Christian democratic parties, including the Partido Nacionalista Vasco, the Unió Democrática de Catalunya and the Unió Democrática del Pais Valenciá—several of whose members were elected to the Congress of Deputies—but this coalition did nothing to strengthen the FDC in the great majority of Spain's provinces.

The disastrous defeat of the FDC in the 1977 elections must be attributed as well to its serious infrastructural inadequacies. As described by Tusell, the Equipo was primarily "an urban group with scarce implantation in those areas which one would logically expect would support it."[176] Even though such parties as the Izquierda Democrática had existed for decades, they never became more than small clusters of individuals. On the eve of the 1977 elections, the Izquierda Democrática had no more than 600 members,[177] very few of whom resided in the religious and conservative rural provinces whose populations were most predisposed to support a Christian democratic party. Indeed, the Equipo could not even present lists of candidates in three provinces of Old Castile (Palencia, Segovia, and Soria), three provinces of New Castile (Guadalajara, Ciudad Real, and Toledo), nor in Albacete, Cáceres, Lugo, Las Palmas, Santa Cruz de Tenerife, Teruel, Ceuta, and Melilla.[178] It was precisely in these areas that the UCD benefitted most from the infrastructural reinforcement provided by the "independents" of Suárez and Martín Villa—assistance that was explicitly rejected by the April 27 vote of the FDC Political Council.

For the parties that explicitly appealed to religious sentiments, the absence of endorsement by the Church was an additional handicap. Not only did the Episcopal Conference abstain from formally intervening in the campaign, but, according to elite sources, there were relatively few instances in 1977 of local priests taking an electoral stance. When they did, such involvement normally took the form of attacks on parties of the left, rather than explicit endorsements of specific parties.[179] A principal reason for the electoral neutrality of the Church was the leadership of Cardenal Enrique y Tarancón as president of the Episcopal Conference. Tarancón believed that the Church should break from its past tradition of political involvement and remain strictly neutral during the transition to democracy. This policy denied Spanish Christian democratic parties the kind of infrastructural support enjoyed by their German and Italian counterparts in the aftermath of Would War II. As Fernando Alvarez de Miranda lamented upon the dissolution of his PDC (in a step toward fusion with the UCD in December 1977), "We are no longer in the time of De Gasperi and Adenauer. Spain is moving irremediably toward laicism."[180] The political neutrality of the Spanish Church proved to be of short duration, but it nonetheless had a profound impact on the 1977 elections. The temporary nature of the Church's noninvolvement in politics suggests a more cynical interpretation of that policy: given the existence of several parties purporting to defend the interests of the Church (the UCD, the AP, and the FDC), as well as initial uncertainty concerning which of them would have the best electoral prospects, it would have been difficult for the Church to intervene explicitly on behalf of any one of them.

Finally, the FDC was defeated as a result of the leftist ideological thrust of its campaign, which was inappropriate for the relatively conservative Christian democratic electorate of Spain. Under the leadership of Ruiz Giménez, the FDC stressed in its electoral appeals such themes as workers' "self-management in business firms, federalism as the structural formula for the state, and collaboration with socialists and communists as an immediate political objective."[181] The result, in the words of a member of a UCD provincial executive committee, was that the FDC "could not satisfy the traditional Christian democratic voters in Spain because it was too progressive; but neither could they satisfy socialist voters."

The ultimate consequence was that the Christian democratic parties which initially appeared to have had such strong prospects were totally shut out of the new Cortes.[182] As Tusell (himself a former member of the FDC) concludes:

> The Equipo de la Democracia Cristiana one year before the elections was in a position to convert itself into one of the fundamental axes of Spanish political life, since opinion polls gave it 16 percent of the electorates, but its sectarianism and its identification, on occasions, with the left, which its own electorate repudiated, reduced it to a purely testimonial position.[183]

Independent liberal and social democratic parties also fared poorly for a variety of reasons. Some of the parties that wanted to join the UCD (such as the Reforma Social Española of Manuel Cantarero del Castillo) were not invited to do so. Presumably their electoral resources were regarded as insufficient to justify their inclusion, when weighed against the costs that would be incurred by displacing other candidates from the coalition's electoral lists. Others, such as the Partido Liberal of Enrique Larroque, left the coalition in anger because of the low positions given to their candidates on UCD lists. The most common cause of the isolation and ultimate extinction of other moderate parties was their opposition to the idea of collaborating with the founders of the UCD. The devastating consequences of such strict adherence to principle were sometimes clearly anticipated by leaders of these parties. In an interview in June 1981, one leader shrugged and sadly concluded: "I met with Calvo Sotelo, and told him we would not enter [the UCD]. Why? Because we were not going along with *Franquismo* after having been in opposition to *Franquismo.* That would be an outrage. We were going to die (as a party), and we knew that we were going to die, but. . . ."

CHAPTER FOUR

Party Development in the Era of Consensus

THE YEARS BETWEEN the 1977 and 1979 parliamentary elections were important both for the major parties of Spain and for the prospects for survival of the new democratic regime itself. For the parties, this was a period in which they addressed the various dilemmas of institutionalization and adjustment to the context of a new political regime. This involved efforts to absorb the remains of parties defeated in 1977, to expand or establish their organizations throughout Spain, to alter or establish party ideologies, and, finally, to consolidate or improve their positions vis-à-vis the voting public.

This period was even more crucial from the standpoint of the regime as a whole. Indeed, the principal task to be undertaken was to write a new constitution—to create and legitimate new political institutions, which, if the regime were to survive over the long run, had to be acceptable to all important segments of society. A failure to secure a broad-based consensus on basic constitutional issues could lead to rejection of the new regime by significant groups, to polarization of both elite and mass opinions over latent and potentially explosive cleavages, and even perhaps to the collapse of the regime— as had occurred in the aftermath of the constituent process of 1931–1932.

The fates of the individual parties were, as we shall see in this chapter, closely intertwined with the political events of this period and were particularly affected by the specific roles that party leaders had played in the constituent process. The quasi-consociational practices adopted at the elite level to secure interparty agreement over most basic constitutional issues, as well as to address a growing economic crisis, were to be particularly beneficial to the governing UCD, and, to a somewhat lesser extent, to the PCE. Widespread popular acceptance of the new Constitution in the referendum of December 1978 enabled the Suárez government to claim credit for the successful establishment of a democratic regime and served as a springboard into the election campaign of winter 1979. As for the PCE, it capitalized on the stabilizing and constructive role it had played in the constituent process and in implementation of the Pacts of Moncloa as evidence of its committment to the new democracy and to help shed the negative image it had inherited from the past. But these events were not uniformly beneficial to all major parties. A lack of agreement over the Constitution within the leadership of the AP, for example, led to the breakup of that party and to hasty efforts to reconstitute a center-right coalition on the eve of the 1979 election. And lack of agreement with Basque nationalists over the devolution of limited self-government authority to the regions contributed to the fragmentation and polarization of the Basque party system and to an ever-increasing cycle of violence in Euskadi.

THE POLITICS OF CONSENSUS

THE CONSTITUTION

The principal task confronting the newly democratic Cortes that assembled in the summer of 1977—the writing of a constitution— required the new political elites of Spain to address several historically divisive issues. These included the relationship between Church and state, the role of the monarchy, and the degree of political and administrative autonomy of the various regions. It was clear that the manner in which these and other issues were addressed would have profound implications for the legitimacy and stability of the new regime. But compromise over these issues would be as difficult to achieve as it was essential. Continuation of the privileged status of the Catholic Church, the bans on divorce and abortion, and criminal sanctions for cohabitation and adultery were certain to offend liberals and the left. At the same time, adoption of an anticlerical constitutional text could provoke the Church into withdrawing its support from the regime, as it had in 1931. Similarly, the rejection of appeals for regional autonomy would undoubtedly alienate Basques and Catalans, while extensive concessions to regionalists might provoke opposition from Spanish nationalists in the military. And antilabor statutes could lead to labor unrest and seriously damage an already sagging economy.

Differences over these issues were clearly reflected in the party system that had emerged from the 1977 election. The economic and labor-related articles of the Constitution pitted the PCE and PSOE (which had their own trade unions) against the other four major parties—the UCD, AP, and the Basque and Catalán nationalist parties (each of which received some electoral support from business groups). Concerning Church-state relations and the monarchy, the traditionally anticlerical and republican PCE and PSOE initially opposed the preferences of the other major parties, although the PCE quickly adopted nonconflictual stands on both issues. Center-periphery conflicts arrayed the Basque and Catalán nationalist parties against the UCD and the intensely Spanish-nationalist AP, while the Socialists and Communists shifted positions from one relevant constitutional article to the next.

By joining forces with the AP, the UCD could have had enough votes in the Cortes to enact a partisan constitutional text favoring the Church, business groups, and the perpetuation of a centralized Spanish state.[1] Indeed, as public debate over the Constitution began in the constitutional committee of the Congress of Deputies, the division of the vote at first conformed to this pattern.[2] Continuation of this trend might have pleased the conservative and center-right clienteles of these two parties, but the enactment of a constitution with the support of this narrow "mechanical majority" and without the approval of regionalist or leftist parties would have had grave implications for the legitimacy of the new regime.

Instead, a new decision-making style was initiated on May 22, 1978—the eve of committee deliberations over the potentially explosive article governing the education system. On that night four UCD representatives met privately with four Socialist deputies at a Madrid restaurant to attempt to resolve their outstanding differences. By the next morning they had reached compromise agreements concerning all major religious issues (disestablishment, education, divorce, and abortion), labor relations, conscientious objection to military service, and constitutional provisions governing the proper role of the state in the economy. Although the Communists and the Catalans did not play direct roles in the negotiations of May 22, they had previously consulted with the UCD and had given their approval to this private bipartite negotiation. As the Communist spokesman Jordi Solé Tura explained in an interview in June 1981, "faced with the danger of a breakdown, we preferred at that moment to enter into the game of nocturnal consensus." In light of the success of "the night of José Luis" (the name of the restaurant), all serious differences among Socialists, Communists, Centrists, Catalans and, at times, Basques were subsequently dealt with in accord with quasi-consociational "rules of the game."[3] Only the deputies of AP and of parties represented by just one or two elected officials were systematically excluded from what was called "the politics of consensus," and only the issue of regional autonomy for Euskadi was not resolved through this procedure.

The patterns of elite interaction characteristic of the politics of consensus had certain procedural features conducive to conflict regulation. First, negotiations involved the direct participation of representatives of all groups crucially affected by, or interested in, the issue in question. Accordingly, five of the six major parties were represented in the subcommittee that wrote the first draft of the Constitution.[4] In later deliberations over still unresolved questions the principal protagonists changed, depending on the issue. Negotiations over Church-state relations, for example, involved only the UCD and PSOE. Similarly, deadlocked articles dealing with regional autonomy gave rise to bilateral negotiations between the UCD and PNV. Direct face-to-face negotiation over critical issues increases the probability of agreement; conversely, the exclusion of relevant groups may lead them to deny the legitimacy of the deliberative process and to reject its outcome.[5] In accord with these hypotheses, it is important to note that the only significant blocs of deputies who did not vote in favor of the Constitution were those of the PNV (which had not been represented in the drafting subcommittee) and about half of those of AP (which had been excluded from all of the nocturnal negotiations of the "politics of consensus").

At the same time, the desire to be all-inclusive had to be balanced against a second important consideration: the size of the bargaining units had to be held down to a manageable level. Numerous experiments in social psychology have demonstrated that decision making is easier when the number of participants is reasonably small.[6] The optimum size for reaching collective decisions appears to be about six; larger groups tend to dissolve into debating societies and reach decisions only with great difficulty.

A third crucial feature of the politics of consensus was that negotiations took place in private, and not in public arenas. Privacy shields party representatives from the scrutiny of their respective supporters and electoral clienteles, and thus facilitates the making of concessions central to compromise agreements. Deliberations in public forums provide incentives toward demagogic posturing and reduce the willingness of political elites to make embarrassing concessions.[7] Accordingly, after May 22 serious negotiations took place in private. Open debates in the committees and on the floor of the Congress were brief, perfunctory, and avoided rancorous exchanges whenever possible.

The most important ingredients of the politics of consensus were the historical memories, basic values, political objectives, and behavioral styles of the relevant sets of party elites. Care must be taken to avoid tautological arguments involving these kinds of variables,[8] but it can be stated in the abstract that negotiations involving pragmatic political figures, whose historical memories lead them to perceive potential threats to system survival and who wish to preserve important features of that system, are more likely to culminate in satisfactory conflict resolution than will negotiations among dogmatic individuals, who are unaware of the fragility of the system or who have no stake in its preservation.

One of the most fundamental of these elite characteristics is the "historical memory" of each key party leader. Interviews with and numerous public statements by those who played the most crucial roles in the politics of consensus clearly revealed that recollections of Spanish history profoundly affected interpretations of contemporary political reality. Leaders of the Communist party, in particular, frequently spoke and wrote about how the miscalculations of the Republican era, the horrors of the Civil War, and the repression of the Franquist era dictated prudent and pragmatic behavior in founding a new regime. It would be difficult to overstate the importance for the transition of the fact that the leaders of the largest party of clandestine opposition to the former regime adopted and implemented a policy of national reconciliation and firmly rejected rancorous and uncompromising behavior during this critical constituent period. Similarly, the moderate and constructive role played by the Catalán leader Josep Tarradellas (who, like Santiago Carrillo, had been active in politics during the Republican and Civil War eras) greatly facilitated negotiations with representatives of the Spanish state. And, although Adolfo Suárez was too young to have personally experienced the Civil War, he nonetheless was keenly aware of the potentially explosive cleavages in Spanish society and how they had been activated and intensified by the political elite of Spain's last democratic regime. Indeed, Suárez believed that at the time of Franco's death the principal concern of the Spanish people was the fear of a new civil war. Accordingly, the avoidance of confrontations among political groups was one of his overriding objectives. The UCD elite also included some for whom the memories of the past were more vivid and personal: on the eve of public deliberations over the Constitution in the Congress of Deputies, the president of that body's constitutional committee delivered an impassioned speech warning current constituent elites not to forget the mistakes of their predecessors.[9]

The manner in which Spanish party elites defined their tasks in the constituent process also profoundly affected the success of those deliberations. The key participants in the successful negotiations over religious issues, for instance, defined their goals not as the maximization of the interests of their respective clienteles, but rather as the creation of a legitimate and stable regime within which their supporters' interests would merely be "satisficed" (to use Herbert Simon's term). This was most clearly stated by Adolfo Suárez in a speech before the Cortes in April 1978. "During a constituent process," he said,

> the government must restrict its options to those which would not produce dissensus, because that is the only way to avoid what would be the gravest danger to the body politic: the lack of a concord rooted in the country and [lack of] respect for the basic elements of national coexistence.... The Constitution, as the expression of national concord, must be obtained by consensus."[10]

Similarly, the PSOE representative in the *Ponencia* (drafting subcommittee), Gregorio Peces-Barba, said on the eve of Cortes deliberations that it was necessary to secure a constitutional consensus, consisting of "not in being in agreement with everything, but [in the fact] that the Constitution would not contain any aspect which would be absolutely unacceptable to any political group."[11] These attitudes played an important part in the satisfactory resolution of differences between the governing UCD and the Socialist and Communist opposition parties, in particular, and precluded the possibility that a lack of agreement would lead significant groups to deny the legitimacy of the new regime. Conversely, representatives of the Basque Nationalist party (PNV) did not regard endorsement of the Constitution by consensus as an important political objective. Indeed, interviews with two high-ranking members of the PNV revealed that the party would not have voted for ratification of that document regardless of the outcome of interparty negotiations. As a PNV deputy stated in a 1981 interview, "We would not approve the Constitution, in fact, ever . . . because it is a *Spanish* Constitution."

The pragmatism of the negotiating elites also affected the outcome of the constituent process. Indeed, according to a 1981 interview with a key participant in the negotiations, this personality characteristic was explicitly taken into consideration in the appointment of most party representatives in the subcommittee which produced the first draft of the Constitution: the Socialists and Communists chose as their representatives Gregorio Peces-Barba and Jordi Solé Tura, both of whom are regarded as among the most moderate and pragmatic members of their parties; Catalans were represented by Miguel Roca i Junyent, who subsequently acquired a reputation for close collaboration with UCD governments in Madrid; and when the UCD representative Miguel Rodríguez Herrero de Miñón exhibited symptoms of dogmatism and rigidity, he was removed from the UCD negotiating team and temporarily replaced, at a particularly crucial point in the negotiations, by the more pragmatic José Pérez Llorca. It is also noteworthy that the dynamic and strong-willed AP representative, Manuel Fraga Iribarne, was systematically excluded from the later stages of private negotiations during the politics of consensus as a means of facilitating compromise among the other parties. Finally, one factor that perhaps impeded negotiations between the UCD and PNV in July 1978 was that the Basque representative in those deliberations was the former Jesuit Xabier Arzallus—reputed to be one of the least moderate, least flexible members of the party hierarchy.

The constituent process of 1977–1978 met with mixed success in addressing traditionally divisive issues. Total conflict resolution was achieved concerning the position of the monarchy, legalization of political parties, and constitutional enshrinement of basic civil and political rights. Consensus over the constitutional treatment of these issues was so widespread and irrevocable that these have ceased to be objects of political controversy. Of these, the status of the king is the most secure: none of the major parliamentary parties following the 1978 constitutional referendum articulated republican sentiments. Only small parties of the extreme right (represented in the 1979–1982 Cortes by just one deputy) and perhaps some within the officer corps of the army openly expressed hostility toward King Juan Carlos.

Compromises over religious issues, the electoral law, and economic matters (labor relations and the role of the state in the economy) are examples of what can best be described as "satisfactory conflict regulation." In these cases the major protagonists reached sufficient agreement over general principles pertaining to these matters so as to neutralize them as potential obstacles to widespread acceptance of the Constitution. But, though the consensus over these principles eliminated them as constitutional conflicts that might, by themselves, threaten the legitimacy of the new regime, implementation of these vague statements would continue to generate considerable (but, so far, manageable) interparty conflict. This is most obvious with regard to economic matters: budgetary and planning decisions in democratic regimes always give rise to clashes between left and right, between government and opposition. Similarly, the parties disadvantaged by a particular electoral system will usually issue demands for reform. In these respects, Spain is no different from other democratic systems. Subsequent conflicts over implementation of constitutional articles dealing with religion, however, have been rather intense and have disrupted the stability of the party system (as will be discussed in our final chapter). To some extent, this was inevitable, insofar as the compromise language of the Constitution mainly functioned to postpone decisions on such matters as legalization of divorce and abortion, and state regulation of and subsidies to the private sector of education. Despite later conflicts over implementation of these general principles, the 1977–1978 constituent process must, nevertheless, be regarded as successful in addressing these traditionally divisive issues.

Resolution of center-periphery conflict through these negotiations was more difficult to secure. Considerable success was achieved in deliberations between Catalán nationalists in the Convergència Democràtica and representatives of the Spanish state. Negotiations with Basque nationalists, on the other hand, never resulted in widespread acceptance of any compromise proposal. The differences between the two cases illustrate the importance of both procedural and attitudinal factors in favoring a positive outcome.

Steps toward decentralization of the Spanish state had, in fact, begun prior to the formulation of a Constitution. On September 28,

1977, the Suárez government signed an agreement in France with Josep Tarradellas, president of the Catalán government-in-exile, which provisionally reestablished the Generalitat under the presidency of Tarradellas. According to the terms of that agreement, the members of the Catalán delegation to the Congress of Deputies would function as elected representatives of the Catalán populace, pending negotiation and approval of a permanent statute of autonomy and the holding of regional elections. In the meantime, the Generalitat entered into direct talks with various ministries of the Spanish state administration with the goal of transferring some governmental functions from Madrid to the region. This "preautonomy" agreement temporarily satisfied Catalán nationalist aspirations. Basque nationalists also secured an interim regional government through preautonomy negotiations, but these agreements were not widely regarded as satisfactory, and their legitimacy was challenged. The most overt challenge came from Francisco Letamendía, then an Euskadiko Ezkerra deputy, who boycotted the negotiations with the Spanish government and subsequently refused to participate in the interim regional institutions. Although favorable to the idea of preautonomy, even the moderate PNV was hostile to the actual institutions that emerged, given their severely limited powers. To this hostility was added the resentment over the election as regional president of Ramón Rubial, a Socialist, rather than someone from their own ranks.

The same pattern carried over into negotiations over the writing of the Constitution. Catalán nationalists promptly endorsed compromise language concerning regional provisions in the new Constitution.[12] Article 2, for instance, "recognizes and guarantees the right of autonomy of the nationalities and regions" but balances this concession with a reaffirmation of "the indissoluble unity of the Spanish nation, common indivisible fatherland of all Spaniards." Recognizing that this and other articles represented the most extensive acknowledgment of the rights of regional minorities ever included in a Spanish constitution, the CDC voted in favor of the text and actively campaigned in support of its ratification in the referendum of December 1978. In contrast, PNV deputies abstained from the vote on article 2, and Letamendía rejected the text altogether, demanding, instead, explicit recognition of the right of self-determination for all regions. "The right to self-determination," he argued, "is a fundamental democratic right, without which the Constitution has no meaning for us. If the Basque people, someday, were to face this alternative, you can be sure that Euskadiko Ezkerra would vote for independence. . . . Euskadi is not a region, but rather a nation divided into two halves."[13] The most serious obstacle to consensual acceptance of the Constitution arose out of a deadlock between the PNV and UCD over a *disposición adicional* to the Constitution concerning restoration of Basque *fueros* (historic rights). That provision expressed "respect for the historic rights of the *foral* territories," the realization of which "will be accomplished . . . within the framework of the Constitution and of the statutes of autonomy." The PNV was particularly opposed to the phrase "within the framework of the Constitution," arguing that the *fueros* were historic rights that took precedence over the Constitution and that the present constituent elites even lacked the authority to "concede" the restoration of those rights.[14] The UCD was equally vehement in opposing an unmitigated restoration of the *fueros*, because, historically they included an implicit acknowledgment of the right to self-determination. This understanding of the *fueros* was shared by many Basque nationalists. As PNV Deputy Xabier Arzallus stated at a party rally: "Ancient Basques lived within an ensemble of kingdoms that were later called Spain . . . and as a guarantee that its way of life would be respected, the right of secession was always reserved. We also reserve [that right], be it or not in the Constitution."[15]

These differences could not be resolved. The PNV delegation walked out of the Congress of Deputies just before that body approved the existing text of the Constitution, abstained from the final Cortes vote on the Constitution, and the party campaigned for abstention in the Constitutional referendum. Euskadiko Ezkerra voted against the Constitution and campaigned against its ratification in the referendum. As a result, less than half of the Basque electorate voted in that referendum (46 percent, compared with a turnout of 68 percent throughout Spain). Only 68.8 percent of those who voted, moreover, cast favorable ballots—some 20 percent less than the national average. In Catalunya, by way of comparison, the turnout was 68 percent, and the affirmative votes (90.4 percent) exceeded the national average.[16]

Several departures from the rules of the politics of consensus contributed to the lack of agreement with Basque nationalists. The absence of a PNV representative in the *Ponencia* that drafted the initial text made it politically difficult for Basque nationalists to endorse in public deliberations a text they had had no hand in writing.[17] The lack of willingness on the part of PNV representatives to compromise—to accept a text which would merely "satisfice"—further reinforced this deadlock. Similarly, the absence of a PNV committment to securing a consensual constitution contributed to this failure.

Whatever may have led to the PNV's stance, its ambiguity toward the new Constitution and the outright hostility of more extreme Basque nationalists posed a regional challenge to the legitimacy of the new regime. This contributed, in turn, to an atmosphere of increasing tension, violence, and uncertainty about regime stability.

ECONOMIC CRISIS AND THE PACTS OF MONCLOA

Another threat to the new democracy came from deteriorating economic conditions in the second half of the 1970s. Just as the Great Depression of the 1930s complicated the tasks of creating and consolidating the Second Republic, a severe economic decline, triggered by the massive increase in Spain's energy costs in 1974, imposed an added burden on political elites.[18] As can be seen in table 7, beginning in 1974, Spain's economic performance increasingly lagged behind that of the 1964–1973 period, during which real economic growth had averaged 7.3 percent and the inflation rate averaged 7.7 percent per year. The extreme difficulty of dealing simultaneously with high levels of unemployment and inflation almost certainly contributed to an undermining of public perceptions of the efficacy of government performance over the long term. In the short run, however, efforts to address the economic crisis created an opportunity for face-to-face negotiations among leaders of government and opposition parties. One positive consequence of this was increased respect and good will among party elites, including both those with roots in the former regime and those from the clandestine opposition. In October 1977 Prime Minister Suárez initiated a round of discussions among the major party leaders at his residence, the Moncloa Palace. The resulting Pacts of Moncloa pledged the government to a continuing program of reforms of political institutions, the social security system, and the regressive taxation system inherited from the Franquist regime; to government controls on price increases; to democratization of the education system; and to certain other policy changes. In exchange, the Socialist and Communist parties promised to induce those trade unions over which they had influence to refrain from excessive strike activity, limit demands for pay increases to 22 percent, and accept more restrictive monetary and expenditure policies. The first major step toward implementation of the pacts was enactment of tax reform legislation by the Suárez government. The long-term consequence of this fiscal policy was the alienation from the UCD of numerous big businesses and wealthy Spaniards—many of whom had taken advantage of the defects of the former taxation system and had made tax evasion what one finance ministry official described as a "national sport" under Franco.[19] The UCD benefitted in the short run, however, by convincing many in the electorate of its reformist intentions and by inducing

TABLE 7
A PORTRAIT OF STAGFLATION

	Growth rate (%)	Unemployment	Inflation (%)	Foreign exchange deficit (in millions)
1974	5.4	430,000	17.9	$3,245
1975	1.1	624,000	14.1	$3,488
1976	2.9	699,000	19.8	$4,294
1977	2.6	831,000	26.4	$2,294

Source: Cambio 16, Dec. 29, 1980: 28.

the Socialist and Communist parties to persuade their trade unions to abide by the terms of the pacts.

The performance of the economy following the pacts was mixed. On the positive side, the rate of inflation fell to 16.5 percent in 1978 and to 15.6 percent in 1979, and balance-of-payment surpluses were recorded in both years. On the other hand, unemployment increased to 1,083,000 in 1978, to 1,334,000 in 1979, and to an estimated 1,634,000 in 1980, while the rate of economic growth declined from 3.1 percent to 1.5 percent during this period.[20] These high levels of unemployment, coupled with the lack of fulfillment of some promised reforms by the UCD government, gave rise to complaints from workers that they had been asked to make sacrifices without gaining much in return and ultimately generated conflict between the two parties of the left and their respective trade unions. But, from the standpoint of regime legitimacy and stability, the immediate political impact of these negotiations was unambiguously positive. The pacts were, as described by Santiago Carrillo in a Cortes speech, "an act of national responsibility in order to restore democracy."[21] There could be no greater symbol of change in the Spanish political system than that of Santiago Carrillo (who, less than one year earlier, had been arrested and jailed on returning to Spain) emerging from the presidential palace after deliberations over a wide range of government policies— except perhaps for his cordial introduction to an exclusive public affairs club, the Club Siglo XXI, by none other than Manuel Fraga Iribarne in Madrid in the autumn of 1977.

The political developments of the 1977–1979 period, in particular the writing of the Constitution and the Pacts of Moncloa, had a considerable impact on the strategies adopted by the parties in attempting to transform themselves into stable institutions and to extend their organizational reach. They also had an effect on each party's success in such endeavors. The UCD and PCE were able to capitalize on these developments and to translate them into short-term electoral advantages. AP and the Basque Euskadiko Ezkerra, on the other hand, were polarized and suffered schisms as a direct result of the constituent process.

THE UCD: FROM COALITION TO PARTY

The party that confronted the most extensive tasks in institution building was the UCD. Indeed, when the first democratic Cortes convened in the summer of 1977, the UCD was not even a political party: it was still only an electoral coalition, totally lacking a common organizational framework, a statement of ideological principles, or a mass-membership base. But it was also the governing party, whose leaders held important posts in the state administration, and which could determine or, at least, influence the legislative agenda of the new parliament and even the rules that would govern its deliberations. With these resources, it was able to construct an impressive organizational structure that could penetrate into all parts of the country by the time of the next election. However, its ideological and programmatic heterogeneity—which enabled the UCD to appeal to a broad segment of the Spanish electorate—proved to be an obstacle to the harmonious development and functioning of party institutions and ultimately caused disruptive conflict among its "political families."

The first formal steps in the construction of a party organization involved the designation of Adolfo Suárez as president of what would become a single party structure, and the creation in September 1977 of two governing bodies. The first was a political council composed of representatives of the regional committees of the UCD coalition, its floor leaders in the Cortes and "barons" of the party (those individuals primarily responsible for forming the initial coalition, who by now held major ministerial posts). The second was a smaller interim executive committee. In December 1977 the political council announced that each of the component parties in the coalition must cease to exist as autonomous organizations and merge into one single party apparatus.

Once that was accomplished, a secretary general and a more permanent executive committee were appointed, as well as a committee charged with the task of writing a formal ideological declaration. The heterogeneity of the party was clearly reflected in the composition of both committees. The executive committee appointed in May, for instance, included two social democrats (Luís Gámir and Arturo Moya), a liberal (Antonio Fontán), two centrist independents (Manuel Núñez and Jesus Viana), one demochristian-independent (Guillermo Medina), and three Christian democrats (Luís de Grandes, Enrique Galavis, and Javier Rupérez), who were, respectively, centrist, conservative, and progressive in ideological orientation. Similarly, the committee that drafted the party's ideological statement included three social democrats, two conservative Christian democrats, three liberals, and two independents.[22] It is not surprising, therefore, that the document issued on May 12, 1978, was vague and eclectic, and paid lip service to each of the major ideological families. A slightly revised version, ratified in the first party congress in October of that year, embraced a "liberal, progressive and pluralist conception of life and culture" and, to further satisfy the liberal faction, stressed the value of the individual. For Christian democrats there was a "proclamation and assumption of humanist values and the ethic of the Christian tradition." And, in a bow to social democrats, the societal model it advanced included "a corrected and socially advanced market economy, understanding that it is the obligation of public powers to assure the predomination of general interests over private interests, as well as [to provide] fundamental services characteristic of modern society, and to guarantee justice and social equality."[23]

Although no UCD candidate, from any faction, would have difficulty standing for office under that ideological banner, the above statement did little to conceal the real incompatibilities among the programmatic demands of these three factions. Most observers would acknowledge that it would be difficult to reconcile the legalization of divorce (not to mention abortion), which was favored by liberals and social democrats, with the desires of Christian democrats to defend the interests of the Church and "the family." Similarly, it would not be easy to implement the social-democratic call for "a sufficient and adequate public sector which would serve for a much more egalitarian and solidary distribution of income, wealth and social power" without alienating liberals and some Christian democrats who favored a smaller public sector and the strict autonomy of a "free market economy."[24]

Through the appointment of Rafael Arias Salgado as the first secretary general of the party in May 1978, however, Adolfo Suárez attempted to orient the party more decisively toward the center-left. Arias Salgado had been active in the "moderate opposition" to the Franquist regime and had been a founding member of the executive committee of the Partido Social Demócrata of Francisco Fernández Ordóñez. Although he pledged to govern the party apparatus impartially and in a manner that would make the distinctions among the UCD's components disappear, he also wasted no time in expressing his belief that the UCD had to be a reformist, not a conservative party. In his first press conference as secretary general, he stated that the social structure of Spain was "profoundly unjust" and that the UCD "assumed responsibility for implementing the Pacts of Moncloa, with all the profound reforms implied by them."[25] The center-left orientation of the two most prominent party officials at first provoked only murmurs of protest from other factions. The bulk of the abstentions in the political council's vote confirming Arias Salgado in his post came from liberals, who had favored the nomination of their own Antonio Fontán to head the party. But, even though opposition to Suárez and his leadership of the party would not pose a serious threat until 1980, the evidence of an incipient right-wing rebellion against his center-left orientation could be seen at the very first UCD Party Congress in October 1978. On that occasion, the conservative Christian Democrat José Luís Alvarez and others mobilized against the party executive and proposed a series of amendments to its ideological and programmatic statement.

The October party congress did serve a positive function in the process of institutionalizing the new party, however. The formal election of Adolfo Suárez as UCD president and the ratification of the party's program by elected delegates legitimated the recently created party institutions in accord with basic democratic principles. Until that time the UCD was frequently attacked by rival parties as an undemocratic façade created by an entrenched governing elite. Even AP, which held its second national congress in January 1978, could claim to be democratic, while criticizing the UCD for remaining an authoritarian creation "from above." The local-level election of delegates to the UCD congress and the open debate over party principles helped to lay such criticisms to rest.

THE ABSORPTION OF SMALLER PARTIES

Over five thousand candidates had stood for election to the Congress of Deputies in the 1977 elections. Many unsuccessful candidates simply retired from active involvement in political affairs, but other talented individuals still aspired for office or sought out important roles in political life. Such opportunities could be provided by their incorporation within the victorious parties, which at the same time were attempting to expand their infrastructures. In the case of the UCD, organizational weaknesses were particularly severe in such regions as Euskadi and Catalunya. In the Basque province of Guipúzcoa, for example, the UCD could not even field a slate of candidates in 1977. One means of dealing with these infrastructural problems was to absorb smaller parties, incorporating their memberships and using the talents of the "unemployed" political elites who had made the mistake of backing the wrong party in 1977. Given ideological similarities between the UCD and several social democratic, liberal, Christian democratic, and regional groups, there appeared to be few inherent obstacles to these mergers. With the passage of time following the fusion of parties, some problems began to surface, but, at the outset of the first interelection period, the UCD and the PSOE (which also suffered from infrastructural weaknesses) undertook steps to absorb the shattered remains of the losers of 1977.

The governing UCD and the PSOE together held over 80 percent of the seats in the Congress of Deputies elected in 1977. In establishing parliamentary regulations and laws providing for funding of political parties, they had, therefore, the opportunity to consolidate their positions. The UCD and PSOE collaborated in a series of decisions concerning committee chairs and assignments, the minimum number of representatives needed to form a parliamentary group, and certain other matters. The selection of fifteen deputies and ten senators as the minimum for each parliamentary delegation constituted a serious setback for small parties. It placed them at a distinct disadvantage in terms of representation in committees, the order of speakers in debate, presentation of party positions on the state-run television system, and, consequently, their visibility to the general public.[26]

Far more devastating for smaller parties were the consequences of the laws enacted to compensate parties for their campaign expenses and to help them maintain their parliamentary delegations in Madrid. Rather than paying parties in accord with a formula based on the number of votes received—or some other proportional allocation scheme—the campaign financing law enacted in March 1977 reflected the biases inherent in the electoral law and thus favored the larger, more successful parties. Parties received subsidies in accord with the number of seats that they won in the preceding election (1 million Pesetas for each congressional and Senate seat), and for each *voto útil* (that is, 45 Ptas. for each vote for successful candidates for the Congress and 15 Ptas. for each vote for successful Senate candidates). According to this formula, the UCD collected 698 million Ptas., the PSOE received 543 million, while the PCE and AP received only 75 million and 55 million Ptas., respectively. Parties that did not elect a single deputy or senator received nothing. In short, the rich got richer, and the poor were driven to bankruptcy. Similarly, the law passed in December 1978, which reimbursed parties for their annual operating expenses, worked to the detriment of smaller parties. Despite efforts in the Senate to bring about a more egalitarian distribution of such funding, the Cortes enacted a law that granted 1 million Ptas. to each parliamentary group annually, plus 60,000 Ptas. for each deputy and senator.[27]

Faced with these institutional constraints, leaders of small parties could either resign themselves to a purely testimonial role or join forces with larger parties. There were significant differences among the major parties with regard to how they undertook such mergers:

the PSOE and AP chose to negotiate formal terms of merger with smaller parties, but the UCD simply incorporated leaders and members of those other groups on an individual basis. This brought into the UCD many persons formerly affiliated with the Christian democratic Equipo, as well as various social democratic parties, and greatly strengthened the UCD in Euskadi and Catalunya, in particular, where it had been quite weak. In Guipúzcoa, for example, Jaime Mayor Oreja, a former Senate candidate of a Basque Christian democratic party, played a leading role in bringing his former collaborators into the UCD and creating a viable branch of the party.[28] The only exception to this process of incorporating the elites of smaller parties on an individual basis occurred in Catalunya. Here the UCD opted for the "formal merger" process used by the PSOE and AP: a coalition was formed for the 1979 elections, which brought into a new "Centristes de Catalunya" prominent members of the Unió del Centre de Catalunya (a liberal party with close ties to Catalán big business leaders) and the historic leader of the Christian democratic Unió Democràtico de Catalunya, Antón Canyellas. The incorporation within the UCD of such prominent Catalans as Canyellas, Carlos Güell, and Joaquim Molins did a great deal to erase the public perception of the party as nothing more than a clone of the governing party in Madrid and significantly contributed to development of its organizational and financial resources.

Although the UCD was anxious to absorb the fragments of Christian democratic, social democratic, and regional parties, it vigorously rejected all attempts at closer association with the AP. In accord with Manuel Fraga's unceasing calls for the formation of a great party of the center and right (a "Gran Derecha") and, probably in response to the institutional pressures toward coalescence described above, representatives of the AP often proposed closer collaboration and even fusion between the two parties. All such suggestions were brusquely rejected. As Adolfo Suárez stated in response to one such proposal, "Neither the UCD nor I want that, because we are a party of the center-center, and want to continue to be so."[29] These proposals were, in part, rejected for reasons of abstract considerations of ideology, differences in programmatic preferences, and personal antipathy. Strategic considerations also played a role: as long as the AP existed as a rival party, it could continue to serve as a lightning rod, deflecting accusations of *"Franquismo"* from vulnerable segments of the UCD. As an example of this UCD hostility toward closer association with the AP and the former regime, Licinio de la Fuente, a popular and relatively progressive former Franquist minister, who had defected from his provincial AP branch because of its increasing conservatism on economic matters, was refused admittance to the UCD.

DEVELOPMENT OF
A MASS-BASED CATCH-ALL PARTY

What kind of organizational structure would the UCD create following the fusion of the original 13 component parties, and what long-term strategies would it employ for the attraction of a stable electoral clientele? Duverger[30] and Weiner and La Palombara[31] have suggested that bourgeois parties, or "internally created" parties will shun the formation of a large base of dues-paying militants and will opt, instead, for small, elitist "cadre" structures. Bartolini suggests, moreover, that in the era of television and mass-media campaigns and public financing of political parties, the classic supportive functions of mass-based political parties have become less important.[32] However, one might argue that there is nothing inherently incompatible between the strategies and activities of modern catch-all parties and the creation of a large base of dues-paying members. It is likely that the very blandness and vague statements of ideology by such parties may make it difficult to sustain the active involvement of party militants, but this is a minor practical problem rather than an explicit inconsistency between two incompatible models of political parties.[33] The combination of catch-all electoral strategies and a mass-based organizational structure can significantly enhance the electoral resources at the disposal of a party: income from members' dues, voluntary activities, and person-to-person proselytism. In addition, given the formula for public financing of political parties, a stable base of dues-paying members could function as a "safety net" for catch-all parties should they suffer short-term electoral setbacks. In establishing an organizational structure for the UCD, Rafael Arias Salgado and Adolfo Suárez were more persuaded by the potential benefits of a mass base of party members than they were by the conventional wisdom that bourgeois catch-all parties should be content with a cadre structure alone.

Several different methods were employed in building and institutionalizing a mass-based party. The first of these was a continuation of the process through which the party had been born: party leaders and elected officials used personal friendships, acquaintances, and family relations in an effort to attract new supporters to the party. The most important role was played by the members of parliament elected from each district, who served as the core of, first, a provincial executive committee and, then, a growing cluster of party affiliates. The party's financial resources were of great benefit in building provincial infrastructures. Among other things, the money that flowed to the party made it possible to hire persons to perform basic organizational tasks. Most commonly a *gerente* (manager) was employed full time to manage party affairs on behalf of a part-time executive committee. In one of our sample provinces, an entire executive committee received financial inducements in exchange for their services. This practice was not without its risks, however: one UCD official who had been "hired" in this manner admitted in an interview that he was not even a supporter of the party but, instead, was a member of the Partido Socialista de Galicia (PSG), and that he had accepted the UCD's offer because of its financial rewards and because he thought that his experiences within the party could serve as the basis of a book.

A second resource was the UCD's status as the governing party. Individuals, most importantly local notables, interested in forging or maintaining connections with important centers of governmental decision making were induced to join the UCD because it was the party in power. In the parts of the country where *caciquismo* persisted, local notables who had earlier been linked to Manuel Fraga and the AP or who had been politically unaffiliated moved into the UCD in the period following the 1977 elections in order to preserve

their roles as "intermediaries" between the central government and
their local clienteles. As a party official with long experience in politics explained in an interview:

> I would say that today the majority of the *caciques* are linked to the
> UCD. They are linked to the UCD for a very logical reason: because
> the *cacique*, if he does not have the instruments of power to resolve
> [local] problems, ceases to be a *cacique*. If you take away his tie to the
> command center, to the powers above, he is no longer a *cacique*. Thus,
> *caciques*, when they glimpse [impending] political change, switch their
> support from one political option to another, if the latter is that which
> has the greatest possibilities of ruling. Thus, we have seen in Galicia
> many people who were friends of Fraga, when he was Minister of the
> Interior, and who had and certainly have sympathies for him, but who
> have subsequently seen that Fraga has been left out of the government,
> have left Fraga, and now support Suárez.

Similarly, a UCD *gerente* in a Castilian province (who personally disapproved of such "feudal" relationships between local notables and
ordinary citizens) stated that a significant number of local notables
abandoned the AP following the 1977 elections and offered their
services to the UCD instead.

The usefulness of *caciquismo* to the UCD should not be overstated.
It was prevalent only in certain regions, and even there its potential
for attracting a stable mass base was limited. It could, moreover, be
detrimental to the party's image over the long term. For example, ties
to such personalistic networks in Galicia were "indispensable for win-
ning the first elections," according to a high-ranking UCD leader, but
they were incompatible with the progressive and reformist image
that the party wished to project. Thus, he continued, ties to *caciquismo* "will be progressively negative in successive elections, because
democracy, insofar as it functions as a system of liberty, makes what is
in essence a system of abuse and domination stand out all too clearly.
Thus, the UCD, if it wants to continue to progress in such areas as
Galicia, must necessarily divest itself of that baggage." Consequently,
the UCD did not cultivate such networks in most parts of Spain, although local notables would naturally gravitate to the UCD as the
party of government.

A major thrust of the party's institutionalization strategy involved the political recruitment of individuals to serve as local elites in the soon-to-be democratized municipal governments. This process of local elite cooptation was also facilitated by the UCD's status as the governing party, which enabled it to set the dates for both general and municipal elections. The UCD had been subjected to considerable pressures concerning the convocations of those elections. Both the PSOE and PCE hoped that their strength in Spain's larger cities would produce a victory at the local level that would create a "bandwagon" effect that would spill over into the parliamentary elections. Over the long term, moreover, this would provide them with numerous power bases and considerable patronage, which would facilitate their accession to power at the national level. Thus, for tactical reasons, the UCD did not wish to hold municipal elections prior to parliamentary elections. On the other hand, the continued existence of Franquist municipal governments well after the ratification of the Political Reform Law was proving to be a political embarrassment. By setting March 1 as the date of the general election, and April 3 for the municipal elections, the UCD government resolved its dilemma: by convoking the local elections prior to the parliamentary election, it eliminated the possibility that opposition parties could accuse it during the parliamentary campaign of wanting to perpetuate Franquist authoritarianism at the local level, but, by holding municipal elections after the parliamentary vote, it denied the PSOE and PCE the power bases they hoped to create.

The 1979 municipal elections greatly contributed to the expansion of the UCD's mass-membership base and to the development of its organizational infrastructure. Through the cooptation of local elites, the UCD was capable of turning its initial organizational weakness (with no more than 70 thousand party members in all of Spain)[34] into a distinct advantage. The elections for city councils in Spain's 8,100 municipalities opened up over 60 thousand local government seats. Thus, given that the UCD's membership was not evenly distributed geographically, persons who were not then party members would have to be recruited to stand as UCD candidates.

These new UCD candidates (over 54 thousand of them), together with their close friends and families, were given a considerable personal stake in the outcome of the elections and were therefore (despite their earlier passivity or apathy) induced to work hard for what had been an organizationally weak party. This was most important in small towns in isolated rural areas, where political awareness and political involvement had traditionally been low and where no UCD branches existed. Through the selection of certain kinds of persons, moreover, a local-level UCD "image" could be created that would be especially attractive to electoral "target groups" in the various socioeconomic segments of each province. Given the social heterogeneity of the population, no single national-level party image (such as that projected through television broadcasts by party leaders) could successfully appeal to all relevant target groups. The remolding or local adjustment of the UCD image through the selection of different kinds of elites in different areas, however, served to broaden this appeal considerably. Through the selection of conservative candidates in conservative areas and progressive candidates in others, the recruitment of candidates for the municipal elections enabled the UCD to strengthen its basis of support. Finally, the cooptation of prestigious individuals within communities added a new dimension to the dynamics of both electoral campaigns: the personal appeal of these candidates drew to the UCD voters who were otherwise ignorant of or inattentive to more abstract ideological or programmatic information.

For the UCD this process of local elite cooptation was time-consuming and involved considerable effort. A high-ranking UCD strategist described how this recruitment took place in his province:

> We had one month before the convocation of the municipal elections during which we prepared these candidatures. That is, we went out hunting for and capturing these candidates—the majority of whom were not militants or affiliates of the party. But we had to find him— the man ideologically just so, the "robot" whom we had designated as that ideal man. We went out after him through direct and indirect questionnaires, through informal chats, through interviews in his house. We practically had to extract from their houses with corkscrews

many persons who are today mayors and councilmen. The only difficulty was that our ideal man had never wanted to have anything to do
with politics, because he had been taught that politics was something
bad, or something for politicians, and that he should be a man dedi-
cated to his business, to his industry or farming exclusively, and not to
public administration.[35]

The end result of this process was the transformation of the UCD
from a tiny coalition of political elites into a mass-based party with
an organizational presence in all parts of Spain. Affiliation with the
UCD increased from 60 thousand in 1978 to 144 thousand in 1981.[36]
By that time the UCD had surpassed even the PSOE in terms of nominal affiliation (the Socialist party had only 107 thousand members)
and claimed to be the second largest mass-membership party in
Spain—behind the PCE, with 160 thousand members.[37] It is noteworthy that in 1981 about one-quarter of all UCD members held elective office at the local, provincial, or national level.[38]

Incumbency aided the party-building efforts of the UCD in several ways, but it was disadvantageous insofar as it attracted to the
party many individuals who were more interested in personal prestige or influence than in advancing the interests of the party. Thus,
even though the UCD could claim a high level of party affiliations,
the quality of that mass militancy was sometimes doubtful. One
former high-ranking party leader strongly criticized, in a 1983 interview, the "opportunists" who joined the party in order to share the
benefits of incumbency. Just as among the *caciques* who had abandoned the AP after its 1977 election defeat, the loyalty of this more
heterogeneous cluster of local elites to the UCD was highly conditional on its continued electoral success. In several areas where the
UCD had attracted many such persons, the party built its infrastructure on a shifting and unreliable base. An impending downturn in
the party's electoral fortunes could produce significant defections of
UCD municipal councilors and other local elites to rival parties (as
eventually occurred in 1982).

Under the leadership of Adolfo Suárez and Rafael Arias Salgado,
the UCD functioned as a catch-all party—electorally, structurally,

and as the party of government. In both the 1977 and 1979 parliamentary election campaigns, the party made broad appeals for voter support and avoided narrow, particularistic appeals that would have alienated voters. Indeed, if any segment of the electorate was singled out for special attention, it was not (as we shall see in the following chapters) the relatively conservative, religious, rural voter who constituted the core of UCD support in many parts of the country but, rather, the well-educated, progressive voter of the center to center-left, who might be drawn to vote for either the UCD or the PSOE, but whose support could spell the difference between electoral victory and defeat. Structurally, the party avoided explicit institutionalized ties to secondary organizations.

Finally, as the party of government during the most crucial early stages of the transition from authoritarianism to democracy, the UCD avoided a stout defense of the particularistic interests of its electorate, preferring, instead, to seek interparty compromises in dealing with basic constitutional or economic issues. This was certainly the case in the manner in which the party's spokesmen dealt with religious issues during the constitutional deliberations of 1977–1978: after briefly articulating demands in support of Church interests, the party's negotiators abruptly adopted compromise positions, which laid to rest fears that religious conflicts would impede widespread support for a consensual constitution. Similarly, rather than narrowly defending the interests of the businesses and upper socioeconomic groups that had supported the UCD, the Suárez government promptly enacted (at first, by an emergency decree law!) a reform of the inadequate and regressive taxation system and entered into the Pacts of Moncloa—a "social contract" with Socialists and Communists.

THE ROOTS OF CONFLICT

Despite its electoral success and its impressive infrastructural development, the national-level leadership of the UCD was badly divided over several important features of party structure, strategy, and ideology. Although the destructive consequences of these internal differences would not become obvious until well after the 1979 elections, the seeds of this discord were sown in the earliest stages of the party's development.

One of the most pervasive sources of tension was also the first to emerge. This involved the organizational structure and leadership of the party. Indeed, conflict over this issue erupted even before the creation of a unitary party. As one of the founders of the UCD stated in an interview:

> Within the coalition, even before [the creation of] the party, a clear position was taken by the Christian Democrats, who did not want to enter into a unitary party with other groups, liberal or social democratic. From the very first moment they stated their reservations. When I asked them to sign the document which established the general outlines of the electoral coalition . . . Fernando Alvarez de Miranda [indicated] that he did not want to commit himself to converting that coalition into a party. . . . They wanted to maintain their independence, to maintain their own ideological contour and probably their own foreign relations—ties to the Christian Democratic International and to Christian Democratic parties in other countries, mainly the German party.

Alvarez de Miranda's group ultimately consented to its dissolution and integration within the UCD in late 1977, but many Christian democrats continued to prefer a federal structure for the party. Such an option was completely unacceptable to Adolfo Suárez, in part for reasons of state. As a high-ranking party leader explained in 1983, "That appeared to me to be very grave. The task of creating a new state, such as the *estado de las autonomías* which we were designing, required the existence of very strong political parties at the national level. If there had been small *partiditos*, we would have run the risk of instability and polarization [*movimientos pendulares*]. I opposed that, and they maintained their position."

Closely related to this tension between those favoring a unitary leadership structure and those defending the positions of the various "political families" was the issue of "internal democratization" versus the alleged personal domination of the party's leadership. As an important party leader stated in an interview, "I believe that Adolfo Suárez did not truly want to have a party—at least a modern party. He had a conception of the party which was that of a party of personal adherence—of personal devotion to him. He really did not facilitate the functioning of the party, because he thought that the more the party grew, the weaker would be his own position of power." Following the 1979 elections, increasing numbers of *críticos* (critics) within the party's political council demanded that Suárez relinquish much of his control over the UCD apparatus, although by no means was there any consensus over the kind of party leadership that should emerge.

Tensions between Suárez and the various political families were further complicated as a result of the UCD's awkward status as the party of government (and, thus, with ministerial posts and other patronage to dispense) without a parliamentary majority (and, thus, needing every vote it could muster in order to pass its legislation). Each political family or personalistic faction insisted upon adequate representation within the Council of Ministers and upon its "fair share" in the distribution of other prestigious positions. The implicit competition among factions led to the adoption of a rigid proportionality as a de facto decision-making principle. One former minister, in an interview in Madrid in July 1983, explained that "party directives were formulated as a function of quotas derived from the various ideological families—according to which it was necessary to have so many social democrats, so many Christian democrats, so many liberals, so many independents." Few party leaders regarded this as a desirable formula for governing. It reduced the government's flexibility in recruitment and policy formulation and, in some instances, gave rise to the perpetuation of practices characteristic of the Franquist past: as under the former regime, the education ministry, for example, was always under the control of Christian Democrats or others closely linked to the Church.[39]

Perhaps even more seriously, these practices institutionalized and deepened the divisions among factions. But, in the absence of a parliamentary majority, the prime minister had no choice but to dispense this patronage to each and every faction, regardless of its size: because every deputy's vote was needed to enact legislation, the "blackmail potential" of each faction was enormous. As a party leader lamented in an interview in Madrid in July 1983: "The very moment I would get rid of some member of those sectors of the party, there would be deep resentment of the government in parliament; the deputies dominated by that person would stop attending sessions, would suffer from strange illnesses, would have 'other obligations.' So I always had to include representatives of all groups." Even then, squabbles would erupt whenever a faction "felt that it was not sufficiently represented. There were occasions [for example] when the Christian democratic sector felt that it was not represented within the government, while, from my point of view, there were four or five Christian democratic ministers. They were just not the ministers that the demochristian sector wanted."

The concessions made to opposition parties in the course of the politics of consensus further intensified hostility among factions and toward Adolfo Suárez. This was particularly true with regard to liberals and conservative Christian democrats close to big-business organizations who were outraged by the 1977 tax reform and other facets of the Pacts of Moncloa, as well as some Christian democrats who preferred a stronger defense of Church interests in the constituent process. In the view of Suárez and his collaborators, those factions were pushing for adoption of a more partisan constitution, which would have conformed to the historical practice of using such documents to "impose dogmatically the preferences of one sector of Spanish society on the rest" (interview with party leader in Madrid in July 1983). "Suaristas" did acknowledge that the concessions made during the constituent process represented the temporary abandonment of one of the main functions of political parties in democratic regimes: during the politics of consensus, one collaborator of Suárez stated in 1981, "parties were not functioning as channels for social demands from the various sectors of society." Nevertheless, they concluded that the constituent process required "a certain consensus among political parties. This is the only way to construct a country in a civilized manner. It can't be any other way. We cannot risk a radical confrontation."

An additional source of conflict among the party's national-level leaders was disagreement over the party's development strategy and its relationship with secondary associations. From the very beginning, Suárez's catch-all strategies were opposed by some (particularly conservative Christian democrats) who preferred that the UCD develop in accord with what might be called a "holding company" type of political party. One of the leaders of the *críticos* claimed in a 1981 interview:

> Adolfo [Suárez], basically does not know what a real and modern political party is and never thought about constructing a political party of that kind. The model that he had in mind was, in fact, the Movimiento Nacional, since there is no other model that he followed. It's not just that he rejected support from the social infrastructure of people who are moved by religious inspirations, but that he rejected the support of any preexisting social infrastructure. . . . That is, he rejected the support of teachers' associations—one of the most important social networks in the country, which is very traditional and reaches even the smallest villages. He rejected the possibility of support from the movements of small agricultural proprietors. He rejected the possibility of support from the small business movement. He rejected the possibility of grouping with an independent trade union. He has systematically closed the doors, because he didn't want to create a party, he wanted to create a pseudo-party.

In the view of these critics, the party should not have stressed the building of an autonomous organization, but rather the creation of a "holding company" that would rely on a number of affiliated secondary organizations. From this perspective, electoral campaigns would be fought primarily by mobilizing the resources of those secondary organizations. The process of party building, then, would consist mainly of forging institutionalized linkages with existing interest groups, such as religious, professional, business, and community organizations. They would be expected to contribute personnel and money to the party at election time and mobilize their members in support of the party. In return, the party would represent their particularistic interests in parliament and formulate public policies on their behalf.

In the abstract, this type of party need not necessarily be associated with a narrow range of secondary organizations and thus could appeal to broad segments of the electorate. Many of the *críticos*, however, favored the conversion of the UCD into a conservative, clerical "holding company" variety of party. Although Suárez and Arias Salgado tried to establish cordial, collaborative but informal relationships with many secondary associations (through tactics to be described in chaps. 5 and 6), they believed that explicit organizational links between the party and interest groups could reduce the attractiveness of the UCD by giving it a narrow, sectarian image. Formal ties with religious institutions, for example, could alienate nonreligious voters from the UCD.[40] Such overt links to particularistic interests, moreover, might unduly constrain its ability, as the governing party, to shift position on various issues or to enter into compromises with other political groups. Were the UCD to be formally associated with big business groups, for example, the obligation to articulate or defend their interests could substantially undermine the party's maneuverability on economic issues. As a high-ranking party leader summarized these concerns: "What one cannot do is to convert the UCD into a party which represents the most conservative interests of the Catholic Church or the most reactionary sectors of the Spanish business class. With that representation one could not win elections."

Finally, one should not dismiss personal ambition as a major cause of conflict within the UCD's elite. When asked to interpret the intraparty struggles that beset the party throughout its existence, one Suárez collaborator flatly stated: "The so-called barons, at least some of them, were simply fighting to become president of the government. For me, this was a pure struggle for power." In return, many party leaders interviewed in 1983 questioned Suárez's motives in his running battle with the barons of the party. In their view, he was simply striving to reinforce his dominant position and eliminate all potential rivals within the party.

In the period between the 1977 and 1979 elections, the UCD developed impressively as an electoral organization. A large and well-

financed infrastructure was established in all parts of the country—
even in parts of Euskadi and Catalunya where the party had scarcely
existed in 1977. A mass-membership base was created that, despite a
quality of militancy perhaps inferior to that of other parties, constituted a valuable electoral resource and even suggested that the party
was well on its way to full institutionalization.

The party's leaders in Madrid, however, were badly divided with
regard to their ideological stands, their programmatic preferences,
and their basic conceptions of the party and what it should become.
The heterogeneity that resulted from the headlong mergers among
political families that founded the UCD on the very eve of the 1977
elections may have helped the party to appeal to a broad segment of
the electorate over the short term, but it was also the source of destabilizing and debilitating conflicts. The hasty "improvisation" of a
party in May 1977, in the absence of an organizational model or consensus on basic ideological tenets,[41] had important long-term consequences. The resulting heterogeneity among political families precluded the formulation of a more coherent ideology. Thus, what
emerged from the First Party Congress in October 1978 was "not an
ideological synthesis, but rather," as described by a party leader, "an
accumulation of ideologies." That heterogeneity also meant that
conflicts over the party's institutional development and basic strategies would remain unresolved and would be intensified by the
stresses of the constituent process.

Thus, by 1979 the UCD had become, for increasing numbers of
militants in most provinces, an object of increasing loyalty and affec-
tion. For historians it was a party that presided effectively over the
creation of a new democracy. But for far too many of its own leaders
(such as a former minister interviewed in July 1983): "It was not a
party but a cluster of groups, united by electoral victory, united by
the attractive image of Adolfo Suárez, but nothing more."

THE PCE: DEMOBILIZING A
MASS-MOBILIZATION PARTY

After the 1977 election, the PCE sought to pursue three sets of
political objectives simultaneously. The first of these was to contrib-

ute to the stabilization of the democratic regime, or, at the least, to avoid behavior that could be used as a pretext for a coup d'état by right-wing elements in the military. The second objective was to further institutionalize party organizations throughout the country, primarily along the lines of the "mass-mobilization" party model. And the third was to transform the public image of the party so as to maximize its voter appeal in future elections. The simultaneous pursuit of some of these objectives gave rise to considerable tension and overt conflict within the party. Although the full consequences of such intraparty struggles did not become visible to outside observers until well after the 1979 elections, their origins lay in the long-term strategies adopted in 1977 and 1978.

THE CONSOLIDATION OF DEMOCRACY

PCE leaders stated on numerous occasions during the period between the 1977 and 1979 elections that the principal political objective of the party was "the consolidation of democracy." In light of the moderate and largely nonconflictual role played by the party in the constituent process, its active support for the Pacts of Moncloa, and the general restraint exercised by its supporters, one must conclude that, for the most part, the behavior of the PCE during the transition was consistent with those verbal committments.

The values, historical memories, and perceptions of the precarious status of the emerging democratic regime on the part of Communist leaders contributed to this cautious and largely constructive behavior. Unlike all the other parties in the constituent Cortes of 1977–1978, the PCE leadership included and, in many respects, was dominated by individuals who had been politically active at the time of the Civil War (see appendix B). The behavior of the PCE elite was profoundly affected by an awareness of the mistakes that culminated in the Civil War and by painful memories of suffering under the Franquist regime. Indeed, among the PCE elites that we interviewed were several individuals who had been imprisoned, one who had been sentenced to death, and one who had been tortured so severely by the police that he was physically deformed. As a member of the

PCE Secretariat, an important historic figure within the party, explained in an interview in July 1979:

> This memory of the past obliges us to take these circumstances into account, that is, to follow a policy of moderation. We feel responsibility for this process [of democratization, and] the need to make a superhuman effort so that this process is not truncated. This is a unique moment in Spanish history. After more than a century of civil wars and a vicious cycle of massacres among Spaniards, which began after the war of independence and ended in June 1977 with the first elections based on universal suffrage, this is the moment when it is possible to end this cycle and open a period of civilized life, politically speaking. In this sense we cannot allow ourselves the luxury of expressing opinions which might be misunderstood, which could be, or appear to be, extremist. Thus, we have a very prudent policy, very closely adapted to the realities of today, and we make efforts to demonstrate that we really want to institutionalize democracy. We don't want this process to be interrupted.[42]

On numerous occasions, PCE leaders publicly warned of the fragility of the current democratic experiment and criticized other parties for their occasional lack of restraint. Santiago Carrillo, for instance, at a pro-Constitution rally in 1978, criticized the parties "which have not had the same sense as we have and the same awareness of the dangers which threaten our society . . . [instead] they have accused us of being catastrophists. . . . The current democracy, which is still ugly, is a thousand times better than the buried past."[43]

These historical memories and concern over the fragility of the new regime conditioned the short-term tactics and objectives of the PCE and differentiated it from the PSOE. The PSOE often attacked the UCD government in persistent efforts to topple it, thereby becoming the "alternative in power," but the PCE preferred the formation of a broad-based coalition government, including all significant parties except the AP. A key PCE strategist in Madrid explained in an interview in 1979:

> We thought that the position of the PSOE of regarding itself as the alternative in power was an erroneous analysis, was wrong: the country was not then, nor is it now in a situation of moving toward a clearly leftist government or to a clearly socialist government. Instead, the

force of the workers had to be manifested in some kind of coalition. And there should be no attempts to impose on the country a leftist program, but rather we should negotiate with the right for a more economically advanced policy.

He further argued that these differences in intermediate objectives—between the PCE's government of national concentration and the PSOE's *alternativa de poder*—led to a whole series of differences in policy stands and style of behavior: to much greater support for the Pacts of Moncloa from the CCOO than from the UGT; to earlier concessions by Communists on divisive constitutional issues; and to a different style of interaction among party elites. "The principal party of the opposition, the PSOE, preferred to play electoral games," he claimed, "[while for us] the stability of the country was fundamental for everything we did."

ORGANIZATIONAL DEVELOPMENT

In terms of party institutionalization, the PCE appeared to have a considerable advantage over all its rivals. Even prior to the Political Reform Law, it had established branches in all the provinces of Spain and, as the principal clandestine opposition force, had attracted a substantial number of party members. This initial advantage was further strengthened as a byproduct of the 1977 election campaign. Communist party officials in several regions reported that during the campaign itself large numbers of persons joined the party and contributed their support to its campaign efforts. In Catalunya, for example, membership increased from about 12 thousand just prior to the legalization of the PSUC to about 40 thousand by late 1977; in Madrid PCE affiliates increased from about 7 thousand to about 32 thousand.[44] The excitement of the campaign and, more generally, the transition from Franquist authoritarianism to democracy were cited by several elite respondents as factors contributing to this development. The recruitment efforts of the party led to a rapid increase in total PCE and PSUC membership to over 200 thousand by the end of 1977.[45] This rapid expansion, however, created problems for the party. As a member of the executive committee of the PSUC complained in a 1978 interview, "We have 30 thousand new members who are not in the habit of regular participation." Many of the new members were less committed to the party and less active in its affairs. This caused some consternation among long-standing party members: "What kind of Communists are these?" lamented a party official. Indeed, after the initial excitement of the transition had worn off, a significant number of new members became inactive or dropped out of the party altogether.

Nonetheless, a large membership base not only constituted a valuable electoral resource but was an essential component of the "mass-mobilization" nature of the party.[46] Under the greatly altered political circumstances of the postelectoral period, however, the functions to be performed by party members were to be considerably different from those of party militants under the Franco regime. This transformation caused confusion and some problems. A PCE official in Galicia explained in an interview:

> During clandestinity, the main task of party militants was to mobilize against the Spanish state. That is not going to solve any problems today and is not suited for our present democratic system. What we need to do is formulate solutions to real problems. Demonstrations won't help in that regard. Moreover, they will have serious negative side effects. They would dishearten the population and could lead to political polarization. It is easy to organize a demonstration and very difficult to study specific problems and suggest solutions.

Thus, the PCE found itself in a somewhat awkward position. On one hand, it wished to retain many of the organizational features of the mass-mobilization party and certainly wanted to expand its membership base. In working toward democratic stability, however, party leaders sought to restrain the activities of militants—to discourage them from engaging in disruptive protest activities and to induce them to accept compromises with the right concerning basic constitutional and economic issues. In essence, this would create a partially "demobilized mass-mobilization party."

The principal thrust of this effort involved careful attempts to channel the activities of party militants. During elections, to be sure, attempts were made to mobilize all party members for various campaign activities. But the PCE had no intention of becoming a purely electoral party. Party members were expected to be active throughout the year in establishing a party "presence" in many of the more important secondary organizations. As described by Ramón Tamames, "the main line of party activity today is in the worker movement, is in the student movement, in the movement of professionals and technicians, and in the citizen movement."[47] Party members were encouraged to join secondary organizations in these sectors, to assume leadership positions within them, and to induce them to act generally in accord with the party's program and overall interests. These efforts did not, however, constitute formal cooptation of the relevant secondary organizations. Again citing Tamames:

> In all of these movements the party cannot attempt to convert itself into the center of thoughts and decisions. These are autonomous movements; and especially on the road to democracy [and] to the consolidation of political and social democracy and of socialism in liberty, it would be a grave error by the party to try to monopolize [them] or even to exercise some type of hegemony. One must let these things grow, grow with autonomy, so that they acquire their own personalities, and even enter, on many occasions, into contradictions with the party.[48]

Rather than relying on pressure or formal institutional ties, the party sought to exert its influence within these organizations by means of personal influence. Given the substantial number of persons who had entered the party via its university cells under the Franquist regime, the party could count on the prestige and the varied professional skills of its members in other secondary associations as resources for creating a favorable party image and attracting additional supporters. As Tamames claimed, "What doubt is there that within the citizen movement one must count on good jurists, on experts in administrative law and on good sociologists and architects, that is, on good technicians who know how to channel the needs of their fellow citizens?"[49] These party members could translate their personal prestige and public services performed on behalf of various social groups into a generalized sense of positive affect toward the party and into the belief that it was deeply committed to solving the daily problems of ordinary citizens. Such activities by popular party members could also undermine the credibility of the demonic image of the party, which had been so widely disseminated through decades of Franquist propaganda.

The two principal arenas for such activities by party members were the CCOO (which will be discussed more fully in a later chapter) and neighborhood associations (*asociaciones de vecinos*). Neighborhood associations emerged during the final years of the Franquist regime and reached their peak of organizational strength in the 1975–1976 period.[50] Such groups were tolerated under the Franquist regime because they were ostensibly nonpolitical and indeed, often dealt with relatively noncontroversial local issues, such as the location of traffic lights.[51] But, in the absence of effective channels for political participation under the former regime, neighborhood associations took on other functions as well. As the secretary general of a large regional branch of the PCE explained in an interview in Madrid in July 1979: "In the final years of the dictatorship, the neighborhood associations were fundamentally a cover for clandestine political activity. There were many kinds of activity: there was the more or less consistent defense of the interests of the neighborhoods, but fundamentally they were platforms for political struggle against the regime."

These organizations were never uniformly under the control of the PCE: interviews with provincial party leaders in 1978 indicated that some neighborhood associations were dominated by persons on the extreme left, and in other areas they were controlled by persons who would ultimately join such parties as the UCD and the PNV. But, as our PCE respondent continued, "we had a great deal of strength [within the neighborhood associations], because we were practically the ones who created them." These organizations declined in political importance after the demise of the Franquist regime:

Once liberty had been achieved, a large number of militants who had undertaken political activities through the neighborhood associations left them to join political parties—ours and other parties. Thus, dur-

ing [a period of] almost two years, the life of the neighborhood associations almost stopped, and they lost their most able members. Just
recently, [in the spring of 1979], they have acquired a new vigor, within
a more normal context; now their legal status is not used as a political
cover, but now that parties exist, neighborhood associations are beginning to truly function to perform their role in the defense of neighborhoods. (All preceding quotations from ibid.)

Despite the relative depoliticization of neighborhood associations and their loss of status as the nearly exclusive channels for citizen participation, they were still regarded as politically significant
bodies within which the PCE sought to establish a "presence." Involvement by PCE members in such organizations provided access to
a significant bloc of the Spanish populace: according to our 1979
survey, 10 percent of all respondents claimed to be members of
neighborhood associations.

In accord with the party's strategy of establishing a "presence"
within various social groups, and in stark contrast with the exception-
ally low levels of institutional affiliation characteristic of most Spaniards, PCE members were very active within a wide range of secondary organizations. A poll of delegates attending the Fourth Congress
of the PSUC, for example, revealed that 77.7 percent of them were
members of trade unions (most of them, not surprisingly, of the
CCOO), 68.5 percent claimed to be members of neighborhood associations, 19 percent of cultural organizations, 14.2 percent of sports and
recreation associations, 6.9 percent of cooperatives, 4.6 percent of
feminist organizations, 3.3 percent of parent-teacher associations,
and 3 percent claimed to belong to professional associations.[52]

BROADENING ELECTORAL APPEAL

The third set of long-term strategic decisions made during the
interelection period involved adjustments in the party's formal ideology in order to broaden its appeal to the overwhelmingly moderate
and democratic Spanish electorate. These modifications, carefully
orchestrated by Santiago Carrillo and his Eurocommunist supporters within the PCE, were approved by substantial majorities at
the Ninth Congress of the party in April 1978. They succeeded in

depriving the principal rivals of the PCE (most importantly, the PSOE) of electoral weapons that could have been used to deter potential voters from the PCE. Many aspects of the party's earlier ideological declarations were incompatible with the moderate and democratic image it wished to project.

The most prominent ideological change involved removal of the term "Leninist" from the party's formal self-description. The PCE would no longer be a "Marxist-Leninist" party. Instead, resolution 15 declared that "the Communist Party of Spain is a Marxist, revolutionary and democratic party, which is inspired by the theories of social development elaborated by the founders of scientific socialism, Marx and Engels, and by its method of analysis."[53] The resolution pointed out that the party was not totally repudiating Leninism, but merely reducing its status from that of an exclusive and orthodox party ideology: "In the PCE the Leninist contribution, insofar as it continues to be valid, is retained, along with the other revolutionary ones, but on the basis that today there is no room for the maintenance of the restrictive idea that 'Leninism is the Marxism of our epoch.'"[54] Going even further, the resolution declared that "The PCE rejects every dogmatic conception of Marxism,"[55] thus formally legitimizing the presence within the party of intellectuals with somewhat eclectic ideologies.

A second set of changes reaffirmed the party's committment to a democratic political system. For outside observers the most significant aspect of this committment involved a recognition that sometimes "the forces favorable to socialism can suffer electoral defeats. And in that case, respecting the popular verdict, they would have to leave the government and pass into the opposition in order to gain anew the confidence of the country."[56] The party further pledged to act "within the framework of democratic legality."[57]

The final change adopted at the Ninth Congress was one that, Carrillo's critics would later allege, was never fully implemented. This concerned certain attempts to bring about a greater degree of internal democratization of the party's decision-making procedures. Numerous statements were approved at the congress affirming that "the functioning of the party is governed by democratic rules."[58] The famous resolution 15 claimed that "We reject as something alien to Marxism the phenomenon of bureaucratization and Stalinism.... Such antidemocratic phenomena [have undercut] ... the influence of revolutionary Marxism among workers in advanced capitalist societies. We Spanish Communists have self-critically overcome, in its fundamentals, Stalinism, and are recovering the democratic and antibureaucratic essences of Marxism."[59] The party did not, however, totally repudiate "democratic centralism." Instead, it claimed that "the principal of democratic centralism by which we govern ourselves, adapted to the conditions of legality and of our epoch, will facilitate the flourishing of internal democracy."[60] Given this ambiguous committment to internal democracy, the tradition of authoritarian rule within the party, and the potential sanctions placed at the disposal of the executive by article 11 of the party's statutes,[61] it is not surprising that Communists would disagree with one another about principles governing the internal functioning of the party.

INCOMPATIBILITIES AND CONFLICTS

Many of the strategic decisions made in the aftermath of the 1977 elections by the leadership of the PCE constituted adjustments to the new environment of a democratic Spain. There is no doubt that they were successful in achieving some important objectives. The moderate and constructive role played by the party in the constituent process and in implementing the Pacts of Moncloa contributed to the legitimacy and stability of the new regime. These accomplishments spilled over into the electoral arena by increasing the visibility and popularity of such key actors in the transition as Jordi Solé Tura (the Communist representative in most deliberations over the Constitution) and Carrillo himself. Finally, ideological changes enacted at the Ninth Congress and the party's role in "the politics of consensus" facilitated PCE efforts to project a more moderate electoral image. But, in several respects, the development strategy implemented after the 1977 elections created serious new problems and internal conflicts.

Some of these difficulties had origins that predated the transition to democracy in Spain and arose out of ongoing efforts to transform the PCE from a closed "devotee" party into a mass-mobilization party. One consequence of this transformation was the coexistence in the party of two generations of Communists with completely different and often conflicting views of how the party should be run. The old generation (of Dolores Ibárruri, Santiago Carrillo, Pere Ardiaca, Gregorio López Raimundo, and others) had entered the party when it was still a devotee organization. The authoritarian traditions of the PCE at that time instilled into those individuals the expectation that party militants would be devoted, disciplined, and united in support of the policies of the executive committee. The more recent generation of Communists (e.g., Ramón Tamames, Roberto Lertxundi, Antoni Gutiérrez Díaz, and Jaime Sartorius) entered the party with greatly different expectations concerning the proper relationship between leaders and rank-and-file militants. In particular, those who had entered the party as a byproduct of student mobilizations against the Franquist regime, many of them with advanced university degrees, were reluctant to accept the passive and obedient role envisaged for them by those of the older generation. Insofar as these two cohorts held conflicting views of the party's decision-making procedures, the transformation of the PCE from devotee to mass-mobilization party sowed the seeds of internal conflict. Specifically, these groups clashed over the meaning of the ambiguous (if not contradictory) formulations concerning "internal democratization" of the party made at the Ninth Congress: the younger generation stressed the formal commitments to change in decision-making practices, while the behavior of older generations clearly indicated that "democratic centralism" had not been abandoned.

Conflicts over formal statements of party ideology interacted with these differing organizational preferences, but in a rather complex fashion. Many older Communists remained loyal to the party's former Marxist-Leninist ideology and to the principle of close collaboration with the Communist party of the U.S.S.R. They never supported the formal abandonment of Leninism and resented Santiago Carrillo's frequent attacks against the excesses of Soviet communism. The first sign of overt disagreement over Carrillo's ideological reforms was opposition from the PSUC against removal of the term "Leninism" at the Ninth PCE Party Congress. In fact, given the institutional autonomy of the PSUC from the PCE, the Catalán branch of the party was able to retain its Marxist-Leninist self-designation throughout the interelection period. The most embarrassing example of such disagreement was a statement made by Dolores Ibárruri (the PCE president) to an American journalist in 1978: "We have not renounced the dictatorship of the proletariat."[62] Many of the same persons who opposed Carrillo on ideological grounds, however, also believed most strongly in the principle of "democratic centralism." Out of respect for Carrillo's leadership position and this tradition of discipline, they refrained from open attacks on his version of Eurocommunism until well after the 1979 elections.

Thus, the party projected an external image of unity. The consensus, however, was fragile. As Juan Linz has pointed out, Carrillo benefitted over the short term from a stalemate within the party between two (or more) groups holding different views of Spanish communism: on the one hand, Carrillo received support from younger Communists, who favored his strategic and ideological reforms, but who later challenged his authoritarian leadership style; many older Communists, on the other hand, opposed his Eurocommunist ideology but deferred to him out of respect for the tradition of democratic centralism.[63] Ultimately, Carrillo would come under fire from both sectors. Carrillo's difficult situation can best be appreciated by examining the fate of his Catalán counterpart, Antoni Gutiérrez Díaz, a Eurocommunist who greatly relaxed the internal authoritarianism of the PSUC. This liberalization permitted a pro-Soviet minority within the party to gain control of its secretariat of organization, to undermine his leadership position, and, in 1980, to temporarily replace him with a coalition of pro-Soviets and Leninists.[64]

The party's role in the politics of consensus also gave rise to internal tension and conflict as a result of its incompatibility with the intrinsic requirements of the "mass-mobilization party" model. As

Joaquín Sempere wrote in a 1981 issue of the party newspaper *Nuestra Bandera*, "the policy of moderation and consensus, especially visible on the occasion of the Pacts of Moncloa, was perceived as a loss of the Communist identity,"[65] especially in light of the economic crisis and extremely high levels of unemployment of recent years. The ultimate consequence has been "disenchantment within and outside of our ranks, on the observation, apparently, that all parties are saying the same thing, and that there is no clear Communist identity in the PSUC or in the PCE."[66] The secrecy of the elite negotiations that were part of the politics of consensus, the marginalization of party militants from this decision-making process, the granting of concessions to opposition parties in the interest of reaching compromises, and the imposition of restraints on the activities of trade union allies—all contributed to the satisfactory outcome of the constituent process and to the stabilization of Spanish democracy. But, at the same time, they disappointed and alienated party militants more accustomed to confrontational rhetoric, the manipulation of ideological symbols, and the excitement of clandestine mobilization against the former regime.[67] This exacerbated latent conflict over role expectations implicit in the two party models that uneasily coexisted in the PCE.

Finally, and somewhat surprisingly, the change in the party's basic unit of organization from the cell to the neighborhood branch served to diminish the appeal of PCE membership to highly educated professionals and technicians. That structural alteration had been undertaken in an effort to make the party appear to be more open and democratic. An unintended consequence of that policy was that the party's basic organizational units became more socially and occupationally heterogeneous. With small cells as the principal unit, the workplace, rather than the residential neighborhood, served as the common denominator for membership.[68] Under those conditions, personal friendships and the sharing of professional interests reinforced the value of participation in party affairs. After the shift to more heterogeneous neighborhoods, however, members of party branches had little in common with one another except party membership, per se, and that was often an insufficient incentive to remain active. This decline in the personal appeal of party membership for intellectuals and professionals was exacerbated by their resentment against the party's authoritarian decision-making style and contributed to the exodus of such persons from the PCE after the 1979 elections. With their departure, the party lost one of its greatest assets and its "presence" in many sectors of society, which it had so carefully cultivated during the final years of the Franquist regime.

Although the origins of these ultimately devastating internal conflicts were implicit in some of the strategic decisions made in the period between the first two democratic elections, the ultimate consequences of these tensions and incompatibilities were not apparent to outside observers until well after the 1979 elections. Prior to that time, only the party's successes were easily visible: the party's stable and disciplined behavioral style remained undisturbed; its moderate and constructive role in the transition was regarded as unambiguously positive; its intellectuals, professionals, and technicians still maintained their highly visible "presence" in many arenas; its ideological reforms had apparently been implemented without much overt opposition (except from the PSUC); and its regional and provincial branches were much larger and better developed than those of any other statewide party (only the PNV was as fully institutionalized, but within a much smaller geographical area). All of these would prove to be valuable resources in the 1979 parliamentary and municipal elections.

THE PSOE: THE CRISIS OF RAPID GROWTH

The strong showing of the PSOE in the 1977 election was a pleasant surprise for its leaders.[69] The PSOE had not been the most prominent party of opposition under the Franquist regime, nor was it particularly well organized. Yet it had emerged from the first democratic election as by far the dominant party of the left. The major task confronting the PSOE was to expand its network of provincial- and local-level party branches, capitalizing on its electoral gains and consolidating its position in the party system.

In some respects, membership growth was the almost automatic product of the transition to democracy and of PSOE success in the 1977 election. The legalization of the party in early 1977 removed a serious impediment to affiliation, and its electoral victory was a magnet that attracted many persons on the left of center who wished to back a winner. Party membership increased from 8 thousand in December 1976 to over 50 thousand on the eve of the 1977 election. By the end of 1978, there were about 100 thousand dues-paying members and a much larger number of nominal affiliates holding party cards.[70]

The PSOE's party-building efforts included, as well, incorporation of other socialist parties, which had competed with the PSOE in 1977—most importantly, the PSP of Enrique Tierno Galván and numerous regional socialist parties. If all the votes for these socialist parties could be added to those received by the PSOE, the Socialist vote total would exceed 6 million, placing it very close to the strength of the UCD in 1977. It was further believed that the expansion of the party's organizational structure resulting from the entry into the PSOE of former militants of other socialist parties would enable it to campaign more successfully in the future. Perhaps most importantly, successful implementation of the strategy would clear the political landscape of potential rivals for socialist votes in the future.

The major target of these efforts was the PSP. Even though it had been reasonably successful in electing six deputies in 1977, the institutional context structured by the PSOE and UCD left it little choice but to abandon its independence. With the establishment of a 15-seat minimum, it was incapable of forming its own parliamentary delegation and was thrown into a "mixed group" with a motley assortment of other parties. The exclusion of Tierno Galván from the *Ponencia* that drafted the Constitution robbed the PSP of prestige and visibility. And the laws governing financial support for parties left the PSP with an enormous and unpayable debt following the 1977 campaign.[71] Thus, as Tierno recalled explaining to his followers in March 1978:

> If we continue, you must understand that it will be a long march through the desert.... We owe many millions, and we have no money.

And they are not going to give us any. We are an annoyance, and annoyances are eliminated. They are going to eliminate us, and so we must choose: . . . Join the PSOE, which is where you will be most sheltered, best protected, and with the best prospects.[72]

The process by which the PSOE sought to absorb other parties was significantly different from the manner in which the UCD swallowed up the remains of Christian democratic, social democratic, and liberal groups. Instead of merely encouraging individual members to affiliate with the UCD, the PSOE opted for formal mergers with the elites of smaller socialist organizations. In most cases, the incoming group, in exchange for dissolving its independent party organization, was granted reserved seats on provincial or regional executive committees. By mid-1978 the PSOE had joined forces with many of its former rivals: the PSP of Tierno Galván, the Partit Socialista del País Valencià, the Partido Socialista de Aragón, the Movimiento Socialista Andaluz, and segments of the PSG (Partido Socialista Galego). In addition, the PSOE transformed what had been an electoral coalition with the Partit Socialista de Catalunya—Congrés into a formal federation.[73] At the same time, it incorporated into the resulting Partit dels Socialistes de Catalunya, PSC-PSOE the smaller, social democratic Partit Socialista de Catalunya-Reagrupament (PSC-R). The latter had broken away from the main bloc of the PSC, partly because of its more moderate ideological stance and partly as a result of a personal rivalry between its former leader, the late Josep Pallach, and the leader of the PSC Congrés, Joan Reventós. Ostentatious displays of socialist solidarity, involving ceremonies attended by internationally prominent figures such as François Mitterand and Mario Soares, accompanied the more important of these mergers.

The PSOE gained some immediate benefit from these fusions. Its parliamentary delegation grew from 118 to 123 through the incorporation of the deputies of the PSC-R,[74] as well as some of the deputies of the PSP. In addition, by eliminating most of its potential rivals, the PSOE reduced the possibility that in future elections socialist votes would be scattered among several socialist parties and thus "wasted." Finally, its merger with the PSC enabled the party to shed its traditional image in Catalunya as a Spanish-centralist party and to extend its appeal beyond the immigrant community to include native-born Catalans.

These mergers, however, produced neither the electoral nor the organizational advantages that had been anticipated. It was perhaps unreasonable to expect that all those who had voted for other socialist parties in 1977 would shift their support to the PSOE in subsequent elections. In several areas (especially Andalucía), the regionalist sentiments that had led voters to support the Unidad Socialista coalition in 1977 could lead them to shift to other regionalist or micronationalist parties instead. Even in such areas as Madrid, where regionalist sentiments were either nonexistent or compatible with support for the PSOE, former PSP voters would be subjected to considerable cross pressures. Most PSP supporters who belonged to a trade union were affiliated with the CCOO. This could lead them to vote for the Communists, rather than the Socialists. At a minimum, PSOE statutes requiring party members to affiliate with the UGT could prevent a former PSP supporter wishing to remain loyal to CCOO from joining the PSOE. Furthermore, survey data clearly indicated that many PSP voters had perceived their party as being closer to the center of the ideological spectrum than the PSOE.[75] These social-democratic or centrist voters might switch to the UCD in subsequent elections. Indeed, our survey data show that only 41.1 percent of former PSP voters chose the PSOE in 1979. The remaining PSP supporters who did not abstain voted for the PCE (11.5 percent), the UCD (7.1 percent), or other regional socialist parties (14.2 percent).[76] Thus, the electoral benefits to the PSOE of these mergers were limited.

The organizational benefits of fusing with smaller socialist parties were also less than anticipated. The most notable disappointment for PSOE leaders in this regard was, again, the merger with the PSP. As one Socialist provincial leader complained in a 1979 interview:

> We encountered a double surprise in uniting with the PSP. [The first] is that no party existed. The PSP had a very attractive, decorative, even honorable figure, Professor Tierno Galván, who *was* the party. In

uniting with the PSP we thought that, given the cultural deficiency of
our base [of party members], it would make a strong contribution of
intellectuals and might even bring about a strong ideological revital-
ization. But it hasn't turned out that way.

Another PSOE respondent was equally disparaging in discussing the
results of those mergers: "We found that either the PSP had no militants, or they simply refused to join the PSOE. The idea that there
was a massive merger of these parties is utterly false. In this province,
only about 20 PSP members joined. The MSA [Movimiento Socialista Andaluz] is also supposed to have merged with the PSOE, but
they had no militants either." Only 1 of the 12 provincial-level socialist leaders interviewed in 1979 claimed that the merger with the PSP
had led to a significant increase in the number of party militants. In
almost all geographical areas, elite-level respondents reported that
estimates of the size and effectiveness of the PSP infrastructure had
been greatly exaggerated.

Indeed, because representation on most provincial or regional executive committees was established in proportion to the total number of members each party would bring into the new coalition, PSP
leaders (and others) in many provinces intentionally exaggerated
their membership statistics in an effort to secure for themselves a
leadership role in the new party. In short, the terms of these mergers
gave the leaders of smaller parties an incentive to make their respective organizations appear to be larger or stronger than they actually
were. The use of this "Potemkin villages" strategy was a common
bargaining technique under these circumstances. In one extreme
case, it turned out that the PSP had only six members in the entire
province, only three of whom actually joined the PSOE. Nonetheless,
one of those three succeeded in negotiating for himself a seat on the
provincial executive committee and a favorable place on the PSOE
1979 municipal election list. In Catalunya, where it was unclear
whether the regional federation of the PSOE or the PSC-Congrés
had the larger base of party militants, it appears that both parties
greatly exaggerated their membership claims. In that region the
composition of the future executive committee was not automati-

cally set in accord with the number of affiliates of each party but was, instead, to be determined by a joint party congress. The size of delegations to that congress from each prospective partner in the new coalition, however, was a direct function of levels of affiliation with each party. On the eve of the 1978 merger, both the PSOE and PSC-Congrés claimed to have between 11 thousand and 12 thousand members each. In combination with the 1 thousand members of the PSC-Reagrupament, this would have given the new Partit dels Socialistes de Catalunya (PSC) about 25 thousand affiliates.[77] The official party census, which determined the size of each provincial or regional delegation to the Twenty-Eighth Congress of the PSOE, however, revealed that there were only 5 thousand dues-paying members of the PSC-PSOE throughout Catalunya.[78]

Organizational benefits were further reduced by the fact that the incorporation of other party elites often increased the level of conflict within the PSOE. As one party official said of the merger with the PSP: "It has brought problems—economic problems [the PSOE assumed the PSP's 1977 campaign debt],[79] and the problem that those persons who have joined the PSOE have not been totally integrated and, in some respects, continue to act like a party within our party."[80] Lingering party loyalties were one source of tensions. Other socialist officials indicated that old party images die hard and that they had not forgotten their resentment over Tierno's reference to his supporters (as compared with those of the PSOE) as the "vote of quality." For their part, long-time PSOE members often referred to PSP supporters as effete "cafe radicals." Such party ties often interacted with ideological predispositions to intensify intraparty conflicts. Some former members of the PSP—the most prominent being Tierno himself—had more orthodox Marxist beliefs than their PSOE counterparts. This exacerbated the internal struggles over efforts to moderate the formal ideological stance of the PSOE.

Finally, mergers with micronationalist or regionalist parties introduced an additional component into this complex pattern of intraparty conflict. The struggles between regionalists and Spanish centralists that were present in the constituent process also erupted

within the party itself. In Galicia clashes between Gallego nationalists and the Madrid central office over the formulation of lists for the
1979 elections culminated in a series of resignations, schisms, and
expulsions, which undermined the party's campaign performance.[81]
In Catalunya ongoing tensions between former members of the Catalán federation of the PSOE and former leaders of the PSC reflected
in microcosm the basic tensions between native Catalans and the
Spanish immigrant community.

The federal structure of the party has been only partly successful
in helping to regulate these center-periphery conflicts. On the one
hand, the existence of autonomous or semi-autonomous regional
branches has helped to prevent regional conflicts from disrupting
the basic functions of the party's central organs. As long as the federal executive committee eschews involvement in fights between
Catalán nationalists and immigrants, for example, there is no inherent obstacle to continued close cooperation between the dominant
ex-PSC leadership of that regional branch and PSOE leaders in Madrid. On the other hand, as Jorge de Esteban and Luis López Guerra
suggest, the very existence of regional party branches helps to perpetuate the center-periphery cleavages dating from the merger of
the PSOE and regional socialist parties.[82]

By the end of this series of interparty mergers in mid-1978, only
the positive aspects of the PSOE's rapid organizational expansion
were easily visible. These short-term successes of the party, accompanied by much "triumphalist" rhetoric, led Socialist leaders to conclude that they could immediately challenge the UCD as its "alternative in power."[83] Indeed the party's accomplishments over such a
short period were impressive. In just one year, it had quadrupled its
nominal membership, thereby ostensibly overcoming the PCE's initial advantage as the largest party organization on the left; it had
eliminated nearly all of its socialist competitors, thereby firmly establishing itself as the only viable statewide socialist party; and it had
merged with several regional socialist parties, thereby helping to
erase its historic image as a defender of Spanish centralism. But these
accomplishments also created new problems that would plague the

PSOE during the 1979 campaign and reach crisis proportions during the six months after that election.

UNEASILY STRADDLING TWO PARTY MODELS

One basic problem for the PSOE was a direct consequence of its rapid growth.[84] The recent creation of local party branches and the infusion of vast numbers of new members caused difficulties associated with low institutionalization.[85] Since 95 percent of its card-carrying members (or 90 percent of its dues-paying members) had not been party affiliates before 1977, a widespread consensus over basic decision-making procedures, the proper roles of militants and officials, party tactics and strategies, and even the party's ideology had not had sufficient time to develop. This gave rise to chaotic "assembly government" within some local branches that was more typical of a student protest movement than a modern political party. As late as February 1981, official party publications expressed deep concern over "internal divisions, confrontations and aggressiveness, the existence of factions, the lack of discipline and the lack of solidarity."[86] This, in turn, disheartened party members and led many of them to withdraw from active involvement in its affairs.

These difficulties were exacerbated by the party's de facto evolution during the 1977–1980 period from a "mass mobilization" party to a predominantly "catch-all" organization. The resulting strains were particularly severe because no consensus existed among party leaders as to which of these two was the preferable model for the PSOE. Inconsistencies between certain basic features of these two types of party were not adequately addressed until autumn 1979. As a result, serious internal conflicts erupted over the party's future tactics, strategies, and ideology.

The emergence of the PSOE as a radical mass-mobilization party, and the ratification of that model at the 27th Party Congress in December 1976, were the products of several factors. First, this type of party was most compatible with the behavior and rhetoric associated with clandestine opposition to the Franquist regime (particularly on university campuses) and of the many public demonstrations that took place during the highly ambiguous early stages of the transition to democracy. The apparent success of the Communist party also contributed to retention of the mass-mobilization model by the PSOE. The PCE's status as the largest and best-established party of opposition led many socialists to wish to emulate its tactics. Finally, and most importantly, this model made sense in light of the widespread expectation among socialists that democratization could only take place by means of a *ruptura* forced upon an unyielding oligarchy by a fully mobilized population.

Although this scenario may have underpinned the beliefs of most PSOE militants, it was by no means universally shared. According to some key respondents, Felipe González himself is reported to have always thought that Generalísimo Franco would die in bed and that his regime could not be displaced by mass mobilization alone.[87] He is reported to have believed that the PSOE's clandestine opposition to *Franquismo* was "an operation which could not destabilize the regime," and that no party, not even the much larger PCE, was "minimally capable" of doing so. According to this version of PSOE history, he was unable to prevail over those Socialist leaders (particularly Luis Gómez Llorente and Pablo Castellano, who dominated the large Madrid federation) who unquestioningly defended the "ruptura" scenario. González was also reported to have departed from the majoritarian view concerning the PSOE's electoral prospects. Many socialists emphasized mass-mobilization activities over electoral campaigns because they were pessimistic over the party's chances of success. Such beliefs were quite widespread even among members of the Socialist International: during a pre-election conversation with François Mitterrand and Hans Matthöver (of the SPD), González was told that it was unlikely that the PSOE would receive more than 14 percent of the popular vote. Given its greater organizational resources, the PCE was regarded by many as having better electoral prospects. And by the end of winter, 1977—just a few months before the first democratic election—few inside the PSOE were even confident that they would surpass the PSP as the largest party of the socialist left. (Some respondents have challenged the veracity of certain aspects of this historical account. They claim that Felipe González himself had been instrumental in converting the PSOE into a radical mass-mobilization party, pointing to the fact that this transformation took place at precisely the same time as González was consolidating his control over the Socialist party apparatus at the 1974 congress at Suresnes. They claim that González substantially changed his stance as the transition proceeded, and they reject the notion that he had always preferred the moderate catch-all party model. This controversy is irrelevant for our purposes, however, since both historical accounts agree that by the summer of 1977 González clearly favored a substantial moderation of the PSOE's programs and behavioral style, but was opposed by other party members.)

The impressive showing of the PSOE in the 1977 election resolved this uncertainty and laid to rest such pessimism. It also greatly strengthened the hand of Felipe González in his efforts to redirect the strategies and tactics of his party. By this time he could point to the political reforms of early 1977 and the openness of the June elections as evidence that a significant democratization of Spanish politics could be achieved through negotiation, compromise, and reform. Moreover, given that the PSOE was now firmly established as the second largest party in the Cortes, it faced the very real prospect of coming to power through entirely electoral means. González firmly believed that the voter appeal of the PSOE could be enhanced if the party could be induced to evolve toward the catch-all model. An abandonment of mass-mobilization rhetoric and radical ideological commitments was dictated by "the very moderation of the Spanish populace."

Throughout the 1977–1979 interelection period, however, efforts to project a more moderate image were undercut by the rhetoric and occasionally rancorous behavior of some party members. On the one hand, the highest-ranking PSOE leaders played crucial roles in "the politics of consensus," both in attempting to secure UGT compliance with the Pacts of Moncloa and in negotiating a consensual constitution. On the other hand, the Socialist party leadership was occasionally unsuccessful in assuming a consistently moderate public posture and in making sure that party militants behaved in strict accord with that image. As late as May 1, 1978, for example, the PSOE reaffirmed that "the force of the left cannot reside in electoral results alone, but in the capacity for mobilization of an organized people."[88] Although the party never actually ordered its supporters into the streets during the interelection period, its leaders sometimes threatened to do so, even in relatively minor disputes with the UCD government (such as over the timing of municipal elections). Opponents of the PSOE in the press, the UCD, and even the PCE seized upon such opportunities to denounce the Socialist party as irresponsible and as undermining the stability of the new democracy.[89] The use of threats to mobilize the masses in an effort to "conquer liberty"[90] was not only counterproductive electorally, but also did not fit with the marked transformation of the political climate of the times. As a Socialist leader has written, "After the elections of 1977, the dynamics of the 'directed mobilization' lost impetus. The loss of capacity for pressure 'from below' on the part of leftist organizations in the two years following July 1977 [now] appears clear."[91] He further argued that continued mass mobilizations "would have increased the probability of a coup."[92] By not rigorously abandoning the rhetoric of mass mobilizations, the PSOE remained vulnerable to accusations by its UCD and PCE rivals of irresponsibility and of contributing to regime instability.

Maintenance of the party's Marxist self-designation and pseudorevolutionary ideological declarations posed an even greater threat to successful implementation of a catch-all electoral strategy. Felipe González was quite aware of the electoral disadvantages for the party of these formal declarations. Therefore, on May 8, 1978, he stated at a press conference in Barcelona: "At the next congress of the PSOE, I am in favor of proposing the elimination of the term 'Marxism' from the programmatic declaration of my party."[93] These changes would not constitute a sharp lurch to the right but were oriented toward restoring Marxism to the position it had held prior to 1976. As a party official explained in an interview, "Felipe didn't want to reject Marxism. He just did not want the party to call itself Marxist. That does not mean that the party was in no way Marxist—those are two different things." According to this interpretation, the changes were designed to move the party away from an exclusively Marxist self-designation to a position of accepting Marxism as one among several bodies of thought within the party: from orthodox Marxism to a situation in which Marxism would be retained as a "method of analysis."[94] In short, he was following in the footsteps of Santiago Carrillo, who had similarly diminished the status of "Leninism" within the PCE just two weeks earlier.

This attempt, however, clashed with the ideological predispositions of many party leaders, and even with recent statements by González's closest collaborators: just five months earlier Alfonso Guerra had flatly asserted in a televised and published debate, "The PSOE has been, from its beginnings, a Marxist party in the purest sense of the word; it has been the only party based on a declaration of Marxist principles."[95] In combination with the low levels of party discipline and ideological consensus within the PSOE, and with its "assembly government" style, the immediate response to González's suggestion was a firestorm of criticism and conflict in the party's local branches. Numerous local and regional branches of the party passed resolutions reaffirming the party's Marxist self-designation and/or censuring its secretary general.[96] Several prominent national-level figures contradicted González's interpretation of the PSOE's ideology and criticized him for raising this issue in the presence of the "bourgeois" press. The party's honorary president, Enrique Tierno Galván, for example, stated, "Those of us who are in this party are Marxists . . . we defined ourselves at the XXVII Congress, which made it very clear that this party is Marxist, and that this cannot be altered."[97] And socialists attacked González, in an article published in *Posible*, "Rebellion at the Socialist Grassroots: Felipe Betrays the PSOE," not only for his attempts to move the party toward social democracy, but also for his "personalistic" leadership style.[98]

This conflict remained totally unresolved throughout the following year and led to polarization within the party. On one side were the *críticos*, who favored retention of the term "Marxism," more radical policy stands, more direct attacks on the UCD government, closer cooperation with the PCE, a reduction of the power of the party executive committee, and greater "internal democracy."[99] On the other side was an "*oficialista*" or "*Felipista*" faction, whose members, whether they considered themselves Marxists or not, defended the leadership position of Felipe González. This unresolved struggle undermined the Socialist party's electoral chances in 1979 and culminated in the temporary resignation of González as party leader in May 1979.

THE AP: REBUILDING A SHATTERED PARTY

Despite the miscalculations and setbacks of 1977, one objective of Manuel Fraga remained the same: just as in early 1976, he wished to build a large party of the center-right that would serve as the principal bulwark against the left in a two-party or two-bloc system. During the 1977–1979 period, AP party-building efforts were twofold: to moderate the ideology of the party, and to merge with other groups. The adoption of this course of action was rooted in the outcome of the 1977 election. The success of the UCD had demonstrated that more votes were to be gained by moving toward the center than by remaining on the right. The financial and infrastructural damage resulting from the defeat of the AP in 1977, moreover, made it advisable to join forces with other parties: something had to be done to reduce the AP's large unpaid campaign debt and to compensate for the loss of local elites, some of whom had defected to the UCD. Party rebuilding took on an added note of urgency when, as a byproduct of the constituent process, an elite-level schism within the AP led to the breakdown of the original coalition and the wholesale departure of the party's right wing.

The first incremental steps toward modification of the AP's ideology were made at the Second Party Congress in January 1978. Many party leaders were well aware that the 1977 defeat was due, in part, to its unattractive public image. In an interview in Galicia in July 1979 with a provincial-level official, he said: "Alianza Popular was the ogre of the country, which was going to devour its democracy and everything else, and this image had to be changed." The initial thrust of these alterations involved removing the defensive, alarmist, authoritarian language from the party's ideological declarations. Indeed, such statements abounded in the manifesto adopted at the First AP National Congress. Its description of the transition to democracy, for example, stated (in AP's translation):

> We are living a process of POLITICAL CHANGE, which because of the contradictions in the ways it has been stated, because of the imbalance created between reality and legality at all levels, because of the proliferation of political groups and the intransigence of their positions, because of the excessive concessions to attitudes of revenge, erosive of peace and order, disruptive for the national integrity, are creating a climate of confusion which weighs decisively on national problems in other spheres, impeding their solution and even aggravating them. . . . Extremist groups take advantage of such conditions and the crisis of authority at all levels to create a climate of social and labor conflictivity [sic] which, in addition to constituting a threat and a danger for the security of persons themselves, attacks the fundamental liberty to work, shakes the cohesion of companies and makes impossible the improvement of social well-being. . . . The SENSATION OF INSECURITY is increasing. The deterioration of public order, the unnecessary acceptance of disruptive ideas, the predominance of permissive attitudes and an excessive preoccupation with internal and external opinions which are more apparent than real. . . . All of this produces, among other serious consequences, a CRISIS OF CONFIDENCE at the historic moment in which it is most needed.[100]

Compounding the image problems that might have been produced by such language, the manifesto included defensive references to the Franquist past: "We reject any form of *ruptura*, and we demand respect for the work of a whole people over nearly half a century."[101] The disappearance of all such language from the ideological declarations adopted at the Second National Congress in January 1978 reflected an effort to modify the party's image. The AP continued to stress the preservation of civil order and national unity, but it did so using much more moderate terminology and added: "Alianza Popular is not to be confused, in any way, with the extreme right. We accept neither their integralist objectives, nor their violent means. . . . We believe that any radicalization is counterproductive."[102]

The second major aspect of the AP's rebuilding strategy was summarized in an interview with a high-ranking party leader in May

1978: "We believe that, by way of coalitions or mergers, the current party system should be simplified and nationalized, in order to present real options to the Spanish people. We will accept any formula that moves us in this direction." A national-level party official added in an interview in Madrid in May 1978: "We are committed to forming a new center, a new majority, to fully implant democracy in Spain. Fraga has publicly stated that we will merge with any party that is not Marxist, nor separatist, nor anarchist. Aside from those conditions, we will accept a fusion with any party. For reasons of its own, which I do not understand, the UCD had refused to join such a movement."

Several other parties, however, particularly those small centrist and conservative groups, which either had been excluded from the UCD coalition or had stood alone in 1977, were greatly interested in the creation of a *gran derecha*. They undertook steps to create the impression that they were formidable political organizations who would contribute a great deal to such a coalition. The first step involved the forging of coalitions or unified organizations among small personalistic clusters sharing common ideological orientations. The most important was the creation of Acción Ciudadana Liberal (ACL) in January 1978 by José María de Areilza. The ACL was formed through the merger of five previously independent liberal "parties."[103] The second step of this strategy typically used "Potemkin village" tactics designed to make the new party appear to be large and with great financial resources at its disposal. Most commonly, representatives of the press were invited to attend expensive dinner meetings of these parties and their supporters held at prominent Madrid hotels.[104] The purpose of these ostentatious gatherings appears to have been to enable the organizers of these "parties" to negotiate their entry into Fraga's "new majority" from a position of strength.

Efforts to merge these parties were greatly accelerated following the decomposition and collapse of the original AP coalition in the summer and fall of 1978. The breakup of the AP resulted from conflicts over constitutional compromises reached through the politics of consensus. In more general terms, this breakdown may be regarded as the result of the incompatibility between the conservative, but democratic followers of Manuel Fraga and the more antidemocratic segments of the party's right wing. The right-wing members of the AP delegation, under the leadership of Silva and Fernández de la Mora, voted against the text of the Constitution, primarily on the grounds that regional political decentralization and recognition of the multinational character of the population of Spain went too far toward destruction of the "unity of the Spanish nation." They also objected to some of the compromises reached concerning religious issues. Manuel Fraga also had reservations about the manner in which the Constitution dealt with regional matters, divorce, the education system, certain economic matters, and the electoral law, but he nonetheless led the rest of the AP Cortes delegation and the executive committee of the party to support the Constitution in the December referendum.[105] This decision provoked the departure of Silva, Fernández de la Mora, and their followers from the AP federation, and split the AP delegation in the Congress of Deputies exactly in half.[106]

The dissolution of the AP federation on November 1, 1978, coupled with widespread expectations that new elections might be held immediately after ratification of the Constitution, meant that Manuel Fraga would have little time to form a new party or electoral coalition. At the same time, the departure from the AP of its most right-wing leaders presented Fraga with an opportunity to undo the mistakes of the past and move his party toward the center-right.[107] With great haste a new Coalición Democrática (CD) was formed. Its main components were Fraga's AP, the ACL of José María de Areilza, Alfonso Osorio's tiny Christian democratic PDP (Partido Demócrata Progresista), the Partido Popular de Cataluña, Renovación Española, Reforma Social Española, and segments of the Demócratas Independientes Vascos.[108] Thus, the Coalición Democrática consisted of parties and factions spanning the ideological space between the "democratic right" and conservative centrism.

It was believed that this coalition would perform several different functions in a party rebuilding process. The first and most important involved the reshaping of the AP's image in a manner that might appeal to the targeted center-right electorate. By joining forces with persons who had somewhat more progressive reputations, who were unambiguously perceived as democrats, and who had played some role in the transition to democracy, it was hoped that the linkage in the public's view between AP and the Franquist past could be expunged. An AP official explained in a 1979 interview: "For the press and for many ordinary people, AP represented the integralist right, an intransigent right, the nondemocratic right. The presence of Areilza and Osorio in Coalición Democrática has served to remove the harshness from our public image." It was further believed that the supporters of these prestigious individuals could be attracted to the Coalición. It was sometimes claimed, for example, that Areilza had a large personal following, which had "sat out" the 1977 election following his ouster as head of the Centro Democrático and which might be induced to return to active involvement in electoral politics. Finally, formation of the Coalición Democrática was regarded as a means of increasing the financial resources available to the AP. The extremely expensive campaign undertaken by the AP in 1977 cost an estimated 1,000 million Ptas.,[109] and that party's crushing defeat meant that it would receive only 55 million Ptas. in state subsidies. Thus, the AP was ill-prepared to finance another campaign. Because both Areilza and Osorio had close connections with Spain's largest business firms and banks,[110] it was believed that their addition would increase the flow of voluntary contributions and bank credits to the party.

The image of the AP was further modified in the course of merging with these center-right forces. Doubts about AP's committment to democracy were greatly reduced by the departure of its right wing and by Fraga's steadfast support of the Constitution, despite some personal misgivings and despite the damage to his own party that he knew would ensue. In terms of electoral strategy, moreover, the presence of other groups on the party's right flank meant that AP leaders could demonstrate their committment to democracy by attacking those parties, thus using them as a foil in much the same manner that the AP had been used by the UCD in 1977.[111]

The direction of change in the party's ideology was not, however, uniformly toward the center. Indeed, the campaign conducted by Coalición Democrática initiated a significant shift in economic policy toward the right—toward a "classical-liberal" defense of free-market capitalism and a reduction in the economic role to be performed by the state. Support for neoliberal economic policies had been much weaker within the AP during the previous two years, partly because the original AP coalition included people who were relatively progressive in their economic policy preferences (e.g., Licinio de la Fuente) and partly because the traditional Spanish right had never embraced Adam Smith. Instead, religious devotion, Spanish nationalism, order, and authority had been more central elements in the belief systems of the founders of the Alianza Popular. Accordingly, the formal ideology adopted at its first two national congresses endorsed the market economy but at the same time called for greater economic equality and stressed the important economic roles of cooperatives and the state. Its 1977 economic reform program endorsed

> the socioeconomic model of the market, based on free initiative, the participation of the public sector, and the intervention of social sectors through a democratic planning of economic activity . . . a fiscal policy oriented toward guaranteeing a high level of investment and employment, and the securing of a more just redistribution of national income and wealth [and] . . . an agricultural policy based on private property and free entrepreneurial initiative, compatible with the promotion of cooperatives and of public or communal property.[112]

The original manifesto of the party adopted in 1977 included attacks on "monopolistic or speculative phenomena in vital goods such as food, salaries and housing."[113] It further stated: "The state of law that we propose will not admit unfair inequalities or privileges and will promote to the maximum social justice and equality of opportunity. The fight against speculation and corruption will be a permanent objective."[114]

The departure of many traditional rightists from the AP, coupled with the incorporation of Areilza, Osorio, and several business leaders (such as the Basque industrialist Luís Olarra), shifted the economic policy preferences toward the neoliberal right. The stout defense of free-market capitalism had been stressed by Areilza's ACL in particular,[115] and these themes were a central focus of the Coalición Democrática campaign in 1979. CD candidates attacked the economic policies of the UCD, arguing that the UCD had betrayed its center-right electorate by numerous compromises with Marxist parties and by its own drift to the center-left.[116] These stands were incorporated within the formal ideology of the AP itself. The program adopted at the Second National Congress in January 1978 had stated, for example, that "Alianza Popular is not an instrument at the service of pure capitalism, but it does believe that the free enterprise system is superior to state capitalism."[117] The corresponding statement adopted at the AP's Third National Congress simply stated, "Alianza Popular believes that the free enterprise system is superior to state capitalism."[118]

The attempt by Fraga and his collaborators to forge a stable coalition and rebuild a party almost in the midst of an election campaign was beset with numerous conflicts and difficulties. Indeed, given its history of conflicts among Fraga, Areilza, and Osorio, it was remarkable that their efforts were even marginally successful.[119] The most important source of conflict in the creation of the Coalición Democrática was the preparation of electoral lists. Even though most of the founders of the AP had left the party, the infrastructure of the AP was still largely intact.[120] In preparing for the 1979 elections, this was a mixed blessing, since it meant that many AP loyalists would have to be displaced in order to provide for the incorporation of new coalition partners. In several provinces (such as Barcelona, Santander, Murcia, Granada, and Sevilla), hasty and ill-conceived efforts to place followers of Areilza, Osorio, and others on CD lists provoked deep hostility on the part of the existing AP organization. In Barcelona, for example, one of the "Magnificent Seven," Laureano López Rodó, abandoned the AP because he had been displaced from the top of the provincial list by Areilza's collaborator, Antonio de Senillosa. Overall, only 43 of the 350 candidates the AP had nominated for the Congress of Depu-

ties two years before were present on the lists of Coalición Democrática in 1979. Struggles over the selection of candidates in many
areas produced formal ruptures between factions and/or gravely undercut the mobilization of party militants for the 1979 campaign.

These conflicts were intensified by some of the terms of the Pact of
Aravaca, which created the Coalición Democrática. Alianza Popular
still possessed an extensive provincial infrastructure and could count
on the services of many experienced campaign organizers, but the
followers of Areilza and Osorio were few in number and without
campaign experience. Nonetheless, management of the 1979 campaign was largely entrusted to the AP's new coalition partners. A
new, totally inexperienced team appointed by Osorio was given responsibility for the coalition's campaign efforts, and the campaign
headquarters were physically moved to the ACL office of Areilza, a
fact of considerable symbolic significance. These agreements left the
AP's infrastructure "immobilized, neutralized and marginalized," as
one embittered AP official said in 1979. In the opinion of most AP
elite respondents, the AP did not gain much over the short term from
the coalition, and it paid a high price. One deputy complained:
"Areilza really didn't have a party, and the party of Osorio is not a
mass party, but a cadre party, which has followers in a few isolated
places. These were not important contributions. . . . Alianza Popular was tricked by Areilza and Osorio. . . . Coalición Democrática is
practically [nothing more than] the old Alianza Popular—decreased
in size, because many elements have left the party." Two vice presidents of the AP nearly resigned in protest over what they regarded as
excessive concessions to their new coalition partners.[121] But, as an AP
leader said in an interview:

> What else were we to do? We had just lost much of our right flank, with
> the departure of Silva and de la Mora, and we had to do something to
> strengthen the party. Compromises and concessions had to be made,
> and I, as leader of a large party, was the only one who was in a position
> to do something. Neither Areilza nor Osorio had any parties at all.
> They were important, prestigious personalities but had little that they
> could give away. I made these concessions as a magnanimous gesture
> that was necessary to create a new political force.

CHAPTER FIVE

Social Class and
the 1979 General Election

S PAIN'S NEW CONSTITUTION entered into effect on December 29, 1978. On the same day, prime minister Adolfo Suárez announced in a televised speech that he had asked the now-constitutional monarch, King Juan Carlos I, to dissolve the Cortes and convoke new elections. In accord with his request, a new senate and congress of deputies would be chosen on March 1, 1979, and municipal elections would be held on April 3. The ostensible purposes of holding early elections, Suárez claimed, were to give "popular legitimacy" to the country's political institutions and to clear the way for a new government to address many unresolved problems in a bold manner, "without the conditions and limitations inherent in a period of transition."[1] Left unstated was the belief that the UCD might gain significant electoral benefit from the atmosphere of good will and accomplishment produced by the recent endorsement of a consensual constitution in the referendum of December 6. Its principal electoral rivals, moreover, faced some short-term difficulties that might redound to the benefit of the UCD. Negotiations over creation of a Coalición Democrática had just been completed, and the new partners had little time to rebuild an organization in advance of elections. The PSOE, meanwhile, had not yet held its Twenty-Eighth Congress, and thus many strategic and ideological disputes remained unresolved.

The outcome of the 1979 election for the Congress of Deputies (table 8) indicated a marked stability of the Spanish electorate in the first two years of democracy. No major changes in the relative strength of the parties took place. Some consolidation of the party system was also apparent: at least partly as a result of the absorption of smaller parties, the share of the total vote obtained by the UCD, PSOE, PCE, and AP (Coalición Democrática) increased from 80.1 percent in 1977 to 82.5 percent in 1979, and the two largest parties increased their joint share of the total national vote from 62.8 percent to 65.6 percent.

The overall stability of the electorate notwithstanding, there were some winners and some losers in 1979. The biggest winner was the UCD. In spite of the outgoing government's inability to reverse

TABLE 8
RESULTS OF 1977 AND 1979
ELECTIONS FOR CONGRESS OF DEPUTIES

Party	1977 valid votes	1977 valid votes (%)	1977 seats won	1979 valid votes	1979 valid votes (%)	1979 seats won
UCD	6,309,991	34.0	165	6,291,312	35.1	168
PSOE	5,371,466	28.9	118	5,476,969	30.5	121
PSP-US	816,582	4.4	6	---a	---	---
PSA	---	---	---	325,842	1.8	5
PCE-PSUC	1,709,870	9.2	20	1,939,387	10.8	23
AP-CD	1,488,001	8.0	16	1,094,438	6.1	9
PDC-CIU	514,647	2.8	11	483,353	2.7	8
ERC	143,954	.8	1	123,482	.7	1
PNV	314,272	1.7	8	296,597*	1.7	7
EE	64,039	.3	1	80,098*	.4	1
HB	---	---	---	172,110	1.0	3
Others	1,853,448	10.0	4	1,649,332	9.2	4
Total	18,586,270		350	17,932,890		350

UCD	Unión de Centro Democrático and Centristes de Catalunya, CC-UCD
PSOE	Partido Socialista Obrero Español and Socialistes de Catalunya
PSP-US	Partido Socialista Popular-Unidad Socialista
PSA	Partido Socialista Andaluz
PCE-PSUC	Partido Comunista de España and Partit Socialista Unificat de Catalunya
AP-CD	Alianza Popular and Coalición Democrática
PDC-CiU	Pacte Democràtic per Catalunya and Convergència i Unió
ERC	Esquerra de Catalunya and Esquerra Republicana de Catalunya amb Front Nacional de Catalunya i Partit Social Democrata de Catalunya
PNV	Partido Nacionalista Vasco (*includes Nacionalistas Vascos in Navarra)
EE	Euskadiko Ezkerra (*excludes Nacionalistas Vascos in Navarra)
HB	Herri Batasuna

Sources: Ministerio de la Gobernación, Dirección General de la Política Interior, Elecciones Generales 1977; and Ministerio del Interior, Dirección General de Política Interior, Elecciones Generales 1979.
aParty did not exist at the time.

Spain's serious economic decline or to put a stop to ever-increasing terrorist violence, the UCD enlarged both its share of the popular vote and the size of its Cortes delegation. Most noteworthy were the party's gains in Catalunya, where the new Centristes de Catalunya (CC-UCD) added three new seats to the nine that the UCD had won in 1977. Another winner was the PCE, which picked up over 200 thousand new voters and three seats in the Congress.

The big loser was the Coalición Democrática. Rather than increasing its number of deputies to 30, as some party officials had expected,[2] its parliamentary delegation was cut almost in half. CD failed to attract new voters dissatisfied with the policies of the UCD government and received almost 400 thousand fewer votes than the AP had attracted in 1977. Indeed, the behavior of former AP voters was the only significant nationwide exception to the overall pattern of electoral stability. According to our survey data, over 90 percent of those who voted for the UCD, PSOE, or PCE in 1977 chose the same party in 1979. In contrast, only 65 percent claimed to have voted for the AP in both 1977 and 1979. Over one-quarter of AP's 1977 voters shifted their support to the UCD in 1979. In the aftermath of what he perceived to be a devastating defeat, Manuel Fraga resigned as the head of his party. Another reflection of deep disappointment was the withdrawal of CD candidates from the April municipal elections.

Lying somewhere between these extremes of victory and defeat was the PSOE: the PSOE received more votes and a larger share of all valid votes than it had in 1977, but mergers with its former rivals did not bring it as large a bloc of new supporters as it had expected. Indeed, a comparison of its 1979 vote total to that of the combined support for the PSOE and PSP in 1977 shows that the "socialist vote" declined by over 700 thousand persons. These losses were most severe in Euskadi and Andalucía—two of the PSOE's traditional strongholds. In the latter region, the appearance of a newly revitalized Partido Socialista Andaluz (PSA, which had been part of the Unidad Socialista coalition in 1977) contributed to this development. The magnitude of the PSA's financial and organizational resurrection provoked numerous speculations that the PSA had been assisted by the UCD as part of a strategy of undermining the governing party's principal rival.[3]

Although the results of the 1979 election were a reaffirmation of the strength of moderate political forces in the new party system, unmistakable signs of polarization could be seen in Euskadi. The extreme Basque nationalist coalition, Euskadiko Ezkerra (EE), had received only 64 thousand votes and elected only one deputy in 1977. Prior to the 1979 election a schism within the EE led to formation of a more extremist coalition, Herri Batasuna, several of whose candidates conducted their campaigns from the jail cells where they were interned for alleged involvement in terrorism. The combined vote total for Euskadiko Ezkerra and Herri Batasuna in 1979 exceeded 250 thousand, 25 percent of the total regional vote. This reflected a significant polarization within Euskadi, which bode ill for the possible stability of the new democratic regime.

CLASS DIVISIONS AND PARTY STRATEGIES

One of the important decisions to be made by newly emerged political parties is what social groups they wish to attract as stable electoral clienteles. Numerous choices concerning organizational strategies, party penetration into secondary organizations, and short-term electoral tactics are all closely related to, if not directly derived from, this basic determination. These decisions are of consequence for each party and, taken together, affect the character of the party system as well. Were the parties to focus on relatively narrow target groups and be successful in their search for a homogeneous following, the unavoidable result would be a higher degree of class polarization.

In making decisions about target groups, parties are constrained by a number of factors. The first of these is the nature of the system of social stratification—primarily, how many identifiable strata there are, and how large they are. The second has to do with the party's self-image, which is rooted in its history and ideology. This self-image can be gradually modified: some aspects can be stressed and others deemphasized, but it is unlikely that the image can be changed abruptly. Among other things, this could create internal tensions and offer a convenient target to political adversaries. Finally, party elites are also constrained by the images of their party that are diffused throughout society. These, too, are hard to alter in the short run.

In the campaign of 1979 the four major Spanish parties adopted remarkably similar strategies with respect to the identification of social targets. Despite differences among their ideologies and initial self-images, during the campaign they adopted broad rather than narrow designations and sought votes from a wide spectrum of social locations.

There were two kinds of departures from this general approach. First, though electoral efforts were geared toward maximizing the party's appeal to the largest possible range of social groups, certain occupational groups were frequently earmarked for special attention. The identity of these sectors was largely a function of the socioeconomic context within which the parties operated in each province. In predominately agricultural provinces, for instance, all parties appealed to farmers; in provinces heavily dependent on tourism special attention was paid to owners of small businesses and service workers in that sector. The second variation was based on the expectation that the party's appeal would meet with a positive response within a more restricted range of social groups. Thus, AP officials believed that the comfortable middle class would be more likely to vote for the party than unskilled workers. These perceptions affected campaign decisions. In allocating scarce financial and organizational resources, party officials would be inclined to devote them to geographical areas most likely to respond favorably to the party's appeals. Accordingly, the PCE campaign in Madrid placed much greater stress on its activities in the peripheral working-class suburbs of Móstoles, Getafe, and Alcobendas than it did in upper- and upper-middle class neighborhoods, such as the Salamanca district. The roles of a party's ideology and its societal image can best be appreciated by considering the parties separately.

THE INTERCLASSIST PARTIES

For the UCD and AP, ideology posed no difficulty. In formal ideological statements, both parties explicitly defined themselves as interclassist.

The UCD behaved as a catch-all party par excellence. In keeping
with its eclectic ideology, the Unión de Centro Democrático strove to
attract support from all socioeconomic groups. The UCD explicitly
stated in its first formulation of ideology of January 1978 that it is "at
the service of the diverse peoples of Spain and of all social, generational, and human sectors."[4] In line with this announcement, all of
our elite-level respondents in that party stated that they wished to
attract persons from all social classes. Although they frequently expressed the belief that their greatest support could be found in the
middle classes, they added that they wished to expand this potential
base to include large segments of the working class. Thus, the appeal
set forth by the UCD during the 1979 general election, as described
in a postelection interview with a high-level party strategist, "was not
a message directed toward any specific sector of the public. It was
destined somewhat in search of the common denominator of all social positions of all regions in Spain and therefore was very general."

Similarly, AP defined itself as "interclassist,"[5] though party officials
were somewhat more likely than the UCD to make specific reference
to the middle class. As one high-ranking official put it, "We have always defined ourselves as an interclassist party, but it is true that, in
effect, we feel more comfortable with the so-called middle class." Interviews with AP officials also revealed another slight difference from
the orientation of the UCD. The overall interclassist stance of the AP
was related to its explicit rejection of the very concept of class struggle.
One high-ranking party official stated in a preelection interview: "A
political party should not represent one class or another, one social
group or another. I think almost all persons could be integrated into
the kind of political party that I would like to see in Spain. . . . We have
no intention of representing the interests of any particular class, of
being a party of any particular class. We do not believe in the class
struggle." This position was a reflection of official party ideology. The

Ponencia Política adopted at the Second Congress of the party in January 1978 stated, *"No lucha de clases: sociedad de clases medias"* ("No class struggle: [for] a society of middle classes").[6]

The two parties of the center-right, however, had some problems projecting an interclassist image. These difficulties lay in the widely shared perceptions that the parties of Suárez and Fraga were forces catering to the upper classes. Awareness that this societal image constituted a handicap was often found in our interviews. As one AP official put it, "The working classes and lower middle classes do not support us because they erroneously believe that we are a party of big capital and industrialists, and that is not true. We do have many party members who are in the liberal professions, but they are not of the great economic oligarchy. We do not discriminate against anyone. We want to attract more persons in the working class and especially those in the agricultural sector."

Nonetheless, both parties defined themselves formally as "interclassist," and their leaders repeatedly stated that they wished to attract an electorate that would transcend class boundaries by conducting catch-all campaigns.

"CATCH-ALL" WORKING-CLASS PARTIES

For the two major parties of the left, the PCE and the PSOE, the adoption of a broad target strategy required a redefinition of the notion of the working class. But the manner and timing of these efforts differed, and had consequences for both their conduct of the campaign and its outcome.

In accord with the self-description traditionally associated with Communist parties, the statutes adopted at the Party Congress of 1978 refer to the PCE as "the vanguard political organization of the working class," but also of "the progressive forces of Spain. In it are voluntarily integrated men and women proceeding from the working class, the peasantry, the forces of culture, and from other sectors of the population."[7] One high-ranking veteran Communist leader told us: "We think that in our party today there is room for sectors [ranging] from the middle classes and small industrialists, businessmen and merchants to workers." This substantially enlarged definition of the party's constituency was adopted at all levels within the party's hierarchy and in all geographical areas. Thus, whereas nearly all PCE leaders interviewed referred to "the working class" in describing their electoral target groups, in all but one case they enlarged that description with a long list of other social groups.

Perhaps the most significant addition to the PCE's list of target groups was the small and medium business sector. The rationale behind this broadened appeal was twofold. The first relates specifically to electoral strategies: a Eurocommunist party that aspires to come to power through democratic means cannot afford to ignore such a large sector of Spanish society. As resolution 16 adopted at the Ninth PCE Party Congress contends:

> Small and medium business and self-employed workers constitute an important sector . . . whose conditions of existence have worsened notably throughout recent years, due particularly to the policy practiced by *Franquismo* and the process of capitalist concentration, aggravated by the economic crisis. A cursory analysis of small and medium business and independent workers confirms that objectively their interests are in contradiction with those of monopoly capital and, in general, with those of big capital. . . . The economic crisis that weighs so heavily on the backs of the workers also weighs profoundly on these sectors, endangering their very existence.[8]

The second line of argument that led the PCE to appeal to owners of small and medium-sized businesses involved the economic and political role envisioned for them during the transition to socialism. As resolution 16 of the Ninth Party Congress explains:

> An important aspect of the advance toward political and social democracy will also be the protection and assistance of small and medium business, which will coexist with the public sector. This attitude does not reflect consideration of political tactics. In Spain, small and medium businesses are necessary to meet a series of production needs and services, and to aid them is not incompatible with the interests of workers and the conservation and improvement of their living standards.[9]

PCE efforts to attract the support of small business groups—or at least to neutralize them—met with some success in 1979. Most busi-

ness groups tend, not surprisingly, to side with parties of the right.
Indeed, the group representing big business interests, the Confederación Española de Organizaciones Empresariales, supported the UCD
and was reported to have channeled considerable financial resources
to it.[10] Breaking from this normal pattern, the Catalán association of
small and medium businesses (the Asociació de Comerciants Auto-
noms Petits i Mitjans Industrials de Catalunya) recommended that its
members vote for Socialist or Communist parties and against the governing UCD, which it alleged had abandoned their interests in favor of
those of large industrial firms. Similarly, its Spanish counterpart, the
Confederación Española de Pequeña y Mediana Empresa, refused to
endorse either the AP or the UCD and remained silent during the
campaign.[11]

The landowning peasantry was another recent addition to the
Communist party's list of target groups. PCE officials in agricultural
provinces explicitly referred to owners of small and medium-sized
farms as one of the groups they wanted to attract. Again, this was not
inconsistent with official party policy. Resolution 9 adopted at the
Ninth Party Congress claims:

> The PCE has always defended the just demands of peasants and
> herders, of agricultural workers, and of all classes and social levels of
> the countryside, exploited or despoiled, and most particularly those of
> the family-landowning peasantry.... The unjust distribution of land
> ... continues to be one of the capital evils of our agriculture. On the
> contrary, the great landowners in general have been favored by that
> policy of support for monopolies, to which they are linked by numer-
> ous ties.... The principal contradiction today in the agricultural and
> herding sector is therefore that farmers and herders are confronted
> with that monopolistic domination.[12]

What social groups, then, did the PCE not want to attract during
the 1979 campaign? Several respondents indicated that they had no
desire to attract the support of "capitalists." Their descriptions of
that group, however, departed markedly from those used by more
orthodox Marxists but were consistent with ideological revisions
adopted at the Ninth Party Congress: resolution 16 implicitly
defined as "capitalists" those owners of businesses who employ more

than 50 workers.[13] Thus, the concept of "working class" was revised to include all those who make a living by dint of their own labor. A member of the executive committee of the PSUC attempted to clarify this point by adding, "I include all those persons who actively produce the wealth of this country, whether this be in the form of professional activities or intellectual creativity." This helps to explain how various professional groups (lawyers, medical doctors, architects, technicians, and university professors) and "the forces of culture" (artists, writers, and performers) were included within the "working class," as were owners of small and medium-sized businesses and farms. Thus, the list of social groups that the PCE excluded from its potential following was rather short. When pressed, most elite respondents rejected only latifundist landowners, *rentiers*, and owners of business enterprises employing more than 50 persons.

Why exclude anyone? Apart from the negative but central role played by "monopoly capitalism" in defining a Communist party's raison d'être, interviews with party elites suggested several reasons. The first was based on sheer negative feelings toward what was perceived to be an oppressive class enemy—an enemy, moreover, that had profited greatly under the previous authoritarian regime. A second consideration was purely electoral: the excluded economic elite could serve as a foil, against which a wide range of social groups could be rallied by the party. One final explanation was set forth by an official in the Madrid branch of the party: "We have nothing at all against their integration. . . . Some persons, in fact, are directors of industry and are active in the Party. It's just that we don't have much hope of attracting these individuals, given that we have a socialist ideology."

The PCE entered the 1979 general election campaign with a list of socioeconomic target groups, which departed from the requirements of a pure "catch-all" designation only in that a small economic elite was rejected in principle. Like both the UCD and AP, however, though the PCE desired in general terms to attract support from nearly all social groups, most respondents stated that they gave highest priority to those groups from which they expected to receive the greatest support—in this case, the traditional "working class."

The Socialist party, the PSOE, has also historically defined itself as a party of the working classes, and, as recently as its Twenty-Seventh Congress (in December 1976), it set forth a maximalist ideology interpreting the concept of working class in a traditional and rather narrow sense.[14] Using language unchanged since the nineteenth century, the party's declaration of principles states:

> Considering: that this society is unjust because it divides its members into two unequal and antagonistic classes: one the bourgeoisie, which, possessing the instruments of labor, is the dominant class; the other, the proletariat, which, not possessing anything but its vital force, is the dominated class: that the economic subjugation of the proletariat is the primary cause of enslavement in all forms of social misery, intellectual degradation, and political dependence: that the privileges of the bourgeoisie are guaranteed by political power, which is used for the domination of the proletariat . . . The Socialist Party declares that it has as its aspiration: (1) The possession of political power for the working class. (2) The transformation of individual or corporate ownership of the instruments of labor into collective, social or common property. . . .[15]

Felipe González and Alfonso Guerra attempted to soften this exclusionary language. In 1977 they wrote: "Today the concept of the working class is updated by the inclusion within it of the totality of those salaried persons who, occupying an indirect place in the productive process, have been incorporated into the fight to build a more just and egalitarian society for all. Thus, employees, medical doctors, lawyers, writers, and engineers may be found today in a process of 'salarization' which places them together with manual laborers."[16] Although most elite respondents continued to describe the PSOE's electoral clientele as the "working class," it was clear that a greatly broadened redefinition of that concept had been employed. As a regional-level party leader (later elected mayor of a large city) described it, "We can consider the working class as reaching from the dean of a university faculty to the student, from the liberal professional and the executive to the carpenter, fisherman, laborer, or bricklayer."

What was most striking was that, within the general context of a catch-all campaign, the greatest emphasis was to be given to efforts to attract middle-class support. Another party leader in Andalucía stated in 1978:

> After the [1977] election, we undertook a series of studies to find out what group had supported us. We found that we had received support from the traditional clientele of the PSOE: manual laborers, the poor, industrial workers, agricultural workers. Following the election, Felipe González decided that we should attempt to widen the base of the party by attracting, in particular, small farmers, small businessmen, and members of the liberal professions. . . . We want to attract a larger proportion of those social groups without at the same time abandoning our traditional appeal.[17]

Indeed, an interview at the highest level of the party confirmed that this was a correct identification of the target groups to be given highest priority in the forthcoming campaign:

> If one imposes a sociological definition of the left, that is, if one defines voters of the left as those of low incomes, then we do have some prospects [for expanding the PSOE electorate]. Those persons with the lowest incomes in this country are peasants. In the last election, paradoxically, we won in rich areas—in the cities—and we lost in poor areas, that is, in the countryside. Economically speaking, these persons should be voters of the left.

Thus, the PSOE targeted for the 1979 campaign large sectors of the Spanish electorate that are conventionally defined as middle-class social groups. The inconsistency between this catch-all electoral strategy and the party's exclusionary working-class ideology led to considerable intraparty tension between two different conceptions of society and the role of the Socialists. This juxtaposition was clearly reflected in the remarks of a party official in Andalucía:

> One is a concept in which the party would continue to be Marxist, in the most dogmatic sense of that word, and which would defend only and exclusively the rights of the proletariat, understanding as "proletariat" the manual laborer. There is another group of persons who think that, when the party was founded, that was fine; there was a very strong proletariat, a practically nonexistent middle class . . . and that as a consequence we should be concerned with that class. A century has passed now since the founding of the Socialist party. The situation has changed. Nowadays, indisputably, from the teacher to the archi-

tect, we're all proletarianized. We see that the subjective interests of
this group can coincide with socialism, and we think that the obligation of the Socialist party should be to transform these subjective interests into objective interests. We think that it would be a fatal error if
these persons were not with us. Our objective should be to steal from
the UCD that million votes from workers, lower professionals, bank
employees, teachers, medical doctors. . . . I, personally, am a Marxist.
What I believe now is that one should not be a dogmatic Marxist.

This ambiguity undercut the PSOE's catch-all appeals. The strident
steam-age rhetoric of its formal ideological statements was manipu-
lated most effectively by UCD candidates in an attempt to frighten
away those middle-class voters that the Socialists wanted to attract.

THE SOCIAL BASES OF CATCH-ALL STRATEGIES

The remarkably similar strategies adopted by the four major parties with respect to the identification of electoral targets can be explained, in part, in terms of the constraints imposed by the system of
social stratification. In modern societies no single social group can
by itself provide a sufficiently large bloc of voters to allow a party to
play a major role. Although Spain lags somewhat behind other more
advanced European countries in its level of development, its social
structure has undergone considerable transformation in the past 30
years. The shrinking of the agricultural sector and the growth of the
tertiary sector have brought about an increase in the size of the middle strata. The classification of heads of household in terms of occupation reported in table 9 shows that by the mid-1970s the traditional working class did not exceed one-third of the total. A grouping
of Spaniards in terms of social strata drawn from the same study
shows that the middle class and the lower-middle class together com-
prise over 50 percent of the total (table 9). In addition, the diffusion
of more homogeneous life-styles in large sectors of society has
tended to blur traditional class lines. Hence, it would make little
sense for any major or aspiring party to limit its appeal to a relatively
narrow target, especially because it is unlikely that any one appeal
would succeed in attracting all the voters of a given group. In short,
simple social arithmetic helps to explain the broad designation of
social groups as electoral targets.

TABLE 9
CLASSIFICATIONS OF HEADS OF HOUSEHOLD
BY OCCUPATIONAL GROUPS AND BY SOCIAL STRATA, 1974

Occupational groups (%)		Social strata (%)	
Executives	1.8	Upper and	5.0
Businessmen	2.7	upper-middle	
Professionals	4.8	Middle	35.0
Mid-Level	4.2	Lower middle	20.3
White-collar	14.3	Working	33.6
employees		Poor	6.1
Civil servants	9.6	N	(3007)
Self-employed	14.7		
(small business,			
proprietors,			
merchants)			
Workers	34.2		
Farmers	7.5		
Farm laborers	6.1		
N	(2849)		

Source: Fundación Foessa, *Informe Sociológico sobre la situación social en España*, 1975, pp. 761 and 763.

Perhaps equally important was the elite's belief that a straightforward class appeal was not likely to resonate favorably with the electorate. Narrow class appeals might in fact constitute a liability if, in the prevailing political culture, they are seen as self-serving and divisive. Indeed, our 1979 sample of Spanish voters expressed an overwhelming sentiment in favor of the proposition that "parties should represent the interests of all social classes" (76 percent). Among leftist voters a narrow class perspective was somewhat more popular, but even within this group it was a point of view shared by a minority. Only 34 percent of the sympathizers of the extreme left, the PCE, and the regional left favored the notion that "parties should represent the interests of only one social class." Moreover, the feeling of belonging to a social class, a prerequisite for successful class appeals, was shared by only slightly more than 40 percent of the electorate.

CLASS DIVISIONS AND PARTY PREFERENCE

To what extent were parties successful in attracting support from a broad spectrum of social groups? More specifically, how did different social strata divide their votes among the parties, and what was the resulting social composition of the different partisan groups?

The analysis of the relationship between class and party preference is complicated by the multifaceted nature of social stratification and the different kinds of indicators of social position that one might use. Because no single approach is entirely reliable, it is preferable to attack the problem from different viewpoints. A first and somewhat oversimplified measure of a person's class position is the distinction between the occupational roles of the self-employed and those who work for others. To be sure, the latter category now includes some people, for example, those in the middle and upper white-collar occupations, who certainly do not fit the traditional notion of "working class." Yet this distinction is meaningful insofar as it sets apart two groups of people who relate to their means of livelihood in sociologically distinct ways, such as proximity to and involvement in one's job, risk taking, fluctuation in income, and organizational constraints. A second simple distinction is that between manual and nonmanual labor. In the earlier stages of economic development, the differentiation between white- and blue-collar occupations constituted a good approximation of the working-class/middle-class classification. With the increase of the tertiary sector and the swelling of lower-level clerical jobs, however, it is doubtful that the manual/nonmanual distinction can by itself capture a person's class position with precision. Clearly, there are highly skilled manual occupations that rank higher than some white-collar jobs in terms of both prestige and monetary compensation. Nevertheless, this second distinction also contributes to the identification of status position.

How closely associated with partisan preference were these two criteria of class position when considered jointly? As one might expect, Socialists, Communists, and other parties of the left did much better among manual laborers than among voters of the other three groups (table 10). Within this traditionally defined working class, the left, taken together, held a clear majority. It did less well, but still better than in the electorate as a whole, among white-collar workers. Among the self-employed the picture was reversed: most preferred the UCD or other parties of the center-right. The AP did particularly well among the nonmanual self-employed—professionals, executives, entrepreneurs, and the like. Two points clearly emerge from these data. The first is that occupational status was definitely linked to partisan leanings. Both of our indicators of status—and particularly the dichotomy self-employed/works for others—identified subgroups of Spaniards with rather different party preferences. When taken together, these two measures of status showed an even sharper differentiation of the partisan preferences of our respondents. The second point is that, though a relationship did exist, there was hardly a full coincidence between the voters' status and their electoral choices in 1979. Over one-third of the people in manual occupations who worked for others chose a party of the center or right and, conversely, almost 40 percent of self-employed voters in nonmanual professions chose a party of the left. Clearly, status made a difference in voting behavior, but it was not the only significant factor.

TABLE 10

PARTY PREFERENCE AND OCCUPATIONAL STATUS

	Work For Others (%)		Self-Employed (%)	
	Manual	Nonmanual	Manual	Nonmanual
Party Preference[a]				
Extreme and regional left	5.0	6.8	2.1	4.5
Communist	13.8	9.8	5.5	6.6
Socialist	44.9	33.7	22.7	27.4
Total left	63.7	50.3	30.3	38.5
Regional moderates	3.6	4.6	1.8	4.6
UCD	31.1	36.2	65.2	47.7
AP (CD)	1.3	6.1	2.2	7.8
Extreme right	0.3	2.8	0.5	1.4
Total center-right	36.3	49.7	69.7	61.5
N	(1035)	(1178)	(291)	(762)

(a) Party groups include the following:
  Extreme left: ORT, EMK-OIC, LKI-LCR, PTE, PTA, OCE-BR
  Regional left: EE, HB, BEAN, BNPG, UPC
  Communist: PCE, PSUC
  Socialist: PSOE, UG, PSA
  Regional moderates: PNV, CiU
  Extreme right: UN, FN, FEJ

A more detailed classification of voters in different occupational strata reveals that no party enjoyed a monopoly of support from any one social group (table 11). Even within the lower strata there were a considerable number of UCD voters. Similarly, over 30 percent of the top strata had leftist leanings. The weakness of the connection between partisan choice and class is quite apparent from the social composition of the different party groups shown in figure 3. To be sure, those in the lower and top social layers were heavily represented among PCE and AP-CD electors, respectively. The overall differences in social status among the different groups of partisans, however, tended to be modest. This was particularly true in the case of the two larger parties. Some differences did exist in the social bases of the UCD and PSOE: within the ranks of the latter, industrial and agricultural workers occupied a more prominent position than in the UCD (42.4 percent vs. 25.5 percent). Conversely, farmers and, to a lesser extent, middle-class people were more heavily represented in the UCD than among the Socialists. Nevertheless, a comparison of the social composition of the PSOE and the UCD is striking more in its similarity than in its difference.

One might object that these results are a function of our classification of occupations and that a more refined scheme would have produced a better fit between the two variables. Conceivably, alternate classifications might lead to slightly different results. There is no reason to believe, however, that the overall picture would be greatly modified. Analysis of the political leanings of specific subgroups, such as skilled workers or those in high prestige occupations, shows that the members of these groups split their vote among the different parties in proportions that differ only marginally from those already discussed. In particular, the two major parties appeared to be popular within a wide variety of social segments, ranging from the higher to the lower occupational groups. In the latter, support for the UCD was more pronounced among the less skilled subgroups, especially in the agricultural sectors. The UCD received 46 percent of the unskilled agricultural workers; only 30 percent of these voted for the PSOE. Among skilled nonagricultural workers, the percentages were 21 for the UCD and 48 for the PSOE.

TABLE 11
DISTRIBUTION OF PARTY PREFERENCES
AMONG DIFFERENT STATUS LEVELS
(in percentages)

Status level[a]		Extreme left	Regional left	Communist	Socialist	Regional Moderate	UCD	CD	Extreme right
I	(N=462)	1.0	2.2	7.8	21.5	3.2	48.9	11.2	4.2
II	(N=755)	3.5	5.0	10.4	33.8	4.6	34.2	6.8	1.6
III	(N=577)	0.8	3.6	6.4	26.4	5.1	50.6	5.3	1.8
IV	(N=288)	2.5	2.7	10.7	35.7	5.1	39.2	2.6	1.5
V	(N=313)	0.6	1.2	4.7	23.0	2.2	65.7	2.1	0.5
VI	(N=677)	2.4	3.1	16.1	42.8	4.9	29.0	1.2	0.6
VII	(N=548)	1.8	1.9	12.5	42.1	2.3	37.9	1.4	—
All respondents (N=3670)		2.0	3.1	10.4	33.3	4.0	41.4	4.5	1.4

Note: Status level based on the occupation of the respondents or of the head of household.
[a]The composition of the seven status groups is as follows:
  I Entrepreneurs, professionals, landowners, high-level public and private executives
 II Mid-level public and private employees, technical professions
III Owners, small businessmen, independent artisans
 IV Low-level white collars, sales and supervisory personnel
  V Small farmers
 VI Skilled workers in agriculture and industry
VII Unskilled workers in agriculture and industry

The fact that class divisions were reflected in the party system in a relatively weak manner raises the question of whether the class cleavage, a traditionally important one in Spanish society, is becoming less salient. A full answer to this question could come only from a longitudinal study. We can speculate about the possibility of such a trend, however, by looking at the linkage between occupation and party preference in different age groups (table 12). No uniform trend can be discerned. In all three age groups, people classified as manual workers were slightly more likely to favor one of the two major leftist parties, but the difference was most noticeable among the middle-aged group. If anything, the most notable findings are the pronounced preference of the older cohort for center-right parties and the leftist predisposition among the young.

The profiles of the major Spanish parties in terms of occupational groups are thus rather mixed. There were differences in the composition of the various partisan groups, but they were not overwhelming. The profiles, moreover, appear to be quite similar to those of other major European parties belonging to the same "political fam-

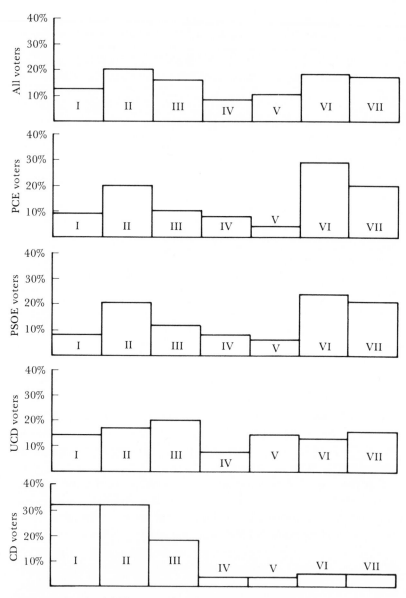

FIGURE 3. Social Class Profiles of Partisan Groups

Note: The seven strata are those defined at the bottom of table 11.

TABLE 12
PREFERENCE FOR THE SOCIALIST AND
COMMUNIST PARTIES AMONG MANUAL AND NONMANUAL
WORKERS IN DIFFERENT AGE COHORTS (in percentages)

	Manual Workers	Nonmanual Workers
Younger cohorts (18–29 yrs.)	77.8	69.3
Middle cohorts (30–49 yrs.)	59.3	40.8
Older cohorts (50 yrs. and older)	42.0	32.9

ily." This is apparent from table 13 in which the pattern of plusses and minuses summarizes the differences between the composition of the different partisan groups, on one hand, and the respective national samples, on the other. As one can see, the PCE deviates from the Spanish sample in a manner that is very similar to the deviation of the Italian Communist party (PCI) from the Italian sample. Similarly, the social profile of the PSOE is similar to that of the British Labour Party and the German Social Democratic party (SPD), while the composition of UCD voters resembles reasonably well that of the Italian Christian Democrats. Finally, though AP has a profile more heavily skewed toward the higher social strata, it fits reasonably well into the family that also contains the British Conservative Party and French center-right parties.

The data discussed thus far refer to the linkage between partisan orientations and status defined in relatively objective terms. But what of the subjective aspects of social class?

Given the historical connection between the working-class movement and the parties of the left in Spain, one might expect that awareness of class divisions and identification with the working class would be related to leftist leanings. The connection between these two variables is, of course, quite commonly made in Spanish political discourse: it can be found in conversations, political messages, speeches, newspaper commentaries, and elsewhere. In our own survey, many people provided definitions of "left" and "right" that were clearly rooted in a classist view of society.

TABLE 13
OCCUPATIONAL PROFILES OF PARTY
FOLLOWERS IN EUROPEAN DEMOCRACIES

Parties	Occupational Groups[a]				
	I	II	III	IV	V
PCF	− 8.8	−2.9	−6.1	+25.6	−7.8
PCE	− 3.6	−6.0	−0.4	+14.6	−4.6
PCI	− 3.7	−5.6	−2.5	+14.6	−2.8
Labour	− 6.5	−4.1	−5.2	+16.2	−0.4
PSOE	− 4.4	−3.0	+0.5	+ 9.8	−2.9
SPD	− 1.9	−3.8	+0.4	+ 6.6	−1.3
PSI	+ 1.7	+0.2	+1.3	− 0.1	−3.1
FDP	+ 4.3	+3.2	+1.7	− 9.7	+0.5
PRI-PSDI-PLI	+10.0	+5.4	+5.5	−18.0	−2.9
CDU-CSU	+ 1.1	+3.7	−0.6	− 5.0	+0.8
DC	− 0.9	+1.3	+0.5	− 5.4	+4.5
UCD	+ 1.9	+3.5	−4.7	− 5.7	+5.0
RPR	+ 5.6	+3.3	+4.1	−11.5	−1.5
UDF	+10.4	+4.3	− − −	−14.8	+0.1
Cons. (U.K.)	+ 6.2	+3.8	+7.8	−18.3	+0.5
AP (CD)	+18.5	+3.1	+6.6	−23.3	−4.9

PCF	French Communist party	PSDI	Italian Social Democratic party
PCI	Italian Communist party	PLI	Italian Liberal party
Labour	British Labour party	CDU-CSU	German Christian Democratic party
SPD	German Social Democratic party	DC	Italian Christian Democratic party
PSI	Italian Socialist party	RPR	French Rally for the Republic
FDP	German Free Democratic party	UDF	Union for French Democracy
PRI	Italian Republican party	Cons. (U.K.)	British Conservative party

Source: Data drawn from the Eurobarometre surveys nos. 9, 10, 10a, 11, and 12 conducted from spring 1978 to fall 1979. The five data sets were pooled, yielding a combined sample of 5,472 cases.

Note: Figures are the differences between the percentage of the entire national samples and each of the party groups falling within the various occupational categories.

[a]Occupational groups are as follows: I, Professionals and executives; II, Merchants, shopkeepers; III, White-collar workers; IV, Blue-collar workers; and V, Farmers.

Some definitions of the "left" in class terms included the following:

"Embodiment of the popular conscience and organization of the working class"

"The working class—those of us who are against the capitalist oligarchy"

"It benefits the working class"

"The way to achieve a society without classes and without exploitation"

Similarly, definitions of the "right" touched on class structure:

"The upper social class"
"The right looks after the interests of business"
"It does not defend the workers"
"The defense of capital"

Moreover, a fair proportion of respondents explained their preference for a party in terms of the defense of particular group or class interests. However, this sort of political imagery, this way of conceptualizing society, was not dominant. Indeed, a narrow, strictly classist view was rather infrequently found among the voters. Only one-fifth of our sample favored the idea that parties "should represent only one class." When our respondents were asked whether they belonged to a social class, only four out of ten people said that they did. When asked to choose from among a specific list of social classes, however, a large majority had no difficulty in assigning themselves to one of the several alternatives provided (working class, middle class, upper class). It is clear, therefore, that subjective class varied in salience, ranging from those with a narrow classist view—only a modest segment of the electorate—to those who denied the very notion of class divisions.

One reason for keeping separate the objective and the subjective dimensions of class is, of course, that, though a certain overlap between the two exists, there is certainly no full coincidence. In Spain, as in other countries, working-class identification is by no means to be found only among the occupational groups that are traditionally regarded as "working class." In our sample, self-assignment to the working class was fairly common among white-collar employees and other groups: among the former, working-class identification reached 49.6 percent. Conversely, many people of lower status did not necessarily see themselves as belonging to the working class. About 17 percent of the skilled workers identified with the middle class. Given these discrepancies, one might legitimately expect to find that the predisposition to prefer a party of the left or of the center-right would be greater among those groups in which objective position and self-identification coincided. One would also expect to find that the subjective dimension is the stronger of the two, overriding, so to speak, the impact of the first. This was indeed the case. As table 14 indicates, subjective class identification made a great deal of difference *within* each of the status levels. The proportion of voters who favored parties of the left was always larger among the subgroup of working-class identifiers than among those who identified with other classes, even when they shared the same objective status.

Subjective class identification was more widespread among younger people, 53 percent of whom identified with a class, than among respondents belonging to the middle and older age groups (48 and 38 percent, respectively). Perhaps this finding can be explained by reasoning that the older cohorts were more successfully socialized under the Franquist regime—a regime that deemphasized class divisions and stressed social solidarity. But the finding could also be accounted for by the greater propensity of younger Spaniards to identify with the working class *and* to vote for parties of the left. As table 15 shows, age played an independent role in shaping party preference even when class identification was held constant. Thus, differ-

TABLE 14
POLITICAL LEANINGS BY OBJECTIVE
AND SUBJECTIVE SOCIAL CLASS (in percentages)

	Subjective class identification		
Status levels	Upper or middle class	Lower middle class	Working class
I	23.6	42.3	49.1
II	39.5	44.4	65.8
III	25.8	37.1	43.3
IV	39.3	51.4	54.4
V	0	22.0	30.6
VI	54.5	53.6	67.7
VII	29.6	39.2	62.3

Note: Figures are percentage preferring a party of the left in each subgroup.
aStatus levels defined in table 11.

ences in rates of class identification could be the product of different partisan preferences.

This second interpretation raises the question of the direction of the linkage between class and voting choice. The assumption often implicit in many analyses is that class is the independent variable, the "cause" of different partisan leanings. Although there can be little doubt on the direction of causality when the variable in question is class (measured by some objective indicators, such as occupation or income level), in the case of "subjective class" the matter is not so simple. It could be argued that the awareness of class divisions and the feeling of belonging to a class are not always antecedents of partisan preference but can be, rather, a consequence of it. This is particularly plausible in the case of citizens who, for a variety of reasons, are close to or sympathetic toward a party whose ideology and rhetoric place a great deal of emphasis on class and on class conflict. The flow of communication emanating from the party—or from allied organizations, such as trade unions or youth associations—can clearly be an important factor for awakening class awareness and cementing it to partisan orientations. It is true that class identification can develop

TABLE 15
SUBJECTIVE CLASS IDENTIFICATION AND PARTY
PREFERENCE AMONG DIFFERENT AGE COHORTS
(in percentages)

	Party preference			
	PCE	PSOE	UCD	AP (CD)
Younger cohorts				
Working class	19.9	45.9	15.7	1.0
Lower middle class	17.3	40.1	24.3	2.3
Middle or upper class	10.0	30.5	31.7	8.4
Middle cohorts				
Working class	12.3	39.8	37.9	2.4
Lower middle class	4.4	31.5	48.4	4.8
Middle or upper class	4.0	22.6	50.3	12.9
Older cohorts				
Working class	7.6	31.7	52.1	2.3
Lower middle class	2.4	24.7	57.0	8.2
Middle or upper class	4.8	11.3	59.2	19.5

spontaneously and independently from one's partisan leanings, but it cannot be denied that parties can play an important role in fostering its development or in crystallizing latent sentiments.

THE ROLE OF TRADE UNIONS

Many Western European political parties have traditionally attempted to attract voters or recruit new members, especially from the working classes, through links with trade unions. The leaders of Spain's leftist parties agreed with their European counterparts and regarded trade unions as essential in translating objective socioeconomic factors into subjective party loyalties and political behavior. A Communist party strategist argued in an interview,

> The organized working class is that which votes for the left. The non-organized working class votes for the right, just as peasants vote for the right. . . . On the other hand, the most conscious, the most secure vote, which is most forcefully expressed, election after election in exactly the same form, is very much a function of the workers' organization, of trade union organization. In those areas where there is heavy industry and a good trade union organization, there is a tremendous vote for the left, and it is moreover a vote which is maintained [over time].

A Catalán Socialist leader was even more explicit in arguing that trade unions play the most decisive role in channeling the working-class vote toward one party of the left, as opposed to its leftist rivals. The pronounced variation in shares of the vote received by the PSC-PSOE and the PSUC in specific districts of the working-class "red belt" of Barcelona, he argued, is entirely a function of trade union organizational strength: where the CCOO were strongest, the PSUC had an electorally hegemonic position; working-class neighborhoods where the UGT was stronger gave relatively greater support to the Socialists. He concluded, "the unions are the main source of working-class support for this party."

In 1979 all significant "working-class" parties were closely associated with a trade union organization: the Sindicato Unitario (SU) was linked to the Organización Revolucionaria de Trabajadores; the Confederación de Sindicatos Unitarios de Trabajadores (CSUT) was associated with the PTE (Partido del Trabajo de España); the UGT (Unión General de Trabajadores) was tied to the PSOE; and the CCOO (Comisiones Obreras) were generally regarded as a Communist (PCE) trade union. To outside observers, these connections appeared to be very close, and, indeed, leaders of the UCD and AP, as confirmed in an interview with a UCD official in 1978, contemptuously referred to these trade unions as being "nothing more or nothing less than the human transmission belts, which have been developed by the parties of the left." Socialist and Communist respondents rejected these claims, steadfastly asserting that the UGT and CCOO were completely independent. The truth lay somewhere between these contradictory views. The UGT and CCOO usually supported, and were supported by, their respective political parties, but such relationships could not be taken for granted in all parts of the country or at all times. There are subtle but important distinctions, moreover, between the manner in which the PCE and PSOE formally related to their respective trade union organizations, which sometimes had significant consequences, as in the 1979 elections.

In some respects, claims of "complete independence" on the part of Spain's two largest trade union organizations verged on the preposterous: in one province, for instance, it was necessary to pass through the office of the UGT in order to reach the PSOE office. In other respects, however, these assertions were correct. In a formal, institutional sense, there were no explicit organizational ties between the PSOE and UGT or the PCE and CCOO. Although the composition of the national and provincial executive committees often resembled an "interlocking directorate," this was more the result of informal practice than of statutory provision. Organizationally there was nothing comparable to the close institutional interpenetration between the British Labour Party and the Trades Union Congress. In an informal sense as well, it would be a mistake to assume too close a relationship between party and trade union. In Navarra, for instance, the CCOO were by no means under the effective control of the PCE: instead, the CCOO were dominated by members of the Movimiento Comunista and former members of various left-wing Catholic labor organizations that flourished under the Franquist regime (the HOAC, JOC, and VO). Similarly, in Alava control of the UGT was the object of bitter conflict between members of the PSOE and the Trotskyite Liga Comunista Revolucionaria. But overall, in most of Spain the CCOO supported the PCE, and the UGT supported the PSOE.

The more subtle, indirect, and complex of these relationships is between the CCOO and the PCE. Partly as a result of continuity with the historical origins of the CCOO and, more importantly, as the product of rational calculations concerning the memberships of the two organizations, the PCE took great care to preserve a semblance of independence of that trade union from the party. Indeed, the CCOO began as totally nonpartisan. In the late 1950s and early 1960s, ad hoc shop floor workers' committees (*comisiones obreras*) emerged as a result of frustration with treatment by the corporatist vertical syndicates established by the Franquist regime.[18] These committees were created in response to specific plant-level grievances and at first tended to dissolve when the dispute was resolved.[19] By the mid-1960s, however, it was decided to form a permanent confederation of workers' committees and to use it as an organizational framework for seizing control of the shop-floor institutions of the vertical syndicates themselves.[20] This strategy was consistent with a long-standing PCE policy of working through existing organizations rather than creating separate underground organizations. Consequently, the Communist party turned its full attention to the Comisiones Obreras as the principal means of organizing Spain's working classes.[21] A smashing success was scored by the CCOO in the 1966 elections of shop stewards (the *enlaces sindicales* of the vertical syndicates), by which time the PCE had succeeded in securing the nomination of large numbers of party members as CCOO candidates.[22] This gave Communists and other regime opponents a legal or semi-legal façade behind which an effective infrastructure could be established for future trade union activity. The following year, however, the regime initiated a crackdown and outlawed the CCOO. Over the following several years, their leaders were arrested and sentenced to long prison terms.[23] Ironically, this served to increase popular support for the workers' committees by converting many of their leaders (including the present CCOO secretary general Marcelino Camacho) into martyrs and popular heroes.[24]

At the beginning, the leadership of the Comisiones Obreras was overwhelmingly noncommunist.[25] With the passage of time, however, PCE members became progressively more influential within the organization and now predominate in most areas. A series of schisms within the CCOO had resulted in the departure of the elites who might have pulled the organization in somewhat different directions.[26] After the departure of most noncommunist leaders, the PCE by 1976 had established a hegemonic position within the national leadership of the CCOO and controlled 21 of 27 seats on the CCOO executive committee.[27] The CCOO won about 40 percent of the votes in the 1978 trade union representation elections, in part because of its organizational head start over the UGT, which won about 30 percent.[28] This gave the PCE a potential electoral resource.

The PCE was cautious, however, in its relations with the CCOO. The resolution on syndical policy adopted at the Ninth Party Congress contains language that unequivocally supports the CCOO but circumscribes those statements with numerous assertions of CCOO independence:

> Within the context of syndical liberty and pluralism, the PCE supports the syndical confederation of the CCOO, as much for its tradition of struggle against *Franquismo* as for its new and profoundly renovating conception of syndicalism. . . .[29]

> CCOO is the trade union where members of the Partido Comunista de España and other parties, at the side of the great mass of independents

without a party, explain and defend their points of view. These may be accepted or not by the base and the directive organs of the CCOO. This does not involve a transmission belt or an organic relationship, but a real, complex, and on occasions contradictory relationship between political parties and the trade union, based on the strictest respect—by the party—for the independence of the trade union and the mass movement.[30]

The statutes of the PCE encourage party members to join the CCOO but do not require them to do so.[31] One example of the implications of this flexibility was volunteered by an official of the Balearic branch of the party (the Partit Comunista de les Illes Balears), who stated, "some of the most veteran and respected members of the PCIB are members of the UGT. They had been members of the UGT during the Republic and therefore have strong sentiments toward the UGT. We respected those personal desires, and no pressures have been placed upon them to change their trade union membership."

In the absence of a formal institutional linkage between party and trade union, one PCE official claimed: "Whatever influence we exert is through our militants who are members of the Comisiones, who set forth our proposals, which are then voted upon. Sometimes they win, but often our proposals are defeated. There are never any joint meetings of the two executive committees, nor are there any organizational ties."

These informal influences, however, were most effective in determining the activities of CCOO provincial branches. In most provinces, most of the leaders of the union were PCE members. Thus, a PCE leader in Galicia argued, in an interview, that

> there is a great deal of consistency in our policies, because many Comisiones Obreras leaders are Communists and they apply the same general principles to the solution of problems. Only three to four thousand Communist party members are active in the Comisiones Obreras [which have 80 to 90 thousand members throughout Galicia]. But they are those individuals who are most active. There are never joint meetings between the two executive committees, but some persons in the Comisiones Obreras are members of the central committee of the party, including the secretary general of the Comisiones Obreras.

In the 1977 elections the role of the CCOO was cautious in the extreme: the trade union did little more than recommend that its members vote for democratic parties and for parties that would defend workers' interests.[32] No explicit endorsement of the PCE or Communist candidates was made. In 1979 the party made greater use of the CCOO, employing two tactics. First, the union wrote a socioeconomic and political program (which bore a remarkable resemblance to that of the PCE), and then, according to a high-ranking PCE leader in an interview, it recommended that CCOO members "vote for the parties that defend the program of the Comisiones." Second, a large number of CCOO leaders were nominated to stand as PCE candidates. Comisiones members were then merely asked to "support the candidacies that contained CCOO leaders on its lists," according to the secretary general of a regional PCE branch, interviewed in July 1979. The PCE campaign manager in a populous province explained, "What we did was exploit during the campaign the prestige of the Comisiones Obreras—the prestige of those Communists who are leaders in the Comisiones. That is how we attempted to win the workers' vote for the Communist party." Although the electoral implications of these endorsements were clear, they were nonetheless consistent with the formally unaffiliated, pseudo-independent status of the Comisiones Obreras that the Communist party wished to maintain. Maintenance of that status, however, was not without its risks, particularly insofar as it left noncommunist CCOO leaders open to similar cooptive efforts by other parties: in one exceptional case, a Comisiones Obreras leader in Málaga even stood as a candidate for the UCD in the 1979 general election.

Why, then, did the PCE not more openly and formally associate itself with the CCOO? A PCE official provided one answer in a post-election interview:

> If we were to use the trade union for political ends, we would wind up sinking the Comisiones Obreras, because if the CCOO were clearly identified with the Communist party ... the process would not be that workers in the Comisiones would vote Communist, but rather that the workers who don't vote Communist would stop voting for the Com-

isiones Obreras. . . . Insofar as we are a much smaller party than the
PSOE, we are most interested in preserving syndical independence in
order to guarantee the continued syndical hegemony of the CCOO.

This strategy was rooted in the realization that the membership of
the CCOO was quite mixed in its political preferences. Indeed, a
survey of trade union members undertaken in 1978 revealed that
only 39 percent of the affiliates of the CCOO had voted for the PCE
in 1977, while 45 percent had cast ballots for the PSOE.[33] Under
these conditions, an attempt to force CCOO members to join the
PCE or a blatant effort to induce them to vote for the Communist
party could have led large numbers of union members to abandon
the Comisiones Obreras. A more subtle use of Communist strength
within the CCOO, however, could attract to the PCE an ever-growing
bloc of new supporters: even if only a portion of the more than one
million CCOO members and their families were attracted to the
party, this was a sizable segment of its support base. The specific
means by which the PCE used its "presence" within the Comisiones,
moreover, fit well with the preferences of the workers themselves.
The PCE strategy sought to capitalize on the personal popularity
and prestige of its members who had acquired leadership positions
within the union. This largely personalistic attraction was consistent
with the opinions of the vast majority of workers polled (80.3 percent of the 1978 sample) who claimed that they were attracted to
their union because it was led by "persons who inspired their confidence"; only 17.4 percent stated that they had selected their union
because they agreed with its ideology.[34] Finally, the absence of formal ties between the CCOO and the PCE was consistent with the
Comisiones' longstanding objective of forming a *sindicato unitario*—a
single trade union that would represent all workers.

In some respects, the relationship between the UGT and the
PSOE was comparable to that between the PCE and the CCOO. The
UGT also claims to be a nonpartisan trade union; party-union coordination was based principally on the influence exerted by party
members within the union, and, like their Communist counterparts,
there is a great deal of personnel overlap between the executive com-

mittees of the two organizations, both at the national and provincial levels. The relationship between the UGT and the PSOE, however, was much more direct. First, PSOE members are required by party statutes to join the UGT and to work actively within the trade union.[35] Second, according to elite interview respondents in most provinces, joint meetings of the UGT and PSOE provincial executive committees were sometimes held, a practice not found in the case of the CCOO and the PCE. Third, the PSOE was much more active in its overt support of the UGT in syndical elections, and in return the UGT was more open about its links to the party. As an American observer wrote of the 1978 syndical representation elections: "The Socialist General Union of Workers (UGT) ... played up its party links, arguing that the Socialist Workers Party (PSOE) is the wave of the future ... [while] the Communist workers' commissions ... played down their Communist party (PCE) link and stressed their individual 'heroes' like their chief, Marcelino Camacho."[36]

National and provincial-level PSOE leaders expected support from the UGT during election campaigns and phrased these expectations much more bluntly than their PCE counterparts. A high-ranking party leader said in an interview, "The UGT's role is to criticize the government on occasion, even if it is a Socialist government, but to support the PSOE." A Socialist deputy explained that "the UGT is walking along the same road as we are. They are an extension of the party. We want them to attract new members to the party, and we in turn want to strengthen the UGT." Still another PSOE deputy referred to the link between the party and its union as a "command" relationship. In the 1979 elections, propaganda of various kinds, stressing that "UGT supports the PSOE," was sent out to provincial branches of both union and party. Most provincial and regional committees of the UGT explicitly endorsed the PSOE's lists of candidates and asked their members to support the party.

The party, however, was not always successful in gaining compliance with these "commands." In some provinces, small-scale rebellions erupted. On the eve of the formal start of the campaign in Vizcaya (where a UGT regional congress had decided seven months ear-

lier to require union members to support the PSOE), 44 UGT members, including 10 members of the executive committee, were
suspended by both the PSOE and UGT for refusing to support the
PSOE.[37] In Santander, the regional committee of the UGT pointedly
refused to support the PSOE in protest over their failure to place a
UGT leader in the second position on the PSOE list.[38] In Zamora, 80
UGT members, angered over the exclusion of a UGT leader from
the party list after he had served as a senator in the previous Cortes,
conducted an anti-PSOE campaign in which they smeared the capital city of that province with hostile graffitti. The UGT Teruel
branch also refused to support the party.[39]

Why was the UGT-PSOE relationship so tumultuous on occasion?
One explanation was suggested by a Communist official: "Part of the
UGT is not pro-PSOE, and seeing itself forced to vote for the PSOE
in a bureaucratic manner—forced by the union directors—made
that sector of the UGT vote for the PCE, for the UCD and for other
parties, but not for the PSOE." Another explanation, given by a
PSOE official, involved the extremely rapid rate of growth and per-
sisting underinstitutionalization of these bodies:

> I lived and worked in Germany for 16 years. During this time I became
> used to relatively united efforts by Spanish immigrants and German
> trade unions. I could not imagine the total lack of coordination that
> exists in this province today. This is not quite a situation of conflict
> between the UGT and the PSOE, but it is certainly one of a total lack of
> coordination. The roots of this problem can be found, I suppose, in
> that the UGT increased very rapidly, much more rapidly than the
> growth of the PSOE.

Despite the long association between the UGT and PSOE (dating
back to 1888), most union branches had been reactivated for only a
short time. Thus, the sudden involvement in partisan politics of such
rapidly expanding organizations placed great stress on them before
mutual expectations and norms governing the party-union relationship had stabilized. The PCE, by way of comparison, with more than
a decade of clandestine trade union activity, had greater experience
and skill in organizing and coordinating mass efforts of this kind.

A third explanation for the sometimes conflictual relationship between the Socialist party and the UGT concerns the trade union affiliation of the members of smaller parties that had merged with the PSOE in 1978, such as the PSP, PSC, and PSPV. These mergers were complicated by the fact that new PSOE members would have to join the UGT, though many of them had previously belonged to other trade unions: considerable numbers of PSP and PSPV members belonged to the CCOO and USO, while most PSC-Reagrupament and PSC-Congrés members were affiliates of the CCOO, USO, CNT, or the Unió de Rabassaires. In Catalunya, in particular, many new Socialists viewed the UGT contemptuously as a union for non-Catalán immigrants. These persons were forced to make a difficult choice between switching to a new party and maintaining loyalty to their trade union, with many (especially in the PSP) apparently choosing the latter. The UGT in Catalunya, moreover, ultimately became an organizational base from which old PSOE members attacked the hegemony established within the party by the former PSC leaders.

Despite these occasional difficulties, both Socialist and Communist party leaders regarded support from their respective trade unions as a valuable asset in electoral competition.

Why, then, did the UCD and AP not make use of trade union ties? In part, differences of opinion among the leaders of the parties prevented them from taking concerted action. Some leaders favored the creation of "cooperative" trade unions, others strongly opposed any form of affiliation with unions, and still others expressed a general interest in forging party-union ties but were dissuaded by the practical difficulties involved.

Strongly negative opinions concerning union ties were frequently expressed by AP respondents. As a national leader flatly stated, "We do not believe in *sindicatos* which are tied to political parties." On occasion, right-wing members of that party would issue more blanket condemnations of trade unions of any kind. One provincial-level official said, "Whether they are vertical *sindicatos* or horizontal *sindicatos*, I don't like them." Although most AP leaders favored the concept of completely independent, non-Marxist trade unions, without any direct involvement in politics, some were in favor of actively collaborating with non-Marxist unions, or (in the case of one respondent) even creating a union directly linked to the AP.

Opinions within the UCD leadership were also mixed but on balance reflected a more serious interest in the creation of a centrist union that might support the party or at least help to check the advances made by the PCE and PSOE in attracting working-class support. One UCD provincial official claimed, "Public opinion polls have shown that 85 percent of the labor force is not Marxist, nor do they want to belong to Marxist unions. In the abstract, it would be beneficial to form a purely professional trade union." Another added, "I think it is absolutely essential to prevent the PSOE from dominating the labor movement and radicalizing the working class. We would like to preserve these persons as social democrats and not Marxists."

However, at least through 1979, the UCD refrained from open trade union involvement as a result of several related concerns. The first was that a UCD union could be perceived as a "yellow" union, in collusion with business. Given that the UCD was often seen as a middle-class and not a working-class party, the formation of a UCD *sindicato* could generate suspicions among workers that might backfire against the party. Even worse, such a trade union could make the party appear as if it were implementing a Franquist labor policy, thereby highlighting one aspect of the party's image that it wanted the public to forget. Another form of association was precluded by the ideological heterogeneity of the party. In several continental European democracies, the principal rivals to Marxist trade unions are Christian democratic unions. Because the UCD was not formally a Christian democratic party, but rather a coalition of liberal, social democratic, independent, and Christian democratic factions, the creation of a Christian union would have provoked considerable intraparty conflict. For these reasons, the UCD, after considerable study and discussion, took no steps toward the creation of an association trade union before the 1979 elections. It did, however, establish informal contacts with numerous smaller "independent" trade unions, and it was rumored that the party was contemplating the cooptation of the USO.

Thus, the two major parties of the left fought the 1979 campaign with the help of potentially important allies, while the UCD and the AP (CD) lacked such channels for attracting popular support. How significant were the trade unions in mobilizing the vote in favor of parties of the left?

In evaluating the role of unions, one must bear in mind that, although these are large secondary organizations, their potential "reach" within the electorate is limited. Union members represented approximately 11 percent of our sample, a figure consistent with the 4 million estimate of union affiliates derived from other sources.[40] This is a large number of voters, but it represents only a segment of the electorate, even considering the families of those affiliated with trade union organizations.

The percentage of union members in different subgroups of voters varied somewhat. It was higher among males, (17.4 percent) than females (4.4 percent), a reflection of the different position of these two subgroups in the occupational structure. Union membership was also more common among younger (13.2 percent) than older (6.8 percent) voters, and in the cities (12.3 percent) than in the countryside (9.8 percent). As one might expect, rates of union affiliation varied in different occupational groups: the highest percentage was among skilled workers (30.2 percent), followed by unskilled laborers (21.6 percent). But there were also significant rates of union affiliation among low-level white-collar workers (19.7 percent) and middle-level public and private employees (17.0 percent). Even among the top occupational groups, one voter in ten declared affiliation with a trade union. Thus, although the unions' potential effectiveness was greater among traditional working-class groups, its reach was by no means confined to them.

As was believed by party leaders, union affiliation was clearly associated with a classist view of society, and union members in our mass sample were more likely to have subjective class identification than nonmembers (66.5 percent vs. 40.4 percent) and to identify more frequently with the working class than with nonunion members (81.5 percent vs. 62.0 percent). In part, of course, these differences were due to the positions occupied by union members in the economic structure. But not entirely: within the same status group unionized respondents were definitely more likely to identify with a class than nonunion members.

Given the leftist parties' ties to the unions and the association of union membership with working class identification, it is not surprising that union affiliates cast their votes overwhelmingly for the Socialist and Communist parties (84.5 percent). Party choice, moreover, was clearly related to membership in one or another of the two major unions (table 16). Almost 90 percent of UGT affiliates voted for the PSOE, and 62 percent of the CCOO members chose the PCE. In both cases, this represented a significant increase in the mobilization of union members in support of the parties. In 1977 only 39 percent of CCOO affiliates had voted for the PCE, and 72 percent of UGT members had chosen the PSOE.[41] The continuing greater ability of the UGT to harness the vote for the Socialists can be attributed to two factors. First, the CCOO were from the beginning more heterogeneous ideologically, and thus their members were more difficult to "move" in a specific partisan direction. Second, the PCE strategy of union-leader cooptation may have been relatively ineffective because of the low visibility of CCOO affiliates who joined the PCE electoral lists. As a Socialist party official in Andalucía argued:

> I believe that this policy has not produced favorable results for the PCE nor for the Comisiones Obreras in the general election campaign, among other reasons, because the number of Comisiones leaders which could be placed on the PCE lists was quite small. Many of them might have been well-known at the middle- and upper-levels of the trade union's hierarchy, but not at the base of that *sindicato.* Either that, or the name [of the candidate] was known, but nobody really knew what his union activity consisted of.

The insufficient visibility of these individual Comisiones leaders limited the effectiveness of this PCE strategy in the 1979 elections. This same official, however, argued that the municipal elections that followed, in which 60 thousand elective positions were at stake, did permit the kind of grassroots penetration that this largely personalistic strategy required.

TABLE 16
UNION MEMBERSHIP AND PARTY PREFERENCE
(in percentages)

Union membership	PCE	PSOE	Other parties
CCOO (N=184)	62.9	26.3	10.8
UGT (N=155)	3.7	87.1	9.2
Other unions (N=125)	6.4	31.2	62.4

The overall influence of trade unions in harnessing the vote for parties of the left was considerable, as shown in figure 4. Quite clearly, the number of electors affiliated with one or another of the two major unions who did not vote for the Socialist, Communist, or other leftist party was small. Moreover, the same data show that, in the presence of union affiliation, differences in occupation mattered little. Non-manual workers differed only slightly from people with manual occupations in terms of their propensity to favor a leftist party.

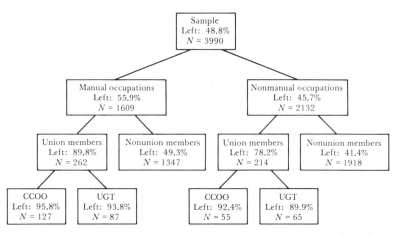

FIGURE 4.   Preference for Leftist Parties, Occupation, and Union Membership

Note: Percentage left is the percentage of voters within each subgroup voting for the PCE, PSOE, or other leftist parties. Classification of occupations based on the profession of the respondent or of the head of the household.

Although union affiliation was in and of itself an important means for harnessing the vote of certain segments of the electorate, it should not be considered in isolation because it was part of a larger cluster of interrelated variables, including structural factors (occupational status, income, manual/nonmanual labor), and attitudes bearing on class cleavage. A number of questions concerning such orientations were posed to our mass sample. Voters were queried about the fairness of income distribution in Spanish society, their feelings toward the unions and big business, their attitudes toward the *sindicatos* of the Franquist regime, and their preference for "private property" versus "nationalization." (See appendix E.) The pattern of responses shows that these orientations were by and large coherent. Thus, for example, voters who were less hostile toward big business were also likely to give a more positive evaluation of the Franquist unions, tended to favor private property over nationalization, and to be less critical about the distribution of wealth in Spanish society. These orientations were also related to the structural aspects of class but to a lesser degree; coherence was much more pronounced for the more attitudinal aspects of class. Not surprisingly, supporters of the major parties tended to differ with respect to these class-related orientations, and the distribution of attitudes among groups was very much in line with the traditional left-right ordering of the parties (table 17). In some cases attitudinal differences were more marked, and in others less, but there is little doubt about the existence of a linkage between partisan preference and attitudes bearing on class divisions. To be sure, there was no unanimity within any of the partisan groups, and, in the case of the larger ones, the UCD and PSOE, opinions were considerably mixed. Thus, class-related issues did not divide the Spanish electorate in two homogeneous blocs but rather generated a certain amount of differentiation among the various groups of voters.

What specific aspects of this issue differentiated the supporters of the various parties? Analysis of the linkage between class and partisanship, taking simultaneously into account all the class-related vari-

TABLE 17
CLASS-RELATED VARIABLES AND PARTISAN PREFERENCE
(in percentages)

Class-related variables	Extreme left	Regional left	PCE	PSOE	Regional Moderate	UCD	AP	Extreme right
Manual occupations	40.7	32.2	52.0	49.1	36.4	41.4	13.7	10.7
Self-employed	16.0	27.8	20.2	24.1	30.8	42.1	43.2	26.1
Identifying with working class	73.8	67.8	75.0	69.4	53.7	58.1	29.4	18.0
Union members	28.9	21.7	33.7	16.9	12.8	2.6	2.5	13.5
Having a classist view of parties	33.9	33.7	34.8	22.1	18.6	12.4	17.3	7.1
Feeling that income distribution unfair	86.7	92.4	88.0	80.1	70.2	64.7	41.1	46.6
In favor of Franquist *sindicatos*	0	2.3	2.1	3.9	5.9	20.7	48.7	81.1
Preferring private property over nationalization	8.5	12.1	7.6	16.6	37.8	48.0	65.8	71.7
Extremely hostile to big business	67.3	45.6	49.6	27.3	17.2	12.3	5.8	16.2

ables, suggests a number of observations concerning the differences among the groups and the relative importance of the factors considered. The figures reported in the last column of table 18 (standardized discriminant coefficients), provide an indication of the relative weight of the variables included in the analysis in separating the followers of the four major parties from one another. It is clear that what best distinguished the four groups of voters were the subjective aspects of class rather than the actual position of the respondents in the social structure. When all the variables are taken into account, the distinction between manual and nonmanual labor and income differential becomes irrelevant. Similarly, working class identification and the classist view of political parties lose much of their importance. The same cannot be said, however, of union membership and of the distinction between people who are self-employed and those who worked for others. Examination of the coefficients for the three pairs of party groups (PCE-PSOE, PSOE-UCD, UCD-AP/CD) suggests that some aspects of the class cleavage were important in differentiating between some groups of voters but not others. For example, income level was of little importance for the comparison between the PCE and the PSOE group, but it was a critical factor in separating the UCD respondents from those followers of AP. Similarly, union membership was significant for setting apart the PCE from the PSOE and the PSOE from the UCD, but of no consequence for the UCD-AP comparison. As to the overall level of similarity between the different pairs, the values at the bottom of the table confirm what the univariate analysis had already shown, namely, the relative proximity of the PCE and the PSOE groups, and of the UCD and the AP/CD supporters. In terms of the objective and subjective aspects of the class cleavage, the largest distance was that which separated the two more central parties. As we have seen, the class cleav-

TABLE 18
RELATIVE IMPORTANCE OF CLASS-RELATED
VARIABLES IN DISTINGUISHING AMONG
PARTISAN GROUPS

Class-related variables	Pairs of Party Groups			All four partisan groups
	PCE-PSOE	PSOE-UCD	UCD-AP	
Manual vs. nonmanual status	.04	.01	.11	.02
Self-employed vs. works for others	.04	.23	.05	.18
Income level	.11	.13	.48	.06
Working-class identification	.08	.14	.12	.13
Union membership	.47	.29	.01	.29
Classist view of parties	.30	.10	.15	.12
Opinion re wealth distribution	.05	.21	.25	.21
Feelings toward unions vs. Franquist sindicatos	.12	.37	.65	.40
Favoring private property or nationalization	.36	.52	.03	.48
Sympathy for big business	.50	.31	.05	.33
Wilks' Lambda	.91	.69	.88	.54

Note: Figures are standardized coefficients obtained through discriminant analysis; they measure the contribution of each variable in distinguishing one group from another. Italicized figures identify variables that are particularly important in distinguishing groups. The values of Wilks' Lambda measure the overall degree of separation between or among the groups; the lower the lambda, the greater the separation between groups.

age did not divide the party system into two blocs, but the major division was that between the PSOE and the UCD. This line of division, however, was much more apparent in terms of attitudes than it was in terms of structural factors. To put it differently, PSOE and UCD voters differed much more in terms of their ideas about class than in terms of their objective position in the class structure.

The interclass appeals of the four major parties did succeed to some extent in attracting to each of them blocs of voters that were heterogeneous in their occupational composition. Nevertheless, the historical images of the PCE and PSOE as working-class parties, coupled with their use of organizational channels of voter mobilization, which penetrated most directly into organized labor, somewhat differentiated their clienteles from those of the two center-right parties. At the same time, appeals by the UCD and especially the AP to working-class voters were undercut by their public images as representing more advantaged social groups, by their more conservative stands on socioeconomic issues, and by their lack of ties to trade union organizations. The only significant social group that voted overwhelmingly for one party were small farmers, who gave their support to the UCD. This was a severe disappointment for the PSOE, insofar as they had made concerted efforts to make inroads into this relatively low-income social group. As a PSOE deputy from a province with a large number of small landowners lamented in an interview: "This is not fertile soil for the cultivation of socialism."

It would be a mistake, however, to conclude on the basis of the occupational composition of partisan groups that class divisions played a limited role in Spanish politics. The subjective dimension of the class cleavage was strongly related to partisan preference. Class images of parties and sharply divided opinions about class-related issues interacted with each other to produce a closer alignment between parties and segments of the electorate. Class consciousness did matter.

CHAPTER SIX

Religion and Politics

Rᴇʟɪɢɪᴏᴜs ᴅɪᴠɪsɪᴏɴs in Spain have long been a source of political conflict and contributed decisively to the outbreak of the Civil War (chap. 2). With the reemergence of democracy, one could well wonder whether this deeply rooted and divisive cleavage would resurface and pose as serious a threat to stability as it had in the past. Competitive politics under the new democratic regime got off to a good start in this regard. In the 1977 parliamentary election, the Church maintained a neutral stance. Except in some geographically isolated areas, the Church did not overtly intervene in any way (chap. 3). This did not mean, however, that religion would play no role in the politics of the new regime.

The first explicit interjection of religion into politics occurred in the course of intraparty negotiations over the Spanish Constitution, specifically over those articles dealing with Church-state relations and other matters of religious significance.[1] In staking out positions on these issues, parties either antagonized or implicitly allied themselves with religious interests. The PSOE initially adopted an anticlerical stance: it advocated total separation of Church and state, favored constitutional provisions that would legalize divorce and abortion, and proposed the elimination of state subsidies to Church schools and ultimately "the progressive disappearance of private education."[2] The AP and UCD, on the other hand, favored an increase of religious freedom but demanded that the Church retain a privileged status under the new Constitution,[3] steadfastly opposed legalization of abortion and a liberal divorce law, and, most importantly, favored continued state subsidies to religious schools with a mini-

220

mum of state regulation. The PCE maintained an almost neutral stance throughout these debates. It sided with the PSOE on divorce and abortion but voted in favor of continued state subsidies to religious schools and special mention of the Catholic Church in the constitutional text. Overall, it played a relatively passive role in these deliberations, as Santiago Carrillo acknowledged: "We have attended these debates as spectators."[4] The rationale given by the PCE for its nonconflictual stance was to avoid clashes that might polarize Spanish society (as in the constituent process of 1931) and ultimately rebound against parties of the left.[5] Achievement of an acceptable compromise over these matters temporarily laid to rest fears that the new regime would follow in the footsteps of the Second Republic.[6] In addressing these fundamental constitutional issues, however, party elites were forced to clarify their stands regarding the role of religion in Spanish society. The result was a party system in which two parties were clearly identified with Church interests (the UCD and AP), one political group had emerged as the principal antagonist of the Church during those deliberations (the PSOE), and one party (the PCE) was still perceived as anticlerical, in spite of its efforts to avoid conflict with the Church.

ORGANIZATIONAL CONTACTS

Although both the AP and UCD actively sought the support of religious segments of the electorate, both parties avoided the establishment of formal ties with religious and quasi-religious organizations. "Our party is not confessional," stated a high-ranking AP leader, "even though it does defend the great Christian tradition of Spain." This statement would be equally valid for the UCD and succinctly described the nature of the relationship between the Church and the two parties on the center and right. Linz has argued that this lack of institutional ties may have deprived these parties of valuable organizational support, such as "the network of Catholic organizations existing in Italy and nurtured by the Vatican during the Fascist years, [which had] provided the DC with a ready-made cadre of lead-

222

RELIGION AND POLITICS

ers at the level of each parish [and] many potential party members."[7] Such formal ties were not politically feasible in Spain, however, given the heterogeneity of the elites of these parties, especially the UCD. Several UCD officials opposed the establishment of ties to religious organizations both as a matter of principle and as necessary in order to avoid a reoccurrence of the tragic events of the 1930s. This did not preclude all forms of contact between these parties and religious groups, however. Informal and personal contacts between local party branches and religious organizations were frequent. Party members were among the most important leaders of those groups, the most politically significant of which were the Padres de Alumnos (Parents of Students) associations. These contacts were particularly important during the constituent period of 1977–1978. At that time parties were keenly aware of the necessity of stabilizing their electoral support. UCD and AP members mobilized these groups on behalf of the private sector of education (regulated by article 27 of the Constitution), thereby demonstrating that their parties were serving as defenders of religious interests.

Given their constitutional stands and their less religious clienteles, the Socialists and Communists could not hope to gain much from such contacts. Both parties greatly desired to neutralize this incipient relationship between religiosity and partisanship, however, and hoped to pick up some electoral support from religious Spaniards. Socialist party leaders in northern provinces, in particular, stated that they wished to attract those who had voted for the Christian democratic Izquierda Democrática in the 1977 elections. Different avenues were pursued toward this goal. The first involved the establishment of a "dialogue" with the Church and religious organizations. Socialists and Communists took advantage of all opportunities to appear in public forums with religious leaders or to reach religious audiences. The most common occasions were public discussions of various portions of the Constitution organized by Church groups. Similarly, during the election campaign, leftist leaders participated in discussions broadcast over the Church's radio network. The overriding purpose of these contacts was to allay historic fears that Socialists or Communists were church-burning fanatics, and to create an image of moderation and civility. Sometimes these tactics were regarded as successful, but a respondent conceded that they were sometimes a dismal failure— "unfortunately they [continue to] regard us as the living incarnation of the devil." Quite possibly, such failures were a response to the similarly unchanged views of leftists. As a Socialist leader confessed, "we regard them as the resurrection of the Inquisition."

The second tactic used to bridge the gap between Catholics and parties of the left built upon the popularity of religious persons and groups that had been active in opposition to the Franquist regime and that were both Catholic and supporters of the left, such as the "Christians for Socialism" movement in Catalunya. A more overt attempt to co-opt religious figures to undermine perceptions of incompatibility between religiosity and leftist politics was the nomination of priests as party candidates or their election as party officials. In some provinces this was carried to an extreme. The two most prominent leaders of the PSOE in Navarra were both priests; one was a member of the Congress of Deputies and the other a senator. The Catalán branch of the Communist party was also quite successful in implementing this tactic: the PSUC candidate for mayor of Santa Coloma de Gramanet (one of the largest working-class suburbs of Barcelona) was a priest, as were about 25 local-level party officials throughout the region and one member of the party's executive committee. The purpose of such efforts was to demonstrate, in the words of a PCE official, that there was "no inherent division in society between believers and nonbelievers. The only major social differences are between those who are exploited and those who are the exploiters."

THE CAMPAIGN

The efforts by the parties of the left to neutralize the influence of religiosity on electoral politics were given a sharp setback by the active intervention of the Church hierarchy.[8] On the second day of the campaign (February 8) the permanent committee of the Episcopal Conference issued a statement entitled "The Moral Responsibility of

the Vote," which called upon Catholics to assess carefully the programs of the various parties in light of their "ideological or operative
commitments which affect religious values or fundamental human
rights." This statement did not endorse any party by name, but it
implicitly condemned so many parties as to virtually preclude a vote
(at the national level) for any but the UCD or AP. The bishops' declaration rejected parties with "materialistic ideologies," a phrase that
excluded the parties of the left and extreme left; it criticized parties
with totalitarian models of society or those that advocated terrorism
or violence as a political method, thereby ruling out electoral support for parties at the extremes of the political spectrum and the
Basque separatist parties.

Perhaps most devastating for the PSOE and PCE was the document's condemnation of "the proposal to legalize abortion, which
figures in some [party] platforms, and certain plans for a divorce law
and an educational system which would restrict the right of parents
to select the type of education that their children should receive."
The Episcopal Conference was abandoning its previous impartiality,
the statement claimed, because the Church "cannot be indifferent to
the destiny of our people" and "could not feel neutral when faced
with possible threats against ethical values or human rights."[9] It is
also believed that the Episcopal Conference document was a means
of forestalling a more virulent anti-Marxist crusade by extreme
right-wing Church leaders. These included the Cardenal Primate
and the bishops of Burgos, Vitoria, Sigüenza, Orense, Ciudad Ro-
drigo, Tenerife, Orihuela-Alicante, and Cuenca, who had earlier
campaigned against ratification of the Constitution.[10] That the
Church document ultimately released was more moderate in tone
than other forms of intervention might have been was small comfort
to the PCE and PSOE, whose leaders perceived this document as
electorally damaging.

Both the UCD and CD were quick to take advantage of this situation. Slogans articulated by party candidates and in newspaper advertisements capitalized on the themes introduced by the bishops.
The CD used such phrases as "the Christian concept of the family

and the right to life" and "*libertad de enseñanza*" (which implied generous state subsidies for private schools and minimal state regulation), while the UCD pledged "protection of the family" and of the private sector of education, and alluded to the "Christian humanist" component of its ideology.[11] The most significant of these appeals was made by Adolfo Suárez in the final television broadcast of the campaign, in which he posed a choice between "the perspective of Christian humanism which inspires the UCD (and) . . . the materialism of the Marxist, Socialist, or Communist parties." He especially singled out for criticism the PSOE, whose "program of the Twenty-Seventh Congress defends free abortion and the disappearance of religious education."[12] In some provinces, UCD candidates used even stronger language. As a Socialist deputy described it, in his province the UCD used a "terminology from the time of the Civil War. Themes such as divorce were phrased like 'They're going to destroy the family. They want your children to be in schools like concentration camps.' You had to see it in order to believe it."

The response of the parties of the left was cautious and oriented toward minimizing the political impact of the bishops' declaration. The PCE issued several statements immediately following the bishops' declaration, but then studiously ignored the religious issue for the duration of the campaign. The Communist response, moreover, was carefully worded so as to criticize the intervention of the bishops, but to avoid attacks on the Church per se. An editorial in *Mundo Obrero* stated, for example:

> The electoral holy water the bishops have thrown at us with their declaration appears to proclaim that the ecclesiastical hierarchy prefers to resuscitate anticlericalism rather than to face the growing indifference in which they have been confined in their isolation from the people. But neither the right nor their Episcopal arm will succeed in arousing anyone with that old baggage—not even Christians, many of whom today see in the Communist and Socialist priests the cleaner face of the church. (Feb. 13, 1979: 7)

Public statements by Santiago Carrillo sought to minimize the differences between the PCE and the Church. In a speech at Aranjuez, for example, he argued that, because the PCE had already endorsed constitutional provisions to protect the private education system and Church spokesmen had previously hinted that a restricted divorce law might be acceptable,[13] the Communists and the Church really disagreed only about the legalization of abortion.[14] Otherwise PCE candidates and party leaders ignored the bishops' statement. In none of the party's three nationwide television broadcasts was any mention made of religious issues. The party's campaign behavior was best summarized by a provincial leader in Andalucía, who said:

> Undoubtedly, we did not make any kind of frontal attack, absolutely not. We think that there have already been enough historical experiences with clericalism/anticlericalism here. We may criticize aspects of the Church which, at some times, we think are linked with the interests of big capital, but we have absolutely avoided this dynamic of Christians vs. atheists. . . . Instead we deal with the daily problems of Christians, which are the same as those of any other worker.

The Socialists also largely ignored the bishops' declaration. In only a few instances did party officials or candidates refer to it, and religion was not mentioned in any of the three televised speeches allocated to the PSOE.[15] A communique released by the party the day after the bishops' declaration criticized their return to political activism, complaining that "when the Church takes a specific position, it is always in favor of conservative parties." In an attempt to distinguish between its criticism of the Church hierarchy and religious Spaniards in general, it added: "Catholics . . . may ask themselves, on whose side is the Church as an institution: on the side of the humble or the powerful?"[16]

The measured response by Socialists and Communists to Church interference in this election was probably motivated by several different concerns. The first was an awareness of the disruptive potential of renewed clerical-anticlerical conflicts in Spain. PCE leaders, in particular, had keen historical memories and frequently expressed the desire to avoid clashes with the Church of the kind that contributed to the destruction of the Second Republic.[17] To do otherwise, they reasoned, would destabilize the present democratic regime and could bring about a return to the authoritarianism of the recent past. Such sentiments were particularly common among the older leaders who had suffered at the hands of the Franquist regime. Straightforward calculation of electoral gain was a second reason for Socialist and Communist restraint. An anticlerical campaign was likely to alienate progressive Catholics who otherwise might be induced to vote for parties of the left on the basis of social or economic issues. By largely ignoring the bishops' declaration, the parties of the left hoped to diminish its salience and prevent it from emerging as a divisive campaign issue, which could only damage their prospects. Finally, any verbal attacks on the Church might alienate younger and more progressive segments of the clergy itself, many of whom could be useful allies in the future.

The overall impact of the bishops' intervention was blunted by the social and political heterogeneity of the Spanish Church. A high-ranking electoral strategist for the Communist party claimed in an interview that "the division within the Episcopal Conference, between the more 'ultra' and the more centrist sectors, makes the Church somewhat incapacitated to intervene electorally. This is not an optimal position, because it did have some influence, there's no doubt about that. . . . But one cannot believe that in Spain there is a dangerous electoral belligerency of the Church. All of this is contained within that [range] which we judge to be desirable." This same opinion was expressed by a politician at the other end of the spectrum. As a Coalición Democrática deputy claimed:

> What is curious is that in some places it exerted influence in favor of the AP, in others in favor of the UCD, in others in favor of the Communist party or the Socialist party, such that the Church divided its influence among various sectors, because it really depended upon the ideology of each parish. But the Church did play an influential role, although not uniformly nor institutionally influential, but rather the various personalities of the Church exerted a very important influence during these elections.

This heterogeneity can be illustrated by examining the Church's stand in several different areas. At one end of the political spectrum are provinces such as Orense, in which the clergy was overwhelming conservative. The bishop of Orense, a right-winger who was not satisfied with the document issued by the Episcopal Conference, released a pastoral letter of his own that was much more extreme in tone. Among other things, it flatly stated that "no Catholic can support candidates of the left, because they are opposed to the Catholic creed."[18] A regional-level Socialist leader in Galicia claimed in an interview that many parish priests joined in this anti-leftist crusade: "From the pulpits Socialism was attacked under the horrifying flag of Marxism." In part, he maintained, such behavior was motivated by the fact that priests continue to perform the traditional role of *cacique* in that region. A similar pull toward the right or extreme right at the behest of conservative bishops was apparent in Santa Cruz de Tenerife, Cuenca, and Toledo—the province of the Cardenal Primate, whose "main task," in the opinion of a Socialist leader, "appears to be to purge progressive priests from this province."

At the other end of the spectrum were provinces such as Málaga, where the bishop was centrist and the political center of gravity of the Church was distinctly left of center. The only complaint concerning the bishop's campaign behavior came from a PCE leader and focused on the bishop's demand that two priests temporarily relinquish their parishes while they were running for office on Communist lists. But the loudest protests about the political involvement of the Church in Málaga came not from parties of the left, but rather from the UCD, and concerned the leftist political activism of many parish priests. As one UCD official complained in an interview, "priests in many villages, I would say in 80 percent of the villages, are tilted toward the left. In those villages, they have behaved more like politicians than priests." Most respondents claimed that priests throughout Andalucía tended to be rather progressive, if not leftist. Because of the existence of large numbers of progressive priests, the statement of the Episcopal Conference was less influential, even less credible, than it otherwise could have been in these areas.

Navarra provides the best example of a divided province. As the heartland of Carlism, the Navarese Church was heir to a reactionary social and political tradition (which, as late as 1876, favored restoration of the Inquisition). But Navarra had also produced Spain's most radical young clergy, many of whom were present in surprising numbers within the leadership of Herri Batasuna, the CCOO, the PSOE, and various parties of the extreme left in Navarra. There were, indeed, campaign posters and billboards, which stated: "The bishops recommend that you not vote for parties of the left," and pamphlets were distributed at private schools calling for a vote for parties of the center and right, but the extreme heterogeneity of the Church in Navarra meant that its net political influence was greatly reduced.

Finally, in Madrid the elite respondents who complained most bitterly about Church intervention in the campaign were not Socialists or Communists (who regarded the Church in that province as centrist), but rather were AP officials. Their complaints were not directed against the Church hierarchy per se, but against the religious publishing house, Editorial Católica. "The influence of the Church was manifested fundamentally through the attitude of Editorial Católica," explained one high-ranking AP official. "The Church *Ya* [daily newspaper] was inexplicably belligerent in favor of the UCD." AP leaders believed that several articles published by *Ya* had greatly undermined the party's electoral chances. In conjunction with the publication of public opinion data (of questionable validity), which suggested the possibility of a PSOE victory in the forthcoming election,[19] *Ya* published a series of editorials that strongly supported the UCD's *voto útil* strategy: they recommended that the best means of forestalling this ominous prospect would be to vote "for the party which has the best possibility of victory, that is, in favor of the so-called *voto útil*, as an elemental demand of common sense."[20] More specifically, these editorials added that votes for CD would be wasted votes and would not contribute to the defense of religious interests. AP leaders were outraged by this stand.[21]

Overall, however, Spanish political elites chose not to emphasize the religious dimension of politics in the campaign because religious issues had been so explosive in the past.

The potential for polarization along religious lines, which some members of the elite viewed with apprehension, was, in fact, quite evident at the mass level. In spring 1979, the Spanish population was sharply divided in terms of religiosity, feelings toward the Church, and opinions on the role of the Church in society. At one extreme of the religiosity continuum 27 percent of the sample professed to be "nonpracticing," "indifferent," or "atheist"; at the other end, about 12 percent defined themselves as "very good Catholics." Two other groups were in the middle: "practicing Catholics" (38 percent), and people who practiced only occasionally (22 percent).

The division in terms of feelings toward the Church was even more clear-cut. Less than one-fourth of the people interviewed professed neutrality toward the Church; the remainder were split between voters with positive (45 percent) and negative (31 percent) orientations. Views concerning the influence of the Church varied. For one resident of Madrid, the Church was still all powerful: "The power of the Church is enormous . . . the Church is the maximum power in Spain, without any doubt . . . more than the army, more than the parties, more than anybody else. . . . Its influence is through the 'politics of the confessional' or the politics of the pulpit. . . . A statement by Monsignor Tarancón is enough to put thousands of Spaniards on the warpath."[22] Another individual, a Communist, bitterly commented on the long-lasting mark left by the Church on her life:

> We have all received a religious education, we have all passed through the martyrdom of sin and of terrorizing confessions, when they said that they were going to send us all to hell . . . and this created traumas. It does not make any difference how old you are, whether you are Communist, Socialist, or whatever . . . it is a Freudian thing. I think that those Spaniards who have received an education through the Church have been marked for life.

As to the direction of the Church's influence, the electorate was rather polarized: approximately four respondents in ten believed that the Church had a "beneficial influence," while the rest either thought that the Church "had no influence" (27 percent) or that it had a "harmful influence" (27 percent). The electorate, moreover, was sharply divided with respect to one issue that traditionally has been part of the clerical-secular cleavage—the role of religious institutions in education. Asked whether they favored compulsory public

education, those in our sample who expressed an opinion split 56 to
44 percent in favor of the proposition. The electorate was also divided in terms of favoring or opposing state subsidies to private (and
overwhelmingly religious) schools: 58 percent were for subsidies,
and 42 percent against.

These different facets of the religious cleavage were interrelated
in a rather marked manner (fig. 5). Generally speaking, people classified as "good Catholics" tended to have more favorable views of the
Church, felt that the Church played a positive role in Spanish society, and were more frequently in favor of private education and state
subsidies than were less religious voters. Indeed, among the latter the
prevailing orientation was markedly anticlerical. The overlap among
these different components of the religious cleavage was not complete, however. Not all good Catholics expressed warm feelings for
the Church; similarly, some support for private education came from
nonreligious respondents; and evaluations of the role of the Church
did not always correspond with the position taken on the issue of
state subsidies to private schools. Overall, however, the indicators
pointed to the existence of a bloc of devout or traditional Catholics
facing a bloc of voters with fairly strong anticlerical sentiments.

As in other European countries, religiosity varied somewhat as a
function of the socioeconomic characteristics of the voters. Proclerical stances were more frequent among older cohorts, women, and
residents of rural areas, as table 19 shows. One might be tempted to
regard age-related differences as an indicator of a trend toward a
greater secularization of Spanish society. The fact that the level of
religiosity was higher in the rural and less modern areas lends some
strength to this supposition. As one conservative citizen lamented:
"We are in the middle of a clear process of secularization even though
the country is theoretically Catholic. . . . People go to church less and
less, possibly because the clergy has lost the trust of the people. . . .
They cannot attract the young generations. . . . In our country we are
moving toward a dangerous lack of religiosity."

Yet, in the absence of longitudinal data that would allow one to
separate the "life-cycle" from the "generational" component of the
phenomenon, no firm conclusion can be drawn. It seems likely, how-

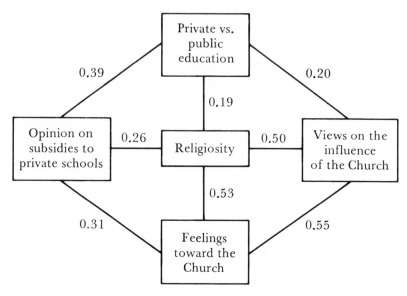

FIGURE 5.   Intercorrelations Among Aspects of the Religious Cleavage

Notes: Figures are Pearson's correlation coefficients.

ever, that the systematic differences among the various age cohorts reflect the more secular orientation of the generations born and socialized in recent decades, as well as a greater preoccupation with religious values on the part of the older cohorts who occupy a different position in the life cycle.

No systematic relationship emerged between the social status of respondents and their degree of religiosity. There were some differences among the various occupational groups, but they did not appear to be directly linked to the system of social stratifications. Rather, religious feelings and positive views of the Church seemed to be related to political traditions, rooted in the voter's family or in the history of the country. The level of religiosity of the respondent's father and family sympathies for the nationalist camp during the Civil War emerged from the analysis as strong predictors of the voters' degree of religiosity, their views of the Church, and their opinions on other related issues. This evidence points to the persistence of

TABLE 19
DEGREE OF RELIGIOSITY IN DIFFERENT SOCIAL GROUPS
(in percentages)

Age		Subjective class identification	
Younger cohorts	22.8	Working class	40.9
Middle cohorts	41.6	Lower middle class	42.0
Older cohorts	54.7	Middle and upper class	43.6
Community Size		Religiosity of father[b]	
Urban	31.2	Higher	73.0
Rural	49.1	Middle	11.3
Sex		Lower	8.7
Men	31.7	Sympathies of family in	
Women	49.1	the Civil War	
Status Level[a]		Nationalist camp	58.6
I (highest)	45.3	Neutral	41.1
II	37.3	Republican camp	19.7
III	42.6		
IV	35.0		
V	63.0		
VI	33.0		
VII (lowest)	41.0		

Note: Figures are percentages of "good Catholics" and "practicing Catholics" within each subgroup.
[a]Status levels defined in table 11.
[b]"Higher" includes "good Catholics" and "practicing Catholics"; "Middle" includes "nonpracticing Catholics"; "Lower" includes "indifferent" and "atheists."

a religious subculture linked in definite ways to politics and with its roots in the past.

Subcultures of this kind can make a difference politically, if not necessarily in attracting votes directly, then at least in terms of constraining voters' choice, by removing some parties from the range of acceptable alternatives. The mechanism through which these constraints on electoral decisions operate is the perception of incompatibility between religiosity and belonging to, or supporting, certain political groups—an incompatibility, rooted in history, ideology, and images of the parties. Preclusions of this sort have been documented for other countries, notably Italy, and it would not be surprising if they existed in the Spanish context as well.[23] For a variety of historical reasons, the parties that were more likely to be the objects of these preclusions were those of the left, especially the Communist party. The preoccupation of PCE leaders with not antagonizing Catholic segments of the Spanish electorate was quite realistic, and PCE efforts to alter the anticlerical image of the party reflected orientations widespread at the mass level. In our sample, four persons out of ten believed that "one cannot be a good Catholic and a good Communist." Another 20 percent of the respondents did not know what position to take on the issue. This latter group were less constrained, but lingering doubts prevented these voters from being entirely free in their choices. Overall, the pool of voters for whom the linkage between religiosity and communism was irrelevant amounted to about 40 percent of the electorate.

In contrast, the degree of perceived incompatibility between socialism and Catholicism was less pronounced. Eight voters out of ten did not find anything objectionable in the hypothetical combination of religion with militancy in, or support for, a socialist party. This is perhaps surprising in view of the fact that, of the two major leftist parties, it was the PCE that had done the most to modify its anticlerical posture of past decades. Evidently, these images were deeply rooted and difficult to change. Moreover, the segments of the population in which communism was perceived as being more incompatible with Catholicism were made up of older people, women, and rural residents, that is, precisely those groups that were also less likely to be exposed to the stimuli of political communication.[24] Quite possibly, either the new image that the PCE attempted to project never penetrated into these groups, or, if it did, it often met with considerable skepticism.

As one might expect, these perceptions of incompatibility between Catholicism and communism or socialism were particularly common among the more religious segments of the electorate— those who classified themselves as "good Catholics" and "practicing Catholics." But some objections also existed among people for whom religion was irrelevant or who were outright antireligious. Although the logic of these aversions was probably different in the two cases, their impact was the same: a fairly drastic reduction of the number of potential voters who might have otherwise supported parties of the left, particularly the PCE. As the figures of table 20 indicate, only a small percentage of those who had a religious preclusion against communism voted for the PCE. The same tendency was evident with regard to the PSOE among electors who considered Catholicism and socialism incompatible. The parties of the center-right were the beneficiaries of these mass-level orientations, and they received overwhelming support from those voters more sensitive to the religious issue. The strategies of those parties were clearly intended to capitalize upon these sentiments. As a Madrid resident said in a conversation with one of the authors:

> Look at the statement made by Suárez two nights before the election . . . it was a declaration similar to those that traditionally have been made by Christian democratic parties . . . he said that his party was the party of the Catholics. Against Marxism, against divorce and abortion . . . and above all against communism. . . . Perhaps the formal declaration of the Conference of Bishops did not count very much, directly. It worked better through Suárez who was the catalyst for the declaration.

To be sure, objection to the Communist party on religious grounds was not the only significant factor drawing voters away from the PCE, but clearly it mattered. In combination with other significant factors, opinions on the compatibility of Catholicism and communism had a considerable impact in harnessing or, conversely, deterring votes for leftist parties. This is illustrated in figure 6, in which the sample is progressively divided into subgroups of respondents on the basis of their degree of religiosity, the Communist-Catholic issue, and age. It is quite clear that the two "extreme" groups were worlds apart in terms of their propensity to favor parties of the left.

Assessing the specific impact of this factor is difficult, in part, because religious-based animosities toward the PCE and the PSOE were related to respondents' views on other aspects of the religious cleavage. Thus, rejection of the PSOE and the PCE by the Catholic subculture cannot be neatly separated from respondents' views on the influence of the Church in society or its role in education. But whether it was hostility toward leftist parties or the attractiveness of the "Christian humanism" appeal of center-right parties, the fact remains that the various partisan groups tended to have conflicting views with respect to all the different aspects of the religious dimen-

TABLE 20
PERCEIVED COMPATIBILITY
BETWEEN CATHOLICISM AND COMMUNISM
(OR SOCIALISM) AND PARTY PREFERENCE
(in percentages)

| | Party preference | | | | |
	Extreme left/ regional left	PCE	PSOE	All center-right parties	(N)
Can a good Catholic be a good Communist?					
Yes	6.2	17.9	45.9	30.1	(1608)
It depends, no answer	4.0	6.5	34.0	55.6	(769)
No	3.0	3.8	21.7	70.5	(1571)
Can a good Catholic be a good Socialist?					
Yes	5.3	13.3	44.2	37.3	(2331)
It depends, no answer	3.8	6.1	24.1	65.4	(847)
No	4.5	4.7	14.5	76.3	(776)

sion. As table 21 indicates, whether one considers religiosity, feelings toward the Church, subsidies to private schools, etc., the result is the same: the followers of the different parties tended to have distinct points of view, and the ordering of partisan groups in terms of this cleavage is, once again, consistent with the left-right axis.

Despite the systematic differences among partisan groups, one should not underestimate the degree of heterogeneity *within* them. In all groups, and particularly within the UCD and the PSOE, there were sizable minorities not aligned with the majority opinion. Among UCD voters, for example, the majority objected to compulsory public education, but one out of three UCD voters held the opposite point of view. Similarly, feelings toward the Church among centrists tended in general to be rather positive, but for a minority of UCD sympathizers the Church did not elicit much sympathy. To a somewhat lesser extent, this is also true of Socialists. In the case of the two smaller parties, however, there was a higher degree of internal homogeneity.

The heterogeneity of partisan groups meant that there was at least some overlap among them in terms of the religious cleavage.

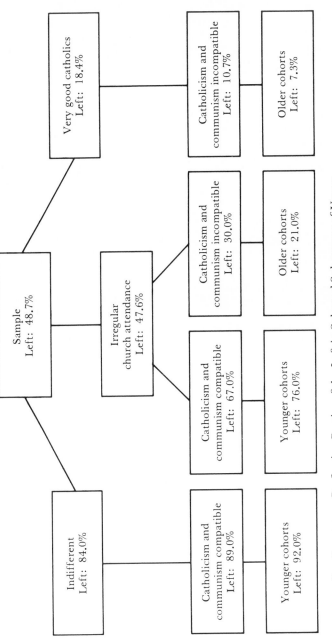

FIGURE 6.   Percentage Preferring Parties of the Left in Selected Subgroups of Voters

TABLE 21
RELIGION-RELATED
VARIABLES AND PARTISAN PREFERENCE
(in percentages)

Religion-related variables	Extreme left	Regional left	PCE	PSOE	Regional moderate	UCD	AP/CD	Extreme right
"Good Catholic" or "practicing Catholic"	9.3	20.9	11.8	23.6	60.0	61.9	63.6	63.2
Positive feelings toward the Church	3.2	13.5	12.3	32.3	46.8	69.8	66.7	64.2
Believing that the Church has beneficial influence in society	3.6	13.1	11.9	27.2	50.7	63.2	58.0	54.0
Agreeing that a good Catholic can be a good Communist	47.0	54.2	71.9	54.5	33.0	24.3	13.6	8.7
Agreeing that a good Catholic can be a good Socialist	62.3	65.6	77.3	76.1	59.2	42.8	28.9	25.4
In favor of private schools	7.1	12.6	6.7	14.3	32.2	34.9	53.7	60.8
Against state subsidies to private schools	65.8	65.4	69.1	55.1	35.1	25.9	24.2	24.5

Note: Figures are percentages *within* each of the partisan groups.

Just how much overlap there was can be seen in figure 7, which summarizes in graphic form the result of a multivariate analysis of the relationship between party preference and the religious cleavage, taking into account simultaneously all the facets of this dimension. Paired distributions of partisans on this overall clerical-secular dimension show that differences between UCD and AP-CD followers were rather modest. The two groups overlapped to a large extent: as far as religion is concerned, these voters could as easily have chosen one or another of the center-right parties. Clearly, whatever drew them to the UCD or the AP-CD was something other than differences connected to religiosity. To a lesser extent, this is also true for the comparison between Socialist and Communist voters. Clearly,

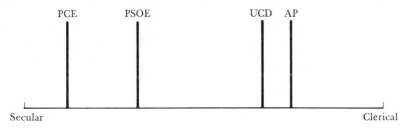

Secular   Clerical

Mean Positions of the Four Major Groups of Partisans

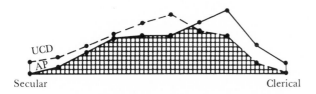

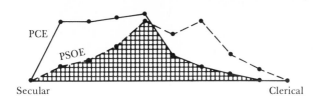

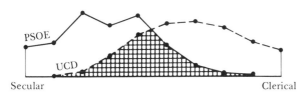

Overlap of the Distributions of the Four Major Groups

FIGURE 7.   Distribution of Partisan Groups on the Clerical-Secular
            Dimension

Note: Findings based on multiple discriminant analysis. The position of each respondent and of
the four partisan groups on the clerical-secular dimension was obtained by pooling information
from all relevant items, i.e., "religiosity," "sympathy for the Church," "opinion on the role of the
Church in Spanish society," and the other variables discussed in the text.

the overlap is not nearly as extensive as in the case of the first two groups, but it is nevertheless considerable. It is the last comparison, that between PSOE and UCD voters, that brings out the sharpest differences. To be sure, even in this case, there was no total separation between Socialists and centrists: there were PSOE voters who, in terms of the clerical-secular dimension, hardly differed from some supporters of the UCD *(ucedistas)*. This is not surprising, considering the presence within the ranks of the centrist party of a social democratic and liberal component, in addition to the Christian democratic faction. Nevertheless, if one were to draw a line demarcating the border between the clerical and the secular subcultures, it would fall somewhere near the center of the political spectrum, between the two largest parties. But it would not be a sharp line separating two totally distinct segments of the electorate. As in the case of class-related attitudes, differences between neighboring parties regarding religious issues were a matter of degree.

CHAPTER SEVEN

The Regional Question

SPAIN IS SIMILAR to most Western European countries in the role that class and religious divisions play in partisan politics. It differs considerably from most other European societies, however, in the extent to which center-periphery cleavages are sources of political conflict—at the national level, between the culturally and linguistically distinct minorities and the Castilian majority, and even within the peripheral regions themselves. Because of the demands for autonomy by regional forces, the structure of the future democratic regime became a crucial issue that had to be dealt with during the constituent process. The four major national parties were forced to take stands on this issue and came into frequent conflict, not only with one another but also with Catalán and, especially, Basque nationalist groups. Even after the principle of autonomy had been agreed on and incorporated in the new Constitution, center-periphery relations remained a source of partisan conflict. Elite and mass-level divisions over the regional question were (as will be shown in chapter 9) most evident and intense in the culturally distinct regions and led to the emergence of regional party systems whose dynamics differed substantially from that of the Spanish party system as a whole. The question of center-periphery relations was also a major issue nationwide and divided Spanish left parties from those of the center-right during the 1979 election. More fundamentally, the lack of resolution of the disputes over center-periphery relations threatened the legitimacy of the new democracy and raised questions about its stability.

241

Both linguistic diversity and competing national loyalties have long been the bases of micronationalist challenges to the Spanish state. Conflict between the Castilian center and culturally distinct regions was one of the major causes of the outbreak of the Civil War and the subsequent demise of the Second Republic. Emerging victorious, Franco made concerted efforts to repress cultural and linguistic diversity and to eradicate distinctive regional loyalties, thereby eliminating what he perceived to be direct challenges to his vision of Spain as "complete, with a single language, Castilian, and a single personality, Spanish."[1] Basques and Catalans were the prime targets of such repression. "Those abominable separatists do not deserve to have a homeland. . . . Basque nationalism must be ruined, trampled underfoot, ripped out by its roots," said the Spanish military governor of the Basque province of Alava during the Civil War.[2] In both Euskadi and Catalunya, public use of the regional language was banned. The teaching of the vernacular was prohibited in public and private schools. Cultural associations were declared illegal. Names were Castilianized and, in Euskadi, all inscriptions in Euskera (the Basque language) were ordered removed from tombstones, funeral markers, and public buildings.[3] Even in Galicia, Franco's region of birth, the government capitalized on widespread feelings of cultural inferiority by plastering buildings with signs saying "Don't be a country bumpkin! Speak Spanish!"[4] In a 1978 interview, an official of the PSOE in the province of Pontevedra recalled that as a young student he was slapped on the hand by his teacher for speaking Gallego, and was instructed to "speak in Christian."

Basque and Catalán nationalists' stress on language as being at the core of group membership notwithstanding, modernization and the assimilationist policies of the Franquist regime succeeded in promoting both a decline in literacy rates in the regional languages and an increase in the use of Castilian. In the 1970s, literacy in Euskera, Catalán, and Gallego was not widespread, and the overwhelming majority of these regional populations were conversant in Castilian.[5] Knowledge and use of the regional language persisted, however, and in our survey substantial numbers of Basques,[6] Catalans, and Gallegos expressed a preference for the use of the regional language as opposed to Castilian.[7] The extent to which the regional language was spoken varied. In Galicia, 86 percent of respondents claimed to speak the regional tongue.[8] In Catalunya, 78 percent of the entire sample (97 percent of those native to the region and 38 percent of those born in other parts of Spain), said that they spoke Catalán. Euskera was far less widely spoken. Just 4 percent of those born outside of the Basque provinces claimed to speak the regional language; but even among natives the proportion increased to only 46 percent. Given the findings of other studies,[9] these figures for the use of Euskera may be exaggerated, but they, nevertheless, reflect a perpetuation of the regional language in the Basque provinces.

Franquist efforts to eradicate distinctive national loyalties and self-identities were also not altogether successful and, indeed, may have been counterproductive. Respondents in the three regions were asked whether they felt "Spanish only," "more Spanish than . . . [Basque, Catalán, Gallego]," "equally Spanish and . . . [Basque, etc.]," "more . . . [Basque, etc.] than Spanish," or " . . . [Basque, etc.] only." As can be seen in figure 8, national self-identity was a source of division in each of the three regions: sizable minorities were at opposite poles and considered themselves to be solely Spanish or solely Basque [or Catalán or Gallego]. An exclusive identity with the regional group was especially pronounced in Euskadi, in which approximately one-third of all respondents claimed to feel "Basque only." The perception that regional groups were indeed different, Basques in particular, was shared by other Spaniards. A resident of Madrid, for example, remarked in an in-depth interview:

> Basques are very nationalist, or maybe it is not that they are nationalist, but rather that they love their country very much. They identify totally with their country. Even so, a majority of Basques still feel Spanish. One is Basque and still knows that it [the Basque country] is a province of Spain, like others are from Madrid, and others are from Valencia. But perhaps they identify themselves more with Euskadi than do others, because Basques have a very ancient spirit. . . . They stick together, and it is very hard to come into a group of Basques.

Another said: "The Basques have absolutely nothing to do with the center, nothing to do with the rest of Spain.... They're of another race."

There were also large numbers of individuals in Euskadi, Catalunya, and Galicia who expressed varying attachments to both Spain and the regional group. Such divided loyalties could, as some have argued, serve to soften polarization over center-periphery relations. But depending on whether nationalist leaders were effective in their efforts to mobilize regionalist sentiments, they could serve instead as a basis from which to draw increasing support for micronationalist demands.

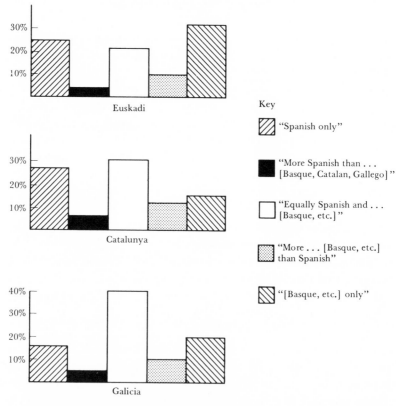

Key

▨ "Spanish only"

■ "More Spanish than . . . [Basque, Catalan, Gallego]"

□ "Equally Spanish and . . . [Basque, etc.]"

▦ "More . . . [Basque, etc.] than Spanish"

▨ "[Basque, etc.] only"

FIGURE 8.   National Self-Identification in Euskadi, Catalunya, and Galicia

Regional identities and loyalties persisted throughout the Franquist era and, even prior to the Caudillo's death, were manifested in the desire on the part of significant segments of these populations for a restructuring of the centralized state,[10] in the formation of regional opposition groups (see chap. 9), and, most virulently, in terrorist activities by the Basque separatist organization Euzkadi ta Askatasuna (ETA), founded in 1959 by young radical members of the PNV. When Franco died, popular aspirations for varying degrees of autonomy or for independence were reflected in the reemergence of historic regional parties, like the PNV and the Catalán Esquerra Republicana, and the appearance of new regional political forces, like the CDC and the radical Euskadiko Ezkerra, Herri Batasuna, and the Bloque Nacional Popular Gallego. Basque and Catalán nationalist parties, in particular, began to assert demands for the reestablishment of regional governments and control over language, educational policy, and tax revenues. In the case of the more extreme groups, additional demands were made for the release of political prisoners, the removal of police forces from the regions, and the recognition of the right of self-determination itself.

In response to such pressures, the UCD government elected in 1977 enacted preautonomy statutes for Euskadi, Catalunya (which had enjoyed a modicum of self-government in the past), and certain other regions. And the 1978 Constitution was the first of the modern era to acknowledge explicitly the multinational and multilingual character of Spanish society and to establish the principle of governmental decentralization.[11] Specifically, article 148 listed an extensive array of governmental functions (in such crucial areas as education and culture) that could, through the enactment of autonomy statutes, be transferred to regional governmental bodies.

However, the restructuring of the state, described by a UCD minister as "the most profound transformation in the history of Spain in the past two centuries,"[12] by no means resolved the regional question. During the constituent process, there was considerable conflict among political elites over center-periphery issues, particularly those dealing with the recognition of the existence of nationalities in

Spain. These struggles continued, even after the principle of autonomy had been established, and concerned the extent, pace, and manner in which decentralization should take place, and, indeed, whether it should take place at all. Regional sentiments, moreover, spread to other parts of Spain, like Andalucía, which, prior to the creation of the new democracy, had never laid claim to separate regional identity or articulated mass demands for autonomy. And finally, the partial attainment of Basque objectives regarding self-government did not stem terrorist activities by ETA; indeed, the transition to democracy and decentralization were accompanied by an increase of violence—from 29 deaths in 1977, to 88 in 1978, to 131 in 1979.[13] Violence was particularly marked during the months between the constitutional referendum campaign and the 1979 parliamentary election and generated considerable political tension, particularly in the Basque country, during the campaign itself.

At the time of the 1979 election, the precise nature and extent of regional autonomy were still open and conflictual questions. The Constitution had established the general principle of decentralization, but it did not determine which regions were to be given autonomy, the actual scope and degree of decision-making power to be devolved to future autonomous regions, the nature of relations between the central and regional governments, and the financial arrangements by which to sustain effective regional government.

At the time of the election, moreover, there were considerable differences of opinion at the mass level concerning even the general question of whether to maintain a centralized state or to grant autonomy. In our survey, respondents were asked a series of questions concerning the desirable structure of the Spanish state, ranging from centralism, to the granting of either limited or extensive autonomy, to outright independence for regional minorities.[14] Throughout almost the entire country, including the linguistically distinct regions, majorities expressed a preference for either limited or extensive autonomy, but this was an issue that divided certain parts of Spain from others (fig. 9). In contrast to the rest of the Spanish electorate, Basques, Catalans, and Gallegos were much more disposed toward independence for regional groups and, conversely, much less likely to favor a centralized state. Also apparent was the recent emergence of autonomist sentiments in Andalucía. In 1977 a majority of Andaluz respondents favored centralism[15]; by 1979, this view was held by less than one-third.

The differences in the distribution of opinion between the linguistically distinct regions and certain others can more clearly be seen in figure 10. Most striking was the contrast between Basques, 23 percent of whom favored independence and only 17 percent, centralism, and those living in Old Castile, 69 percent of whom preferred a centralized state and only 2 percent, independence. As figure 10 also makes clear, the question of autonomy divided the linguistically distinct populations as well. Polarization was most pronounced in the Basque country. The least polarized of the three was Catalunya, although even there centralism and independence were choices preferred by sizable minorities of 21 percent and 11 percent, respectively. In Galicia, opinion was also divided, but in this region, preferences for a centralized state outweighed those for either extensive autonomy or independence.

Overall, survey data indicate that, between the 1977 and the 1979 elections, there was a perceptible decline in support for centralism (from 42 to 33 percent), and a commensurate increase in support for varying degrees of autonomy, including independence for certain regional minorities (from 3 to 7 percent).[16] Nonetheless, in 1979 there was still a considerable division of opinion in the electorate as a whole concerning the structure of the state. A near majority (47 percent) preferred limited autonomy, but the remainder were divided between centralism (30 percent) and extensive autonomy or independence (15 percent). In short, there was no widespread consensus among Spaniards concerning the principle of limited autonomy, which, only a few months earlier, had been ratified in the constitutional referendum. Disparate views regarding the regional question were clearly reflected in in-depth interviews with residents in Madrid. One said, for example, "I believe that one should not talk about independence in any manner at all. We ought to shoot them [*indepen-*

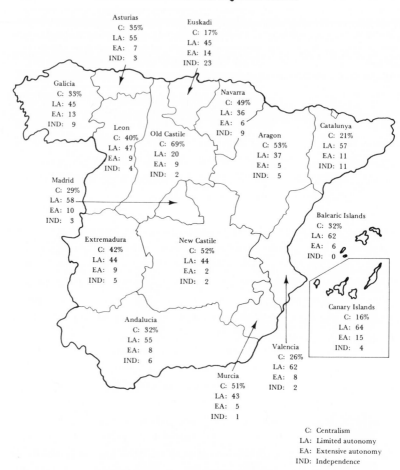

Asturias
C: 35%
LA: 55
EA: 7
IND: 3

Euskadi
C: 17%
LA: 45
EA: 14
IND: 23

Galicia
C: 33%
LA: 45
EA: 13
IND: 9

Navarra
C: 49%
LA: 36
EA: 6
IND: 9

Leon
C: 40%
LA: 47
EA: 9
IND: 4

Old Castile
C: 69%
LA: 20
EA: 9
IND: 2

Aragon
C: 53%
LA: 37
EA: 5
IND: 5

Catalunya
C: 21%
LA: 57
EA: 11
IND: 11

Madrid
C: 29%
LA: 58
EA: 10
IND: 3

Extremadura
C: 42%
LA: 44
EA: 9
IND: 5

New Castile
C: 52%
LA: 44
EA: 2
IND: 2

Balearic Islands
C: 32%
LA: 62
EA: 6
IND: 0

Canary Islands
C: 16%
LA: 64
EA: 15
IND: 4

Andalucia
C: 32%
LA: 55
EA: 8
IND: 6

Valencia
C: 26%
LA: 62
EA: 8
IND: 2

Murcia
C: 51%
LA: 43
EA: 5
IND: 1

C: Centralism
LA: Limited autonomy
EA: Extensive autonomy
IND: Independence

FIGURE 9.   Proportions of Regional Populations Favoring Varying Degrees of Autonomy (Missing Excluded)

dentistas]. Autonomy is okay for those who want it. But they have to maintain their solidarity with the Spanish state." Another argued that the answer to the regional question lay in the establishment of a kind of confederation of states:

Catalunya would be Catalunya, the Basque country, as well as all regions that want to constitute themselves nations. It seems absurd to me that we keep on defending archaic values, such as the unity of the Fatherland. To me, the unity of the Fatherland is not very important. What matters to me is to have a decent country, tranquil, happy and in which people live well. It would be easy to grant autonomy, to establish a type of confederation in which there would be neither frontiers nor customs, in which there would be cultural and political intercommunication. . . .

But that same respondent also voiced concern about the inequality between richer and poorer regions of Spain:

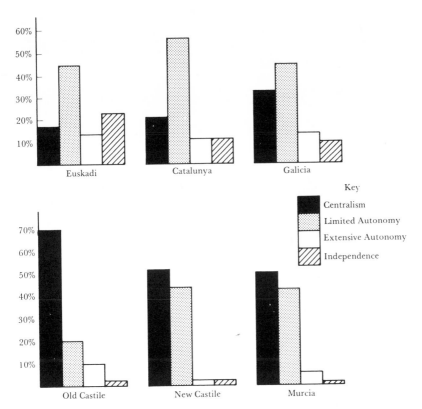

FIGURE 10.   Preferences Concerning the Structure of the State in Selected Regions

> It's marvelous that Catalunya and Euskadi have autonomous budgets, but to leave poor Andalucía with its own budget would be to crush it. There would also have to be economic intercommunication, so that the central government would help the development of the poorest regions, but not only the central government—the richest regions as well.

Given such differences of opinion about the structure of the state, it is not surprising that respondents also disagreed about the likely consequences of autonomy for interregional conflict, the unity of Spain, and inequality between rich and poor areas of the country: 32 percent believed that autonomy would increase regional conflict, 41 percent said that it would not, and 19 percent were ambivalent. About one-quarter of all persons interviewed claimed that autonomy would destroy the unity of Spain, and another 20 percent were undecided. Even higher proportions believed that autonomy would not reduce inequality between rich and poor regions.

Concern for interregional inequality, in particular, was often mentioned by individuals during mass-level in-depth interviews as a reason for their disapproval of autonomy for Euskadi and Catalunya: "The best would be a centralized state. But it should treat all regions equally. There should not be a central power like the former one, which only protected those regions that screamed the loudest. As for autonomy, autonomy should be given to all regions. There should not be privileged regions." Another Madrid resident favored administrative decentralization, but not autonomy, because it would be inefficient and costly:

> Independence is absurd, absurd from all points of view. There must, though, be decentralization of the apparatus of the state. It's absurd that, to solve a problem having to do with imports or exports, I have to trek all the way to Madrid to settle it. But autonomy—no one really knows what it will lead to. I believe that it will be too expensive, that it will produce a double, even triple bureaucracy. For example, when Catalán autonomists say that the Generalitat will not impose any higher financial burden on Catalans, I wonder who will pay for the Generalitat? The Catalans will pay a small part, but also the man in Extremadura, the man in Cádiz, and the man in Almería.

Views concerning autonomy were not uniformly distributed throughout the electorate. Religious Spaniards, for example, were more than twice as likely to be *centralistas* than were nonpracticing voters (fig. 11). Indeed, among practicing Catholics the proportion favoring a centralized state was almost equal to that favoring limited autonomy. Among the nonreligious, in contrast, the number disposed toward independence was only slightly less than that preferring centralism. Support for varying degrees of autonomy, therefore, was clearly related to secularism in 1979. As figure 11 also shows, autonomist sentiments were more prevalent in urban rather than in rural Spain. And finally, support for autonomy was most pronounced among the young: 29 percent of those 30 years and younger, compared with 13 percent and 19 percent of the two older cohorts, favored either extensive autonomy or independence; the proportions holding the opposite view were 18, 31, and 45 percent, respectively. Support for decentralization, however, was related neither to objective nor subjective class position (table 22). Only among small-scale farmers was there a majority in favor of centralism, rather than limited autonomy. Otherwise, the distributions of opinion among upper and lower status occupational groups were remarkably similar.

PARTISAN DIVISIONS
AND THE REGIONAL QUESTION

The regional question in its multiple manifestations was a source of division at both the elite and mass levels. Not unexpectedly, polarization was most evident between regional and Spanish or statewide parties, and between extreme and more moderate regional groups. In Euskadi, for example, where such polarization was most intense, two radical Basque nationalist parties, Herri Batasuna and Euskadiko Ezkerra, had urged their supporters to vote "no" during the constitutional referendum. The PNV, often regarded as the most moderate of Basque nationalist parties, also challenged the legitimacy of the Constitution by refusing to endorse it in the Cortes and by advocating abstention in the referendum.

In general, the four major national parties supported decentralization during the 1979 campaign. They did so, however, to varying degrees and with differing programmatic emphases. In a complete

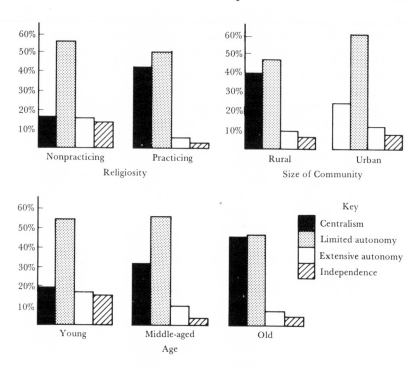

FIGURE 11.   Preferences Concerning the Structure of the State by Religiosity, Size of Community, and Age

reversal of the traditional centralist stances taken by the Spanish left, contemporary leaders of the PSOE and PCE came to regard political decentralization as an integral part of the process of democratization and were the most ardent supporters of autonomy and of the recognition of the multilingual and multinational character of Spanish society. The PSOE even articulated demands for a thorough federalization of the state and, accordingly, structured its own party organizations along federal lines. Both the Socialists and Communists advocated obligatory bilingualism (the learning of and instruction in the regional languages) in regional school systems. The pro-autonomy stances of the PCE and PSOE were somewhat tempered, however, by the perceived conflict between class-related issues and the regional question. This ambivalence was reflected in remarks made by Txiki Benegas, leader of the Basque Socialists. On one hand, he refuted the portrayal by Basque nationalists of his party as centralist:"Socialists are the authentic autonomists ... because we are the only ones to have defended and will continue to defend the statute of Guernica, both against the centralism of the UCD and against independentist tendencies. . . ."[17] On the other hand, he lamented that the "national problem has obscured the problems of class."[18] In addition to the leftist Spanish parties' concern that the regional question would overshadow problems of class-based inequality, they were troubled about the implications of autonomy (and regional control over taxation and spending) for interregional inequality. The PCE and PSOE came out in opposition, therefore, to the restoration of the historic *conciertos económicos* to the highly developed and rich provinces of Euskadi.[19]

UCD leaders were more cautious in their attitudes toward decentralization, because of fear that it would lead to increased interregional conflict and to a weakening of the state. The UCD's electoral program states: "The process toward self-government of the autonomous communities must take into consideration ... the delicate problem of the replacement of a strongly centralized state while assuring that no vacuums or disturbances will be created in the functioning and effectiveness of state institutions."[20] But at the same time, they acknowledged the necessity of moving away from a highly centralized state, in light of popular preferences, which were especially strong in the peripheral regions.

In general, AP was negative in its stand toward autonomy. It regarded concessions to some regional demands, such as the inclusion of the term *nacionalidades* in article 2 of the Constitution, as being tantamount to the recognition that Spain was not a single, unified nation, but rather a composite of several nations whose loyalty to Spain might be weakened by autonomy. As a high-ranking AP leader emphatically stated in an interview, "A nation cannot exist inside another nation." The strong opposition voiced by AP leaders during somewhat by the time of the election, however, because of the inclusion into the electoral coalition of more moderate leaders, such as Areilza and Senillosa.

Thus, at the time of the 1979 election, a certain consensus had emerged, at least at the elite level, over the general principle of autonomy and some related policy issues. All were in favor, for example, of coofficiality of Castilian and the regional language, and of either the obligatory study of the regional vernacular in the school system (in the case of the PCE and PSOE) or its voluntary use (in the case of center-right parties). Finally, the four parties were in substantial agreement in their opposition to terrorism as a means of achieving self-government.

Despite elite-level consensus over the desirability of regional autonomy, the followers of the four major national parties differed substantially from one another in their stances toward this issue (table 23). They did so in a manner that conformed with the party elites' relative committments to the principle of autonomy. Only among Communists and, to a lesser degree, Socialists were there majorities in favor of limited autonomy, and overall the distribution of opinion of these two groups was similar to that of supporters of the Catalán Convergènc+ cia i Unió (CiU).[21] *Ucedistas* were almost evenly divided between *centralistas* and limited autonomists, and two-thirds of AP partisans favored the status quo ante. The followers of Blas Piñar's Unión Nacional were at one with his view of "*la lealtad como norma*" (loyalty as a norm). Not surprisingly, *independentistas* were most prominent among supporters of more extreme regional parties; they were also a significant minority among partisans of the most moderate of Basque nationalist groups, the PNV. The regional question, as table 23 shows, was also a source of considerable disagreement within most partisan groups, including Bloque Nacional Popular Gallego, Bloc d'Esquerra d'Alliberament Nacional (BEAN), and the *abertzale* (nationalist) left in Euskadi. Only among AP and extreme right voters was there a clear consensus in favor of centralism. Thus, the electorate was deeply divided about this crucial aspect of the new regime.

TABLE 22

OPINIONS CONCERNING REGIONAL AUTONOMY AND OCCUPATIONAL STATUS OF RESPONDENT OR OF HEAD OF HOUSEHOLD (in percentages)

Opinion	Status level of respondent[a]							All respondents
	I	II	III	IV	V	VI	VII	
Centralism	33	26	37	27	54	27	31	32
Limited autonomy	51	53	49	52	34	59	55	52
Extensive autonomy	10	12	7	11	8	9	9	9
Independence	6	9	7	10	4	5	5	7
N	(620)	(1027)	(742)	(364)	(364)	(836)	(718)	(4671)

[a]Status levels are:
I   Entrepreneurs, professionals, landowners, high-level public and private executives
II   Mid-level public and private employees, technical professions
III Owners, small businessmen, independent artisans
IV   Low-level white collar workers, sales and supervisory personnel
V   Small farmers
VI   Skilled workers in agriculture and industry
VII Unskilled workers in agriculture and industry.

TABLE 23

OPINIONS CONCERNING REGIONAL AUTONOMY AND PARTISAN PREFERENCE (in percentages)

Opinion	Partisan preference									All respondents
	Extreme left	Regional left	Communist	Socialist	PNV	CiU	UCD	AP/CD	Extreme right	
Centralism	9	3	8	17	11	13	45	61	76	30
Limited autonomy	34	23	55	63	48	66	43	29	21	47
Extensive autonomy	28	23	22	10	13	10	3	3	0	9
Independence	24	44	11	5	21	6	1	1	2	6
No answer	5	7	4	5	7	5	8	6	1	8
N	(73)	(120)	(400)	(1354)	(79)	(77)	(1658)	(173)	(45)	(5439)

These general predispositions toward autonomy were in accord with the views of the different partisan groups concerning the implications of decentralization for interregional conflict, the unity of Spain, and the extent of inequality between poorer and richer parts of the country. Table 24 presents the proportions of each partisan group, as well as of the electorate as a whole, who gave unequivocally positive assessments of the likely effects of the granting of autonomy. Consistent with their general antipathy toward autonomy, AP and extreme right partisan groups saw dire consequences ensuing from it: majorities of both groups claimed that autonomy would destroy the unity of Spain or at least lead to increased conflict and that it would not lessen interregional inequality. *Ucedistas*, given their luke-warm support for decentralization, were slightly less negative in their appraisals of its effects: only 30 percent said that autonomy would destroy the unity of Spain, but another 23 percent gave the equivocal response, "it depends."

All other partisan groups, especially Communist voters, tended to be far more sanguine concerning the impact of autonomy on levels of conflict. Its effect on interregional inequality, however, generated greater disagreement, both among and within these partisan groups. Only among followers of the extreme left and the PCE did a majority claim that autonomy would reduce inequality. Supporters of regional parties and of the PSOE were less certain. Their scepticism concerning the equalizing consequences of autonomy may have been based on widespread suspicions that greater regional control over taxation and spending on the part of Basque and Catalán governments could widen the gap between these two wealthy regions and the less-developed parts of Spain. The lessening of the flow of revenue to the state could reduce the level of resources available for redistribution to poor regions. This might be compounded by the granting of autonomy to poorer areas, such as Galicia and Andalucía, insofar as they would be more dependent on their own scarce resources. Thus, the implications of autonomy for regional inequality were not straightforward and clearly had not been settled during the constituent process.

Despite these partisan differences at the mass level concerning the fundamental issue of the structure of the state, there was greater consensus on other aspects of the regional question. Widespread agreement, for example, was apparent over language policy. Although complex stands were taken by party elites concerning the relative status of the regional language versus Castilian, a majority of the electorate and of most partisan groups favored the obligatory learning of both languages in the linguistically distinct regions (table 25). Only regional leftists and supporters of the extreme right deviated in a predictable manner from this broad consensus.

An even greater degree of consensus emerged in attitudes toward terrorism. As the most violent of separatist groups, ETA was an object of intense hostility on the part of all voters. When asked to indicate their feelings toward ETA on an 11-point "feeling thermometer," 90 percent of respondents placed themselves at the most negative position on the scale. Even supporters of extreme micronationalist parties, many of whom shared with ETA the ultimate goal of regional independence, were almost equally divided between those sympathetic and those hostile to that terrorist organization: 42 percent had positive feelings, while 37 percent were negative. Regional moderates were considerably less favorable: 70 percent expressed negative feelings, and only 9 percent were sympathetic. For example, a person of Basque origin, who was sympathetic to Basque grievances and desires for autonomy, was extremely negative toward ETA because of what its terrorist activities would lead to:

> I don't understand at all the way they behave, because the only thing that the Basques will achieve with independence is a military coup. They will suffer unemployment; they will not only lose their independence, but also their autonomy and liberties, including the recognition of their own language. We will go back to the way it was in the past.

Among Communists, the least negative of supporters of the four major Spanish parties, only 5 percent considered themselves to be positive toward ETA.

Despite increasing ETA violence and widespread hostility toward it, only a small minority of all voters and of each partisan group attributed mounting violence to micronationalist forces. Partisan groups differed considerably, however, as table 26 shows, in their

TABLE 24
PARTISAN GROUPS SAYING THAT AUTONOMY WILL HAVE POSITIVE CONSEQUENCES
(in percentages)

	Partisan preference									
Opinion	Extreme left	Regional left	Communist	Socialist	PNV	CiU	UCD	AP/CD	Extreme right	All respondents
Autonomy *will not* increase interregional conflict	57	65	69	55	55	49	27	22	13	41
Autonomy *will not* destroy the unity of Spain	66	53	72	64	63	62	38	28	17	49
Autonomy *will* decrease inter-regional inequality	62	44	51	40	38	31	26	21	24	33
N	(73)	(120)	(400)	(1359)	(79)	(77)	(1650)	(173)	(56)	(5439)

TABLE 25
OPINIONS REGARDING THE OBLIGATORY LEARNING
OF THE REGIONAL LANGUAGE VERSUS CASTILIAN, AND PARTISAN PREFERENCE
(in percentages)

	Partisan preference								
Opinion	Extreme left	Regional left	Communist	Socialist	Regional moderates[a]	UCD	AP/CD	Extreme right	All respondents
Regional language only	8	24	6	4	5	2	3	5	4
Both	86	74	82	79	92	66	53	48	73
Castilian only	6	2	12	17	3	32	44	47	23
N	(73)	(120)	(396)	(1343)	(156)	(1633)	(169)	(56)	(3944)

[a]Because PNV and CiU supporters were highly similar in their preferences, they have been combined.

TABLE 26
ATTRIBUTIONS OF RESPONSIBILITY FOR TERRORIST VIOLENCE, AND PARTISAN PREFERENCE
(in percentages)

Responsibility for terrorism	Partisan preference									All respondents
	Extreme left	Regional left	Communist	Socialist	PNV	CiU	UCD	AP/CD	Extreme right	
Micronationalist forces	16	6	11	14	11	27	21	31	20	17
Extreme left	24	18	24	38	48	48	57	62	70	43
Extreme right	58	46	56	52	60	55	40	30	11	45
The government	48	58	40	26	60	21	13	21	25	24
Police	22	46	17	9	36	2	4	4	6	10
Students, youth	4	4	2	4	6	2	9	9	16	7
Franco regime	51	59	50	35	55	12	12	7	4	25

Note: Percentages do not total 100 percent because respondents were permitted to give multiple responses.

TABLE 27
OPINIONS REGARDING GOVERNMENTAL RESPONSE TO TERRORISM, AND PARTISAN PREFERENCE
(in percentages)

Preferred governmental response	Partisan preference									All respondents
	Extreme left	Regional left	Communist	Socialist	PNV	CiU	UCD	AP/CD	Extreme right	
Accept terrorist demands	10%	13%	4%	1%	0%	1%	1%	0%	0%	2%
Negotiate with ETA	23	67	32	21	56	5	6	5	5	16
Maintain order, within the law	55	17	52	58	43	79	58	45	20	55
Make war on terrorism	6	2	10	16	1	13	26	34	48	20
Establish military rule	6	0	2	4	0	2	10	16	27	7
N	(66)	(108)	(381)	(1265)	(72)	(74)	(1544)	(153)	(56)	(3718)

opinions on who to blame. Predictably, majorities of UCD, AP, and extreme right supporters blamed the extreme left, while many followers of extreme left parties, the PCE, and the PSOE tended to hold the extreme right, the government, and the Franco regime culpable for violence. PNV and CiU voters were also quite different from each other in their responses.

Similarly, there was great variation both among and within partisan groups as to how the government ought to respond should terrorist violence continue (table 27). When presented with the following alternatives—accept terrorist demands, negotiate with ETA, maintain order within limits set by law, wage a full-scale war on terrorism, or establish military rule—80 percent of regional party leftists chose either of the two most conciliatory responses, as did 56 percent of *peneuvistas* (supporters of the PNV). In contrast, 50 and 75 percent of AP and extreme right voters, respectively, chose either of the two most "hard-line" (and unconstitutional) options. Majorities of all other partisan groups, including supporters of the CiU, said that the government should take all legal measures to maintain order. At the same time, sizable minorities of these same partisan groups (with the exception of *ucedistas* and moderate Catalán nationalists), took the position that the government ought to enter into negotiations with terrorists.

Differences among partisan groups with regard to the regional question were, in part, a reflection of the relative support given to autonomy by the various party elites. Among Spanish party sympathizers, PSOE and PCE supporters, like Socialist and Communist leaders, were the most favorable toward decentralization. AP voters were outflanked only by extreme rightists in their centralist leanings. Differences among party elites and among their respective followers were also due to a fundamental transformation of the ideological underpinnings of support for decentralization, both in Spain as a whole and, to an even greater extent, in the peripheral regions. In the 1930s, none of the major nationwide parties had been a staunch advocate of autonomy, but today the formerly antiregional parties of the left have clearly identified themselves with autonomist sentiments. Whether as a cause of, or in response to, this change at the elite level, voters most likely to support leftist parties in 1979 were also the most likely to favor varying degrees of autonomy (see chap. 8).

Thus, the regional question had a divisive influence on the Spanish party system as a whole. Its fullest impact, however, was most clearly evident in the culturally distinct regions themselves. It led to the emergence of regional party systems, with their own particular dynamics and within which micronationalist groups, especially in the Basque country, competed successfully with the four major nationwide parties. (The party systems of Euskadi, Catalunya, and Galicia will be discussed in detail in chap. 9.)

CHAPTER EIGHT

Left-Right, the Structure of Competition, and the Role of Leadership

In two-party systems, electoral competition is relatively straightforward, and the choice offered to voters is simple. In multiparty systems, the electorate is provided with a wide array of alternatives, and the structure of partisan competition is, in principle, more complex and less well defined. In reality, however, political competition is constrained by a number of factors, even in multiparty systems. In Spain, divisions based on class, religion, and center-periphery relations were certainly important components of the parties' electoral strategies and voter choices, but such divisions were by no means the only elements that conditioned and structured political conflict. There was also a more purely political aspect to political competition, both at the elite and mass level. In Spain, as in other Western European countries, there was and is a widely shared notion that the world of politics can be understood in terms of a left-right dimension. Whether in a more sophisticated or more simple manner, the left-right cleavage underlay the elites' perceptions of their own and other parties, the voters' images of themselves as political actors, and the public's image of important political objects. As a consequence, political divisions, understood in left-right terms, helped to shape the parties' electoral strategies and to restrict voters' choices.

262

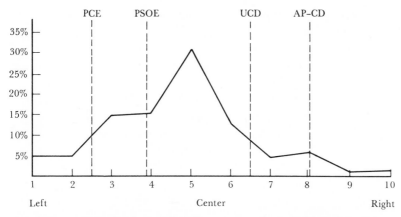

FIGURE 12.   Distribution of the Electorate on the Left-Right Continuum
and Perceived Mean Position of the Four Major·
Parties in 1979

Note: The mean left-right locations of the parties are as follows: PCE, 2.50 (N=5058); PSOE,
3.89 (N=5043); UCD, 6.44 (N=5076); AP-CD, 7.97 (N=4809).

The key elements of this structure of competition were: the distribution of voters on the left-right continuum; their perceptions of
where the parties stood in this space; and elite awareness of the location of voters and their own inclinations to play the electoral game in
left-right terms. Voters and parties came to the 1979 contest with a
vision of the party system shaped in a manner similar to that depicted in figure 12.[1] For voters, this meant a considerable simplification of choice on election day. For parties, the awareness that the bulk
of the electorate was located at the center and intermediate positions
of the spectrum imparted a centripetal thrust to competition.

IDEOLOGICAL TARGET
GROUPS AND SPATIAL STRATEGIES

All parties designated the moderate segments of the electorate as
their principal target groups and attempted to alter their images to
gain the support of such voters. This, together with the left-right

ordering of parties, meant that each was primarily concerned with its two neighboring competitors and paid greatest attention to the one closer to the center. When parties did focus on the more "extreme" of their neighbors, it was primarily to point out the wastefulness of voting for a minor party (*voto útil*).

UCD officials interviewed in 1978 and 1979 were consistent in their descriptions of the ideological target groups that they wished to attract: voters toward the center of the political spectrum, bounded at one end by the "democratic right" and at the other by non-Marxist social democracy. They were also in agreement in explicitly rejecting support from the extreme right and from the Marxist left. These two "negative target groups" played, for the UCD, the same role of "foil" that "monopoly capitalism" played for parties of the left. There was no serious expectation that support would ever be received from these groups but explicitly rejecting this imaginary offer of support was of some strategic value in its own right. The ideological territory staked out by the UCD was thus both broad and densely populated. Studies available to elites prior to the election indicated that in 1976 less then 10 percent of the Spanish electorate defined themselves as "Marxists," and just 17 percent placed themselves on the "right."[2] Furthermore, in a July 1978 survey, 38 percent placed themselves in the two center categories on a ten-point left-right scale.[3]

There was considerable variation in the ideological center of gravity of the party from one region to another. The party's slate of candidates and overall image ranged from center-left in some provinces to downright conservative in others.[4] But the main thrust of the campaign waged by the UCD at the national level (especially in television and radio broadcasts) was directed toward one specific segment of this broader potential audience—moderates on the center-left. This group was given highest priority on the basis of the expected strong showing by the PSOE and on the belief, expressed in a preelection interview by a UCD official in Madrid, that "one-third of the electorate of the UCD and the PSOE are in fact interchangeable—they constitute a fluid, fluctuating vote." The basic UCD strategy was explained by a high-ranking party official as follows:

In Spain there is emerging a two-party hegemony between the UCD and the PSOE. One of these two parties or the other will win the next election. In order to do so, they will have to attract 10 percent of the vote at the center of the political spectrum. This bloc of votes could either go to the UCD or the PSOE. In order to win, the UCD must get these votes and possibly attract PSOE voters. At a minimum, we must prevent the PSOE from stealing votes from us. In order to do so, we must avoid an image of being a conservative or right-wing party. We must receive support from progressive voters.

Thus, the UCD, a party whose leadership was predominantly to the right of center, placed greatest emphasis in its national-level campaign on its efforts to draw votes from the center-left.

Motivated by the same reasoning, the PSOE adopted a similar strategy. As Maravall writes,

Competition for the center/moderate vote followed from the decisive weight of this section of the electorate: 43 percent of the total, of which only 8 percent had supported the PSOE in 1977. A left-wing electoral victory necessarily required the displacement of this moderate electorate towards the Socialist party. . . . The PSOE hoped to win ground here since this moderate electorate was often represented by small peasants and lower-level nonmanual workers whose vote was mostly of a deferential kind and could be attracted in the short run by a Socialist party with a strong local presence and by an adequate campaign.[5]

This was more succinctly stated by a PSOE provincial-level official in Andalucía: "Our objective is, indisputably, to steal votes from the UCD."

This decision constituted a partial step toward social democracy and away from maximalism, and ultimately contributed to intraparty conflict. Not all PSOE militants supported this strategy. For many Socialist militants, the term "social democrat" was an insult, and the thought that the PSOE might one day transform itself into something like the German SPD was utterly abhorrent. As a regional-level official said of the national leadership:

Let them form their own party. There is no room in the PSOE for them. I am fully opposed to the efforts of Felipe and Múgica. The Congress of this party officially proclaimed it to be a class party and a Marxist party. There is no room for social democrats. If they were to enter the party, they would say that we should abandon the class struggle. We should never abandon that position. My own personal view is that, rather than trying to take votes from the right, we should attempt to get votes from the left—to move more toward the Communist party.

In the 1979 elections, however, the moderate, center-seeking strategy of González and Guerra prevailed and was implemented everywhere by the party apparatus. The success of this strategy was undermined somewhat by the opposition of certain party militants and leaders.

The ideological targets of the AP-CD and the PCE were determined partly in response to the struggle between the PSOE and the UCD over the center of the political spectrum. As the two larger parties moved toward the center, the two smaller parties followed in their wake, hoping to fill what they perceived to be the "political space" being vacated on either flank of the two more centrist groups.

The PCE hoped that, as the PSOE drifted toward the center, the Socialists who disapproved of social democracy would defect to the Communist party. On the eve of the general election campaign, Madrid party leader Simón Sánchez Montero publicly stated that the PCE would give highest priority to attracting dissatisfied former PSOE supporters,[6] and throughout the campaign (e.g., Santiago Carrillo's televised speech of February 26) explicit appeals were made to Socialists asking them to switch sides.

Similarly, CD hoped to attract center-right voters who felt abandoned by the leftward drift of the UCD. Thus, a party usually perceived as a party of the right moved toward the center to attract support from former UCD voters, redefining itself, in the process, as a party of the center-right. Some AP elites clearly did not approve of this shift. One provincial-level official persisted in describing the AP's clientele as "the traditional Spanish right." Others went along with this reorientation, but without much enthusiasm. An AP official (and candidate in the municipal elections) in Old Castile said:

> The formation of the Coalición Democrática, with the formulation of the center-right strategy of capturing that nucleus of UCD voters . . . has moved us toward the center. We do not like to speak of the center. We [would prefer] to remain on the right—the right that we understand as the democratic right; the right that respects the Constitution . . . the

progressive right; but not the center. . . . Alianza Popular cannot stop calling itself the right; basically its postulates are based on the right.

Similarly, an important national-level official stated:

> We want to continue to say that we are at the service of Spain, that national unity is our primary point, that we want a free-market economic model, that we want public order, citizen security, that we are against the excess of pornography, that we want *libertad de enseñanza,* etc. All of these things are traditionally of the right. But all of this, I insist, within the Constitution, with respect for its institutions, and, of course, accepting the democratic game.

The tactics designed by the parties to attract voters from these specific segments of the political continuum were remarkably similar. First, each party attempted to mold its image in such a fashion as to conform to the perceived political preferences of its ideological target group. Accordingly, AP, PSOE, and PCE toned down the more distinctive and extreme aspects of their ideologies so as to be more acceptable to voters toward the center. The secretary general of a provincial branch of the PSOE explained:

> We are altering the tone of political discourse within the party, both at the national level and within this province. The party began in clandestinity and during this period developed its own vocabulary, which is no longer appropriate for a modern, democratic state. Therefore, we are changing this tone of discourse and offering a broader image of the party—one with a real capacity to govern.

Because the UCD had a vague, eclectic ideology to begin with, it did not have to alter or conceal its ideological precepts. Instead, it chose to stress the social, economic, and political reforms it had brought about and to draw attention away from the Franquist political backgrounds or conservative political values of many of its candidates. This behavior is clearly distinguishable from that which one would expect to find in a "centrifugal" party system, in which party elites emphasize their ideological *distinctiveness* as a means of appealing to their respective clienteles.[7]

The second characteristic of the electoral strategies employed in 1979 was to focus attacks primarily on neighboring parties toward the center of the spectrum, to ignore groups toward the extremes, and never to attempt to "outbid" those parties for the support of voters located toward the extremes. Thus, the PCE attacked the PSOE and, less frequently, the UCD, and rarely mentioned the ORT, PTE, and other parties to its left; the AP attacked the UCD, not the fascist and parafascist parties in the Unión Nacional to its right; and the UCD and PSOE attacked each other. On those few instances when extreme parties were criticized, such attacks were sharply restricted to appeals for the *voto útil*—that is, an appeal based on the argument that votes for the extreme party would be "wasted votes." A national-level strategist for the PSOE explained that "from the beginning of the campaign we thought that the worst thing we could do would be to respond directly to the PCE." Socialist candidates behaved in almost strict accordance with that policy.

Indeed, the national media reported only two major instances when the PSOE attacked the PCE.[8] Neither of these attacks could be regarded as attempts to outbid the PCE for votes on the Socialists' left flank, except insofar as to claim that the PCE was dividing the left, diluting its parliamentary representation, and thereby undercutting the Socialists' chances of becoming the "alternative in power." After making the second of these attacks, Felipe González refused, at the last PSOE rally of the campaign, to respond in kind to the criticisms of Santiago Carrillo and his party: "I have not answered him, and I will not answer him tonight,"[9] he stated. In his television broadcast of February 16 (the only one of the three PSOE broadcasts to refer even indirectly to the PCE), González quickly dismissed "those parties that say that they have done everything with 15, 20, 26 deputies, or even 2" and drew the viewer's attention instead to "the debate between the only two parties that are capable of undertaking this task of government—of directing the destiny of Spain during the next four years—UCD and PSOE."

The UCD behaved in a similar fashion by focusing its attention on the Socialists and, at least initially, ignoring the AP-CD. A high-ranking party strategist stated that prior to the start of the campaign it was decided "to give battle to the PSOE. We were not at all worried about the right, because we knew that the AP was going to disintegrate. . . . Neither did we want to give much weight to the *voto útil,* but in the end we opted for it. . . . At the start we planned not to use the *voto útil* very much." Adolfo Suárez made no reference whatsoever to the party on his right during his three televised speeches (February 15, 23, and 27). CD, for its part, adopted a similar approach: "The only conflict was toward our left, with the center. Concerning the conflict toward our right, with the party of Blas Piñar—we did not reply to Blas Piñar in any manner; that is, we followed a policy that did not take into account the presence of Piñar on our right . . . and as a consequence our campaign centered fundamentally in trying to take votes from the center."[10] Finally, Santiago Carrillo, in the only PCE attack on parties of the extreme left, criticized the ORT and PTE on the grounds that their very existence divided the left, depriving the PCE of the votes needed to exert a powerful influence on Spanish politics. These groups, he said, preferred to be "the head of a rat, rather than the tail of a lion."[11]

The third tactic was to exaggerate certain aspects of the ideological stands and image of the principal rival of each party in an effort to frighten voters away from that competitor. Accordingly, the PCE exaggerated the drift of the PSOE toward social democracy in order to pick up voters on the left of the Socialist party. For instance, Santiago Carrillo claimed on February 26 that "the UCD [which he further described as 'a monocolor government of bankers, industrialists and representatives of multinationals'] and the PSOE will have to govern together after the election; that is, they are the same option."[12] Similarly, the PSOE attempted to portray the UCD as a conservative party. In one Socialist leader's view, "the right is the UCD, the center is the PSOE, and the left is the PCE." Socialists also cast aspersions on the Franquist backgrounds of many prominent UCD politicians, although during the campaign itself they relied more on subtle innuendo than on the flamboyant language of the past. (Less than a year earlier, for example, Alfonso Guerra stated to the press that Prime Minister Adolpho Suárez had crawled "from the sewers of fascism.")[13]

The UCD countered by denying that the PSOE was becoming a social democratic party, insisting instead, that it was Marxist, revolutionary, and dangerous. Finally, the AP first depicted the UCD as of the center-left: Alfonso Osorio characterized the UCD as being "in the hands of social-democrats."[14] The following day, his fellow CD candidate, the Basque industrialist Luis Olarra, went even further by claiming that "the (UCD) government has not made policies of the center-left, but rather of the left. If the UCD wins again, it could deliver Spain to a third-world situation."[15] This strategy fit rather well with the normal tendency of voters to visualize the party system as a function of their own positions. (See fig. 13.) Right-wingers tended to place Socialists and Communists toward the far left portions of the ideological spectrum, while the extreme left portrayed those same two parties as moderates of the center-left. The obverse obtained, as figure 13 shows, in the case of the placement of the UCD and AP by left-wing voters. Clearly, it could be advantageous, at least in some cases, to play up to the voters' predisposition to visualize the party system in such a deformed manner.

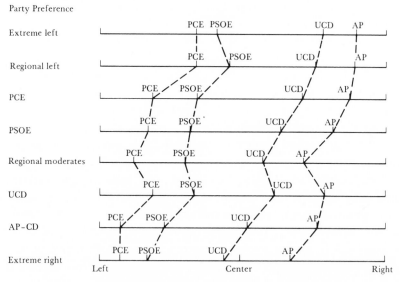

FIGURE 13. Mean Positions Assigned to the Four Major Parties on the Left-Right Continuum by Different Partisan Groups

The use of these tactics by all parties was the product of rational and informed calculations of maximum electoral advantage. First, leaders regarded as their primary competitors only the contiguous parties because they were not likely to capture votes from more distant segments of the political spectrum. Indeed, these expectations were quite correct. When survey respondents were asked whether there were parties for which they would never vote, about 75 percent mentioned at least one party as unacceptable. Their responses were largely a function of their self-placement on the left-right continuum. The parties most frequently singled out were the PCE and the AP, but even the more moderate parties were so designated, especially by those at the extremes. (See fig. 14.) This constraint on voter choice was clearly perceived by party elites. A high-ranking UCD strategist explained why a party like the PCE could best maximize votes by attacking the Socialists, and not the UCD or AP: "The PCE did not really attack us, it ignored us. Its tactic was clear. . . . They knew perfectly well that by attacking us they could not pick up any votes and could not steal our clientele, because we are far from them. We also chose not to attack them." Significant shifts of votes were more likely to take place between ideologically contiguous parties than between parties with different images and ideologies. As a provincial-level Socialist party leader explained, "We believe that the electorate of the PCE is identical to our electorate. We are trying to attract votes from the same social groups. . . . We're struggling for the same political space." The left-right self-placements of those who actually voted for one of the four major parties in 1979 confirmed the correctness of the parties' perceptions and strategies. (See Figure 15.)

The limitation of interparty attacks to contiguous groups, it should be noted, distinguished the 1979 general election campaign in Spain from that of 1977. In that earlier campaign, most parties, including the PCE, concentrated their fire on the AP. The source of this difference between campaigns is the fact that the 1979 contest took place under relatively normal circumstances, in which short-term vote maximization was of primary importance, while the main concern of many party elites in the first election was to prevent the

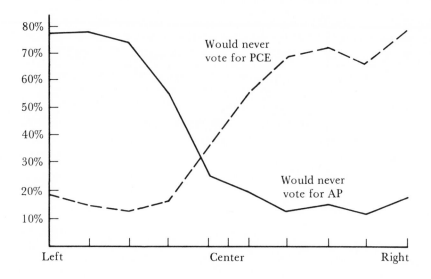

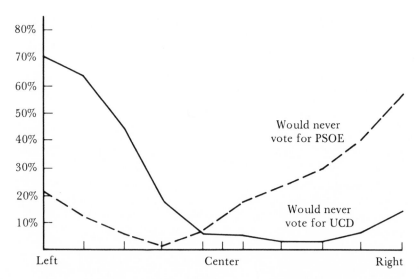

FIGURE 14. Negative Party Preference and Voters' Locations on the Left-Right Continuum

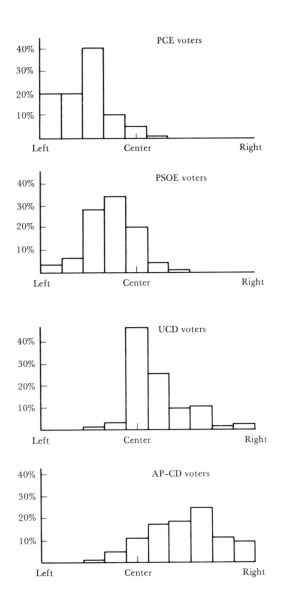

FIGURE 15.   Distribution on the Left-Right Continuum of the Four Major
            Partisan Groups

Note: The mean left-right locations of the parties are as follows: PCE, 2.74 (*N*=364); PSOE,
3.89 (*N*=1233); UCD, 5.90 (*N*=1469); AP-CD, 7.09 (*N*=158).

return to power of those who might impede rapid progress toward full democratization. As the secretary general of a regional branch of the Communist party explained, "in 1977 our efforts were fundamentally to clear away the danger represented by Alianza Popular and Fraga as those who would perpetuate the Franquist regime."

If elites in each of these parties believed that they were engaged in what was fundamentally a two-front electoral battle, why did they focus their campaign attacks on only one front? Outside of the campaign itself, party leaders did not hesitate to launch verbal attacks against parties on either flank. In spring 1978, the then-president of the Federación Socialista Madrileña of the PSOE, Alonso Puerta, in the course of a vicious criticism of the PCE explained to a neighborhood meeting of party militants (which one of us attended) that "The PCE can only gain strength by drawing votes from us. They can only expand their electoral support by moving into our political space. Thus, we must struggle both against enemies on the right and also against adversaries in the PCE itself." And yet during the following year's electoral campaign the PSOE scarcely mentioned the PCE. The answer to this puzzle has to do with the belief that more votes were to be gained from the center than from the left, coupled with the practical difficulty of appealing during an election campaign to two distinctly different clienteles and at the same time not appearing to be inconsistent and untrustworthy. A Socialist effort to increase its appeal to voters on its left flank would require that party to reestablish its Marxist ideological credentials and actively convince that target group that it was not, as the PCE suggested, drifting dangerously toward social democracy, but rather that it would continue to press for radical changes in Spanish society. Such statements would almost certainly play into the hands of UCD strategists, would clash with the PSOE's attempts to portray itself as a moderate party, and might frighten away centrist voters. Instead, PSOE strategists decided that, though the PCE might make some inroads into the segment of the electorate to the Socialists' left, those marginal losses would be more than offset by larger gains toward the center of the political spectrum. PSOE strategists, in fact, concluded that defections to the left would be minimal. One of them explained in an interview: "We had a study [undertaken] in advance, and we knew that there would be an almost equal transfer of votes from one to another—that we would take almost as many from them [the PCE] as they would take from us."

The only departure from this pattern was the appeal for the *voto útil*. Given the deviations from strict proportionality inherent in the electoral law, a UCD candidate in a small province could point out to center-right voters, for example, that the CD candidate had no real chance of being elected. Thus, the votes cast by conservatives that did not go to the UCD would be tantamount to abstention, which, in turn, might result in the election of a Marxist. This form of attack on the extreme party would not undermine the moderate image that the party wished to project. Only cautious use was made of this strategy, however, because frequent references to that party would only call attention to it and increase its visibility as a serious competitor. As a Socialist deputy stated: "We attacked the UCD, but at no time did we touch the PCE, because we thought that what the PCE really wanted was for us to talk about them."

THE LEFT-RIGHT
CONTINUUM AND THE VOTERS

The salience of the left-right dimension at the elite level was fully matched by the widespread use of this imagery at the mass level. First, few electors in our 1979 survey had difficulty in assessing their position in left-right terms: only 13.9 percent either refused to place themselves on a 10-point left-right scale or said that they were apolitical. Second, voters had little difficulty in placing parties on the left-right continuum: less than 10 percent failed to do so. From the point of view of interparty competition, this was certainly as important as their ability to locate themselves on the political spectrum. Third, a substantial majority of the voters polled was willing and able to provide a definition of the terms "left" and "right." The referents of the terms, culled from answers to open-ended questions, varied considerably. For some people, these terms were merely synonyms for parties. For others, the referent was somewhat more abstract (fascism, communism, capitalism, socialism). Still others made reference to the history of the country (describing the right as "*franquistas*," "blue shirts," and the left as "the Republicans," "those who lost the war") or to social classes ("the defense of capital," "the upper classes," "workers," "the poor," "those who fight against monopoly capitalism"). The definitions were often colored by the respondent's own position, as is evident in the case of those respondents who defined "right" as "order, peace and prosperity" and left as "those who defend human rights." In many cases, the definitions provided were simplistic and rather sketchy. Nevertheless, the left-right imagery appeared to be, for most voters, a device that allowed them to make sense of the political world, to relate to it, and to provide a basis for evaluating significant political events, actors, and issues.

Analysis of the respondents' left-right scores shows that they were meaningfully related to the voters' orientations in a variety of areas (table 28). As we noted earlier, "negative party preference"—the exclusion of one or more parties from the range of acceptable choices—was a function of political distance as measured on the left-right scale. And, as one might have supposed, left-right scores were also strongly related to the voters' feelings toward parties and party leaders. Although this assessment was not as multifaceted as might have been desirable, positive or negative feelings toward Santiago Carrillo, Felipe González, Adolfo Suárez, and Manuel Fraga were quite closely related to the respondents' own positions on the left-right spectrum. Indeed, one can gauge rather accurately the feelings of a group of voters toward the leader of the Communist party, for example, on the basis of their left-right locations. One is not surprised that leftist voters felt greater sympathy for Carrillo than for Suárez or Fraga because the finding "makes sense," that is, because left-right is politically meaningful for the observer, no less than for the citizen.

If the left-right scale measured only attraction or dislike for partisan objects, it could be treated as another measure of general political leanings or party preference, and it would be of lesser signifi-

TABLE 28
CORRELATIONS BETWEEN VOTERS' LEFT-RIGHT
SELF-LOCATIONS AND VARIOUS ATTITUDES

Class cleavage	
Feelings toward the unions	−.43
Feelings toward big business	.41
Subjective class identification	.18
Social status	−.12
Religious cleavage	
Feelings toward the Church	.51
Religiosity	−.48
Opinions on the influence of the Church	.44
Opinions on compulsory public education	−.14
Opinions on subsidies to private schools	−.13
Incompatibility Catholic/Communist	.25
Incompatibility Catholic/Socialist	.23
Regional cleavage	
Preferred solution to the regional problem	−.44
Feelings toward ETA	−.33
Political antagonism	
Feelings toward the UCD	.50
Feelings toward A. Suárez	.54
Feelings toward the PSOE	−.25
Feelings toward F. González	−.28
Feelings toward the PCE	−.44
Feelings toward S. Carrillo	−.48
Feelings toward CD/AP	.56
Feelings toward M. Fraga	.57
UCD unacceptable voting choice	−.44
AP unacceptable voting choice	−.44
PCE unacceptable voting choice	.39
PSOE unacceptable voting choice	.19

Note: Figures are product moment correlations.

cance. But this is not the case: left-right self-locations were also strongly related to the positions taken by the respondents on a variety of different issues. The correlation coefficients reported in table 28 show that attitudes related to class, religious, and center-periphery cleavages were associated with the left-right scale. The relationships between certain variables were stronger; in other cases, less pronounced. Overall, however, the left-right dimension appeared to capture, if not all nuances, at least major attitudinal differences. In a sense, a voter's self-placement on the left-right scale constituted a summary measure of his or her position vis-à-vis the three major dimensions of conflict in Spanish politics. Thus, a particular position chosen on the continuum was not just a nominal category but tended to coincide with a cluster of viewpoints on various issues. Centrist voters were more likely than leftists or rightists to exhibit less intense feelings of sympathy or hostility toward various political actors and to take middle-of-the-road stands on specific issues.

In large measure, this was due to the internal coherence of the respondents' attitudes, that is, to the fact that there was a definite linkage among the various dimensions of cleavage. Class, region, and religion, although analytically separable, were not empirically disconnected. On the contrary, proclerical stands tended to go together with conservative positions on the class cleavage and with a definite procentrist stance on the question of the organization of the Spanish state. And these interrelations were clearly reflected in the overall orientations of the voters expressed in left-right terms (table 29). Thus, as crude and imperfect as the left-right scale is, to know a person's position on the continuum is to have a rather good knowledge of his or her views on the three major cleavages, as well as of the more explicitly "political" or partisan dimensions of conflict, such as "negative party preference," or views of parties or politicians. It is not surprising that these last orientations were reflected more clearly on the left-right dimension, because, after all, this is primarily a political rather than a social domain.

It should be added that left-right differentiations operated in the Spanish populace *within* as well as across partisan groups: the scale is

TABLE 29
INTERCORRELATIONS AMONG CLEAVAGE DIMENSIONS

	Feelings toward big business	Feelings toward the Church	Preferred solution to regional problem	Left-right self-locations
Feelings toward big business	—	.45	.29	.41
Feelings toward the Church	—	—	.37	.52
Preferred solution to regional question			—	.44
Left-right self-locations				—

Note: Figures are Pearson correlation coefficients.

useful not only for distinguishing among the various partisan groups, but also for identifying different segments within each of them. The shades of opinion that existed within groups (described in previous chapters) were reflected rather well in the self-placements of voters who shared a preference for the same party. These differences are displayed for UCD voters in table 30. The *ucedistas'* degree of religiosity, perceptions of incompatibility between Catholicism and communism, hostility to big business, feelings toward the unions, and other attitudes varied in a systematic manner as a function of the position occupied by the respondents on the left-right spectrum. Clearly, voters who placed themselves at positions 4 and 5, the social-democratic or progressive wing of the UCD, were different in terms of their orientations from those who belonged to more conservative factions and who occupied positions toward the right end of the spectrum.

Much the same can be said for Socialist voters, as table 31 shows. These figures indicate that the opinions of PSOE voters varied con-

TABLE 30
OPINIONS OF UCD VOTERS BY LEFT-RIGHT LOCATIONS
(in percentages)

Opinions	Positions on the left-right scale					
	Left 1–4	5	6	7	8	Right 9 or 10
Favorable to unions	70	56	52	38	32	34
Very hostile to big business	31	13	9	7	10	7
Very good Catholic	11	13	21	19	20	40
Very favorable to Church	18	30	32	42	52	66
Church has positive influence	31	62	66	66	78	69
Would never vote PSOE	1	9	20	20	23	42
Would never vote PCE	36	45	61	73	76	79
Would never vote AP	41	19	17	10	10	5
Possible to be Catholic and Communist	45	23	21	30	22	20
Very hostile to PSOE	0	9	6	10	12	22
Very hostile to PCE	30	32	40	42	58	74
Very hostile to CD	42	16	9	7	6	4

siderably and systematically and that sizable differences separated the "radical" wing from the more moderate social democratic component. Indeed, the data suggest that this last group of voters had a lot in common with the left wing of UCD. This partial attitudinal overlap of the left wing of one party with the right wing of a contiguous party existed also in the case of the PCE with the PSOE group, and of AP-CD with the UCD group.

In sum, there can be no doubt about the significance of the left-right dimension at the mass level. Political cognitions were clearly organized in left-right terms. Voters' evaluations of parties and politicians and their attitudes related to the major cleavages were clearly reflected in their self-location on the political spectrum. As party elites set out to seek votes in the course of the campaign, they were confronted not with an amorphous electorate with ill-defined and contradictory notions, but with people whose maps of the political world, likes, and dislikes had clearly recognizable contours.

THE 1979 CAMPAIGN

These spatial strategies were implemented by parties in various ways during the 1979 campaign. In its efforts to become "the alterna-

TABLE 31
OPINIONS OF PSOE VOTERS BY LEFT-RIGHT LOCATIONS
(in percentages)

			Positions on the left-right scale			
Opinions	Left 1	2	3	4	5	Right 6 or higher
Favorable to unions	89	86	88	79	73	69
Very hostile to big business	56	42	38	22	18	13
Not practicing, indifferent or atheist	69	71	60	48	32	28
Very hostile to Church	39	28	20	7	7	3
Would never vote for UCD	59	54	38	16	11	12
Would never vote for PCE	9	9	11	13	24	37
Would never vote for AP	65	75	72	55	39	42
Very hostile to UCD	49	29	22	10	7	12
Very hostile to PCE	5	5	6	8	12	24
Very hostile to CD	68	68	59	39	25	30

tive in power," the PSOE conducted a campaign intended to convince voters that it was more capable of governing Spain than was its principal rival, the UCD. Socialist candidates criticized the incumbent government for its various shortcomings over the past two years—most importantly, for high levels of unemployment and inflation, and for the government's inability to end terrorist violence. They also attacked UCD incumbents for administrative inefficiency, and for policy failures in the areas of health, housing, education, agriculture, and protection of less-advantaged social groups (young people, women, the rural population, and retired persons). These criticisms, however, were tempered by the overriding desire to appear moderate. Specific policy proposals, moreover, did not constitute a radical socialist alternative but, indeed, were quite similar to those of the UCD.[16] The only significant differences between the two parties were that the PSOE regarded unemployment as a more serious economic problem than inflation, stressed public investment rather than private investment as a means of reviving the economy, and favored nationalization of the high-voltage electricity-transmission network (which the UCD had proposed over a year earlier but later abandoned).

In its efforts to appear stable, responsible, and qualified to govern, the image that the party projected through its billboards, posters, and pamphlets was sober, almost somber. The most widely disseminated poster included a black-and-white photo of Felipe González, uncharacteristically wearing a tie. As one observer has noted, his serious and worried expression was the exact opposite of "the jovial, youthful and happily unconcerned image that was used in the 1977 campaign. . . . They attempted to inculcate the idea that the elections were reduced to an almost personal choice between Suárez and González, and . . . to highlight the presidential capacity of the latter, suppressing every detail (excessive youth, partisanship, etc.) which might alienate one single vote."[17] The basis of virtually all the slogans was "Un Gobierno Firme" ("A Firm Government"), which was usually followed by a reference to a specific policy (e.g., "to reduce unemployment" or "for a safe/secure country").

Perhaps more important was the complete abandonment of references to its Marxist, revolutionary, and classist ideology. Indeed, in

no PSOE slogan or poster did the word "socialism" appear.[18] In order to attract centrist voters, especially in rural areas targeted by
party strategists, it was decided to avoid all references to Marxism or
to other terms that might frighten them away. As a Socialist deputy
in a conservative rural constituency explained,

> It was necessary to break with the 'Red' image that the Socialist party
> had in this province, and to some extent still has. That is, to break with
> the image of a revolutionary party. Thus the campaign was very pru-
> dent, tremendously conservative in word and in appearance, not at all
> aggressive—to the contrary—we gave an image of prudence, even
> when faced with the UCD, which was terribly, terribly aggressive.

Another Socialist deputy reported,

> There is no doubt that our campaign was very moderate, because we
> were interested in attracting votes from the great majority of the peo-
> ple in this province, who are moderate. We were interested, for exam-
> ple, in attracting the vote of religious persons—not from priests, but
> from the great mass of religious persons in this province—so our cam-
> paign was very moderate and respectful of everybody.

There were occasional slip-ups in this regard during the campaign, most prominently by the honorary president of the party,
former PSP leader Enrique Tierno Galván. In keeping with his
Marxist beliefs (and, presumably, a lower level of committment to a
party he had joined less than one year earlier), he was somewhat inconsistent in adhering to this aspect of the campaign strategy. On
February 12, for example, he said: "We Socialists are so humble that
we need the help of everyone, including the honorable right. . . . We
want the citizen on the right to come to socialism, attracted by our
honor."[19] The very next day he undercut his own appeal for conservative support by saying that the PSOE wants to build a "powerful and
revolutionary socialism."[20] On earlier occasions he had explicitly rejected the notion that the PSOE was a social democratic party.[21] The
ambivalence of Tierno and some other Socialists undermined the
moderate image that campaign strategists wished to project.

The UCD's 1979 electoral strategy entailed both long-term and
short-term elements. The long-term or precampaign effort to attract

its targeted "interclassist" bloc of centrist supporters was described in a 1978 interview with a high-ranking national leader of the party. When asked how the UCD planned to gain the support of these groups, he responded: "by being a reformist and progressive party; by bringing about social policies that are clear and effective; by offering concrete results with regard to the redistribution of national wealth." Another member of the UCD national executive committee concurred, using almost the same words in a preelection interview: "by bringing about a profound reform of the economic and political structure of this country; by offering a program of change that will be accompanied by justice and liberty. This is more a strategy of deeds than of ideology." Thus, the "politics of consensus" practiced by the UCD government following the 1977 elections—in constitutional negotiations, in its fiscal reform policies and in the Pacts of Moncloa—served a dual purpose: it helped to stabilize the new democratic regime by satisfying the basic interests of most significant social groups or, at least, by not totally alienating any significant sector of society; and it attracted to the party voters who might have been repulsed by more conservative social or economic policies or by adoption of a partisan, one-sided Constitution. Thus, the UCD began to publicize its accomplishments through the release of propaganda well in advance of the 1979 election campaign.[22]

During the campaign itself, this thrust of the UCD strategy was embodied in the two most widely publicized UCD slogans: "Dicho, y Hecho" ("Said, and Done"), and "UCD Cumple" ("UCD Fulfills" [its promises]). A key electoral strategist pointed out: "We were trying to explain that thanks to the UCD it has been possible to bring about the transition from an autocratic or dictatorial regime to a more democratic system ... (and) toward a regime progressively more open, more liberal and more of free commerce, without the trauma of a civil war, nor *pronunciamientos*, nor victims, other than those of terrorism." Antonio Fontán's opening speech of the campaign[23] and the first two televised broadcasts by Suárez (February 15 and 23) were among the best examples of this emphasis on progressive reform. They dealt almost exclusively with the achievement of a consensual constitution, economic policies that attempted to deal with inflation in a balanced and nonpartisan manner (especially through the Pacts of Moncloa), the prompt enactment of a tax reform, steps toward judicial reform, and progress toward decentralization of the Spanish state.[24] The specific objectives of the first two television broadcasts by Suárez were explained by a key UCD official: In the first, "We tried to explain what President Suárez said in 1977 he was going to do, and that, in effect, he did it. . . . That was the point of departure, which gave credibility to what the party would say in the campaign. The second broadcast tried to describe the fundamental problems that would confront the government in the next four years."

But, in the second phase of the campaign, the UCD employed a markedly different, more overtly conflictual tactic, which represented a departure from "the politics of consensus." The party attacked the PSOE, accusing it of being dangerous, unstable, Marxist, revolutionary, and certainly not social democratic. This attack exploited the ideological ambivalence of the Socialist party and the revolutionary rhetoric of some of its militants. An example of the use of this tactic was described by a UCD candidate:

> We made a great deal of the term "Marxist" and of the declarations of the Twenty-Seventh Congress of the PSOE. We even read literally from its self-definition as a "revolutionary, Marxist, *autogestionario* [workers' self-management], class party." We literally quoted from what they had said at their meetings. Especially when a Socialist or Socialist party sympathizer would show up, saying that he was a social democrat, then we would use the argument that he, personally, may be a social democrat, but that his party, according to its statutes and according to its ideological declarations from the Congress was not. We even read from the book from the Twenty-Seventh Congress of the PSOE so that there would be no doubt. We really clobbered them that way [he chuckled].

Beginning in the second week of the campaign, numerous UCD leaders (including Calvo Sotelo, Arias Salgado, Sánchez Terán, Martín Villa, Pérez Llorca, Ruíz Navarro, Cabanillas, and José Luis Alvarez) joined this attack against their Socialist rivals.[25] As Sánchez Terán described it, the PSOE campaign "lacks credibility: it uses campaign slogans of the right, an electoral program copied from the center, and has a party program of the left."[26] This thrust of the UCD campaign was inadvertently made more credible by the behavior of a handful of PSOE militants, who formed part of a hostile, jostling mob that threateningly surrounded President Suárez at campaign appearances in Badajoz and Atarfe (Granada). UCD secretary general Rafael Arias Salgado and campaign media director Federico Ysart responded by holding a press conference at which they displayed pictures of the incidents and claimed that unruly behavior of this kind was typical of the unstable PSOE and its "mass mobilizations," and linked this campaign theme to the growing public concern over terrorism and increases in crime and delinquency.[27]

The most devastating of these assaults was launched by Adolfo Suárez himself, in his last television appearance of the campaign. One observer went so far as to claim that "in reality, Adolfo Suárez won the election for UCD in those ten minutes,"[28] and, indeed, elite interview respondents in all political parties asserted that that final speech was the single most decisive act of the 1979 campaign. The prime minister tensely and melodramatically set forth the choice between the UCD's societal model and the revolutionary Marxist model of the PSOE—a decision that would determine whether "Spain would be a western country, or would march toward collectivism."[29] According to a Socialist rival, Suárez "appealed to the vote of fear. He tried to instill a suspicion and fear of what would happen if the PSOE were to come to power." Another Socialist deputy added: "I met an old woman who asked me if we were going to take her pension away, as the men of the UCD had said. I met another person who asked, if the Socialists won, was it going to become more or less like it was in China, if it was going to be decided what each person would wear, if we were all going to look the same, if we were not going to have cars or televisions." The most startling example of the impact of this tactic was the response of a member of an AP provincial executive committee, who claimed that he had been so frightened by that speech and the prospect of a Marxist government that he voted for the UCD, rather than for the candidates of his own party.

How is this phase of the UCD campaign to be interpreted? These attacks on the radical Marxist features of the PSOE ideology served three functions. The first was to appeal to persons of the right, such as the AP respondent mentioned above. Our survey data suggest that this tactic was most successful: 33 percent of those respondents who claimed to have voted for the AP in the first parliamentary election shifted their support to the UCD in 1979. The second function was to retain the support of moderate voters by offering them the prospect of continued reforms, while, at the same time, frightening them away from the PSOE. Frequent reminders of the Socialist party's Marxist ideology, moreover, could also encourage the defection of persons on the center-left who had voted for the PSOE in 1977: a preelection study of public opinion revealed that only about one-quarter of those PSOE voters identified themselves with the term "Marxist."[30] At the same time, this tactic did not require the UCD to adopt right-wing policy positions, which might have alienated centrist voters. Finally, this alarmist tactic was oriented toward encouraging active electoral participation by large numbers of persons who were (according to preelection polls)[31] initially predisposed to abstain from involvement in this election. As described by a UCD provincial secretary general, the principal target "is fundamentally the apolitical person, the person who really wants tranquility, who wants confidence/security, who wants to be able to work . . . with the maximum guarantees possible."

Some of the concerns and strategies of the two smaller parties were similar to those of their larger competitors. Given their positions on the left-right continuum, however, their strategies were somewhat distinct. The image projected by the PCE was one centered on the themes of moderation and responsibility. It portrayed itself as a serious, stable, democratic party. In no PCE slogan did the word "communism" appear.[32] One poster (observed in Toledo in June 1979) did mention the name "Marx," but that referred to Groucho, Chico, and Harpo—a party branch was showing *A Day at the Races* at a local festival. A UCD official said of the PCE campaign: "They appeared as the Little Sisters of Charity."

Moderation was a central feature of the PCE campaign for two reasons apart from those that constrain any party attempting to pursue a "catch-all" strategy. The first concerned its continuing efforts to erase the perceptions of the party that had emerged from the Civil War and were reinforced by the Franquist regime. For many people these memories were still quite vivid. The intensity of such feelings was clearly reflected in comments made by ordinary citizens in conversations in Madrid with one of the authors.[33] One person said, for example,

> In the civil war my family was totally wiped out, all dead. My mother died when I was four years old, they killed my father in the war, all of the males in my family were killed in the war . . . murdered . . . because we were a family with lots of money. . . . I remember well . . . the disappearance of the members of the family, the attacks on the house, the shots, the bombs . . . the way they came and took them away . . . and they also wanted to take my brothers and me. . . . We children were going to end up in Russia. . . .

For others, however, these memories had faded, and a new party image was beginning to emerge. As another Madrid resident said: "In the past in Spain to call someone 'Red' or 'Communist'. . . was terrible . . . like the devil or something like that. . . . Now it is less so because we have seen Santiago Carrillo appear on television and talk just like all the others. . . . Before, to talk about Carrillo was a terrible thing . . . he *was* the devil. . . ." In spite of these changes, there remained some basic suspicions about the true intentions and ideological commitment of the party. Asked about the "Eurocommunist" stance of the PCE, one person stated: "They're still Communists. They are not Russian Communists, certainly, nor Bulgarian Communists, nor Polish Communists. They are Spanish Communists with their own set of solutions. But clearly, undoubtedly, with a Marxist theory. . . . I have not the slightest doubt. . . . They can call it Eurocommunism, they can call it anything they want, but it is still communism."

Despite the widely publicized ideological changes undertaken by the Eurocommunist PCE and the deterioration of its relationship with the Soviet Union, there were some who insisted that no real change had taken place: "It is nothing but a tactic. . . . I am convinced that Carrillo is still thinking about the dictatorship of the proletariat and is still profoundly pro-Russian. . . . Whatever they might say, and even if they were to appear as nuns, as the very model of charity. . . ." For another person, however, these changes had gone too far:

> The PCE is no longer a Marxist-Leninist party. They now want to arrive in power via proper channels. It is necessary to wear the sheepskin. . . . At the moment they were legalized, everything was softened, to collaborate, to reduce to the minimum anything that would perpetuate the legend that Communists had horns and tails—to make people believe that they were normal persons, but above all, to become a party, like in Italy, of a Berlingueresque Eurocommunism . . . trying to come to power, but denying all their beliefs. For me, this is false, totally false. For me, they are social democrats.

PCE restraint, apart from its key role in the party's electoral strategy, was also a product of the belief that Spain was still passing through a difficult and sensitive period of transition. Under such circumstances, the party argued that partisan conflict should be minimized. Indeed, the initial PCE position was that the holding of early elections would needlessly polarize political life, possibly destabilizing the new regime. Once elections were called, the PCE would have to attack other parties but, according to this line of reasoning, should do so in a manner sufficiently moderate so as not to foreclose the possibility of interparty collaboration or coalescence after the election. As Santiago Carrillo is reported to have argued before the central committee: "We will have to criticize the PSOE, but preserving the perspective of unity, taking into account that an advance in democracy is impossible without the Socialists. But we have to criticize them, because we are competing parties."[34]

The PCE's attacks against the PSOE and UCD were consistent with its calls for a larger share of the vote and subsequent inclusion into a PCE-PSOE-UCD coalition government. The UCD government was criticized for its failure to solve the dual crises of terrorism and economic decline. These problems could only be solved if the PCE were included in a broad government of national concentration, and would never be resolved under a UCD government with its narrow and conservative bases of support—a government (Carrillo repeatedly claimed) of "bankers, industrialists, and representatives of multinationals."[35] Neither could these crises be satisfactorily addressed by a two-party UCD-PSOE coalition. In such a government, according to Communist leaders, the PSOE would be quickly coopted by the UCD, and this would only further the Socialist party's drift to the right. Indeed, in the party's appeal to its principal target group—Socialists of the left—PCE spokesmen frequently argued that the best way to check the PSOE's drift toward social democracy was to vote Communist.[36]

These attacks notwithstanding, the most noteworthy feature of the PCE campaign was its stress on the need for continued interparty collaboration during a crucial period of transition. As described by a key party strategist, the PCE program "was not a maximalist position, but was disposed to place before all other questions the priority objective of the consolidation of democracy in Spain." In keeping with its moderate stance and its efforts to diffuse voters' fears, the PCE deliberately avoided presenting a choice between two drastically different models of society. In his concluding remarks in a televised speech of February 26, Santiago Carrillo said:

> Many of you have told me, "I don't share your ideas, but I admire what you do. You are a serious responsible party without demagoguery that deals with reality." Well, good for all of you that think this way. I say to you that it does not come down to voting for a capitalist or Communist regime. No, that will happen some day in the future.... Today the question is if democracy is going to be consolidated, if liberties are going to be assured, if the welfare of the people will be a reality, if the economic crisis will continue to gnaw away at us—not only the workers, but also small and medium businessmen and the marginal sectors. To solve these problems, this year and a half you have seen that the Communist party is a serious party that can resolve this problem—not only for the Communists—but for all Spaniards. Therefore, for those that think that way, although you may not share our ideas, I tell you, voting Communist is voting for what you want for this country.

To a greater extent than the Socialists, Communist party leaders were successful in implementing their campaign strategy, to which its party candidates and militants adhered more consistently. This was due in part to the greater discipline nurtured within the party during the years of clandestinity and in part to special efforts oriented toward projecting a uniform image. The secretary general of an Andaluz party branch explained: "The proposals that were elaborated by the central committee were discussed extensively in all provincial and local organizations; the precampaign was a campaign of ideological intensification within the party, which motivated a great homogenization of the positions of all Communists vis-à-vis this electoral program." Communist party leaders were keenly aware that immoderate or inconsistent behavior before the campaign could seriously undermine its centripetal electoral strategy. The manager of a Communist campaign in one of Spain's most populous regions stated in an interview: "The electoral campaign is not undertaken for one month every four years but is always going on. The electoral campaign itself is just one moment of a campaign that lasts forever, and that is to explain the policies of the party. Parties that change their policies at election time have no credibility."

The tasks that confronted the Coalición Democrática were made more difficult by the timing of the election. Negotiations over the creation of the CD practically coincided with the opening of campaign hostilities. This meant that the new alliance would have to simultaneously assemble a new organization, alter its public image and ideology, formulate an electoral strategy, and draw up lists of candidates from among the elites of three different parties. This was too much, too soon.

The basic CD strategy, as described by a high-ranking AP leader, was "the idea of amplifying the image of the party by not presenting it as a party of the right, but attempting to broaden it into a party of the center-right." One observer went so far as to write that "the primary objective of the campaign consisted in erasing, as much as possible, the image of Alianza Popular after [its] defeat in the elections of June 15 [1977]."[37] Some of the subsequent efforts to alter the image of the party appear in retrospect to have been excessive and counterproductive. The symbol and colors of the party were changed, in some respects to their disadvantage—the new "CD" easily became confused with "UCD," and the once vibrant AP colors were replaced by a pasty, washed-out green. The composition of its lists of candidates was drastically altered, producing numerous internal conflicts. And, perhaps most importantly, control of the campaign was turned over to a new team associated with Osorio, marginalizing the stronger and more experienced AP infrastructure in many areas. The inexperience of the new campaign managers led them to commit a series of tactical and strategic blunders that may have done serious harm to the coalition's efforts. One oft-cited example concerns a widely used campaign slogan—"Para Ordenar Bien las Cosas" ("To Arrange Things Well" or, more figuratively translated, "To Set Things Straight")—this provoked fits of sniggering throughout the country because, first, it had a distinctly authoritarian air about it that was precisely what the new coalition was trying to avoid, and, second, it was easy prey for graffiti artists, who changed the verb to "ordeñar," which means "to milk or strip." Several of these measures were later acknowledged by the AP leadership to have been disastrous mistakes. As one party leader argued:

> In the past campaign, we could have maintained the image of Alianza Popular and added to this . . . [a new component], but not eliminating the image of Alianza. The name Alianza Popular-Coalición Democrática, AP-CD, would have been much more advantageous. Maintaining the initial colors of the party, red and yellow, which are colors incorporated now into the mentality of the people, perhaps uniting them with another color, would have been more useful than the total change of colors, which produced great confusion. . . . Our appearance with a new name that could not be identified by the electorate, especially in rural areas, was not beneficial. It is obvious that, for our most loyal public, the conservative agrarian public, the new image did not sink in.

In its attempts to attract more moderate voters, the CD softened the traditional rightist themes associated with the AP. During the campaign the Coalición continued to defend Spanish national unity against threats posed by regional separatists; it still spoke out in favor of state subsidies to church schools, "in defense of the family," and against abortion; it reiterated its warning against the advance of Marxism; and it reissued its call for a crackdown on crime and terrorism. But, unlike during the preceding year of constitutional debates, it articulated these themes in a more consistently restrained fashion. And, unlike in the 1977 election campaign, it explicitly favored some moderate decentralization of the Spanish state through the granting of limited autonomy to several regions; it attempted to lay to rest lingering doubt about its committment to democracy; and it studiously avoided defensive references to the accomplishments of the Franquist regime.

THE VOTERS' CHOICES:
LEFT-RIGHT CONSTRAINTS

How did voters respond to the campaign, and how did they make up their minds in favor of a particular party? For some voters, the voting decision was no choice at all. Clearly, party members, militants, and "strong identifiers" had few doubts about what they would do on election day. The voting choice was also an irrelevant problem for another group of voters—those who were going to defer to others and when asked about the reasons for their choice responded: "My son told me how to vote," "I voted like my husband," "My friends suggested this party to me," and the like. But neither "precommitted" voters nor the "indifferent" voters represented a significant segment of the electorate, and, in any event, from the point of view of the voting decision their cases are of little interest. For the motivations behind the voters who did have to make a choice, some indications come from answers to open-ended questions on why they voted the way they did.

One of the largest block of answers (17 percent) referred to one or more specific qualities ascribed to the party chosen. The most frequently used term was "moderation," but also frequently cited were "seriousness," "responsibility," "balance," "experience," and "reasonableness." Other voters stressed "sincerity," "newness," and "capacity to struggle." About 10 percent of our respondents emphasized the importance of party leaders in general or mentioned the names of specific politicians. Suárez alone was mentioned by 6 percent of the sample as the major reason for voting UCD. Another block of answers made reference to the political tendency of the party (Communist, Socialist, etc.), to its left-right position, or to the fact that the party was against other political groups (anti-Communist, anti-fascist). References to the defense of class or group interests, usually the "working class," accounted for 12 percent of the total. Another 10 percent of the answers singled out the accomplishments of a particular party as the primary reason for the voter's choice, and 6 percent cited the party's position on the regional issue as the decisive factor. Finally, there were those (10 percent) who could not come up with any specific reason and gave vague answers: "I liked everything in the party," "It was the best," or, in a number of cases, "it was the one I dislike the least!"

This catalog of explicitly formulated motivations does not, however, shed much light on the direction of the choices made by the voters. Clearly, the same quality can be invoked to justify or explain a variety of different choices. For explanations of the direction of choice, we must turn to other considerations.

There are reasons to believe that a number of voters framed their voting decision in terms of a left-right conceptualization. One citizen, for example, in a wide-ranging conversation explained his voting choices as follows:

> In the election of June 1977, I voted for the Center . . . and I did so in spite of the fact that all my friends voted for AP. . . . I voted UCD for a fundamental reason. . . . I believed that it would be bad for Spain to be polarized and that there was a need for a center-right and a center-left. . . . And since there was already a Socialist party I voted for what I thought would be a center-right party. . . . Then in 1979 I voted for Coalición Democrática. Why? Because I thought that a stronger right was needed. I did not think that the UCD government was behaving as a center-right government. . . . I thought . . . well, there is a Communist group in the Cortes, and so there should also be a right-wing group. . . .

In conversations with other electors, it became apparent that, though they were often less articulate, the left-right spectrum frequently underlay their descriptions of events and their interpretations of political phenomena. However sketchy and inarticulate their notions of "left" and "right" may have been, this terminology provided a meaningful imagery and a significant frame of reference for most citizens.

It could also be argued that the existence of widespread perceptions of the political world and of evaluations of political protagonists in left-right terms constituted a powerful set of constraints on voters' choices even when notions of left and right held by the voters were sketchy and inarticulate. Once voters placed parties and themselves on the continuum, they inevitably found themselves closer to some political groups and more distant from others. Hence, the many options available in the voting booth were narrowed down, in most cases, to only two. In the regional party systems, as we shall see, the presence of micronationalist parties somewhat complicated the choice, but there too, an ordering of the parties on the relevant space simplified the choice considerably. For voters placing themselves on the right or center-right segment, perceived distances between themselves and the various parties excluded from the range of options the PSOE, the PCE, and other smaller parties of the left. For these voters, then, the only realistic alternatives were the UCD and the AP-CD. Similarly, for electors at the other end of the scale, to vote for the parties of Suárez or Fraga was unthinkable. For centrist voters, the ordering of parties led to the exclusion of all but the UCD and the PSOE.

Thus, at a minimum, the left-right structuring brought about a simplification of the picture. But it could be argued that it did more than that, that the left-right logic compelled the voter even further. As the data in table 32 show, in many cases there was a party that the electors perceived as being the closest to their own position and that, therefore, constituted a logical or "natural" choice. Perhaps in many cases the "closest" party was not entirely satisfactory to the voter in terms of ideology, programs, or policy stands. Perhaps the closest party was simply the least objectionable choice, but even in that case the choice would be based on proximity. How well does a least-distance model account for the vote of Spaniards in 1979? Our analysis indicates that the proximity criterion held for most voters. The mean distances between voters in the various groups of partisans and the four major parties reported in figure 16 are totally congruent with the least-distance hypothesis. There was a remarkable symmetry, moreover, in the evaluation of the distance between the "self" and each of the parties. Clearly, perceptions of political distance were systematically reciprocated, and they were very much in line with the structure of competition between adjacent parties illustrated earlier in this chapter.

It would be misleading to suppose, however, that the left-right logic accounted for every single vote. For one thing, a least-distance criterion did not always provide an unambiguous choice. Some people failed to locate some of the parties, others placed two parties at exactly the same position, still others saw themselves as being equidistant from two political groups. For another, although a vision of the world in left-right terms was widespread, it was not universally shared and, when it existed, did not necessarily overshadow all other elements. Clearly, some people also took into consideration other aspects. In particular, our data suggest that, together with left-right identifications, images of party leaders played a critical role in shaping voting choices.

TABLE 32

PERCEIVED DISTANCE BETWEEN RESPONDENTS AND THE FOUR MAJOR PARTIES BY LEFT-RIGHT LOCATIONS

Left-right distance between	Respondents' Left-Right Self-Locations									
	1	2	3	4	5	6	7	8	9	10
Self and PCE	2.2	1.5	1.1	1.6	2.7	3.7	5.1	6.2	7.4	8.3
Self and PSOE	3.4	2.2	1.2	0.7	1.4	2.2	3.5	4.4	5.7	7.2
Self and UCD	7.1	5.6	4.1	2.5	0.9	0.8	1.2	1.6	2.6	3.6
Self and AP-CD	8.2	7.0	5.9	4.5	2.7	2.2	1.5	1.5	1.4	2.4

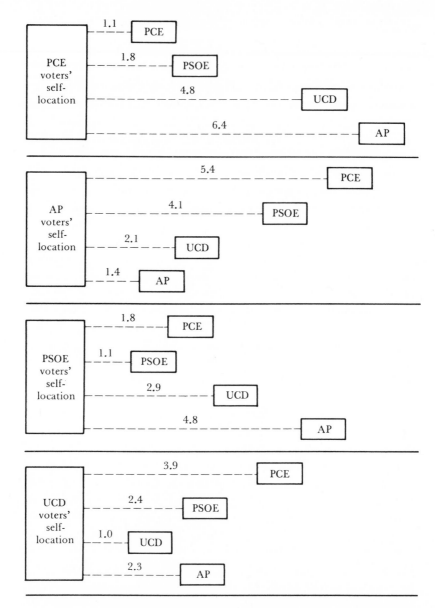

FIGURE 16. Left-Right Distance Between the Mean Locations of Partisan Groups and the Mean Perceived Location of the Four Major Parties

IMAGES OF PARTY LEADERS

Although at the time of the 1979 election the democratic regime was less than two years old, party elites, and especially the leaders of the four major parties, were well known by large segments of the electorate. For different reasons, Adolfo Suárez, Felipe González, Santiago Carrillo, and Manuel Fraga enjoyed widespread popularity. Suárez, as our mass survey shows, was correctly identified as the prime minister by over 95 percent of the voters polled. His past record under the Franquist regime was also known by a fair number of Spaniards, but by 1979 he had become primarily identified as the head of the government under which the transition to democracy had been accomplished. We have no precise estimates of the familiarity of the mass public with the other three major leaders, but it can be safely assumed that they, and the roles they occupied in the political system, were also quite well known. At the least, people associated them correctly with their respective parties and had some minimal ideas about their politics. Both Fraga and Carrillo were familiar faces—individuals who had played highly visible and significant, if very different, roles, during the Franquist era and in the early phases of the transition. As for Felipe González, his youthful image had appeared on countless posters throughout Spain; he had been seen repeatedly on television and had emerged in the eyes of the voters as the indisputable leader of the second largest party.

The public's knowledge of political leaders was tightly linked to positive and negative feelings toward the major politicians. For many voters, the heads of the four major parties were not just salient political "objects," but also figures that elicited positive or negative feelings, sometimes of strong intensity. Political passion, however, did not prevent people from seeing positive qualities in leaders with whom they had little in common politically. Our informal interviews with Madrid residents indicate that some personal characteristics of political leaders were so visible and pervasive as to be perceived, and appreciated, by voters of different ideological predilections. People frequently expressed respect, and sometimes also admiration, for political protagonists they considered far removed from their own point of view. Some center-right voters, for example, made the following comments about Carrillo:

> Carrillo is an extremely able man . . . and he knows a lot. . . . And considering that he has much less political strength than the others, he is doing an excellent job, nothing less than Berlinguer or Marchais. He is a true party leader, and everybody can respect him. . . . Furthermore, he has a great sense of humor.

> I believe that Carrillo is one of the most intelligent political personalities of Spain. He is moving slowly, doing his thing. I believe he is convinced that Communist votes will increase. . . . Well, this has always been the posture of the Communists—a drop here, a drop there, and finally we get a lake.

> Carrillo, I will define him as a good politician, as a very good politician, one who went through a lot . . . and who is now much more tranquil . . . because he is older now, and he has suffered, and he does not have the strength now to spend another 40 years like the last ones. . . .

Some citizens with leftist leanings characterized Fraga in the following terms:

> Mr. Fraga, in spite of his ideas which I personally dislike, absolutely dislike . . . well, I see him as a very intelligent type . . . very intelligent, but it is an intelligence not well employed. . . .

> Mr. Fraga is a politician *par excellence.* . . . As a person and as a politician he seems like a good person, but he is too unstable to be trusted with power.

> Fraga for me is perhaps the most intelligent politician that has come out so far. Maybe his reactions to things are his weak point; I think he is honest, but his violent reactions. . . . Besides, he is very authoritarian. . . . He is well prepared, well prepared . . . but he could be more careful. . . .

The owner of a small store in downtown Madrid, who claimed to have been a centrist from the very beginning, added another telling and even-handed comment: "The best politicians? I believe that Santiago Carrillo is one of those who knows most about politics. . . . He and the other one, Fraga, they are the best, they are fabulous. . . . Now, one might go for one or the other depending on one's ideas, but they are both excellent. . . . "

In spite of the voters' objectivity in evaluating political figures, the overall pattern of feelings toward leaders was closely aligned, as we have seen earlier, with the left-right dimension. Right-wing and left-wing Spaniards tended to have extremely negative feelings toward Carrillo and Fraga, respectively. Positive and negative evaluations of Suárez and González followed basically the same pattern but, as figure 17 shows, the intensity of sympathy or hostility was far less pronounced. In particular, Suárez appeared to be liked, or at least accepted, by a broad spectrum of voters stretching from the center to the extreme right. Felipe González too, although less popular than the prime minister, was clearly liked much more than either Carrillo or Fraga.

These general measures of overall feelings do not directly address the question of the qualities ascribed to the leaders and of the importance of these traits in the eyes of the public. Our general impression is that a number of different components—some more purely political, others strictly personal, others related to the performance of the politicians—entered into the leaders' overall images. Some indications of the wide range of factors involved can be gleaned from the opinions expressed in informal interviews with Madrid residents.

Suárez has many qualities. . . . He has an appealing physique, that is, neither good looking nor ugly, agreeable, a good voice so that one feels inferior to him. . . . He is a great actor, to pretend to be social democratic to deceive. He has the ability to change his face and go with the wind. . . .

Yes, I think that Suárez is a progressive type. . . . He is young, and he has shown that he is a good politician. . . . He obtained power and used it . . . yes I see him as a liberal. . . .

Suárez as a politician, well I do not think much of him. . . . He did manage to "change his jacket" at the right time, to be sure.

Yes, I do like Suárez. . . . I like the way he looks and furthermore it seems to me that he has done a lot . . . he put himself in the middle and he said: "Let's try to do something moderate". . . those on the left say he is a right-winger and those on the right say he is a leftist. . . . I have heard him talk, and he is very convincing.

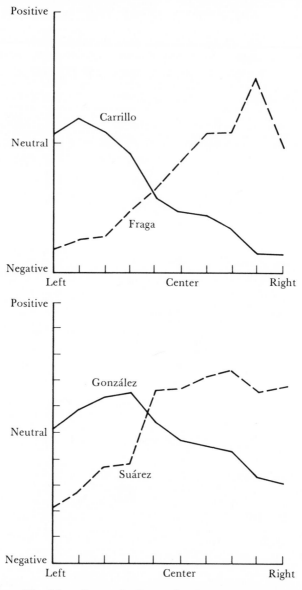

FIGURE 17. Mean Sympathy Scores for the Four Major Party Leaders by
Left-Right Location of Respondents

Adolfo Suárez is a person who speaks to everybody and has a more representative demeanor than González, not to mention Guerra. I do not really know who is the better one, but there is one obvious fact, the way they look.

Suárez is a leader, a man who, independently of his ideas which I do not like, is a person who makes people think ... and he makes people listen.... They say he is an idiot, that he says stupid things, but they listen....

Suárez is a rather intelligent man, but in spite of his intelligence he is still a right-winger. Fundamentally on the right.... Yes, he is very able, one cannot deny that....

I do like Felipe González because of his ideas. However, I think he is too young, not mature enough to lead a party.... For example, Tierno Galván has much more experience; Felipe does not have too much experience, and that is not good.

Felipe González behaved like a man during the last congress. I like him; he showed the world that he can handle himself. He has shown that he is really the best politician there is in Spain.

I think that Fraga is a magnificent politician but he has a very serious defect for a politician.... He does not take kindly to the ideas of other people or groups. He is not very diplomatic, and in politics without a little bit of diplomacy one does not go too far....

For me the party of Sr. González is a party of people who promise a lot ... and I do not like people who promise a lot because then they will not deliver.... And there is another thing, too: I never liked people from Andalucía.... Felipe is very ambitious, lusting for power.

Of Felipe I think this: This guy ... well I saw him on TV yesterday and he spoke very well, very well. He said that it is not a question of bringing about a type of socialism that has been put into a bottle a long time ago; no, one must go further ... one must change.... he seems like a very good speaker ... and besides he is well known abroad; he goes and talks to Willy Brandt and to Mario Soares, and all this means experience.

Felipe González seems to me to be a very able speaker. He knows how to talk and how to convince people. But I do not know whether he really knows where he is heading. They say that because he is young, he is not mature. I am not sure about that.

Alfonso Guerra uses too harsh a language. . . . One cannot go around attacking people in a violent and rough manner for a whim, or without a purpose. . . . No, man, there are other interests, higher interests. . . . It might have been O.K. during the clandestinity but not now, now that he represents the second largest party in the country.

How important were the qualities ascribed to the major leaders in influencing voters' choice? And what was the relative importance of these qualities compared to the voters' left-right identifications and their attitudes toward the parties? These are difficult questions to answer because of the high degree of connection among the variables involved. Clearly, a positive or negative view of, say, Fraga had a great deal to do not only with the respondents' left-right scores, but also with their general attitudes toward AP and their perception of where this party stood on the political spectrum. Disentangling this complex set of relations among several variables and ascertaining the direction of causality is impossible with the data at our disposal. Perhaps in some cases it was the approval of the political position of a party—stemming from the voter's own self-location—that spilled over and colored favorably the image of its leader. In other cases, it might well have been the other way around, given the high visibility and influence of political elites. Although these variables can be sorted out conceptually by an outside observer, it is by no means certain that a neat separation existed in the minds of the people themselves. Indeed, the strong correlation among them suggests that they might have been perceived by the actors as slightly different aspects of the same thing.

Our supposition is that the left-right dimension provided voters with a general map of the party system—a map in which they could locate the various politically relevant actors, events, and issues as well as themselves—while their feelings toward parties and leaders helped in a more direct manner in choosing between two contiguous voting alternatives. For voters located on the *same* position on the left-right continuum, the decisive "pull" or "push" came from their views of the key politicians of adjacent parties. Our survey data are fully consistent with this interpretation. As table 33 shows, the relationship

TABLE 33
EVALUATIONS OF ADOLFO SUÁREZ
AND FELIPE GONZÁLEZ BY LEFT-RIGHT PLACEMENT
OF VOTERS AND VOTING CHOICES OF PSOE AND UCD VOTERS

	4 (N=462)		5 (N=900)		6 (N=347)	
	Evaluations of		Evaluations of		Evaluations of	
	Suárez	González	Suárez	González	Suárez	González
PSOE voters	4.7	7.3	5.8	7.4	5.4	7.3
UCD voters	7.0	5.6	7.7	4.9	7.6	4.5

Note: Figures are mean sympathy scores for the two leaders within each subgroup of voters, on a "sympathy" scale of 0 to 10.

between feelings toward the two major leaders and the vote remained strong even after controlling for the voters' location on the left-right spectrum. The electoral choice of respondents who occupied the same position on the continuum and who, therefore, did not differ in their "ideological" stands, was definitely in line with their feelings toward González and Suárez. The same holds for the other pairs of adjacent parties, that is, PCE-PSOE and UCD-AP. While these data do not allow us to assess in a precise manner the influence of party leaders in shaping voting behavior, the figures strongly suggest that images of key politicians played a significant role.

THE STRUCTURE OF MASS ATTITUDES

The evidence we have reviewed indicates that within the Spanish electorate there was a coherent structure of attitudes and that party preference was a "natural" component of this configuration of orientations. The fundamental axis of this structure was a left-right view of the political world in which evaluations of parties, party leaders, and other politically relevant groups clustered in a meaningful manner. In addition to items related to the three major cleavages, these clusters included attitudes toward groups and institutions, such as ETA, the police, the king, the leader of the right-wing Fuerza Nueva (Blas Piñar), and respondents' choices between juxtaposed ideological concepts such as "monarchy vs. republic," "Marxism vs. no-Marxism," "Franquism vs. anti-Franquism," and "friendship toward the U.S.A. vs. friendship toward the U.S.S.R." Practically all of these orientations were related to the left-right identifications of respondents, as well as to their more explicitly partisan attitudes. Figure 18 depicts a number of these small subclusters of congruent orientations. They constituted, so to speak, the tiles of a mosaic that summarizes the views of the Spanish electorate in the late 1970s. Although none of these relationships comes as a surprise, the coherence of these patterns indicates the existence of a high degree of structuring of political perceptions and evaluations. The strong identification existing in the citizens' minds of AP and Fraga with the symbols of the past regime might have served to attract some nostalgic voters to AP-CD, but it certainly alienated many others. Similarly, in the case of the PCE the persistent coupling in the public's eyes of Carrillo and his party with anticlerical postures and Marxism did little to help the PCE penetrate the more moderate segments of the electorate.

Further analysis of these intercorrelations revealed a meaningful pattern. The points plotted in figure 19 represent the positions of the different "objects" in the attitudinal space created by factor analysis. Several observations are suggested by the distribution of the points in the space generated by the first two factors. This simplified version of the "firmament" of Spanish politics contains a clear demarcation of its elements in two general areas that could be roughly identified as containing rightist and leftist elements. These two broad areas are defined not only by the presence of elements pertaining to the political realm, but also by the evaluation of groups, such as big business, the Church, and the unions. Thus, the picture incorporates social as well as political cleavages. Within the two major groupings, moreover, specific clusters exist. Indeed, the existence of these clusters is as significant as the overall partition. The first includes elements associated in the public's mind with the previous regime (Franco, Blas Piñar, Fraga, and AP). The second might be said to symbolize the "establishment" (Suárez, the Church, the police, and UCD). Last, the leftist elements of the picture are subdivided into a Socialist and a Communist subgroup. Because the analysis was carried out for the entire sample, the "map" of the political world in figure 19 is a composite picture that reflects

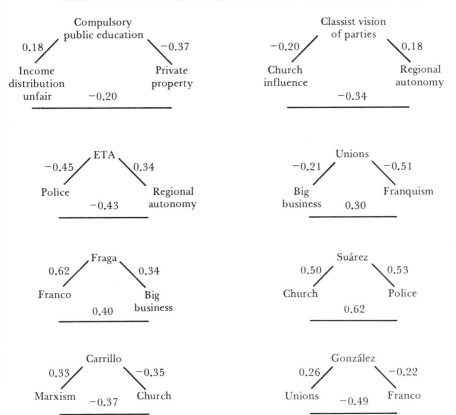

FIGURE 18.   Clusters of Attitudinal Variables

Note: Figures are zero-order correlation coefficients between "feeling thermometer" scores for the items indicated in the figure.

the partisan coloration of the sample. An examination of these cognitive-evaluative structures carried out separately for different partisan groups indicates that they differ in significant (and interesting) details, but the broad outlines of the pattern of antagonism remain largely unchanged.

It is interesting to note that the evaluation of the king is almost equidistant from the voters' attitudes toward the two major groupings. The king was not identified in any way with the previous re-

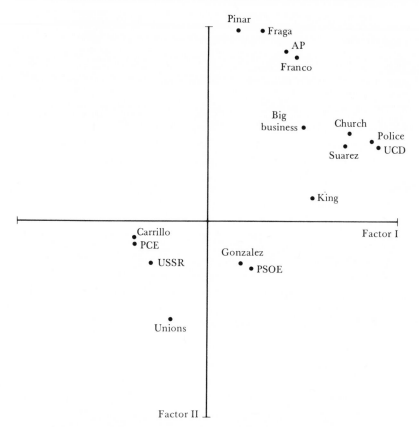

FIGURE 19. The Structure of Mass Evaluations of Sixteen Political
Objects

Note: Based on factor analysis of "feeling thermometer" scores for the items that appear on the chart. The two axes correspond to the first two factors.

gime, but located approximately halfway between the leaders of the two major parties. Clearly, the combined popular evaluation of the king and his performance are less tightly bound to the structure of attitudes toward other elements of the political world. In the eyes of the mass public, Juan Carlos appeared to be "above the factions" or, at least, not clearly identified with any specific partisan cluster.

Overall, evaluations of the king's performance in the first few years of the new regime were positive. Only about 8 percent of our mass level respondents gave a negative assessment. An examination of these evaluations indicates that this minority of negative opinions came from both the most extreme elements of the left, where republican sentiments were still strongly rooted, and from the far right. In these latter quarters, there was some resentment toward what was perceived as a "betrayal" of Franco's mandate by Juan Carlos. These three statements drawn from conversations with Madrid residents are illustrative of this point of view.

> It seems to me that the king perjured himself. To my mind, a person does not have to swear on the Gospel, but if he does that, well, he should keep his word.... Leaving aside the fact that he is not too smart.... But that is not important, really. The fact is that Franco treated him very well, like a son, I would say even better than his own daughter. Well, anyhow all that the king has done is to destroy everything that Franco had built....

> I am a monarchist by tradition. But I must say that I do not like Juan Carlos. In the first place, I do not consider him a very intelligent man. I feel that he has been too involved in politics. Maybe because of the influence of certain cliques, I do not know. In any event, I feel that he should have changed less brusquely.... Perhaps he is under the influence of his father who strongly resented the previous regime....

> The king has permitted regions to be introduced in Spain. He has broken the country into little pieces, and this I cannot forget or forgive.

In contrast, leftist, but not extreme leftist, voters often expressed positive, if cautious, evaluations of the king. A PCE voter, for example, said:

> Well, I believe that Juan Carlos has played a very important role in the development of democracy in Spain. I do believe that he, really, is not a man of the right.... He has demonstrated that. No, he is not a right-winger, but neither is he a leftist. In many ways he has been helpful in ushering in the new democratic system.... And this has been a very important factor. Furthermore, because of the support of the king for the new regime, people have felt encouraged....

A left-wing Socialist added,

The king? If he had not existed we should have had to invent him. Let me tell you something. In the last years of Franquism, Tierno Galván used to say "The monarchy is not the solution but it is a way out" (*salida*). . . . And my father, for example, who has been a socialist militant throughout his life, has always had a rather positive image of Juan Carlos. . . . Sometimes he says that Juan Carlos is not very smart, but he adds that he is carrying out his role pretty well and that it is his father who is guiding him. That is to say, people like us, the left, we are aware that we wanted much more than what we got. At the same time, if it had not been for the king we would have had to fight much more to achieve what we have achieved. . . .

And a school administrator and long-time activist in the PSP said:

The king has done pretty well. He deals well with foreign relations. He has a decent family, they live a normal life, I know for sure his son is treated like everybody else in the school he attends. . . . Politically, he has surrounded himself with good people, at least until now. . . . I think that in a situation of crisis he would behave in a manner favorable to democracy. . . .

The left-right structuring of the behavior of political elites and the mass public is fully confirmed by the analysis of shifts in voting choices from 1977 to 1979 and from the parliamentary election of March 1979 to the nationwide municipal elections of April 1979. A left-right constraint implies that in moving away from a party a voter would generally not go to a "distant" group, but rather to a "neighboring" party. Thus, shifts in voting choice from one election to another would be accounted for primarily by lateral "moves" rather than by "jumps." The pattern of voters' response to a question on how they voted in 1977 and in 1979 conforms, to a large extent, to this hypothesis (table 34). Perhaps the respondents exaggerated the continuity of their behavior over time, but this is not of great concern. What is significant is not the high level of stability evident from table 34, but rather the pattern of shifts. The flow of voters clearly conforms to the argument we have been making in this chapter. Competition was not a war of all against all, but an orderly and selective war of attrition between pairs of adjacent parties. Most voters confirmed the choice they had made two years earlier; those who did not moved to a "nearby" party. There are some exceptions to this conduct, but they are few indeed, and it is significant that in such a large sample there was not even one voter who reported shifting from the PCE to the AP, or vice versa. Analysis of the shifts between the parliamentary and the municipal elections of 1979 confirms these findings (table 35). When those who had voted for the PCE at the beginning of March shifted in April, they went overwhelmingly for the PSOE, and vice versa. Shifts involving other parties exhibited the same pattern.

TABLE 34
VOTE STABILITY, 1977 TO 1979
(in percentages)

Vote in 1979	Vote in 1977			
	PCE	PSOE	UCD	AP
PCE	92.8	2.6	0.4	0
PSOE	6.0	93.6	6.8	2.2
UCD	1.2	3.2	91.0	33.3
CD	0	0.6	1.8	64.5
N	(250)	(833)	(1461)	(141)

TABLE 35
VOTE STABILITY BETWEEN THE PARLIAMENTARY
AND MUNICIPAL ELECTIONS OF 1979
(in percentages)

Municipal elections	Parliamentary elections			
	PCE	PSOE	UCD	CD
PCE	89.7	2.4	0.7	0.9
PSOE	7.8	90.8	5.1	2.0
UCD	1.9	6.6	90.3	47.6
AP-CD[a]	0.6	0.2	3.9	49.5
N	(319)	(1007)	(1286)	(105)

[a]Most CD slates of candidates withdrew prior to the municipal election, which contributed to the decline in support for that party.

Micronationalism and the Regional Party Systems of Euskadi, Catalunya, and Galicia

The building of a state composed of autonomous regions is our only way out of Spain's current problems, but it is also the principal risk that threatens our fragile democracy.
— *Prime Minister Adolfo Suárez*[1]

As a clear reflection of the salience of the regional question and its potentially destabilizing influence on the new regime, distinct regional party systems emerged in the first democratic election in 1977. In Euskadi, Catalunya, and Galicia, the four major statewide parties competed for electoral support with relatively moderate nationalist* parties (e.g., the PNV and the CDC) and more extreme groups (e.g., Euskadiko Ezkerra and the Gallego BNPG). A process of consolidation of the regional party systems took place between the 1977 and 1979 elections (table 36). In Euskadi and Galicia, regional parties as a whole improved their position considerably; in Catalunya, their proportion of the total vote

---

*The terms "nationalist" and "micronationalist" will be used interchangeably in this chapter to refer to orientations and behavior based on the idea that Basques, Catalans, and Gallegos constituted groups distinct from that of Castilian Spaniards and wanted to secure regional autonomy or independence. Regional parties or groups, as distinct from regional branches of statewide parties, that made demands for autonomy or independence are also labeled "nationalist" or "micronationalist."

TABLE 36

1977 AND 1979 PARLIAMENTARY ELECTION
RESULTS IN EUSKADI, CATALUNYA, AND GALICIA
(in percentages)

	1977	1979
Euskadi		
Regional parties		
PNV	30.0	27.6
EE	6.5	8.0
HB	—	15.0
Total	36.5	50.6
Statewide parties		
AP (GU)/UFPV	7.2	3.4
UCD	12.9	16.9
PSOE (PSE)	26.7	19.1
PCE	4.6	4.7
Total	51.4	44.1
Catalunya		
Regional parties		
PDC/CiU	17.0	16.4
ERC	4.7	4.1
BEAN	—	1.6
Total	21.7	22.1
Statewide parties		
AP/CD	3.6	3.7
UCD/CC-UCD	17.0	19.4
PSC-PSOE	28.7	29.8
PSUC	18.4	17.4
Total	67.7	69.3
Galicia		
Regional parties		
PSG/UG	2.4	5.4
BNPG	2.0	5.9
Total	4.4	11.3
Statewide parties		
AP/CD	13.2	14.2
UCD	53.9	48.3
PSOE	15.6	17.4
PCE (PCG)	3.0	4.2
Total	85.7	84.1

PNV	Partido Nacional Vasco
EE	Euskadiko Ezkerra
HB	Herri Batasuna
AP(GU)/UFPV	Alianza Popular (or Guipúzcoa Unida) in 1977; Unión Foral del País Vasco (AP party label in Euskadi in 1979)
PDC/CiU	Pacte Democràtic per Catalunya/Convergència i Unió
ERC	Esquerra Republicana de Catalunya
BEAN	Bloc d'Esquerra d'Allíberament Nacional
UCD/CC-UCD	In Catalunya, the UCD ran under the label Centristes de Catalunya
PSUC	Partit Socialista Unificat de Catalunya (Communist party of Catalunya)
PSC-PSOE	Partit dels Socialistes de Catalunya– Partido Socialista Obrero Español
BNPG	Bloque Nacional Popular Gallego

Sources: Ministerio de la Gobernación, Dirección General de la Política Interior, *Elecciones Generales 1977;* and Ministerio del Interior, Dirección General de Política Interior, *Elecciones Generales 1979.*
Note: Percentages do not add up to 100 because only the votes for major statewide and regional parties are presented.

remained unaltered. The results of the two elections also indicated that, though a process of crystallization toward a four-major-party system had taken place in Spain as a whole, in the Basque country the party system had become increasingly fragmented and polarized. A new *abertzale* left coalition, Herri Batasuna, competed for the first time and emerged with 15 percent of the vote. Herri Batasuna and the radical Euskadiko Ezkerra obtained almost as many votes as the historic and more moderate PNV.

The 1979 election also demonstrated that, though some support for micronationalist forces existed in all three culturally and linguistically distinct regions, the nature and extent of such support varied markedly from one area to another. There were a number of significant differences among the Basque, Catalán, and Gallego party systems. The most obvious of these was the far lesser degree to which the party system in Galicia was organized around the regional question. The preconditions for micronationalist movements were (as we have seen in chap. 7) present in all three regions: each exhibited linguistic diversity, divided national loyalties, and preferences for varying degrees of autonomy. Nevertheless, the Gallego nationalist parties received only 11.3 percent of the vote in the 1979 election, compared with totals of 50.6 percent and 22.1 percent for such groups in Euskadi and Catalunya, respectively. The regional party systems also differed in the relative strength of leftist versus center-right forces. In Galicia, center-right parties clearly dominated, whereas in Catalunya the Communist PSUC and the Socialist PSC-PSOE together obtained a near-majority of the popular vote. The Basque system was the most fragmented: support was split between leftist regional and statist parties, and between Basque and Spanish centrist or center-right groups. The three party systems differed as well in their levels of polarization: Basque politics was the most polarized, due to the strong presence of Herri Batasuna, an explicitly antisystem party.

This chapter will compare the party systems of Euskadi, Catalunya, and Galicia. To account for the similarities and differences

among them, we will focus primarily on the nature of micronationalism in each and the centrality of the regional question as a source of
partisan conflict among both elites and voters. We argue that the
variations among the three regional party systems were due to a
complex set of factors. The first and most obvious concerns the differing nature and intensity of micronationalist sentiments in the
three regions. These, in turn, cannot be accounted for by any single
determinant. One might have expected, for example, that, because
regional language usage was most widespread in Catalunya and Galicia, preferences for extensive autonomy or independence and support for nationalist parties would have been most evident in these
two regions. Instead, it was the Basque country, in which Euskera was
spoken by less than one-quarter of the population, where micronationalist sentiments were most intense. Similarly, one might have anticipated that Gallegos, the population that felt the greatest degree
of attachment to the regional group and the most discriminated
against by other Spaniards,[2] would have been the most politicized
with regard to the center-periphery cleavage. Clearly, these expectations were not met.

Finally, according to Hechter's argument concerning the decisive
influence of "internal colonialism" for the emergence of micronationalist movements,[3] one might have assumed that Galicia, as the
least economically developed of the three regions and, indeed, as
one of the poorest areas of the country (see table 37), would have
been the most vociferous in its demands for autonomy. Yet it was in
the two richest regions of Spain that such demands were made. Thus,
none of these factors in and of itself—the extent of objective differences between the regional group and Castilian Spaniards, the degree of perceived national distinctiveness, or the extent to which the
minority population felt subject to discrimination—is sufficient to
explain the degree to which the center-periphery cleavage had become a source of political conflict. None of them individually, moreover, helps to account for the specific sets of issues or demands that
became politically salient and divisive.

TABLE 37
INDICATORS OF ECONOMIC DEVELOPMENT, 1975

	Per capita income (in ptas.)	Work force engaged in agriculture (%)	Work force engaged in industry (%)	Work force engaged in service sector (%)
Spain	144,731	22.9	37.9	39.2
Euskadi	190,963[a]	10.1	52.6	37.2
Catalunya	184,414	6.9	54.4	38.7
Galicia	110,464	50.3	23.7	26.0
Andalucía	103,103	27.4	29.1	43.5

Sources: Per capita figures from Banco de Bilbao, Renta Nacional de España y su Distribución Provincial, 1978, p. 85. Regional percentages were obtained from Carles Gispert and Josep Mª Prats, España: Un Estado Plurinacional, Barcelona: Editorial Blume, 1978, pp. 134–36; Percentages for Spain came from Alfonso Magariños, Quienes somos los gallegos?, Epidauro, 1979, p. 112.
[a]Euskadi and Navarra were combined in the table from which these figures were obtained.

We contend, instead, that variations among the three regions, with regard to both their micronationalist phenomena and their party systems, are attributable to the degree to which objective differences and diffuse regionalist sentiments were found within the regional populations *and* the extent to, and manner in, which these were translated at the mass level into more overtly political orientations and specific policy demands regarding the regional question. The relative level of economic development of a region, moreover, served either as a limiting condition for extensive mass mobilization of any kind (Galicia) or as a facilitating condition for such mobilization (Euskadi and Catalunya).

Finally, we argue that the particular configuration of political parties found within each region and the extent to which political elites articulated nationalist sentiments and mobilized voters on the basis of nationalist appeals had an independent effect on micronationalist phenomena.[4] Each contributed to the degree to which center-periphery cleavages, compared with other salient divisions, became a source of political conflict at the mass level. As an AP leader from Galicia stated in 1981 in an interview concerning the sources of micronationalism: "The will to be a nation is, indeed, the product of a tradition, of a culture, of a history, but also of the particular politics at a given moment."

THE NATURE AND INTENSITY OF MICRONATIONALIST ATTITUDES

The tasks confronting nationalist parties in the three regions were twofold: to make more politically salient the linguistic and perceived cultural distinctiveness of regional populations; and to mobilize diffuse regionalist sentiments in support of regional forces and their micronationalist demands. These tasks were compounded in Galicia by the traditional passivity of its population, which historically has worked to the advantage of conservative political forces. They were made more complex in Euskadi and Catalunya for an altogether different reason. As highly developed regions, both have long been areas of massive immigration of Castilian-speaking Spaniards seeking employment and an improved standard of living: for example, 35 percent of our Basque and Catalán respondents were born in other parts of Spain. Thus, the center-periphery cleavage that divides these two regions from the rest of the country is replicated, but in reverse within each. Basque and Catalán nationalists, therefore, had to promote an identification with regional aspirations, or at least to forestall their rejection, among those in their societies who did not speak the language, did not descend from a native family, or were born outside of the region. In short, given the presence of sizable immigrant communities in their midst, as well as the large number of native-born Basques who did not speak Euskera, Basque and Catalán nationalists were forced to formulate their appeals more on the basis of a voluntaristic identification with the "nation" and less on the basis of "primordial" attachments to language and place of birth.[5]

LANGUAGE, BIRTHPLACE, AND NATIONALISM

The difficulties confronting Basque and Catalán nationalists in fostering such a voluntaristic identification among immigrants, as well as their potential success among those segments who spoke the regional language and who were native-born, can be seen in table 38.

In Euskadi and Catalunya (the two regions in which there is substantial variation in language usage), there were marked differences in subjective national identity between those who claimed to speak the regional language and those who did not. The differences in national self-identity between Catalán and non-Catalán-speaking immigrants suggests that the learning and usage of the regional language may serve to foster new attachments and to erode old ones. At the same time, it should be noted that in Euskadi a strong sense of "Basqueness" among the native-born has often led to the learning of Euskera by those whose first language was Castilian. Thus, the causal relationship between language usage and subjective national identity is not unidirectional. Nevertheless, as table 38 indicates, place of birth[6] was more closely linked to a sense of primary or exclusive loyalty to the regional group.[7]

The greater importance of birthplace as compared with language usage in defining national self-identity in Euskadi and Catalunya was further evidenced by the pattern of responses, shown in table 39, of both native and immigrant groups to a series of three questions concerning what it takes to be a member of the Basque or Catalán community. In comparison with "being born in the region or descended from a Basque or Catalán family" and "living and working in the region," "speaking the regional language" was the least frequently mentioned requirement among both natives and immigrants. Apart from this similarity, the patterns of responses in the two regions were somewhat different. Although both natives and immigrants most often mentioned ascriptive rather than voluntaristic criteria for membership in the community, this was less pronounced in Euskadi than in Catalunya. Almost twice as many Basque as Catalán natives opted for the most inclusive or assimilationist definition—living and working in the region.[8] Immigrants in Euskadi were also more likely to choose voluntaristic criteria than were their Catalán counterparts.

These attitudinal differences as well as the similarity in the perceived lesser role attributed to language usage were somewhat unexpected, given the distinct images of the two societies and the contrasting nature of their traditional nationalist ideologies.[9] Catalunya

TABLE 38
SUBJECTIVE NATIONAL IDENTIFICATION BY PLACE OF BIRTH AND LANGUAGE USAGE
(in percentages)

Sense of group identification	Euskadi[a]				Catalunya[b]			
	Native speakers	Native nonspeakers	Immigrant nonspeakers	All respondents	Native speakers	Immigrant speakers	Immigrant nonspeakers	All respondents
"Spanish only"	3	15	61	25	15	54	71	31
"More Spanish than Basque (Catalán)"	1	21	7	3	4	12	12	7
50-50	10	37	24	24	43	25	15	36
"More Basque (Catalán) than Spanish"	15	14	2	11	17	5	0	12
"Basque (Catalán) only"	72	32	6	37	21	4	1	15
N	(268)	(302)	(268)	(856)	(748)	(150)	(188)	(1122)

[a] Immigrant speakers of Euskera are omitted. They are only 4 percent of the sample in Euskadi; they are included, however, in the total N.
[b] Native nonspeakers of Catalán are omitted. They are only 4 percent of the sample in Catalunya; they are included, however, in the total N.

TABLE 39
ASCRIPTIVE AND VOLUNTARISTIC
CRITERIA FOR MEMBERSHIP IN THE
BASQUE (CATALÁN) COMMUNITY BY BIRTHPLACE
(in percentages)

	Euskadi		Catalunya	
	Natives	Immigrants	Natives	Immigrants
Ascriptive Criteria				
Born in the region or descent +				
speak the regional language +				
live and work in the region	25	15	18	14
Birth + language	2	5	4	5
Birth + live and work in the region	16	15	11	18
Born in the region or descent	17	33	41	43
Total	60	68	74	80
Voluntaristic Criteria				
Live and work in the region				
+ language	4	5	6	2
Speak the regional language	1	1	1	0
Live and work in the region	35	25	19	18
N	(508)	(284)	(770)	(402)

has long been viewed and has been depicted by Catalans themselves as the more tolerant, open, and integrationist of the two societies. A CDC leader interviewed in 1978 described his society in the following way:

> Virtually all cultures of any importance in the Mediterranean have passed through Catalunya at one point or another. The Phoenicians, Greeks, Carthagenians, Romans, Moors. This is a very mixed culture. It has acquired a character of compromise. It is not closed and racist. . . . We are not interested in any form of purity in our culture.

Basque society and culture, in contrast, are widely perceived as being parochial, defensive, and even hostile to the cultural diversity introduced by immigrants.

These images of the two societies are, in turn, congruent with the contrasting definitions of Basque and Catalán national identity contained in the late nineteenth-century formulations of their respective nationalist ideologies. For the founder and principal ideologue of the Basque Nationalist party, Sabino de Arana y Goiri, and his early followers, "race" lay at the core of Basque national identity. As Evangelista de Ibero, author of an important nationalist tract, wrote in 1906:

> What is a nation? The ensemble of men or people who have the same origin, the same language, the same character, the same customs, the same fundamental laws, the same glories, the same tendencies and aspirations, and the same destinies. Of all those properties, which constitutes essentially a nationality? In the first place, the blood, race, or origin; in the second place, the language. The other qualities are nothing but the consequences of the other two, most specifically of the first.[10]

The chief objective of the Basque nationalist movement, historically, was to revive and defend the purity of the "Euskeran race" from contamination by *maketos* (Spaniards).[11] Language, by serving as a barrier to the mixing of the two groups, was largely seen as an instrument to achieve these goals. Catalán nationalist ideologies tended, instead, to define Catalán national identity in terms of language and culture.[12] Hence, "Catalanism" could be preserved and enhanced not only by the continued use of Catalán in daily life, but also by teaching the immigrant community the Catalán language and customs. In general terms, then, the formal ideology of Catalán nationalism favored (or at least posed no hindrance to) the integration of immigrants, while early Basque nationalism was overtly exclusionary. Arana was well aware of this difference between the two. He wrote:

> Catalán politics ... consists in attracting to it other Spaniards, whereas the Vizcayan program is to reject from itself all Spaniards as foreigners. ... The Catalans want all Spaniards living in their region to speak Catalán; for us it would be ruin if the *maketos* resident in our territory speak Euskera. Why? Because purity of race is, like language, one of the bases of the Vizcayan banner. So long as there is a good grammar and a good dictionary, language can be restored even though no one speaks it. Race, once lost, cannot be resuscitated.[13]

Although there continue to be traditionalist Sabiniano factions (followers of the party's founder) within the PNV, the early emphasis on "race" as the central defining characteristic of Basque identity has been considerably muted in the ideologies of contemporary Basque nationalist groups, especially the more radical of these. In the past several years, both Basque and Catalán nationalist leaders have often expressed the desire to prevent the division of their respective societies into two hostile communities of natives and immigrants, and have shown an awareness of the potential problems for Castilian-speaking immigrants posed by the granting of regional autonomy. Accordingly, nationalist leaders have more and more frequently mentioned voluntaristic criteria of membership in the Basque or Catalán community—the "willingness" to be Basque or Catalán—rather than such primordial "traits" as birthplace, ancestry, or language usage.[14] A member of the Euskadi Buru Batzar (the national executive committee of the PNV), for example, said in an interview in 1978, "To be Basque . . . is a matter of self-definition, of self-designation." In a more emphatic and exclusionary manner, Heribert Barrera, leader of the Esquerra Republicana de Catalunya (and, as of 1980, president of the Generalitat) stated: "He who merely lives and works in Catalunya is not Catalán; only he who has the will to be Catalán. The others are strangers."[15]

The slightly greater degree of identification with the region among immigrants in Euskadi (table 38), compared with their counterparts in Catalunya and the greater frequency with which native Basques mentioned "living and working in the region" as opposed to birthplace as the criterion for group membership suggest—in a reversal of the implications of traditional Basque and Catalán nationalist ideologies—that the native-immigrant cleavage might be bridged more successfully in the Basque area. This, in turn, might lead one to expect that Basque nationalist groups would be more effective than Catalán parties in gaining the support of the immigrant community on behalf of nationalist goals.

The likelihood of greater political integration (or of lesser polarization) in the Basque region is given further support by native and immigrant group preferences concerning language policy. There were fewer differences of opinion in 1979 between natives and immigrants regarding the exclusive use of Euskera as the language of instruction in schools. Immigrants in Catalunya were more likely than any of the other groups to prefer Castilian monolingualism and to reject either bilingualism or the exclusive use of the regional language. Similar patterns were found in response to a question concerning the obligatory study of the regional language (as opposed to the mandatory learning of Castilian or both). Regional differences were smaller, however, with regard to whether or not mayors should be obliged to know the regional language: 52 percent of native Catalans said "yes," in contrast to 33 percent of those born elsewhere. In Euskadi, the difference between the two communities was slighter: 48 percent of native Basques said that mayors should be required to know Euskera, as compared with 34 percent of the immigrant group.[16]

The critical question of regional autonomy, however, produced far greater polarization of opinion between natives and immigrants in Euskadi (fig. 20). Three times as many of those born in the Basque country as those born outside the region expressed a preference for outright independence. Almost twice as many immigrants as natives favored a centralized state. In contrast, the distributions of opinion among immigrants and natives in Catalunya with regard to autonomy were virtually identical. These findings, together with the far greater degree of differentiation in Euskadi between the two groups' national loyalties (the somewhat stronger attachment to the region of Basque compared with Catalán immigrants, notwithstanding), suggest that efforts by Basque political elites to mobilize the immigrant community on behalf of *explicitly* nationalist objectives might prove to be less effective than was initially supposed. The member of the Euskadi Buru Batzar who was earlier quoted as saying that "to be Basque is a matter of self-identification," also stated: "It [being Basque] is the acknowledgment of the right of self-determination for individuals themselves. . . . In addition, there are certain factors which we all share. . . . The most important of these, however, is the subjective demand or desire to be independent and the efforts expended in this struggle for independence."

The implications for regional politics of the relationship between birthplace and attitudes toward autonomy are not clear-cut. Insofar as the two regional party systems were internally divided on the question of autonomy, the Basque party system would be the more likely

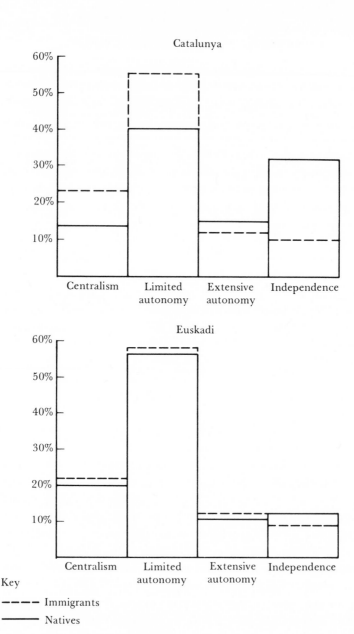

FIGURE 20. Distribution of Preferences Regarding Regional Autonomy Among Natives and Immigrants in Euskadi and Catalunya

of the two to reflect and mobilize the native-immigrant cleavage, rather than to diffuse it. One might suppose, therefore, that in the 1979 election Catalán nationalist groups, like the CiU and ERC, were in a better position to gain the support of immigrants than were radical Basque parties or even the more moderate PNV. The relative advantage of Catalán nationalist parties in this regard, however, may have been undermined insofar as statewide parties, whose ideological and class appeals better resonated with immigrant workers, *also* identified themselves with nationalist aspirations.

The general point to be made here is that the presence of cultural and linguistic minorities introduced considerable complexity and division in Euskadi and Catalunya, societies in which even the native-born were often in substantial disagreement over center-periphery issues. The effects of the immigrant presence on their politics and party systems, moreover, were variable, and depended (as we shall see later) on the particular interactions among the native-immigrant cleavage, ideological and class-based divisions, and the stances and strategies adopted by competing political elites in each region.

THE ATTITUDINAL
STRUCTURE OF MICRONATIONALISM

The critical question of regional autonomy generated considerable division in Euskadi, Catalunya, and Galicia, as well as in Spain as a whole. (See table 40.) Although limited autonomy was supported by a plurality of Basques and Gallegos, and by a majority of Catalans, large numbers of people in all three regions expressed preferences for the two extreme positions: a centralized state or independence. Polarization was most pronounced in the Basque region, and least in Catalunya. Birthplace and language usage, as we have seen, were strongly associated with views regarding autonomy. But, as one observer of micronationalist phenomena stated, "What is fundamentally involved in such (ethnic) conflict is that divergence of basic identity which manifests itself in the us-them syndrome."[17] Greater identification with the regional group than with Spain was strongly related to preferences for extensive autonomy or independence in all three regions (and among immigrants as well as the native-born in Euskadi and Catalunya). The association between the two was especially pronounced in Euskadi, as the data in table 40 indicate. A majority of those claiming to feel "Basque only" stated a preference for regional independence; only 6 percent favored centralism. The relationship was weakest in Galicia. Although those who identified solely with the region were almost six times as likely to favor extensive autonomy or independence than were those who felt "Spanish" or "more Spanish," Gallego regionalists were rather evenly divided in their views: 20 percent favored centralism, and 28 percent preferred independence. Thus, in Galicia, a sense of exclusive attachment to the region was not translated into preferences for regional self-government to the same extent as in Euskadi and Catalunya. One other important point should be drawn from the data in table 40. Those who felt equally Spanish and Basque or Catalán, a minority within their respective regions, were most in favor of limited autonomy. Such divided loyalties would seem, therefore, to have predisposed individuals to adopt the most moderate stance regarding the structure of the Spanish state.

When the feeling of belonging to a distinct minority is coupled with a sense of group discrimination—thus implying not merely mutually acknowledged differences but perceived inequalities—one might expect that the desire for regional autonomy would increase considerably. In addition to being subject to political, cultural, and linguistic discrimination, nationalists in all three regions have claimed that each has suffered from economic discrimination, either as a result of governmental policies or as a consequence of the actions of industrial and financial elites. The underdevelopment of Galicia, which led to the emigration from Spain of one out of every eight Gallegos between 1962 and 1974, has been attributed to long-standing governmental neglect, to external control of its resources and factories, and to extraction of capital for investment in more industrial regions.[18] In the instances of the far more developed regions of Euskadi and Catalunya, nationalists have often argued that, despite their wealth, these two

TABLE 40
SUBJECTIVE NATIONAL IDENTIFICATION BY PREFERENCES
FOR REGIONAL AUTONOMY BY REGION (in percentages)

Subjective national identification	Centralism	Limited autonomy	Extensive autonomy	Indepen- dence	N
		Stance toward regional autonomy			
Euskadi					
"Spanish" or "more Spanish"	36	56	7	1	(220)
50-50	15	62	13	10	(199)
More regional than Spanish	9	42	24	25	(83)
Regional only	6	27	16	51	(275)
Total region	17	45	14	24	(777)
Catalunya					
"Spanish" or "more Spanish"	39	54	5	3	(410)
50-50	16	69	10	5	(382)
More regional than Spanish	9	45	26	20	(126)
Regional only	7	45	11	37	(161)
Total region	22	57	10	11	(1079)
Galicia					
"Spanish" or "more Spanish"	48	43	7	2	(102)
50-50	39	53	6	2	(193)
More regional than Spanish	6	56	32	6	(57)
Regional only	20	29	23	28	(104)
Total region	33	46	13	9	(456)
Spain as a whole	33	51	9	7	(4984)

regions suffered from economic discrimination at the hands of the state because of the inegalitarian impact of Spanish taxation and spending policies. Although such claims have been the subject of considerable debate and supportive evidence is ambiguous, nationalist leaders have long maintained that revenues derived from the Basque area and Catalunya have far exceeded the value of public services received by them.[19] An official of the CDC (the dominant party in the CiU coalition), for example, said in an interview in 1978 that one way by which the party attempted to gain supporters was by claiming that

there is a tremendous negative balance of taxes over expenditures by the state in this region. Overall, the net loss in this balance of taxes over expenditures amounts to 10 percent of the net wealth of Catalunya. We are in favor of improving economic and social conditions in Extremadura and Andalucía. But we are against working hard through our own labors only to finance high living by bureaucrats in Madrid.

Not surprisingly, given the discriminatory policies of the Franquist regime and the efforts by nationalists to mobilize voters on the basis of perceptions of group disadvantage, a sense of unjust treatment of the regional group by other Spaniards was found to varying degrees in all three regions in 1979: 56 percent of respondents in Galicia, 48 percent in Euskadi (58 percent of native Basques), and 24 percent in Catalunya (30 percent of the native-born) said that their group was treated unfairly.[20] Those who identified primarily or exclusively with the region were particularly likely to express a sense of group discrimination (65 percent in Euskadi and in Galicia and 45 percent in Catalunya). The expected relationship between a sense of group discrimination and a desire for extensive regional autonomy or independence was evident, however, only in Euskadi and Catalunya: those who felt disadvantaged were three times as likely to be *independentistas* as *centralistas* in the Basque region, and twice as likely to be so in Catalunya. In Galicia, among those who said there was discrimination against the regional group, 29 percent favored a centralized state, and only 12 percent independence.

The weaker association in Galicia between a sense of group discrimination and preferences for regional self-government may be due to the fact that there was no widespread belief among Gallegos in general, and among those who felt discriminated against in particular, that autonomy would result in a discernible reduction in the degree of inequality between rich and poor regions. Only 33 percent of all respondents in Galicia said that autonomy would reduce such inequality. Among those who felt that there was discrimination, 40 percent believed that autonomy would be beneficial in this regard, a proportion only slightly higher than the 34 percent of those who perceived no discrimination. This skepticism on the part of Gallegos about the economic benefits to be derived from autonomy was based, undoubtedly, on the same sort of reasoning that led the Spanish left to voice its concern in this regard. With autonomy, the poorer regions might experience economic losses, given that they would be more dependent on their own limited resource base and that the central government would be constrained, due to its own reduction in revenues, in providing compensatory funding to the less developed areas of the country. Irrespective of the accuracy of such perceptions, what appeared to be lacking in Galicia, at least in 1979, was an important element for mass mobilization in support of nationalist goals—the widespread expectation that the achievement of regional autonomy would satisfy long-standing grievances based on economic disadvantage.[21]

As we have seen, in all three regions, a sense of group discrimination and, in particular, self-identification as a Basque, Catalán, or Gallego were translated, but to varying degrees, into preferences for autonomy or independence. These two attitudes were also positively related to other micronationalist orientations—preferences regarding regional language policy, feelings toward ETA, and views concerning the appropriate governmental response to the continuation of terrorism in Spain. At the same time, the varying extent to which these different orientations were linked to one another to form a coherent attitudinal structure of micronationalism demonstrated, once again, that politicization of the center-periphery cleavage was most pronounced in Euskadi and least in Galicia.

Not unexpectedly, Basques, Catalans, and Gallegos tended, in comparison with other Spaniards, to be more in favor of the exclusive use of the regional language in schools and by elected officials or, at the least, of cooficiality of the regional language and Castilian. Basques, in particular, were less hostile toward ETA and more favorably disposed toward the government's acceptance of terrorist demands or negotiation. At the same time, the regional populations, like the Spanish electorate as a whole, were divided in their opinions about these issues. As one might expect, those in the regions who adopted these micronationalist stances were more likely to identify themselves primarily or exclusively with the region, to perceive group discrimination, and to prefer extensive autonomy or outright independence than were those who held opposing views. A substantial majority of *independentistas* in all three regions, for example, said that should terrorism continue the government ought to either accede to the demands of terrorists or negotiate with them. In contrast, a majority of both *centralistas* and limited autonomists favored restoring order but within the guidelines provided by the Constitution.[22]

There are additional examples of the linkages between attitudes related to the regional question, but, to summarize our findings, the correlations among all such items for the three regions are presented in table 41. Only a few points need be mentioned about these data. First, in all but a small number of instances, the various indicators of the center-periphery cleavage were related. Because such correlations, when applied to survey data, tend to understate the strength of relationships, most of the links between the various attitudes were stronger than is apparent. Second, regionalist attitudes tended to cohere most strongly in Euskadi and least in Galicia (although in Galicia the relationships were by no means weak). The somewhat "looser" associations in Galicia derived primarily from the fact that identification with the region was not as readily translated into overtly political orientations regarding the regional question, and a sense of group discrimination was translated hardly at all. This overall slippage in support for regionalist demands among those who felt a sense of strong regional identity and of shared grievances helps to explain the relative weakness of support for nationalist parties in Galicia, compared with that in Catalunya and especially in the Basque country. This slippage requires some explanation, however, as does the intensity of micronationalist sentiments in Euskadi.

One may, to a certain extent, attribute differences in the politicization of the center-periphery cleavage to varying historical traditions of regional self-government. Both Euskadi and Catalunya had,

TABLE 41
CORRELATION MATRIX AMONG ATTITUDES RELATED TO THE REGIONAL QUESTION

	Attitude on autonomy	Sense of group discrimination	Language of instruction	Learning of regional language	Language of mayor	Feeling toward ETA	Government action on terrorism
Euskadi							
Subjective national identification	.57	.24	.40	.34	.32	.45	.44
Attitude on autonomy		.30	.35	.37	.23	.47	.43
Sense of group discrimination			.24	.19	.18	.26	.25
Language of instruction				.38	.21	.24	.37
Learning of regional language					.20	.23	.30
Language of mayor						.19	.27
Feeling toward ETA							.37
Catalunya							
Subjective national identification	.44	.27	.50	.42	.40	.19	.31
Attitude on autonomy		.22	.25	.34	.16	.21	.45
Sense of group discrimination			.15	.09	.26	.19	.14
Language of instruction				.55	.33	.21	.28
Learning of regional language					.30	.11	.27
Language of mayor						.02	.10
Feeling toward ETA							.29
Galicia							
Subjective national identification	.38	.18	.31	.37	.31	.36	.27
Attitude on autonomy		.15	.33	.35	.24	.46	.38
Sense of group discrimination			.02	.02	.12	.05	.14
Language of instruction				.43	.21	.33	.30
Learning of regional language					.17	.37	.24
Language of mayor						.16	.07
Feeling toward ETA							.46

Note: Figures are Pearson r simple correlations. In Euskadi, the correlation analysis was based on $N = 541$; in Catalunya, on $N = 865$; and in Galicia, on $N = 354$.

as recently as the period of the Second Republic, experienced some modicum of autonomy. Regional institutions associated with autonomy, like the Basque *fueros* and the Catalán Generalitat, served as symbols for renewed mobilization in support of autonomy even before the transition to democracy had begun. Because Galicia has been an integral part of the Castilian state for centuries, such historical memories are absent in Galicia.[23]

One might nevertheless have expected, following Hechter's thesis on internal colonialism,[24] that the relative economic and social underdevelopment of Galicia, together with the prevalence of diffuse regionalist sentiments and perceptions of group disadvantage, would prove to be fertile soil for micronationalist orientations and movements. But the comparison of such phenomena in Spain proves otherwise.[25] In direct contrast to Hechter's argument, an important explanation of the relative weakness of micronationalist movements in Galicia is its level of development. In contrast with Euskadi and Catalunya, Galicia has historically been a region of emigration by the more dynamic segments of the working and lower-middle classes. This, together with the integration of the regional socioeconomic and political elites into the dominant Castilian culture, served to deprive Galicia of both a well-organized leadership and a mass base for nationalist movements. Further impeding mass mobilization are the geographical dispersion of the largely agricultural population into small, not easily accessible villages, the poorly developed communications and transportation infrastructures, and the low level of education in the rural sector of society. These characteristics of underdevelopment have facilitated the perpetuation of *caciquismo* which, in turn, reinforces the relative lack of politicization at the mass level, especially among the agricultural poor.[26] In both Euskadi and Catalunya, a high level of social and economic development has served to promote mass mobilization around center-periphery issues, not least of all because it has made them magnets for immigration from other parts of Spain, thus resulting in the creation of culturally divided societies.[27]

A subjective component of socioeconomic modernization may

also play a role in accounting for regional differences. According to a 1981 interview with an AP leader from Galicia:

> In the Basque country, they are conscious of having come to be the social vanguard of Spain. In Galicia, in contrast, the great majority of the population have the sense of being the tail end of Spain. Thus . . . in Galicia, rural people commonly speak in Gallego among themselves, but when I speak with them, for example, I who am a gentleman from Madrid, they try to speak in Castilian, and they speak Castilian poorly . . . they are ashamed of speaking Gallego. The Basques, in comparison, don't know Basque, yet they have contrived a language in order to appear Basque, because they are proud of their language.

A similar contrast might be made between Gallegos and Catalans.

But, if traditions of self-government as well as socioeconomic development have facilitated the politicization of regionalist sentiments in both Euskadi and Catalunya, other explanations must be sought for the greater coherence and particular intensity of micronationalist attitudes in the Basque country. One reason often suggested by elite respondents was the pervasive sense of a culture and language threatened by extinction, due to both the assimilationist policies of the state and the heterogeneity introduced into Basque society by the immigrant presence. In the words of a UCD official in Guipúzcoa in 1981: "There is greater anguish in their [Basque] demands, because there are greater threats to the survival of their culture. . . . If you believe that Basque culture is most incompatible with the Spanish, then this exacerbates the sense of injury in the community."

Catalans, perhaps even more than Basques, perceive their regional language to be the crux of their national identity. But since Catalán is considerably more thriving a language than Euskera—there exists a substantial volume of literature in Catalán and virtually all native Catalans and a sizable segment of immigrants in the region know the language—its preservation, unlike that of Euskera, is not seriously in doubt. The Basque language, in contrast, has been declining in use over the past millenium. Historically, it was never used as a language of governmental administration, even when the region enjoyed considerable autonomy from the Spanish state.[28] Basque literature is by no means as extensive as Catalán;[29] and only a minority of the native-born and a miniscule portion of immigrants in Euskadi claim to speak the language.

Still another explanation of the differing degrees to which the center-periphery cleavage has become politicized in the three regions has to do with the social and ideological bases of support for micronationalism, as well as with the relative size of those social and ideological segments of the electorate holding pro-autonomist views.

THE BASES OF SUPPORT
FOR REGIONAL AUTONOMY

The dominant regional parties from the turn of the twentieth century until the demise of the Second Republic—the PNV and the Catalán Lliga—are widely believed to have drawn their support from the ideologically conservative, middle and upper socioeconomic strata. The urban working class, in contrast, are thought to have given its support to the traditionally highly centralist Socialist party and, in Catalunya, to anarchosyndicalist movements as well.[30] Since the 1930s, a major realignment in the socioeconomic and political bases of support for nationalist objectives has taken place in all three regions, but this transformation has occurred to varying degrees and in differing contexts, further contributing to regional differences in the intensity of micronationalism, especially between Galicia, on one hand, and Euskadi and Catalunya, on the other. Micronationalism is no longer a pronouncedly middle-class phenomenon. In Euskadi and Catalunya, the relationships between occupational status and preferences regarding regional autonomy were positive, but relatively weak. In Galicia, there was no relationship whatsoever between the two.[31] A few points should, nevertheless, be made about the distribution of opinion among occupational groups, because of its possible bearing on the class basis of support for different regionalist and statewide parties (table 42). Upper-middle and middle-level occupational strata stood out somewhat, because of their greater support for a level of self-government beyond that of limited autonomy. Unskilled workers in Euskadi and Catalunya and farmers in all three

TABLE 42

MEAN POSITION ON REGIONAL AUTONOMY BY OCCUPATIONAL STATUS
OF RESPONDENT OR OF HEAD OF HOUSEHOLD IN EUSKADI, CATALUNYA, AND GALICIA

Status level[a]	Euskadi			Catalunya			Galicia
	Total regional population	Natives (N)	Immigrants (N)	Total regional population	Natives (N)	Immigrants (N)	Total regional population (N)
	2.45	2.64 (507)	2.10 (283)	2.13	2.16 (726)	2.07 (393)	2.01 (418)
I	2.48	2.66 (51)	2.05 (20)	2.08	2.11 (80)	2.01 (39)	2.02 (64)
II	2.61	2.84 (139)	2.15 (69)	2.27	2.29 (162)	2.22 (70)	2.09 (91)
III	2.58	2.70 (95)	2.26 (37)	2.26	2.28 (122)	2.21 (39)	2.05 (92)
IV	2.35	2.54 (58)	1.94 (27)	2.24	2.26 (95)	2.17 (40)	2.02 (18)
V	2.17	2.28 (13)	2.00 (9)	1.83	1.87 (53)	1.60 (10)	1.83 (60)
VI	2.42	2.64 (105)	2.14 (81)	2.08	2.04 (140)	2.14 (102)	1.92 (56)
VII	2.04	2.13 (48)	1.93 (39)	1.95	2.04 (74)	1.88 (93)	2.11 (37)

Note: The higher the mean (which can range from one to four), the more the group favors more extensive degrees of autonomy.
[a]Status levels are:

I   Entrepreneurs, professionals, large landowners, high-level public and private executives
II   Mid-level public and private employees, technical professions
III   Owners, small businessmen, independent artisans
IV   Low-level white collar workers, sales and supervisory personnel
V   Small farmers
VI   Skilled workers in agriculture and industry
VII   Unskilled workers in agriculture and industry.

regions also deviated somewhat from the norm, because of their weaker support for autonomy. Thus, though the desire for regional autonomy was no longer a view isolated to middle strata, these occupational groups tended to hold more extreme views regarding self-government.

The relative lack of support among workers in Euskadi and Catalunya for more extensive levels of autonomy might plausibly be attributed to the fact that immigrants were more likely to occupy lower status positions than were the native-born. In Euskadi, 45 percent of immigrants, compared with 29 percent of natives, were either skilled or unskilled workers. In Catalunya, the relationship between occupational status and place of birth was even stronger: 50 percent of immigrants versus 30 percent of natives were manual workers. The low level of support for extensive autonomy or independence among unskilled workers and among the skilled in Euskadi was, to a certain degree, attributable to the large number of immigrants among them. Nonetheless, even within the indigenous population, unskilled workers tended to be among the groups least favorably disposed toward autonomy. Immigrant skilled workers in Catalunya, however, were slightly more supportive of self-government than were their native-born counterparts.

There has also been a reversal, at least at the mass level, of the traditional link between clericalism and nationalism in the Basque region. In Catalunya and Galicia (in which micronationalism historically has been a secular phenomenon), as well as in Euskadi, nonpracticing Catholics were far more likely to prefer extensive autonomy or independence than were religious voters (fig. 21). The relationship between secularism and pro-autonomist sentiments was strongest in Galicia, but, because this close association occurred in a society in which less than one-third of the electorate claimed to be nonpracticing, the support given by this group to more radical versions of self-government meant that their views counted for very little. The secular basis of micronationalism was weakest in Euskadi. This reflects the fact that historically the Church and religious persons were at the forefront of Basque nationalism. A party official, interviewed in Guipúzcoa in June 1979, said:

The Church has been the spiritual reserve of nationalism. All of the current boom in nationalism, including that of ETA and ultranationalist forces that support violence, are heirs of a tradition that was fundamentally preserved by religious persons in seminaries.... Modern priests have always been nationalistic, and under the dictatorship were those who preserved and promoted Basque culture. In Guipúzcoa, the nationalist movement was, in large part, fomented by the Church.

Indeed, at the time of its founding, the PNV's platform stated as one of the party's objectives the establishment of Euskadi "with the complete and unconditional subordination of the political to the religious, of the State to the Church."[32] Religion no longer plays such a preeminent role in the party's ideology, but the PNV retains a significant Christian democratic component and it continues to be affiliated with the Christian Democratic International. Although in our survey the nonreligious segment of the Basque population was most supportive of extreme degrees of autonomy, practicing Catholics in Euskadi, unlike their counterparts in Galicia, by no means rejected such options, and, indeed, 18 percent claimed to be *independentistas*. Overall, the weak relationship in Euskadi between religiosity and opinion regarding the structure of the state would suggest that the secular-clerical cleavage would have a discernible impact primarily on electoral competition between the PNV and the *abertzale* left: insofar as there existed a Basque nationalist party associated, at least historically, with clericalism and widespread support for autonomy among practicing Catholics, there would be no need for believers to "cross over" and vote for center-right Spanish parties.

A rupture of another sort has taken place in the bases of support for micronationalism. In 1979 the more extreme demands for autonomy were not being made by those who personally experienced the short period of regional autonomy during the Second Republic, but rather by those who came to political maturity during the last years of the Franquist regime or during the transition to democracy.[33] (See fig. 22.) Because there were strong relationships in all three regions between age and religiosity, the association between secularism and pro-autonomy orientations may be due to the fact that nonpracticing voters tended to be young. In examining the relationships among age, religiosity, and preferences toward regional self-government, it is clear

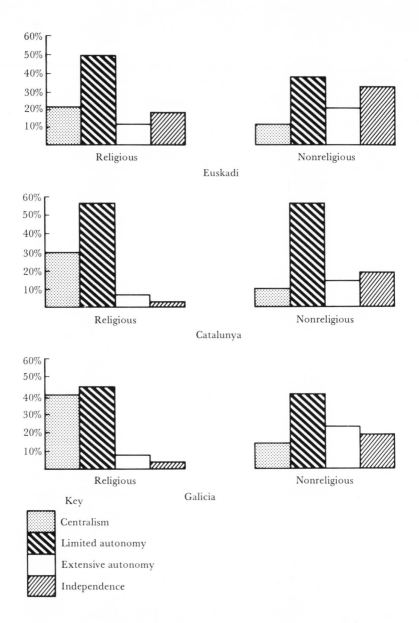

FIGURE 21. Opinions Concerning the Structure of the State Among Religious and Nonreligious Segments of Regional Populations

that, though part of the relationship between religiosity and these preferences was attributable to the age factor, whether a respondent was a practicing or nonpracticing Catholic had an independent effect on his or her views regarding autonomy.

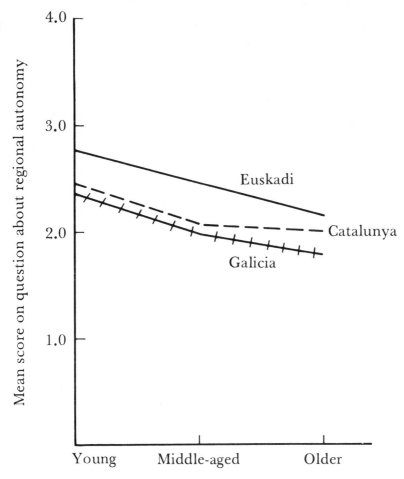

FIGURE 22.   Mean Position on Regional Autonomy by Age in Euskadi, Catalunya, and Galicia

Note: The higher the mean, the more the group favored more extreme degrees of autonomy.

One final but important transformation that has also occurred is the reversal of the historical ideological underpinnings of micronationalism. At the mass level, aspirations for regional autonomy were clearly associated with leftist or center-left political beliefs. As the mean scores of self-placement on the ten-point left-right continuum indicate, *centralistas* either placed themselves at the center of the political spectrum or, in the case of Galicia, to the right of center (table 43). *Independentistas,* on the average, identified themselves as being considerably to the left in their ideological predispositions. But even those favoring limited autonomy tended to be slightly left of center in their political leanings. Overall, the relationship between general ideological tendencies and attitudes toward autonomy was quite strong and uniformly greater than those between autonomist preferences, on one hand, and age and religiosity, on the other.

Whether as a cause of, or as a response to, this change at the mass level, a similar realignment has come about among political parties. The formerly conservative PNV has in the past several years taken more progressive stances, while recently emerged regionalist groups (such as the Catalán CDC) have adopted either social democratic programs or are avowedly Marxist (such as certain elements in Herri Batasuna and Euskadiko Ezkerra). At the same time, the formerly antiregionalist Socialist and Communist parties have come to identify themselves with autonomist (but not separatist) sentiments. As we have seen, the two center-right parties, in contrast, were less enthusiastic in their advocacy of decentralization.

TABLE 43

MEAN POSITION ON TEN-POINT LEFT-RIGHT
SCALE BY PREFERENCES FOR REGIONAL
AUTONOMY IN EUSKADI, CATALUNYA, AND GALICIA

	Euskadi	Catalunya	Galicia
Centralism	5.5	5.5	6.2
Limited autonomy	4.4	4.3	5.1
Extensive autonomy	3.6	3.4	4.0
Independence	2.9	2.4	3.4

Although the ideological transformation of micronationalism has taken place in all three regions, it is congruent with the ideological climates of only Euskadi and Catalunya. As figure 23 shows, 55 percent of the Catalán and 54 percent of the Basque electorates identified themselves as being left of center, and only 9 and 8 percent, respectively, claimed to be on the right. Given these distributions of opinion and the identification of the Socialist and Communist parties with autonomist aspirations, it is not surprising that in these two regions leftist statewide and nationalist parties enjoyed a considerably greater degree of success in the 1979 election than did Spanish parties of the center-right and that, furthermore, there was substantial fragmentation of support for these political forces.

In marked contrast to Basques and Catalans, Gallegos were decidedly moderate or conservative in their ideological leanings. Only 35 percent identified themselves as being left of center. Thus, the hegemony of center-right groups in the 1979 election is not at all surprising, but the dominance of statewide center-right parties was reinforced by two factors: the center-right tendencies of those who supported limited autonomy, and the absence of nationalist parties

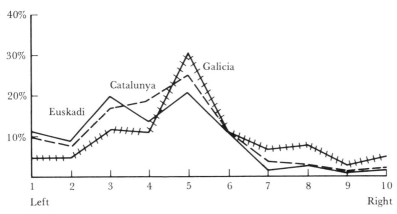

FIGURE 23. Percentages of Regional Populations on a Ten-Point Left-Right Scale

located in that portion of the political spectrum. As a Gallego AP deputy to the Cortes said in a 1979 interview:

> Nationalism is not politically represented in Galicia as it is in Catalunya and the Basque region, where the people can vote nationalist and also according to their ideology. Here, the one who wants to vote nationalist has to go to a specific ideology, because neither in the center, nor on the right, nor even including the Socialist party . . . is there nationalism. Hence, many people have to make an ideological leap in order to place their vote with a Gallego party.

This cogent explanation for the lack of support for nationalist parties in Galicia and, implicitly, for the presence of such support in Euskadi and Catalunya points to the importance of other determinants of regional differences in the politicization of the center-periphery cleavage, apart from the nature and bases of support for micronationalist orientations. These factors concern the political parties themselves and the interaction between elite and mass-level partisan divisions.

THE CENTER-PERIPHERY
CLEAVAGE: PARTIES AND VOTERS

The center-periphery cleavage was a major, if not the most important, source of partisan division in all three regions in the 1979 election. In none of the three regions, however, was the battle line clearly drawn between those who wanted to maintain a centralized state and those who favored autonomy: in the campaign, all major statewide parties—from the AP to the PCE—supported regional autonomy, notwithstanding their pejorative portrayal by regional political elites as *centralistas* or *sucursalistas* (branch offices). Leaders of all four major statewide parties in Euskadi, Catalunya, and Galicia tended, moreover, to be more sympathetic to regionalist sentiments and demands than their fellow party leaders elsewhere, not only because they had to be responsive if they hoped to compete successfully with regional parties, but also because they were members of the particular regional group whose electoral support they sought.

Nonetheless, competition between regional and Spanish parties, between more autonomist and less autonomist statewide groups, and between more radical and more moderate nationalist forces meant that in the three regions the 1979 election was a multifaceted conflict with regard to the center-periphery cleavage. It involved a complex array of choices offered to the voters concerning the nature, degree, and manner of implementation of autonomy. The results of the election demonstrated that the response of the voters to these choices was equally complex and differed across the regions. The divergent outcomes of the 1979 election and, more fundamentally, the differing regional party systems themselves can be explained by three sets of factors: (1) the nature and degree of polarization at both the elite and mass levels with respect to various dimensions of the regional question; (2) the extent to which partisan divisions coincided with other political and socioeconomic cleavages; and (3) the salience of the center-periphery cleavage, compared to the others, in voters' decisions.

POLITICAL PARTIES IN EUSKADI

The Basque party system in 1979 was structured by the center-periphery cleavage and reflected divisions over the regional question to a far greater extent than either the Catalán or Gallego party system. Basque nationalist parties became increasingly dominant between the 1977 and 1979 general elections: their proportion of the vote grew from 36.5 to 50.6 percent. The PNV garnered a majority of the votes going to regional parties and a plurality of the total votes cast in each of the two elections (30 and 27.6 percent, respectively), but support for the more extreme nationalist groups increased substantially during this time. In the first contest Euskadiko Ezkerra obtained 6.5 percent; in 1979 (in which Herri Batasuna fielded candidates for the first time), 23 percent of the vote went to more extreme groups.[34] Thus, there was no hegenomic regional party in Euskadi.

The most startling feature of the increase in votes for the *abertzale* left was the degree of support given to the more extreme of the two, Herri Batasuna, which was founded in 1978 as a coalition of avowedly separatist and Marxist-Leninist groups.[35] It advocated a "no" vote in the constitutional referendum and active abstention in the autonomy statute referendum. It did so, according to HB leaders, because neither document acknowledged the right of Basque self-determination or considered Navarra as an integral part of the Basque nation (which they defined as consisting of Alava, Guipúzcoa, and Vizcaya, in addition to Navarra and the three Basque departments in France). Although Herri Batasuna has fielded candidates (some of whom were in prison) in all elections since March 1979, its elected representatives have refused to take their positions, either in central or regional governmental bodies. Moreover, even though the party presently bases its strategy on political struggle, it "does not," according to HB leader Francisco Letemendía, "rule out any form of struggle which could bring about an advance for the people."[36] Thus, violence is not eschewed as a means of achieving its goals and, indeed, in 1979 HB was reputedly connected with ETA *militar*, the more extreme and violent wing of the Basque terrorist organization.

Unlike Herri Batasuna, Euskadiko Ezkerra (EE) urged a "yes" vote on the forthcoming autonomy statue, and its elected officials have played active roles in parliamentary affairs both within Euskadi and in Madrid.[37] Although EE leaders believed that the existing representative bodies represented "neither the liberty nor the authentic democracy for which we are struggling," nonetheless, they regarded them as a "valid tool with which to bring about a progressive development of the statute, in order to improve conditions of working life, and to achieve Basque industrial modernization."[38] Illustrative of the difference between the two *abertzale* left groups was EE's motto during the 1979 electoral campaign: "To construct Euskadi brick by brick; and not by bricks."[39] Euskadiko Ezkerra and Herri Batasuna were alike, however, insofar as they both called for a "no" vote on the Constitution, advocated obligatory learning of the Basque language, total amnesty for political prisoners, the removal of Spanish police forces from Basque territory, and support for the *conciertos económicos*. And both groups sought to gain the support of the immigrant as well as the indigenous Basque working class, whom they saw as being equally exploited by capitalists and by the "forces of oppression" controlled by the state. Thus, despite its more moderate and pragmatic stance, regional autonomy for Euskadiko Ezkerra was only a short-term goal: "Today we fight for the autonomy statute and tomorrow we will do it for the sovereignty and self-determination of Euskadi."[40]

The most moderate of the Basque nationalist parties with respect to both regional and left-right issues was the Partido Nacional Vasco (PNV). It was founded in 1893 by Sabino de Arana as a nationalist, clerical, and bourgeois party, and it competed in provincial elections for the first time in 1898. During the Second Republic, the PNV was the most successful of Basque regional groups. Thus, it has a long history as the most important Basque party and, as a result, is deeply rooted in Basque society—it views itself as both a party and a community (*partido-comunidad*).[41] Unlike HB and EE, the PNV did not feature demands during the 1979 campaign for the release and full pardon of ETA prisoners; though it regarded Navarra as part of the Basque country, it did not emphasize this claim during the campaign; and it opted, at least in the short term, for the coofficiality of Euskera and Castilian and for a free choice between the two as the language of instruction in schools. In general, the PNV sought to appeal to as many voters as possible by portraying itself as the sole Basque party capable of achieving in a responsible manner the "restoration" of Basque national and political identity. In an interview with a member of the Buru Batzar in 1978, he noted that the PNV tended to ignore all ideological appeals, other than those based on nationalism: "We are the spokesman for the national claims of our people. We are representative of an entire people, and not a spokesman for an ideological tendency. As a result, we really don't have an ideology. We have always attempted to attract to this party all those persons of varying ideological tendencies who are part of the Basque population."

At the same time, however, characterizations of the PNV by statewide parties as harboring separatist tendencies and, thus, as posing a serious threat to the legitimacy of the regime were frequently borne out by certain actions of the PNV and by statements made in interviews with PNV leaders. The PNV called for active abstention in the constitutional referendum, because it does not recognize the legal precedence of the *fueros*. According to PNV leader Carlos Garaikoetxea, later elected head of the Basque government, "Basque *foral* rights are fundamental rights, which at no time were granted by the state, but have always been consubstantial with the Basque people."[42] One PNV elite in a 1978 interview frankly stated that the party's long-range goal was "to reunify the Basque provinces so that we can join our brothers in France." A member of the Euskadi Buru Batzar affirmed this point in another interview: "The Basque nation consists of four Spanish provinces and three French provinces. We are very much aware, however, of the slight possibility of uniting this territory in the short term. Nevertheless, we are in the long run still in favor of this unification. We see this within the context of European unity." Nonetheless, he went on to say, "we are not *independentistas*."

The ambiguity of the PNV was also reflected in statements by elites concerning terrorism and ETA. A party official, when asked about terrorism in an interview in Guipúzcoa in 1979, angrily replied: "I remember perfectly French patriots who fought against Pétain. . . . Then, they were called terrorists. Well, the Vichy government spoke of terrorists. Today they are patriots. Hence, everything is very relative. They speak of the terrorism of ETA, but I would never speak of ETA terrorism." Another said in a 1978 interview, "We must bear in mind that ETA was born out of the violence of the Franco regime, but this very clearly is not a sufficient excuse for their present acts." Nevertheless, "As long as the Spanish state does not take effective and clear steps designed toward reversing discrimination against Basque culture, it will be very difficult for us to explain to ETA why they should lay down their guns." Ambivalence toward ETA may have stemmed from the ambiguity of long-range PNV goals or from internal divisions. It may also have derived, as Linz has suggested, from a sense of tolerance among older *peneuvistas* of their children's sympathy for or active involvement in more radical Basque organizations.[43] It should also be remembered that ETA was formed by a group of radical young PNV members who abandoned the party in July 1959.[44]

In sum, "For the three [Basque] parties, the question of independence continues to be a persistent backdrop, both as something to be achieved and a danger to be avoided."[45]

Statewide parties, not unexpectedly, were less autonomist than regional parties. They all favored limited autonomy, however, and were more sympathetic to Basque aspirations than were their counterparts in other parts of Spain. During the 1979 election, each Spanish party (with the exception of the UCD) ran under a regional party label—Partido Socialista de Euskadi, Partido Comunista de Euskadi, and Unión Foral del País Vasco (AP-CD)—in an attempt to present a regional image to voters. All made explicit efforts in the campaign to mobilize the support of the native population, although the two leftist parties were constrained in such attempts because of their fear of losing the votes of the immigrant working class whom they perceived to be their traditional base of support. All four parties were similar in their advocacy of the study of Euskera and Castilian in schools, although both the UCD and AP tended to emphasize the voluntary learning of the regional language.

Paradoxically, it was the two center-right parties, rather than the more autonomist PCE and PSOE, which favored the restoration of the *conciertos económicos*. Thus, in the case of the two leftist parties, concern over regional inequality within Spain as a whole curtailed their support for a critical aspect of Basque autonomy demands. At the same time, the two center-right parties' emphasis on maintaining the integral unity of Spain served to constrain their support for another essential feature of Basque nationalism, the *fueros*. These "historic rights" of the Basque people were perceived as implying the right of self-determination. As a UCD official said in an interview in Guipúzcoa in 1978: "We are in favor of equality of regions, but we reject the PNV's claim that this area has special historic rights. These historic rights have been superceded by the passage of history itself." Consequently, the same UCD respondent said that his party sought to "attract Basques who don't follow the *independentista* line of the PNV but who instead favor a more moderate autonomy," as well as to gain the support of former Alianza voters, and nonleftist immigrants. Coalición Democrática adopted a contradictory position with regard to the *fueros*. By calling itself Unión Foral del País Vasco, AP meant to suggest that it sought the "defense of the *fueros,* but all the while within the unity of Spain," according to an AP elite interviewed in Guipúzcoa in 1978. This explicitly contradictory stand might be explained by the Coalición's desire, mentioned by several party officials, to draw the votes of traditional Carlists, a group historically identified with support of the *fueros* against a centralized, liberal, and secular Spanish state.

POLITICAL PARTIES IN CATALUNYA

Unlike in the Basque provinces, in no election (with the exception of those for regional government bodies) did all regional parties combined gain even a plurality of votes in Catalunya. Regional party support, moreover, was far less fragmented than in Euskadi. The largest regional group received between 16 and 17 percent of the votes cast in the two general elections. (In 1977 this group was called the Pacte Democràtic per Catalunya (PDC), of which the CDC was the nucleus. In 1979, it ran under the label Convergència i Unió (CiU), and was a coalition comprised of Jordi Pujol's CDC and portions of the Christian democratic Unió Democràtica de Catalunya.)[46] Esquerra Republicana de Catalunya (ERC), founded in 1931 and one of the most important parties of the Second Republic and, under the current leadership of Heribert Barrera, more stridently nationalist than the CiU, only obtained 4.7 percent and 4.1 percent of the vote in the 1977 and 1979 elections, respectively. The separatist Catalán party, Bloc d'Esquerra d'Alliberament Nacional (BEAN), gained only minimal support (less than 2 percent of the vote). CiU did emerge with a plurality (28 percent) in the regional election of March 1980, thus besting the PSOE, which had previously been the plurality party, and the ERC increased its level of support to 9 percent. Still, statewide parties were predominant. What is striking about Catalunya, therefore, when compared with Euskadi, was the extensive degree of penetration achieved by statewide parties, particularly those of the left, despite widely held regional attachments and micronationalist views. This both reflected and contributed to the lesser degree of polarization of the Catalán party system, compared to the Basque.

The contrast between the two party systems may partially be explained by the histories, organizational characteristics, and images of statewide parties in Catalunya. Of the most important regional parties, only Esquerra Republicana de Catalunya has a history going back to the Second Republic, but it did not remain as well implanted in society during the Franquist era as did the PNV. The Communist party in Catalunya, the PSUC, however, operated in clandestinity throughout the Franquist years and emerged in the late 1960s as one of the most ardent advocates of Catalán autonomy. During negotiations over the Constitution, a PSUC leader, Jordi Solé Tura, was a leading spokesman (along with Convergència representatives) on behalf of regional self-government. Branches of statewide parties in Catalunya, moreover, have greater organizational autonomy compared with party branches elsewhere, including Euskadi. The epitome of such independence is the PSUC: though affiliated with the PCE, it is fully autonomous.[47] Finally, statewide parties in Catalunya have sought to strengthen their identities and electoral appeal by merging with distinctive regional groups. The Catalán branch of the PSOE, in comparison with the PSUC, was historically more closely tied to the statewide party, and its image was that of a Spanish rather than a regional political force. But in 1977 it formed an electoral alliance with regional socialist groups, and in July 1978 it merged with the PSC. By the 1979 election, members of the PSC dominated both the party organization and its leadership, and the party ran under the label PSC-PSOE.[48] Even the UCD in the 1979 election adopted the name Centristes de Catalunya and chose as head of the party a prominent Catalán regionalist, Anton Canyellas.

The moderation of contemporary Catalán nationalism, in comparison with that of the Basques, has also contributed to the lesser degree of polarization between regional and Spanish parties and to the ability of statewide political groups to mobilize widespread support among Catalán voters. The concept of transcendent historic rights, with their implication of national sovereignty, for example, has been muted in present-day Catalán nationalist rhetoric. Thus, although UCD officials on several occasions branded the Convergèn- cia and the Esquerra as separatist parties, there was little ambiguity, at least in statements made by CDC elites, about their desire for re- gional autonomy within the limits set by the Constitution. As a CDC elite respondent remarked in a 1978 interview:

> Catalán nationalism is fundamentally different from Basque national- ism. . . . There will never be an ETA associated with our movement. That is not our style. . . . The ideology of this party is a national ideol- ogy. But we do not want to tear Catalunya apart. We want to preserve our solidarity with other regions in Spain. We do not want to convert this region into another Ulster.

The lesser degree of polarization between Spanish and Catalán nationalist parties concerning the regional question was manifested at the time of the 1979 election in the substantial agreement among party leaders over the desirable scope and nature of autonomy. Even policy stands with respect to so important a dimension of Catalanism as language usage produced only mild partisan disagreement during the 1979 electoral campaign. ERC and CiU leaders, as one might ex- pect, were most in favor of the obligatory learning of Catalán by all, and ultimately of the use of Catalán as the exclusive language of in- struction. Sensitive to the problems this would pose for immigrants, however, they advocated a choice with regard to the language of in- struction, at least in the short term. This stand toward language pol- icy was explained at great length by an official of the CDC in an inter- view in 1978:

> We are in favor of teaching in Catalán because Catalán is the weaker of the two languages and needs to be protected. . . . Language is the key to one's community and national identity. But we have serious prob- lems with immigration within this region. Children of immigrants don't naturally speak Catalán, and there may be some difficulty when they enter school. But, I don't think that's a serious problem. My chil- dren did not know Castilian and were forced to learn Castilian in school in order to take courses. I would be in favor of a gradual change to teaching in Catalán. In my view, a monolingual policy is ideal, but we must take into consideration the presence of these immigrants.

PSUC and PSOE leaders also advocated the coofficial status of Catalán and Castilian, and the obligatory learning of Catalán at the primary level of education. Only the UCD stood out in opposition; though it favored the voluntary learning of Catalán, Castilian was given priority. A UCD respondent provided the following explanation: "We ought not to consider the Castilian languge as a foreign language as do some nationalists. . . . This is an aberration, and we ought not to accept it." Instead, he argued that Catalán should be taught and learned as a second language, like French or Italian.

In Catalunya, then, there were few substantial differences either between the two major regional political groups or between them and statewide parties with respect to the regional question. Regional parties tended, therefore, to make primarily symbolic appeals to the electorate by stressing their solely Catalanist character and by accusing Catalán branches of statewide parties of being *sucursalistas.* One of the campaign slogans of the Convergència, for example, was "Catalunya cannot be a dependency." In general, as we will show, partisan divisions concerning socioeconomic issues and ideological tendencies appeared to be more salient than those based on the center-periphery cleavage.

POLITICAL PARTIES IN GALICIA

The Gallego party system was the least politicized of the three with respect to the regional question. Gallego demands for regional autonomy were articulated during the 1979 campaign by a relatively moderate coalition, Unidade Galega (UG), which included both socialist and center-left regional parties; more extreme Gallego nationalism was voiced by the leftist Bloque Nacional Popular Gallego (BNPG).[49] There were no Gallego political forces at the center or to the right of center where, as we have seen, the vast majority of Gallegos placed themselves on the political spectrum. In the 1977 parliamentary election, support for UG and BNPG was rather evenly divided, but amounted to only about 4 percent of votes cast in the region. Two years later, support for the two groups increased, but they still gained only 11.3 percent of the total vote. In neither election did Gallego regional parties gain representation in the Cortes.

Statewide parties of the center-right, particularly the UCD, emerged with a clear majority of votes and seats.

For the most part, there were few differences between Unidade Galega on one hand and the Communist and Socialist parties on the other with respect to regional autonomy. All three took the position that Galicia should obtain a degree of self-government equal to that proposed for Euskadi and Catalunya. All three advocated the coofficiality of Gallego and Castilian and bilingualism in the school system. The stated long-term objective of UG, however, was the creation of a federal Spanish state and, in the case of the BNPG, a federal Europe in which Galicia would be a member state.

The stands taken by center-right statewide party elites toward regional autonomy ranged from ambiguity on the part of the UCD to serious reservation by AP. In an interview in Pontevedra in 1978, a UCD provincial-level official summarized his party's position succinctly: "Each member of the Cortes has his own personal views. Some are for it, others against it." A high-ranking member of AP, interviewed in 1979, took a decidedly negative view: "In Galicia, there is no popular nationalism, but a nationalism of an intellectual elite . . . which, to the extent that it is concerned with the defense of Gallego culture and language . . . is splendid." He then proceeded to criticize political autonomy for Galicia or for any other region of Spain because, in his view, it would lead to the disintegration of the state.

The point on which all party elites agreed was the difficulty of mobilizing the Gallego population behind either regional or class issues. Indeed, the rate of abstention in the March 1979 election was the highest in all of Spain. Slightly more than 50 percent of the Gallego electorate did not vote.[50] All elite respondents mentioned as factors responsible for this the dispersal of the agricultural population into over 40 thousand physically isolated communities, its lack of education and familiarity with democracy, and its traditional social and political conservatism. At the same time, leftist statewide party leaders noted in interviews that, when Gallegos did participate, their activity was channelled by *caciques* and thus served to benefit center-right forces, rather than micronationalist or leftist groups. A

Communist party leader, for example, mentioned that: "The UCD and CD control the *cacique* network, in their capacity as mayors and as municipal officials, as well as leaders of agricultural associations that distribute both farm subsidy payments and pensions."[51]

The lack of popular support for pro-autonomy parties in the 1979 election meant that the UCD was to play the major role in subsequent negotiations over the Gallego autonomy statute. No Gallego nationalist group participated. All pro-autonomy parties initially rejected the UCD's proposed statute. The dispute between statewide leftist and center-right parties was not so much over the content of the draft statute, but rather over the procedure by which autonomy would be granted to Galicia (via article 151 of the Constitution, via the "rapid route" the PCE and PSOE preferred, or via article 143 endorsed by the UCD and AP).[52] Regional parties, however, opposed the statute because, as a leader of Unidade Galega stated, it "provides for only a minimal level of political self government. It removes from the hands of future autonomy institutions the necessary economic power to end dependency and under-development and, as a result condemns autonomous government in the future to a lack of popularity and prestige."[53] Not until concessions were made by the UCD concerning the manner in which Galicia would obtain autonomy did the Socialists and Communists accept a revised statute and advocate a "yes" vote in the 1980 referendum. The BNPG and UG, however, remained opposed and urged that the electorate vote "no."

THE CENTER-PERIPHERY CLEAVAGE
AND PARTISAN ALIGNMENTS AT THE MASS LEVEL

Inter- and intra-regional variations among party elites paralleled to a considerable degree the nature of voter alignments in the 1979 election. Those who spoke the regional language, who identified themselves as being primarily or exclusively Basque (or Catalán or Gallego), who favored extensive autonomy or independence, and who held other micronationalist views were more likely to support regional parties, especially extreme groups. Leftist parties were preferred over those of the center-right among voters with these characteristics who supported Spanish rather than regional political forces. Just as the level of polarization among party elites was the most pronounced in Euskadi, divisions among partisan groups in the Basque country were considerably more intense than those in Catalunya and Galicia.

The claims made by regional parties that they were the "true" representatives of the Basque or Catalán or Gallego people appeared to resonate with voters' perceptions of regional as opposed to Spanish parties. Both birthplace and language usage were associated with partisan preferences in Catalunya and especially Euskadi (table 44).[54] Seventy-seven percent of all native Basques (and 66 percent of Euskera-speakers) favored nationalist forces, whereas 67 percent of immigrants sympathized with statewide parties, particularly those of the left. Of those immigrants who supported regional parties, 59 percent claimed to be partisans of the leftist *abertzale* groups. Basque-born children of immigrant parents were even more likely to support Herri Batasuna and Euskadiko Ezkerra. Linz suggests that this is reflective of "the success of the combination of nationalism and social radicalism" in integrating a sizable segment of the immigrant community, especially younger first-generation Basques into the political community.[55] Such a combination of appeals was evidently lacking in Catalunya: only 8 percent of immigrants favored BEAN, ERC, or CiU. Use of the Catalán language, moreover, only marginally increased regional party support among immigrants. Nevertheless, differences in the partisan preferences of the various groups in the Catalán electorate were less pronounced than those in Euskadi. Even though almost three times as many natives as immigrants supported regional parties, three-quarters of those born in Catalunya stated a preference for Spanish parties, particularly the PSUC and PSOE.

The greater importance of the native-immigrant cleavage in the Basque party system, compared with that in Catalunya, did not stem, however, from any dramatic difference in the relative ability of Basque and Catalán nationalist parties to mobilize immigrant voters. As table 45 shows, the proportions of immigrants among their respective followings were virtually identical. Instead, the contrast was the result of the greater success of the Catalán Socialist and Communist parties,

TABLE 44
BIRTHPLACE AND LANGUAGE USAGE BY PARTISAN PREFERENCE (in percentages)

Euskadi[a]	HB	EE	PNV	Total regional parties	PCE	PSOE	UCD		N
Native speaker	28	13	49	90	0	5	2		(190)
Native nonspeaker	19	10	37	66	2	10	18		(225)
Immigrant nonspeaker	14	4	15	33	5	33	23		(187)

Catalunya[b]	BEAN	ERC	CiU	Total regional parties	PSUC	PSC-PSOE	UCD	AP-CD	N
Native speaker	17	7	15	23	11	35	25	4	(594)
Immigrant speaker	1	4	8	13	18	46	20	3	(139)
Immigrant nonspeaker	1	1	3	5	15	47	27	2	(182)

Note: Percentages do not always add up to 100 because preferences for "other parties" are not presented.
[a] Immigrant speakers of Euskera are omitted. They are only 4 percent of the sample in Euskadi; they are included, however, in the total number of cases.
[b] Native nonspeakers of Catalán are omitted. They are only 3 percent of the sample in Catalunya; they are included, however, in the total number of cases.

TABLE 45

PARTISAN PREFERENCE BY LANGUAGE USAGE AND BIRTHPLACE IN EUSKADI AND CATALUNYA

(in percentages)

Euskadi[a]	Partisan Preference						
	HB	EE	PNV	PCE	PSOE	UCD	Total
Native speaker	43	44	45	0	10	3	31
Native nonspeaker	35	41	41	29	24	47	37
Immigrant nonspeaker	22	15	14	71	66	50	30
N	(122)	(55)	(207)	(14)	(93)	(87)	(616)

Catalunya[b]	BEAN	ERC	CiU	PSUC	PSC-PSOE	UCD	AP-CD	Total
Native speaker	56	85	85	54	58	66	75	63
Immigrant speaker	13	11	10	21	18	12	13	15
Immigrant nonspeaker	31	4	5	25	24	22	12	19
N	(8)	(47)	(105)	(116)	(357)	(224)	(32)	(943)

[a]Immigrant speakers of Euskera are omitted. They are only 4 percent of the sample in Euskadi; they are included, however, in the total number of cases.
[b]Native nonspeakers of Catalán are omitted. They are only 3 percent of the sample in Catalunya; they are included, however, in the total number of cases.

TABLE 46
PARTISAN PREFERENCE BY NATIONAL SELF-IDENTIFICATION IN EUSKADI, CATALUNYA, AND GALICIA
(in percentages)

Partisan Preference

Euskadi	HB	EE	PNV	Total regional parties	Communist	Socialist	UCD	AP-CD	N
"Spanish" or "more Spanish"	4	1	14	19	4	31	42	5	(151)
Equally Spanish & Basque	15	4	35	54	4	24	12	3	(141)
"More Basque than Spanish"	25	17	46	88	0	8	4	3	(65)
"Basque only"	35	16	44	85	0	3	0	2	(230)

Catalunya	BEAN	ERC	CiU	Total regional parties	Communist	Socialist	UCD	AP-CD	N
"Spanish" or "more Spanish"	0	3	4	7	9	38	34	5	(302)
Equally Spanish & Catalán	0	4	16	20	11	37	27	3	(322)
"More Catalán than Spanish"	1	13	27	41	10	31	16	3	(106)
"Catalán only"	4	9	6	19	23	47	8	2	(128)

Galicia	BNPG	UG	Total regional parties	Communist	Socialist	UCD	AP-CD	N
"Spanish" or "more Spanish"	1	1	2	1	12	69	13	(66)
Equally Spanish & Gallego	1	5	6	3	16	66	9	(148)
"More Gallego than Spanish"	2	20	22	7	39	24	2	(44)
"Gallego only"	26	9	35	8	26	24	3	(83)

Note: Percentages do not always add up to 100 because preferences for "other parties" are not presented.

compared with their Basque counterparts, in gaining the support of the indigenous community. One further point is revealed by the data in tables 44 and 45. Extremist regional parties were not any more successful in recruiting the native-born and regional-language speakers than were the more moderate PNV, ERC, and CiU.

The patterns of partisan support among voters differentiated according to their national self-identities were quite similar to those based on the objective dimensions of the center-periphery cleavage. Although a relationship between partisan preference and subjective national identity existed in all three regions, Catalán parties were far less successful than their Basque or Gallego equivalents in attracting the support of voters whose attributes would be expected to have led them to favor regional, rather than Spanish, political forces. As table 46 reveals, regional parties were far more popular among those identifying themselves as "more Catalán than Spanish" than they were among voters who felt exclusively Catalán, although even among the former group less than a majority were partisans of the CiU, ERC, or BEAN. Among those who said that they were "Catalán only," 80 percent favored the parties of the Spanish left. In Galicia, and especially in Euskadi, those with an exclusive attachment to the region were far more likely to support regional parties, and in particular the more extremist of these, than were voters with divided or exclusively Spanish loyalties.

A sense of group discrimination was strongly associated with regional party support only in Euskadi: 76 percent of those claiming unfair treatment of the regional group, compared with 49 percent of those who said that none occurs, identified with Basque parties. In Catalunya and Galicia, those who perceived discrimination were only marginally more likely to support regional parties. Among this group, Socialists and Communists tended to be disproportionately favored to the detriment of the UCD and AP.

The relationships between partisan preference, on one hand, and birthplace, language usage, and subjective national identity, on the other, clearly suggest that the success of nationalist parties in mobilizing their natural bases of support varied markedly across the three regions. In Euskadi, Basque natives and Euskera speakers, in particular, overwhelmingly concurred with the claims made by nationalist parties that they were the "true" spokesmen for the interests of the "national community." The left *abertzale* parties were especially successful in gaining the support of those with an exclusive attachment to the region. In Galicia, regional parties were only able to gain the support of about one-third of those who felt exclusively Gallego. The remainder were rather evenly divided in their preferences for Spanish left and center-right parties. Nationalist parties did least well in Catalunya in attracting those who would be expected to be the most disposed to vote for them. The PSUC and especially the PSC-PSOE were by far the preferred parties of the native-born and of those who identified most strongly with the region. Thus, the assumption of regional identities and autonomist stands by the two Spanish leftist parties in Catalunya and Galicia was not only more successful in terms of gaining electoral support than in Euskadi but also contributed to the lesser degree of polarization within these two electorates and the party systems as a whole with regard to both the objective and subjective dimensions of group membership. The relative lack of success of Spanish leftists in mobilizing the support of the indigenous population in Euskadi was acknowledged by a Socialist party official in a 1979 interview: "One reason for [our] loss of votes was the failure to respond to the specific set of problems in Euskadi. . . . In the future, we will have to emphasize much more the necessity of autonomy in Euskadi, and, in any case, the image of the party will have to be made much more Basque, much more national[ist] in Euskadi." To have done so, however, might have alienated a significant number of immigrants from supporting the Socialist party, 66 percent of whose electorate in Euskadi were drawn from this segment of the population. At the same time, to have identified more closely with Basque nationalism probably would not have attracted sufficient numbers of native-born voters away from nationalist parties to the PSOE.[56]

These distinct patterns were also apparent with regard to the relationship between partisan preference and attitudes toward the structure of the state (table 47). In Euskadi, opinions concerning

TABLE 47
PARTISAN PREFERENCES OF VOTERS WITH DIFFERING OPINIONS
REGARDING THE STRUCTURE OF THE STATE IN EUSKADI, CATALUNYA, AND GALICIA
(in percentages)

Partisan Preference

Euskadi	HB	EE	PNV	Total regional parties	Communist	Socialist	UCD	AP-CD	N
Centralism	4	6	23	33	2	18	44	7	(96)
Limited autonomy	9	6	39	54	4	24	15	2	(255)
Extensive autonomy	27	11	35	73	1	18	2	3	(79)
Independence	49	16	28	91	2	1	0	2	(148)

Catalunya	BEAN	ERC	CiU	Total regional parties	Communist	Socialist	UCD	AP-CD	N
Centralism	0	4	8	12	4	21	45	7	(172)
Limited autonomy	0	5	13	18	10	24	45	2	(561)
Extensive autonomy	2	7	11	20	24	40	11	3	(97)
Independence	6	10	7	23	33	37	2	2	(92)

Galicia	BNPG	UG	Total regional parties	Communist	Socialist	UCD	AP-CD	N
Centralism	0	2	2	0	8	74	14	(97)
Limited autonomy	3	9	12	2	25	54	7	(153)
Extensive autonomy	15	15	30	20	26	21	0	(46)
Independence	37	11	48	4	19	17	0	(30)

self-government were related to support for regional versus Spanish parties and support for extreme groups versus the PNV. In Galicia, too, the more autonomist one's views, the more likely one was to favor regional parties, especially the BNPG. Unlike in Euskadi, however, Spanish parties of the left were also disproportionately favored by those who preferred extensive regional autonomy. In Catalunya, support for regional versus Spanish parties was only marginally associated with orientations toward autonomy. Such attitudes were, instead, much more strongly linked to support for the Spanish left versus the Spanish center-right.

Differences in the distribution of opinion regarding autonomy among the various partisan groups reflect these regional contrasts (table 48). In Euskadi there was a marked difference between the attitudes of regional party supporters and Spanish party sympathizers, but there was almost as sizable a difference between supporters of Herri Batasuna and those of the PNV. A majority of HB sympathizers were *independentistas;* a majority of *peneuvistas* favored limited autonomy. (Still, slightly more than one-fifth of PNV supporters desired independence, evidence at the mass level of this party's ambivalence toward the resolution of the Basque question.) Thus, both the pronounced degree of polarization of the Basque electorate as a whole and that of party leaders were mirrored in the opinions of differing partisan groups at the mass level. In Catalunya, an equally sharp distinction existed between the views of the small extremist Catalán partisan group and those of ERC and CiU supporters. In contrast to Euskadi, however, the opinions of moderate regional party supporters and those of the PSUC and PSOE were rather similar.[57] Thus, the same tendency for a convergence between regionalists and Spanish leftists apparent earlier was evident as well in their preferences concerning the structure of the Spanish state. Voter alignments in Galicia with regard to autonomy resembled in some respects those of Catalunya and in others, those of Euskadi. In the aggregate, supporters of the PCE and PSOE were not unlike UG sympathizers in their opinions concerning regional self-government, but there was, as in the Basque provinces, a marked contrast between the views of the more extreme and the more moderate regional partisan groups. Finally, though UCD and AP supporters in all three regions were less favorably inclined toward a centralized state than were their counterparts in the rest of Spain, center-right party voters clearly stood out in their pro-centralist views. In short, divisions at the mass level were congruent with those among party elites.

This was true as well with regard to opinions about the use of violence to achieve nationalist goals. There were sharp contrasts between extremist and more moderate regional party supporters; still sharper differences between these two groups and partisans of the center-right; and a certain degree of convergence toward the middle

TABLE 48

PREFERENCES CONCERNING REGIONAL
AUTONOMY BY REGION AND PARTISAN SUPPORT (in percentages)

				Partisan Preference				
Euskadi	HB	EE	PNV	Communist	Socialist	UCD		Total Region
Centralism	3	11	11	12	18	52		17
Limited autonomy	19	29	53	63	65	46		44
Extensive autonomy	17	16	14	7	15	2		14
Independence	61	44	22	18	2	0		25
N	(120)	(54)	(191)	(14)	(94)	(83)		(577)
Catalunya	BEAN	ERC	CiU	Communist	Socialist	UCD	AP-CD	Total Region
Centralism	9	13	13	6	10	34	40	19
Limited autonomy	12	55	65	49	69	60	44	61
Extensive autonomy	25	14	11	20	11	5	9	10
Independence	63	18	11	25	10	1	6	10
N	(8)	(49)	(151)	(119)	(359)	(228)	(31)	(922)
Galicia	BNPG		UG	Communist	Socialist	UCD	AP-CD	Total Region
Centralism	0		7	0	13	42	57	30
Limited autonomy	19		52	21	60	49	43	47
Extensive autonomy	31		28	69	19	6	0	14
Independence	50		13	10	4	3	0	9
N	(22)		(25)	(13)	(64)	(169)	(24)	(317)
Rest of Spain[a]				Communist	Socialist	UCD	AP-CD	Total
Centralism				8	21	56	73	39
Limited autonomy				62	65	40	24	50
Extensive autonomy				23	10	3	3	8
Independence				7	3	1	0	3
N				(140)	(424)	(598)	(64)	(1279)

[a]Data for Navarra and Valencia are not included.

ground on the part of all moderate regional and all Spanish leftist party supporters. The magnitude of differences among the various partisan groups varied, however, depending on the particular question asked of respondents.

Table 49 presents the mean scores of regional populations and party sympathizers within the regions on a "feeling thermometer" measuring affect toward ETA. (The higher the mean, the more sympathetically ETA is viewed.) There was widespread hostility toward ETA on the part of all voters, except for supporters of Herri Batasuna and Euskadiko Ezkerra (whose means scores of 6.49 and 5.00, respectively, reflected positive and neutral attitudes). However, when it came to opinions concerning what the government ought to do about terrorism (a highly salient issue in the early months of 1979 because of increasing ETA violence), there were, with only a few exceptions, sharp differences across partisan groups in terms of the proportions saying that the government should either accept the demands of terrorists or negotiate with them (table 50). But, apart from the sharper interpartisan differences, one other noticeable deviation from previous patterns is apparent in tables 49 and 50. Communist and Socialist party sympathizers differed considerably from each other in their views regarding terrorism. Of the two groups, Communists were less hostile toward ETA and more favorably disposed toward a conciliatory response on the part of the government to terrorism. Indeed, they were more likely to hold these views than were supporters of moderate regional parties in Catalunya and Galicia.

The most noteworthy findings that emerge from these data, however, concern the overall climate of opinion in the Basque region. No doubt due to the direct impact of ETA violence on Basque society and the greater intensity and polarization of the regional question in Euskadi, Basques were the most divided in their feelings toward ETA. At the same time, they were also the most sympathetic and the most willing to see the government grant concessions to terrorists: 57 percent of all Basques said that the government ought either to accept the demands of terrorists or to negotiate with them. An identical proportion of *peneuvistas* took this stance, once again a reflection at the mass level of the ambivalent feelings toward ETA expressed by the PNV leadership.

TABLE 49
MEAN SCORE ON "FEELING THERMOMETER"
TOWARD ETA BY REGION AND PARTISAN PREFERENCE

				Partisan Preference				
Euskadi	HB	EE	PNV	Communist	Socialist	UCD		Mean Region
	6.49	5.00	3.01	3.07	1.62	0.82		3.86
N	(123)	(53)	(178)	(11)	(91)	(81)		(558)
Catalunya	BEAN	ERC	CiU	Communist	Socialist	UCD	AP-CD	Mean Region
	3.53	1.74	1.34	1.86	1.41	0.66	0.16	1.25
N	(8)	(49)	(102)	(116)	(348)	(226)	(31)	(908)
Galicia	BNPG		UG	Communist	Socialist	UCD	AP-CD	Mean Region
	4.28		2.02	2.06	0.69	0.13	0.00	0.80
N	(21)		(24)	(14)	(68)	(170)	(25)	(330)
Rest of Spain[a]				Communist	Socialist	UCD	AP-CD	Mean
				1.53	0.79	0.34	0.14	0.65
N				(141)	(438)	(644)	(68)	(1354)

Note: The higher the mean, the more sympathetically ETA is viewed by a particular group.
[a]Data for Navarra and Valencia are not included.

TABLE 50
PERCENTAGE IN FAVOR OF ACCEPTING DEMANDS OF OR
NEGOTIATING WITH TERRORISTS, AMONG PARTISAN GROUPS

				Partisan Preference				
Euskadi	HB	EE	PNV	Communist	Socialist	UCD		Total Region
	83	87	57	40	40	21		57
N	(128)	(56)	(187)	(11)	(89)	(74)		(547)
Catalunya	BEAN	ERC	CiU	Communist	Socialist	UCD	AP-CD	Total Region
	72	20	7	36	18	2	0	15
N	(7)	(120)	(101)	(120)	(340)	(215)	(27)	(883)
Galicia	BNPG		UG	Communist	Socialist	UCD	AP-CD	Total Region
	81		35	48	24	7	9	21
N	(23)		(25)	(14)	(66)	(162)	(24)	(321)
Rest of Spain[a]				Communist	Socialist	UCD	AP-CD	Total
				36	19	5	4	14
N				(138)	(421)	(611)	(60)	(1289)

[a]Data for Navarra and Valencia are not included.

There was far less division among partisan groups with regard to language policy—another important issue related to the regional question. During debates over the Constitution and the 1979 campaign, party leaders in all three regions expressed general support for the principle of bilingualism. However, complex and differing stands were taken by political elites, even within the same party, concerning the specifics of language policy: the voluntary or obligatory study of the regional language; the use of the regional tongue, Castilian, or both as the language(s) of instruction; and the primacy of one or the other at various levels of education. In general, Catalán and Basque nationalist leaders differed from each other in their stands on these issues. Given the low level of knowledge of Euskera, Basque nationalist party elites tended to advocate a more voluntaristic approach to the study and usage of the regional language. But even among Catalán nationalist leaders, there was considerable divergence in their language policy proposals. Socialist and Communist party leaders in the regions tended to advocate the obligatory learning of both Castilian and the regional language in primary schools, in order to promote the integration of children of immigrants into Basque or Catalán society, but, at higher levels of education, they argued for voluntarism. Center-right parties, as we have seen, also supported the principle of bilingualism but emphasized the primacy of Castilian throughout the school system.[58]

At the mass level, however, majorities in all regions and among all partisan groups, (with the sole exception of BNPG supporters), favored the obligatory study of both languages in the school system. The degree of consensus shown with respect to this aspect of language policy broke down somewhat, however, when respondents were asked their preference concerning the thornier issue of the obligatory language of instruction (table 51). Although there were still sizable majorities in each region who favored mandatory bilingual instruction, there was somewhat of a decline among most partisan groups in the proportions taking this stand and, depending on the particular set of voters, a commensurate increase in the numbers favoring the sole use of the regional language or of Castilian. In general, supporters of Spanish leftist parties were less favorably disposed toward the use of both languages in instruction than they were toward the mandatory learning of both languages: the proportions opting for "Castilian only" increased. This shift was also apparent, but to a greater degree, among center-right party sympathizers. Among regional party supporters, the change was in the opposite direction: higher proportions favored the exclusive use of the regional tongue as the language of instruction.[59] The most important finding that emerges from these data, however, is that, at the general level to which these questions were addressed, there was a broad consensus in 1979 concerning the desirability of bilingual education. This could serve to temper political conflict, once autonomous regional governments began to enact and implement concrete language policy.[60]

There was far less agreement, however, regarding the question of whether mayors should be obliged to speak the regional language. Not only were voters as a whole sharply divided on this issue, (bare majorities in all three regions said "no"), but most partisan groups were internally divided to the same degree.[61] With the exceptions of Gallego and Catalán extreme nationalist party sympathizers, Basque Socialists, and UCD and AP supporters, slight majorities of all other groups said that mayors should speak the regional language, thus resulting in relatively small interpartisan differences.

In sum, the patterns of opinion among partisan groups toward the regional question were quite varied. With regard to certain aspects of micronationalism, like language policy in the school system and ETA, there was, in general, widespread agreement among the different groups. Other aspects, like the crucial issue of the structure of the state, generated considerably greater partisan division. And with regard to the objective as well as the more diffuse attitudinal manifestations of the center-periphery cleavage, voters, particularly in Euskadi, tended to be divided along a single axis—supporters of regional parties versus supporters of Spanish parties.

These differing patterns at the mass level were for the most part congruent with those existing among the various party leaders. It

TABLE 51

PREFERENCES CONCERNING THE OBLIGATORY
LANGUAGE OF INSTRUCTION BY REGION AND PARTISAN PREFERENCE (in percentages)

Partisan Preference

Euskadi

	HB	EE	PNV	Communist	Socialist	UCD	Total for Region
Regional language only	11	14	3	0	0	0	5
Bilingualism	87	82	90	80	76	48	79
Castilian only	3	5	7	20	24	52	16
N	(131)	(56)	(205)	(14)	(91)	(82)	(601)

Catalunya

	BEAN	ERC	CiU	Communist	Socialist	UCD	AP-CD	Total for Region
Regional language only	64	13	9	16	12	1	3	9
Bilingualism	36	81	85	72	70	77	63	73
Castilian only	0	6	6	12	18	22	34	18
N	(8)	(48)	(106)	(120)	(361)	(227)	(31)	(929)

Galicia

	BNPG	UG	Communist	Socialist	UCD	AP-CD	Total for Region
Regional language only	59	23	20	7	4	4	12
Bilingualism	37	75	67	79	69	55	68
Castilian only	4	2	13	14	27	40	21
N	(25)	(26)	(14)	(71)	(173)	(25)	(342)

would appear that, where opinions in the population as a whole were considerably polarized and parties offered clear and analogous choices to the electorate (as in Euskadi), attitudinal differences at the mass level were readily translated into sharply defined partisan alignments. Where, on the other hand, both the electorates and party leaders were less polarized in their views (as in Catalunya and Galicia), the distinction between regional and statewide partisan alignments were blurred, and thus the potential for significant political conflict over the regional question was moderated even further.

Despite the congruity of opinion between political elites and their supporters at the mass level in all three regions, the fact remains that, in Catalunya and Galicia, individual characteristics and opinions that one would expect would lead to support for regional parties were *not* translated to a significant degree into support for regional political forces. Catalán and Gallego parties did not receive majority support, let alone a monopoly of support, from the native-born or speakers of the vernacular (in the case of Catalunya), self-identified regionalists, those favoring the sole use of the regional language, autonomists, or even *independentistas*. Noteworthy as well is the fact that in Galicia, 24 percent of those who identified themselves as "Gallego only" did not express any partisan preference whatsoever, nor did 26 percent of those who favored regional autonomy of whatever degree. The failure of nationalist parties in these two regions to mobilize such potential support more effectively and thus to protect their political space can, in part, be explained by the success of the Communists and Socialist parties in assuming regional identities and identifying with Catalán and Gallego communal sentiments and nationalist goals. It can also be attributed to the fact that, unlike in Euskadi, native Catalans and immigrants with both leftist leanings and intense regionalist viewpoints had no regional party alternative to the PSOE and PSUC comparable to Euskadiko Ezkerra and Herri Batasuna. Finally, in Galicia, the moderate or conservative ideological tendencies of many Gallego voters evidently precluded them from supporting the leftist BNPG and even the center-left Unidade Galega.

THE SOCIAL AND IDEOLOGICAL
BASES OF THE REGIONAL PARTY SYSTEMS

The regional question was not the only source of partisan division in Euskadi, Catalunya, and Galicia. As in Spain as a whole, class, religious, generational, and ideological cleavages were also reflected to varying degrees in the self-images, stands, and strategies adopted by party elites and in the choices made by Basque, Catalán, and Gallego voters. A fuller understanding of the regional party systems must, therefore, take into consideration the extent to which these societal divisions structured party competition and affected partisan choice.

CLASS, PARTIES, AND PARTISAN CHOICE

In the general election campaign of 1979, the four major Spanish parties pursued, as we have seen, remarkably similar strategies with respect to the identification of socioeconomic target groups. Despite differences in their ideologies and initial self-images, they adopted broad rather than narrow designations of class groupings and sought votes from a wide array of social groups. The deemphasis by political elites of divisions along class lines found a considerable degree of correspondence at the mass level, and the overall differences in objective social status among the various groups of partisans tended to be small. Similarly, no party enjoyed a monopoly of support from any one social stratum.

Both the catch-all strategies of parties and the interclassist basis of partisan support were evident in the three regions as well. Officials of the PNV and CiU, for example, expressed the desire to gain the support of virtually all social groups and made note of the social heterogeneity of their sympathizers. As a spokesman for the PNV in Guipúzcoa remarked in a 1978 interview: "We want to attract the entire population, except big capital, because that would give this party a bad image. Big capitalists in this region are not nationalists, anyway." Regional parties of the left were more pointed in their rejection of financial and business elites, whom they identified as the exploiters of both the native and immigrant working class and the oppressors of the Basque, Catalán, or Gallego people.

The absence of narrow class appeals to voters coincided with the relatively modest relationship between class divisions (as measured by occupational status) and partisan preference. In all three regions, the proportions supporting regional versus Spanish parties, for example, were remarkably similar from one occupational group to another (table 52). Even in Euskadi, where differences were most marked, the percentages favoring regional parties ranged from a low of 54 percent in the case of unskilled workers to a high of 71 percent among artisans and owners of small businesses—the traditional bases of support for the PNV. This disparity in the two groups' degree of support for Basque parties persisted among the native-born population as well.[62]

Not surprisingly, there was a stronger relationship between partisan preference and subjective class identification. Class awareness, and especially a sense of belonging to the working class, tended to be associated with support for leftist parties. In both Euskadi and Galicia, those who identified with the working class disproportionately favored parties of the left, especially regional leftist groups. Among Gallego working-class identifiers, for example, 17 percent claimed to be BNPG partisans, while only 7 percent of all voters supported that party; among their Basque counterparts, 42 percent favored the *abertzale* left. In Catalunya, however, only the PSUC and PSC-PSOE were given disproportionate support by self-identified members of the working class; among this group, regional parties fared less well than they did in the total electorate. This, once again, is a reflection of the absence of apparently viable leftist nationalist alternatives to the Communist and Socialist parties.

RELIGIOSITY, AGE, AND PARTISAN CHOICE

Party elites in the regions, as in Spain as a whole, made concerted efforts during the campaign to downplay their differences regarding religious issues. For example, a spokesman for the PSUC in Barce-

TABLE 52
STATUS LEVEL OF RESPONDENT OR OF HEAD OF HOUSEHOLD BY PARTISAN PREFERENCE IN EUSKADI, CATALUNYA, AND GALICIA (in percentages)

Partisan preference	Status Level [a]							All respondents
	I	II	III	IV	V	VI	VII	
Euskadi								
HB	23	24	18	22	11	24	24	22
EE	9	11	10	5	7	13	9	10
PNV	24	33	43	39	42	29	21	33
Total regional parties	56	68	71	66	60	66	54	65
PCE	0	2	2	6	0	3	3	2
PSOE	11	18	11	15	19	19	13	13
UCD	27	9	14	10	14	9	25	25
N	(49)	(158)	(108)	(61)	(19)	(125)	(62)	(581)
Catalunya								
BEAN	0	3	2	0	0	0	0	1
ERC	4	7	7	4	3	6	4	5
CiU	15	12	13	7	12	12	8	11
Total regional parties	19	22	22	11	15	18	12	17
PSUC	5	12	12	15	14	16	16	13
PSC-PSOE	28	25	25	45	35	46	51	39
UCD	31	29	29	25	36	16	20	24
AP-CD	8	5	7	0	0	2	0	3
N	(95)	(163)	(122)	(118)	(43)	(211)	(144)	(896)
Galicia								
BNPG	3	10	7	3	9	5	11	7
UG	9	9	9	7	5	5	6	8
Total regional parties	12	19	16	10	14	10	16	15
PCE	9	3	3	3	0	5	5	4
PSOE	10	29	22	17	31	21	18	22
UCD	55	41	48	60	42	51	57	49
AP-CD	12	6	9	0	13	7	3	8
N	(46)	(69)	(71)	(14)	(32)	(46)	(29)	(307)

Note: Percentages do not always add up to 100 because preferences for "other parties" are not presented.
[a] The composition of the seven status groups is as follows:
   I   Entrepreneurs, professionals, large landowners, high-level public and private executives
  II   Mid-level public and private employees, technical professions
 III   Owners, small businessmen, independent artisans
  IV   Low-level white-collar workers, sales and supervisory personnel
   V   Small farmers
  VI   Skilled workers in agriculture and industry
 VII   Unskilled workers in agriculture and industry.

lona, interviewed in 1978, mirrored comments made by Communist elite respondents elsewhere, when he claimed that "there was no inherent division between believers and nonbelievers." A UCD official in Guipúzcoa stated that his party was a-confessional and that in his province there had been no contacts between the UCD and the Church. He went on to say, however, that this was due, in part, to the fact that virtually all religious organizations were strong supporters of the PNV, a party with a long historical association with the nationalist clergy and deep penetration into the religious segment of Basque society. The religious dimension, however, did at times intrude into the campaign. Some CDC officials, for example, accused Esquerra Republicana of being anticlerical. On the other hand, a Catalán Socialist respondent, interviewed in Barcelona in 1978, reasserted the traditional stance of the PSOE when he stated emphatically that his party, unlike the PSUC, was anticlerical and ought to remain so.

The parties' downplaying of the religious cleavage notwithstanding, these images, the historical links between certain regional parties and the Church or practicing Catholics, and the varying positions adopted by the parties during the constituent process all colored voters' perceptions and were reflected in sharp partisan differences between the religious and nonreligious (table 53). In Euskadi and Catalunya, the religious cleavage was not reflected in differences in support for regional versus statewide parties. Instead, its greatest impact was manifested in preferences for leftist versus moderate or center-right political groups: religious voters were far more likely to prefer the PNV, CiU, UCD, and AP than were the nonreligious. In Galicia, however, the degree of religiosity was associated with support for regional versus Spanish parties. The religious segment of the electorate rejected Unidade Galega, as well as the BNPG, and overwhelmingly supported Spanish center-right parties. The strong relationship between religiosity and voter choice was reflected as well in the composition of the various partisan groups. Nonpracticing Catholics constituted a majority only among supporters of regional left parties, Communists, and Catalán Socialists.

TABLE 53

DISTRIBUTION OF PARTISAN PREFERENCES AMONG
PRACTICING AND NONPRACTICING CATHOLIC VOTERS
(in percentages)

Partisan Preference								
Euskadi	HB	EE	PNV	Total regional parties	PCE	PSOE	UCD	*N*
Practicing	14	7	41	62	1	14	20	(390)
Nonpracticing	34	14	21	69	4	18	4	(223)
Catalunya	BEAN	ERC	CiU	Total regional parties	PSUC	PSC-PSOE	UCD	AP-CD	*N*
Practicing	0	2	15	17	5	31	37	5	(469)
Nonpracticing	1	8	8	17	21	46	12	2	(472)
Galicia	BNPG		UG	Total regional parties	PCE	PSOE	UCD	AP-CD	*N*
Practicing	4		6	10	1	15	63	10	(237)
Nonpracticing	15		11	26	11	32	24	1	(107)

Note: Percentages do not always add up to 100 because preferences for "other parties" are not presented.

Given the strong association between age and degree of religiosity, as well as the leftist leanings of both younger and nonreligious voters, the young were far more likely to support leftist parties, either regional or Spanish, than were older voters (table 54). Indeed, a majority or near-majority of left *abertzale* groups and PCE supporters in Euskadi, BEAN sympathizers, and BNPG, UG, and PCE voters in Galicia were 18 to 29 years of age. In contrast, middle-aged and older cohorts made up two-thirds or more of every other partisan group. But, as in the case of the religious cleavage, age differences had little bearing in Euskadi and Catalunya on preferences for regional versus statewide parties: about 64 percent of all three age groups in Euskadi and 17 percent in Catalunya favored regional parties. Age, however, did have a significant impact on voters' preferences for the PNV or the *abertzale* left. In Galicia, regional parties, especially the BNPG, were favored in significant numbers only by the young. The UCD

TABLE 54

DISTRIBUTION OF PARTISAN PREFERENCES AMONG
AGE GROUPS IN EUSKADI, CATALUNYA, AND GALICIA
(in percentages)

Euskadi	Partisan Preference							
	HB	EE	PNV	Total regional parties	PCE	PSOE	UCD	N
Young	40	17	8	65	5	17	9	(167)
Middle-aged	17	8	38	63	1	19	14	(257)
Older	10	5	49	64	1	10	23	(188)

Catalunya	BEAN	ERC	CiU	Total regional parties	PSUC	PSC-PSOE	UCD	AP-CD	N
Young	2	7	10	19	22	40	12	2	(222)
Middle-aged	0	4	12	16	13	42	23	4	(373)
Older	1	6	11	18	8	34	34	4	(347)

Galicia	BNPG		UG	Total regional parties	PCE	PSOE	UCD	AP-CD	N
Young	16		18	34	8	24	20	4	(85)
Middle-aged	4		8	12	5	19	57	7	(127)
Older	5		0	5	0	20	66	10	(132)

Note: Percentages do not always add up to 100 because preferences for "other parties" are not presented.

and AP enjoyed almost a complete monopoly of support among both middle-aged and older voters.

How might one account for these differences in the social bases of partisan support between Euskadi and Catalunya, on one hand, and Galicia, on the other? The explanation lies, in large part, in the structuring of the regional party systems along the left-right continuum and the overall ideological leanings of the respective electorates.

IDEOLOGY, PARTIES, AND VOTERS

In the regions, nationalist parties, like the four major Spanish parties, adopted distinct ideological stands and positioned themselves differently on the political spectrum. The radical nationalist parties made their leftist views clear in the 1979 campaign, although in ideological terms they differed little from the Communists. Some leaders of the CDC and PNV, on the other hand, attempted to portray themselves as falling between the Spanish Socialists and the UCD, that is, slightly to the left of center. A CDC official, for example, said in a 1978 interview: "We are a center-left party between the Socialists and the UCD. We are in favor of reformist and progressive policies that would transform our society into something like Sweden or Norway."

UCD officials, however, in both Euskadi and Catalunya claimed that there were no major differences in social and economic policy between their party and that of moderate regional forces, and the only issue that divided them was the regional question. Socialist party leaders, as well as those of the extreme nationalist groups, tended to concur with UCD elites in this regard: they saw the PNV or CDC as bourgeois, center-right parties. The array of parties and the clear distinctions drawn within both regional and statewide party camps in their self-images and electoral appeals meant that in Euskadi and Catalunya voters could find a party that was compatible both with their ideological predispositions[63] *and* their opinions regarding the regional question. Moderate Catalans who supported limited autonomy could, for example, choose the CiU rather than the more center-left ERC. Leftist Basque *independentistas* could select either Euskadiko Ezkerra or Herri Batasuna, rather than the PNV. Similarly, immigrants in Catalunya who were leftist and supportive of limited autonomy could opt for either the PSUC or the PSC-PSOE.

Gallego voters, however, were far more limited. The BNPG was clearly a party of the extreme left. Unidade Galega, the more moderate of the two nationalist parties with regard to the regional question, also portrayed itself as a party of the left. Thus, the great majority of Gallego voters who, as we have seen, were both religious and center-right in their political leanings had little alternative but to support Spanish parties of the center-right. The fact, moreover, that 61 percent of those who favored limited autonomy supported either the UCD or AP suggests that Unidade Galega could not overcome its leftist image in the eyes of these voters.

The ideological self-designation of the various parties closely corresponded to the political leanings of their respective followers, as the data in figures 24, 25, and 26 show. HB and PNV voters clearly differed from each other. In general, CiU and PNV supporters placed themselves between Socialists and *ucedistas*. And Unidade Galega sympathizers were, on the average, virtually identical to Gallego Socialists in their left-of-center leanings. Two findings emerge from these data, however, that deserve further comment. While CiU voters did lie between Socialist and UCD sympathizers on the left-right spectrum, most Convergència partisans were clearly centrist rather than center-left, and they were much more similar to UCD partisans than to PSC-PSOE voters in their ideological predispositions. This might help to account for the greater appeal of the PSUC and especially the Socialist party among pro-autonomists, the majority of whom were left of center. The second is the striking similarity between ERC and PSC-PSOE voters. If anything, ERC sympathizers were slightly more to the left of center than were Socialists. Why, then, did leftist, pro-autonomy voters support the PSUC and PSOE rather than the ERC? This puzzle cannot be answered by our data. But a partial explanation may be that in the first election of the post-Franco era the ERC allied itself with the extreme-left Partido del Trabajo de España (PTE), whose program combined Maoist and

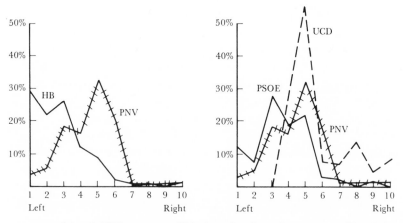

FIGURE 24.   Self-Placement of Various Partisan Groups on a Ten-Point Left-Right Scale in Euskadi

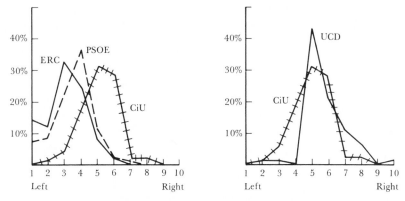

FIGURE 25.   Self-Placement of Various Partisan Groups on a Ten-Point Left-Right Scale in Catalunya

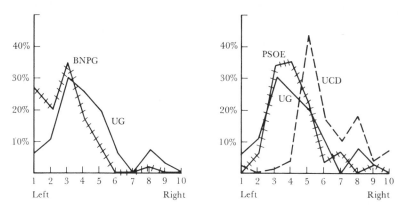

FIGURE 26.   Self-Placement of Various Partisan Groups on a Ten-Point Left-Right Scale in Galicia

Marxist-Leninist elements. This strange electoral alliance may have undermined the ERC's potential for becoming the leading regional party within Catalunya. A further explanation may lie, once again, in the apparent success with which Spanish leftist parties assumed regional identities and made credible their regionalist stands.

EUSKADI, CATALUNYA, AND GALICIA

It is clear that, in addition to the center-periphery cleavage, there were a number of other societal divisions that helped to structure partisan competition and to affect voter choice in the three regions. It is further evident that these various divisions were related to each other. In all three regions, pro-autonomists tended to be more leftist in their political leanings; religious voters were more conservative; and the young were less religious than older cohorts.

It is often argued that the impact of societal divisions on political conflict may be magnified or reduced depending on the degree to which salient cleavages are connected: cross-cutting divisions tend to mitigate conflict, whereas reinforcing cleavages tend to exacerbate tensions.[64] In these three regions of Spain, the subjective dimensions of class, religion, regional cleavages, and left-right divisions were associated with each other. But as the data in table 55 demonstrate, the strength of the various relationships differed: overall, the linkages were weakest in Euskadi and strongest in Catalunya. On the basis of these data alone, one might conclude that politics in the Basque

TABLE 55

CORRELATIONS AMONG LEFT-RIGHT SELF-PLACEMENT AND SUBJECTIVE INDICATORS OF CLASS, RELIGIOUS, AND REGIONAL DIVISIONS IN EUSKADI, CATALUNYA, AND GALICIA

	"Class"	"Religion"	"Region"	Left-Right
Euskadi				
"Class"		.39	−.17	.29
"Religion"			−.29	.49
"Region"				−.42
Catalunya				
"Class"		.52	−.40	.46
"Religion"			−.48	.52
"Region"				−.49
Galicia				
"Class"		.45	−.29	.41
"Religion"			−.36	.52
"Region"				−.42

Note: Correlations are Pearson's r. Indicators of religious and class divisions are feelings toward the Church and big business, respectively, as measured by an 11-point "feeling thermometer." The indicator of the regional cleavage is preference regarding the structure of the state.

country was the most moderate, and politics in Catalunya, the most conflictual. The potentially moderating effect of cross-cutting cleavages, however, may not be felt if one societal division is particularly salient and generates especially intense views. It may be sufficiently potent in and of itself to lead to considerable polarization at both the elite and mass levels. This appeared to be the case in Euskadi.

When these various cleavages are assessed jointly, by means of discriminant analysis, to determine their relative weight with respect to partisan divisions, the regional question stood out as a major source of partisan differentiation, irrespective of the particular pair of parties being considered (table 56). Certain aspects of the center-periphery cleavage differentiated regional party supporters from Spanish party sympathizers; other aspects distinguished between extreme and moderate nationalist party voters. Differences on the left-right continuum also remained an important source of differentiation between most pairs of partisan groups. But, apart from these similarities, there emerged from the discriminant analysis certain regional variations in the relative importance of these disparate factors that suggest that the underlying bases of political conflict differed across the regions. The analysis also demonstrates the existence of regional variations in the overall degree to which these issues served to polarize one partisan group from another.

In Euskadi, there were sharp differences between extreme and moderate regionalist groups, between Spanish party sympathizers, and between supporters of Basque and statewide political forces. The summary statistics (Wilks' Lambdas) presented in table 56, in fact, confirm earlier findings that partisan groups were most polarized in Euskadi. In addition, the analysis shows that in the Basque country center-periphery issues (especially attitudes toward ETA and subjective national identity) tended to overshadow all others as sources of partisan division. This was particularly the case for the paired groups for whom ideological differences were relatively small (e.g., HB versus EE, PNV versus PSOE, regional left versus Spanish left), but the center-periphery dimension remained the most signifi-

TABLE 56

RELATIVE IMPORTANCE OF VARIOUS SOCIETAL DIVISIONS
IN DISTINGUISHING BETWEEN PARTISAN GROUPS IN EUSKADI, CATALUNYA, AND GALICIA

	Pairs of Partisan Groups					
Euskadi	HB vs. EE	Regional left vs. PNV	Regional left vs. Spanish left	PNV vs. PSOE	PNV vs. UCD	PSOE vs. UCD
Birthplace	**.25**	.07	.07	.08	.11	.14
Speaking regional language	.13	.07	.04	.06	.01	.14
Subjective nat'l. identification	**.35**	.12	**.43**	**.66**	**.76**	**.32**
Opinion on autonomy	**.61**	**.22**	.17	.13	**.21**	.19
Sense of group discrimination	.08	.04	**.28**	**.47**	.17	.01
Language of instruction	**.50**	.10	.19	**.24**	**.25**	.02
Study of regional language	**.33**	.06	.08	.15	.18	.02
Mayors should know regional language	.11	**.23**	.08	**.25**	.08	**.20**
Attitude toward ETA	**.67**	**.50**	**.54**	**.38**	.03	.13
Gov't. response to terrorism	.05	**.26**	.16	.03	.06	.06
Status (objectively defined)	**.29**	**.27**	.12	.04	.12	.19
Subjective class identity	**.27**	.11	.04	**.36**	.10	**.48**
Attitude toward big business	.08	**.26**	.17	.09	.07	.07
Age	.02	**.32**	.09	**.69**	**.27**	**.35**
Degree of religiosity	.01	.08	.16	**.51**	.00	**.30**
Attitude toward Church	**.35**	**.24**	.16	**.47**	.01	**.23**
Left-right self-placement	**.38**	.15	**.26**	**.50**	**.22**	**.73**
Wilks' Lambda	.78	.52	.41	.50	.45	.36

Note: Figures are standardized coefficients obtained through discriminant analysis and measure the contribution of each variable in distinguishing one group from the other. Wilks' Lambda measures the overall degree of separation between groups; the lower the lambda, the greater the separation between groups. Those coefficients that are .20 or higher are highlighted.

TABLE 56 (cont.)

			Pairs of Partisan Groups			
Catalunya	ERC vs. GiU	ERC vs. PSUC	GiU vs. PSOE	ERC+ GiU vs. Spanish left	GiU vs. UCD	PSOE vs. UCD
Birthplace	**.23**	**.54**	**.43**	**.54**	.14	**.21**
Speaking regional language	.08	.18	.03	.02	.19	.15
Subjective nat'l. identification	.10	.02	.04	.02	**.29**	.08
Opinion on autonomy	.08	.17	.14	.09	**.24**	.03
Sense of group discrimination	.03	.11	.13	.12	.06	.13
Language of instruction	**.21**	.07	.13	.11	.10	.07
Study of regional language	**.23**	**.49**	.01	.16	.07	.05
Mayors should know regional language	.02	.13	.10	.17	.11	.01
Attitude toward ETA	**.23**	.16	.06	.00	.07	.03
Gov't. response to terrorism	**.22**	.14	.05	.03	**.21**	.02
Status (objectively defined)	.07	**.44**	.02	.02	**.33**	**.21**
Subjective class identity	.05	**.37**	**.32**	**.43**	.09	**.23**
Attitude toward big business	.05	.05	**.32**	**.29**	**.22**	.03
Age	.05	**.35**	.05	.08	**.24**	.13
Degree of religiosity	**.36**	.01	**.24**	.13	.08	.11
Attitude toward Church	.11	**.26**	**.25**	**.25**	**.39**	.14
Left-right self-placement	**.81**	**.59**	**.76**	**.65**	**.41**	**.79**
Wilks' Lambda	.57	.59	.68	.74	.68	.47

TABLE 56
RELATIVE IMPORTANCE OF VARIOUS SOCIETAL DIVISIONS IN DISTINGUISHING
BETWEEN PARTISAN GROUPS IN EUSKADI, CATALUNYA, AND GALICIA (cont.)

	Pairs of Partisan Groups				
Galicia	BNPG vs. UG	BNPG vs. PSOE	UG vs. PSOE	UG vs. UCD	PSOE vs. UCD
Subjective nat'l. identification	**.36**	.01	.16	.17	**.28**
Opinion on autonomy	**.59**	**.42**	**.29**	**.20**	.18
Sense of group discrimination	.08	.05	.21	.03	.12
Language of instruction	**.26**	**.21**	**.39**	**.33**	.08
Study of regional language	**.89**	.16	.12	.05	.07
Mayors should know regional language	.19	.10	**.22**	.10	.19
Attitude toward ETA	**.87**	.00	**.37**	.19	.01
Gov't. response to terrorism	**.31**	**.23**	.11	.03	.12
Status (objectively defined)	**.65**	**.54**	.04	.10	.14
Subjective class identity	**.38**	.11	**.51**	**.34**	**.28**
Attitude toward big business	**.21**	.13	**.55**	**.32**	.09
Age	.06	**.59**	**.51**	**.52**	.14
Degree of religiosity	**.27**	**.22**	**.52**	.11	**.34**
Attitude toward Church	**.42**	.07	**.34**	**.30**	.19
Left-right self-placement	**.65**	**.48**	**.41**	**.33**	**.68**
Wilks' Lambda	.43	.46	.61	.49	.50

cant cleavage, even for the partisan groups that differed considerably from each other in their left-right views (e.g., the regional left versus the PNV). The sole exception to this pattern in Euskadi occurred with respect to the most distinct pair of partisan groups— *ucedistas* and Socialists. The most important source of differentiation between these two groups of Spanish party voters was self-placement on the left-right spectrum, and center-periphery issues were relatively minor sources of division compared with subjective class identification and age.

On the whole, partisan groups were only slightly less polarized in Galicia than in Euskadi. Unlike in the Basque country, however, other issues such as left-right self-placement, class, religion, and, for certain groups, generational differences rivaled the regional question in importance. Only among supporters of the two Gallego nationalist parties did center-periphery issues overshadow all others, and these differences, together with others, served to make BNPG and UG voters the most distinct pair of groups shown in table 56. The least distinct set of party supporters were those of the UG and the PSOE, further evidence of the tendency toward convergence between moderate nationalist and Spanish leftist groups in Galicia.

In Catalunya, ideological differences and, to a lesser extent, class divisions were almost as important, if not more important, than the regional question in separating partisan groups. This was the case not only between Spanish-party supporters (*ucedistas* versus Socialists) and between ERC and CiU sympathizers, but also between partisans of regional versus statewide parties. The convergence over center-periphery issues between regionalists and Spanish leftists, in particular, is once again clearly evident. The only significant aspect of the center-periphery cleavage that distinguished the CiU from the PSOE or the ERC and the CiU from the Spanish left at the mass level was place of birth. Indeed, as the Wilks' Lambda statistics indicate, the latter two sets of voters were the most alike of all the paired groups, notwithstanding their differences in self-placement on the left-right spectrum. Overall, the data shown in table 56 support the argument that mass politics in the three regions was least polarized in Catalunya.

OTHER NATIONALISMS

Although we have focused on micronationalism and the regional party systems of Euskadi, Catalunya, and Galicia, such phenomena were by no means confined to these three areas of Spain. Preferences for varying degrees of autonomy and even for independence, as well as support for regional parties, were not only present in other culturally and linguistically distinct regions, such as Navarra, Valencia, and the Balearic Islands, but also existed in such Castilian-speaking areas as Andalucía and the Canary Islands with no previous aspirations for, or historical experiences with, self-government. (See fig. 9.) In none of the regions did the politicization of the center-periphery cleavage reach the level of intensity of that in Euskadi. Indeed, in some, micronationalist parties did not even gain 5 percent of the regional vote in 1979. In others, however, notably Navarra and Andalucía, the regional question was highly salient during the second parliamentary election and had repercussions that far transcended internal regional politics.

Of these other regions, Navarra approached the Basque country in the complexity and intractability of the regional question. Whether Navarra should be a region in and of itself or should be incorporated with neighboring Euskadi has been a heated issue, both within Navarra and between the Basques and certain segments of the Navarro population: "In some respects Navarra can be regarded as straddling the boundary of two historical linguistic and cultural communities, and thereby as the object of an irredentist struggle [on the part of the Basques] within the Spanish state."[65] This was manifested in the 1979 survey in the lack of consensus over national self-identification; 52 percent of respondents in Navarra said that they felt "Navarro," 26 percent claimed to be Spanish, and 15 percent regarded themselves as "Basque." In addition, 12 percent of the respondents claimed to speak Euskera. According to a 1980 study, those who said that they spoke Euskera and who identified themselves as Basque tended to favor the incorporation of Navarra into either an autonomous or independent Euskadi.[66] All the Basque nationalist parties, both in Euskadi and in Navarra, have set forth the same demand. They have, moreover, called for a referendum in Navarra on this issue, even though some of these groups, most notably Herri Batasuna, have stated that they would not consider a negative result binding.[67] A large segment of the Navarra population, however, was adamantly opposed to the inclusion of the province into Euskadi.[68] For this group, Navarra's long history of autonomy within the Spanish state[69] justifies the demand that it should constitute a distinctive self-governing region, on a par with Euskadi, Catalunya, and Galicia. Whether Navarra should be a singular autonomous community or a part of Euskadi was not the sole source of division in the Navarro electorate, however. In 1979, 46 percent of our respondents rejected the very notion of autonomy and expressed a preference for a highly centralized state.

The lack of agreement over center-periphery issues, particularly the institutional status of the province, was reflected in the highly polarized and fragmented outcome of the 1979 election. Herri Batasuna, the PNV, and the extreme left Euskadiko Mugimendua Komunista–Organización de Izquierda Comunista (EMK-OIC)—the parties that claimed Navarra as an integral part of the Basque country—obtained 9 percent, 8 percent, and 1 percent of the vote, respectively. The parties most clearly opposed to such a claim, most notably the very conservative and anti-Basque Unión del Pueblo Navarro and the UCD, received 11 percent and 32 percent, respectively. The remainder of the vote was divided between the Socialists (who in the 1979 campaign took a more ambivalent position on Navarra's future),[70] the extreme-left PTE, and the Partido Carlista. Thus, the 1979 election hardly resolved the issue of Navarra. It may indeed be insoluble, given the likely persistence of irredentist claims by Basque nationalists and their rejection by significant segments of the Navarra political elite and mass public.

One of the most startling results of the 1979 election was the success of the Partido Socialista de Andalucía (PSA).[71] Under the leadership of Alejandro Rojas Marcos, this self-proclaimed Andaluz nationalist party received 11 percent of the vote in Andalucía and obtained 5 out of the 59 seats allotted to the region. The meteoric rise of the PSA was the most dramatic instance of the spread of demands for autonomy in Castilian-speaking and indisputably "Spanish" regions of the country. The considerable increase in autonomist sentiments in Andalucía and elsewhere may have been a response to the arguments made by certain regional elites that continuing support for Spanish parties would reduce Andalucía and others to the status of second-class regions, compared with the more economically and politically advantaged soon-to-be autonomous communities of Euskadi and Catalunya. The unexpected success of the PSA, in particular, was also due to the support given to the party by the UCD in an effort to undercut the PSOE in that region.[72] The success of the PSA and its cooperation with the UCD led the PSOE, the plurality party in the region, to emphasize Andaluz demands for autonomy more strongly. This meant that Andalucía would become the next to achieve autonomy after the three "historic" regions of Spain. But, as is discussed in our concluding chapter, the achievement of Andaluz self-government was difficult and had severe repercussions for the UCD and for the future of the autonomy process itself.

The Canary Islands, despite its full integration into Castilian culture and language, also experienced a significant rise in mass preferences for autonomy and support for regional groups.[73] Although statewide parties, especially the UCD, prevailed in both parliamentary elections, a complicated and shifting array of regional parties increased their support considerably, from a total of 6.8 percent of the vote in the first contest to 14.5 percent in the second. Among regional parties, leftist nationalist groups dominated, and in 1979 the coalition Unión del Pueblo Canario (with 11 percent of the vote) was able to attain one seat in the Cortes. As in Andalucía, this increase in micronationalism appears to have been fueled by a combination of underdevelopment, a sense of relative deprivation, and appeals to the electorate on the basis of Third World *dependencia* or "internal colonialism" rhetoric. Unlike in Andalucía, however, extreme micronationalist views were reflected in the emergence of a separatist organization, Movimiento para la Autodeterminación e Independencia del Archipiélago Canario, which has been responsible for a number of terrorist activities. But, according to our 1979 survey, its objective of independence was shared by only 4 percent of the electorate.

In contrast with the indisputably "Spanish" regions of Andalucía and the Canary Islands, linguistically distinct Valencia and the Balearic Islands have thus far manifested only negligible support for micronationalist parties.[74] This is the case in spite of the rejection of a centralist Spanish state by majorities in both regions. In Valencia, there has been an ongoing debate among those intellectuals and political elites who favor autonomy as to whether Valencia should constitute a separate autonomous community or whether, given the belief by some that Valenciano is a variant of Catalán, the region should be incorporated within a larger self-governing Catalunya. The latter view appears to have gained little currency among voters, however: only 2 percent of our respondents claimed to feel "Catalán," while the remainder were rather evenly split between those who felt "Spanish" and those who identified themselves as "Valenciano." Despite this sharp differentiation in national self-identity, center-periphery issues appear to be of low salience at the mass level. The four statewide parties totally dominated politics in the region, and Valenciano parties fared even less well in the 1979 election than they did two and a half years earlier. Their combined vote declined from 5 to 2.3 percent. Regional parties in the Balearic Islands, where there is almost universal usage of the vernacular (a dialect of Catalán), also experienced a similar loss of support from 5.5 to 3.4 percent of the vote between the two parliamentary elections.

THE REGIONAL PARTY SYSTEMS: AN OVERVIEW

The linguistic and cultural distinctiveness of the Basque, Catalán, and Gallego electorates, the widespread sense of belonging to the regional group, and the generalized desire for autonomy have all resulted in the emergence of regional party systems in Spain. The three party systems differed markedly from one another, however, as did the extent of their dissimilarity from the statewide party system and their implications for Spanish politics as a whole.

In Catalunya the regional question was a major element of political conflict in 1979, and was reflected in interpartisan disagreements, disputes between regional elites and the government in Madrid, and tensions between the native and immigrant communities. But a number of factors combined to mitigate the divisive impact of the center-periphery cleavage on partisan politics. First, a clear majority favored limited autonomy, a moderate stance that precluded support for extreme or anti-system micronationalist parties equivalent to Euskadiko Ezkerra or Herri Batasuna. Second, divisions based on ideology and, secondarily, the subjective dimensions of class were, in addition to center-periphery issues, also major foci of electoral competition and bases of voter choice. Hence, given the center-left tendencies of the Catalán electorate, together with Spanish leftists' effective identification with Catalanism, the PSUC and especially the PSC-PSOE were able to mobilize the support of a majority of Catalán autonomists. They were able to do so, moreover, without forfeiting the votes of significant numbers of immigrants, at least in the 1979 election.

Thus, the relative similarity between micronationalist and Spanish leftist parties concerning the regional question served to moderate center-periphery conflicts in Catalunya and to bridge a potentially wide gap between regional and statewide political forces at both the elite and mass levels. At the same time, the absence of extreme micronationalist forces and, hence, of the potential for outbidding among parties over center-periphery issues also served to reduce polarization. This would make it possible for the CiU to negotiate with the Suárez government with greater flexibility than would be the case for its Basque counterpart, the PNV. The relative ideological proximity of the CiU and certain segments of Centristes de Catalunya (UCD) helped in this regard as well. In sum, despite the existence of widespread micronationalist parties, the dynamics of the Catalán party system were quite similar to those of the Spanish party system as a whole.

A variety of factors different from those in Catalunya also operated in Galicia to lessen the potentially divisive impact of the center-periphery cleavage. Notwithstanding the preponderance of Gallego speakers in the electorate, widespread attachment to the region, and pro-autonomist views, micronationalist forces fared poorly, as did even the pro-autonomist Spanish left. These parties were constrained in a number of ways in their efforts to metamorphose these attitudes into electoral support. Social and economic underdevelopment hampered mass mobilization around either center-periphery or class-based issues. Also undermining their success, particularly that of the BNPG and UG, was widespread skepticism that the establishment of self-government would do much to alleviate the disadvantaged position of the region. But the most important impediment to the success of micronationalist or autonomist Spanish parties was that the widespread conservative and clerical sentiments of the Gallego electorate appeared to preclude significant levels of support for regional or Spanish leftist groups. Center-right and less pro-autonomist forces prevailed.

The Basque party system stood out from the other regional party systems, both because of the far greater strength of micronationalist parties and because of its greater degree of polarization and fragmentation. A dynamic of polarization over center-periphery issues existed not only between statewide parties and the more strident nationalist forces of Euskadi, but also among Basque groups themselves. Indeed, the nationalist bloc encapsulated within itself all other salient societal cleavages—left-right, class, clerical-secular, and generational, in addition to divisions over the regional question. Given this, the majority of Basques who identified strongly with the region and who favored varying degrees of autonomy could remain within the regionalist camp and did not have to cross over to Spanish parties because of ideological, class, or religious considerations. But, though this contributed to the overall strength of Basque parties relative to statewide groups, the wide differences among micronationalist forces with regard to a host of issues made it impossible for them to develop a consensus over Basque autonomy. In addition, these intense divisions made it extremely difficult for the largest and the historic Basque party, the PNV, to make binding commitments on behalf of Basque nationalists in its negotiations over autonomy with the central government. Rivalry between the PNV and Herri Batasuna also meant that the PNV would find it difficult even to enter into pragmatic bargaining with Madrid political elites because of its vulnerability to charges by the *abertzale* left of abandoning the fundamental claims of the Basque nation. Finally, the rancorous rhetoric and disruptive behavior of PNV elites during the constituent process contributed significantly to tensions over the regional question, despite the party's more moderate position regarding self-government.

Polarization of the Basque party system was reinforced further by the distinct context of partisan politics in Euskadi. Unlike in Catalunya and Galicia, conflicts over the regional question were played out both in escalating acts of terrorism on the part of ETA and in frequent street confrontations between Basque nationalists and the Spanish police. The impact of such violence was not only to fuel already heightened emotions among all segments of Basque society, but also to effectively disenfranchise many voters who, out of fear of reprisal, stayed in their homes rather than come out in open support of the UCD or AP.

These characteristics of Basque politics and society all contributed to the emergence in Euskadi of a highly distinct party system. The distinctiveness of the Basque party system and the critical importance of the center-periphery cleavage within it lay at the heart of the regional question in Spanish politics and posed the most serious challenge to the legitimacy and stability of the new democratic regime.

CHAPTER TEN

Conclusion and Epilogue

THE MODERATELY FRAGMENTED
four-party system that emerged at the national level in Spain following the death of Francisco Franco was one in which expressions of
conflict were restrained and the structure of partisan competition
was centripetal. These characteristics greatly facilitated the difficult
task of founding a new political regime. One party, the centrist UCD,
held power throughout the 1977–1982 period by means of single-
party minority governments. Its principal rival, the PSOE, became
increasingly moderate during this protracted constituent period.
And neither of the two more extreme nationwide parties, the PCE
and AP, threatened to polarize or destabilize the system—indeed,
they occasionally played crucial and positive roles in founding the
new regime. Two distinct regional subsystems also emerged, due to
the intensity of micronationalist sentiments in Catalunya and, especially, in the Basque country. The six-party system of Catalunya was
slightly more fragmented than that of the national level, and its underlying structure of social and cultural cleavages was more complex,
but it too could be characterized throughout this period as only
moderately polarized and as centripetal in its structure of competition. The party system of Euskadi, however, was marked by sometimes violent conflict among greatly divergent alternatives. The degree of polarization along the center-periphery cleavage was
extreme, and the centrifugal drives inherent in the region actually
led to increased political fragmentation with the formation of the
anti-system Herri Batasuna in 1978. The existence of these two regional party systems greatly complicates Spanish politics and adds
considerably to its overall level of polarization and fragmentation.

In this book we have sought to explain how and why this complex party system came into existence. We have argued that no single element can adequately account for the outcome. It was, instead, the product of an interaction among several factors. More specifically, our research suggests that the characteristics of the party system that emerged in the 1976–1979 period were the product of six factors: (1) the interaction of the voters' attitudinal predispositions with their perceptions of each party's ideological stance; (2) voters' feelings toward party leaders; (3) the effects of electoral laws; (4) the strength of each party's infrastructural organization; (5) the nature of the post-Franco transition to democracy; and (6) the advantages of incumbency and the politics of consensus.

The first factor is *the attitudinal predispositions of the voters interacting with their perceptions of the ideological stance of each party.* (The term "ideological" is used here loosely: it refers to the general idea of whether a party is progressive or conservative, democratic or authoritarian, etc. and does not necessarily reflect the exact content of a party's electoral program or formal ideological declarations.) In Spain in 1977 and 1979 most voters were moderately progressive in their political values. The electoral success of the UCD can be attributed in large measure to the fact that its leaders were able to assemble a broad centrist coalition, draft a vague but decidedly moderate statement of principles, and, most importantly, behave in a manner consistent with those reformist principles. The image thereby projected fit well with the political predispositions of the largest bloc of voters. The PSOE was also perceived by the electorate as being a relatively moderate option and as a result did quite well. The PCE and AP, however, were regarded by most voters as belonging to extreme segments of the political spectrum. Certainly, the historical memories and negative images inherited from the past played a key role in affecting popular perceptions of the positions of these two parties. By 1979 these images were in some respects out of date and did not reflect the parties' recent behavior, but they, nevertheless, led most voters to view the AP and PCE as nonviable voting choices.

In Euskadi and Catalunya the most notable feature of public opinion was the presence of highly salient micronationalist sentiments. The persistence of Basque and Catalán national identities served as bases for the emergence or reemergence of both moderate and extreme nationalist parties. Closely related to these attitudes were varying preferences concerning the restructuring of the Spanish state. The complete absence of consensus and the wide divergence of such preferences in Euskadi (where nearly one-quarter of the population favored independence from Spain) led to a polarization of politics in the region and the fragmentation of its party system. The overwhelming consensus of opinion in support of intermediate levels of autonomy for Catalunya, on the other hand, provided little basis for the electoral success of a Catalán *independentista* party and contributed to the relative moderation of politics in that region.

The *popular images of party leaders* are empirically associated with, but conceptually distinct from, the ideological factor mentioned above. Voters on the left were, of course, more disposed to like the leaders of leftist parties and dislike conservative leaders, and vice versa. But the attractiveness of party leaders can play an independent role in inducing voters to cast ballots for specific parties. This is especially true for electors who are more or less equidistant from two parties and for whom the personal attractiveness of a party's national leader may serve as a deciding and decisive factor. In the 1977–1979 period both Adolfo Suárez and Felipe González were very popular and certainly contributed to the success of their respective parties. As in other countries, the age of television has brought about a personalization of politics. The 1979 campaign, in particular, was presidential in its focus and gave great emphasis to the leadership qualities of Suárez and González. The attractiveness of the other two party leaders was not as widespread and was confined, mostly, to the voters on the left and right ends of the spectrum. Both Carrillo and Fraga, moreover, tended to elicit strong antagonistic feelings and thus polarized voters much more than Suárez and González. This was especially true in the case of Fraga who was the object of intense devotion on the part of the conservative elements and of intense hostility on the part of progressive Spaniards.

The *electoral law and institutions* regulating party financing gave disproportionate representation and public funds to the two largest parties. The smallest political groups were devastated by these institutional arrangements: they were denied representation in visible political arenas, thus reinforcing their position of inferiority, and were driven to bankruptcy. The characteristics of the electoral law gave the larger parties the opportunity to issue campaign appeals for the *voto útil,* that is, to attract those voters who might prefer to cast ballots for ideologically proximate but smaller parties on the grounds that such votes would be "wasted." At the national level, the electoral system greatly benefitted the UCD and the PSOE, worked to the detriment of the PCE and AP, and virtually wiped out smaller parties with geographically dispersed bases of support. If its purpose was to reduce the degree of fragmentation of the party system, it certainly succeeded. At the regional level, especially in Euskadi and Catalunya, electoral institutions generally favored the two largest, moderate micronationalist groups, the PNV and the CDC-led coalitions, although the extent of representational bias depended on the size of the province.

The fourth factor was the *party organization infrastructure.* The four nationwide parties that emerged from the 1977 election with significant parliamentary representation all possessed organizational infrastructures that enabled them to field candidates and conduct campaigns in all parts of the country (the sole exception being the UCD in Guipúzcoa). In Euskadi the PNV was also well developed organizationally. Most of the numerous parties that performed badly in 1977 suffered from organizational deficiencies, sometimes so severely that they were unable to present lists of candidates in many important areas. In some cases, organizational weakness was sufficient to offset other, normally powerful advantages. Thus, the PSP, led by the prestigious and popular Enrique Tierno Galván and perceived by most voters as close to the modal center-left segment of the political spectrum, was routed by its socialist rival, the PSOE, which had mounted a more extensive and better-financed campaign. Similarly, the UCD, with a far superior organizational network, totally destroyed its social democratic and Christian democratic competitors, even though they occupied the same basic "political space" and in some cases were led by highly visible and popular figures.

Organizational development and effectiveness, however, cannot automatically be equated with electoral success. To be sure, parties must have a certain minimal level of organizational presence in many areas in order to be taken seriously or even simply to be visible to voters. Parties that do not go beyond such a minimum organizational threshold (for example, the PSP and the various liberal, social democratic and Christian democratic parties) are all too easy victims of *voto útil* appeals by their larger rivals. Once this threshold is surpassed, however, the relationship between organizational advantage and electoral success tends to weaken considerably. This is so because the advantage of party organization is offset by other factors, such as the preexisting negative image of the party or the lack of broad appeal of its leaders. In 1977, for example, the Communist party had by far the most well-developed organizational infrastructure of any party in Spain: the largest membership, the most skilled and experienced local leadership, the most thorough geographical coverage, the largest trade union, and the most visible "presence" in many influential sectors of society. Yet, in spite of all this, it received less than one-third of the votes won by the less well-organized PSOE. Clearly, there are limits to what party organization can accomplish.

The *peaceful character of the transition to democracy* greatly affected the electoral fortunes of the four nationwide parties. It reinforced the moderate political predispositions of the electorate; it enabled the governing elite to take credit for the successful dismantling of an authoritarian regime; and the initial uncertainty about its ultimate outcome confounded the strategic choices made by other parties at earlier stages in the transition. In 1976 it was by no means clear how (and even if) a transition to democracy would be accomplished. The leaders of the Socialist and Communist parties, completely skeptical of the reformist intentions of Adolfo Suárez, formulated their partisan strategies on the assumption that the transition would either be accomplished by means of an abrupt break or not at all. Accordingly, they relied heavily on the rhetoric and actual use of mass mobilizations against what they feared would be a perpetuation of the Franquist regime. Much to the surprise of the parties of the left, Adolfo Suárez and several other founders of the UCD succeeded in dismantling the Franquist regime via *reforma,* rather than the more potentially tumultuous *ruptura,* which they had anticipated.

This peaceful process of change fit well with most Spaniards' preferences for peace and order and reinforced the moderate character of public opinion. It is likely that a more abrupt regime transformation, accompanied by higher levels of disorder and violence, would have polarized public opinion and created a situation much less favorable to a moderate reformist party, such as the UCD. Instead, the nature of the transition undercut the mass-mobilization strategies of the PCE and PSOE, as well as the electoral chances of parties (such as the AP) that might have benefitted from a backlash against the turmoil that a *ruptura* would have entailed.

The sixth factor is the effect of *incumbency and the politics of consensus.* In much the same way, "the politics of consensus," which characterized the interelection period of 1977–1979, redounded to the immediate benefit of the UCD. Despite expectations that the "automatic majority" held in the Cortes by the UCD and AP would lead to adoption of a conservative, proclerical Constitution, a relatively progressive, nonclerical (but not anticlerical) Constitution was adopted—one that, in addition, gave far more explicit recognition of the multinational character of Spain (and implied a much more extensive decentralization of the Spanish state) than had been anticipated. Thus, Adolfo Suárez and the UCD were able to go into the first two democratic elections claiming credit for the significant political changes accomplished in the relative absence of violence and upheaval. In addition, since they, as the incumbent government, were able to control both the direction and pace of political developments (including the convoking of elections), they could formulate short-term electoral strategies in the face of less uncertainty than that confronting other parties.

In Euskadi this picture was quite different. Neither the new Constitution nor the Statute of Autonomy was fully acceptable to all Basque nationalist parties. The extended constituent period of 1976 through 1979 was one marked by incessant mass mobilizations and a self-reinforcing cycle of violence. In some cities (such as Pamplona, San Sebastián, and Rentería), violent clashes between pro-ETA demonstrators and Spanish police were almost daily occurrences, as were assassinations of Spanish police and army officers. These highly visible and emotive events increased the level of hatred and distrust among competing groups. Under these circumstances, an already fragmented and polarized regional party system became even more so as the transition unfolded.

It is clear from this brief summary that the behavior of political elites was by far the most important factor in the emergence of the new party system. Electoral and party financing laws were the product of conscious deliberations and negotiations among party leaders. Elites were the driving force behind the creation or expansion of party organizational infrastructures. Their electoral strategies determined the ideological stance and overall image they would present to the voters. Moreover, in the role of electoral strategists political elites determined how organizational resources would be deployed. As founders of a new political regime they also greatly affected the nature of the transition, and in doing so they influenced the nature of public opinion itself. Finally, in the absence of long-standing partisan attachments, and in the age of television, party leaders themselves served as significant objects of popular identification and electoral support.

This conclusion about the crucial role played by party elites might not hold in the case of an older party system in which long-standing partisan attachments at the mass level reduce the malleability of the electorate. In the process of founding a new party system, however, particularly when it is accompanied by a major change of regime, the political values and predilections of the population serve only to establish general parameters. Within these, the balance of forces is determined most directly by political elites.

Changes in the behavior of these same party elites after 1979 help to explain why the Spanish party system was altered in 1982. But, before turning to post-1979 developments, it is important to stress that party elites during the transition were simultaneously pursuing three sets of objectives not always compatible with one another: short-term electoral victory, the long-term institutionalization of party structures, and the establishment of a legitimate and stable political regime. A brief review of the manner in which elites addressed the major political and social issues reveals that, with the exception of the center-periphery cleavage, political leaders were more or less successful in pursuing vote-maximizing strategies that simultaneously contributed to the stability of Spain's democracy. In doing so, however, they sometimes sowed the seeds of discord, which ultimately grew into intense intraparty conflict and threatened the survival of some parties.

This tension between the requirements of different goals can be seen most clearly in the manner in which party elites dealt with ideological divisions within the polity. The centripetal thrust of the first two campaigns, and especially that of 1979, contributed to regime stability and, from the standpoint of the four nationwide parties, also represented rational vote-maximizing electoral strategies. Given the unimodal center-left distribution of public opinion, the efforts of the UCD and PSOE to attract moderately progressive voters and the parallel drives of the PCE and AP, which deemphasized appeals to the extremes, represented a pure application of Downsian strategic principles. They also led to a moderation of postures and to a softening of ideological conflict, which redounded to the benefit of the democratic regime as a whole. In this respect, comparative data suggest that, though Spain was more polarized in left-right terms than other stable Western European regimes, such as Great Britain, West Germany, and the Netherlands, it was less so than France, Italy, and Finland.[1]

These center-seeking drives, however, gave rise to intraparty conflict. By including within the initial coalition representatives of diverse political families, the UCD was able to attract a broad range of voters in the first two elections. Moreover, the party's heterogeneity and the lack of a clear ideological stance defused potential interparty clashes during the most crucial stages of the transition. But this same heterogeneity made the formulation of policy proposals a difficult and conflictual task, as decisions on crucial issues produced intense dissatisfaction on the part of one political family or another. And these incessant intraparty struggles contributed decisively in the end to the breakup of the UCD. The moderation of ideological stands had similar, if less dramatic, consequences for the other nationwide parties. The staking out of an unequivocal democratic position led to the collapse of the original AP coalition. The abandonment of Marxism-Leninism by the PCE and the efforts to downgrade the status of Marxism within the PSOE also generated intraparty conflict, with the most visible manifestations of those tensions apparent after the 1979 election.

Much of the same can be said with reference to class divisions. The electoral strategies of the four major nationwide parties were to a varying degree interclassist, and so was the composition of their electorates. AP and UCD supporters were, to be sure, more often middle class than were Socialist and Communist voters, but no party could claim to speak exclusively on behalf of one social class—nor would they want to, because a too close identification with any one social group might make the party unattractive to voters from other social strata. Consequently, the articulation of class conflict by party elites was rather muted, with stabilizing implications for the regime as a whole. This downplaying of the class dimension, however, generated strong tensions, particularly within the two leftist parties. Efforts to define more broadly the notion of the "working class" produced lively and sometimes rancorous debates, particularly within the PSOE. The most serious manifestations of such conflict arose out of beliefs within the UGT and the CCOO that they were being asked by the two leftist parties to make sacrifices in adhering to the Pacts of Moncloa and were getting little in return. In Catalunya class-related tensions interacted with the center-periphery cleavage, as the UGT emerged as an organizational stronghold for the immigrant working class within the PSC-PSOE. Finally, class-based tensions also manifested themselves within the UCD. Prompt enactment of tax reform legislation and other initiatives related to "the politics of consensus"

led part of the business community, and ultimately its major association, the Confederación Española de Organizaciones Empresariales,
to regard the UCD, especially Adolfo Suárez, as traitors who had
failed to protect the interests of the upper social strata that had supported the centrist party.

Given Spain's record, the transition could have been imperiled by
the politicization of religious divisions. As we have shown, the potential for exacerbating conflict over religious issues certainly existed.
Communist voters were overwhelmingly secular and displayed anticlerical attitudes; the PSOE electorate was divided in its religious values
and practices; and AP and UCD voters were predominately religious
and pro-Church in their sentiments. Despite this sharp differentiation,
however, party elites chose not to exploit fully the clerical-
secular cleavage. The gravest threat to a revival of religious conflict
was presented by the constituent process itself. Fortunately, implementation of the "politics of consensus" during constitutional deliberations over Church-state relations laid to rest fears that the religious issue would pose a direct threat to the legitimacy and stability
of the new regime. And in the election that followed, party elites did
not overly stress differences over religious matters. Indeed, Communist and Socialist party elites sought to neutralize such issues, even
though they were directly attacked by the Spanish Episcopal Conference. For its part, the UCD, though portraying itself as a defender of
Christian humanism, by and large did not overly stress this appeal to
the electorate. Elite behavior served to soften interparty differences
and, thus, to stabilize the new regime, but the religious issue nonetheless proved to be a critically divisive one in the years that followed
for the UCD. Once such issues as legalization of divorce, abortion,
and the public financing of private schools came to the fore, differences among the UCD political families exploded and contributed
significantly to the party's demise.

Despite the concerted efforts by most political elites during the
transition to meet the demands for regional autonomy, the center-
periphery cleavage, unlike others, remained a serious threat to the

survival of the new regime. Most Catalán nationalists regarded the Constitution as satisfactory, and the principal Catalán party campaigned on behalf of its ratification, but the same could not be said for the PNV. It refused to endorse the Constitution in the Cortes, its parliamentary delegation walked out as ratifying votes were taken, and its supporters (at the urging of the party leadership) abstained in the December 1978 referendum. By themselves, these actions by the most moderate and largest of Basque parties constituted a serious challenge to the fledgling democracy. However, a more ominous threat from the standpoint of regime stability came from the strengthening of the political forces that favored Basque independence and from the escalation of ETA violence.

The lack of satisfactory resolution of center-periphery issues created, in turn, another potentially explosive situation. Because military and police officers were the principal targets of ETA assassinations, any concessions to micronationalist demands by the democratic regime led to heightened perceptions on the part of some key segments of society, the military in particular, that democracy meant the dismemberment of Spain itself. As the neo-Fascist newspaper *El Alcázar* (read by many army officers) ominously stated on the eve of Basque and Catalán autonomy referenda in autumn 1979: "Today it is decided whether Spain should exist or commit suicide."[2] Given the history of military interference in Spanish politics, such views raised the specter of a military overthrow of the new regime. Thus, the combination of irreducible micronationalism and the inflexible centralist posture of other minorities exacerbated already difficult attempts by political elites to deal effectively with the regional question.

Efforts to come to terms with this explosive issue also led to internal party conflicts, particularly between national party elites and the leadership of regional branches of statewide political forces. Given their different constituencies and the need of regional party leaders to emphasize autonomist demands and assume more overt regional identities in order to compete successfully with micronationalist groups, conflicts over the extent, substance, and pace of regional self-government occurred within the statewide parties themselves. These led, as we shall see, to schisms within the Communist party and to significant electoral defeats for the UCD in regional contests, which foreshadowed the governing party's collapse in 1982.

EPILOGUE: THE REALIGNMENT OF 1982

By the end of 1979 Spain's new democratic regime and its party system appeared to be moving toward consolidation. The Constitution and the basic political institutions of the parliamentary monarchy were accepted as legitimate by all political groups with the exception of some Basque nationalist forces and a tiny group of extreme right-wingers. Traditionally explosive class, religious, and ideological conflicts were being expressed in a moderate fashion and contained within proper institutional channels. With the approval of Catalán and Basque autonomy statutes in the autumn referenda (the latter with the endorsement of both the PNV and Euskadiko Ezkerra, and opposed by only Herri Batasuna), even the regional question appeared to be on its way to resolution.[3] By the end of the year 1979, one could argue that the transition to democracy had been completed and the institutional framework for more normal politics and further consolidation of the regime had been established.

The party system too seemed to have reached a stable configuration. The 1979 general election reaffirmed the simplification of the party system and the strength of the two major moderate parties, the UCD and PSOE. The success of those two forces, coupled with the weakness of extremist and antisystem parties (except in Euskadi), seemed to preclude any serious polarization. In addition, the low volatility of the electorate (again, with the exception of Euskadi) seemed promising evidence for the future stability of the party system. The April 1979 municipal elections reflected a shift of the vote somewhat toward the left, which had the effect of incorporating the Socialists and Communists into positions of governmental responsibility without placing any additional stress on the system.

During the following three years, however, some of these trends were reversed. The regional question was reopened as the result of a shift from the quasi-consociational practices of "the politics of consensus" (which had been revived and used in the course of successful negotiations over the Basque and Catalán autonomy statutes) to a more legalistic and majoritarian style of decision making in dealing with center-periphery relations. Similarly, elite-level restraint concerning religious matters broke down on two important occasions—during enactment of the statute regulating public and private education and the legislation legalizing divorce—with rancorous inter- and intraparty conflict as the end product. Finally, and most dramatically, on February 23, 1981, segments of the paramilitary Civil Guard and the army (including several high-ranking generals) attempted to topple the new regime through a coup d'état. Although public support for a democratic political system remained high, concerns about the efficacy of political leaders and institutions in solving basic problems, as well as grave doubts about the continuing loyalty of the armed forces, made consolidation of the regime more doubtful.[4]

Developments affecting the party system were even more dramatic. After 1979 the party system entered into a process of decomposition at the elite level, which culminated in a partisan realignment of massive proportions in the general election of 1982. The governing UCD suffered perhaps the single greatest electoral disaster ever to befall a contemporary Western European party. Its share of the vote plunged from 35 to 6 percent and its delegation in the Congress of Deputies shrank from 168 to 11 seats. The PCE lost over 80 percent of its parliamentary delegation, and, in the face of this disaster, Santiago Carrillo resigned from the post of secretary general. One big winner was the Socialist party, which gained 16 percentage points and enough seats to form the first single-party Socialist government in Spanish history. Another was AP (a gain of 19 percent of the vote), which surged from 9 seats in 1979 to 107 in 1982 (table 57).

How and why did this realignment take place? We believe that these more recent events are the outgrowth of trends and potential problems inherent in the party development strategies that we have analyzed in this book. Indeed, the way in which the 1982 realignment came about reaffirms our conclusion about the importance of the role played by party elites in the development of the Spanish party system. Briefly put, in the period between the 1979 and 1982 elections, each of the four largest parties experienced crises of major proportions, the seeds of which have been described. The two parties that triumphed in 1982, the PSOE and AP, had successfully resolved their internal problems early in the interelection period. On the other hand, the defeated UCD and PCE were caught in the throes of divisive intraparty struggles on the eve of the 1982 election, and their images in the eyes of the electorate were badly damaged. These differences in intraparty dynamics stand out clearly from even a cursory examination of the problems encountered by the leadership of the four major parties between 1979 and 1982 and the ways in which they were met.

TABLE 57

RESULTS OF 1977, 1979, AND 1982 ELECTIONS
FOR CONGRESS OF DEPUTIES

Party	1977: Pct. of Total Valid Votes	1977: Seats Won	1979: Pct. of Total Valid Votes	1979: Seats Won	1982: Pct. of Total Valid Votes	1982: Seats Won
UCD	34.0%	165	35.1%	168	6.3%	11
PSOE	28.9	118	30.5	121	48.4	202
PCE-PSUC	9.2	20	10.8	23	4.1	4
AP	8.0	16	6.1	9	26.6	107
CDS					2.9	2
PNV	1.7	8	1.7	7	1.8	8
PDC/CiU	2.8	11	2.7	8	3.7	12
Others	15.6	12	13.1	14	6.3	4

UCD   Unión de Centro Democrático and Centristes de Catalunya, CC-UCD
PSOE   Partido Socialista Obrero Español and Socialistes de Catalunya
PCE-PSUC   Partido Comunista de España and Partit Socialista Unificat de Catalunya
AP   Alianza Popular (in 1979, Coalición Democrática; in 1982 includes AP-PDP-PDL-UCD coalition in Euskadi)
CDS   Centro Democrático y Social
PNV   Partido Nacionalista Vasco (includes Nacionalistas Vascos in Navarra)
PDC/CiU   Pacte Democràtic per Catalunya (1977) and Convergència i Unió (1979 and 1982)

Sources: Ministerio de la Gobernación, Dirección General de la Política Interior, *Elecciones Generales 1977;* Ministerio del Interior, Dirección General de Política Interior, *Elecciones Generales 1979;* and Alejandro Muñoz Alonso, *Las Elecciones del Cambio,* Barcelona: Editorial Argos Vergara, 1984, p. 229.

THE SOCIALIST PARTY:
FROM OPPOSITION TO GOVERNMENT

In the very dynamics of a party, they say, there is first the
hour of the mystics, and then the hour of the politicians.
When the mystics of the epoch of clandestinity no longer
fit with the needs of the party, the politicians will
devour the mystics.

—*from an interview with a*
PSOE provincial leader, 1979

The first Spanish party to experience a crisis was the PSOE. In the preceding chapters we have explored the origins of these struggles. In both the 1977 and 1979 elections, the party leadership adopted "catch-all" electoral strategies, intended to increase the appeal of the party to moderate voters by softening its programmatic and ideological stands and by demonstrating that the PSOE was stable, responsible, and prepared to govern. Those appeals had been undercut, however, particularly in the 1979 election, by the maximalist rhetoric of the party's formal ideological declarations, by its unstable "assembly government" style of internal deliberations, and by the electorate's fear that "mass mobilizations," which party leaders sometimes threatened to unleash, could seriously destabilize the new regime. One observer flatly asserted: "Socialists attributed their defeat in March 1979 to the persistence of an image too radical for most moderate voters, which hindered its presentation as a real alternative in power and created contradictions between its theoretical declarations and its electoral program, which were skillfully taken advantage of by its competitors in the campaign."[5] Thus, Felipe González proposed the adoption of certain changes in the party's formal ideology. His efforts were cut short, however, by fierce opposition from many party militants and by the convoking of general elections. An attempt to secure formal endorsement of these modifications through a party congress had to be postponed from December 1978 until May 1979. It was at that Twenty-Eighth Party Congress that these internal struggles came to a head.

In an effort to secure massive support for their proposed ideological changes, González and Guerra negotiated a compromise with the various ideological factions represented on the party's executive committee. The resulting text was, nevertheless, rejected by the congress. Instead, the declaration passed by the delegates reaffirmed the PSOE's character as a Marxist party.[6] This was not the only defeat suffered by the party leadership. The official candidate for the presidency of the congress, Gregorio Peces-Barba (one of the seven authors of the initial text of the Constitution), was rejected in favor of a Marxist. The party leadership was criticized for its "lack of understanding" of regional-autonomist aspirations, and a resolution was passed calling for "the recognition of the multinational reality of Spain [and] the right to self-determination of its peoples."[7] And a proposal to permit the organization of ideological factions within the party (which would give maximalists an organizational base from which to attack the moderating efforts of the party executive) was narrowly defeated in a committee vote. The overall atmosphere of the congress served to punish and embarrass the González-Guerra leadership team for their efforts to abandon the maximalist stands adopted in 1976: most heavily applauded were references to Marxism, attacks on efforts to lower its formal status, and the introduction of visiting delegations representing the Cuban Communist party, the pro-independence party of Puerto Rico, and the Polisario Front; speeches by Felipe González and others favoring ideological moderation received tepid applause, at best.[8] The various efforts of most delegates to "teach a lesson" to the party's executive led one high-ranking party leader to describe the congress as a "Freudian" phenomenon.

In response to this disaster, Felipe González and Alfonso Guerra resigned from the executive committee of the party. They did not, however, retire from active involvement in party affairs, nor did they passively accept the verdict of the Twenty-Eighth Party Congress. Instead, they succeeded in halting the formal closure of the congress (thereby preventing its resolutions from becoming official) and in convoking an "Extraordinary Congress" for September, when these issues would be addressed anew, but by a different set of delegates. In the four months between the Twenty-Eighth Congress and the Extraordinary Congress, González and Guerra traveled extensively throughout the country, holding meetings with provincial executive committees (which were much more "Felipista" than the majority of delegates to the Twenty-Eighth Congress) and coordinating their efforts to control more effectively the selection of delegates to the Extraordinary Congress. They were greatly assisted in these endeavors by the implicit blackmail of the party inherent in González's resignation: given his enormous prestige within the party and his great popularity among Spanish voters, it was clear that a PSOE without Felipe González as its leader would not be in a position to challenge the UCD as an "alternative in power" in the foreseeable future. As a result of their efforts, González and Guerra were in a position to dominate the Extraordinary Congress and secure approval of changes in the party's ideology.

The most visible of these modifications lowered the status of Marxism from an official doctrine to that of one among several intellectual traditions represented within the party. The Twenty-Seventh Congress of the PSOE had formulated a description of the party in 1976 as a "class party, and therefore of the masses, Marxist and democratic." The corresponding declaration adopted in September 1979 describes the PSOE as a "class party, of the masses, democratic and federal."[9] This change, however, did not by any means constitute a complete rejection of Marxism. At least partly to mollify maximalist militants, the ideological resolution retains Marxism as a "method of analysis" and calls for a substantial transformation of Spanish society.[10]

A second significant change was the formal transformation of the party from a "mass movement" to something closer to the "catch-all" model described in earlier chapters. The political resolution adopted at the Twenty-Eighth Congress had formally acknowledged the mass-mobilization character of the party.[11] The corresponding statement endorsed at the Extraordinary Congress totally excludes all mention of "popular mobilization" as a medium for party activity. This formal declaration was accompanied by a notable change in the strategies and style of the party. Thereafter, party leaders completely abandoned threats of street mobilizations as a means of attempting to influence government policy (the only exception being collaboration with other parties in organizing massive prodemocracy rallies and marches in the aftermath of the February 23 coup attempt).

Finally, and perhaps most importantly, much higher levels of discipline were established within the party: it ceased to resemble a student protest movement or an assembly government in its internal deliberations. To some extent, this resulted from increased vigilance and authoritative (some might say authoritarian) behavior on the part of party executives in the aftermath of the Twenty-Eighth Party Congress debacle. It is also likely that the normal tendency of party militants to become demobilized and apathetic as political life becomes more routine (as compared with the excitement of the early states of the transition to democracy) further contributed to this development. The end result was that, by the time of the Twenty-Ninth Congress in November 1981, Felipe González and Alfonso Guerra had secured full control of a disciplined party. Where the Twenty-Eighth Congress had been described as "Freudian," the 1981 party meeting was unflatteringly compared to congresses of the Franquist Movimiento Nacional and the Bulgarian Communist party.[12] Nonetheless, the establishment of internal party discipline almost certainly aided the PSOE in implementing its "catch-all" strategy in the 1982 parliamentary election.

ALIANZA POPULAR: FROM MARGINALITY TO RELEVANCE

We have always had the same objective. In 1977 we wanted
to lay down the bases of a future party like the British
Conservative party and the American Republican party.
We continue to hold that idea. That is our objective, and
there is no other.
—*from a 1981 interview with
an Alianza Popular leader*

For Manuel Fraga and the AP, the most serious crisis was the outcome of the 1979 election itself. In the aftermath of its defeat in the general election and the withdrawal of most of its candidates from the municipal elections, the party and its leadership were demoralized and greatly reduced in political resources. Fraga resigned as party leader immediately after the March election, handing control of the party to one of his long-time collaborators, Felix Pastor. Return visits by one of the authors to 15 provinces for postelection interviews revealed that many party militants dropped out of active involvement in its affairs, some local notables had shifted their support to the victorious UCD, and several party offices were vacant or rarely open for business.

But the 1979 election setback was only one of a series of crises, which began with the disappointing election results of 1977 and intensified with the schism over endorsement of the Constitution and the creation of Coalición Democrática (CD). These crises involved two different factors: the first, and by far the most important, was the ideology of the party, and the second concerned its organizational structure. Some of these problems had been resolved by the time of the 1979 elections. Doubts about the party's committment to democracy were assuaged by the 1978 departure of the more extreme right-wing members of its founding elite and by its active support for the Constitution in the December 1978 referendum. The clientelistic nature of the party that entered the 1977 elections was no longer a significant characteristic: many *caciques* had departed by mid-1979, and the AP began to rely more heavily on its own organizational resources. But some questions still remained unanswered. These were, for the most part, resolved by the time of the Third Party Congress in December 1979.

Many within the AP felt uncomfortable with the concessions their party had made in the process of creating the CD. They resented the disappearance of the party's identity within the new coalition, its ideological redefinition as of the "center-right," and the prominence given to Areilza and Osorio during the campaign (and the concomitant reduction in that of Manuel Fraga). Electoral defeat in 1979 led to a reassessment of those decisions. The first matter to be resolved was the reaffirmation of the AP's future as an independent party. Since many within the AP apparatus believed that the formation of the CD had merely confused voters and led a sizable segment of the AP's electorate to sit out the 1979 election, plans to merge formally with the parties of Osorio and Areilza were quietly abandoned. Thenceforth, the Coalición Democrática was regarded as merely the name of a delegation to the Congress of Deputies, and not as the framework for a future unified party. Since the center-right self-designation used in 1979 was also regarded as having caused confusion and alienated conservative voters, that change was effectively repealed by the political resolutions adopted at the Third Congress, even though many of the programmatic modifications (such as a clearer defense of business interests and a free-market economy) were retained.

Finally, Manuel Fraga reemerged as the unchallenged leader of the party. The congress ratified the presidential (if not personalistic) structure of the party apparatus. Resignations on the eve of the congress by Felix Pastor and two AP vice presidents further indicated that Fraga would assume full control of the party apparatus. Over an extended period of time, Fraga asserted his public status as the dominant figure to the right of the UCD. Areilza and his collaborator, Antonio de Senillosa, were so effectively displaced that they abandoned the CD and joined the UCD just before the 1982 election. Thus, by the early 1980s, the AP had eliminated many of the inconsistencies that plagued it in the past. It emerged as a party of the democratic right—not of the authoritarian right nor of the center-right. It relied more fully on its own organizational resources—not those of local notables nor those of partners in a loose coalition. And it was led by only one person, Manuel Fraga, who no longer shared the limelight or control of his party with other dignitaries—neither from the Franquist regime nor from the transition.

THE COMMUNIST PARTY: DISUNITY AND DEFEAT

When a party, in three years, loses 120 thousand members, when it loses 200 thousand votes, when we have open crises everywhere, you must conclude that we did something wrong—by definition, right? And Carrillo keeps saying,

"I wasn't wrong, and I'm still right." Well *something* must
have been done badly!
—*from a 1983 interview with a PCE
leader opposed to Santiago Carrillo*

The model of a party open to everybody is cute, but very
confusing. A deideologized, lay party, within which you
can think anything, do anything, and say anything is no
longer a Communist party. There must be a minimum
of political and ideological coherence, and of acceptance
of basic principles.
—*from a 1983 interview with a
supporter of Santiago Carrillo*

The fortunes of the PCE, by way of contrast, deteriorated markedly during this same period. In the immediate aftermath of the
1979 elections, Communists had reason to feel optimistic about the
future. The party had scored significant electoral gains in the parliamentary election and very substantial gains in the municipal elections, which enabled the PCE to enter into governing coalitions in
most of Spain's largest cities. This government experience, coupled
with the moderate and constructive role played by the party's representatives in the constituent processes of 1977–1979, gave the PCE a
new respectability in the eyes of many Spaniards, which could have
contributed to further incremental advances in subsequent elections.
Instead, in the two years preceding the 1982 elections, the party was
rent by factional fights, expulsions, desertions of prominent leaders,
regional tensions, and bitter attacks on the leadership of Santiago
Carrillo. The end results were an electoral rout in 1982 and Carrillo's
resignation as secretary general.

The origins of these destructive internal conflicts are enormously
complex and are related to the party's heterogeneous composition,
which resulted from the recruitment of persons from vastly different backgrounds and with different political values over its extended
period of organizational expansion. In sociodemographic terms,
these may be regarded as struggles between intellectuals and working-class cadres, between different generations, between center and
periphery, and between groups who had entered the party through

different organizational channels. In terms of ideological factions, Carrillo was attacked by pro-Moscow groups (often called *afganos*), Eurocommunists who favored a thorough democratization of the party and resented the authoritarian style of Carrillo (the so-called *renovadores*), Leninists (who attempted to stake out an intermediate position between the *afganos* and the *renovadores*), and leaders of regional Communist parties, especially the Basque PCE-EKP, who demanded independence from Madrid in establishing basic policies. In short, the Eurocommunist consensus so carefully constructed by Carrillo over more than two decades totally broke down.

A harbinger of things to come was the leadership struggle that broke out within the Catalán PSUC in late 1980. A pro-Soviet faction (which had gained control of the secretariat of organization and, according to a PCE leader, received funds and assistance from the Russian embassy) joined with a Leninist faction to topple the Eurocommunist executive committee of Antoni Gutiérrez Díaz. Within a few short months, the Leninists abandoned that alliance and joined forces with the Eurocommunists, eventually expelling the leaders of the pro-Soviet faction from the party. This culminated in a formal schism and the creation of a rival Communist party.

Carrillo had long struggled against pro-Soviet sectors of the party in his efforts to move the PCE toward adoption of a Eurocommunist ideology and a mass-mobilization (not devotee) structure. With the massive influx into the party of university students, technicians, and professionals, a new potential conflict was created: these individuals tended to support Carrillo's ideological reforms but also expected that the internal democratization of the party would be fully implemented. Instead, the authoritarian leadership styles inherited from the Franquist past did not disappear. By the time of the Tenth PCE Congress in August 1981, these tensions were clearly apparent. Votes taken during that meeting indicated that about 26 percent of the party's elite favored a "renovation" of the party leadership (continuation of Eurocommunism, but under a different leader with a more democratic leadership style), while about 6 percent favored the pro-Soviet stance. Carrillo still retained majority support, but his efforts to retain leadership of the party (in large part, by attacking the *renovadores* as heretical social democrats) contributed to a polarization among the various factions.

These tensions came to a head following an attempt by the Communist party of Euskadi to fuse with the Basque nationalist Euskadiko Ezkerra. This gave rise to subsequent waves of expulsions, not only of the offending Basque leaders, but of distinguished and highly visible *renovadores* (including five members of Madrid's city council), who had organized a public forum in Madrid for the Basques. Accompanying the separation from the party (both voluntary and involuntary) of prominent leaders, large numbers of party militants terminated their membership or ceased to play active roles in its affairs. Thus, by the time of the 1982 elections the membership base of the party (its prime electoral resource) had been reduced; its image of stability, moderation, and responsibility was greatly damaged; rival Communist parties had emerged to challenge it; and the respect or admiration won by Santiago Carrillo in many quarters had been displaced by distrust and hostility.

THE CENTRIST PARTY:
FROM GOVERNMENT TO OBLIVION

Q. "How would you explain the demise of the UCD?"
A. Ortega y Gasset, while speaking about the decadence of Spain, once asked: why are there so many books about the historical decadence of Spain? What one must explain is the Siglo de Oro. The exceptional thing was the Siglo de Oro, the sixteenth century. Well, I now say to you, why should we ask ourselves about the decadence of the UCD? We should be asking ourselves about the success of the UCD. The rare fact is that a group, which had neither unity nor solidity, which had no history, nonetheless had an almost absolute majority in two elections. Why? That is what we must ask. The other is easy."
*—from an interview
with a former UCD president*

The lack of internal cohesion was from the beginning a major problem for the UCD. Tensions among party leaders increased in the immediate aftermath of the 1979 election. In an apparent effort to gain greater control over the UCD, Adolfo Suárez appointed a team of ministers that excluded several of the "barons" of the party, most importantly, Francisco Fernández Ordóñez, Rodolfo Martín Villa, Pío Cabanillas, and Landelino Lavilla (the leader of the Christian democratic faction of the party, who was appointed, instead, to the largely symbolic post of speaker of the Congress of Deputies). This cabinet reshuffle had no immediate impact on party unity but, over the following year and a half, led to a growing resentment among barons of all ideological factions against what they regarded as the personalistic leadership style of Suárez.

A second source of conflict within the party stemmed from the belief that the process of granting autonomy to regions was largely ad hoc—that decentralization policies had been shaped, willy nilly, through sets of bilateral negotiations with representatives of the regions in question, and not in light of any clear understanding of what kind of state structure was likely to emerge. Further adding to these concerns was the belief that other regions, not wishing to appear as "second class" in comparison with Euskadi and Catalunya, would make unreasonable demands on the state. As a means of stopping this growing competition among regions for extensive autonomy statutes and in an effort to impose a coherent framework upon a future *estado de las autonomías,* the leaders of the UCD and PSOE reached a private agreement that would have slowed down the autonomy process for other regions and would have increased the roles in autonomy negotiations of the Cortes and the relevant *diputaciones provinciales.*[13]

The PSOE, however, backed out of that agreement and began to campaign publicly on behalf of more rapid and extensive grants of autonomy for Galicia and Andalucía.[14] It also attacked the UCD, claiming (unfairly) that the governing party was a rigid defender of centralism and that it was seeking to impose second-class status on the other regions. The UCD suffered significant damage from its stance. A prominent party leader, Minister of Culture Manuel Clavero Arévalo, angrily resigned from the party and attempted to form his own centrist party in Andalucía. The UCD also lost heavily

in the 1980 Basque and Catalán regional elections, at least partly because of the anti-autonomy image it had inherited from the struggles over Galicia and Andalucía. Although these electoral setbacks
were not very significant in themselves (the PSOE also suffered substantial defeats in the Basque and Catalán elections), they triggered a
serious crisis of confidence within the governing party and promoted the first of a series of attacks on the leadership of Adolfo
Suárez from both inside and outside of the party.

The most devastating conflicts among UCD elites involved the enactment of legislation dealing with divisive religious issues. The first
of these was an Estatuto de Centros Docentes, a statute that regulates
both public and private educational institutions. The text proposed
by the Christian democratic Minister of Education Otero Novas was
regarded by many within the UCD, as well as by the Socialist and
Communist delegations in the Cortes, as so extreme in its defense of
Church interests as to be unconstitutional. Debate in the Congress of
Deputies over this statute was the most rancorous since the creation
of the new regime. Even more explosive was passage of a bill legalizing divorce in Spain for the first time in four decades. It was almost
inevitable that the legalization of divorce would bring to the surface
latent conflicts between religious and nonreligious or anticlerical
segments of the UCD elite, but this conflict was further exacerbated
by two developments. The first was the election of Pope John Paul II
and his appointment of a new, more conservative Nuncio in Madrid.[15] The Spanish Church began to intervene in political matters
more overtly: in February 1981, for example, the Episcopal Conference issued a statement roundly reaffirming the indissolubility of
marriage and opposing the divorce bill prepared by the UCD Minister of Justice.[16] The second development, which contributed to polarization over this issue, was the replacement of the Christian democrat Iñigo Cavero as Minister of Justice by the social democrat
Francisco Fernández Ordóñez. Cavero's original text of the divorce
bill was liberalized by the new minister. Although the somewhat
more restrictive bill initially proposed was supported by many Christian democrats and appeared to have the grudging endorsement of

the Church, the new text provoked outright rejection by those quarters. Struggles over the wording of the bill led to the breakdown of voting discipline within the UCD delegation in the Cortes and to a marked increase in hostility among factions, especially between Christian democrats, on the one hand, and social democrats and *suaristas*, on the other.

In the face of growing criticism of his allegedly personalistic style of leadership, of regional autonomy policies, and of this "betrayal" of conservative and religious UCD voters, Adolfo Suárez resigned as both President of Government and as head of the UCD on the eve of the party's Second Congress in January 1981. Suárez did not, however, abandon hopes of returning to these positions of power. Indeed, Suárez loyalists retained positions of great strength within the party apparatus: the new party leader was his own brother-in-law, and *suaristas* solidified their control of provincial branches of the party in local congresses held throughout the following summer. These efforts met with increasingly organized opposition within the party. The formal institutionalization of a conservative Christian democratic faction calling itself the Plataforma Moderada in August was one step taken toward excluding Suárez from the party leadership. In retrospect, however, it can be regarded as the first decisive step toward the disintegration of the UCD as a political party.

The decomposition of the UCD accelerated in November 1981 with the departure of Fernández Ordóñez and a small group of social democratic deputies, and their formation of a new Partido de Acción Democrática. Several months later a schism from the right wing of the party led to the formation of a predominately Christian democratic Partido Democrático Popular. Finally, in August 1982 Adolfo Suárez himself left the party, forming a center-left Centro Democrático y Social.

Now lacking a working majority in the Cortes, and in an effort to stem the tide of defections from what remained of the UCD, the prime minister, Leopoldo Calvo Sotelo, asked the king to dissolve the Cortes and hold new elections on October 28, 1982. The result of that contest was a devastating defeat for the UCD. Not even Calvo Sotelo was able to secure a seat in the new Cortes.

CONCLUSION AND EPILOGUE 415

PARTIES, VOTERS, AND
TRANSFORMATION OF THE PARTY SYSTEM

An explanation of the 1982 realignment is clearly beyond the scope of this book,[17] but a prima facie exploration indicates that many of the factors that led to the success of the UCD and PCE in earlier elections were also responsible for their defeat in 1982. A preliminary analysis of survey data gathered shortly after the 1982 election and an additional round of elite interviews conducted in the spring of 1983 also suggest that the origins of that realignment lay at the elite level. Profound changes in the images projected by those elites led to defections by the great majority of 1979 PCE and UCD voters. In 1979 the PCE had carefully cultivated an image of stability, responsibility, moderation, and committment to democracy, and on that basis had gained in popular support. The image it projected later, however, was one of a party wracked by dissension, led by an authoritarian despot, and containing sizable pro-Soviet and perhaps antidemocratic factions. Similarly, the UCD had become Spain's dominant party in the first two democratic elections by filling a broad and heterogeneous "ideological space" and by cultivating the populist appeal of Adolfo Suárez. The centrist party that appeared before the electorate in 1982, however, had been decimated by conflicts over incompatible tenets of the party's all-too-eclectic "ideology" and had recently deposed its most popular leader.

Data from the 1982 survey of the Spanish electorate reveal that, as in earlier elections, most voters cast ballots for those parties to which they were closest on the left-right continuum. One factor that might have contributed to the decline of the PCE was that, following the resignations and expulsions of many ideologically moderate *renovadores*, the Communist party was seen by the voters as being more extreme than it had been in 1979, and hence more distant from the moderate majority of the electorate.[18] It is also possible that a slight shift of voters away from the exact center of the continuum may have contributed marginally to the decline of the UCD. But the data suggest that the 1982 realignment was *not* primarily due to fundamental ideological shifts among voters. The proportion of voters located on the more central segments of the political spectrum remained identical from 1979 to 1982 (53 percent). The fact that large segments of former UCD voters shifted to the PSOE or to AP, notwithstanding the fundamental stability of their position in left-right terms, implies that other variables, notably the leadership factor, determined the outcome of the 1982 contest.[19]

An examination of "feeling thermometer" ratings of political leaders strongly suggests that their varying degrees of personal popularity were clearly relevant to these electoral changes. In 1979 the UCD was led by the popular Adolfo Suárez (whose mean feeling thermometer rating was 5.5 on the 11-point scale); the UCD leader at the time of the 1982 election was Landelino Lavilla (a mean rating of 3.3), and the outgoing UCD prime minister was Leopoldo Calvo Sotelo (3.1)—both of whom were less popular than Francisco Franco (3.8)! Similarly, 16 percent of our respondents in 1979 had positive attitudes (ratings of 7 through 10) toward Santiago Carrillo; positive opinions had fallen to 7 percent by 1982, and his mean thermometer rating stood at 2.9. More direct evidence of the impact of party leadership on the 1982 election results can be seen in a similar examination of persons who had cast ballots for the UCD in 1979: those who shifted to the AP in 1982 rated Manuel Fraga much more positively than any other political leader; former UCD supporters who defected to the PSOE had much more favorable attitudes toward Felipe González than the others; and those who remained loyal to the UCD liked Landelino Lavilla better than any other politician.

Finally, the reasons set forth by former UCD and PCE voters themselves for abandoning their respective parties suggest that leadership struggles and the decline in prestige of centrist and Communist elites contributed to their poor showing in 1982. When presented with a closed-ended list of ten reasons that might explain a shift away from the UCD, a considerable plurality (41 percent) of former centrist voters selected "its style of governing (indecision, lack of seriousness, etc.)." When combined with the other "party leadership" responses ("It's a party in which they were always fighting among themselves" and "It did not have leaders who inspired confidence"), it would appear that 53 percent of our respondents who had voted for the UCD in 1979 shifted their support to another party in 1982 because of their rejection of the leadership style of the outgoing UCD government. Similarly, 38 percent of the respondents who had voted for the PCE in 1979 claimed that they quit the party in 1982 because of leadership defects ("Many of its most attractive figures abandoned the party," "I don't like Carrillo," "It didn't have leaders who inspired confidence," or "It's a party in which they were always fighting among themselves"). In short, these and other data suggest that the 1982 party-system realignment reflected a mass-level repudiation of the UCD and PCE elites in response to their conflictual and seemingly irresponsible behavior of the preceding three years.

Other party and electoral-system characteristics examined in this book also contributed to the massive changes in 1982. The opportunistic "local notables" who were attracted to the governing UCD in 1979 began to drift away from the party as its electoral defeat became increasingly likely. The organizational and financial resources at the disposal of the UCD and PCE were reduced, as compared with those employed in the 1979 campaign. And many of the electoral institutions created by the UCD (at least partly structured in accord with its own partisan interests) ultimately worked to its disadvantage: the electoral law that had once overrepresented the large centrist party now disproportionately diminished its representation in the new Cortes, and, as the ultimate irony, the campaign financing law that had channelled vast resources to the party in 1979 drove the party into bankruptcy after the next election—the UCD ceased to exist as an organized political party in February 1983.

In the 1982 election, the configuration of the Spanish party system was substantially altered at the national level. Due to the disappearance of the UCD and the decline of the PCE, some simplification of the party system has occurred. This, coupled with the only modest show of strength of Suárez's centrist CDS, appears to have pushed the party system in the direction of bipolarity. The reduced strength of the PCE would seem to lessen the overall left-right distance among the major parties following the election. But, at the same time, an analysis of our 1982 survey data indicates a significant increase in the level of polarization between the two major political forces themselves. PSOE and AP voters are far more distant from each other than were Socialists and UCD supporters, not only with regard to their ideological predispositions, but also with respect to religion and attitudes toward the regional question.[20] Thus, though the Spanish party system after 1982 has come to resemble more closely other "two-plus party" systems of Western Europe, it does not appear to be characterized by the moderate degree of polarization typical of other bipolar systems, such as those of West Germany and Great Britain in the 1960s and 1970s.[21] The increasing polarization of Spanish politics may be a temporary phenomenon, but it is nevertheless a disturbing characteristic when one considers the disparity in strength between the two forces. A dominant majority facing a frustrated AP that may have little chance of reversing roles, at least in the short term, raises new questions about the stability of the regime.

The implications of the transformation of the party system have been the subject of heated debate among political elites. Some have argued that the transition is complete and that the continuation of centrism and "the politics of consensus" is both unnecessary and undemocratic—"the betrayal by a political party of its electorate," as one critic has described it. In his view, "the need for a center party has ceased to exist."[22] On the other hand, others have argued that, in light of the polarization that destroyed Spain's last democratic regime, a confrontation between two blocs would produce a similar tragic outcome. Rafael Arias Salgado, for example, has stated: "To divide a country like Spain into blocs of left and right would not only ignore the complex social stratification of an industrial society—which is serious enough—but would ignore what has always been and could again be the Spanish reality—which would be more than serious, it would be unpardonable."[23]

Whatever the implications of the 1982 realignment may be, it is clear that the transition to democracy in Spain has been a remarkable achievement. A new political order was created with little disruption or violence, despite unfavorable economic circumstances attending its birth. Political elites of the old regime either found their place in the new system or returned to private life. No vengeance was wreaked, and no one was ostracized for serving the old master. Although outside help and sympathy were given to facilitate democratization, the new regime was not imposed from without; it was largely the product of internal development, unlike those of Italy, West Germany, and Japan. Although the founding of the democracy was primarily the work of political elites, ordinary Spaniards also contributed to the success of the transition. Despite years of socialization under authoritarianism, most quickly adapted to the new rules of the game, turned out in large numbers for referenda and elections, and voiced their support for the new regime when it was threatened during the attempted 1981 coup. No one can fully gauge the depth of popular attachment to a democratic ethos, but citizen behavior and attitudes would appear to be congruent with the new political regime. Finally, the success of the transformation is reflected in the peaceful rotation of national governing elites in 1982, and even earlier at the municipal level. This stands in sharp contrast to the experience of industrialized democracies created after World War II. It took twenty years for such an alternation to occur in West Germany, while it has yet to take place at the national level in Italy and Japan.

Successful beginnings, however, do not necessarily imply that the consolidation of the new democratic regime will be completed without difficulty. Spain still faces considerable challenges. But the positive outcome of this first stage augurs well for the future.

Occupations of Party Elites

The following table gives the occupation—i.e., apparent principal sources of income—of each party's delegation in the Congress of Deputies, as well as of members of executive committees in a sample of 16 Spanish provinces (Málaga, Sevilla, Córdoba, Granada, Toledo, Madrid, Segovia, Navarra, Guipúzcoa, Barcelona, Gerona, La Coruña, Pontevedra, Zamora, Valencia, and Baleares). Provincial executive committee data were presented orally by respondents interviewed in those provinces or were copied directly from party membership cards on file in provincial party offices. "Upper-level professionals" include medical doctors, lawyers, tenured university professors, engineers, architects, chemists, physicists, geologists, and skilled technicians. "Business" refers to ownership of industrial, commercial, or agricultural properties, or seats on boards of directors of large corporations. "Intellectual middle class" refers to teachers (at levels up to and including university PNNs), students, journalists, translators, librarians, school administrators, and persons whose occupations were vaguely referred to as "licenciado en. . . ." "Blue-collar workers" includes manual laborers (skilled and unskilled) in industrial and agricultural sectors.

	PCE		PSOE		UCD		AP	
	Exec. Comm. (%)	Con- gress (%)	Exec. Comm. (%)	Con- gress (%)	Exec. Comm. (%)	Con- gress (%)	Exec. Comm. (%)	Con- gress (%)
Upper-level professionals	24	32	31	51	45	39	35	38
Business	2	0	8	3	21	22	26	44
Government functionaries	1	0	2	4	1	16	7	13
Housewives	1	0	1	0	2	0	5	0
Intellectual middle class	19	26	26	11	20	9	13	6
White-collar employees	13	5	18	16	8	4	10	0
Blue-collar workers	40	37	13	14	4	0	5	0
N	(172)	(19)	(179)	(118)	(168)	(165)	(120)	(16)

Sources: For Congress of Deputies: Equipo de Documentación Politica, *Radiografia de las Neuvas Cortes* (Madrid: Sedmay, 1977). Because multiple occupations were listed for several deputies (mostly from the AP and UCD, where prior government service was followed by employment with private business firms), the "most likely principal source of current income" was used as a classification criterion, that is, where a deputy began his career as a lawyer, then served for some time in government, but now sits on the boards of directors of a half-dozen business firms, it is clear that current business ties now generate the great bulk of that person's income. In cases of this kind, the individual was classified as "business." (No such ambiguity existed at the provincial level, where only a single occupation was presented by respondents or listed in the party's membership files.)

For provincial-level elites: interviews undertaken in 1978 and 1979. Data for UCD, PSOE, and PCE from all provinces listed above, except (for UCD) Baleares, where no UCD interviews were held, and (for PCE and PSOE) Gerona and Pontevedra (where in Galicia and Catalunya, those parties have regional structures and do not have provincial committees). Given a large number of follow-up interview refusals by AP respondents, these data are only for the provinces of Pontevedra, Guipúzcoa, Zamora, Valencia, Toledo, Baleares, and Madrid.

APPENDIX B

Ages of Party Elites

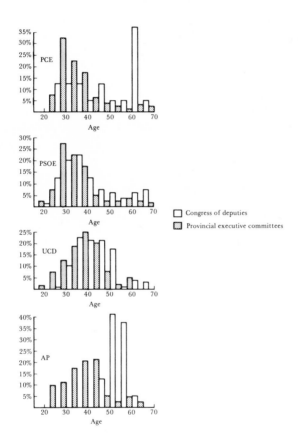

Sources: For Congress of Deputies: Equipo de Documentación Política, *Radiografía de las Nuevas Cortes;* for provincial executive committees: interviews and party documents in elite-interview sample of 16 Spanish provinces.

Provinces in the Elite-Interview Sample

Provinces were selected for inclusion in the elite-interview sample in such a manner as to provide both regional and socioeconomic balance. Clustered by regions, the provinces in the sample were as follows:

Andalucía—Sevilla, Córdoba, Málaga, and Granada
New Castile—Madrid and Toledo
Old Castile and León—Segovia and Zamora
Navarra
Euskadi—Guipúzcoa
Catalunya—Barcelona and Gerona
Valencia—Valencia
Balearic Islands
Galicia—Pontevedra and La Coruña

Broken down by per capita income quintiles (for 1977), the provinces in the sample are as follows (Banco de Bilbao 1980):

I (richest) Madrid, Barcelona, Guipúzcoa, Gerona, Baleares, and Navarra
II Valencia
III Segovia, La Coruña, and Pontevedra
IV Sevilla, Málaga, and Toledo
V Zamora, Córdoba, and Granada

Given the overriding necessity of including within the sample provinces within which micronationalism was politically significant (such as Barcelona, Guipúzcoa, Gerona, and Navarra), there is an imbalance between the provinces in the two richest income quintiles.

The Mass Survey

The mass survey was carried out in April-May 1979 by trained interviewers supervised by DATA S. A. of Madrid. The questionnaire was developed by the authors in consultation with DATA and was pretested in 1978.

The survey sample was stratified by region and size of community. For purposes of sample construction, the regions were defined as follows: Madrid, Barcelona, Catalunya without Barcelona, Basque provinces, Navarra, Andalucía, Aragón, Asturias, Balearic Islands, Canary Islands, Castilla la Nueva (New Castile) without Madrid, Castilla la Vieja (Old Castile) and León, Extremadura, Galicia, Murcia, and Valencia. Communities were divided into metropolitan areas: (1) with more than 2,000,000 inhabitants; (2) with 50,000 to 100,000 people; and communes with (1) over 100,000 people; (2) from 50,000 to 100,000; (3) from 10,000 to 50,000; (4) with less than 10,000.

The number of interviews to be administered in each stratum was determined with probability proportional to the number of inhabitants. After establishing a total of 200 sampling points within the strata, tracts and households were randomly selected and individuals were randomly selected within households.

The design of the sample also took into account the desirability of having a sufficient number of respondents in certain parts of the country in which the regional autonomy issue was very important. Therefore, after drawing the stratified sample, a number of additional interviews were assigned to sampling points in the regions of Euskadi, Catalunya, Galicia, Navarra, and Valencia. A total of 5,439 interviews were carried out. They were divided among the regions as follows: Euskadi, 928; Navarra, 322; Catalunya, 1,230; Galicia, 516; Valencia, 565; the rest of Spain, 1,778. The analysis pertaining to all of Spain was based on a data file constructed so as to compensate for the oversampling of the regions listed above.

The Mass-Level Questionnaire

The following questionnaire was administered to respondents in Catalunya. It includes all items asked of respondents in the entire Spanish sample, as well as the additional items asked only of respondents in the five oversampled regions of Euskadi, Catalunya, Galicia, Valencia, and Navarra. The latter are the final thirteen questions.

1. Si un amigo de fuera de España le pidiese un juicio sobre la situación *Económica* actual española, ¿qué le diría? (Leer lista)

   Todavía quedan muchos problemas por resolver, pero en conjunto no nos podemos quejar 1   (12)

   La situación va haciéndose cada vez más grave, no se puede continuar así 2

1a. Y si un amigo de fuera le pidiese un juicio sobre la situación *política* actual española, ¿qué le diría? (Leer lista)

   Todavía quedan muchos problemas por resolver, pero en conjunto no nos podemos quejar 1   (13)

   La situación va haciéndose cada vez más grave, no se puede continuar así 2

2. De esta serie de formas en que la gente intenta de influir en las autoridades, ¿cuál cree vd. que es la más eficaz? (Tarjeta)

2a. Y ¿cuál cree es la menos eficaz?

	La más eficaz	La menos eficaz
a. Organizar un grupo con amigos y vecinos	1 (14)	1 (15)
b. Actuar a través de un partido político . .	2	2
c. Escribir cartas o hacer visitas a las autoridades	3	3
d. Actuar a través del sindicato o grupo profesional al que pertenezca	4	4
e. Participar en huelgas, manifestaciones, sentadas, etc.	5	5

3. Aquí tenemos unas frases sobre la política. Quisiera que me dijera, para cada una, si está de acuerdo con ella o no.

		Acuerdo	Desacuerdo	Depende	
a.	Un acuerdo negociado es la mejor forma de solucionar un conflicto	1	2	3	(16)
b.	El gobierno y la política a veces paracen tan complicados que una persona como yo no puede saber lo que está pasando . .	1	2	3	(17)
c.	La democracia es el mejor sistema de gobierno conocido	1	2	3	(18)
d.	Los políticos toman las decisiones solamente en defensa de los intereses de su partido	1	2	3	(19)
e.	La distribución de los ingresos entre personas en España es *totalmente* injusta	1	2	3	(20)

4. Ahora quisieramos conocer sus opiniones sobre algunas instituciones políticas. ¿Quiénes piensa vd. que hiciéron una mejor labor para resolver los problemas de la sociedad española en cada momento: los sindicatos verticales de la época de Franco o los actuales sindicatos?

Los sindicatos verticales de la época de Franco 1

Los actuales sindicatos 2

(21)

5. A su juicio, ¿como diría que lo está haciendo el Rey, muy bien, bien, ni bien ni mal, mal o muy mal?

Muy bien . . . 1   Bien . . . 2   Ni bien ni mal . . . 3   Mal . . . 4   Muy mal . . . 5   (22)

6. Hablando de temas políticos en general, ¿cuál de las dos frases siguientes corresponde mejor con sus ideas?

a. Monarquía o República?

Monarquía 1   (23)
República 2

Ambas, ninguna 3

b. Socialismo o propiedad privada?

Socialismo 1   (24)
Propiedad privada 2

Ambas, ninguna 3

c. Marxismo o no marxismo?

Marxismo 1   (25)
No marxismo 2

Ambas, ninguna 3

d. Franquismo o anti-Franquismo?

Franquismo 1   (26)
Anti-Franquismo 2

Ambas, ninguna 3

e. Mantener la propiedad privada o nacionalizar las empresas?

Mantener la empresa privada 1   (27)
Nacionalizar las empresas 2

Ambas, ninguna 3

f. Amistad con los Estados Unidos o amistad con Rusia?

Los Estados Unidos 1   (28)
Rusia 2

Ambas, ninguna 3

g. Libertad de creación de colegios privados o enseñanza obligatoria a través de los centros del Estado?

Libertad colegios privados . 1 (29)
Enseñanza obligatoria
centros del Estado 2

Ambas, ninguna 3

h. Ayuda estatal a los colegios privados o ninguna ayuda a los colegios privados?

Ayuda colegios privados . . . 1 (30)
Ninguna ayuda colegios
privados 2

Ambos, ninguno 3

7. Y ahora, quisieramos saber sus sentimientos respecto a algunos grupos e instituciones en la España de hoy. Aquí tiene una tarjeta con una escala de 0 a 10, que queremos que vd. utilice para indicarme sus reacciones hacia cada grupo mencionado. El 0 indicaría hostilidad extrema hacia ese grupo o institución. Un valor 5 indicaría que se siente neutral hacia ese grupo, y el 10 que siente una gran atracción. (Entregar tarjeta)

Primero, ¿qué piensa acerca de la UCD?

	0	1	2	3	4	5	6	7	8	9	10	
a. La UCD	00	01	02	03	04	05	06	07	08	09	10	31,32
b. La policía	00	01	02	03	04	05	06	07	08	09	10	33,34
c. El PSOE	00	01	02	03	04	05	06	07	08	09	10	35,36
d. El PCE	00	01	02	03	04	05	06	07	08	09	10	37,38
e. La Iglesia	00	01	02	03	04	05	06	07	08	09	10	39,40
f. ETA	00	01	02	03	04	05	06	07	08	09	10	41,42
g. Las grandes empresas	00	01	02	03	04	05	06	07	08	09	10	43,44
h. Coalición Democrática . .	00	01	02	03	04	05	06	07	08	09	10	45,46

8. Existe muchas maneras de que las personas puedan demostrar su desacuerdo con las acciones o la política del gobierno. De la siguiente lista, quisieramos que me dijese si las aprueba o las rechaza.

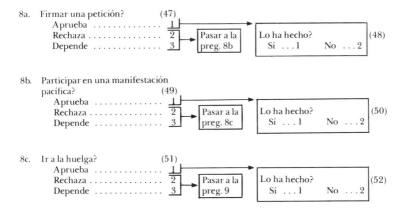

8a. Firmar una petición?   (47)
Aprueba 1
Rechaza 2   Pasar a la   Lo ha hecho?   (48)
Depende 3   preg. 8b   Sí . . . 1   No . . . 2

8b. Participar en una manifestación pacífica?   (49)
Aprueba 1
Rechaza 2   Pasar a la   Lo ha hecho?   (50)
Depende 3   preg. 8c   Sí . . . 1   No . . . 2

8c. Ir a la huelga?   (51)
Aprueba 1
Rechaza 2   Pasar a la   Lo ha hecho?   (52)
Depende 3   preg. 9   Sí . . . 1   No . . . 2

9. Hay muchas asociaciones en la España de hoy. ¿Es vd. miembro de algún sindicato o asociación o colegio profesional?

(53)   Sí, de un sindicato 1

(54)   Sí, de una asociación profesional................ 1

(55)   Sí, de un colegio profesional 1

(56)   No 1

¿De cuál sindicato?   57,58

¿De cuál asociación profesional?   59,60

¿De cuál colegio profesional?   61,62

Pasar a la pregunta 10

A todos

10. ¿Es vd. miembro de alguna asociación religiosa?

Sí 1   No..........................2   (63)

10a. ¿Es vd. miembro de alguna asociación de vecinos?

Sí 1   No..........................2   (64)

10b. ¿Es vd. miembro de alguna asociación regional o cultural?

Sí 1   No..........................2   (65)

Quisiéramos ahora hablar de algunas personas importantes de la actualidad política en nuestro país.

11. Por ejemplo, ¿sabe vd. el nombre del Presidente del Gobierno? (Anotar literalmente la respuesta)   (66)

11a. ¿Puede vd. decirme el nombre del secretario general de Comisiones Obreras? (Anotar literalmente la respuesta)   (67)

11b. ¿Podría decirme el nombre del Presidente del Congreso de los Diputados? (Anotar literalmente la respuesta)   (68)

12. Mucha gente, cuando piensa en la política, usa las palabras "izquierda" y "derecha." Aquí tiene una escala con una fila de casillas que van de "izquierda" a "derecha." De acuerdo con sus opiniones políticas, ¿en qué casilla se colocaría vd.? (Entregar Tarjeta)

Izquierda   1   2   3   4   5   6   7   8   9   10   Derecha   69,70

13. Cuando utiliza las palabras "izuierda" y "derecha" ¿qué quiere vd. decir? Primero,   *Ficha II*
     ¿qué significa la palabra "izquierda"? (Profundizar)

_____

_____   10–25

_____

_____

13a. ¿Alguna cosa más?_____

_____

14. Ahora referente al significado de la palabra "derecha." (Profundizar)   26–41

_____

_____

_____

14a. ¿Alguna cosa más?_____

_____

15. Teniendo en cuenta esta misma tarjeta, ¿en qué casilla situaría vd. a la UCD? (Pre-
     guntar por cada uno hasta terminar la lista)

		Izquierda									Derecha	
		1	2	3	4	5	6	7	8	9	10	
a.	UCD = Unión de Centro Democrático	01	02	03	04	05	06	07	08	09	10	42,43
b.	PSOE = Partido Socialista Obrero Español	01	02	03	04	05	06	07	08	09	10	44,45
c.	PCE = Partido Comunista de España	01	02	03	04	05	06	07	08	09	10	46,47
d.	CD = Coalición Democrática	01	02	03	04	05	06	07	08	09	10	48,49

16. ¿Votó vd. en las elecciones al Congreso de Diputados del primero de marzo de
     1979?

     Sí 1   No 2   No reunía las condiciones 3   (50)

         ┌──────────────────────────┐   ┌──────────────────────────┐
         │   Pasar a la preg. 18   │   │   Pasar a la preg. 18a   │
         └──────────────────────────┘   └──────────────────────────┘

17. ¿Por qué partido votó vd. en esas elecciones? (Entregar tarjeta)

     Centristas de Cataluña—UCD 1   (51,52)
     Socialistas de Cataluña—PSC/PSOE 2
     PSUC 3
     Convergència i Unió 4
     Coalición Democrática 5
     Esquerra Republicana 6
     Bloc d'Esquerra D'Alliberament Nacional 7
     Otro Partido (Anotar)_____
     _____ A

17b. ¿Qué fue lo que más le gustó de ese partido?

     _____   (53–68)

         ┌──────────────────────────┐
         │   Pasar a la pregunta 19 │
         └──────────────────────────┘

18. ¿Por qué no votó?
     • Porque no creo en democracia 1   (69)
     • Porque no me convence ni me interesa la política 1   (70)
     • Porque tenía mucho trabajo y no disponía de tiempo libre 1   (71)
     • Porque las elecciones no se hacen de una manera auténtica y demo-
        crática, con libertad y participación de todos los partidos 1   (72)
     • Porque los partidos políticos no me dicen nada que me atraiga 1   (73)
     • No veía ninguno que me inspirase confianza 1   (74)
     • Mi voto no servía para nada; los que han salido elegidos van a hacer lo
        que quieran sin tener en cuenta mi voto 1   (75)
     • No veía que los partidos políticos defendieran mis intereses 1   (76)
     • Otras (Especificar)

     _____
     _____ A

18a. Aunque no haya votado a las elecciones del Congreso del 1 de marzo, ¿se considera   *Ficha III*
      vd. simpatizante o partidario de un partido político en particular?

      Sí 1   No 2   (8)

         ┌──┐
         │ 18b. ¿De cuál partido?   (9,10)   │
         │   │
         │ _____│
         └──┘

19. Votó vd. en las primeras elecciones al Congreso de Diputados del 15 de junio de 1977?

Sí 1   No 2   No reunía los requisitos 3

Pasar a la pregunta 20

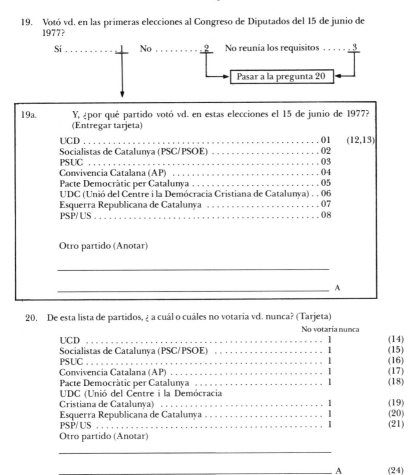

19a.   Y, ¿por qué partido votó vd. en estas elecciones el 15 de junio de 1977?
           (Entregar tarjeta)

UCD 01   (12,13)
Socialistas de Catalunya (PSC/PSOE) 02
PSUC 03
Convivencia Catalana (AP) 04
Pacte Democràtic per Catalunya 05
UDC (Unió del Centre i la Demócracia Cristiana de Catalunya) . . 06
Esquerra Republicana de Catalunya 07
PSP/US 08

Otro partido (Anotar)

_____

_____ A

20. De esta lista de partidos, ¿ a cuál o cuáles no votaría vd. nunca? (Tarjeta)

                                                                          No votaría nunca
UCD 1   (14)
Socialistas de Catalunya (PSC/PSOE) 1   (15)
PSUC 1   (16)
Convivencia Catalana (AP) 1   (17)
Pacte Democràtic per Catalunya 1   (18)
UDC (Unió del Centre i la Demócracia
Cristiana de Catalunya) 1   (19)
Esquerra Republicana de Catalunya 1   (20)
PSP/US 1   (21)
Otro partido (Anotar)

_____

_____ A   (24)

No rechazo a ningún partido 0   (25)

21. ¿Votó vd. en el referendum sobre la Constitución de diciembre de 1978?   (26)

Sí 1
No 2   Pasar a la
No reunía los requisitos 3   preg. 22
No se acuerda 4

21a.   ¿Qué votó vd. en el referendum?
        Sí 1   No 2   En blanco 3   (27)

Hablando de los partidos políticos, tenemos algunas preguntas más.

22. Quisiera leerle algunas frases referentes a los partidos políticos. Dígame si está de acuerdo o en desacuerdo con cada frase.

	Acuerdo	Desacuerdo	Depende	
a. Los partidos políticos tienden a crear conflictos donde no los hay . .	1	2	3	(28)
b. Los candidatos políticos son más importantes que los programas del partido	1	2	3	(29)
c. La democracia funciona mejor cuando hay mucha competencia entre los partidos	1	2	3	(30)
d. Los partidos políticos hacen posible que se oigan distintas opiniones en la política	1	2	3	(31)

Ahora me gustaría hablar con vd. sobre la participación de los ciudadanos en la política.

23. ¿Con qué frecuencia sigue vd. las noticias de la política por la radio, TV., o la prensa? ¿Las sigue todos los días, con bastante frecuencia, solo de vez en cuando, casi nunca o nunca?

Todos los días 1   (32)
Con bastante frecuencia 2
Solo de vez en cuando 3
Casi nunca 4
Nunca 5

24. Normalmente, ¿con qué frecuencia habla vd. de política con su familia? Con mucha frecuencia, bastante frecuencia, solo de vez en cuando, casi nunca o nunca?

Con mucha frecuencia 1   (33)
Con bastante frecuencia 2
Solo de vez en cuando 3
Casi nunca 4
Nunca 5

25. ¿Diría vd. que en su familia hay preferencias por un partido político, hay preferencias por más de un partido político o no prefieren a ningún partido político?

Un partido 1   Más de un partido . . 2   Ningún partido 3   (34)

Pasar a la
preg. 26

25a. ¿A qué partido (o partidos) político(s)?   (35,36)

    (37)

26. En general, ¿diría vd. que está muy al corriente, bastante, poco o nada de lo que sucede en la política?

   Muy al corriente . 1   Bastante 2   Poco 3   Nada 4   (38)

27. Durante la campaña electoral, ¿cuáles de estas cosas hizo vd.?

27a. ¿Ha trabajado para un partido durante la campaña?

   Sí 1   No 2

27b. ¿Ha asistado a mítines, charlas u otros actos políticos?

   Sí 1   No 2

Pasando a otros temas.

28. Cuando tiene que resolver un asunto de tipo oficial, ¿qué cree vd. que hace la mayor parte de la gente? (Leer lista)

   Tratar de resolverlo personalmente 1   (41)
   Utilizar amistades o hacer regalos 1   (42)
   Buscar una recomendación 1   (43)
   Seguir los trámites normales 1   (44)
   Encargárselo a un abogado o gestoría 1   (45)

29. ¿Se ha puesto vd. alguna vez en relación con un funcionario o político por problemas personales?

   Sí 1   No 2   (46)

30. Se dice que algunas personas tienen miedo de participar activamente en la política. ¿Diría vd. que en *esta localidad* en general la gente tiene mucho temor, bastante, poco o ningún temor a participar activamente en la política?

   Mucho   Bastante   Ningún
   temor 1   temor 2   Poco 3   temor 4   (47)

Hablemos ahora de las autonomías regionales.

31. Vea estas dos frases que dicen dos personas con actitudes diferentes ante el regionalismo. (Entregar tarjeta)

   Sr. García: Lo mejor es mantener la unidad del país y limitar lo más posible a las regiones.
   Sr. Pérez: En España hay regiones o nacionalidades y lo lógico es darle *autonomía* a cada una de ellas, para que resuelvan por sí mismas una parte de sus propios asuntos.

   Dígame por favor, ¿con cuál está vd. más de acuerdo?

   Sr. García 1   Sr. Pérez 2   (48)

   | Pasar a la pregunta 34 | | Pasar a la pregunta 32 |

32. Vea ahora estas otras dos actitudes igualmente diferentes. (Entregar tarjeta)

Sr. López: Hay que dar más autonomía a las regiones para que gestionen sus propios asuntos, e incluso hay que dejarles que cada una haga sus propias leyes.

Sr. Fernández: Me parece bien dar más autonomía a las regiones para sus asuntos internos, siempre que se respete la unidad política del país.

¿Con cuál está vd. más de acuerdo?

Sr. López 1   Sr. Fernández 2   (49)

Pasar a la
preg. 34

33. Volvamos a ver estas otras dos actitudes, igualmente diferentes. (Entregar tarjeta)

Sr. Martínez: Soy partidario de que las regiones tengan sus propias leyes, pero siempre debe haber algunas cosas como el ejército, las relaciones internacionales, etc., que tiene que depender del gobierno central.

Sr. Sánchez: Las regiones son verdaderas nacionalidades que, aparte de sus propias leyes, deben tener incluso su ejército, aduanas, etc., es decir, que deben ser estados totalmente independientes.

¿Con cuál está vd. más de acuerdo?

Sr. Martínez 1   Sr. Sánchez 2   (50)

34. En las regiones donde hay una lengua distinta, ¿cree vd. que en las escuelas debería ser obligatorio aprender la lengua de la región, que solamente debería ser obligatorio aprender el castellano o que debería ser obligatorio aprender la lengua de la región y el castellano?

Solo la lengua de la región 1   (51)
Solo castellano 2
Ambas 3

35. ¿Cree vd. que si en una región hay una mayoría que quiere la independencia de esa región, se le debe conceder?

Sí 1   No 2   (52)

36. ¿Cuáles de las siguientes cosas cree vd. que pasará ahora que algunas regiones tienen autonomía?

	Si	No	Depende
a. Que aumentarán los conflictos entre las regiones	1	2	3 (53)
b. Que disminuirán las diferencias entre las regiones ricas y las regiones pobres	1	2	3 (54)
c. Que se perderá la unidad de España	1	2	3 (55)

37. Quisieramos saber sus sentimientos hacia algunas figuras políticas destacadas en España de hoy y del pasado. Aquí tenemos una escala que va de 0 a 10. (Tarjeta). Si se siente muy favorable hacia esa persona puede darle la valoración más alta de 10; si se siente hostil hacia esa persona puede darle la valoración de 0 (la más baja posible); si se siente absolutamente neutral hacia esa persona, puede darle una valoración de 5. Empecemos por Felipe González. (Ir leyendo la lista hasta el final)

	Hostil									Favorable		
	0	1	2	3	4	5	6	7	8	9	10	
a. Felipe González	00	01	02	03	04	05	06	07	08	09	10	(56,57)
b. Adolfo Suárez	00	01	02	03	04	05	06	07	08	09	10	(58,59)
c. Santiago Carrillo	00	01	02	03	04	05	06	07	08	09	10	(60,61)
d. Manuel Fraga Iribarne	00	01	02	03	04	05	06	07	08	09	10	(62,63)
e. Francisco Franco..................	00	01	02	03	04	05	06	07	08	09	10	(64,65)
f. Blas Piñar	00	01	02	03	04	05	06	07	08	09	10	(66,67)

38. ¿Cree vd. que cada partido político debe representar los intereses de una clase social, o debe representar los intereses de todas las clases?

Los intereses de una clase 1   Los intereses de todas las clases ... 2   (68)

39. En su opinión, ¿puede una persona ser un buen Católico y un buen Comunista?

Sí 1   No.............. 2   Depende 3   (69)

40. Y qué diría referente a un buen Católico y un buen Socialista?

Sí 1   No.............. 2   Depende 3   (70)

41. En general, ¿diría que en España la Iglesia tiene una influencia beneficiosa para la sociedad, una influencia perjudicial para la sociedad o no tiene influencia?

Beneficiosa 1   Perjudicial 2   No tiene influencia .. 3   (71)

Pasando a otros temas.

42. Pensando ahora en las personas que están comprometidas en el terrorismo, ¿cuál de los siguientes términos las describe mejor, en su opinión? (Entregar tarjeta)

Patriotas 1   (72)
Idealistas 1   (73)
Manipulados por otros 1   (74)
Locos 1   (75)
Criminales comunes 1   (76)

43. En su opinión, ¿qué grupos tienen la responsabilidad principal por el desorden y la violencia con que se está enfrentando España? (Leer lista) (Puede dar más de una respuesta).

Ficha IV

Grupos políticos de extrema izquierda	1	(10)
Grupos políticos de extrema derecha	1	(11)
Grupos regionalistas o nacionalistas	1	(12)
El gobierno central	1	(13)
La policía	1	(14)
Los estudiantes y jóvenes	1	(15)
La dictadura pasada	1	(16)

44. Si el terrorismo continuase, ¿cuál de las siguientes acciones apoyaría vd.? (Entregar tarjeta).

El gobierno debería aceptar la demanda de los terroristas 1 (17,18)
La negociación y el diálogo con los terroristas 2
El gobierno debería mantener la autoridad y el orden, respetando los derechos humanos básicos 3
El gobierno debería declarar la guerra al terrorismo usando todos los medios posibles 4
Deberían establecerse medidas militares 5

Ahora quisiera hacerle unas preguntas sobre vd.

45. ¿Qué interés por la política tenían sus padres cuando vd. tenía 14 o 15 años? ¿Hablaban de política muy a menudo, de vez en cuando, casi nunca o nunca?

Muy a   De vez en
menudo 1   cuando 2   Casi nunca ..3   Nunca 4   (19)

46. Por lo que vd. sabe, haya vivido o no en esos años, ¿con cuál de los dos lados simpatizaba vd. o su familia en la guerra de 1936: con el Frente Nacional o con el Frente Popular?

Frente Nacional (los de Franco)	1	(20)
Frente Popular (los Republicanos)	2	
Ambos lados	3	
Ningún lado	4	

47. En cuestión de religión, se considera vd. . . .? (Entregar tarjeta)

47a. Y cuándo vd. tenía 15 o 20 años, ¿como consideraría que era *su padre* en cuestiones religiosas?

	El	Su padre
Muy buen Católico	1 (21)	1 (22)
Católico practicante	2	2
Católico no muy practicante	3	3
Católico no practicante	4	4
Indiferente	5	5
Ateo	6	6
Creyente de otra religión	7	7

48. ¿Cuál diría que es el nivel económico de su familia en comparación a las otras familias de la ciudad donde vd. vive? (Leer lista)

Mucho mejor que mayoría 1   (23)
Mejor 2
Ni mejor ni peor 3
Peor 4
Mucho peor 5

49. ¿Se siente vd. identificado con alguna clase social?

Sí 1   No 2   No sabe 3   (24)

49a. ¿A qué clase social diría vd. que pertenece su familia? (Leer lista)

Alta 1   Media-alta . . 2   Media-baja . . 3   Trabajadora 4   (25)

50. ¿Cuál diría vd. que es la cantidad que entre todos y por *todos* los conceptos ingresan vds. al mes por término medio? Dígame la letra que corresponda a la cantidad. (Entregar tarjeta).

A. Más de 250.000 ptas 1   E. De 30.001 a 50.000 ptas 5   (26)
B. De 100.000 a 250.000 ptas. 2   F. De 20.001 a 30.000 ptas 6
C. De 70.001 a 100.000 ptas. 3   G. De 10.001 a 20.000 ptas 7
D. De 50.001 a 70.000 ptas. 4   H. Hasta 10.000 ptas 8

51. ¿En qué provincia nació vd.?

En ésta 1   Otra (Anotar)_____   (27,28)

Si es diferente a la provincia de la entrevista, preguntar: (31,32,33)
51a. Aproximadamente, ¿cuánto tiempo lleva vd. viviendo aquí en esta provincia?
Años:_____   Meses:_____

52. ¿En qué provincia nació su padre?

En ésta 1   Otra (Anotar)_____   (34,35)

53. ¿En qué provincia nació su madre?

En ésta 1   Otra (Anotar)_____   (36,37)

54. ¿En qué año nació vd.?

En el año:_____   (38,39)

55. ¿Está vd. trabajando ahora?

Sí 1   No . . . . 2 → Pasar a la pregunta 56   (40)

55a. ¿Ha estado vd. en los últimos años, parado (desempleado) más de un mes, alguna vez?
Sí 1   No 2   (41)
55b. ¿Trabaja vd. por cuenta propia o por cuenta ajena?
Por cuenta propia 1   → Pasar a la pregunta 57   (42)
Por cuenta ajena 2

56. ¿Podría decirme que hace vd.?
    Soy ama de casa 1
    Soy estudiante . . . . 2 ── ▶ │ Pasar a la preg. 58 │   (43)
    Estoy buscando trabajo
    por primera vez . . . . 3 ── ▶ │ Pasar a la preg. 59 │
    Estoy parado 4
    Estoy jubilado 5

56a. ¿Trabajaba vd. antes por cuenta propia o por cuenta ajena?	(44)
Por cuenta propia . . . . 1 Por cuenta ajena 2	

57. ¿En qué trabaja (o trabajaba) concretamente?

Trabaja por cuenta ajena: - Directores de empresa, directivos 01   (45,46)
    - Empleados a nivel superior 02
    - Funcionarios de nivel alto (con titulación
       superior) 03
    - Jefes y Generales de las Fuerzas Armadas 04
    - Oficiales de las Fuerzas Armadas 05
    - Técnicos medios 06
    - Funcionarios a nivel medio 07
    - Empleados a nivel medio 08
    - Vendedores, agentes comerciales, etc. 09
    - Empleados subalternos, (conserjes, etc.) 10
    - Capataces, encargados, contramaestres 11
    - Suboficiales de las Fuerzas Armadas 12
    - Obreros cualificados agrícolas 13
    - Obreros cualificados de la industria y servicios 14
    - Peones y obreros sin calificar del campo 15
    - Peones y obreros sin calificar de la industria,
    - Personal manual de servicios no
       calificados 16
    - Otra ocupación por cuenta ajena ¿Cuál?
      (Anotar)

    _____

    _____ A

Trabaja por su cuenta: - Empresario agrario, propietario o arrendatario
      agrícola (de tipo medio y grande) 20
    - Agricultores, propietario o arrendatario
      agrícola (de tipo pequeño) 21
    - Empresario de la industria, el comercio u
      otra actividad de servicios (de tipo medio
      y grande) 22
    - Industrial comerciante o empresario de otra
      actividad de servicios (de tipo pequeño) 23
    - Profesional liberal 24
    - Trabajador independiente, autónomo,
      artesano 25
    - Otra ocupación por cuenta propia, ¿Cuál?
      (Anotar)

    _____

    _____ A

THE MASS LEVEL QUESTIONNAIRE   441

Solo a estudiantes y amas de casa

58. Ha trabajado vd. alguna vez?

Sí 1   No..............2 ├──► Pasar a la preg. 59   (47)

58a. ¿En qué trabajos, fijos o eventuales?   (48)

Fijos 1   Eventuales 2

59. ¿Es vd. el cabeza de familia?

Sí ....1 ├──► Pasar a la preg. 62   No..............2   (49)

60. Digame, ¿cuál es el empleo u ocupación principal del cabeza de familia?   (50)

Está empleado/a ....1 ├──► Pasar a la preg. 61

Trabaja por su cuenta ....2 ├──► Pasar a la preg. 61

Está jubilado/a y antes
   estaba empleado/a ....3 ├──► Pasar a la preg. 61

Está jubilado/a y antes trabajaba
   por su cuenta ....4 ├──► Pasar a la preg. 61

En paro ....5 ├──► Pasar a la preg. 61

Estudiante ....6 ┐
                              ├──► Pasar a la preg. 62
Sus labores ....7 ┘

61. ¿A qué actividad se dedica (dedicaba) el cabeza de familia? (Anotar con detalle)

_____

_____

Trabaja por cuenta ajena: - Directores de empresa, directivos 01 (51,52)
                             - Empleados a nivel superior 02
                             - Funcionarios de nivel alto (con titulación
                                superior) 03
                             - Jefes y Generales de las Fuerzas Armadas 04
                             - Oficiales de las Fuerzas Armadas 05
                             - Técnicos medios 06
                             - Funcionarios a nivel medio 07
                             - Empleados a nivel medio 08
                             - Vendedores, agentes comerciales, etc. 09
                             - Empleados subalternos, (conserjes, etc.) 10
                             - Capataces, encargados, contramaestres 11
                             - Suboficiales de las Fuerzas Armadas 12
                             - Obreros cualificados agrícolas 13
                             - Obreros cualificados de la industria y servicios 14
                             - Peones y obreros sin calificar del campo 15
                             - Peones y obreros sin calificar de la industria,
                                personal manual de servicios no calificados . 16
                             - Otra ocupación por cuenta ajena ¿Cuál? (Anotar)

_____

_____ A

Trabaja por su cuenta: - Empresario agrario, propietario o arrendatario
agrícola (de tipo medio y grande) 20
- Agricultores, propietario o arrendatario
agrícola (de tipo pequeño) 21
- Empresario de la industria, el comercio u
otra actividad de servicios (de tipo medio
y grande) 22
- Industrial comerciante o empresario de otra
actividad de servicios (de tipo pequeño) 23
- Profesional liberal 24
- Trabajador independiente, autónomo,
artesano 25
- Otra ocupación por cuenta propia, ¿Cuál?
(Anotar)

_____

_____ A

62.   ¿Qué estudios tiene vd.?

62a.   ¿Y cuáles su padre?

	El	Su padre
Ninguno	1 (53)	1 (61)

62b. ¿Pero sabe leer y escribir?		El padre
	El	
Sí	1 (69)	1 (70)
No	2	2

	El	Su padre
Escuela maternal o parvulario	1 (54)	1 (62)
Escuela primaria	2	2
Formación profesional, aprendizaje de un oficio	1 (55)	1 (63)
Cultura general	2	2
Mecanografía, secretariado, idiomas	3	3
Formación profesional industrial: iniciación o aprendizaje	1 (56)	1 (64)
Formación profesional industrial: oficialía industrial	2	2
Formación profesional industrial: maestría industrial	3	3
Formación profesional naútico-pesquera	4	4
Escuela de capacitación agraria	5	5
Escuela de artes aplicadas y oficios artísticos	6	6
Conservatorio de música (grado elemental y profesional, conocimientos de solfeo y música)	7	7
Bachillerato elemental	1 (57)	1 (65)
Bachillerato superior	2	2
Escuela de asistentes sociales	1 (58)	1 (66)
Oposiciones banca y otras parecidas	2	2
Escuela social (graduados sociales)	3	3
Ayudantes técnicos sanitarios	4	4
Escuela de idiomas..............................	5	5
Magisterio	6	6
Peritaje mercantil..............................	7	7

Escuela técnica de grado medio (antiguos aparejadores
y peritos) 8   8

Conservatorio superior de música 1 (59)   1 (67)
Escuela superior de bellas artes 2   2
Escuela superior de arte dramático 3   3
Profesorado mercantil 4   4
Facultad universitaria 5   5
Escuela técnica superior (antiguos arquitectos e ingenieros)
.... 6   6
Estudios de especialización superior (investigación,
doctorado, etc.) 1 (60)   1 (68)
No sabe   9

63. ¿Cuál era la ocupación principal de su padre cuando vd. tenía 14 ó 15 años?

Director de empresa, directivos 01   (71,72)
Empleados a nivel superior 02
Funcionarios de nivel alto (con titulación superior) 03
Jefes y Generales de las Fuerzas Armadas 04
Oficiales de las Fuerzas Armadas 05
Técnicos medios 06
Funcionarios a nivel medio 07
Empleados a nivel medio 08
Vendedores, agentes comerciales, etc. 09
Empleados subalternos (conserjes, etc.) 10
Capataces, encargados, contramaestres 11
Suboficiales de las Fuerzas Armadas 12
Obreros cualificados agrícolas 13
Obreros cualificados de la industria y servicios 14
Peones y obreros sin calificar del campo 15
Peones y obreros sin calificar de la industria, personal
manual de servicios no calificados 16
Otra ocupación por cuenta ajena ¿Cuál? (Anotar)

_____

_____ A

Trabaja por su cuenta:

Empresario agrario, propietario o arrendatario agrícola (de
tipo medio y grande) 20
Agricultores, propietario o arrendatario agrícolas (de tipo
pequeño) 21
Empresario de la industria, el comercio u otra actividad de servicios
(de tipo medio y grande) 22
Industrial, comerciante o empresario de otra actividad de servicios
(de tipo pequeño) 23
Profesional liberal 24
Trabajador independiente, autónomo, artesano 25
Otra ocupación por cuenta propia, ¿Cuál? (Anotar)

_____

_____ A

64. ¿Ha estudiado vd. en un colegio del estado, o lo ha hecho en un colegio privado?
Del estado 1   Privado 2   Los dos 3 (73)

> 64a. ¿Religioso o no religioso?
>
> Religioso 1   No religioso 2   Ambos 3

(74)

65. Anotar el sexo del entrevistado.

Varón 1   Mujer 2 (75)

66. Y para terminar, ¿me podría decir a qué partido votó en las pasadas elecciones municipales? (Anotar con la máxima precisión)

Ficha IV

Votó a: _____   (76,77)

1. ¿Qué lengua o lenguas se hablaba en su casa cuando vd. estaba creciendo?

Ficha V

Castellano 1 (10)	Gallego 1	(13)
Catalán 1 (11)	Vasco 1	(14)
Valenciano 1 (12)	Otra, ¿Cuál?_____ A	(15,16)

2. ¿Qué lengua utiliza normalmente en el trabajo?

Castellano 1 (17)	Gallego 1	(20)
Catalán 1 (18)	Vasco 1	(21)
Valenciano 1 (19)	Otra, ¿Cuál?_____ A	(22,23)

3. ¿Qué lengua prefiere vd. usar?

Castellano 1 (24)	Gallego 1	(27)
Catalán 1 (25)	Vasco 1	(28)
Valenciano 1 (26)	Otra, ¿Cuál?_____ A	(29,30)

4. (Si no mencionó el *Catalán* en ninguna de las preguntas 1, 2 o 3). ¿Entiende vd. el catalán?

Sí 1   No 2   (31)

> 4a. ¿Lo habla vd.?   (32)
>
> Sí 1   No 2

5. Con respecto a la lengua de enseñanza, en el estudio de matemáticas, historia, etc. piensa vd. que deberían estudiarse (Leer lista)

Solo en Catalán 1   Solo en Castellano . . 2   En ambas lenguas . . . 3   (33)

6. Hoy se habla mucho de las nacionalidades. ¿Diría vd. que se siente . . . (Leer lista)

Español 1   (34)
Más español que catalán 2
Tanto catalán como español 3
Más catalán que español 4
Catalán 5
Otro (Especificar)

_____ A

7. ¿Cuales de las siguientes condiciones son necesarias para que una persona pueda considerarse catalán?

	Sí	No	
a). Vivir y trabajar en Cataluña	1	2	(35)
b). Hablar Catalán	1	2	(36)
c). Descender de una familia catalana y haber nacido en Cataluña ...	1	2	(37)

8. Para ser alcalde o concejal de esta ciudad, ¿debería ser obligatorio hablar catalán?

Sí 1   No 2   (38)

9. Algunas personas dicen que los catalanes son tratados injustamente por el resto de los españoles. ¿Está vd. de acuerdo con esta afirmación?

Sí 1   No 2   (39)

10. Algunas personas dicen que en Cataluña los inmigrantes son tratados injustamente. ¿Está vd. de acuerdo con esta afirmación?

Sí 1   No 2   (40)

11. Cataluña ha sido una región con mucha inmigración de otras partes de España. ¿Con cuáles de estas opiniones está vd. de acuerdo o en desacuerdo?

Acuerdo Desacuerdo

a). Los catalanes deben tratar de limitar el número de los emigrantes de otras partes de España 1   2   (41)

b). Los catalanes deben permitirles a los emigrantes mantener sus propias formas de vida, idiomas y costumbres regionales 1   2   (42)

12. Pensando ahora en sus íntimos amigos, ¿diría vd. que todos o casi todos son catalanes, que algunos son catalanes o ninguno?

Todos o casi todos . . 1   Algunos 2   Ninguno 3   (43)

13. Y de sus vecinos, ¿diría vd. que todos o casi todos son catalanes, que algunos son catalanes o ninguno?

Todos o casi todos . . 1   Algunos 2   Ninguno 3   (44)

Muchas gracias por su colaboración.

Notes

CHAPTER ONE: INTRODUCTION

1. Giovanni Sartori, "The Sociology of Parties: A Critical View," in Otto Stammer, ed., *Party Systems, Party Organizations, and the Politics of the New Masses*, Committee on Political Sociology of the International Sociological Association, 1968, p. 22.

2. Excerpt from a statement by Fraga before the Comisión de Asuntos Constitucionales y Libertades Públicas on May 5, 1978 (Cortes Españolas, *Diario de Sesiones del Congreso de Diputados*, no. 59, May 5, 1978, p. 2044).

3. For an excellent statement of the role of party elites as "translators" of conflict, see Samuel Barnes, "Ideology and the Organization of Conflict," *Journal of Politics*, vol. 28, 1966.

4. For statements of the importance of party elites in determining the degree of group hostility in divided societies, see, e.g., Arend Lijphart, *The Politics of Accommodation*, Berkeley and Los Angeles: University of California Press, 1968; G. Bingham Powell, *Social Fragmentation and Political Hostility*, Stanford, Calif.: Stanford University Press, 1970; Robert Putnam, *The Beliefs of Politicians: Ideology, Conflict and Democracy in Britain and Italy*, New Haven: Yale University Press, 1973; and Joseph La Palombara, "Italy: Fragmentation, Isolation, Alienation," in Lucien Pye and Sidney Verba, eds., *Political Culture and Political Development*, Princeton, N.J.: Princeton University Press, 1965.

5. See Robert A. Dahl, "Governments and Political Oppositions," in Dahl, *Regimes and Oppositions*, New Haven: Yale University Press, 1973.

6. Powell, *Social Fragmentation*.

CHAPTER TWO: PAST AS PROLOGUE

1. *Informaciones*, July 22, 1978, p. 2.

2. For some of the many excellent studies of the collapse of the Second Republic, see Stanley G. Payne, *The Spanish Revolution*, New York: Norton, 1970; Gabriel Jackson, *The Spanish Republic and the Spanish Civil War: 1931 – 1939*, Princeton, N.J.: Princeton University Press, 1965; Edward Malefakis, *Agrarian Reform and Peasant Revolution in Spain: Origins of the Civil War*, New Haven: Yale University Press, 1970; and Gerald Brenan, *The Spanish Labyrinth*, New York: Cambridge University Press, 1943 (also in paperback, 1974). For analyses of the Franquist regime, see Kenneth Medhurst, *Government in Spain: The Executive at Work*, Oxford: Pergamon Press, 1973; Juan J. Linz, "An Authoritarian Regime: Spain," in Erik Allardt and Stein Rokkan, eds., *Mass Politics*, New York: Free Press, 1970 (also in Erik Allardt and Yrjö

Littunen, eds., *Cleavages, Ideologies and Party Systems*, Helsinki: Westermarck Society, 1962); Stanley G. Payne, *Franco's Spain*, New York: Crowell, 1967; and Richard Gunther, *Public Policy in a No-Party State: Spanish Planning and Budgeting in the Twilight of the Franquist Era*, Berkeley and Los Angeles: University of California Press, 1980. For extensive descriptions and/or analyses of the transition to the current democracy, see Raymond Carr and Juan Pablo Fusi, *Spain: From Dictatorship to Democracy*, London: George Allen and Unwin, 1979; and José María Maravall, *La Política de la Transición, 1975–1980*, Madrid: Taurus Ediciones, 1981.

3. An additional cleavage in Spanish history, which also contributed to serious polarization, but which we do not examine in this book, is the issue of monarchy vs. republic. The role of the monarchy in the current transition to democracy in Spain has been explored by two other groups of researchers: one includes Samuel Barnes and Peter McDonough of the University of Michigan, and Antonio López Pina of the Universidad Complutense de Madrid; the other is led by Dieter Nohlen and Carlos Huneeus of the Universität Heidelberg.

4. As Stanley Payne has described that style: "Its pattern was that of moralistic French ideological politics rather than the conciliatory Anglo-Saxon empiricism of the former official parties and the Reformists" (*The Spanish Revolution*, p. 85). For a discussion of precisely how this behavioral style hindered conflict regulation, see Richard Gunther and Roger A. Blough, "Conflicto Religioso y Consenso en España: Historia de dos Constituciones," in *Revista de Estudios Políticos*, no. 14, March–April 1980, pp. 89–90.

5. For a brief overview of the Church-state relationship, see Jaime Vicens Vives, *Approaches to the History of Spain*, trans. and ed. by Joan Connelly Ullman, Berkeley and Los Angeles: University of California Press, 1967. For more detailed discussions of this relationship over the past two centuries, see Raymond Carr, *Spain: 1808–1939*, Oxford: Clarendon Press, 1966; Richard Herr, *Spain*, Englewood Cliffs, N.J.: Prentice Hall, 1971; Brenan, *The Spanish Labyrinth*, chap. 3; and Guy Hermet, *Les Catholiques dans l'Espagne Franquiste*, Paris: Presse de la Fondation Nationale des Sciences Politiques, 1980.

6. For detailed discussions of conflicts over religion in writing the Constitution of the Second Republic, see Gunther and Blough, "Conflicto Religioso"; José Ramón Montero Gibert, *La CEDA: El Catolicismo Social y Político en la II Republica*, 2 vols., Madrid: Ediciones de Revista de Trabajo, 1977; Fernando de Meer Lecha-Marzo, *La Cuestión Religiosa en las Cortes Constituyentes de la II República Española*, Pamplona: Ediciones Universidad de Navarra, 1975; Arturo Mori, *Crónica de las Cortes Constituyentes de la Segunda República Española*, Madrid: M. Aguilar, 1933; Luis Jiménez de Asua, *Proceso Histórico de la Constitución de la República Española*, Madrid: Editorial Reus, 1932; José María Gil Robles, *No Fue Posible la Paz*, Barcelona: Ediciones Ariel, 1968; and Juan-Simion Vidarte, *Las Cortes Constituyentes de 1931–1933: Testimonio del primer secretario del Congreso de Diputados*, Barcelona: Ediciones Grijalbo, 1976; and Santiago Varela, *Partidos y Parlamento en la Segunda República*, Madrid: Editorial Ariel, 1978.

7. Such violence increased in the spring preceding the outbreak of the Civil War. In a speech before the Cortes in June 1936, Gil Robles claimed that 160 churches had been destroyed since February (J. W. D. Trythall, *Franco: A Biography,* London: Rupert Hart-Davis, 1970, p. 38). For more data, see Ramiro Cibrián, "Violencia Política y Crisis Democrática: España en 1936," in *Revista de Estudios Políticos,* vol. 6, Nov.–Dec. 1978.

8. José María Maravall claims that the CNT had 1,577,547 members in 1933 (*Dictatorship and Political Dissent: Workers and Students in Franco's Spain,* London: Tavistock, 1978, p. 67). Two other studies claim that CNT membership ranged between 500,000 and 1 million during the period 1931–1936. See Antonio Elorza, *La Utopía Anarquista bajo la II República Española,* Madrid: Ayuso, 1973, p. 351; and Alfons Cucó, "Contribución a un Estudio Cuantitativo de la CNT" in *Saitabi,* vol. 20, 1970, pp. 181–202. Also see Antonio Bar, *La CNT en los Años Rojos: Del Sindicalismo Revolucionario al Anarcho-sindicalismo, 1920–1926,* Madrid: Akal, 1981.

9. Excellent discussions of CNT ideology and behavior may be found in Brenan, *The Spanish Labyrinth,* chaps. 4, 7, and 8.

10. Maravall (*Dictatorship and Political Dissent,* p. 67) claims that the UGT had 1,444,474 members in 1933; Alba (*El Partido Comunista,* p. 177) puts UGT membership in 1936 at 2 million; and Malefakis (*Agrarian Reform*) states that by 1933 the UGT had 1 million members among the peasantry.

11. Luís Gómez Llorente claims that the UGT statutes were reformist by nature and did not represent the "programa máximo" of the PSOE (*Aproximación a la Historia de Socialismo Español,* Madrid: Cuadernos para el Diálogo, 1976, p. 102).

12. Payne, *The Spanish Revolution,* p. 179, and elsewhere.

13. See Brenan, *The Spanish Labyrinth,* part 2, "The Condition of the Working Class."

14. Payne (*The Spanish Revolution,* p. 156) writes: "There had been nothing like the Asturian revolt in Spanish history, or in that of the rest of Western Europe since the Paris Commune." Estimates of the number of persons killed (including many workers executed without trial) range from 1,200 (Payne, ibid.) to over 3,000 (Elena de la Souchere, *An Explanation of Spain,* New York: Random House, 1964, p. 160). For another example of the use of violence by employers against their unionized employees, see Brenan's discussion of the "war of pistoleros" in Catalunya, *The Spanish Labyrinth,* pp. 67–69. Also see Juan J. Linz, "From Great Hopes to Civil War: The Breakdown of Democracy in Spain," in Juan J. Linz and Alfred Stepan, *The Breakdown of Democratic Regimes,* part 2, Baltimore: Johns Hopkins University Press, 1978.

15. Bogdan Zaborski classifies Basque as an Asianitic language, related to Caucasian (spoken in an area east of the Black Sea) and Burushaski (spoken near the border of Pakistan and the U.S.S.R.). (See Edward B. Espenshade, Jr., ed., *Goode's World Atlas,* 13th ed., 1970, p. 31.) Statistics concerning the current usage of these languages may be found in our chap. 7.

16. For histories of these movements, see Stanley G. Payne, "Basque and Catalán Nationalism," *Contemporary History,* 6, no. 1, 1979; Payne, *Basque Na-*

tionalism, Reno: University of Nevada Press, 1975; and Jordi Solé Tura, *Catalanismo y Revolución Burguesa,* Madrid: Editorial Cuadernos para el Diálogo, 1974.

17. An excellent history of state building in Spain may be found in Juan J. Linz, "Early State-Building and Late Peripheral Nationalism Against the State: The Case of Spain," in Stein Rokkan and S. M. Eisenstadt, *Building States and Nations,* Beverly Hills, Calif.: Sage, 1973. Historical discussions of the *fueros* may be found in Jaime Ignacio del Burgo, *El Fuero: Pasado, Presente, Futuro,* Pamplona: EUNSA, 1975; Elias Amezaga, *1000 Años con Fueros y 100 sin,* Bilbao: Editorial la Gran Enciclopedia Vasca, 1976; and Pedro Novia de Salcedo, *Defensa Histórica, Legislativa y Económica del Señorío de Vizcaya y Provincias de Alava y Guipúzcoa,* Bilbao: Librería de Delmas e Hijo, 1851.

18. The electoral districts were Spain's eight largest cities (Madrid, Barcelona, Bilbao, Valencia, Malaga, Murcia, Sevilla, and Zaragoza), the surrounding areas in each of those provinces, the remaining 42 provinces of Spain, and its two Moroccan territories (Ceuta and Melilla).

19. A description of how many seats constituted a "majority" in each district may be found in Juan J. Linz and Jesus M. de Miguel, "Hacia un Analisis Regional de las Elecciones de 1936 en España," in *Revista Española de la Opinión Pública,* no. 48 April–June 1977, p. 29.

20. Brenan, *The Spanish Labyrinth,* n. 1, p. 266.

21. The partisan composition of those legislatures is presented in Juan J. Linz, "The Party System of Spain," p. 260; and Santiago Varela, *Partidos y Parlamento en la Segunda República,* pp. 69–74.

22. Payne, *The Spanish Revolution,* p. 174.

23. Giovanni Sartori, "European Political Parties: The Case of Polarized Pluralism," in Joseph La Palombara and Myron Weiner, eds., *Political Parties and Political Development,* Studies in Political Development no. 6, Princeton, N.J.: Princeton University Press, 1972, p. 159 (paperback ed.). Also see Maurice Duverger, *Political Parties,* 2d ed., New York: John Wiley and Sons, 1959, p. 388.

24. Victor Alba, *El Partido Comunista en España,* Barcelona: Planeta, 1978, pp. 166–67.

25. Statement by Niceto Alcalá-Zamora, cited in Mori, *Crónica de las Cortes,* vol. 3, pp. 128–29.

26. The impact of this lack of proportionality on the constitutional deliberations of 1931 is discussed in Gunther and Blough, "Conflicto Religioso," pp. 93–97.

27. See Brenan, *The Spanish Labyrinth,* chap. 11; Payne, *The Spanish Revolution,* p. 132; Herr, *Spain,* pp. 174–75; and Jackson, *The Spanish Republic,* pp. 124 and 170–71.

28. See Payne, *The Spanish Revolution,* pp. 190–91; and Jackson, *The Spanish Republic,* pp. 123 and 169–70.

29. Payne, ibid., p. 162.

30. See Joseph La Palombara, "Distribution: A Crisis of Resource Man-

agement," in Leonard Binder et al., *Crises and Sequences in Political Development,* Princeton, N.J.: Princeton University Press, 1971, pp. 233–82.

31. For example, left-wing anticlerical Spaniards were represented by the PSOE; bourgeois anticlerical Spaniards could support Azaña's Left Republicans; and left-wing anticlerical Catalán nationalists could vote for the Esquerra. Centrist Catholic Spaniards were represented by Alcalá-Zamora's party; centrist and conservative Basque Catholics could vote for the PNV; and right-wing Catholic Spaniards could support Gil Robles' Confederación Española de Derechas Autónomas (CEDA) or Calvo Sotelo's Renovación Española; etc.

32. Many of the following arguments are set forth in greater detail in Gunther, *Public Policy in a No-Party State,* chap. 1.

33. For more detailed descriptions of the Franquist regime and its relationship with the Church, see Kenneth Medhurst, *Government in Spain: The Executive at Work,* Oxford: Pergamon Press, 1973; and Gunther, *Public Policy in a No-Party State,* pp. 11–13, 32–37, and 173–74.

34. As late as 1961 only 17 percent of high-school students were enrolled in state schools. (Fundación FOESSA, *Estudios Sociológicos Sobre la Situación Social de España, 1975,* Madrid: Editorical Euramérica, 1976, p. 327).

35. See Amando de Miguel, *Sociología del Franquismo,* Barcelona: Editorial Euros, 1975, esp. p. 92; C. Viver Pi-Sunyer, *El Personal Político de Franco, 1936–1945,* Barcelona: Editorial Vicens-Vives, 1978; Juan J. Linz and Amando de Miguel, "La Elite Funcionarial Española ante la Reforma Administrativa," in *Sociología de la Administración Pública Española,* Anales de Moral Social y Económica no. 17, Madrid: Centro de Estudios Sociales de la Santa Cruz del Valle de los Caidos, 1968; and Miguel Jerez, *Elites Políticas y Centros de Extracción en España, 1938–1957,* Madrid: Centro de Investigaciones Sociológicas, 1982.

36. See Gunther, *Public Policy in a No-Party State,* pp. 46–77 and 251–84.

37. See the text of Franco's "Farewell Message," in ibid., p. 285; and excerpts from his final public speech, cited in Carr and Fusi, *From Dictatorship to Democracy,* p. 205.

38. For extensive discussions of the institutions and legitimating principles of the Franquist regime, see Gunther, *Public Policy,* pp. 23–41; and Torcuato Fernández-Miranda Hevia, *El Hombre y la Sociedad,* 6th ed., Madrid: Ediciones Doncel, 1965.

39. For a description and analysis of Franco's role in the policy process, see Gunther, *Public Policy,* pp. 163–74 and 260–84.

40. This concept is derived from Nelson Polsby, "Legislatures," in Fred I. Greenstein and Nelson W. Polsby, eds., *Handbook of Political Science,* vol. 5, Reading, Mass.: Addison-Wesley, 1975.

41. Gunther, *Public Policy,* pp. 161–63 and 285–88.

42. José María Maravall, *Dictatorship and Political Dissent: Workers and Students in Franco's Spain,* Tavistock, London, 1978, p. 4.

43. For descriptions of the composition of the Cortes, see Gunther, *Pub-*

lic Policy, p. 38; and Juan J. Linz, "Legislatures in Organic Statist Authoritarian Regimes: The Case of Spain," unpublished MS, Yale University, 1975.

44. See Linz, "Political Opposition in and Under an Authoritarian Regime: The Case of Spain," in Robert A. Dahl, ed., *Regimes and Oppositions,* New Haven: Yale University Press, 1973.

45. For the most exhaustive history of the Falange, see Stanley G. Payne, *Falange,* Stanford Studies in History, Economics and Political Science no. 22, Stanford, Calif.: Stanford University Press, 1961.

46. For a discussion of this downgrading of the Falange and its ideology, see ibid.; Juan J. Linz, "From Falange to Movimiento-Organización: The Spanish Single Party and the Franco Regime," in Samuel Huntington and Clement Moore, eds., *Authoritarian Politics in Modern Society: The Dynamics of Established One-Party Systems,* New York: Basic Books, 1970; and Gunther, *Public Policy,* pp. 25–31.

47. Cited in Payne, *Falange,* p. 232.

48. Ibid., p. 266.

49. Payne, *The Spanish Revolution,* p. 84.

50. Pedro Schwartz, "Politics First: The Economy after Franco," in *Government and Opposition,* vol. 11., no. 11, Winter 1976, p. 86.

51. Gunther, *Public Policy in a No-Party State,* p. 63.

52. Herr, *Spain,* p. 22.

53. Figures from *1979 World Bank Atlas: Population, Per Capita Produce and Growth Rates,* Washington, D.C.: World Bank, 1979, p. 6.

54. The Instituto Nacional de Estadística (INE), *Anuario Estadístico, 1976* (p. 53), puts that figure in 1930 at 46.1 percent (4.04 million agricultural workers, out of a total work force of 8.77 million). Other studies, however, make higher estimates of the number of agricultural workers, e.g., Antonio de Pablo Masa, "Estratificación y Clases Sociales en la España de Hoy" (FOESSA, *1975,* p. 717), puts that figure for 1930 at 47.1 percent, and Angel Carrión Garzarán et al., in "La Población Española y su Territorio" (ibid., p. 69) makes an estimate of 51.2 percent for 1940.

55. This is reasonably close to similar figures for Italy. In 1961, 29.1 percent of the Italian labor force was engaged in agriculture; in 1971, 17.2 percent. Figures for Spain are from INE, *Anuario Estadístico, 1976,* p. 53; and for Italy, from Corrado Barberis, *La Societá Italiana,* Milano: Franco Angeli Editore, 1976.

56. INE, *Anuario Estadístico, 1976,* p. 56.

57. A provincial-level breakdown of net population loss through migration between 1931 and 1970 for Andalucía is as follows: Huelva 83,049, Cádiz 49,738, Sevilla 31,883, Córdoba 323,462, Jaén 410,609, Málaga 117,948, Granada 342,495, and Almería 173,285 (Carrión Garzarán et al., "La Población Española," p. 70).

58. A province-by-province breakdown of net population loss through migration between 1931 and 1970 for Leon and Old Castile follows: Santander 67,236, Zamora 134,560, Valladolid 42,240, Soria 90,562, Segovia

92,291, Salamanca 139,340, Palencia 97,995, Logroño 43,373, León 126,730, Burgos 144,193, and Avila 114,138 (ibid.).

59. Between 1931 and 1970, the net population losses through migration for the provinces of New Castile (excluding Madrid) were: Albacete 189,155, Ciudad Real 235,767, Cuenca 196,356, Guadalajara 102,726, and Toledo 221,112 (ibid.).

60. Between 1931 and 1970, the province of La Coruña lost 124,218, Lugo lost 165,292, Orense lost 128,786 inhabitants, and Pontevedra suffered a net population loss of 100,056 through migration (ibid.).

61. Between 1931 and 1970, the net population loss through migration was 358,490 for the province of Badajoz, and 248,048 for Cáceres (ibid.).

62. Between 1931 and 1970 the province of Barcelona experienced a net population gain of 1,464,660 persons through internal migration, Madrid gained 1,485,663, Guipúzcoa picked up 134,171, Vizcaya gained 297,138, and Valencia attracted 339,978 migrants from other parts of Spain (ibid.).

63. INE, *Anuario Estadístico, 1976*, p. 54.

64. One study (by Alfonso Pérez Penasco et al., "Educación," in FOESSA, *1975*, p. 212) put the rate of illiteracy in Spain in 1930 at 25.9 percent, while the INE, *Anuario Estadístico, 1976*, places that figure at 31.1 percent (p. 51).

65. The INE figure for 1970 is 8.8 percent (ibid., p. 51); the FOESSA estimate is 8.9 percent (p. 212). Although the remaining illiteracy rate was considerably higher than the average for developed countries (3.5 percent in 1970, according to FOESSA, p. 211), it was well below that of the average of 23.6 percent for Latin America (ibid.).

66. Ignacio Fernández de Castro, "Estratificación y Movilidad Social," in FOESSA, *1975*, p. 982.

67. Antonio de Pablo Masa, "Estratificación," p. 758.

68. Ibid.

69. Ibid.

70. Carr and Fusi, *From Dictatorship to Democracy*, p. 77.

71. The mean of the per capita incomes of the five poorest provinces is only 46.3 percent of the mean of the per capita incomes of the five richest (Banco de Bilbao, *Renta Nacional de España y su Distribución Provincial*, Bilbao: Grijelmo, 1977, p. 33).

72. Maravall, *Dictatorship and Political Dissent*, pp. 41–42. For a history of labor unrest in the 1960s and 1970s, see ibid., pp. 30–37.

73. Carrión Garazán et al., "La Población Española," p. 63.

74. See Juan J. Linz and Amando de Miguel, "La Elite Funcionarial Española ante la Reforma Administrativa"; Amando de Miguel, *Sociología del Franquismo;* and José María Maravall, *La Política de la Transición*, pp. 21–22.

75. See Karl Deutsch, "Social Mobilization and Political Development," *American Political Science Review*, vol. 55, no. 3, September 1961; and Daniel Lerner, *The Passing of Traditional Society*, New York: Free Press, 1958.

76. See, e.g., Lester W. Milbrath and M. L. Goel, *Political Participation*, 2d

ed., Chicago: Rand McNally, 1977, chap. 5; and Norman Nie, G. Bingham Powell, Jr., and Kenneth Prewitt, "Social Structure and Political Participation: Developmental Relationships, Parts I and II," *American Political Science Review*, vol. 6, nos. 2 and 3, 1969, pp. 361–78 and 808–32.

77. States of emergency were declared in Euskadi in 1968 and throughout Spain in 1969 and 1970.

78. Cited in E.J. Heubel, "Church and State in Spain: Transition Toward Independence and Liberty," *Western Political Quarterly*, vol. 30, March 1977, p. 135. Also see Alfred Fierro Bardaji, "Political Positions and Opposition in the Spanish Catholic Church," in *Government and Opposition*, vol. 11, no. 2, Spring 1976, pp. 198–211; and Carr and Fusi, *From Dictatorship to Democracy*, pp. 150–56.

79. Heubel, "Church and State," p. 135.

80. The fact that studies of this kind, dealing with sensitive political issues, could even be conducted gives some indication of the relative "openness" of the situation at that time. Nevertheless, these materials must be taken with some caution. As knowledgeable commentators have pointed out, the conditions and the climate under which the studies were carried out were hardly ideal from the point of view of obtaining an unbiased picture of popular sentiments. (See, e.g., Manuel Gómez-Reino, Francisco Andrés Orizo, and Darío Vila Carro, "Sociología Política," in FOESSA, *1976*, pp. 1168–69.) It is, therefore, quite possible, indeed likely, that the pattern of answers was affected to some extent by a natural reluctance on the part of respondents to divulge information on delicate matters. In spite of these limitations, data gathered in the early 1970s can provide some useful indications concerning the state of mind of the general population toward the end of the Franquist regime.

81. Gómez-Reino, Orizo, and Vila Carro, "Sociología Política," p. 1262. Another study conducted in 1975, which asked respondents the same question, found that 86 percent said that all leaders should be directly elected (Salustiano del Campo, Manuel Navarro, and J. Felix Tezanos, *La Cuestión Regional Española*, Madrid: Editorial Cuadernos para el Diálogo, 1977, p. 59).

82. Gómez-Reino, Orizo, and Vila, "Sociología Política," p. 1184.

83. Juan J. Linz, Manuel Gómez-Reino, Francisco A. Orizo, and Darío Vila Carro, *Informe Sociológico Sobre el Cambio Político en España, 1975–1981*, IV Informe, FOESSA, Madrid: Editorial Euramérica, 1981, p. 14.

84. Del Campo, Navarro, and Tezanos, *La Cuestión Regional*, p. 139.

85. Other survey data pertaining to the structure of public opinion in this period may be found in Rafael López Pintor, *La Opinión Pública Española: Del Franquismo a la Democracia*, Madrid: Centro de Investigaciones Sociológicas, 1982.

86. Gómez-Reino, Orizo, and Vila Carro, "Sociología Política," pp. 1185, 1199.

87. Ibid., p. 1184.

88. Ibid., p. 1215.

89. Del Campo, Navarro, and Tezanos, *La Cuestión Regional,* p. 95.

90. Fraga claims that it was his explicit intention to encourage a flourishing of Catalan literature through enactment of the Press Law (Carlos Sentís, *Manuel Fraga Iribarne, Perfil Humano y Político,* Madrid: Editorial Cambio 16, 1977, p. 17).

91. Maravall, *Dictatorship and Political Dissent,* p. 9.

92. Carr and Fusi, *From Dictatorship to Democracy,* p. 148.

93. Ibid., p. 191.

94. Excerpts from the text of that speech were published in *Informaciones,* Feb. 12, 1974, pp. 18–19.

95. Ibid., p. 19.

96. Carr and Fusi, *From Dictatorship to Democracy,* pp. 204–5. The one group that met all of the requirements of associationism was the Unión del Pueblo Español (UDPE), a Movimiento-sponsored association formed in June 1975 under the presidency of Adolfo Suárez.

97. See Gunther, *Public Policy,* pp. 163 and 286–87.

98. The largest of these was Coordinación Democrática, formed in March 1976. It provided a platform for the coordination of opposition activities of the Communist PCE, the socialist PSOE, the socialist PSP of Enrique Tierno Galván, the leftist Christian Democratic Izquierda Democrática of Joaquín Ruiz Giménez, the Carlists (reincarnated as a leftist socialist party under the leadership of the Pretender Carlos Hugo de Borbón Parma), the social democratic USDE founded by Dionisio Ridruejo, the Basque nationalist PNV, the Labor Party (PTE), and several other small groups.

99. Immediate legalization of the Communist party could have led important sectors of the armed forces to oppose the transition.

100. Giuseppe Di Palma, "Founding Coalitions in Southern Europe: Legitimacy and Hegemony," *Government and Opposition,* 15, Spring 1980, pp. 162–89.

101. José María Maravall, *La Política de la Transción,* p. 27. Elsewhere, Maravall documents the increasing politicization of the objectives of these strikes (ibid., p. 23).

102. Ibid., p. 33.

103. Jordi Solé Tura, "La Constitución y la Lucha por el Socialismo," in Gregoria Peces-Barba, et al., *La Izquierda y la Constitución,* Barcelona: Ediciones Taula de Canvi, 1978, pp. 19–20.

104. These changes were restricted to the political arena (in the narrowest sense of that term) and did not include significant administrative, judicial, or economic changes.

105. Among the negative consequences of the political amnesties was the subsequent discovery that some of those pardoned resumed their involvement in terrorist activities after their release from jail.

CHAPTER THREE:
THE EMERGENCE OF POLITICAL PARTIES

1. Although this description was commonly used by political observers in Spain throughout the period 1979 through 1982, we will not use it here, because it has taken on a specific and somewhat different meaning in describing another party system (Giorgio Galli, *Dal Bipartitismo Imperfetto alla Possibile Alternativa,* Bologna: Il Mulino, 1975).

2. Even though important public financing provisions were included in the 1977 electoral law itself, we will defer our discussion of this factor until chapter 4.

3. For a discussion of the social-psychological dynamics of the inclusion or exclusion of groups from a constituent process, see Richard Gunther, "Constitutional Change in Contemporary Spain," in Keith Banting and Richard Simeon, eds., *The Politics of Constitutional Change in Industrial Nations: Redesigning the State,* London: Macmillan, 1984.

4. Francisco González Navarro, *La Nueva Ley Fundamental para la Reforma Política,* Colección Informe, no. 14, Madrid: Servicio Central de Publicaciones, Presidencia del Gobierno, 1977, p. 430. Also see Pablo Lucas Verdú, *La Octava Ley Fundamental,* Madrid: Tecnos, 1977.

5. The "committee of nine" included representatives of the socialist, social-democratic, communist, liberal, and Christian democratic parties; the three largest trade unions; and moderate Basque, Gallego, and Catalán groups.

6. Ministerio del Interior, Secretaría General Técnica, *Legislación Electoral Española,* March 1979, pp. 25–96. The North African territories of Ceuta and Melilla were given one seat each in the Congress of Deputies.

7. Ibid., pp. 28 and 27, respectively.

8. Douglas W. Rae, *The Political Consequences of Electoral Laws,* New Haven and London: Yale University Press, 1967, p. 33.

9. Ibid., p. 53.

10. Linz, Gómez-Reino, Orizo, and Vila Carro, FOESSA, *Informe 1975–1981,* p. 165.

11. Ibid., p. 161.

12. Ibid., p. 189.

13. Ibid., p. 14.

14. Ibid., p. 162.

15. Ibid., p. 189.

16. Ibid., p. 153–54.

17. Ibid., p. 162.

18. Findings from a 1975 survey concerning mass-level preferences for nationwide versus regional parties suggested that, in Euskadi, Catalunya, and Galicia, small regional parties might also fare quite well, given the biases of the electoral law. When asked if they would vote for a nationwide party or a regionalist group, the latter was chosen by 37, 29, and 43 percent of the Basque, Catalán, and Gallego samples, respectively. See Salustiano del Campo, Navarro, and Tezanos, *La Cuestión Regional,* p. 87.

19. In certain regions, the PCE had different names for regional branches, such as the Partido Comunista de Euskadi (PCE/EKP), and the Partido Comunista de Galicia (PCG). In Catalunya its affiliate, the Partit Socialista Unificat de Catalunya (PSUC), had considerable organizational autonomy.

20. For more detailed histories of the PCE, see Eusebio Mujal-Leon, *Communism and Political Change in Spain*, Bloomington: Indiana University Press, 1983; Mujal-Leon, "The PCE in Spanish Politics," *Problems of Communism*, July–Aug. 1978, vol. 27, no. 4, pp. 15–37; Paul Preston, "The Dilemma of Credibility: The Spanish Communist Party, the Franco Regime and After," *Government and Opposition*, Winter 1976, vol. 11; and Preston, "The PCE's Long Road to Democracy, 1954–1977," in Richard Kindersley, ed., *In Search of Eurocommunism*, London: Macmillan, 1981. For rather polemical views of the PCE's history, see the markedly anticommunist account of Victor Alba, *El Partido Comunista en España*, Barcelona: Planeta, 1978; and the sympathetic account of José Díaz (secretary general of the PCE during the Republic), *Tres Años de Lucha*, Barcelona: Editorial Laia, 1978.

21. See Gabriel Jackson, *The Spanish Republic;* and Stanley Payne, *The Spanish Revolution.*

22. This concept is based upon that originally set forth by Maurice Duverger in *Political Parties*, 2d ed., New York: John Wiley and Sons, 1959, p. 70.

23. J. M. Maravall, *Dictatorship and Political Dissent*, pp. 151–52.

24. Quoted in Eduardo Chamorro, *Ramón Tamames, Perfil Humano y Político*, Madrid: Editorial Cambio 16, 1977, p. 63.

25. Preston, "The PCE's Long Road to Democracy," p. 61.

26. Ibid., p. 58.

27. Carr and Fusi (*From Dictatorship to Democracy*, p. 161) argue that the *guerrilla*, rather than rallying Spaniards against the regime, came to be regarded as common banditry and a nuisance.

28. Alba, *El Partido Comunista*, p. 299.

29. See Maravall's description of these differences in *Dictatorship and Political Dissent*, pp. 146–52.

30. Chamorro, *Tamames*, p. 62.

31. Rafael Rodríguez, *Quienes son en Málaga: Partido Comunista de España*, Málaga: Ediciones Lafer, 1977, p. 30. Also see the speech by Santiago Carrillo to the PCE Central Committee in September 1957, excerpts of which are published in PCE, *Noveno Congreso del Partido Comunista de España, 19–23 Abril, 1978*, Barcelona: Editorial Crítica, 1978, p. 57.

32. Maria Eugenia Yagüe, *Santiago Carrillo, Perfil Humano y Político*, Madrid: Editorial Cambio 16, 1977, p. 58.

33. Ibid., pp. 56–57.

34. Ibid., pp. 57–58.

35. See PSUC, *IV Congrés del Partit Socialista Unificat de Catalunya: Recull de Materials i d'Intervencions*, Barcelona: Edita LAIA, 1978.

36. Preston, "The PCE's Long Road," p. 59.

37. For a detailed history of trade union protests, see Equipo de Estu-

dios (Ignacio Fernández de Castro, director), "El Movimiento Obrero y sus Organizaciones Sindicales en los años 70," in *Documentación Social: Revista de Estudios Sociales y de Sociología Aplicada*, no. 22, April–June 1976, pp. 57–98. Also see Maravall, *Dictatorship and Political Dissent* and chapter 5 of this book.

38. Maravall, ibid., p. 157.

39. These demonstrations and those following the Burgos Trial in 1970 led to the enactment of a new National Defense Law that greatly increased military and police expenditures (Gunther, *Public Policy*, pp. 164–72).

40. José María Maravall, "Transición a la Democracia, Alineamientos Políticos y Elecciones en España," *Sistema*, no. 36, May 1980, p. 75.

41. Maravall, *Dictatorship and Political Dissent*, pp. 157–58.

42. Carlos Elordi ("El PCE por Dentro," *La Calle*, no. 95, Jan. 15–21, 1980, p. 24) reports that party membership in 1975 was 15 thousand; Alba (*El Partido Comunista*, p. 342) records the PCE claim of 20 thousand members at the time of Franco's death.

43. Santiago Carrillo claimed in July 1976 that the party had 100 thousand members (Alba, *El Partido Comunista*, p. 344), while Gerardo Duelo (*Diccionario de Grupos, Fuerzas y Partidos Políticos Españoles*, Barcelona: La Gaya Ciencia, 1977, p. 97) reports that the party had only 90 thousand members in early 1977.

44. Party officials in the following provinces claimed (in interviews conducted in 1978 and 1979) that the PCE had constantly maintained some kind of organizational presence in their respective territories: Madrid, Toledo, Segovia, Málaga, Granada, Córdoba, Sevilla, Valencia, Baleares, Barcelona, Navarra, Guipúzcoa, La Coruña, Pontevedra, and Zamora. Because of the regional structure of the PSUC, no interviews were held in Gerona, the only other province in our elite interview sample.

45. Fernando Jaúregui and Manual Soriano, *La Otra Historia de UCD*, Madrid: Emiliano Escolar Editor, 1980, pp. 167–68.

46. Excerpt from an interview with Santiago Alvarez on June 29, 1979. Victor Alba (*El Partido Comunista*, p. 281) sets forth a similar claim.

47. Carr and Fusi, *From Dictatorship to Democracy*, p. 14.

48. Manuel Pérez Ledesma, "Los Partidos Políticos en la Transción," *Tiempo de Historia*, 72, 1980, p. 56.

49. Ibid.

50. José María Maravall, "La Alternativa Socialista: La Política y el Apoyo Electoral del PSOE," *Sistema*, 35, May 1980, p. 10. Also see Maravall, *La Política de la Transción*, pp. 26–31.

51. Pedro J. Ramírez, *Así se Ganaron las Elecciones*, Barcelona: Planeta, 1977, p. 68.

52. These conclusions concerning Suárez's role in legalizing the PCE were derived from an extensive interview with a former high-ranking UCD leader held in May 1984.

53. Ramírez, *Así se Ganaron las Elecciones*, p. 188.

54. 1936 election data are from Juan J. Linz and Jesus de Miguel, "Hacia

un Analisis Regional de las Elecciones de 1936 en España," *Revista Española de la Opinión Pública,* 48, April–June 1977. The trade union figure is from Maravall, *Dictatorship and Political Dissent,* p. 67.

55. Carlos Elordi ("El PSOE por Dentro," *La Calle,* 115, June 1980, p. 15) claims that PSOE membership in 1972 was 1,500. José María Maravall ("La Alternativa," p. 9) places total membership of the PSOE within Spain in 1974 at 2,000. José Ramón Montero Gibert ("Partidos y Participación Política: Algunas Notas sobre la Afiliación Política en la Etapa Inicial de la Transción Española," *Revista de Estudios Políticos,* 23, Sept.–Oct. 1981, p. 44) lists total PSOE membership in 1975 as 4,000.

56. PSOE officials reported in 1978 interviews that all vestiges of party organization had been eliminated from Segovia, Zamora, Baleares, Navarra, Toledo, Pontevedra, and La Coruña. Those sample provinces in which the party was able to maintain clandestine branches throughout the Franquist regime were Sevilla, Córdoba, Málaga, Granada, Madrid, Guipúzcoa, Valencia, and Barcelona. (Again, because of the regional structure of the PSOE, no interviews could be held in Gerona.)

57. Maravall, *Dictatorship and Political Dissent,* p. 23.

58. Ibid., p. 69.

59. Maravall, "La Alternativa," p. 7.

60. Maravall, "La Alternativa," p. 7.

61. The Basques on the executive committee were Ramón Rubial (who later became party president) and Enrique Múgica; the representatives from Madrid were Francisco Bustelo, Pablo Castellano, and Luís Gómez Llorente (all of whom would eventually form the core of maximalist Socialist opposition to Felipe González's attempts to moderate the party's ideology in 1979); and the Andaluces (all from Sevilla) were Felipe González, Alfonso Guerra, Guillermo Galeote, and Luis Yáñez.

62. Elordi, "El PCE," p. 15.

63. José María Maravall, "Eurocomunismo y Socialismo en España: La Sociología de una Competición Política," *Sistema,* no. 28, Jan. 1979, p. 58.

64. PSOE, Federació Socialista de Catalunya, *El PSOE, Apunte Histórico,* p. 19.

65. Maravall, "La Alternativa," p. 9.

66. Pérez Ledesma, "Los Partidos Políticos," p. 56.

67. PSOE, *XXVII Congreso del PSOE,* Barcelona: Avance, 1977, pp. 115–16.

68. For a specific list of these industries, see Maravall, "Eurocomunismo y Socialismo," p. 67.

69. Javier Tusell, "El Centro Democrático y la Democracia Cristiana en las Elecciones del 15 de Junio de 1977," unpublished MS, 1978.

70. Ramírez, *Así se Ganaron las Elecciones,* 1977, p. 263.

71. Michael Roskin, "Spain Tries Democracy Again," *Political Science Quarterly,* Winter 1978–79, vol. 93, no. 4, p. 646.

72. PCE respondents, by way of comparison, admitted that they re-

ceived advice and borrowed some campaign equipment from the Italian Communist party but denied that they received any significant financial assistance from abroad.

73. SPD financial assistance to the PSOE was confirmed by Willy Brandt in an interview on the CBS television program, *Face the Nation*, on Dec. 8, 1980.

74. PSP, *Resumen del Programa Electoral del PSP*, 1977, p. 6.

75. PSP, "III Congreso del PSP, 1976," cited in Javier Alfaya, *Raul Morodo: Perfil Humano y Político*, Madrid: Editorial Cambio 16, 1977, p. 53.

76. Alfaya, *Raul Morodo*, p. 55.

77. Ibid., pp. 57 and 72.

78. Fernando Ruiz and Joaquín Romero, eds., *Los Partidos Marxistas: Sus Dirigentes Sus Programas*, Barcelona: Editorial Anagrama, 1977, pp. 309–10.

79. Alfaya, *Raul Morodo*, p. 56.

80. Tierno Galván and other PSP leaders often referred to their support as the "vote of quality" (Ramírez, *Así se Ganaron las Elecciones*, 1977, p. 23 and 180), angering Felipe González and others because this implied (in González's words) "five million yokels voted for us" (ibid., p. 180).

81. Ramírez, *Así se Ganaron las Elecciones*, 1977, p. 180.

82. Alfaya, *Raul Morodo*, p. 76.

83. Ruiz and Romero, *Los Partidos Marxistas*, p. 312.

84. Ramírez, *Así se Ganaron Las Elecciones*, 1977.

85. For a description and analysis of López Rodó's policy-making role, see Gunther, *Public Policy*, chaps. 7, 8, and 9.

86. Excerpt from a Jan. 1973 statement by Fraga, cited in Carr and Fusi, *From Dictatorship to Democracy*, p. 192.

87. Statement by Fraga, cited in Carlos Sentís, *Manuel Fraga Iribarne, Perfil Humano y Político*, Madrid: Editorial Cambio 16, 1977, p. 67.

88. Excerpt from the formal ideological declaration of the Reforma Democrática, in GODSA, *Libro Blanco para la Reforma Democrática*, Madrid: GODSA, 1976, p. 22.

89. Jonathan Story, "Spanish Political Parties: Before and After the Elections," *Government and Opposition*, vol. 12, no. 4, Autumn 1977, p. 476.

90. Ibid.

91. Excerpt from a statement by Tamames, in Chamorro, *Tamames*, p. 26. Tamames claims that Fraga's basic orientation toward the reform process was best characterized by his statement, "*I* determine the timing" (ibid., p. 25). In apparent conformity with this statement, he once said to Felipe González, "I want to construct a democracy in which you could be prime minister within four years, but not one day earlier" (Ramírez, *Así se Ganaron Las Elecciones*, 1977, p. 171).

92. Excerpt from an interview with an AP official, held in May 1978. Also see J. M. González Páramo, "El Rapto de la Reforma," in GODSA, *Boletín de Información y Documentación*, nos. 8–9, Jan. 1977.

93. Statement by Fraga, in Sentís, *Manuel Fraga Iribarne*, p. 69.

94. Otto Kirchheimer, "The Transformation of the Western European Party Systems," in Joseph La Palombara and Myron Weiner, eds., *Political Parties and Political Development*, Princeton, N.J.: Princeton University Press, 1966.

95. Carr and Fusi, *From Dictatorship to Democracy*, p. 204.

96. 1978 interview with an AP official who had played a key role in writing the basic ideological and programmatic declaration of that party, the *Libro Blanco para la Reforma Democrática*.

97. See *Cambio 16* (Sept. 27, 1976, p. 15; and Oct. 4, 1976, p. 12); and Story, "Spanish Political Parties," p. 77.

98. José Oneto, *José María de Areilza, Perfil Humano y Político*, Editorial Cambio 16, 1977, pp. 67–68.

99. Fraga's supporters in the Reforma Democrática were alarmed about the consequences of this split in the UDE (*Cambio 16*, Oct. 4, 1976, p. 13, and Oct. 18, p. 15).

100. Amando de Miguel, *Sociología del Franquismo*, Barcelona: Editorial Euros, 1975; and Gunther, *Public Policy*, passim.

101. Survey data gathered in 1977 indicated that only 9 percent of Spaniards polled selected the term "Marxism" over "non-Marxism," either or both. See Linz, Gómez-Reino, Orizo, and Vila Carro, FOESSA, *Informe, 1975–1981*, p. 154.

102. For an excellent survey of these types of relationships, see Keith Legg, *Patrons, Clients and Politicians*, Working Papers on Development 3, Berkeley: University of California, Institute of International Studies, July 1975.

103. Santiago Varela, "La Perspectiva Historica," in Jorge de Esteban, et al., *El Proceso Electoral*, Barcelona: Editorial Labor, 1977, p. 292.

104. Excerpt from an interview with a prominent member of the Communist party in July 1979. For similar statements concerning the mutual utility of such relationships, see William A. Christian, Jr., *Person and God in a Spanish Valley*, New York: Seminar Press, 1972, pp. 173–74; and Varela, op. cit., pp. 290–93.

105. See Javier Tusell, *Oligarquía y Caciquismo en Andalucía (1890–1923)*, Barcelona: Editorial Planeta, 1976; Javier Tusell, "El Sistema Caciquil Andaluz Comparado con otras Regiones Españolas (1903–1923)," in *Revista Española de Investigaciones Sociológicas*, no. 2, 1978; Varela, "La Perspectiva Histórica"; Raymond Carr, *Spain, 1808–1939*, Oxford: Clarendon Press, 1966, chap. 9; Gerald Brenan, *The Spanish Labyrinth*, New York: Cambridge University Press, 1974 (paperback ed.), pp. 6–8; Stanley Payne, *The Spanish Revolution*, pp. 21–22; and José Varela Ortega, *Los Amigos Políticos*, Madrid: Alianza, 1977.

106. Tusell, "El Sistema Caciquil," p. 19.

107. For classic discussions of this aspect of modernization, see Daniel Lerner, *The Passing of Traditional Society*, New York: Free Press, 1958; Karl

Deutsch, *Nationalism and Social Communication,* Cambridge: Massachusetts Institute of Technology, 1953; and Karl Deutsch, "Social Mobilization and Political Development," *American Political Science Review,* vol. 55, no. 3, Sept. 1961.

108. Montero ("Partidos y Participacion") describes the basic character of the "Franquist political culture" as one of "demobilization, depoliticization, apathy" (p. 7).

109. See Gunther, *Public Policy,* chaps. 8 and 9.

110. E.g., in a debate with Enrique Tierno Galván on the television program "Cara a Cara," broadcast Jan. 4, 1978.

111. Statement by Fraga, in Sentís, *Manuel Fraga,* p. 69.

112. Story, "Spanish Political Parties," p. 477.

113. *Cambio 16,* Nov. 8, 1976, p. 24.

114. See *Cambio 16,* Nov. 29, 1976, p. 21; Varela, "La Perspectiva Histórica," p. 295; and Francisco Rubio Llorente, "La Astucia Electoral," in *Cambio 16,* June 14, 1976, p. 27.

115. *Cambio 16,* Nov. 29, 1976, pp. 16–21.

116. Story, "Spanish Political Parties," p. 478.

117. Silva had written numerous articles during the Franquist era calling for democratization (Carr and Fusi, *From Dictatorship to Democracy,* p. 193), and he was among the first to form a political association under the Arias Navarro "reforms" of 1974. His shift to the antidemocratic right was interpreted by one high-ranking leader of the AP (in a 1981 interview) as a reaction against the events surrounding the constituent process of 1978.

118. Ramírez, *Así Se Ganaron las Elecciones,* 1977.

119. Ibid., p. 62.

120. For a more detailed discussion of the candidate selection process, see ibid., pp. 98–105.

121. Ramírez, *Así Se Ganaron las Elecciones,* 1977.

122. Ibid., pp. 60–61.

123. Ibid., p. 50.

124. Ibid.

125. Ibid., p. 132.

126. Ibid., p. 244.

127. Ibid., p. 244; also see p. 305.

128. Ibid., p. 132.

129. Ibid., pp. 305–6.

130. Ibid., p. 236.

131. Tusell, "El Centro Democrático y la Democracia Cristiana," p. 2. Much of the following discussion would not have been possible without the generous assistance of Javier Tusell in making his manuscript available. The authors gratefully acknowledge his contribution.

132. The most famous such incident involved six-month terms of confinement served by several moderate opposition leaders (including the future UCD leaders Iñigo Cavero, José Luís Ruiz-Navarro, and Fernando Alvarez de Miranda) for their participation in an opposition congress held in Munich in 1962.

133. The "Tácitos" were a group of conservative Christian democrats (including two undersecretaries in the state administration—Marcelino Oreja and Landelina Lavilla—and several directors general—e.g., Juan Antonio Ortega y Díaz Ambrona and Luis Jaúdenes) who wrote an extended series of articles in favor of political reform in the early 1970s under the pseudonym "Tácito." See Tácito, *Un Año y Medio de Política Española*, Madrid: Ibérico-European, 1975.

134. Excerpt from a statement by the former UCD Secretary of State for Information, Josep Meliá, cited in Maravall, "La Transición," p. 74.

135. Ramírez, *Así se Ganaron las Elecciones*, 1977, p. 121. Jaúregui and Soriano (*La Otra Historia*, p. 49) report that the German Christian Democratic Union contributed money to Alvarez de Miranda's party, but other sources assert that this financial aid did not begin until after the demise of the Christian Democratic Equipo in the June 1977 elections.

136. A poll taken in February 1977 (cited in Tusell, "El Centro Democrático," p. 16) indicated that Suárez greatly outdistanced other party leaders in terms of popularity and perceived capacity to create a democratic regime. In response to a question about the latter characteristic, for example, 45.4 percent named Suárez as most capable, as compared with 5.9 percent for Felipe González, 4.2 percent for Areilza, 2.5 percent for Fraga, and 2.2 percent for Ruiz Giménez.

137. José Oneto, *José María de Areilza, Perfil Humano y Política*, Madrid: Editorial Cambio 16, 1977, p. 63. Also see José María de Areilza, *Diario de un Ministro de la Monarquía*, Barcelona: Planeta, 1977.

138. Ramírez (*Así se Ganaron las Elecciones*, 1977, p. 121) reports that Suárez's collaborator, Leopoldo Calvo Sotelo, greatly stressed this argument in his negotiations with Centro Democrático leaders over the founding of the UCD.

139. In support of this accusation, an AP leader (who had been a government minister under Franco) stated in a 1978 interview that he knew of several budget items that were so vaguely defined and so poorly controlled that they could easily be "reappropriated" for partisan purposes.

140. The following account is based on interviews with two of the highest-ranking founders of the UCD in the summer of 1983. Unfortunately, much descriptive detail could not be included here because many comments were made strictly "off the record."

141. *Cambio 16*, April 10, 1977, p. 9.

142. Ramírez, *Así se Ganaron las Elecciones*, 1977, p. 30.

143. Ibid., p. 118.

144. Ibid., p. 120-21.

145. Ibid., p. 163.

146. Ramírez (ibid.) reports that 206 of the UCD's candidates for the Congress and Senate were "Independents."

147. Tusell ("El Centro Democrático"), p. 34.

148. These were Manuel Fanjul Sedeño and Fernando Benzo Mestre, who occupied positions nos. 3 and 9, respectively.

149. Tusell ("El Centro Democrático") lists Jaén, Extremadura, Galicia, Valencia, and Navarra as areas of such conflict.

150. Jaúregui and Soriano, *La Otra Historia,* p. 60.

151. For example, Tusell ("El Centro Democrático," p. 34) claims that the UCD was strengthened in Salamanca through the activities of the former Procurador Esperabé.

152. Ibid., p. 35.

153. Maravall, "La Transición," p. 74.

154. 1978 interview with a high-ranking AP official.

155. The two high-ranking party leaders most directly responsible for the incorporation of the "independents" denied, in 1983 interviews, that regime legitimation was a significant party-building criterion at that time. In their view, such considerations ceased to be crucial with the ratification of the Political Reform Law in December 1976.

156. See Juan J. Linz, "The Legacy of Franco."

157. See Juan J. Linz, "The New Spanish Party System," in Richard Rose, ed., *Electoral Participation,* London: Sage, 1980.

158. Among the UCD deputies, 8 had been officers within the Movimiento, 18 had held positions within the vertical *sindicatos,* 8 had served as mayors or city councilmen, and 15 had been procuradores in the Cortes, civil governors, or presidents of diputaciones provinciales (corporatist "provincial legislatures") (Equipo de Documentación Política, *Radiografía de las Nuevas Cortes,* Madrid: Sedmay Ediciones, 1977). We gratefully acknowledge the collaboration of Roger A. Blough in analyzing these biographical data.

159. UCD, *Manual para Veintidos Miliones de Electores,* Madrid: Sucesores de Rivadeneyra, 1977, p. 11.

160. As described by a former secretary general of the UCD in a 1983 interview.

161. Francisco Fernández Ordóñez, *Qué son los Socialdemócratas?,* Barcelona: La Gaya Ciencia, 1976, pp. 14–15.

162. Among the more prominent economically conservative Christian democrats were Alfonso Osorio, Oscar Alzaga, and José Luís Alvarez, all of whom eventually left the party to join Manuel Fraga.

163. Ramon Pí, *Joaquín Garrigues Walker, Perfil Humano y Político,* Madrid: Editorial Cambio 16, 1977, p. 102.

164. Ibid., p. 104.

165. Linz, Gómez-Reino, Orizo, and Vila Carro, FOESSA, *Informe 1975–1981,* p. 163.

166. Tusell, "El Centro Democrático," p. 9.

167. See *ABC,* edición semanal aerea, Feb. 10, 1977, pp. 15–16.

168. Jaúregui and Soriano, *La Otra Historia,* p. 52.

169. Tusell, "El Centro Democrático," p. 23.

170. Jaúregui and Soriano, ibid., p. 55.

171. Ramírez, *Así se Ganaron las Elecciones,* p. 78.

172. Tusell, "El Centro Democrático," p. 23.

173. Ibid.

174. Ramírez, ibid., p. 78; and Tusell, ibid., p. 30.

175. Ramírez, ibid., p. 81.

176. Tusell, ibid., p. 40.

177. Duelo, *Diccionario,* p. 75.

178. For the complete list of candidates participating in that election, see *Boletín Oficial del Estado,* no. 120, May 20, 1977, pp. 11098–11142.

179. This conclusion was drawn from interviews with party officials in 16 provinces in 1978.

180. *Informaciones,* Dec. 13, 1977.

181. Ramírez, *Así se Ganaron las Elecciones,* p. 83. Also see Tusell, "El Centro Democrático," p. 46; Andrés de Blas Guerrero, "UCD, PSOE, PCE y AP: Las Posiciones Programáticas," in Raul Morodo, et al., *Los Partidos Políticos en España,* Barcelona: Editorial Labor, 1979, p. 158; and Juan J. Linz, "The New Spanish Party System."

182. For an early prediction of the possible strength of Christian democratic parties in a post-Franco democracy, see Juan J. Linz, "The Party System in Spain: Past and Future," in Seymour Martin Lipset and Stein Rokkan, eds., *Party Systems and Voter Alignments,* New York: Free Press, 1967.

183. Tusell, "El Centro Democrático," p. 57.

CHAPTER FOUR:

PARTY DEVELOPMENT
IN THE ERA OF CONSENSUS

1. The UCD would have exceeded the minimum "absolute majority" of 176 by combining its 165 deputies with the 16 representatives of AP.

2. See Gunther and Blough, "Religious Conflict and Consensus," p. 399.

3. These practices differed from full-fledged consociationalism, as described by Arend Lijphart (*The Politics of Accommodation,* Berkeley and Los Angeles: University of California Press, 1968) in the following ways. First, Spanish society is not "pillarized" at the mass level. Indeed, levels of affiliation with secondary organizations, in particular, are low in Spain. Second, the elite-level "rules of the game" were restricted to the constituent process and to negotiations over the economic crisis of the late 1970s; they did not carry over into other aspects of governmental decision making and were abruptly abandoned after the 1979 general election (except for their revival for the purpose of negotiating autonomy statutes for Euskadi and Catalunya). Third, there was no widespread proportionality in the distribution of governmental posts or outputs.

Even though participants in the constituent process were keenly aware of the provisions of many democratic constitutions, both past and present (see, e.g., the numerous comparative references made by Oscar Alzaga Villaamil, *Comentario Sistemático a la Constitución Española de 1978,* Madrid: Ediciones del Foro, 1978), those same constituent elites never made references to consociational practices in other countries, as revealed in a thorough survey of constitutional debates published in the press and in Cortes Españolas, *Diario de Sesiones del Congreso de los Diputados, Comisión de Asuntos Constitucionales y Libertades Públicas*, nos. 59–93, May 5, 1978–June 20, 1978; Cortes Españolas, *Diario de Sesiones del Congreso de los Diputados*, nos. 103–116, July 4, 1978–July 21, 1978; and no. 130, Oct. 31, 1978; and Cortes Españolas, *Diario de Sesiones del Senado, Comisión de Constitucion*, nos. 39–67, Aug. 18–Oct. 5, 1978. Several key participants in "the politics of consensus," in the course of in-depth interviews, firmly rejected suggestions that these rules of the game might have been copied from consociational practices elsewhere and indicated, instead, that a particularly Spanish set of political-cultural norms may have led to their adoption. In the final stages of conflict resolution, the shift to private, bilateral negotiations between the parties most directly involved in a dispute was a well-established tradition within the Spanish state administration at least as far back as the Franquist era (Gunther, *Public Policy*). Thus, in sharp contrast with French elite political culture, often characterized by an avoidance of face-to-face negotiations (Michel Crozier, *The Bureaucratic Phenomenon*, Chicago: University of Chicago Press, 1967), Spanish elites were predisposed to enter into private discussions as a means of conflict resolution. As a high-ranking respondent said, when asked why he shifted the negotiations to that format, "It's just my style."

4. The *Ponencia* of the constitutional committee of the Congress of Deputies included Manuel Fraga Iribarne (AP), Gregorio Peces-Barba (PSOE), Jordi Solé Tura (PCE), Miguel Roca i Junyent (Catalán Minority), and Miguel Herrero de Miñón, Gabriel Cisneros, and José Pérez Llorca (all UCD).

5. See Gunther and Blough, "Religious Conflict and Consensus," p. 390.

6. See R. Marriott, "Size of Working Group and Output," *Occupational Psychology*, no. 23, Jan. 1949, pp. 47–57; A. Paul Hare, "A Study of Interaction and Consensus in Different sized Groups," *American Sociological Review*, no. 17, June 1952, pp. 261–67; and B. P. Indik, "Organization Size and Member Participation," paper presented at American Psychological Association meeting, New York, Sept. 1961.

7. As one of the key participants in "the politics of consensus" stated in a June 1981 interview, "Always, when there are public conversations, in the constitutional committee or in a public negotiating forum, the conversations fail to produce results. Under those conditions, the participants express a liturgy . . . each one sticks to his original position without change that would abandon the original meaning of those positions. . . . [To make concessions under those circumstances] would have high political cost, vis-à-vis both party militants and voters."

8. Inferences from observed behavior as "evidence" of pragmatism or dogmatism, for example, would produce a tautological argument. In this study, however, numerous statements made by the relevant elites prior to the start of the negotiations (as well as extensive in-depth interviews with many of those party leaders concerning their perceptions, calculations, and atti-

tudes relevant to the constituent process) constituted independent bases for assessing such attitudes.

9. This speech (attended by one of the authors) was delivered by Emilio Attard Alonso at the Club Siglo XXI on May 8, 1978. Excerpts were published in *Informaciones*, May 9, 1978, p. 6.

10. *Informaciones*, April 6, 1978.

11. *El Socialista*, May 7, 1978, pp. II and III.

12. Catalán nationalist interests in these deliberations were articulated principally by representatives of the CDC (Convergència Democràtica de Catalunya) and ERC (Esquerra Republicana de Catalunya), but also by many leaders of the Catalán branches of the Socialist and Communist parties.

13. Cortes Españolas, *Diario de Sesiones del Congreso de los Diputados: Comisión de Asuntos Constitucionales y Libertades Públicas*, May 8, 1978, no. 60, p. 2084. Also see his statements of May 12, in *Diario de Sesiones*, no. 65, pp. 2263–65.

14. For an example of this argument, see the statement by Carlos Garaicoechea in *Informaciones*, Sept. 28, 1978, p. 4.

15. *Informaciones*, Aug. 9, 1978, p. 2. Also see the statements by Arzallus as reported in *ABC*, edición semanal aerea, Aug. 17, 1978, p. 18.

16. Referendum results from *ABC*, edición semanal aerea, Dec. 14, 1978.

17. In accord with this interpretation, the PNV Deputy Kepa Sodupe said of the breakdown of those negotiations: "A large part of the difficulties that are emerging now arose out of the exclusion suffered by the PNV during the ten months in which the Constitution was being elaborated, during which all the other political groups had opportunities to be heard, to participate in the consensus and to decide by vote" (*Informaciones*, June 20, 1978, p. 5).

18. For data concerning the impact of oil price increases, see Gunther, *Public Policy*, pp. 105–9.

19. For a detailed analysis of the distribution of the tax burden under the Franco regime, see Diego Perona Villarreal, *La Distribución de la Carga Tributaria en España*, Madrid: Instituto de Estudios Fiscales, 1972; also see Gunther, *Public Policy*, chaps. 2 and 3.

20. *Cambio 16*, Dec. 29, 1980, p. 28, and Jan. 4, 1982, p. 42.

21. *ABC*, edición semanal aerea, Nov. 3, 1977.

22. The members of the committee were Rafael Arias Salgado, Arturo Moya, Gonzalo Casado, José Luís Alvarez, Iñigo Cavero, Manuel Clavero, Antonio Fontán, Federico Mayor Zaragoza, Salvador Sánchez Terán, and Leopoldo Calvo Sotelo.

23. UCD, *La Solución a un Reto* (Madrid: Unión Editorial, 1978), p. 149. This statement of principles very closely parallels the May declaration released by Rafael Arias Salgado, the new secretary general of the party, in which the UCD endorsed "the liberal conception of society, the values of Christian humanism and the defense of a social market economy and a social state of law" (*El País*, May 13, 1978, p. 17). It is somewhat more "social-

democratic," however, than the first ideological statement released in January 1978 (ibid.), which had been drafted by a committee that had not included two of the social democrats listed in n. 22 (Arturo Moya and Gonzalo Casado).

24. UCD, *La Solución a un Reto,* p. 157.

25. *El País,* May 12, 1978, p. 11.

26. See Antonio Torres del Moral, "Los Grupos Parlamentarios," *Revista de Derecho Político,* Spring 1981.

27. These operating subsidies are derived from article 6 of the Ley de Partidos Políticos. In the Senate, members of soon-to-be-defunct parties (such as the Christian democratic party of Manuel Villar Arregui) unsuccessfully attempted to modify the law in the interests of smaller parties.

28. Although Mayor Oreja was primarily motivated by the institutional inducements described above, it is also noteworthy that he is the nephew of the UCD Minister of Foreign Affairs Marcelino Oreja.

29. *El País,* May 16, 1978, p. 11.

30. Maurice Duverger, *Political Parties,* New York: John Wiley and Sons, 1959.

31. Myron Weiner and Joseph La Palombara, "Introduction," in *Political Parties and Political Development,* Princeton, N.J.: Princeton University Press, 1966.

32. Stefano Bartolini, "La Afiliación en los Partidos de Masas: La Experiencia Socialista Democrática (1889–1978)," *Revista de Estudios Políticos,* no. 15, May–June 1980.

33. See Richard Gunther, "Conflictos de los Partidos Políticos Españoles," in Dieter Nohlen and Carlos Huneeus, *Problemas de Consolidación de la Monarquía Parlamentaria,* forthcoming.

34. Membership from Montero, "Partidos y Participación," p. 44.

35. Given the large number of personal contacts required for these activities, it is not surprising that other parties attacked the UCD for having used public employees to undertake these efforts. See, e.g., the accusations of Felipe González (*El País,* Feb. 21, 1979, p. 9), Manuel Fraga Iribarne (ibid., Feb. 17, 1979, p. 12), and Santiago Carrillo (ibid., Feb. 23, 1979, p. 14).

36. Montero, "Partidos y Participación, p. 44.

37. Ibid.

38. Ibid., p. 56. The UCD succeeded in electing 29,614 of its candidates as municipal councilors in the 1979 elections (*El País,* April 5, 1979).

39. See Gunther, *Public Policy,* pp. 33–34.

40. Otto Kirchheimer makes this point in "The Transformation," pp. 187 and 193.

41. A key UCD leader stated in a 1983 interview that the shortage of time available for the formulation of the party's electoral lists in 1977 made it necessary to "improvise everything" and that no particular party model was taken into account in making those choices—which, in essence, created the UCD.

42. For a similar statement by Santiago Carrillo, see María Eugenia Yagüe, *Santiago Carillo, Perfil Humano y Político,* p. 11.

43. *Informaciones*, Dec. 5, 1978, p. 4. Also see warnings by Marcelino Camacho about the possibility of the emergence of a "Spanish Pinochet," cited in *Diario 16*, Sept. 1, 1977; *Mundo Obrero* Aug. 16, 1977; and Eusebio Mujal-León, "The PCE," p. 26.

44. The prelegalization data are from interviews with members of PCE provincial executive committees (conducted in late spring and early summer 1978); 1977 membership data are from same sources, confirmed by Carlos Elordi, in "El PCE por dentro," *La Calle*, no. 95, Jan. 15–21, 1980, p. 30.

45. From interviews with PCE officials and Elordi, "El PCE." Much confusion surrounds estimates of membership in the PCE. Some observers have pointed to the discrepancies between the public claims by Communist leaders of 200 thousand party members and the number of delegates permitted to attend party congresses. Because only one delegate could be sent to the party congress for each 100 dues-paying members in the relevant provincial or regional *agrupación* and there were only 1,271 territorial representatives in attendance at the Ninth Party Congress in April 1978, one might conclude that the party could have had no more than 127,100 members at that time. To some extent, these discrepancies were due to the use of different indicators of party membership. Our provincial elite respondents, as well as those party officials claiming 200 thousand members of the party, defined party members as those to whom party cards had been issued. The sizes of provincial or regional delegations to party congresses, however, were determined by the number of members who had paid their dues at the time of the most recent party census. This "hard" measure of party membership (used as a verifiable means of preventing provincial and regional branches from inflating their membership figures and thereby gaining disproportionate voting strength at the party congress) invariably gives rise to lower estimates than does the "card-carrying" indicator because not all party members pay their dues each month and, therefore, are not counted in determining the size of party-congress delegations.

46. As defined by Resolution 15 approved at the Ninth Congress: "The PCE is, at the same time, a party of struggle and a party of government disposed to assume directive responsibilities in the life of the country, and to defend, both in parliament and in the democratic action of the masses, the interests of the working class, of all levels of workers, and of the forces of culture" (PCE, *Noveno Congreso*, p. 156).

47. Chamorro, *Ramón Tamames*, p. 65.

48. Ibid.

49. Ibid.

50. For a brief history of these associations, see Centro de Investigación y Documentación Urbana y Rural, *Las Asociaciones de Vecinos en la Encrucijada: El Movimiento Ciudadano en 1976–77*, Madrid: Ediciones de la Torre, 1977, pp. 11–13.

51. See Gunther, *Public Policy*, p. 309, n. 102.

52. J. Botella, J. Capo, and J. Marcet, "Aproximación a la Sociología de los Partidos Políticos Catalanes," *Revista de Estudios Políticos* (10), July–Aug. 1979.

53. PCE, *Noveno Congreso*, p. 154.

54. Ibid.

55. Ibid., p. 155.

56. Ibid., p. 86.

57. Ibid., p. 169.

58. Ibid., p. 172.

59. Ibid., p. 155.

60. Ibid., p. 157.

61. Article 11 requires that "the minority accept and apply the decisions of the majority" and enables the party's governing organs to suspend any member from his party affiliation (PCE, *Noveno Congreso*, pp. 172-73).

62. See *ABC*, edición semanal aerea, Aug. 17, 1978, p. 19; and *Informaciones*, Aug. 5, 1978, p. 3.

63. Juan J. Linz, "A Sociological Look at Spanish Communism," in George Schwab, ed., *Eurocommunism: The Ideological and Political-Theoretical Foundations*, Westport, Conn.: Greenwood Press, 1981, p. 259.

64. See *Cambio 16*, Jan. 12, 1981, pp. 19-20.

65. Joaquín Sempere, "Un Malestar en Busca de Coordenadas," *Nuestra Bandera*, no. 106, 1981, p. 33. Also cited in Montero, "Partidos y Participación," p. 62.

66. Montero, ibid.

67. Montero ("Partidos y Participación") has pointed out that the normalization of politics during this phase of the transition was inherently unsatisfying to militants in both major mass-mobilization parties—the PCE and PSOE—who were, in essence, demobilized and marginalized from significant political participation except at election time.

68. See Elordi, "El PCE por dentro," p. 38; and Montero, "Partidos y Participación," p. 61. Elordi reports that, of the 2,526 PCE branches that existed in December 1978, only 178 were shop-floor organizations, and only 23 were university branches; all the rest were residential neighborhood branches (p. 25).

69. Mario Caciagli, "Il PSOE," *Il Mulino*, nos. 282-283, July-Oct. 1982, pp. 674-76.

70. Membership statistics (except non-dues-paying cardholders) from Montero, "Partidos y Participación," p. 44; similar statistics in Cacagli, "Il PSOE," p. 695. For a general discussion of the distinction between party membership estimates based on official party censuses of dues-paying members and "softer" estimates based on the distribution of membership cards, see n. 45 above. As in the aforementioned case of the PCE, the distinction between dues-paying and cardholding members has given rise to some public debate about the true size of the PSOE. Rather than step into this debate, we present both types of data. By mid-1978 there were about 100 thousand dues-paying members of the PSOE (in the December census, it was revealed that about 99,500 affiliates had paid their dues). In the spring of 1978, however, some party leaders, such as Alfonso Guerra, were claiming that PSOE membership had reached 200 thousand. At the same time, provincial-level

interviews in 16 provinces generated data that (if extrapolated to the national level) suggested that 163 thousand persons held party membership cards, not all of whom paid their dues with great regularity.

71. Raul Morodo places that campaign debt at 74 million pesetas (*La Vanguardia,* April 30, 1978), but Jorge de Esteban and Luis López Guerra claimed that it totaled 800 million ptas. (*Los Partidos Políticos,* p. 117).

72. *El País,* March 9, 1980, p. 22.

73. For a brief history of the PSC, see Andreu Claret, *Joan Reventós, Perfil Humano y Político,* Madrid: Editorial Cambio 16, 1977.

74. The deputies of the PSC-R had entered the 1977 election in coalition with the CDC and sat with the CDC in the "Catalán Minority" in the Congress.

75. Juan J. Linz ("The New Spanish Party System" in Richard Rose, *Electoral Participation,* London: Sage, 1980) presents data showing that the location of the PSP on a left-right continuum, as perceived by survey respondents, was between the PSOE and the UCD.

76. These data are self-reports of votes cast in the 1977 and 1979 elections by our 5,439 mass-level respondents.

77. These data were volunteered by a member of the PSOE provincial committee in an interview held in Barcelona in July 1978.

78. PSC-PSOE membership was calculated by multiplying the size of that regional branch's delegation (as listed in an unpublished document prepared by the Comisión Organizadora for the Twenty-Eighth Congress of the PSOE) by 100 (1 delegate for each 100 dues-paying party members). This figure is corroborated by Carlos Elordi ("El PSOE por Dentro"), who states that PSC-PSOE membership in September 1979 was 4,664.

79. Raul Morodo flatly asserted at the time of the merger that a major reason why the PSP chose to give up its independence was that the PSOE had promised to absorb its 1977 campaign debt, which he set at 74 million pesetas (*La Vanguardia,* April 30, 1978).

80. 1979 interview with a member of a PSOE executive committee in an Andaluz province.

81. For detailed accounts of these conflicts, see *El País,* Jan. 23, 24, 25, and 27, 1978. Jorge de Esteban and Luis López Guerra (*Los Partidos Políticos,* p. 119) claim that this struggle is responsible for the fact that the Gallego branch of the PSOE had four different secretaries general between 1978 and 1982.

82. Ibid., p. 120.

83. Alfonso Guerra, for example, not only proclaimed the near inevitability of a Socialist victory, but also stated that he could "destroy the UCD" as a party in less than one week (*El País,* May 9, 1978).

84. For an excellent and thorough study of the sociological characteristics of PSOE affiliates, see José Félix Tezanos, *Sociología del Socialismo Español,* Madrid: Tecnos, 1983.

85. See Samuel Huntington, *Political Order in Changing Societies,* New Haven: Yale University Press, 1968.

86. Excerpt from Grupo Federal de Estudios Sociológicos, "Un PSOE Más Unido y Organizado" in *Boletín PSOE,* 10, Feb. 1981, p. 18.

87. The unidentified quotes and overall line of argument included in the next two paragraphs were derived from an extensive interview with a high-ranking PSOE leader held in May 1984.

88. *El País*, May 2, 1978, p. 13.

89. E.g., *ABC*, edición semanal aerea, March 16, 1978.

90. Words used by a high-ranking PSOE leader in a 1978 interview.

91. Maravall, "Transción," p. 77. Also see Montero, "Partidos y Participación."

92. Maravall, "Transción," p. 86.

93. *El País*, May 9, 1978, p. 1.

94. Excerpt from an interview with a national-level PSOE official in June 1981. For a similar interpretation, see *El Socialista*, May 9, 1978; also cited in *El País*, May 10, 1978.

95. "Socialismo y Eurocomunismo: Debate Norberto Bobbio-Alfonso Guerra," *Sistema*, 22, Jan. 1978, p. 98.

96. See, e.g., excerpts from the resolutions passed by the *agrupaciones* of Carabanchel (*El País*, May 10, 1978, p. 11), Vallecas and Móstoles (*El País*, May 11, 1978, p. 11), by the Comité Regional of the Madrid federation of the party (*ABC*, edición semanal aerea, June 1, 1978, p. 18), and by the Congress of the Asturian federation (*El País*, Jan. 14, 1979).

97. *El País*, May 11, 1978, p. 11.

98. *Informaciones*, July 28, 1978, p. 3.

99. Esteban and López Guerra, *Los Partidos Políticos*, pp. 121–22.

100. AP, *What Alianza Popular Is*, Madrid: Afanias, 1977, pp. 12–13.

101. Ibid., p. 14.

102. AP, *II Congreso Nacional de Alianza Popular: Ponencias y Discursos*, Madrid, Jan. 1978, p. 12.

103. Those parties were the Partido Liberal of Enrique Larroque, the Partido Progresista Liberal of Juan García de Madariaga, the Partido Liberal Independiente of Oscar Bernat, the Partido Popular de Catalunya of Antonio de Senillosa, and the Partido Demócrata Gallego of Ramon País. Larroque and Senillosa, it should be recalled, were among those who had quit the UCD in protest over Suárez's changes in that coalition's electoral lists in 1977.

104. E.g., the ACL meeting of May 2, 1978, and the Nueva Derecha meeting of May 10, 1978, both held at the Hotel Meliá Castilla. The Nueva Derecha meeting was part of an attempt to create a single conservative party through a merger among the Unión Regional Andaluza of Luís Jaudenes, Renovación Española of José Antonio Trillo, Carlos Ruíz Soto's Partido Conservador, and the Partido Nacional Independiente of Artemio Benavente.

105. These reservations are outlined in a statement published in *Informaciones*, Oct. 7, 1978, p. 3, and in the formal resolution passed by Junta Nacional of the AP in *Informaciones*, Oct. 31, 1978.

106. Seven AP deputies voted with Fraga in support of the Constitution; five voted against that text (Silva, Fernández de la Mora, Alberto Jarabo, José Martínez Emperador, and Pedro de Mendizabal), and three others abstained

(Licinio de la Fuente, Alvaro Lapuerta, and Modesto Piñeiro) (*ABC*, edición semanal aerea, Nov. 9, 1978).

107. Several former AP leaders, including Silva, Fernández de la Mora, Thomás de Carranza, and José Martínez Emperador, attempted (in December 1978 and January 1979) to forge a right-wing coalition with Blas Piñar's Fuerza Nueva, Raimundo Fernández Cuesta's Falangistas, the Traditionalists of Carlos Sixto de Borbón, and the small conservative parties of Luís Jaudenes and Jesus Barros de Lis.

108. Initially included within the Coalición was the center-left social democratic party of José Ramón Lasuén, as part of a bizarre effort to build a "bridge over the center." Negotiations with Lasuén ultimately broke down, but some members of his party remained in the Coalición, standing as CD candidates in the 1979 election.

109. *El País*, Feb. 4, 1979.

110. Osorio, for example, was vice president of the Petromed group of companies and was closely tied to the bank Banesto (Pedro J. Ramírez, *Así se Ganaron las Elecciones: 1979*, Madrid: Editorial Prensa Española, 1979, p. 46).

111. For an example of the use of this tactic, see Fraga's statements in *ABC*, edición semanal aerea, Jan. 18, 1979, p. 14.

112. Excerpt from "Reforma Económica," in AP, *Qué es Alianza Popular?: Síntesis*, 1977.

113. AP, *What Alianza Popular Is*, p. 12.

114. Ibid., p. 14.

115. These themes were prominent in speeches by all of the founders of the ACL at its "presentation" at the Hotel Meliá-Castilla, Madrid, May 12, 1978, which was attended by Richard Gunther. See press reports of that meeting, e.g., in *Informaciones*, May 13, 1978, p. 4.

116. E.g., see Areilza's statements in *El País* (Jan. 23, 1979, p. 9; and Jan. 31, 1979, p. 11). Also see Joaquín García Morillo, "El Desarrollo de la Campaña," in Jorge de Esteban and Luis López Guerra, eds., *Las Elecciones Legislativas del 1 de Marzo de 1979*, Madrid: Centro de Investigaciones Sociológicas, 1979, pp. 211–12.

117. AP, *II Congreso Nacional de Alianza Popular: Ponencia y Discursos*, p. 121.

118. AP, *III Congreso Nacional*, Madrid, 1980, p. 68.

119. Areilza and Fraga, e.g., had frequently clashed while serving together in the first post-Franco Government, and Osorio had played a major role in dumping Areilza from the presidency of the Centro Democrático in 1977 (Ramírez, 1979, p. 43).

120. Interviews with provincial AP leaders indicated that, in most areas, only a few party members followed Silva, Fernández de la Mora, et al., in abandoning the party, even in Zamora and Pontevedra (their respective bases of support).

121. Ramírez, *1979*, p. 135.

CHAPTER FIVE:
SOCIAL CLASS AND THE 1979 GENERAL ELECTION

1. *Informaciones,* Dec. 30, 1978, pp. 1 and 4.

2. In an interview, a provincial-level AP official in Pontevedra stated that the party leadership expected a victory of that magnitude.

3. A UCD leader confirmed in an interview that the UCD gave assistance to the PSA in the form of poll data and advice but denied that financial assistance was also given.

4. The first ideological declaration of the newly formed UCD contains a close paraphrase of this statement (UCD, Secretaría General de Información, *Documento Ideológico de UCD,* Jan. 1978, p. 7). This particular version was set forth in UCD, *La Solución a un Reto* (p. 151), published immediately after the first party congress in October 1978.

5. AP, *II Congreso Nacional de Alianza Popular, Ponencias y Discursos,* Jan. 1978, p. 13.

6. Ibid.

7. PCE, *Noveno Congreso,* p. 169.

8. Ibid., p. 157.

9. Ibid., p. 91.

10. Eduardo Espín, "Los Medios de la Campaña: La Organización Partidista," in de Esteban and López Guerra, *Las Elecciones Legislativas,* p. 174.

11. Ibid., p. 184.

12. PCE, *Noveno Congreso,* pp. 103 and 105.

13. Ibid., p. 158.

14. See PSOE, *Resoluciones del XXVII Congreso del PSOE,* Madrid, 1977.

15. See *Declaración de Principios y Estatutos del PSOE,* which is also reproduced in Felipe González and Alfonso Guerra, *PSOE* (Bilbao: Ediciones Albia, 1977, pp. 23-24).

16. González and Guerra, *PSOE,* p. 23.

17. For a similar analysis, see Maravall, "La Transición," pp. 92-93.

18. For descriptions of the corporatist *sindicatos* and their role in the policy processes of the Franquist regime, see Gunther, *Public Policy,* pp. 251-59; and chap. 9, passim.

19. Carr and Fusi, *From Dictatorship to Democracy,* p. 144.

20. Ibid.; and Maravall, *Dictatorship and Political Dissent,* pp. 30-31.

21. Maravall, Ibid., p. 30.

22. Ibid., p. 32; and Equipo de Estudios, "El Movimiento Obrero," p. 77.

23. Carr and Fusi, *From Dictatorship to Democracy,* p. 146. The CCOO leaders convicted during the famed "Trial 1001," for example, were sentenced to jail for terms averaging more than 16 years.

24. Ibid.; and Joe Gandelman, "Spanish Unions Compete for Support," *Christian Science Monitor,* Feb. 17, 1978, p. 19.

25. Maravall, *Dictatorship and Political Dissent.*

26. Ibid., p. 31.

27. Eusebio Mujal-León, "The PCE in Spanish Politics," p. 27.

28. Because these syndical elections lasted several months and much confusion was produced by using "closed lists" in larger factories (employing more than 250 workers) and "open lists" in smaller factories, it is difficult to be precise in measuring support for each of these unions. Mujal (ibid., p. 29) claims that the CCOO received 44 percent of the vote, and the UGT received 31 percent. Robert Fishman, however, places these figures at 34.5 percent for the CCOO and 21.7 percent for the UGT ("The Labor Movement in Spain: From Authoritarianism to Democracy," *Comparative Politics*, vol. 14, no. 3, April 1982, p. 290).

29. PCE, *Noveno Congreso*, p. 93.

30. Ibid., pp. 94–95.

31. Resolution 7 asserts that "the PCE has preferred the option of syndical liberty, so that it would be the workers who freely choose the trade union to which they would belong" (ibid., p. 93).

32. Eduardo Espín, "Las Fuerzas Políticas Concurrentes," in Jorge de Esteban and Luis López Guerra, eds., *Las Elecciones Legislativas*, p. 184; also Pedro J. Ramírez, *Así se Ganaron las Elecciones* (1977), p. 161.

33. The remainder of the industrial workers who belonged to the CCOO divided their votes among the PSP (2.4 percent), and the UCD or AP (10 percent). The UGT, by way of comparison, was much more homogeneously socialist: 71.9 percent of its members voted for the PSOE in 1977, while 21 percent voted for the UCD or AP, 2 percent for the PCE, and 2.3 percent for the PSP (Victor Pérez Díaz, *Clase Obrera, Partidos y Sindicatos*, Madrid: Fundación del Instituto Nacional de Industria, 1979, p. 109). These were the results of an Encuesta entre Asalariados del Sector Industrial, which interviewed 4,179 workers in the industrial sector.

34. Ibid., p. 111.

35. See PSOE, *Estatutos del PSOE*, Article 8g. This policy was reaffirmed in the Syndical Resolution adopted at the Twenty-Seventh PSOE Congress (PSOE, *Resoluciones Del XXVII Congreso del PSOE*, 1977, p. 5).

36. Gandelman, "Spanish Unions," p. 19.

37. *El País*, Feb. 7, 1978, p. 19.

38. Ibid.

39. Ramírez, *1979*, p. 87.

40. Pérez Díaz, *Clase Obrera*, p. 88.

41. Due to differences in the sampling procedures used to obtain the figures for 1977 and 1979, caution should be exercised in drawing conclusions about the actual magnitude of change.

CHAPTER SIX:
RELIGION AND POLITICS

1. For a more extensive discussion and analysis of this debate over religious issues in the Constitution, see Gunther and Blough, "Religious Conflict and Consensus."

2. See PSOE, XXVII Congreso, *Programa de Transición: La Enseñanza*, p. 8.

3. Specifically, the UCD and AP representatives in the Ponencia of the Comisión de Asuntos Constitucionales y de Libertades Públicas of the Congress of Deputies added to Article 16 of the Constitution (which disestablished the Church), the following statement: "The public powers will take into account the religious belief of Spanish society and will maintain the consequent relations of cooperation with the Catholic Church and other religions."

4. Cortes Españolas, *Diario de Sesiones del Congreso de los Diputados*, no. 106, July 7, 1978, p. 3993.

5. This rationale was clearly set forth by Santiago Carrillo in a statement before the Congress of Deputies:

> I believe that the religious question has been surmounted in its essentials in this country; we should all do everything to overcome it once and for all. Particularly the forces of progress, the democratic forces, we forces who want socialism, have a special interest in not clashing with the Catholic Church and in not contributing to maintaining any obstacle which could confront these forces, which, let us not forget, gave an ideological basis to the [Franquist] rebellion and "the crusade," and which could still give an ideological basis to a resistance that would be very dangerous for the advance of democracy and socialism. (Ibid., p. 3994)

6. See Gunther and Blough, "Religious Conflict and Consensus," pp. 71–82, for a description of the principal constitutional compromises on religious issues and the stands on these issues taken by the various parties. The Permanent Committee of the Episcopal Conference of the Catholic Church (the supreme body in the Church hierarchy) issued a declaration stating that there was nothing in the Constitution that violated Church beliefs, and left a decision to vote "yes" or "no" on the referendum to each individual citizen (see the text of that declaration in *ABC*, edición semanal aerea, Nov. 30, 1978). However, 8 right-wing bishops (out of about 80) and the Cardenal Primate recommended a "no" vote. (See the Cardenal Primate's statement in *ABE*, edición semanal aerea, Dec. 7, 1978, p. 13.)

7. Juan J. Linz, "The New Spanish Party System" (original manuscript version only).

8. In retrospect, this intervention may be regarded as the first major instance of a return to proconservative political activism under the new Pope, John Paul II. Other prominent examples of electoral intervention are pastoral letters released by Humberto Cardinal Medeiros of Boston (which attempted to influence the outcome of the 1980 Democratic primaries in the 4th and 5th districts of the U. S. House of Representatives) and by West German bishops in the course of the 1980 Bundestag elections (who, far from limiting themselves to religious matters, also attacked the fiscal policies of the SPD government). (See *New York Times*, Sept. 15, 16, and 18, 1980.)

9. Summaries of, or excerpts, from this statement may be found in *El*

País, Feb. 9, 1979, p. 11; *Informaciones*, Feb. 9, 1979, pp. 1 and 31; Espín, "Los Medios de la Campaña," pp. 185–87; Ramírez, *1979*, pp. 162–63.
10. See *El País*, Feb. 8, 1979, p. 14; also Espín, ibid., p. 187.
11. See Miguel Satrústegui, "El Marco Jurídico: La Legislación Electoral," in de Esteban and López Guerra, *Las Elecciones Legislativas*, pp. 141–43; CD advertisements in *Informaciones*, Feb. 15, 1979, p. 8 and Feb. 17, p. 26; UCD advertisements in *Informaciones*, Feb. 24, p. 17 and Feb. 26, 1979; and statements by Suárez (*Informaciones*, Feb. 10, p. 4), Herrero de Miñón (*Informaciones*, Feb. 15, p. 4), Lavilla (*El País*, Feb. 15), Fraga (*Informaciones*, Feb. 19, p. 4), Alvarez de Miranda (*Informaciones*, Feb. 20, p. 5), and Areilza (*Informaciones*, Feb. 23, p. 6).
12. *Informaciones*, Feb. 28, 1979, p. 3; and *El País*, Feb. 28, 1979, p. 10.
13. E.g., Casiano M. Just, the Abad of Monserrat, said, "From the Christian point of view, we know that matrimony is indissoluble; nevertheless, if in the state, in which there are pluralist attitudes, well-prepared laws are written which foresee divorce, I believe that the Church will respect that" (*Informaciones*, March 18, p. 5).
14. See Carrillo's statement in *El País*, Feb. 11, 1979, p. 13.
15. A thorough survey of campaign coverage in *El País* and *Informaciones* revealed only two other instances when PSOE candidates were reported as having referred to the bishops' statement. On February 19, several Catalán socialists joined with other leftists, all of whom described themselves as devout Catholics, in publishing a letter criticizing the trend toward conservatism implicit in the bishops' statement and calling for a return to the laudable political neutrality of 1977 (*El País*, Feb. 20, 1979, p. 13). In the only other instance reported, a PSOE candidate for the Senate in Asturias had no choice but to refer specifically to religious issues—he was speaking at a forum organized by the Church, attended by over 100 priests and nuns (*El País*, Feb. 14, 1979, p. 13).
16. *El País*, Feb. 10, 1979, p. 15.
17. E.g., see Gunther and Blough, "Religious Conflict," pp. 90–93; and the statement by Santiago Carrillo in note 5, above. Similar statements were often made in the course of interviews with PCE officials.
18. *El País*, Feb. 25, 1979, p. 11.
19. A high-ranking AP official complained in an interview that the poll results "have subsequently been demonstrated to have been false—that the French firm which was supposed to have undertaken the survey did not even exist."
20. *Ya*, Feb. 28, 1979, p. 5. Also see the editorials in *Ya* published the following day (election day) March 1, 1979, p. 5.
21. Among other things, the Coalición Democrática filed a complaint about the publication of allegedly fictitious poll results, and its deputies introduced a bill (subsequently passed) that stringently regulated the publication of opinion poll data. That bill requires that publication of poll data in-

clude descriptions of the sample sizes and sampling procedures used, and clearly identify the polling organization. Poll results, moreover, may not be published during the final ten days of an election campaign.

22. This and the following two extensive quotations are excerpts from transcripts of in-depth discussions of politics between Giacomo Sani and a sample of Madrid residents, as described in chapter 1.

23. Giacomo Sani, "Mass-Level Response to Party Strategy: the Italian Electorate and the Communist Party" in Donald L. Blackmer and Sidney Tarrow, eds., *Communism in Italy and France* (Princeton, N.J.: Princeton University Press, 1975), pp. 456-503.

24. Giacomo Sani and Pilar Del Castillo Vera, "El Rol Político de Las Mujeres en la España Actual: Continuidad y Cambio" in *Revista de Derecho Político*, March 1983.

CHAPTER SEVEN:

THE REGIONAL QUESTION

1. Quoted in Robert P. Clark, "Language and Politics in Spain's Basque Provinces," in *Western European Politics*, vol. 4, Jan. 1981, p. 93.

2. Quoted in Norman L. Jones, "The Catalán Question Since the Civil War," in Paul Preston, ed., *Spain in Crisis*, New York: Harper and Row, 1976, p. 236.

3. For a description of Franquist efforts to repress Basque culture and language, see Clark, "Language and Politics," pp. 86-103. With regard to repression in Catalunya, see Jones, "The Catalán Question," pp. 239-41.

4. Carles Gispert and Josep María Prats, *España: Un Estado Plurinacional*, Barcelona: Editorial Blume, 1978, p. 112.

5. See the discussions of literacy rates and language usage in del Campo, Navarro, and Tezanos, *La Cuestión Regional*, 1977.

6. By Basques, we mean individuals living in the provinces of Alava, Guipúzcoa, and Vizcaya.

7. Even large numbers of those who did not speak the regional language expressed a preference for its use, rather than for Castilian.

8. Respondents were categorized as regional language speakers if they answered "yes" to whether they had spoken the language as a child, or to whether they normally use the vernacular at work, or to whether they speak the language.

9. Clark, "Language and Politics"; Roslyn M. Frank, "The Politics of Language and Ethnicity in the Basque Country Today," paper presented at the Sixth European Studies Conference, Oct. 10, 1981, Omaha, Neb.

10. Del Campo, Navarro, and Tezanos, *La Cuestión Regional*, table 5.3, p. 139.

11. Article 2 of the Constitution "recognizes and guarantees the right to autonomy of the nationalities of which it is composed. . . ." Article 3 guarantees "co-official" status for regional languages.

12. Statement by Minister of Finance Jaime García Añoveros, in *El País*, Dec. 28, 1980, p. 15.

13. These figures include all deaths from terrorist violence, the vast majority of which were committed by ETA. For other statistics, see Robert P. Clark, "The Roots of Insurgency: The Social Origins of Euzkadi ta Askatsuna (ETA)," paper presented at the Annual Meeting of the International Studies Association/South, University of Florida, Gainesville, Oct. 3, 1981.

14. The categorization of respondents as favoring centralism, limited autonomy, extensive autonomy, or independence was based on their answers to three questions, each of which asked them to choose which of two alternative statements they agreed with. The first set of alternatives were:

Sr. García: It is best to maintain the unity of the country and to limit the regions as much as possible.

Sr. Pérez: In Spain there are regions or nationalities. It is logical to grant autonomy to each of them, so that they can resolve certain of their affairs by themselves.

Those agreeing with the statement of Sr. García were classified as favoring centralism; those choosing Sr. Pérez were then asked whether they agreed with either of the next two statements:

Sr. López: One must give autonomy to the regions, so that they can manage their own affairs, and must also allow them to make their own laws.

Sr. Fernández: I think it is fine to give more autonomy to the regions regarding their internal affairs, as long as the political unity of the country is always respected.

Those agreeing with Sr. Fernández were categorized as limited autonomists; and those choosing Sr. López were then asked to choose between the following two statements:

Sr. Martínez: I favor the regions having their own laws, but the central government must be responsible for certain things, like the military, foreign affairs, etc.

Sr. Sánchez: The regions are true nationalities which, in addition to their own laws, must have their own military and customs regulations. That is, they must be totally independent states.

Those siding with Sr. Martínez were regarded as favoring extensive autonomy; those agreeing with Sr. Sánchez were classified as favoring independence. It should be noted that, in works by Linz and others who have used these same sets of questions, extensive autonomy is referred to as federalism.

15. Juan J. Linz, "La Crisis de un Estado Unitario, Nacionalismos Periféricos y Regionalismo" in R. Acosta, ed., *La España de las Autonomías (Pasado, Presente y Futuro)*, Madrid: Espasa Calpe, 1981, vol. 2, table 15, p. 706.

16. Ibid.

17. *El País*, March 8, 1980, p. 10.

18. *Informaciones,* Nov. 19, 1979, p. 5.

19. The *conciertos económicos* grant to the Basque regional government exclusive authority to collect and inspect all taxes paid by residents of the region, except for customs duties and excise taxes on tobacco and alcohol. Three times a year, the Basque government will give a portion of those tax revenues to the Spanish state as compensation for the performance of governmental functions not transferred to the regional government.

20. UCD, *Programa Electoral de UCD; Elecciones/79,* p. 19.

21. The CiU was a coalition of the CDC and the Christian democratic Unió Democràtica de Catalunya.

CHAPTER EIGHT:

LEFT-RIGHT, THE STRUCTURE OF
COMPETITION AND THE ROLE OF LEADERSHIP

1. Surveys conducted in July 1976 and January 1977 indicate that the proportion of the population with moderate leanings was approximately the same in 1979 (Linz, Gómez-Reino, Orizo, and Vila, FOESSA, *Informe 1975–1981,* p. 372).

2. Darío Vila Carro, Francisco Andrés Orizo, and Manuel Gómez-Reino, "Sociología del Actual Cambio Político en España," in Fundación FOESSA, *III Informe,* Madrid: Fundación FOESSA, 1978, pp. 707 and 708.

3. Linz, Gómez-Reino, Orizo, and Vila, FOESSA, *Informe 1975–1981,* p. 372.

4. See chapter 4.

5. José María Maravall, "Political Cleavages in Spain and the 1979 General Election," *Government and Opposition,* vol. 14, Summer 1979, pp. 304–5.

6. *El País,* Feb. 7, 1979.

7. See Giovanni Sartori, "European Political Parties: The Case of Polarized Pluralism," in Joseph La Palombara and Myron Weiner, eds., *Political Parties and Political Development,* Princeton; N.J.: Princeton University Press, paperback, 1972, p. 159.

8. These conclusions and others in the following discussion are drawn from a survey of published reports in the two "independent" Madrid dailies, *El País* and *Informaciones,* of campaign speeches made at party rallies and broadcast over television or radio during the campaign (Feb. 7 through 27).

9. *El País,* Feb. 27, 1979, p. 11.

10. Excerpt from an interview with a high-ranking AP leader. On only one occasion (reported in either *El País* or *Informaciones*) did a Coalición Democrática candidate refer to the Unión Nacional or any of its candidates, and that occurred two days before the formal start of the campaign (see Fernando Suárez's attack on Blas Piñar in *El País,* Feb. 6, 1979, p. 12).

11. *El País,* Feb. 28, 1979, p. 13.

12. *El País,* Feb. 27, 1979, p. 13.

13. Ibid., May 9, 1978, p. 13.

14. Ibid., Feb. 16, 1979, p. 12.

15. Ibid., Feb. 17, 1979, p. 12.

16. These are published in PSOE, *Programa: Elecciones 79*, Madrid: Gráficas Reunidas, 1979.

17. Joaquín García Morillo, "El Desarrollo de la Campaña," in de Esteban and López Guerra, *Las Elecciones Legislativas*, p. 213.

18. Ibid., p. 216.

19. *El País*, Feb. 13, 1979, p. 14.

20. Ibid., Feb. 14, 1979, p. 13.

21. See his statements in ibid., May 11, 1978, p. 11; and May 16, 1978, p. 13.

22. E.g., Secretaría de Información, UCD, *Una Política de Hechos*, 1978. In addition, during the December 1978 referendum campaign in support of the Constitution, the UCD also sought to capitalize on popular support for that document (*ABC*, edición aerea semanal, Nov. 16, 1978, p. 27).

23. See *El País*, Feb. 8, 1979.

24. For the most eloquent statement of UCD accomplishments, see the article by Antonio Fontán in *El País*, Feb. 18, 1979.

25. See *El País*, Feb. 15, 1979, p. 11; Feb. 14, p. 15; Feb. 20, p. 14; Feb. 23, p. 15; and Feb. 18, p. 13.

26. Ibid., Feb. 25, 1979, p. 12.

27. Ibid., Feb. 17, 18, and 20, 1979.

28. Ramírez, *1979*, p. 256.

29. Excerpt from televised speech by Adolfo Suárez (*Informaciones*, Feb. 28, 1979, p. 3).

30. In a July 1978 survey, Juan Linz found that, when Socialist voters were asked to choose between the terms "Marxismo" and "No-Marxismo," only 26.7 percent selected "Marxismo," while 39 percent opted for the latter term (Juan J. Linz, "A Sociological Look at Spanish Communism," manuscript version, p. 66).

31. The final poll undertaken by the Centro de Investigaciones Sociológicas caused considerable concern among UCD leaders because it indicated that voter turnout might be very low (*El País*, Feb. 22, 1979, p. 14).

32. García Morillo, "El Desarrollo de la Campaña," p. 216.

33. The following are excerpts from taped conversations with a small sample of Madrid residents that took place between mid-April and mid-June 1979.

34. Ramírez, *1979*, p. 160.

35. See *El País*, Feb. 8, 1979, p. 11; Feb. 9, p. 12; Feb. 18, p. 14; Feb. 27, p. 13.

36. See *El País*, Feb. 8, 1979, p. 11; Feb. 9, p. 12; Feb. 14, p. 12; Feb. 18, p. 14; Feb. 25, p. 15; and Feb. 27, p. 13. Also see García Morillo, "El Desarrollo de la Campaña," p. 216.

37. See column by Camilo Valdecantos in *El País*, Feb. 28, 1979, p. 18.

CHAPTER NINE:
MICRONATIONALISM AND THE
REGIONAL PARTY SYSTEMS OF
EUSKADI, CATALUNYA, AND GALICIA

1. *Deia* (Bilbao), May 21, 1980.

2. According to our survey, 56 percent of respondents in Galicia said that their region was discriminated against by other Spaniards, compared with 48 percent and 24 percent of respondents in Euskadi and Catalunya, respectively.

3. For a provocative attempt to explain the resurgence of ethnic nationalism in the Celtic fringe of northern Europe as a response to discrimination against ethnic minorities in underdeveloped regions of a society, see Michael Hechter, *Internal Colonialism: The Celtic Fringe in British National Development, 1536–1966,* Berkeley and Los Angeles: University of California Press, 1974.

4. For a similar argument, see Derek W. Urwin, "Harbinger, Fossil or Fleabite? Regionalism and the West European Party Mosaic," in Hans Daalder and Peter Mair, eds., *Western European Party Systems: Continuity and Change,* London: Sage, 1983, p. 240.

5. For a discussion of the relative importance of primordial vs. voluntaristic elements in contemporary nationalist movements, see Juan J. Linz, "Peripheries within the Periphery," in Per Torsvik, ed., *Mobilization, Center-Periphery Structures and Nation-Building: A Volume in Commemoration of Stein Rokkan,* Bergen: Universitetsforlaget, 1982, pp. 342–46; Erik Allardt, *Implications of the Ethnic Revival in Modern Industrialized Society: A Comparative Study of Linguistic Minorities in Western Europe,* Helsinki: Societas Scientiarium Fennica, 1979.

6. If one constructs a more complex indicator of native/immigrant status by taking into account, for those born in the region, whether neither parent, either mother or father, or both parents were born in Euskadi or Catalunya, the differences between those born in the region of Basque or Catalán parents and immigrants born elsewhere are even more striking with regard to their attitudes on the center-periphery cleavage. There is no consistent pattern of differences, however, among the remaining groups.

7. For a detailed examination of the relative impact of birthplace and language usage on attitudes and behavior related to the center-periphery cleavage in Euskadi and Catalunya, see Goldie Shabad and Richard Gunther, "Language, Nationalism and Political Conflict in Spain," *Comparative Politics,* vol. 14, no. 4, July 1982.

8. Linz, "Peripheries within the Periphery," pp. 342–46.

9. For a discussion of traditional Basque nationalist ideologies, see Antonio Elorza, *Ideologías del Nacionalismo Vasco,* San Sebastián: Haranburu, 1978; for Catalunya, see Joan F. Marsal, Francesc Mercadè, Francesc Hernández y Benjamín Oltra, *La Nació com a problema: Tesis Sobre el Cas Català,* Barcelona: Edicions 62, 1979; and for both, Santiago Varela, *El Problema Regional en la Segunda República Española,* Madrid: Unión Editorial, 1976; and Payne, "Catalán and Basque Nationalism."

10. An excerpt from *Ami Vasco,* cited in Linz, "Early State-Building," p. 37.

11. Arana and his followers were by no means unique in defining national or ethnic groups in racial terms. Such definitions were widespread in the nineteenth century, and the results of such conceptions in the twentieth century are well known.

12. Shabad and Gunther, "Language, Nationalism and Political Conflict," pp. 446–48.

13. From a 1894 statement, cited in Payne, *Basque Nationalism*, p. 76.

14. Unfortunately, in our survey we did not provide this definition of what it takes to be Basque, Catalán, etc. as an option to respondents. On this point, see Linz, "Peripheries within the Periphery," pp. 342–43, 359.

15. *Informaciones*, Nov. 24, 1979, p. 6.

16. See table 4 and related discussion in Shabad and Gunther, "Language, Nationalism and Political Conflict," with respect to the relative impact of birthplace vs. language usage on preferences concerning language policy.

17. Walker Connor, "Nation-Building or Nation Destroying," in *World Politics*, vol. 24, no. 3, April 1972, p. 34.

18. For data on emigration from Galicia, see Alfonso Magariños, *Quienes Somos Los Gallegos?*, Barcelona: Epidauro, S.A., 1979, pp. 101–9, and for a discussion of the causes of underdevelopment, ibid., pp. 109–21.

19. For a statement and a critical examination of these claims, see Amando de Miguel, *Recursos Humanos, Clases y Regiones en España*, Madrid: Editorial Cuadernos para el Diálogo, 1977; and Robert P. Clark, "Euskadi: Basque Nationalism in Spain Since the Civil War," in Charles R. Foster, ed., *Nations Without a State: Ethnic Minorities in Western Europe*, New York: Praeger, 1980, pp. 83–87; Jones, "The Catalán Question Since the Civil War," p. 259.

20. Perceptions of regional group discrimination were by no means confined to Basques, Catalans, and Gallegos. See data for other regions in Manuel García Ferrando, *Regionalismo y Autonomías en España 1976/1979*, Madrid: Centro de Investigaciones Sociológicas, 1982.

21. Milton J. Esman, ed., *Ethnic Conflict in the Western World*, Ithaca: Cornell University Press, 1977, p. 378.

22. It should be noted that, although those favoring independence were the most likely to favor governmental concessions to terrorists or negotiation with them, the views of terrorists among the *independentistas* varied considerably across the three regions, e.g., 57 percent of *independentistas* in Euskadi said that terrorists were idealists, but in Catalunya, only 33 percent saw them in this light.

23. Linz, "Early State-Building."

24. Hechter, *Internal Colonialism*.

25. For criticisms of Hechter's thesis as applied to Spain and elsewhere, see A. W. Orridge, "Uneven Development: 2," in *Political Studies*, vol. 29, no. 2, June 1981, pp. 181–90; Urwin, "Harbinger, Fossil or Fleabite?" p. 241.

26. Linz, "Early State-Building," pp. 91–92.

27. See Marianne Heisberg, "Insiders/Outsiders: Basque Nationalism," in *European Journal of Sociology*, vol. 16, no. 2, 1975, pp. 169–93.

28. Payne, "Catalán and Basque Nationalism," p. 32.

29. Payne, *Basque Nationalism*, p. 115.

30. Payne, "Catalán and Basque Nationalism"; Linz, "Early State-Building," pp. 57 – 65, 80 – 82; Beltza (pseud. of Emilio López), *Nacionalismo Vasco y Clases Sociales*, San Sebastián: Txertoa, 1976.

31. Weak relationships were also evident even when subjectively defined class position was used as an indicator of class.

32. Heisberg, "Insiders/Outsiders; Basque Nationalism," p. 178.

33. In Euskadi and Catalunya, the importance of age was evident only with regard to the more political manifestations of regional sentiment. Feelings of belonging primarily or exclusively to the regional group were shared by the young and old alike. In Galicia, however, identification with the region was even more a sentiment of the young than was a predisposition for extensive autonomy or independence. Only 23 percent of Gallegos 50 years of age or older felt "Gallego" or "more Gallego," as compared with 35 percent of those in their middle years, and 57 percent of the young.

34. The electoral strength of the various parties and of all regional parties vs. statist parties varied from province to province. See Juan J. Linz, "The Basques in Spain: Nationalism and Political Conflict in a New Democracy," in W. Phillips Davison and Leon Gordenker, eds., *Resolving Nationalist Conflicts: The Role of Public Opinion Research*, New York: Praeger, 1980, pp. 11 – 52.

35. At the time of the 1979 election, Herri Batasuna (HB) consisted of Langille Abertzale Iraultzaleen Alderdi (LAIA), Euskal Sozialista Biltzarrea (ESB), and the nucleus party Herriko Alderdi Sozialista Iraultzaea (HASI). In 1980 LAIA and ESB abandoned the coalition. For a statement of the objectives of the *abertzale* left, see Ortzi (Francisco Letamendía), *Historia de Euskadi: El Nacionalismo Vasco y ETA*, Paris-Barcelona: Rueda Ibérico, 1977; and the interview with HB leader Letamendía in *El País*, March 9, 1979, pp. 12 – 13.

36. *El País*, Feb. 11, 1979, p. 12.

37. In the aftermath of the Assembly VII of ETA held in 1976, a new part, Euskal Iraultzako Alderdia (EIA) was formed. It had no formal organizational ties with armed ETA groups but shared their *independentista* ideology. EIA is the nucleus of Euskadiko Ezkerra.

38. *El País*, March 4, 1980, p. 19.

39. *El Diario Vasco*, Feb. 24, 1979.

40. *El País*, Feb. 20, 1979, p. 17.

41. Payne, *Basque Nationalism*; Javier Corcuera Atienza and Miguel Angel García Herrera, "Sistema de Partidos, Instituciones y Comunidad Nacionalista en Euskadi," in *Revista de Política Comparada*, no. 2, Autumn 1980, p. 155 – 90.

42. *Informaciones*, Sept. 28, 1978, p. 4.

43. Linz, "The Basques in Spain," p. 51. This tolerance for the younger generation's sympathies with left *abertzale* forces was apparent in interviews with rank-and-file members of the PNV in *Cambio 16*, March 30, 1980, pp. 31 – 32.

44. Robert P. Clark, "The Roots of Insurgency: The Social Origins of Euskadi ta Askatsuna (ETA)," paper presented at the annual meeting of the

International Studies Association/South, University of Florida, Gainesville, Oct. 3, 1981; Letamendía, *Historia de Euskadi.*

45. Jorge de Esteban and Luis López Guerra, *Los Partidos Políticos en la España Actual,* Barcelona, Editorial Planeta, 1982, p. 179. See also Ramiro Cibrián, "El Sistema Electoral y de Partidos en Euskadi," in *Papers,* vol. 14, 1980, pp. 69–97.

46. Jones, "The Catalán Question," pp. 256–67; Jordi Pujol, *Una Política per Catalunya,* Barcelona: Nova Terra, 1976.

47. Eusebio Mujal-León, "Cataluña, Carillo and Eurocommunism," in *Problems of Communism,* vol. 30, no. 2, March-April 1981, p. 32.

48. Ismael E. Pitarch, Joan Botella, Jordi Capo, and Joan Marcet, *Partits i Parlamentaris a la Catalunya d'Avui (1977–1979),* Barcelona: Edicions 62, 1980.

49. Manuel Rivas and X. Tairbo, *Os Partidos Políticos na Galiza,* La Coruña: Rueiro, 1977.

50. The high rate of abstention in Galicia was, to a certain degree, exaggerated by outdated electoral lists and by the sizable number of emigrants from Galicia residing and working outside of Spain.

51. Interview with PCE party elite in Pontevedra in 1978. *Caciquismo* as an explanation of both electoral absenteeism and the dominance of conservative forces has been questioned by a Gallego sociologist who has written extensively about Gallego society and politics. He suggests that "the failure to vote (in the 1979 election) signifies that ties to *caciques* have begun to crumble" and that mass "silence" is an important sign of liberation from such political forces (José Pérez Vilariño, "Comportamiento Electoral en Galicia," in *Papers: Revista de Sociologia,* vol. 14, 1980, p. 53).

52. The PSOE leadership had originally reached an agreement with the UCD over this issue but (as we discuss in the concluding chapter) the Socialists abandoned their position as a result of intense opposition from some sectors of the Gallego branch of the party and as a means of turning regionalist sentiments against the UCD.

53. *El País,* July 1979.

54. Table 44 does not report the vote of immigrants and natives in Euskadi and Catalunya, but rather the partisan preference (a combined indicator of reported vote and partisan sympathy). Conclusions concerning varying distributions of support among these two groups remain the same when considering reported vote only. It should be noted, however, that both levels of reported abstention and refusal to answer were higher among Basque than Catalán immigrants.

55. Juan J. Linz, "Immigrantes y Nativos," unpublished monograph, 1982.

56. The PSC-PSOE evidently did not suffer such adverse consequences in the 1979 election from its greater identification with Catalanism. In the 1980 regional election, however, it suffered a considerable loss of support because many immigrants did not vote.

57. There were no significant differences in Catalunya in the distribution of opinion regarding autonomy between native and immigrant supporters of left Spanish parties. Native supporters of moderate regional par-

ties were only slightly more likely to favor extensive autonomy (but not independence) than were native sympathizers of the PSUC and PSOE.

58. For a more extensive discussion of differing party stances toward language policy, see Shabad and Gunther, "Language, Nationalism and Political Conflict," pp. 460–64.

59. In Euskadi and in Catalunya, in particular, there were differences between immigrants and native supporters of the same party with regard to language policy. Among PNV, Socialist, and Communist sympathizers in Euskadi, the native-born were more likely to favor the use of both Castilian and Euskera as languages of instruction, while immigrants were more disposed toward the use of Castilian only. In Catalunya, leftist Spanish party supporters and *ucedistas*, among whom natives and immigrants were both well represented, were internally divided: even though majorities of both natives and immigrants favored bilingualism, sizable minorities of natives favored the exclusive use of Catalán and even larger proportions of immigrants favored "Castilian only."

60. As it turned out, the actions of the Catalán government since 1980 have served to make language policy a highly salient issue and have heightened tensions considerably between natives and immigrants. The Basque government, in contrast, has thus far adopted a more gradual approach to the introduction of bilingualism and, as a result, there is a significantly lesser degree of polarization. See Shabad and Gunther, "Language, Nationalism and Political Conflict," pp. 464–73, on Basque and Catalán governmental language policies and their differing consequences for political conflict.

61. The greater degree of consensus regarding language policy in the school system compared with language policy in the political realm may be the result of the format of the questions asked in our survey. When asked whether local elected officials should be required to speak the regional language, only "yes" and "no" were given as possible answers. With respect to education policy, however, respondents were offered three choices. Of the three, bilingualism is the preference that appears to be a compromise between the two extremes and, therefore, the least discriminatory.

62. Among native-born Basques, the level of support for regional parties ranged from a high of 85 percent in the case of artisans and owners of small businesses (status group III) to a low of 66 percent in the case of unskilled workers (status group VII).

63. Unfortunately, in our survey respondents were not asked to place the full array of parties on the 10-point left-right continuum.

64. See Seymour Martin Lipset, *Political Man*, Garden City, N.Y.: Doubleday, 1963; and Arend Lijphart, *The Politics of Accommodation*, Berkeley and Los Angeles: University of California Press, 1968.

65. Richard Gunther, "A Comparative Study of Regionalisms in Spain," paper presented at the conference of the Society for Spanish and Portuguese Historical Studies, Toronto, Canada, April 1981, p. 12.

66. Linz, Gómez-Reino, Orizo, and Vila, FOESSA, *Informe 1975–1981*, p. 539.

67. Ibid., pp. 537–39.

68. Linz, "Peripheries within the Periphery," table 12, p. 363.

69. Ibid., pp. 353–54; Jaime del Burgo, *Historia de Navarra: La Lucha por la Libertad,* Madrid: Tebas, 1978.

70. After the 1979 election, Socialist party leaders in Navarra adopted a much more overt stand against Navarra's integration into Euskadi.

71. See the discussion of regionalism in Andalucía in Linz, Gómez-Reino, Orizo, and Vila, FOESSA, *Informe 1975–1981,* pp. 568–74.

72. In the aftermath of the 1979 parliamentary election, the PSA promised to vote for Suárez's investiture as prime minister, in exchange for the government's lowering of the number of representatives required to form a parliamentary delegation. This enabled the PSA to have its own parliamentary group of five deputies.

73. Linz, Gómez-Reino, Orizo, and Vila, FOESSA, *Informe 1975–1981,* pp. 577–79; Juan Hernández Bravo de Laguna, "Autogobierno y Política: Sistema de Partidos y Comportamiento Electoral en Canarias," in *Canarias Ante el Cambio,* Santa Cruz de Tenerife: Instituto de Desarrollo Regional, Univ. de La Laguna, Banco de Bilbao en Canarias, Junta de Canarias, Facultad de Ciencias Económicas y Empresariales de la Univ. de La Laguna, 1981.

74. Linz, Gómez-Reino, Orizo, and Vila, FOESSA, *Informe 1975–1981,* pp. 574–76.

CHAPTER TEN: CONCLUSION AND EPILOGUE

1. See table 11.5 in Giacomo Sani and Giovanni Sartori in Hans Daalder and Peter Mair, eds., *Western European Party Systems,* London: Sage, 1983, pp. 322–23.

2. Reported in *the New York Times,* Oct. 26, 1979.

3. For a summary of regional developments since the 1979 general election, see Goldie Shabad and Richard Gunther, "Spanish Regionalism in the Eighties," in Stanley Payne et al., eds., *Europe in the Eighties: A Comprehensive Assessment of Politics, Economics and Culture,* Princeton, N.J.: Karz-Cohl, 1985.

4. For extensive survey data concerning support for Spanish democracy in the aftermath of the February 23, 1981 attempted coup, see excerpts from a study undertaken by DATA in *Cambio 16,* April 6, 1981, pp. 42–45.

5. Pérez Ledesma, "Los Partidos Políticos en la Transición," p. 57.

6. See *El País,* May 19, 1979, p. 1.

7. Ibid.

8. Ibid., May 18, 1979. Similar impressions were drawn by one of the authors from listening to a tape recording of floor speeches made at that congress.

9. PSOE, *Resolución Política del Congreso Extraordinario,* p. 2.

10. That resolution stated:

The PSOE adopts Marxism as a theoretical instrument, critical and nondogmatic, for the analysis and transformation of social reality, recognizing Marxist and non-Marxist contributions which have contributed to making socialism the great emancipating alternative of our time. . . . The society which the PSOE foresees is a total and complete alternative to capitalist society, which is intrinsically unjust and exploitative . . . . [Socialists] wish to radically transform society, rejecting the possibility of merely managing the capitalist system. (*Informaciones*, Oct. 1, 1979, p. 4)

11. The resolution adopted at the Twenty-Eighth Congress stated:

The PSOE defends a dialectical method of the transition to socialism which combines the parliamentary struggle with popular mobilization in all its forms, which seek the deepening of the democratic concept through the overcoming of the necessary but not sufficient character of political liberties of the capitalist state. (PSOE, 28 Congreso, *Resolución Política*, p. 4)

12. E.g., *Cambio 16*, Nov. 2, 1981, p. 40.

13. According to several high-ranking party officials or former officials (including a PSOE regional leader), this agreement would have led to the granting of autonomy to the other regions according to "the slow route" (article 143), rather than through the "fast route" (article 151). Procedurally, this would have shifted the initiative to the *diputaciones provinciales*, (within which the UCD had a majority in Andalucía) rather than an assembly of the region's representatives in the Congress of Deputies and the Senate (which would have produced a partisan line-up of 38 Socialists to 31 *ucedistas*).

14. Three motives were suggested by respondents for the PSOE's abandonment of its agreement with the UCD. First, this shift was a means of placating Gallego regionalists or nationalists within that sometimes chaotic branch of the party. Second, the UCD's disproportionate representation within the *diputaciones provinciales* in several parts of Andalucía would have meant that it would have had much greater influence under article 143 than under article 151 (see the preceding note). Finally, the PSOE's stout defense of Andaluz autonomy was a means of staving off the challenge to one of its strongest bases of support posed by the Partido Socialista de Andalucía. At the same time, support for the UCD within the region could be undercut by portraying it as an enemy of the region.

15. The previous Nuncio, Monseñor Dadaglio, had been a prime mover behind the more progressive stance of the Church between 1969 and 1975. His replacement in autumn 1980 by the conservative Monseñor Inocenti was closely followed by a marked increase in Church involvement in the divorce debate.

16. See *Cambio 16*, Feb. 16, 1981, p. 12.

17. The 1982 party-system realignment is a central focus of the research currently underway by the authors in collaboration with Juan Linz, Hans-Jürgen Puhle, and José Ramón Montero, with financial support from the Stiftung Volkswagenwerk of West Germany and the National Science Foundation (under grant no. SES-8309 162). For preliminary analyses of these data, see Giacomo Sani and Goldie Shabad, "Electoral Change in Spain in 1982: A Polarizing Realignment," in *Revista de Derecho Político*, forthcoming in Spanish

translation; and Richard Gunther, "El Realineamiento del Sistema de Partidos Políticos en España," *Revista de Estudios Políticos*, forthcoming, 1985.

18. The PCE's mean position on the left-right scale shifted from 2.5 to 1.9.

19. Even more revealing is our initial finding that 37 percent of those who had voted for the UCD in 1979 and who still in 1982 placed themselves closer to the UCD than to the PSOE on the left-right continuum defected to the Socialists in 1982. An identical 37 percent of former UCD supporters who remained ideologically closer to the center party than to the AP cast their ballots for the party of Manuel Fraga in 1982. (See Gunther, "El Realineamiento.")

20. See Sani and Shabad, "Electoral Change."

21. Sani and Sartori, "Polarization, Fragmentation and Competition," pp. 307–40.

22. Statement by Carlos Ferrer Salat, in *Cambio 16*, Sept. 13, 1982, p. 20.

23. *Cambio 16*, Jan. 26, 1981, p. 23.

Bibliography

BOOKS AND ARTICLES

Aguilar, M. A., and E. Chamorro. *Felipe González: Perfil Humano y Político.* Madrid: Editorial Cambio 16, 1977.

Alba, Victor. *El Partido Comunista en España.* Barcelona: Planeta, 1978.

Alcalá-Zamora, Niceto. *Memorias (Segundo Texto de mis Memorias).* Barcelona: Editorial Planeta, 1977.

Alfaya, Javier. *Raúl Morodo: Perfil Humano y Político.* Madrid: Editorial Cambio 16, 1977.

Alianza Popular (AP). *Qué es Alianza Popular?: Síntesis.* Madrid: Afanias, 1977.

———. *Qué es Alianza Popular?* 1978.

———. *II Congreso Nacional de Alianza Popular, Ponencias y Discursos.* Jan. 1978.

———. *III Congreso Nacional.* 1980.

Allardt, Erik. *Implications of the Ethnic Revival in Modern Industrialized Society: A Comparative Study of Linguistic Minorities in Western Europe.* Helsinki: Societas Scientiarium Fennica, 1979.

Alvarez, Santiago. *Galicia, Nacionalidad Histórica.* Madrid: Editorial Ayuso, 1980.

Alvira, Francisco, Katharina Horter, Marina Peña, and Ludgerio Espinosa. *Partidos Políticos e Ideologías en España.* Madrid: Centro de Investigaciones Sociológicas, 1978.

Alzaga Villaamil, Oscar. *Comentario Sistemático a la Constitución Española de 1978.* Madrid: Ediciones del Foro, 1978.

———. "Reflexiones Sobre una Crisis Política Grave." *Revista de Derecho Político,* 10, Summer 1981.

Amezaga, Elías. *1000 Años con Fueros y 100 sin.* Bilbao: Editorial la Gran Enciclopedia Vasca, 1976.

Areilza, José María de. *Diario de un Ministro de la Monarquía.* Barcelona: Planeta, 1977.

Banco de Bilbao. *Renta Nacional de España y su Distribución Provincial, 1977.* Bilbao: A. G. Grijelmo, 1980.

———. *Renta Nacional de España: Serie Homogenea, 1955–1975.* Bilbao: Grijelmo, 1978.

Bar, Antonio. *La CNT en los Años Rojos: Del Sindicalismo Revolucionario al Anarcosindicalismo, 1920–1926.* Madrid: Akal, 1981.

Barberis, Corrado. *La Società Italiana.* Milano: Franco Angeli Editore, 1976.

492   BIBLIOGRAPHY

Barnes, Samuel H. "Ideology and the Organization of Conflict." *Journal of Politics*, 28, 1966.

Barnes, Samuel H., Peter McDonough, and Antonio López Pina. "The Development of Partisanship in New Democracies: The Case of Spain." Paper presented at American Political Science Association annual meeting, Washington, D.C., Sept. 1984.

Bartolini, Stefano. "La Afiliación en los Partidos de Masas: La Experiencia Socialista Democrática (1889–1978)." *Revista de Estudios Políticos*, 15, May–June 1980.

Beltza (pseud. of Emilio López). *Nacionalismo Vasco y Clases Sociales*. San Sebastián: Txertoa, 1976.

Botella, J., and J. Marcet. "La Inmigración en Cataluña: Electores, Partidos y Representación Política." *Sistema*, 45, Nov. 1981.

Botella, J., J. Capo, and J. Marcet. "Aproximación a la Sociología de los Partidos Políticos Catalanes." *Revista de Estudios Políticos*, 10, July–Aug. 1979.

Brenan, Gerald. *The Spanish Labyrinth*. New York: Cambridge University Press, (paperback), 1974.

Caciagli, Mario. "Le Risorse e i Ritardi del Partido Socialista Obrero Español." *Il Mulino*, 282–283, July–Oct. 1982.

Carr, Raymond. *Spain, 1808–1939*. Oxford: Clarendon Press, 1966.

Carr, Raymond, and Juan Pablo Fusi. *Spain: From Dictatorship to Democracy*. London: George Allen and Unwin, 1979.

Carrillo, Santiago. *Qué es La Ruptura Democrática?* Barcelona: Editorial La Gaya Ciencia, 1976.

Carrión Garzarán, Angel, et al. "La Población Española y su Territorio." In Fundación FOESSA, *Estudios Sociológicos Sobre la Situación Social de España, 1975*. Madrid: Editorial Euramérica, 1976.

Centro de Investigación y Documentación Urbana y Rural. *Las Asociaciones de Vecinos en la Encrucijada: El Movimiento Ciudadano en 1976–1977*. Madrid: Ediciones de la Torre, 1977.

Centro de Investigaciones Sociológicas. *La Reforma Política de los Españoles*. Madrid: CIS, 1977.

Chamorro, Eduardo. *Ramón Tamames: Perfil Humano y Político*. Madrid: Editorial Cambio 16, 1977.

Christian, Jr., William A. *Person and God in a Spanish Valley*. New York: Seminar Press, 1972.

Cibrián, Ramiro. "El Sistema Electoral y de Partidos en Euskadi." *Papers: Revista de Sociología*, 14, 1980.

———. "Violencia Política y Crisis Democrática: España en 1936." *Revista de Estudios Políticos*, 6, Nov.–Dec. 1978.

Claret, Andreu. *Joan Reventós, Perfil Humano y Político*. Madrid: Editorial Cambio 16, 1977.

Clark, Robert P. "Basque Socialism at the Polls: An Analysis of Four Post-Franco Elections." Paper presented at the Conference of the Council of European Studies, Washington, D.C., Oct. 1980.

―――. "Euzkadi: Basque Nationalism in Spain Since the Civil War." In Charles R. Foster, ed., *Nations Without a State: Ethnic Minorities in Western Europe.* New York: Praeger, 1980.

―――. "Language and Politics in Spain's Basque Provinces." *West European Politics* 4, Jan. 1981.

―――. "The Roots of Insurgency: The Social Origins of Euzkadi ta Askatasuna (ETA)." Paper presented at annual meeting of the International Studies Association/South, Univ. of Florida, Gainesville, Oct. 31, 1981.

Claudín, Fernando. *Eurocomunismo y Socialismo.* Madrid: Siglo XXI de España, 1977.

Connor, Walker. "Nation-Building or Nation Destroying." *World Politics* 24, April 1972.

Converse, Philip E. "Of Time and Partisan Stability." *Comparative Political Studies* 2, 1979.

Corcuera Atienza, Javier, and Miguel Angel García Herrera. "Sistema de Partidos, Instituciones y Comunidad Nacionalista en Euskadi." *Revista de Política Comparada,* 2, Autumn 1980.

Crozier, Michel. *The Bureaucratic Phenomenon.* Chicago: University of Chicago Press, 1967.

Cucó, Alfons. "Contribución a un Estudio Cuantitativo de la CNT." *Saitabi,* 20, 1970.

Dahl, Robert A., ed. *Regimes and Oppositions.* New Haven: Yale University Press, 1973.

DATA, S.A. *Estructura Social Básica de la Población de España y sus Provincias.* Madrid: Confederación Española de Cajas de Ahorro, 1973.

De la Souchere, Elena. *An Explanation of Spain.* New York: Random House, 1964.

Del Burgo, Jaime Ignacio. *El Fuero: Pasado, Presente, Futuro.* Pamplona: EUNSA, 1975.

―――. *Historia de Navarra: La Luncha por la Libertad.* Madrid: Tebas, 1978.

Del Campo, Salustiano, Manuel Navarro, and J. Félix Tezanos. *La Cuestión Regional Española.* Madrid: Editorial Cuadernos para el Diálogo, 1977.

Del Castillo, Pilar. "Unión de Centro Democrático." Unpublished monograph, Ohio State University, June 1981.

Deutsch, Karl. *Nationalism and Social Communication.* Cambridge, Mass.: MIT Press, 1953.

―――. "Social Mobilization and Political Development." *American Political Science Review,* 55, Sept. 1961.

Díaz, Elias. "El Lado Osuro de la Dialéctica: Consideraciones Sobre el XXVIII Congreso del PSOE." *Sistema,* 32, Sept. 1979.

Díaz, José. *Tres Años de Lucha.* Barcelona: Editorial Laia, 1978.

Di Palma, Giuseppe. "Founding Coalitions in Southern Europe: Legitimacy and Hegemony." *Government and Opposition,* 15, Spring 1980.

Duelo, Gerardo. *Diccionario de Grupos, Fuerzas y Partidos Políticos Españoles.* Barcelona: Editorial La Gaya Ciencia, 1977.

Duverger, Maurice. *Political Parties.* 2d ed. New York: John Wiley and Sons, 1959.

Elordi, Carlos. "El PCE por Dentro." *La Calle,* 95, Jan. 15–21, 1980; and 96, Jan. 22–28, 1980.

———. "El PSOE por Dentro." *La Calle,* 115, June 3–9; and 116, June 10–16, 1980.

Elorza, Antonio. *Ideologías del Nacionalismo Vasco.* San Sebastián: Haranburu, 1978.

———. *La Utopía Anarquista bajo la II República Española.* Madrid: Ayuso, 1973.

Equipo de Documentación Política. *Radiografía de las Nuevas Cortes.* Madrid: Sedmay Ediciones, 1977.

Equipo de Estudios (Ignacio Fernández de Castro, director). "El Movimiento Obrero y sus Organizaciones Sindicales en los Años 70." *Documentación Social: Revista de Estudios Sociales y de Sociología Aplicada,* 22, April–June 1976.

Esman, Milton J., (ed.). *Ethnic Conflict in the Western World.* Ithaca: Cornell University Press, 1977.

Espín, Eduardo. "Las Fuerzas Políticas Concurrentes." In Jorge de Esteban and Luis López Guerra, eds., *Las Elecciones Legislativas.*

———. "Los Medios de la Campaña: La Organización Partidista." In de Esteban and López Guerra, eds., *Las Elecciones Legislativas.*

Esteban, Jorge de, and Luis López Guerra, eds.. *Las Elecciones Legislativas del 1 de Marzo de 1979.* Madrid: Centro de Investigaciones Sociológicas, 1979.

———. *Los Partidos Políticos en la España Actual.* Barcelona: Editorial Planeta, 1982.

Fernández de Castro, Ignacio. "Estratificación y Movilidad Social." In Fundación FOESSA, *Estudios Sociológicos, 1975.*

Fernández-Miranda Hevia, Torcuato. *El Hombre y la Sociedad.* 6th ed. Madrid: Ediciones Doncel, 1965.

Fernández Ordóñez, Francisco. *Qué son los Social Demócratas?* Barcelona: La Gaya Ciencia, 1976.

Fierro Bardaji, Alfred. "Political Positions and Opposition in the Spanish Catholic Church." *Government and Opposition,* 11, Spring 1976.

Fishman, Robert M. "The Labor Movement in Spain, From Authoritarianism to Democracy." *Comparative Politics,* 14, April 1982.

FOESSA, Fundación. *Estudios Sociológicos Sobre la Situación Social de España, 1975.* Madrid: Editorial Euramérica, 1976.

Fraga Iribarne, Manuel. *Alianza Popular.* Bilbao: Ediciones Albia, 1977.

Frank, Roslyn M. "The Politics of Language and Ethnicity in the Basque Country Today." Paper presented at the Sixth European Studies Conference, Omaha, Neb., Oct. 1981.

Galli, Giorgio. *Dal Bipartitismo Imperfetto alla Possibile Alternativa.* Bologna: Il Mulino, 1975.

Gandelman, Joe. "Spanish Unions Compete for Support." *Christian Science Monitor*, Feb. 17, 1978.
García Ferrando, Manuel. *Regionalismo y Autonomías en España 1976/1979*. Madrid: Centro de Investigaciones Sociológicas, 1982.
García Morillo, Joaquín. "El Desarrollo de la Campaña." In de Esteban and López Guerra, eds., *Las Elecciones Legislativas*.
Gil Robles, José María. *No Fue Posible la Paz*. Barcelona: Ediciones Ariel, 1968.
Gispert, Carles, and Josep María Prats. *España: Un Estado Plurinacional*. Barcelona: Editorial Blume, 1978.
GODSA. *Libro Blanco para la Reforma Democrática*. Madrid, 1976.
Gómez Llorente, Luis. *Aproximación a la Historia del Socialismo Español*. Madrid: Cuadernos para el Diálogo, 1976.
Gómez-Reino, Manuel, Francisco Andrés Orizo, and Darío Vila Carro. "Sociología Política." In FOESSA, *Estudios Sociológicos, 1975*.
González, Felipe. *España y su Futuro*. Madrid: Cuadernos para el Diálogo, 1978.
————. *Socialismo es Libertad*. Barcelona: Galba Ediciones, 1978.
González, Felipe, and Alfonso Guerra. *PSOE*. Bilbao: Ediciones Albia, 1977.
González Navarro, Francisco. *La Nueva Ley Fundamental para la Reforma Política*. Colección Informe 14, Madrid: Servicio Central de Publicaciones, Presidencia del Gobierno, 1977.
González Páramo, J. M. "El Rapto de la Reforma." In GODSA, *Boletín de Información y Documentación*, 8–9, Jan. 1977.
Grupo Federal de Estudios Sociológicos. "Un PSOE Más Unido y Organizado." *Boletín PSOE*, 10, Feb. 1981.
Gunther, Richard. "A Comparative Study of Regionalisms in Spain." Paper presented at the conference of the Society for Spanish and Portuguese Historical Studies, Toronto, Canada, April 1981.
————. "Constitutional Change in Contemporary Spain." In Keith Banting and Richard Simeon, eds., *The Politics of Constitutional Change in Industrial Nations: Redesigning the State*. London: Macmillan, 1984. (Released in North America under the title *Redesigning the State: The Politics of Constitutional Change in Industrial Nations*. Toronto: University of Toronto Press, 1984.)
————. "Crisis de los Partidos Políticos Españoles." In Dieter Nolen and Carlos Huneeus, eds., *Problemas de Consolidación de la Monarquía Parlamentaria en España*. Forthcoming.
————. "Models—and Crises—of Spanish Political Parties." In Juan Linz and Richard Gunther, eds., *Politics and Society in the New Democratic Spain*. Forthcoming.
————. "Political Evolution Toward Democracy: Political Parties." In John Crispin, José Luis Cagigao, and Enrique Pupo Walker, eds., *Spain 1975–1980: The Conflicts and Achievements of Democracy*. Madrid and México D.F.: Editorial Porrúa, 1982. (Also published as "Evolución Hacia la Democra-

496   BIBLIOGRAPHY

cia: Partidos Políticos." In Crispin, Cagigao, and Pupo Walker, eds., *Los Conflictos y Logros de la Democracia: España 1975–1980.* Madrid and México, D.F.: Editorial Porrúa, 1982.)

————. *Public Policy in a No-Party State: Spanish Planning and Budgeting in the Twilight of the Franquist Era.* Berkeley and Los Angeles: University of California Press, 1980.

————. "El Realineamiento del Sistema de Partidos Políticos en España." *Revista de Estudios Políticos,* forthcoming, 1985.

————. "Strategies, Tactics and the New Spanish Party System: The 1979 General Elections." Paper presented at the International Symposium on Spain and the United States, University of Florida, Gainesville, Dec. 1979.

Gunther, Richard, and Roger Blough. "Conflicto Religioso y Consenso en España: Historia de dos Constituciones." *Revista de Estudios Políticos,* 14, Madrid, March–April 1980. (Also published in English as "Religious Conflict and Consensus in Spain: A Tale of Two Constitutions," *World Affairs,* 143, Spring 1981.)

Gunther, Richard, Giacomo Sani, and Goldie Shabad. "Party Strategies and Mass Cleavages in the 1979 Spanish Parliamentary Election." *World Affairs,* 143, Fall 1980. (Also published as "Estrategias de los Partidos y Escisiones de Masas en las Elecciones Parlamentarias Españolas de 1979." *Revista de Derecho Político,* 11, Fall 1981.)

Hare, A. Paul. "A Study of Interaction and Consensus in Different Sized Groups." *American Sociological Review,* 17, June 1952.

Hechter, Michael. *Internal Colonialism: The Celtic Fringe in British National Development, 1536–1966.* Berkeley and Los Angeles: University of California Press, 1974.

Heisberg, Marianne. "Insiders/Outsiders: Basque Nationalism." *European Journal of Sociology,* 16, 1975.

Hermet, Guy. *Les Catholiques dans l'Espagne Franquiste.* Paris: Presse de la Fondation Nationale des Sciences Politiques, 1980.

Hernández Bravo de Laguna, Juan. "Autogobierno y Política: Sistema de Partidos y Comportamiento Electoral en Canarias." In *Canarias Ante el Cambio,* Santa Cruz de Tenerife: Instituto de Desarrollo Regional, Universidad de la Laguna, Banco de Bilbao en Canarias, Junta de Canarias, Facultad de Ciencias Económicas y Empresariales de la Universidad de La Laguna, 1981.

Herr, Richard. *Spain.* Englewood Cliffs, N.J.: Prentice-Hall, 1971.

Heubel, E.J. "Church and State in Spain: Transition Toward Independence and Liberty." *Western Political Quarterly,* 30, March 1977.

Huneeus, Carlos. "Transition to Democracy in Spain: Dimensions of the Consociational Politics." Unpublished monograph [1982].

————. "La Unión de Centro Democrático, un Partido Consociacional." *Revista de Política Comparada,* 3, 1981.

Huntington, Samuel. *Political Order in Changing Societies.* New Haven and London: Yale University Press, 1968.

Indik, B.P. "Organization Size and Member Participation." Paper presented at American Psychological Association meeting, New York, Sept. 1961.

Jackson, Gabriel. *The Spanish Republic and the Civil War, 1931–1939.* Princeton, N.J.: Princeton University Press, 1965.

Jáuregui, Fernando, and Manuel Soriano. *Lo Otra Historia de UCD.* Madrid: Emiliano Escolar Editor, 1980.

Jerez, Miguel. *Elites Políticas y Centros de Extracción en España, 1938–1957.* Madrid: Centro de Investigaciones Sociológicas, 1982.

Jiménez de Asúa, Luis. *Proceso Histórico de la Consitución de la República Española.* Madrid: Editorial Reus, 1932.

Jiménez Blanco, José, et al. *La Conciencia Regional en España.* Madrid: Centro de Investigaciones Sociológicas, 1977.

Jones, Norman L. "The Catalan Question Since the Civil War." In Paul Preston, ed., *Spain in Crisis.* New York: Harper and Row, 1976.

Kirchheimer, Otto. "The Transformation of the Western European Party Systems." In Joseph La Palombara and Myron Weiner, eds., *Political Parties and Political Development.* Princeton, N.J.: Princeton University Press, 1972.

La Palombara, Joseph. "Distribution: A Crisis of Resource Management." In Leonard Binder et al., *Crises and Sequences in Political Development.* Princeton, N.J.: Princeton University Press, 1971.

————. "Italy: Fragmentation, Isolation, Alienation." In Lucien Pye and Sidney Verba, eds., *Political Culture and Political Development.* Princeton, N.J.: Princeton University Press, 1965.

Legg, Keith. *Patrons, Clients and Politicians.* Working Papers on Development, 3, Institute of International Studies. Berkeley: University of California, July 1975.

Lerner, Daniel. *The Passing of Traditional Society.* New York: Free Press, 1958.

Letamendía Ortiz, Francisco. *Breve Historia de Euskadi: El Nacionalismo Vasco y ETA.* Paris and Barcelona: Ruedo Ibérico, 1977.

Lijphart, Arend. *The Politics of Accommodation.* Berkeley and Los Angeles: University of California Press, 1968.

Linz, Juan J. "An Authoritarian Regime: Spain." In Erik Allardt and Stein Rokkan, eds., *Mass Politics.* New York: Free Press, 1970. (Also in Erik Allardt and Yrjö Littunen, eds., *Cleavages, Ideologies and Party Systems.* Helsinki: The Westermarck Society, 1962.)

————. "The Basques in Spain: Nationalism and Political Conflict in a New Democracy." In W. Phillips Davison and Leon Gordenker, eds., *Resolving Nationality Conflicts: The Role of Public Opinion Research.* New York: Praeger, 1980.

————. "La Crisis de un Estado Unitario, Nacionalismos Periféricos y Regionalismo." In R. Acosta, ed., *La España de las Autonomías (Pasado, Presente y Futuro).* Madrid: Espasa Calpe, 1981, vol. II.

————. "Early State-Building and Late Peripheral Nationalism." In Stein Rokkan and S. N. Eisenstadt, eds., *Building States and Nations.* Beverly Hills, Calif.: Sage, 1973.

————. "The Eight Spains." In Richard L. Merritt and Stein Rokkan, eds.,

Comparing Nations. New Haven: Yale University Press, 1966.

———. "Europe's Southern Frontier: Evolving Trends Toward What?" *Daedalus,* Winter 1979.

———. "From Falange to Movimiento-Organización: The Spanish Single Party and the Franco Regime." In Samuel Huntington and Clement Moore, eds., *Authoritarian Politics in Modern Society: The Dynamics of Established One-Party Systems.* New York: Basic Books, 1970.

———. "From Primordalism to Nationalism." In Edward A. Tiryakian and Ronald Rogowski, eds., *New Nationalisms of the Developed West: Toward Explanation.* Hemel Hempstead: George Allen and Unwin, 1983.

———. "Inmigrantes y Nativos." Unpublished monograph, 1982.

———. "The Legacy of Franco and Democracy." In Horst Baier, Hans Mathias Kepplinger, and Kurt Reumann, eds., *Öffentliche Meinung und Sozialer Wandel.* Westdeutscher Verlag, 1982.

———. "Legislatures in Organic Statist Authoritarian Regimes: The Case of Spain." Unpublished monograph, Yale University, 1975.

———. "The New Spanish Party System." In Richard Rose, ed., *Electoral Participation.* Beverly Hills, Calif.: Sage, 1980.

———. "Opposition In and Under an Authoritarian Regime: The Case of Spain." In Robert A. Dahl, ed., *Regimes and Oppositions.* New Haven: Yale University Press, 1973.

———. "The Party System in Spain: Past and Future." In Seymour Martin Lipset and Stein Rokkan, eds., *Party Systems and Voter Alignments.* New York: Free Press, 1967.

———. "Peripheries Within the Periphery?" In Per Torsvik, ed., *Mobilization, Center-Periphery Structures and Nation Building: A Volume in Commemoration of Stein Rokkan.* Bergen: Universitetsforlaget, 1982.

———. "La Política en Sociedades Multilingües y Multinacionales." In Fundación de Estudios Sociológicos (FUNDES), *Cómo Articular las Autonomías Españolas.* Madrid: FUNDES, 1980.

———. "A Sociological Look at Spanish Communism." In George Schwab, ed., *Eurocommunism: The Ideological and Political-Theoretical Foundations.* Westport, Conn.: Greenwood Press, 1981.

———. "Some Comparative Thoughts on the Transition to Democracy in Portugal and Spain." In Jorge Braga de Macedo and Simon Serfaty, eds., *Portugal Since the Revolution: Economic and Political Perspectives.* Boulder, Colo.: Westview Press, 1981.

———. "Totalitarian and Authoritarian Regimes." In Fred I. Greenstein and Nelson W. Polsby, eds., *Handbook of Political Science,* vol. 5. Reading, Mass.: Addison-Wesley, 1975.

Linz, Juan J., and Amando de Miguel. "La Elite Funcionarial Española ante la Reforma Administrativa." In *Sociología de la Administración Pública Española,* Anales de Moral Social y Económica, 17. Madrid: Centro de Estudios Sociales de la Santa Cruz del Valle de los Caidos, 1968.

———. *Los Empresarios Ante el Poder Público.* Madrid: Instituto de Estudios Políticos, 1966.

Linz, Juan J., and Jesús M. de Miguel. "Hacia un Análisis Regional de las Elecciones de 1936 en España." *Revista Española de la Opinión Pública,* 48, April–June 1977.

Linz, Juan J., and Alfred Stepan. *The Breakdown of Democratic Regimes,* Part 2. Baltimore: The Johns Hopkins University Press, 1978.

Linz, Juan J., Manuel Gómez-Reino, Francisco Andrés Orizo, and Darío Vila Carro. *Atlas Electoral del País Vasco y Navarra.* Madrid: Centro de Investigaciones Sociológicas, 1981.

———. *"Conflicto en Euskadi, Estudio Sociológico Sobre el Cambio Político en el País Vasco, 1975–1980.* Madrid: Espasa Calpe, 1983.

———. *Informe Sociológico Sobre el Cambio Político en España, 1975–1981.* Madrid: Fundación FOESSA, 1981.

Lipset, Seymour Martin. *Political Man.* Garden City, N.Y.: Doubleday, 1963.

Lipset, Seymour Martin, and Stein Rokkan. *Party Systems and Voter Alignments.* New York: Free Press, 1967.

López Pintor, Rafael. *La Opinión Pública Española: Del Franquismo a la Democracia.* Madrid: Centro de Investigaciones Sociológicas, 1982.

Lucas Verdú, Pablo. *La Octava Ley Fundamental.* Madrid: Tecnos, 1977.

McDonough, Peter, Antonio López Pina, and Samuel H. Barnes. "The Spanish Public in Political Transition." *British Journal of Political Science,* 11, 1981.

Magariños, Alfonso. *Quiénes Somos Los Gallegos?* Barcelona: Epidauro, S.A., 1959.

Malefakis, Edward. *Agrarian Reform and Peasant Revolution in Spain: Origins of the Civil War.* New Haven: Yale University Press, 1970.

———. "Peasants, Politics and Civil War in Spain: 1931–1939." In Robert Bezucha, ed., *Modern European Social History.* Lexington, Mass.: Heath, 1972.

Maravall, José María. "La Alternativa Socialista: La Política y el Apoyo Electoral del PSOE." *Sistema,* 35, May 1980.

———. *Dictatorship and Political Dissent: Workers and Students in Franco's Spain.* London: Tavistock, 1978.

———. "Eurocomunismo y Socialismo en España: La Sociología de una Competición Política." *Sistema,* 28, Jan. 1979.

———. *La Política de la Transición, 1975–1980.* Madrid: Taurus Ediciones, 1981.

———. "Political Cleavages in Spain and the 1979 General Election." *Government and Opposition,* 14, Summer 1979.

———. "Students and Politics in Contemporary Spain." *Government and Opposition,* 11, Spring 1976.

———. "La Transición a la Democracia, Alineamientos Políticos y Elecciones en España." *Sistema,* 36, May 1980.

Marriott, R. "Size of Working Group and Output." *Occupational Psychology,* 23, Jan. 1949.

Marsal, Joan F., Francesc Mercadé, Francesc Hernández, and Benjamín Oltra. *La Nació com a Problema: Tesis Sobre el Cas Català.* Barcelona: Edicions 62, 1979.

Medhurst, Kenneth. *Government in Spain: The Executive at Work.* Oxford: Pergamon Press, 1973.

Meer Lecha-Marzo, Fernando de. *La Cuestión Religiosa en las Cortes Constituyentes de la II República Española.* Pamplona: Ediciones Universidad de Navarra, 1975.

Merkl, Peter. *Western European Party Systems.* New York: Free Press, 1980.

Miguel, Amando de. *Recursos Humanos, Clases y Regiones en España.* Madrid: Editorial Cuadernos para el Diálogo, 1977.

———. *Sociología del Franquismo.* Barcelona: Editorial Euros, 1975.

Milbrath, Lester, W., and M. L. Goel. *Political Participation.* 2d ed. Chicago: Rand McNally, 1977.

Montero Gibert, José Ramón. "La Abstención Electoral en las Elecciones Legislativas de 1982: Términos de Referencia, Pautas de Distribución y Factores Políticos." *Revista de Derecho Político,* 21, Summer 1984.

———. "La CEDA y la Iglesia en la II República Española." *Revista de Estudios Políticos,* 31–32, Jan.–April 1983.

———. *La CEDA: El Catolicismo Social y Político en la II República.* 2 vols. Madrid: Ediciones de Revista de Trabajo, 1977.

———. "Partidos y Participación Política: Algunas Notas Sobre la Afiliación Política en la Etapa Inicial de la Transición Española." *Revista de Estudios Políticos,* 23, Sept.–Oct. 1981.

Mori, Arturo. *Crónica de las Cortes Constituyentes de la Segunda República Española.* 13 vols. Madrid: M. Aguilar, 1933.

Morodo, Raúl, et al. *Los Partidos Políticos en España.* Barcelona: Editorial Labor, 1979.

Mujal-León, Eusebio. "Cataluña, Carrillo, and Eurocommunismo." *Problems of Communism,* 2, March/April 1981.

———. *Communism and Political Change in Spain.* Bloomington: Indiana University Press, 1981.

———. "Spain: The PCE and the Post-Franco Era." In David E. Albright, ed., *Communism and Political Systems in Western Europe.* Boulder, Colo.: Westview Press, 1983.

———. "The PCE in Spanish Politics." *Problems of Communism,* 27, July–Aug. 1978.

Muñoz Alonso, Alejandro. *Las Elecciones del Cambio.* Barcelona: Argos Vergara, 1984.

Navarro, Manuel, and J. Félix Tezanos. *La Cuestión Regional Española.* Madrid: Editorial Euramérica, 1981.

Neumann, Sigmund. "Toward a Comparative Study of Political Parties." In Harry Eckstein and David Apter, eds., *Comparative Politics: A Reader.* New York: Free Press, 1963.

Nie, Norman, G. Bingham Powell, Jr., and Kenneth Prewitt. "Social Structure and Political Participation: Developmental Relationships, Parts I and II." *American Political Science Review,* 63, 1969.

Novia de Salcedo, Pedro. *Defensa Histórica, Legislativa y Económica del Señorío de*

Vizcaya y Provincias de Alava y Guipúzcoa. Bilbao: Librería de Delmas e Hijo, 1851.

Oneto, José. *José María de Areilza, Perfil Humano y Político.* Madrid: Editorial Cambio 16, 1977.

Oriol Costa, Pedro. *Jordi Pujol. Perfil Humano y Político.* Madrid: Editorial Cambio 16, 1977.

Orridge, A. W. "Uneven Development: 2." *Political Studies,* 29, June 1981.

Ostrogorski, Moisei. *Democracy and the Organization of Political Parties.* 2 vols. Ed. by Seymour Martin Lipset. Chicago: Quadrangle Books, 1964.

Pablo Masa, Antonio de. "Estratificación y Clases Sociales en la España de Hoy." In FOESSA, *Estudios Sociológicos, 1975.*

Partido Comunista de España (PCE). *Noveno Congreso del Partido Comunista de España, 19–23 Abril, 1978.* Barcelona: Editorial Crítica, 1978.

Partido Socialista Obrero Español (PSOE). *XXVII Congresso del PSOE.* Barcelona: Avance, 1977.

———. *XXVII Congreso del PSOE, 1976, Programa de Transición; La Enseñanza.*

———. *Declaración de Principios y Estatutos del PSOE.*

———. *Estatutos y Funcionamiento Interno, XXVII Congreso.*

———. *Estatutos del PSOE, Aprobados en el XXVII Congreso.*

———. *Manifiesto Electoral, Elecciones 77.*

———. *Programa: Elecciones 79.* Madrid: Gráficas Reunidas, 1979.

———. *Resolución Política del Congreso Extraordinario.* 1979.

———. *Resoluciones del XXVII Congreso del PSOE.* Madrid, 1977.

———, Federació Socialista de Catalunya. *El PSOE, Apunte Histórico,* Barcelona, 1978.

———, Secretaría de Formación y Documentación. *¿Qué es el Partido Socialista Obrero Español?*

Partido Socialista Popular (PSP). *Resumen del Programa Electoral del PSP.* Madrid, 1977.

Partit Socialista Unificat de Catalunya (PSUC). *IV Congrés del Partit Socialista Unificat de Catalunya: Recull de Materials i d'Intervencions.* Barcelona: Edita LAIA, 1978.

Payne, Stanley G. *Basque Nationalism.* Reno: University of Nevada Press, 1975.

———. "Catalan and Basque Nationalism." *Contemporary History,* 6, 1979.

———. *Falange.* Stanford Studies in History, Economics and Political Science, 22. Stanford, Calif.: Stanford University Press, 1961.

———. *Franco's Spain.* New York: Crowell, 1967.

———. *The Spanish Revolution.* New York: Norton, 1970.

———. "Terrorism and Democratic Stability in Spain." *Current History,* 77, Nov. 1979.

Pérez Díaz, Víctor. *Clase Obrera, Partidos y Sindicatos.* Madrid: Fundación del Instituto Nacional de Industria, 1979.

Pérez Ledesma, Manuel. "Los Partidos Políticos en la Transición." *Tiempo de Historia,* 72, 1980.

Pérez Peñasco, Alfonso, et al. "Educación." In FOESSA, *Estudios Sociológicos, 1975.*

Pérez Vilariño, José. "Comportamiento Electoral en Galicia." *Papers: Revista de Sociología,* 14, 1980.

Perona Villarreal, Diego. *La Distribución de la Carga Tributaria en España.* Madrid: Instituto de Estudios Fiscales, 1972.

Pi, Ramón. *Joaquín Garrigues Walker: Perfil Humano y Político.* Madrid: Editorial Cambio 16, 1977.

Pitarch, Ismael E., Joan Botella, Jordi Capo, and Joan Marcet. *Partits i Parlamentaris a la Catalunya d'Avui (1977–1979).* Barcelona: Edicions 62, 1980.

Polsby, Nelson. "Legislatures." In Fred I. Greenstein and Nelson W. Polsby, eds., *Handbook of Political Science,* vol. 5. Reading, Mass: Addison-Wesley, 1979.

Powell, G. Bingham. *Social Fragmentation and Political Hostility.* Stanford, Calif.: Stanford University Press, 1970.

Preston, Paul. "The Dilemma of Credibility: The Spanish Communist Party, the Franco Regime and After." *Government and Opposition,* 11, Winter 1976.

————. "The PCE's Long Road to Democracy 1954–1977." In Richard Kindersley, ed., *In Search of Eurocommunism.* London: Macmillan, 1981.

Pujol, Jordi. *Una Política per Catalunya.* Barcelona: Nova Terra, 1976.

Putnam, Robert. *The Beliefs of Politicians: Ideology, Conflict and Democracy in Britain and Italy.* New Haven: Yale University Press, 1973.

Pye, Lucien, and Sidney Verba, eds. *Political Culture and Political Development.* Princeton, N.J.: Princeton University Press, 1965.

Rae, Douglas W. *The Political Consequences of Electoral Laws.* New Haven and London: Yale University Press, 1967.

Ramírez, Pedro J. *Así se Ganaron las Elecciones.* Barcelona: Planeta, 1977.

————. *Así se Ganaron las Elecciones, 1979.* Madrid: Editorial Prensa Española, 1979.

Rivas, Manuel, and X. Tairbo. *Os Partidos Políticos na Galiza.* La Coruña: Rueiro, 1977.

Rodríguez, Rafael. *Quiénes son en Málaga?, Partido Comunista de España.* Colección Política: Partidos y Hombres, 8. Málaga: Ediciones Lafer, S.A., 1977.

Romero Maura, Joaquín. "After Franco, Franquismo?: The Armed Forces, The Crown and Democracy." *Government and Opposition,* 11, Winter 1976.

Roskin, Michael. "Spain Tries Democracy Again." *Political Science Quarterly,* 93, Winter 1978–79.

Rubio Llorente, Francisco. "La Astucia Electoral." *Cambio 16,* June 14, 1976.

Ruiz, Fernando, and Joaquín Romero. *Los Partidos Marxistas, sus Dirigentes, sus Programas.* Barcelona: Editorial Anagrama, 1977.

Sani, Giacomo. "Mass-Level Response to Party Strategy: The Italian Electorate and the Communist Party." In Donald L. Blackmer and Sidney Tarrow, eds., *Communism in Italy and France.* Princeton, N.J.: Princeton University Press, 1975.

————. "A Test of the Least-Distance Model of Voting Choice: Italy 1972." *Comparative Political Studies*, 7, 1974.

————. "Old Cleavages in a New Democracy: The Mass Bases of Spanish Parties." Paper presented at the International Symposium on Spain and the United States, University of Florida, Gainesville, Dec. 1979.

————. "Partisanship and the Structure of Mass Attitudes in Spain and Italy." Paper presented at the seminar "Encuestas Electorales, Información y Comportamiento Electoral," Madrid, Nov. 1980.

Sani, Giacomo, and Pilar de Castillo Vera. "El Rol Político de las Mujeres en la España Actual: Continuidad y Cambio." *Revista de Derecho Político*, 17, Spring 1983.

Sani, Giacomo, and José Ramón Montero Gibert. "The Left-Right Continuum Revisited: The Case of Spain." Paper presented at annual meeting of European Consortium for Political Research, Salzburg, Austria, April 1984.

Sani, Giacomo, and Giovanni Sartori. "Polarización, Fragmentación y Competición en las Democracias Occidentales." In *Revista del Departamento de Derecho Político*, 7, Fall 1980. (Also published in English as "Polarization, Fragmentation and Competition in Western Democracies." In Hans Daalder and Peter Mair, eds., *European Party Systems*. London: Sage, 1983.)

Sani, Giacomo, and Goldie Shabad. "Electoral Change in Spain in 1982: A Polarizing Realignment." *Revista de Derecho Político*, forthcoming in Spanish translation.

Santamarina, Alvaro. *Enrique Múgica, Perfil Humano y Político*. Madrid: Cambio 16, 1977.

Sartori, Giovanni. "European Political Parties: The Case of Polarized Pluralism." In Joseph La Palombara and Myron Weiner, eds., *Political Parties and Political Development*, Studies in Political Development #6. Princeton, N.J.: Princeton University Press, 1972. Paperback ed.

————. "The Sociology of Parties: A Critical View." In Otto Stammer, ed., *Party Systems, Party Organizations and the Politics of the New Masses*. Committee on Political Sociology of the International Sociological Association, 1968.

Sartorius, Nicolás. *Qué son las Comisiones Obreras?* Barcelona: La Gaya Ciencia, 1976.

Satrústegui, Miguel. "El Marco Jurídico: La Legislación Electoral." In de Esteban and López Guerra, eds., *Las Elecciones Legislativas*.

Schwartz, Pedro. "Politics First: The Economy after Franco." *Government and Opposition*, 11, Winter 1976.

Sempere, Joaquín. "Un Malestar en Busca de Coordinadas." *Nuestra Bandera*, 106, 1981.

Sentís, Carlos. *Manuel Fraga Iribarne, Perfil Humano y Político*. Madrid: Editorial Cambio 16, 1977.

Servicio de Estudios Sociológicos de la Confederación Española de Cajas de Ahorros. *Comentario Sociológico: Estructura Social de España*. 17–18, Jan.–June, 1977, and 19–20, July–December, 1977. Madrid: Confederación Española de Cajas de Ahorros, 1977.

Shabad, Goldie, and Richard Gunther. "Language, Nationalism and Political Conflict in Spain." *Comparative Politics*, July 1982. (Also to appear in Spanish in *Sistema*, forthcoming.)

———. "Spanish Regionalism in the 1980s." In Stanley Payne et al., eds., *Europe in the Eighties: A Comprehensive Assessment of Politics, Economics and Culture*. Princeton, N.J.: Karz-Cohl, 1985.

"Socialismo y Eurocomunismo: Debate Norberto Bobbio-Alfonso Guerra." *Sistema*, 22, Jan. 1978.

Solé Tura, Jordi. *Catalanismo y Revolución Burguesa*. Madrid: Editorial Cuadernos para el Dialógo, 1974.

———. "La Constitución y la Lucha por el Socialismo." In Gregorio Peces-Barba et al., *La Izquierda y la Constitución*. Barcelona: Ediciones Taula de Canvi, 1978.

Story, Jonathan. "Spanish Political Parties: Before and After the Election." *Government and Opposition*, 12, Autumn 1977.

Tácito (pseud.). *Un Año y Medio de Política Española*. Madrid: Ibérico-European, 1975.

Tezanos, José Félix. "Analisis Sociopolítico del Voto Socialista en las Elecciones de 1979." *Sistema*, 31, July 1979.

———. "El Espacio Político y Sociológico del Socialismo Español." *Sistema*, 32, Sept. 1979.

———. "La Crisis de la Conciencia Obrera en la España Actual." *Sistema*, 41, March 1981.

———. *Sociología del Socialismo Español*. Madrid: Tecnos, 1983.

Tierno Galván, Enrique. *Qué son las Izquierdas?* Barcelona: Editorial La Gaya Ciencia, 1976.

Torres del Moral, Antonio. "Los Grupos Parlamentarios." *Revista de Derecho Político*, 9, Spring 1981.

Trythall, J. W. D. *Franco: A Biography*. London: Rupert Hart-Davis, 1970.

Tusell, Javier. "El Centro Democrático y la Democracia Cristiana en las Elecciones del 15 de junio de 1977." Unpublished manuscript, 1978.

———. *Oligarquía y Caciquismo en Andalucía (1890–1923)*. Barcelona: Editorial Planeta, 1976.

———. "El Sistema Caciquil Andaluz Comparado con Otras Regiones Españolas (1903–1923). *Revista Española de Investigaciones Sociológicas*, 2, 1978.

Unión Centro Democrático (UCD). *Documento Ideológico de UCD*. Jan. 1978.

———. *Manual para Veintidós Millones de Electores*. Madrid: Sucesores de Rivadeneyra, 1977.

———. *Una Política de Hechos*. 1978.

———. *Programa Electoral: Elecciones/1979*. 1979.

———. *La Solución a un Reto: Tesis para una Sociedad Democrática Occidental*. Madrid: Unión Editorial, 1978.

Urwin, Derek W. "Harbinger, Fossil or Fleabite? Regionalism and the West European Party Mosaic." In Hans Daalder and Peter Mair, eds., *Western European Party Systems: Continuity and Change*. London: Sage, 1983.

Varela, Santiago. *Partidos y Parlamento en la Segunda República*. Madrid: Editorial Ariel, 1978.

———. "La Perspectiva Histórica." In Jorge de Esteban, Luis López Guerra,

Eduardo Espín, Jaime Nicolás, Francisco Javier García Fernández, Miguel Satrústegui, and Santiago Varela, *El Proceso Electoral*. Barcelona: Editorial Labor, 1977.

———. *El Problema Regional en La Segunda República Española*. Madrid: Unión Editorial, 1976.

Varela Ortega, José. *Los Amigos Políticos: Partidos, Elecciones y Caciquismo en la Restauración (1875–1900)*. Madrid: Alianza, 1977.

Vicens Vives, Jaime. *Approaches to the History of Spain*. Trans. and ed. by Joan Connelly Ullman. Berkeley and Los Angeles: University of California Press, 1967.

———. *An Economic History of Spain*. Princeton, N.J.: Princeton University Press, 1969.

Vidarte, Juan Simeón. *Las Cortes Constituyentes de 1931–1933: Testimonio del Primer Secretario del Congreso de Diputados*. Barcelona: Ediciones Grijalbo, 1976.

Vila Carro, Darío, Francisco Andrés Orizo, and Manuel Gómez-Reino. "Sociología del Actual Cambio Político en España." In Fundación FOESSA, *III Informe*. Madrid: Fundación FOESSA, 1978.

Viver Pi-Sunyer, Carles. *El Personal Político de Franco, 1936–1945*. Barcelona: Editorial Vicens-Vives, 1978.

Weiner, Myron, and Joseph La Palombara. "Introduction." In *Political Parties and Political Development*. Princeton, N.J.: Princeton University Press, 1966.

Wildavsky, Aaron. "A Methodological Critique of Duverger's Political Parties." In Harry Eckstein and David E. Apter, eds., *Comparative Politics: A Reader*. New York: Free Press, 1963.

World Bank. *1979 World Bank Atlas: Population, Per Capita Produce and Growth Rates*. Washington, D.C.: World Bank, 1979.

Yagüe, María Eugenia. *Santiago Carrillo, Perfil Humano y Político*. Madrid: Editorial Cambio 16, 1977.

NEWSPAPERS AND PERIODICALS

ABC. Edición semanal aérea, 1977–1979. Madrid.

Cambio 16. 1976–1984. Madrid.

Deia. 1978–1979, various issues. Bilbao.

Diario 16. 1977–1980, various issues. Madrid.

El Diario Vasco. 1978–80, various issues. Bilbao.

El País. 1978–1984, various issues. Madrid.

Euzkadi. 1978–1980. Bilbao.

Informaciones. 1973–1975, 1977–1980, various issues. Madrid.

Keesing's Contemporary Archives. Vol. 29 (March 1983). Bath, England.

Partido Communista de España (PCE). *Mundo Obrero*. 1978–1979, various issues. Madrid.

———. *Nuestra Bandera*. 1978–1981, various issues. Madrid.

Partido Socialista Obrero Español (PSOE). *El Socialista*. 1978–1979, various issues.

La Vanguardia. 1978–1979, various issues. Barcelona.

SPANISH GOVERNMENT DOCUMENTS

Boletín Oficial del Estado. 120, May 20, 1977, pp. 11098–11142.

Cortes Españolas. *Diario de Sesiones del Congreso de los Diputados.* 103–116, July 4, 1978–July 21, 1978; and 130, Oct. 31, 1978.

————. *Diario de Sesiones del Congreso de los Diputados, Comisión de Asuntos Constitucionales y Libertades Públicas.* 59–93, May 5–June 20, 1978.

————. *Diario de Sesiones del Senado, Comisión de Constitución.* 39–67, Aug. 18–Oct. 5, 1978.

Instituto de Estudios Fiscales, Ministerio de Hacienda. *Contabilidad Nacional de España.* Madrid: Boletín Oficial del Estado, various years.

Instituto Nacional de Estadística, Presidencia del Gobierno. *España: Anuario Estadístico.* Madrid: Boletín Oficial del Estado, various years, 1965–1980.

Ministerio de la Gobernación, Dirección General de la Política Interior. *Elecciones Generales 1977: Resultados Congreso por Provincias.*

Ministerio del Interior, Dirección General de Política Interior. *Elecciones Generales 1979: Resultados Congreso por Provincias.*

Ministerio del Interior, Secretaría General Técnica, *Legislación Electoral Española,* March 1979.

Index

Abril Martorell, Fernando, 104, 106
ACL (Acción Cuidadana Liberal), 172, 173, 176, 177
Alvarez, José Luis, 129, 284
Alvarez de Miranda, Fernando, 94, 96, 110, 140
AP (Alianza Popular)
 origins of, 5, 10, 78–92
 position on electoral law, 43, 84, 88
 and the political reform law, 48, 88, 89
 public image of, 78, 89–92, 99, 103, 170, 173, 174, 184, 218, 219, 290–292, 297, 298, 299, 302, 304
 ideology and program of, 79, 81, 83, 110, 130, 170–176, 183, 184, 220, 221, 266, 267, 340, 345, 346, 350, 397, 407, 408
 composition of elite, 82–84, 87, 88–92, 103, 176–177
 intra-party conflict, 83, 114, 126, 172, 173, 176, 177, 211, 291, 402, 407, 408
 campaign strategies and tactics, 84, 87, 88, 92, 103, 171, 172, 174–177, 183, 184, 219, 224, 225, 266–267, 290–292, 396
 composition of electorate, 99, 180, 182, 193, 194, 197, 218, 219, 224, 225, 238, 260, 360, 370, 372, 397, 398, 416, 418
 role during transition, 115–117, 389, 394
 organizational development strategies, 132, 170–177, 221, 222
 see also Coalición Democrática (CD)
Arana y Goiri, Sabino de, 318, 319, 343
Areilza, José María de, 83, 95–97, 99, 101, 172–177, 254, 407, 408
Arias Navarro, Carlos, 32–33, 34–35, 65, 80, 81, 82, 87, 91, 94, 97, 103

Arias Salgado, Rafael, 94, 105, 129, 134, 138, 144, 284, 285, 418
Army
 and the transition to democracy, 2, 8, 36, 63, 115, 395, 399
 under the Second Republic, 16
Arzallus, Xabier, 120, 123
"Associationism," 32, 33, 81, 82, 87, 94, 95, 455n96

Barrera, Heribert, 320, 346
Basque Nationalism. *See* Language; Micronationalism
BEAN (Bloc d'Esquerra d'Alliberament Nacional de Catalunya), 254, 346, 352, 356, 371
BNPG (Bloque Nacional Popular Gallego), 245, 254, 310, 349, 351, 359, 363, 366, 368, 370, 371, 373, 381, 386
Business organizations, 304, 367
 and partisan involvement, 2, 87, 88, 97, 115, 125, 132, 139, 142, 143, 144, 174, 184–187, 212, 289, 398

Cabanillas, Pío, 83, 87, 95, 96, 284, 412
Cabinet instability
 under the Second Republic, 18
 under Suárez, 141, 144, 413, 414
Caciquismo, 85, 86, 89, 92, 134–135, 228, 330, 350, 351, 407, 461n105, 485n51
Calvo Sotelo, Leopoldo, 99, 100, 104, 112, 284, 414, 416
Camacho, Marcelino, 205, 209
Campaign financing, 96, 97, 131, 174, 186, 417, 468n27
Campaign strategies and tactics, 3–6, 40, 41, 181, 182, 190, 191, 263, 264, 271–274, 367–373, 392, 395, 396

507

Press Law and liberalization, 31, 32,
79, 455n90
"associationism," 32, 33, 82
clientelism, 86
FSD (Federación Social Demócrata),
94, 95, 100
taxation, 125, 467n19
policy process under, 141, 451n39,
474n18
and class divisions, 200
and usage of regional languages,
242–245, 478n3
policies toward micronationalism,
326
Fueros, 123, 330, 344–346, 450n17

Gallego Nationalism. See Language;
Micronationalism
Garrigues Walker, Joaquín, 93, 94,
95, 105
Generalitat, 19, 20, 21, 122, 250,
320, 328
Gil Robles, José María, 15, 93, 107,
108, 109
GODSA, 82
González, Felipe
becoming secretary general of
PSOE, 72
and PSOE in Andalucía, 73
image of, 75, 276, 281, 297, 299–303,
391, 416
with reference to transition, 166, 167
and ideology and program of PSOE,
167, 168, 169, 170, 188, 404–406
and leadership conflict in PSOE, 168,
169, 170, 266, 404–406
with reference to PCE, 268
Gross national product per capita, 24,
25, 26, 453n71
Guerra, Alfonso, 73, 169, 188, 266, 269,
301, 302, 404–406
Gutiérrez Díaz, Antoni, 155, 156, 406

HB (Herri Batasuna)
origins of, 181, 245, 312, 341, 389
composition of elite, 229
stands on Constitution and autonomy
statute, 251, 383, 400

ideology of, 338, 341–343
relationship with ETA, 342, 361
composition of electorate, 352, 359,
366, 373, 377
Herrero de Miñón, Miguel Rodríguez,
120
HOAC (Hermandades Obreras de
Acción Católica), 29, 204
"Holding company" party model, 143,
144

Ibárruri, Dolores ("Pasionaria"), 67,
155, 156
IDC (Izquierda Demócrata Cristiana),
93, 94, 107, 109, 222
"Independents," 97, 99–103, 105–106,
110, 464n155
see also UCD

JOC (Juventudes Obreras Católicas),
29, 204
Juan Carlos I, 13, 120, 178, 305–308
see also Monarchy

Language
language policy under Franco, 8,
21, 32, 242, 243, 245, 478n3
usage of regional languages, 16,
242, 243, 313, 331, 332, 449n15,
478n7, 484n30
language usage and political
attitudes, 242, 246, 313, 315, 316,
319, 323, 331, 351, 352, 356, 357,
366, 381, 382, 385, 482n7,
483n16
treatment of language in 1978
constitution, 245, 351, 363
party stands on language usage, 252,
253, 254, 257, 342, 343, 345,
348–350, 486n58
language policies in autonomous
regional communities, 257, 319,
320, 321, 327, 328, 363, 364
language usage and voting preferences, 385
Larroque, Enrique, 93, 94, 101, 111
Lavilla, Landelino, 104, 412, 416
Left-right orientations
distribution of voters on left-right

Designer: Mark Ong
Compositor: Innovative Media Inc.
Text: VIP Baskerville
Display: Baskerville
Printer: Braun-Brumfield, Inc.
Binder: Braun-Brumfield, Inc.